Men and Masculinities in
Christianity and Judaism:
A Critical Reader

Men and Masculinities in Christianity and Judaism: A Critical Reader

Edited by
Björn Krondorfer

scm press

© Björn Krondorfer 2009

Published in 2009 by SCM Press
Editorial office
13–17 Long Lane,
London, EC1A 9PN, UK

SCM Press is an imprint of Hymns Ancient and Modern Ltd
(a registered charity)
St Mary's Works, St Mary's Plain,
Norwich, NR3 3BH, UK
www.scm-canterburypress.co.uk

British Library Cataloguing in Publication data

A catalogue record for this book is available
from the British Library

978 0 334 04191 7

Typeset by Regent Typesetting, London
Printed in the UK by
CPI Antony Rowe, Chippenham SN14 6LH

Contents

CONTENTS

Acknowledgments

Conceiving the idea of this volume has been a highly pleasurable activity, and equally enjoyable have been the many conversations with colleagues and friends about the project in its various stages. Having had the privilege of connecting with almost every single contributing author by phone conversations or e-mail correspondence was a special source of gratification. I thus renewed contact with old friends and colleagues and, in other cases, spoke to a person for the first time. The sense of mutual respect and affirmation conveyed in these conversations was heartening. I ought to mention here everyone by name, but the reader will meet them all when perusing this book. Everyone was helpful in his or her own ways: responding to my queries, completing missing bibliographical information, re-reading edited versions, initiating contacts to publishers, and extending other gestures of help. I want to thank all my colleagues for the trust in this project and for entrusting me with their texts.

Putting the chapters of the *Critical Reader* into their final form has been a labor of love. There were moments of doubt regarding the effective use of sparse research time when spending endless hours on the mechanical and editorial aspects that need to go into the production of such a project. During these moments, it was only my firm belief that a volume on the critical study of men and religion is desperately needed that kept me moving forward. Currently, no comprehensive volume is available that offers the student of gender and religion an overview of the research conducted in this area, and audiences outside of academia have had only few opportunities to learn about the research done in this field and about the excitement it has generated.

Once I had identified the individual contributions and obtained a good copy of the original, all pages were scanned into pdf files and then saved as a word document. Anyone who has undertaken such data transfer knows how many errors can creep into the generated word files, leaving the editor to battle with illegible sentences, misplaced paragraphs, wrongly reformatted quotes, and missing or changed punctuations. Only through careful and repeated editorial readings does a document emerge that mirrors the original. Luckily, I found a steady and reliable assistant in René Koch, who managed the technical aspects of this process and helped with much of the required manual labor. As a German graduate student at Berlin's Freie Universität, whose native language is not English, he accomplished masterfully the challenging task of doing the initial editorial clean-up. It was a pleasure to work with him.

An equally anxious phase for an editor of such a volume is seeking permission for reprinting the original sources, and then watching the steadily rising amount of permission fees to be paid. This project could have been easily derailed at this juncture, but almost all publishers were willing to listen to my pleas for granting the rights at a reasonable cost or, as it happened in some cases, for free. I thank them for their willingness to work with me. Natalie Watson, my editor at SCM Press, should also be mentioned here. She believed in the project from the very beginning and has been a constant source of good advice, encouragement, and material support.

Very special thanks go to the provost office of St Mary's College of Maryland, and provost Larry Vote. He stepped in with generous support when other sources failed. His immediate signaling of assistance when in need speaks to the fine ethos of a liberal arts college in relation to its faculty, an ethos Larry embodies so well. Also, this project would not have gotten off the ground without having been granted a sabbatical year. Much of the work on this volume was done while on leave in Berlin, Germany, where I found an open door (and office) at the Institute of Protestant Theology at the Freie Universität. Ralf Wüstenberg, chair of the institute, not only made me feel welcome but he and I also shared many good conversations beyond social niceties and academic small-talk.

Of the many people with whom I discussed aspects of the *Critical Reader* – in some cases even before the idea of this volume took on a tangible shape – I want to mention particularly Scott Haldeman, Stephen Boyd, Philip Culbertson, and Norbert Reck. Donald Boisvert offered not only advice but generously took care of the permission rights for his chapter – thank you. E-mail correspondences have the tendency to erase rootedness in geographical localities, so I want to mention how much the idea of this book benefited from perspectives of men located in different parts of the world: Christoph Walser (Switzerland), André Musskopf (Brazil), James Poling (while in Korea), Norbert Reck (Germany) and Philip Culbertson (New Zealand/United States). I had a chance to begin talking about the outlines of this book at a literature and theology conference in Glasgow (UK), at two retreats on questions of gender and religion in Boldern/ Zurich (Switzerland), at the universities of Salzburg (Austria) and Konstanz (Germany), and also, within a broader context, at the annual meetings of the American Academy of Religion in 2006 and 2008. As the book went into its final phase of completion, I was offering my first upper-level religious studies seminar on 'masculinities in Christianity' at my college, where I was testing chapters and ideas contained in these pages on an undergraduate student population. Against my expectation, more students registered for this class than the assigned room was able to accommodate.

I do not claim that the contributors to this volume agree with my definitions or assessments of the field nor that they agree with each other. I owe each of them a great debt, but I take full responsibility for the choices I have made. I tried my best to keep the reprinted texts as close to the original as possible, and I apologize for the inadvertent yet inevitable errors that may have slipped by the many pairs of editorial eyes. Gratitude also goes to Katharina von Kellenbach for her insightful editorial comments regarding all of my introductions. Finally, I want to thank Janet Butler Haugaard for her always reliable editing skills.

Introduction

Priests, rabbis, monks, prophets, disciples, patriarchs, elders, bishops, promise keepers, pastors, TV-evangelists, eunuchs, healers, saints, apostles, cenobites, muscular Christians, yeshiva bokhurs, householders, son(s) of God, wicked sons, male fairies, ascetics, revivalists, reformers, mendicants, theocrats, saviors, scribes, soldiers of Christ, desert fathers, mystics, popes, laymen, Hasids, visionaries, sinners, inquisitors, crusaders, saintly schlemiels, God-inspired vagrants, transvestite celebrants, false Messiahs, perfect servants, slaves of Christ, stylites, hermits, heretics, theologians, celibates, Zaddiks, martyrs, holy men . . . the list would continue for many more lines before we would exhaust the possibilities of men being religious in the Jewish and Christian traditions.

They fasted, prayed, comforted and punished; they decreed, dreamed, blessed, condemned, meditated, obeyed, ruled, rebelled and conquered; they told stories, made creeds, made love, made holy wars, sang hymns, submitted to pain, got circumcised, got baptized, dispensed sacraments, made children, flagellated themselves, were ripped apart by lions, were burnt at the stake, inflicted torture, disciplined their bodies, trained their minds, painted icons, destroyed images, created doctrines, collected charity, built communities . . . this list, too, cannot easily be completed.

Given such an abundance of possibilities and activities for men who were expressing and embodying their religious commitments, one might assume that there is an equivalent body of literature that critically reflects men as gendered beings vis-à-vis Judaism and Christianity. This, however, is not the case. Compared to the many centuries in which men have practiced religion, taught religion, articulated creeds, enforced religious codes and occupied positions of sacred power, the scholarship dedicated to the critical study of men in religion has had only a short lifespan. With the onset of the age of Enlightenment and secularization, men have, of course, also rebelled against religion, investigated religion and developed critical approaches to the study of religion. A critical study of men and religion, however, is not the same as modernity's critique of religion in general. A critical study does not disapprove of religion in general but, instead, questions the implicit and normative gender assumptions of *men* as they engage in, and are engaged by, religious traditions. It is the goal of this *Critical Reader* to present a selection of the best and most representative writings published in this field since its inception in the 1980s.

What Does the *Critical Reader* Want to Accomplish?

Men and Masculinities in Christianity and Judaism: A Critical Reader brings together a selection of contemporary writings from religious studies scholars who address men as gendered beings within the Jewish and Christian traditions. The investigation of the links and relations between men and religion has emerged over the years as a subfield of religious studies. This field takes 'gender' seriously as an analytic category, yielding insights into the variegated ways that men as biologically and socially differentiated beings have appropriated and shaped religious traditions, and how, vice versa, religious traditions have influenced and impacted men's lives and self-perceptions.

An assumption guiding most of the chapters in the *Critical Reader* is that neither 'men' nor 'religion' constitute fixed and predetermined categories. Rather, the critical perspectives brought to bear upon men's studies in religion ascertain the notion that the interrelations between men and religion are dynamic, elastic, complex, creative, and filled with historical and political significance at specific moments in time. Religions create images of men and impose particular modes of being a man; they can also impede or cultivate a man's development and provide alternative pathways for men. This volume on men and masculinities in Christianity and Judaism introduces the student of religion and of gender to the rich complexity of the relations between men and their religious commitments; it also provides an overview of the different themes that emerge in such a study and of the different methodologies applied by scholars of religion.

The contributing authors ask questions, for example, about the significance of the maleness of religious savior figures (such as Jesus Christ) or about the gendered positions that religious men have adopted vis-à-vis God (such as brother, lover, friend, 'woman'). The authors also address the eroticization of spiritual learning (such as Torah study; the devotion to saints; confessional reflections) as well as religious practices that either lock men into a body-repressive politic or invite them to become passionate care-takers. They investigate canonical texts, theorize conceptions of masculinities, and pay attention to how religious ideals have been embodied. Indeed, the (religious) *text* and the (male) *body* are often pivotal in guiding the interpretive and analytic interests of the contributing scholars. This is not too surprising given that Judaism and Christianity are scriptural traditions that understand themselves to be working in and through history, thus assigning the body religious signification. It is in, with, and through our bodies that we express and experience the joys and sorrows of the divine–human encounter as told and preserved in Scriptures that have been considered holy and sacred.

Close readings of canonical and heterodox texts through a consciously male-gendered lens provide new insights into the relationships between men and women, men and men, men and the divine; reinterpretations of historical documents can make us aware of the struggles that went into determining what is considered normative and deviant behavior; a sharpened focus on issues relating to the male anatomy can cull from the historical record neglected aspects of religious concerns (for example, the theological significance of nocturnal emissions). Beyond investigations of textual sources, the male body itself – as experienced in the here-and-now of the present moment – requires critical reflection.

Men (just as women) cannot avoid attending to their bodily needs and desires, and the religious imagination offers them multiple options in how to regulate or liberate, discipline or explore their embodiedness. Religion has the power to rigidify already restrictive social customs, but it can also inspire subversive and transgressive practices.

This *Critical Reader* should not be mistaken for a compilation of primary texts that historically documents the various Jewish and Christian articulations on men. It does not present short readings sampled from the New Testament, the Talmud, Augustine, Maimonides, Calvin, or other such religious sources and figures. Instead, it provides critical reflections put forth by scholars of religion in the last decades. The range of concerns reaches from individual sexual ethics (such as masturbation) to gender justice (such as heterosexism), from the disenchantments with modernity (as articulated, for example, in modern religious men's movements) to issues of communal commitments; the chronological span reaches from biblical time to postmodernity. Such is the breadth and scope of the themes addressed in this volume.

The contributing scholars bring their expertise and academic training to their investigations of the place and role of men as gendered (rather than normative) beings within Christianity and Judaism. At stake is that unacknowledged male gender perspectives within religious discourse have all too often been claimed as normative. Once authorized as norm, religion has the power to legitimize and enforce privileges of certain men in the name of universal truth. The authors chosen for this volume do not, however, legitimize or defend unjust male privileges. They do not argue for stabilizing heterosexual and heteronormative claims. Rather, they have trained their critical eye on the complexity and problematics of the male gender within religious discourse and practices. Critical men's studies in religion, then, is not about a positivist and heteronormative reading of men's presence in religious traditions but, instead, a critical reading of the privileged performances of male gender within those traditions.

Critical Men's Studies in Religion

In order to understand the relevance of investigating men and masculinities within Judaism and Christianity, it is helpful to take a look at how the study of men in religion has evolved in the last three decades.

In the beginning, it had been far from certain whether the scholarly interest in this area would be able to define itself as something distinct from other scholarship that pursues related questions. Would the scattered individual research projects be able to stand on their own? Or would they be subsumed under particular disciplines (like New Testament studies, practical theology, Jewish studies) or absorbed by already established cross-disciplinary research areas, such as women's studies, gender studies or queer studies? Defining and describing the contours of men's studies in religion as a distinct field has met with some difficulties. Is it a study of patriarchy from a man's perspective? Is it a constructive attempt at rebinding men to the church? Is it a feminist critique forwarded by non-patriarchal male scholars? Is it advocacy for men's rights? Is it research on men rigidly adhering to academic standards? Is it political

activism that addresses practical concerns of marginalized men? Is it constructive theology of gay men or men of color? Should it focus on theoretical musings
on 'masculinity' from a religious perspective? Looking at these questions, we
may get a sense of the separate directions that the interest in men and religion
can potentially take. In a 2004 review of books on religion and masculinity, the
reviewer writes, somewhat unfairly, that 'scholarship in masculinity – like the
broader studies of gender that fostered it – remains an ambiguous, ambitious,
interdisciplinary, and immature field of intellectual endeavor.' And she concludes on an acerbic note: 'Rather than a provocative interrogation of gendered
discourse, masculinity studies have become just another way to talk about
white men' (Lofton 2004).

By suggesting that we call the field *critical* men's studies in religion', I would
like to move the intellectual endeavor to a level of sophistication where it can no
longer be confounded with yet 'another way to talk about' privileged men. I also
suggest locating this field primarily within the academic discipline of religious
studies rather than the larger (secular) study of masculinities. Thus identifying a name and setting a perimeter, I wish to demonstrate cohesion to a field,
which, at times, has been unsure of itself. Surely, contributions by colleagues of
other relevant disciplines, such as history, sociology, psychology, anthropology
or art history, are welcome. I do not intend to set up restrictive barriers but to
seek clarity of focus. What the proposed focus brings to the conversation are
an analysis and comprehension of religion that do not conceive of their subject
and object ('religion') as derivative of other forms of social organization and
human behavior (such as economic relations, psychological maladjustment or
demographic statistics). Religion, instead, is viewed as a genuine expression of
human interaction, and while religion remains firmly at the core of the scholarly
agenda, it is viewed as a complex web of phenomena that must be approached
from various angles.

'Critical men's studies in religion' owes a great debt to gender studies. As
a matter of fact, one can arguably locate it as a subcategory within the larger
body of transdisciplinary gender studies. Its historical precedents are secular and religious feminisms, the gay liberation movements and secular men's
studies. Secular gender and men's studies, however, had their own share of
hesitations toward religion, and they generally have not given the religious
dimension sufficient scholarly attention.[1] Hence, the bulk of the material on the
academic study of men and masculinities in religions has been put forth by
religious studies scholars, and the field has found its organizational home primarily within the American Academy of Religion (AAR), the worldwide largest
professional association dedicated to the study of religions.[2]

An early interest in men and religion by religious studies scholars is already
discernible in the 1980s, though it took about ten more years before these scholars began to identify themselves – albeit often tentatively and loosely – as
belonging to a group working on common themes. Realizing that their inquir-
ies were sufficiently differentiated from other approaches to the phenomenon of
religion, a need emerged to search for a classification that would best describe
the thematic unity across a range of applied methodologies. Especially two
groups within the AAR have pushed the scholarly agenda of this field, namely
the Gay Men's Issues in Religion group, founded in 1988, and the Men's Studies

in Religion group, founded two years later. Whereas John Boswell's *Christianity, Social Tolerance, and Homosexuality* (1980) can be seen as an important key to launching the scholarly interest in the study of religion by, for and about gay men (and especially the interest in the study of the history of homosexualities), it took the heterosexual community of male scholars of religion until the mid-1990s to gain a more discernible profile.

In 1996, scholars who belonged to the Men's Studies in Religion group of the AAR (a group primarily, though not exclusively, attended and staffed by the heterosexual community), published two edited volumes, which sketched the possibilities of this emergent field: *Redeeming Men: Religion and Masculinities* (eds Stephen Boyd, Merle Longwood and Mark Muesse) and *Men's Bodies, Men's Gods: Male Identities in a (Post-) Christian Culture* (ed. Björn Krondorfer). Independent of each other, both volumes organized their contributions into six sections, many of which dealt with questions of identity (masculine identity, religious identity, sexual identity). While the second of these works emphasized the significance of the male body within religious practice and discourse, Boyd et al. paid more attention to historical and communal manifestations of masculinities. Between these two volumes, there is little overlap among contributors;[3] some of the authors gathered in these volumes have since ceased to publish in the field of men's studies in religion, while others have steadily advanced their research along the trajectories laid out in these works. Other books that deal with religion and masculinities were, of course, published in the same period – such as Brod's *The Making of Masculinities: The New Men's Studies* (1987), Culbertson's *New Adam: The Future of Male Spirituality* (1992), Eilberg-Schwartz's *God's Phallus: And Other Problems for Men and Monotheism* (1994), and Brod's and Kaufman's *Theorizing Masculinities* (1994). However, both *Redeeming Men* and *Men's Bodies, Men's Gods* remain, arguably, the most distinctive and representative volumes published during the formative stage of men's studies in religion.[4]

Evidence of the formal recognition of a new academic field is, for better or worse, to gain entry into a standard encyclopedia. In 2004, 'men's studies in religion' made its debut as a separate category in such an official archive of knowledge. The editors of Macmillan's second edition of the *Encyclopedia of Religion* asked Philip Culbertson and me to define and describe the contours of this subdiscipline. We wrote:

MEN'S STUDIES IN RELIGION is part of the unfolding concern within religion to address the effects of gender and sexuality upon religious faith and practice. As a new field of scholarly inquiry, it reflects upon and analyzes the complex connections between men and religion, building upon gender studies, feminist theory and criticism, the men's movement, and the increasing number of subdisciplines in the academic study of religion. Methodologically men's studies in religion is an open field; its object of inquiry is 'men' as gendered beings in relation to religion. But the precise delineations of this inquiry are not yet determined. Distinctions between the academic study of men in religion, on the one hand, and affirmation of socially accepted forms of male religiosity, on the other, are not always drawn with sufficient clarity. (Krondorfer and Culbertson 2004, 5861–2)

This opening paragraph summarizes well the state of affairs of men's studies in religion at the turn of the millennium: it had moved out of its early phase of formation and become a recognizable entity. At the same time, it remained resistant to drawing precise boundaries, open to methodological diversity, and permeable to cross-fertilizations by shifting theoretical and practical concerns. Culbertson and I continue:

> Studies in this new field are, on the one hand, critical of normative models of masculinities and, on the other, also supportive of men struggling to find their place in religion and society. These studies may examine male religious authority, analyze societal attitudes toward men, or study religious practices that enforce gender norms. They may probe theologies that justify patriarchal hierarchies or investigate men's participation in religiously sanctified oppression. They may also suggest alternative devotional and spiritual practices for men and reenvision men's roles as caregivers in both the profane and sacred realms. (5862)

Describing the agenda of men's studies in religion as, on the one hand, 'critical of normative models of masculinities' and, on the other, 'supportive of men' reveals a tension at its very core. Is it a critique of masculinities as the latter manifest themselves in specific historical circumstances? Or is it partisan scholarship furthering the cause of men? Once this simmering dissonance is pressed into the dichotomous terms of 'political advocacy' versus 'academic detachment', scholars and practitioners will quarrel over the right understanding of the contours, tasks, and trajectories of this field. If, however, we do not let ourselves be drawn into these polarizing alternatives and, instead, conceive of the inherent tension as a creative tool for advancing a scholarly approach of critical empathy, we might be able to take the wind out of the sails of unproductive disputes.

> Generally speaking, there is a difference between the men's movement (secular and religious) and the academic study of men in religion. Whereas the former tends to favor biological, essentialist, and archetypal models, the latter tends to see men as culturally constructed, gendered, and performing contradictory roles due to constantly changing ideologies of masculinity. Men's studies in religion then analyzes and understands 'the role of religion in supporting or resisting unstable masculine identities' [Boyd et al. 1996, 286]. (Krondorfer and Culbertson 2004, 5862)

Having pointed to the difference between religious men's movements on the one hand, and on the other the academic study of men in religion, Krondorfer and Culbertson proceed to describe four scholarly trends observable within the field:

- 'Men reclaiming religion and faith' (this trend focuses on Christian men's movements).
- 'Spiritual and confessional writings' (this trend is about the wide-ranging literature that blends scholarly analysis and personal reflection).

- 'Theological and biblical reflections'.
- 'Gay and queer studies in religion'.

I have since come to the conclusion that insisting on adding the term 'critical' is crucial. By calling the new field 'critical men's studies in religion', I wish to emphasize that bringing gender consciousness to the analysis and interpretation of men in relation to all aspects of religion is indispensable; otherwise, we might just slip back into a long tradition of reiterations of male dominance within the sphere of religion. In other words, 'critical men's studies in religion' exhibits not only a reflective and empathetic stance toward men as individual and communal beings trying to make sense of their lives within the different demands put upon them by society and religion, but it must also engage these issues with critical sensitivity and scholarly discipline in the context of gender-unjust systems. Such systems – like patriarchy, androcentrism, the oppression of women, heterosexism, masculinist God-language, homophobia, xenophobia, religious discrimination, colonization or enslavement – can operate in subtle and overt ways, and they benefit certain men in certain historical and political circumstances. These systems need to be kept in mind when working in this area.

Scope and Limits of the *Critical Reader*

In the last decade, research on men and masculinities in Christianity and Judaism has proliferated. Various short-term alliances and interdisciplinary collaborations with groups like feminist theology, queer theory, biblical studies and ritual studies have helped to sharpen the profile of this research. Professional organizations like the American Academy of Religion (AAR) and the American Men's Studies Association (AMSA) have provided important venues, and international journals like *Theology & Sexuality*, *Journal of Men's Studies* and, more recently, the online *Journal of Men, Masculinities and Spirituality*, which have played pioneering roles, continue to attract new audiences. A number of monographs and an even greater number of articles scattered around specialized journals have explored the field from heterosexual and gay perspectives. Furthermore, numerous individual chapters dedicated to issues of men and masculinity are buried within edited volumes and anthologies in such fields as women's studies, general men's studies, feminist theological studies, gay studies, queer studies, and theology and sexuality studies. Yet, to date no single volume exists that presents the research on men in religion as a cohesive field. *Men and Masculinities in Christianity and Judaism* intends to remedy this lack by bringing together seminal texts written by religious studies scholars in the last three decades. It offers men and women in academia, seminaries, classrooms, churches, and religious and humanitarian organizations a sourcebook that represents the spectrum, depth and quality of the work accomplished so far. It hopes not only to demonstrate the relevance of this field, but also to stimulate excitement and encourage further explorations.

Three caveats are in order: First, *Men and Masculinities in Christianity and Judaism: A Critical Reader* wants to close the still existing gap between the research done by the heterosexual community of scholars and gay religious studies scholars. This separation can be commonly observed in their respective research agendas and publications; it is mirrored also in the organizational split between the AAR's 'Gay Men's Issues in Religion' and 'Men's Studies in Religion' groups. This gap, I believe, can be bridged. Since the *Critical Reader* does not wish to continue the gay/straight dichotomy, it does not, for example, create separate headings for 'gay theology' or 'queer religious studies' sections (as had still been the case in the encyclopedia entry mentioned above), thus implying that 'men's studies' is normative and gay men's studies derivative. Such a division would diminish and distort the accomplishments of gay scholars and the impact they have had on the field as a whole. This volume, instead, offers a balanced blend of contributors who define their gendered and sexed identities in multiple ways.

Second caveat: *Men and Masculinities in Christianity and Judaism* confines itself, as the title suggests, to research relating to the Jewish and Christian traditions. Given the multiple themes and methodologies already present within these two traditions, the deliberate limitation gives this volume additional cohesiveness. It also reflects accurately the current state of the scholarly engagement of men and masculinities in religion. For example, the first panel on religion and masculinities in Islam did not take place until the AAR in Chicago in 2008. Although a few critical contributions on men in other world religions have been written, they would need to be embedded in their own cultural contexts and politics of knowledge. Such a task would be difficult to handle within one single volume. However, it is certainly my hope that another volume will address those issues in the near future, placing them within a global context of other religious traditions, including research in both local geographies and migrant populations.

Third caveat: *Men and Masculinities in Christianity and Judaism* draws heavily on contributions from the North American continent (including a few works from the United Kingdom and South America) because it is here that the field has emerged in the last decades. Besides social forces, critical men's studies in religion also owes its existence to a North American ethos of academic life that is decentralized and fosters independent thinking; this ethos is also guided by a healthy dose of pragmatism that creates room for individual explorations. No doubt, critical men's studies in religion still lingers at the margins of the academic enterprise, but the North American location provided the spaces for inventiveness and creativity needed for a nascent field to establish itself. There is, of course, a risk that – due to its North American origins – this new field will dominate discourses on masculinities as they emerge in other locations. Linguistic hegemony can be one of the reasons why non-English language research gets ignored in an international context. Only recently, for example, German, Swiss and Austrian scholars have begun to publish in the area of 'kritische theologische Männerforschung' (critical theological research on men).[5] The field of critical men's studies in religion cannot afford to become hegemonic itself; hence, the *Critical Reader* also aims to pave the way for future collaboration among scholars from different linguistic backgrounds and different geographic and cultural locations.

A few final words on how the *Critical Reader* came into being and how to read it: The selection of texts happened in four stages. First, I drew up a preliminary list of contributions I deemed relevant to this volume. Second, I contacted about a dozen scholars who, in the past, have been engaged in the study of men and masculinities in Judaism and Christianity. I asked them a simple question: 'If you would have to name the three most important articles or chapter-length contributions to the field, which ones would you choose?' Their responses helped to cast a wider net and also served as a check against my own scholarly preferences and personal biases. The collegial correspondence created a short-term, virtual community of scholars and also generated a fine and representative list of titles. Third, with a semi-consensual list in hand, I thoroughly scoured the available scholarly writings in men's studies in Christianity and Judaism and came up with material about triple the size of this volume. Finally, for each entry I considered various alternatives. I paid attention to unnecessary repetition and decided to select only one contribution per author – although, certainly, many of the selected authors have produced other noteworthy and excellent work on men and religion. I also shortened the original lengths of several of the contributions (with permission from the authors), indicating the places of missing text by inserting an ellipsis in square brackets, and changed all footnoting and references to adhere to the same format. Not all of the authors I chose for the *Critical Reader* would conceive of themselves as primarily, or necessarily, operating within men's studies in religion. Although I do believe that each of them has made significant contributions to the critical study of men and religion, I do not claim that they agree with my definitions, observations, and descriptions of the field.

The seven parts of this volume are not organized according to methodology, although, at first, I was tempted to do so. I eventually discarded this principle given that the majority of contributions cannot be neatly packaged into method- and discipline-based differences. Most of the research crosses boundaries, driven by several reasons: to get a handle on recalcitrant materials, to delve into counter-normative readings, to deconstruct and reassemble traditionally held assumptions, and to engage creatively the religious imagination. The following brief descriptors may, however, provide a quick orientation:

- Parts 1 and 2 ('In the Beginning' and 'A New Field Takes Shape') assemble introductory materials. Whereas Part 1 offers chapters by four influential thinkers who laid the groundwork for a gendered reading of men and religion, Part 2 traces the beginnings of 'men's studies in religion' as an academic field.
- Part 3, 'Theorizing and Theologizing Alternative Masculinities', offers new theological and theoretical conceptualizations of men and masculinities.
- Part 4, 'Biblical Musings', is more hermeneutic in outlook and contains four thought-provoking chapters on interpreting and appropriating biblical Scriptures.
- With Part 5, 'Masculine Ideals in the Jewish and Christian Traditions', one enters historical territory, stretching from late antiquity to the twentieth century, from Syria to the United States.
- The chapters of Part 6 ('Spirituality and the Intimate Body') engage the modes

of discernment of practical theology, ethical thought and the history of sexuality when tackling concerns regarding male desire and embodiment.
• Finally, Part 7 ('Gender, Justice, and Community') moves within a framework
best described as a blend of social ethics and liberation theology.

This brief overview must be read as signposts that can take the reader only so
far. Hence, each section will begin with a succinct introductory narrative that
addresses the context and background of the debates, challenges, and predica-
ments. Introductory narratives for each author also provide cross-references
between the volume's contributions and, where and when appropriate, point out
how authors have referred to and built upon each other's work. Furthermore, a
list of publications by the same author as well as suggestions for further reading
are provided.

Notes

1 See, for example, Kaufman (1987), Jardine and Smith (1987), Clatterbaugh (1990),
May and Strikwerda (1992), Middleton (1992), Connell (1995), Kimmel (1996), Adams
and Savran (2002), and Hanisch (2005).

2 The American Academy of Religion is a professional association of scholars
and teachers of religion with over 10,000 members. Founded in 1964, the current
mission statement emphasizes the 'critical need for ongoing reflection upon and
understanding of religious traditions' and for the 'furthering of knowledge of religion and religious institutions in all their forms and manifestations'
(www.aarweb.org/About_AAR/Mission_Statement/default.asp).

3 Only two authors, James Nelson and Seth Mirsky, contributed chapters to both
volumes.

4 To avoid duplications, I have decided not to reprint any of the contributions
contained in these volumes, although *Men and Masculinities in Christianity and Judaism*
does include authors who have also written for *Redeeming Men* and *Men's Bodies,
Men's Gods* (in alphabetical order, Garth Baker-Fletcher, Stephen Boyd, Harry Brod,
J. Michael Clark, Philip Culbertson, Howard Eilberg-Schwartz, Scott Haldemann,
Björn Krondorfer and James Nelson). This *Critical Reader*, hence, not only complements *Redeeming Men* and *Men's Bodies, Men's Gods* but also augments, expands,
updates and redefines the status of this field of scholarly inquiry.

5 See Wacker and Rieger-Goertz (2006), Schürger et al. (2007), Fischer (2008),
Mayordomo (2008), and Walz and Plüss (2008).

Literature

Adams, Rachel and David Savran (eds). 2002. *The Masculinity Studies Reader.* Oxford:
Blackwell.
Boswell, John. 1980. *Christianity, Social Tolerance, and Homosexuality: Gay People in
Western Europe from the Beginning of the Christian Era to the Fourteenth Century.*
Chicago: The University of Chicago Press.
Boyd, Stephen B., Merle Longwood and Mark Muesse (eds). 1996. *Redeeming Men:
Religion and Masculinities.* Louisville: Westminster John Knox.

Brod, Harry (ed.). 1987. *The Making of Masculinities: The New Men's Studies*. London: Routledge.

Brod, Harry and Michael Kaufman (eds). 1994. *Theorizing Masculinities*. Thousand Oaks and London: Sage.

Clatterbaugh, Kenneth. 1990. *Contemporary Perspectives on Masculinity: Men, Women, and Politics in Modern Society*. Boulder: Westview Press.

Connell, R. W. 1995. *Masculinities*. Berkeley: University of California Press.

Culbertson, Philip. 1992. *New Adam: The Future of Male Spirituality*. Minneapolis: Fortress.

Eilberg-Schwartz, Howard. 1994. *God's Phallus: And Other Problems for Men and Monotheism*. Boston: Beacon.

Fischer, Martin. 2008. *Männermacht und Männerleid: Kritische theologische Männerforschung im Kontext genderperspektivierter Theologie als Beitrag zu einer Gleichstellung der Geschlechter*. Göttingen: Edition Ruprecht.

Hanisch, Ernst. 2005. *Männlichkeiten: Eine andere Geschichte des 20. Jahrhunderts*. Wien: Böhlan Verlag.

Jardine, Alice and Paul Smith (eds). 1987. *Men in Feminism*. New York and London: Methuen.

Kaufman, Michael (ed.). 1987. *Beyond Patriarchy: Essays by Men on Pleasure, Power, and Change*. Toronto and New York: Oxford University Press.

Kimmel, Michael. 1996. *Manhood in America: A Cultural History*. New York: The Free Press.

Krondorfer, Björn (ed.). 1996. *Men's Bodies, Men's Gods: Male Identities in a (Post-) Christian Culture*. New York: New York University Press.

Krondorfer, Björn and Philip Culbertson. 2004. 'Men Studies in Religion,' in *Encyclopedia of Religion*, 2nd edition (vol. 9), ed.-in-chief Lindsay Jones. Detroit and New York: Macmillan. Pp. 5861–5.

Lofton, Kathryn. 2004. 'The Man Stays in the Picture: Recent Works in Religion and Masculinity.' *Religious Studies Review* 30/1 (January):23–8.

May, Larry and Robert Strikwerda (eds). 1992. *Rethinking Masculinity: Philosophical Explorations in Light of Feminism*. Lanham: Littlefield Adams.

Mayordomo, Moisés. 2008. 'Konstruktionen von Männlichkeit in der Antike und der paulinischen Korintherkorrespondenz.' *Evangelische Theologie* 68/2:99–115.

Middleton, Peter. 1992. *The Inward Gaze: Masculinity and Subjectivity in Modern Culture*. Routledge: London.

Schürger, Wolfgang, Christian J. Herz and Michael Brinkschröder (eds). 2007. *Schwule Theologie: Identität – Spiritualität – Kontexte*. Stuttgart: Kohlhammer.

Wacker, Marie-Theres and Stefanie Rieger-Goertz (eds). 2006. *Mannsbilder: Kritische Männerforschung und theologische Frauenforschung im Gespräch*. Münster: LIT.

Walz, Heike and David Plüss (eds). 2008. *Theologie und Geschlecht: Dialoge Querbeet*. Münster: LIT.

Part 1

In the Beginning

Sometimes, a paradigm shift has to occur before people can embrace radically different approaches to the understanding of already existing issues. At other times, it is the insistent nudging of individuals that eventually entices others to join new scholarly explorations, frequently against the resistance of entrenched positions. In the case of the emergent awareness about 'men' in religion, it was the latter rather than the former that generated change.

In Part 1, we will meet four scholars who have been 'nudging' their colleagues in the 1970s and 1980s to take seriously the gendered experiences of men in religion, at a time before these issues coalesced into their own discrete field of inquiry: specifically, Mary Daly, John Boswell, Michel Foucault and James Nelson. Of these four, it is James Nelson who directly addresses the theological need to reflect on the experiences of heterosexual men. In so many ways, his writings can be seen as precursor to the critical study of men in religion. By contrast, Mary Daly speaks to women's experiences only. In the process of thinking and writing about women, she had come to realize that in order to recover women's way of being in the world she had to resist the infiltration of any patriarchal practices and mentalities into her thought. Her radical critique contains a challenge to the study of men that cannot be ignored. John Boswell's work demonstrates another venue through which the question of men in the history of religion was put on the scholarly agenda. The 1980 publication of his book *Christianity, Social Tolerance, and Homosexuality*, which generated enormous attention, opened the way to the serious study of the history of homosexuality and hence, by extension, to the study of gay religious experiences. Finally, Michel Foucault, philosopher and cultural theorist, must be included among those who have deeply influenced the study of men in religion. In particular, his observations on, and theoretical frameworks about, the Christian roots of modern discourses on sexuality have been picked up in subsequent research on gender and religion.

The Final Cause: The Cause of Causes

Editor's Introduction

Awareness of gender was not first generated by the men's movement. The passionate and radical call for change – a paradigm shift of sorts – occurred when the women's movement in the second half of the twentieth century, in an uphill battle, put women's equality and questions of gender justice on the social and political agenda. The liberal women's movement, guided by practical concerns (suffrage, equal rights, reproductive rights, equal pay, concerns about shared childcare and housework, etc.), based its persuasive appeal on women's experiences, and the radical women's movement, concomitantly, reassessed the grounds from which social and political theory had to be built up. Women put forth a challenge to gender entrenchments in all walks of life, whether the judiciary, the work place, the private home, religious institutions or academic life. Few men were ready to abandon their intellectual positions and their status of unquestioned privilege; hence, the feminist challenge was, for a long time, not reciprocated by men querying critically their own attachments to patriarchal traditions. Change was slow to come (Segal 1990).

Regarding religion, it was also women who first put the question of gender equality and gender justice on the table. There were, of course, women who had worked toward the awareness of women in religion earlier, like the nineteenth-century Elizabeth Cady Stanton, but the movement of feminist theologies did not form until the 1960s, picking up strength and speed in the 1970s (see Grey 1996; May 1996; Plaskow 1996). Christian and Jewish feminists articulated a critique of patriarchy in the history of religions, pointing to the lack of research on women in religion, and suggesting new theoretical and hermeneutical models that would rescue women from oblivion and invisibility. Among the pioneering women scholars of this generation were Letty Russell (1974), Rosemary Radford Ruether (1975; 1983), Carol Christ (1979), Elizabeth Schüssler Fiorenza (1983), Carter Heyward (1984), Judith Plaskow (1990), and, of course, Mary Daly.

Daly promoted perhaps the most radical and uncompromising critique of patriarchal religion. Even though she would not want her work to be understood as a stepping-stone toward a study of *men* and religion, her writings put men into the discomfiting position of explaining what they have so far taken for granted. Back in the early third century, the conservative Latin church father Tertullian had urged the Christian community to 'look to the body' – a 'deceptively simple formula', according to Peter Brown – to provide a vision to the early church by counseling chastity in order to receive the spirit while, at the same time, being able to hold on to the patriarchal household's 'wealth and slaves' and instituting a male 'gerontocracy' (rule of elders) in the church (Brown 1988, 77–9). Now Mary Daly, who herself came from a Catholic background, also looked at the body and formulated, by subverting Tertullian, a similarly effective formula: 'Look to the body: it is male!' When God is conceived as male, then male is divine, with the consequence that women and their experiences are relegated to a subordinate status. Leaving the church, according to the stance that Daly eventually advocated, would be a theologically compelling and reasonable response for women.

In *Beyond God the Father* (1973), a book that has become classic in the literature of feminist theology, Daly argues that the subordination of women has been legitimized through a tangled web of deceptive myths and distorting mirrors. We thus start the *Critical Reader* with a short excerpt from *Beyond God the Father*, in which Daly deconstructs the patriarchal deceptions spun around the biblical myth of creation and, in doing so, shows the generative power of an alternative way of being in this world. Her language in this passage is a fascinating blend of contentious lyricism and poetic analysis, thus counterspinning her own mythic imagery, which she developed further in her later works *Gyn/Ecology* (1978) and *Pure Lust* (1984). The excerpt below appears in the final pages of *Beyond God the Father*, indicating her transition from a critical Catholic theologian – who, in her first book (*The Church and the Second Sex*, 1968), was still somewhat hopeful about positive changes in the church – to a philosophical thinker arguing for the need of the separation of the sexes.

In the chapter below, Daly decries the consequence of deceptions upheld and promoted by religious men: nothing less than the death of all life on this planet! Daly calls upon women to free themselves from these elaborate deceptions – with its 'Magnifying Mirrors', 'Male Mothers' and 'Supernatural Mothers' – and to embrace a different form of living rooted in the restoration of the verb *being*: 'The question–answer is a verb, and when one begins to move in the current of the verb, of the Verb, she knows that she is not a mirror.' Women must extricate themselves from the 'House of Mirrors' that began with the story of Adam and Eve. When women in their sisterhood 'begin to hear and to see and to speak', it will directly affect men: 'Without Magnifying Mirrors all around, men would have to look inside and outside. They would start to look inside, wondering what was wrong with them.' Here, then, lies Daly's profound challenge to men: once the mythic projections are removed, men – the beneficiaries of the old system – lose grip on power and are left with a shattered identity.

For Daly, there is no choice. Not to shatter the House of Mirrors risks the 'freedom-becoming-survival of our species . . . The cost of failure is Nothing.'

Publications by the Same Author

Daly, Mary. 1968. *The Church and the Second Sex*. New York: Harper & Row.
——. 1973. *Beyond God the Father: Toward a Philosophy of Women's Liberation*. Boston: Beacon.
——. 1978. *Gyn/Ecology: The Metaethics of Radical Feminism*. Boston: Beacon.
——. 1984. *Pure Lust: Elemental Feminist Philosophy*. Boston: Beacon.
——. 1992. *Outercourse: The Be-Dazzling Voyage*. San Francisco: HarperSanFrancisco.
——. 1998. *Quintessence . . . Realizing the Archaic Future: A Radical Elemental Feminist Manifesto*. Boston: Beacon.

——. 2006. *Amazon Grace: Re-Calling the Courage to Sin Big*. New York: Palgrave Macmillan.

Further Reading

Brown, Peter. 1988. *The Body and Society: Men, Women and Sexual Renunciation in Early Christianity*. New York: Columbia University Press.

Christ, Carol P. and Judith Plaskow (eds). 1979. *Womanspirit Rising: A Feminist Reader in Religion*. San Francisco: Harper & Row.

Grey, Mary C. 1996. 'Feminist Theologies, European', in *Dictionary of Feminist Theologies*, eds Russell and Clarkson. Pp. 102–04.

Heyward, Carter. 1984. *Our Passion for Justice: Images of Power, Sexuality and Liberation*. New York: Pilgrim.

May, Melanie A. 1996. 'Feminist Theologies, North America', in *Dictionary of Feminist Theologies*, eds Russell and Clarkson. Pp. 106–08.

Plaskow, Judith. 1990. *Standing Again at Sinai: Judaism from a Feminist Perspective*. San Francisco: Harper & Row.

——. 1996. 'Feminist Theologies, Jewish', in *Dictionary of Feminist Theologies*, eds Russell and Clarkson. Pp. 104–06.

Ruether, Rosemary R. 1975. *New Woman, New Earth: Sexist Ideologies and Human Liberation*. New York: Seabury Press.

——. 1983. *Sexism and God-Talk: Toward a Feminist Theology*. Boston: Beacon.

Russell, Letty M. 1974. *Human Liberation in a Feminist Perspective: A Theology*. Philadelphia: Westminster.

Russell, Letty M. and J. Shannon Clarkson (eds). 1996. *Dictionary of Feminist Theologies*. Louisville: Westminster John Knox.

Schüssler Fiorenza, Elisabeth. 1983. *In Memory of Her: A Feminist Theological Reconstruction of Christian Origins*. New York: Crossroads.

Segal, Lynne. 1990. *Slow Motion: Changing Masculinities, Changing Men*. London: Virago.

The Final Cause: The Cause of Causes

MARY DALY

Our planet is inhabited by half-crazed creatures, but there is a consistency in the madness. Virginia Woolf, who died of being both brilliant and female, wrote that women are condemned by society to function as mirrors, reflecting men at twice their actual size. When this basic principle is understood, we can understand something about the dynamics of the Looking Glass society. Let us examine once again the creatures' speech.

That language for millennia has affirmed the fact that Eve was born from Adam, the first among history's unmarried pregnant males who courageously chose childbirth under sedation rather than abortion, consequently obtaining a child-bride. Careful study of the documents recording such achievements of Adam and his sons prepared the way for the arrival of the highest of the higher religions, whose priests took Adam as teacher and model. They devised a sacramental system which functioned magnificently within the sacred House of Mirrors. Graciously, they lifted from women the onerous power of childbirth, christening it 'baptism.' Thus they brought the lowly material function of birth, incompetently and even grudgingly performed by females, to a higher and more spiritual level. Recognizing the ineptitude of females in performing even the humble 'feminine' tasks assigned to them by the Divine Plan, the Looking Glass priests raised these functions to the supernatural level in which they alone had competence. Feeding was elevated to become Holy Communion. Washing achieved dignity in Baptism and Penance. Strengthening became known as Confirmation, and the function of consolation, which the unstable nature of females caused them to perform so inadequately, was raised to a spiritual level and called Extreme Unction. In order to stress the obvious fact that all females are innately disqualified from joining the Sacred Men's Club, the Looking Glass priests made it a rule that their members should wear skirts. To make the point clearer, they reserved special occasions when additional Men's Club attire should be worn. These necessary accoutrements included delicate white lace tops and millinery of prescribed shapes and colors. The leaders were required to wear silk hose, pointed hats, crimson dresses, and ermine capes, thereby stressing detachment from lowly material things and dedication to the exercise of spiritual talent. They thus became revered models of spiritual transsexualism.

These anointed Male Mothers, who naturally are called Fathers, felt maternal concern for the women entrusted to their pastoral care. Although females obviously are by nature incompetent and prone to mental and emotional confusion, they are required by the Divine Plan as vessels to contain the seeds of men so that men can be born and then supernaturally (correctly) reborn as citizens of the Heavenly Kingdom. Therefore in charity the priests encouraged women to throw themselves gratefully into their unique role as containers for the sons of the sons of the Son of God. Sincerely moved by the fervor of their own words, the priests educated women to accept this privilege with awe-struck humility.

Since the Protestant Reformation, spiritual Looking Glass education has been modernized in some roots of the House of Mirrors. Reformed Male Mothers gradually came to feel that Maleness was overstressed by wearing dresses all the time and even decided to include a suitable proportion of females (up to one half of one percent) among their membership, thereby stressing that the time for Male Snobbism was over and the time for Democracy had come. They also came to realize that they could be just as supernatural without being hemmed in by a stiff sacramental system. They could give birth spiritually, heal and console, and give maternal advice. They therefore continued the Looking Glass tradition of Mother Adam while at the same time making a smooth transition to The Modern Age.

Thus, Western culture was gracefully prepared by its Supernatural Mothers called Fathers to see all things supernaturally, that is, to perceive the world backward clearly. In fact, so excellent had been our education that this kind of thinking has become like second nature for almost everybody. No longer in need of spiritual guidance, our culture has come of age. This fact is evident to anyone who will listen to it when it talks. Its statesmen clear-headedly affirm the fact that this is 'the Free World.' Its newscasters accurately report that there has been fighting in the demilitarized zone, that several people were killed in a non-violent demonstration, that 'our nation' is fighting to bring peace to Southeast Asia. Its psychiatrists proclaim that the entire society is in fact a mental institution and applaud this fact as a promising omen of increasing health for their profession.

In the Looking Glass society females, that is, Magnifying Mirrors, play a crucial role. But males have realized that it would serve no good purpose if this were to become known by females, who then might stop looking into the toy mirrors they have been taught to use incessantly. They might then begin looking inside or outside or backward or forward. Instead of settling for the vanity of parakeets they might fall into the sin of pride and refuse to be Magnifying Mirrors any longer.

The females, in the terrifying, exhilarating experience of becoming rather than reflecting, would discover that they too have been infected by the dynamics of the Mirror World. Having learned only to mirror, they would find in themselves reflections of the sickness in their masters. They would find themselves doing the same things, fighting the same way. Looking inside for something there, they would be confused by what at first would appear to be an endless Hall of Mirrors. What to copy? What model to imitate? Where to look? What is a mere mirror to do? But wait—how could a mere mirror even frame such a question? The question itself is the beginning of an answer that keeps unfolding itself. The question–answer is a verb, and when one begins to move in the current of the verb, of the Verb, she knows that she is not a mirror. Once she knows this she knows it so deeply that she cannot completely forget. She knows it so deeply that she has to say it to her sisters. What if more and more of her sisters should begin to hear and to see and to speak?

This would be a disaster. It would throw the whole society backward into the future. Without Magnifying Mirrors all around, men would have to look inside and outside. They would start to look inside, wondering what was wrong with them. They would have to look outside because without the mirrors they would begin to receive impressions from real Things out there. They would even have to look at women, instead of reflections. This would be confusing and they would be forced to look inside again, only to have the harrowing experience of finding *there* the Eternal Woman, the Perfect Parakeet. Desperately looking outside again, they would find that the Parakeet is no longer *out there*. Dashing back inside, males would find other horrors: All of the other Others—the whole crowd—would be in there: the lazy niggers, the dirty Chicanos, the greedy Jews, faggots and dykes, plus the entire crowd of Communists and the backward population of the Third World. Looking outward again, mirrorless males would be forced to see—people. Where to go? Paroxysm toward the Omega Point? But without the Magnifying Mirror even that last refuge is gone. What to do for relief? Send more bombing missions? But no. It is pointless to be killing The Enemy after you find out The Enemy is yourself.

But the Looking Glass Society is still there, bent on killing itself off. It is still ruled by God the Father who, gazing at his magnified reflections, believes in his superior size. I say 'believes,' because the reflection now occasionally seems to be diminished and so he has to make a renewed act of faith in Himself.

We have been locked in this Eden of his far too long. If we stay much longer, life *will* depart from this planet. The freedom to fall out of Eden will cost a mirror-shattering experience. The freedom-becoming-survival of our species will require a continual, communal striving in be-ing. This means forging the great chain of be-ing in sisterhood that can surround nonbeing, forcing it to shrink back into itself. The cost of failure is Nothing.

Is this the war to end wars? The power of sisterhood is not war-power. There have been and will be conflicts, but the Final Cause causes not by conflict but by attraction. Not by the attraction of a Magnet that is All There, but by the creative drawing power of the Good Who is self-communicating Be-ing, Who is the Verb from whom, in whom, and with whom all true movements move.

2

Christianity, Social Tolerance, and Homosexuality

Editor's Introduction

John Boswell, professor of history, died of AIDS-related causes in 1994. He is best known for his book *Christianity, Social Tolerance, and Homosexuality*, which he published in 1980 at the age of 33. It is only fitting to use part of his 'Introduction' in the *Critical Reader* to convey his basic ideas. In 1994, shortly before he died, Boswell published his fourth and last book, *Same-Sex Unions in Premodern Europe*, for which he gained, as with his earlier work, both instant recognition and criticism. Why did his work create such a commotion in the scholarly world and popular press?

The completion of *Christianity, Social Tolerance, and Homosexuality* came at a time when the gay rights movement had taken strident steps toward the recognition and acceptance of gay men within the social fabric of America. The 1969 Stonewall Riots in New York City had triggered an outburst of public visibility and celebration of gay life. Though these advances were accompanied by various assaults on gay men's rights, the AIDS crisis had not yet fully struck the community. In 1980, the year of the book's publication, the first American gay men were already dying from the disease, but the severity of the threat was not yet known. Hence, in 1980 the general population was willing, at least to a degree, to tolerate a different lifestyle, and Boswell's book spoke to both the issue of toleration and the (religious) history of homosexuality. No longer treated as an arcane subject or, equally dismissive, with caution and disdain, homosexuality became 'a legitimate field of historical study' that was as 'useful as a modern gauge of social tolerance as studies of past attitudes toward women or religious minorities' (Kuefler 2006, 2). In a volume appraising and assessing the influence of *Christianity, Social Tolerance, and Homosexuality* 25 years after its publication, Kuefler sums up succinctly Boswell's overall argument:

> There were four main points that form the narrative of the book: First, that Christianity had come into existence in an atmosphere of Greek and Roman tolerance for same-sex eroticism. Second, that nothing in the Christian scriptures or early tradition required a hostile assessment of homosexuality; rather, that such assessments represented a misreading of scripture. Third, that early medieval Christians showed no real animosity toward same-sex eroticism. Fourth, that it was only in the twelfth and thirteenth centuries that Christian writers formulated a significant hostility toward homosexuality, and then

read that hostility back into their scriptures and early tradition ... Taken together, we might consider these arguments as the Boswell Thesis. (Kuefler 2006, 2–3)

Although some of Boswell's historical and theoretical claims have come under critique by his colleagues – among them, for example, David Halperin (1990; see Kuefler 2006, 6–20; also Jordan, chapter 21) – the book's lasting impact may not be grounded so much in the details of its research as in its general encouragement to reassess Christian attitudes toward homoeroticism and, indirectly, to take seriously the spiritual experiences of gay men past and present.

Publications by the Same Author

Boswell, John. 1980. *Christianity, Social Tolerance, and Homosexuality: Gay People in Western Europe from the Beginning of the Christian Era to the Fourteenth Century.* Chicago: Chicago University Press.
——. 1988. *The Kindness of Strangers: The Abandonment of Children in Western Europe from Late Antiquity to the Renaissance.* New York: Pantheon Books.
——. 1994. *Same-Sex Unions in Premodern Europe.* New York: Villard.

Further Reading

Halperin, David. 1990. *One Hundred Years of Homosexuality and Other Essays on Greek Love.* New York: Routledge.
Kuefler, Mathew (ed.). 2006. *The Boswell Thesis: Essays on Christianity, Social Tolerance, and Homosexuality.* Chicago: Chicago University Press.

Christianity, Social Tolerance, and Homosexuality: Introduction

JOHN BOSWELL

Between the beginning of the Christian Era and the end of the Middle Ages, European attitudes toward a number of minorities underwent profound transformations. Many groups of people passed from constituting undistinguished parts of the mainstream of society to comprising segregated, despised, and sometimes severely oppressed fringe groups. Indeed the Middle Ages are often imagined to have been a time of almost universal intolerance of nonconformity, and the adjective 'medieval' is not infrequently used as a synonym for 'narrow-minded,' 'oppressive,' or 'intolerant' in the context of behavior or attitudes. It is not, however, accurate or useful to picture medieval Europe and its institutions as singularly and characteristically intolerant. Many other periods have been equally if not more prone to social intolerance:[1] most European minorities fared worse during the 'Renaissance' than during the 'Dark Ages,' and no other century has witnessed anti-Semitism of such destructive virulence as that of the twentieth. Moreover, treating these two subjects—intolerance and medieval Europe—as if each were in some sense a historical explanation of the other almost wholly precludes understanding of either one. The social history of medieval Europe and, perhaps even more, the historical origins and operations of intolerance as a social phenomenon require far subtler analysis.

This study is offered as a contribution to better understanding of both the social history of Europe in the Middle Ages and intolerance as a historical force, in the form of an investigation of their interaction in a single case.[2] [. . .]

Of the various groups which became the objects of intolerance in Europe during the Middle Ages, gay people[3] are the most useful for this study for a number of reasons. Some of these are relatively obvious. Unlike Jews and Muslims, they were dispersed throughout the general population everywhere in Europe; they constituted a substantial minority in every age—rather than in a few periods, like heretics or witches—but they were never (unlike the poor, for instance) more than a minority of the population. Intolerance of gay people cannot for the most part be confused with medical treatment, as in the case of lepers or the insane, or with protective surveillance, as in the case of the deaf or, in some societies, women. Moreover, hostility to gay people provides singularly revealing examples of the confusion of religious beliefs with popular prejudice. Apprehension of this confusion is fundamental to understanding many kinds of intolerance, but it is not usually possible until either the prejudice or the religious beliefs have become so attenuated that it is difficult to imagine there was ever any integral connection between them. As long as the religious beliefs which support a particular prejudice are generally held by a population, it is virtually impossible to separate the two; once the beliefs are abandoned, the separation may be so complete that the original connection becomes all but incomprehensible. For example, it is now as much an article of faith in most European countries that Jews should not be oppressed because of their religious beliefs as it was in the fourteenth century that they should be; what seemed to many Christians of premodern Europe a cardinal religious duty— the conversion of Jews—would seem to most adherents of the same religious tradition today an unconscionable invasion of the privacy of their countrymen. The intermingling of religious principles and prejudice against the Jews in the fourteenth century was so thorough that very few Christians could distinguish them at all; in the twentieth century the separation effected on the issue has become so pronounced that most modern Christians question the sincerity of medieval oppression based on religious conviction. Only during a period in which the confusion of religion and bigotry persisted but was not ubiquitous or unchallenged would it be easy to analyze the organic relation of the two in a convincing and accessible way.

The modern West appears to be in just such a period of transition regarding various groups distinguished sexually, and gay people provide a particularly useful focus for the study of the history of such attitudes.[4] Since they are still the objects of severe proscriptive legislation, widespread public hostility, and various civil restraints, all with ostensibly religious justification, it is far easier to elucidate the confusion of religion and intolerance in their case than in that of blacks, moneylenders, Jews, divorced persons, or others whose status in society has so completely ceased to be associated with religious conviction that the correlation—even if demonstrated at length—now seems limited, tenuous, or accidental.

Much of the present volume, on the other hand, is specifically intended to rebut the common idea that religious belief—Christian or other—has been the *cause* of intolerance in regard to gay people. Religious beliefs may cloak or incorporate intolerance, especially among adherents of revealed religions which specifically reject rationality as an ultimate criterion of judgment or tolerance as a major goal in human relations. But careful analysis can almost always differentiate between conscientious application of religious ethics and the use of religious precepts as justification for personal animosity or prejudice. If religious strictures are used to justify oppression by people who regularly disregard precepts of equal gravity from the same moral code, or if prohibitions which restrain a disliked minority are upheld in their most literal sense as absolutely inviolable while comparable precepts affecting the majority are relaxed or reinterpreted, one must suspect something other than religious belief as the motivating cause of the oppression.

In the particular case at issue, the belief that the hostility of the Christian Scriptures to homosexuality caused Western society to turn against it should not require any elaborate refutation. The very same books which are thought to condemn homosexual acts condemn hypocrisy in the most strident terms, and on greater authority: and yet Western society did not create any social taboos against hypocrisy, did not claim that hypocrites were 'unnatural,' did not segregate them into an oppressed minority, did not enact laws punishing their sin with castration or death. No Christian state, in fact, has passed laws against hypocrisy per se, despite its continual and explicit condemnation by Jesus and the church. In the very same list which has been claimed to exclude from the kingdom of heaven those guilty of homosexual practices, the greedy are also excluded. And yet no medieval states burned the greedy at the stake. Obviously some factors beyond biblical precedent were at work in late medieval states which licensed prostitutes[5] but burned gay people: by any objective standard, there is far more objurgation of prostitution in the New Testament than of homosexuality. Biblical strictures have been employed with great selectivity by all Christian states, and in a historical context what determines the selection is clearly the crucial issue.

Another advantage in employing gay people as the focus of this study is the continued vitality of ideas about the 'danger' they pose to society. Almost all prejudice purports to be a rational response to some threat or danger: every despised group is claimed to threaten those who despise it; but it is usually easy to show that even if some danger exists, it is not the origin of the prejudice. The 'threat' posed by most groups previously oppressed by Christian society (e.g., 'witches,' moneylenders), however, now seems so illusory that it is difficult for modern readers to imagine that intelligent people of the past could actually have been troubled by such anxieties. In fact one is apt to dismiss such imagined dangers out of hand as willful misrepresentations flagrantly employed to justify oppression. Not only is this untrue; it obscures the more important realities of the relationship between intolerance and fear.

No such skepticism obscures this relationship in the case of gay people. The belief that they constitute some sort of threat is still so widespread that an assumption to the contrary may appear partisan in some circles, and those who subscribe to the notion that gay people are in some way dangerous may argue that for this very reason they are not typical victims of intolerance.

It should be noted that whether a group actually threatens society or not is not directly relevant to the issue of intolerance unless the hostility the group experiences can be shown to stem from a rational apprehension of that threat. Traveling gypsies may actually have been at some point a hazard to isolated communities if they carried infections and diseases to which local residents had no immunity, but it would be injudicious to assume that it was this threat which resulted in antipathy toward them, particularly when it can be shown that such hostility antedates by centuries any realization of the communicability of most infections and when the content of antigypsy rhetoric bears no relation to disease at all.

The claims about the precise nature of the threat posed by gay people have varied extravagantly over time, sometimes contradicting each other directly and almost invariably entailing striking internal inconsistencies. [. . .] It may be worth alluding here to two of the most persistent.

The first is the ancient claim that societies tolerating or approving homosexual behavior do so to their own manifest detriment, since if all their members engaged in such behavior, these societies would die out. This argument assumes—curiously—that all humans would become exclusively homosexual if given the chance. There seems to be no reason to make such an assumption: a great deal of evidence contradicts it. It is possible that the abandonment of social sanctions against homosexuality occasions some increase in overt homosexual behavior, even among persons who would not otherwise try it; it is even conceivable (though not at all certain) that more people will adopt exclusively homosexual lifestyles in societies with tolerant attitudes. But the fact that a characteristic increases does not demonstrate its danger to the society; many characteristics which, if adopted universally, would presumably redound to the disadvantage of society (e.g., voluntary celibacy, self-sacrifice) may nonetheless increase over periods of time without causing harm and are often highly valued by a culture precisely because of their statistical rarity. To assume that any characteristic that increases under favorable conditions will in the course of time eliminate all competing characteristics is bad biology and bad history. No current scientific theories regarding the etiology of homosexuality suggest that social tolerance determines its incidence. Even purely biological theories uniformly assume that it would be a minority preference under any conditions, no matter how favorable.[6]

Moreover, there is no compelling reason to assume that homosexual desire induces nonreproductivity in individuals or population groups.[7] No evidence supports the common idea that homosexual and heterosexual behavior are incompatible; much data suggests the contrary.[8] The fact that gay people (definitionally) prefer erotic contact with their own gender would imply a lower overall rate of reproductive success for them only if it could be shown that in human populations sexual desire is a major factor in such success. Intuition notwithstanding, this does not appear to be the case.

Only in societies like modern industrial nations which insist that erotic energy be focused exclusively on one's permanent legal spouse would most gay people be expected to marry and produce offspring less often than their nongay counterparts, and it appears that even in these cultures a significant proportion of gay people—possibly a majority—do marry and have children. In other societies (probably most literate premodern cultures), where procreation is separable from erotic commitment and rewarded by enhanced status or economic advantages (or is simply a common personal ambition), there would be no reason for gay people not to reproduce.[9] With the exception of the clergy, most of the gay people discussed in the present study were married and had children. The persistence of the belief in the nonreproductivity of gay people must be ascribed to a tendency to notice and remember what is unusual about individuals rather than what is expected. Far fewer people are aware that Oscar Wilde was a husband and father than that he was gay and had a male lover. [. . .]

The second threat which might be adduced as explanation of intolerance of homosexuality relates to its 'naturalness.' May it not be that human society reacts with hostility to gay people because their preferences are inherently 'unnatural'? [. . .] The idea that homosexuality is 'unnatural' (perhaps introduced by a chance remark of Plato)[10] became widespread in the ancient world due to the triumph of 'ideal' concepts of nature over 'realistic' ones. Especially during the centuries immediately following the rise of Christianity, philosophical schools of thought using idealized 'nature' as the touchstone of human ethics exercised a profound influence on Western thought and popularized the notion that all nonprocreative sexuality was 'unnatural.' Although this argument subsequently fell into disfavor, it was revived by Scholastics in the thirteenth century and came to be a decisive, even controlling concept in all branches of learning, from the technical sciences to dogmatic theology. The scientific, philosophical, and even moral considerations that underlay this approach have since been almost wholly discredited and are consciously rejected by most educated persons, but the emotional impact of terms like 'unnatural' and 'against nature' persists. Although the idea that gay people are 'violating nature' predates by as much as two millennia the rise of modern science and is based on concepts wholly alien to it, many people unthinkingly transfer the ancient prejudice to an imagined scientific frame of reference, without recognizing the extreme contradictions involved, and conclude that homosexual behavior violates the 'nature' described by modern scientists rather than the 'nature' idealized by ancient philosophers. [. . .]

In addition to casting a clearer light on the relationship of intolerance and religious beliefs and imaginary dangers to society, the study of prejudice against gay people affords, as the final advantage to be discussed here, revealing insights into the similarities and differences of intolerance toward many different groups and characteristics. In a number of ways the separate histories of Europe's minorities are the same story, and many parallels have been drawn in this study with groups whose histories relate to or reflect the history of gay people. Most societies, for instance, which freely tolerate religious diversity also accept sexual variation, and the fate of Jews and gay people has been almost identical throughout European history, from early Christian hostility to extermination in concentration camps. The same laws which oppressed Jews oppressed gay people; the same groups bent on eliminating Jews tried to wipe out homosexuality; the same periods of European history which could not make room for Jewish distinctiveness reacted violently against sexual nonconformity; the same countries which insisted on religious uniformity imposed majority standards of sexual conduct; and even the same methods of propaganda were used against Jews and gay people—picturing them as animals bent on the destruction of the children of the majority.[11]

But there are significant differences, and these bear heavily on the present analysis. Judaism, for example, is consciously passed from parents to children, and it has been able to transmit, along with its ethical precepts, political wisdom gleaned from centuries of oppression and harassment: advice about how to placate, reason with, or avoid hostile majorities; how and when to maintain a low profile; when to make public gestures; how to conduct business with potential enemies. Moreover, it has been able to offer its adherents at least the solace of solidarity in the face of oppression. Although European ghettos kept the Jews in, they also kept the Gentiles out; and Jewish family life flourished as the main social outlet for a group cut off from the majority at many points in its history, imparting to individual Jews a sense not only of community in the present but of belonging to the long and hallowed traditions of those who went before.

Gay people are for the most part not born into gay families. They suffer oppression individually and alone, without benefit of advice or frequently even emotional support from relatives or friends. This makes their case more comparable in some ways to that of the blind or left-handed, who are also dispersed in the general population rather than segregated by heritage and who also are in many cultures the victims of intolerance. Gay people are even more revealing than most such dispersed minorities, however, because they are usually socialized through adulthood as ordinary members of society, since parents rarely realize that children are gay until they are fully grown. Their reactions and the reactions of those hostile to them thus illustrate intolerance in a relatively uncomplicated form, with no extraneous variable such as atypical socialization, inability to contribute to society, or even visible abnormality. In every way but one, most gay people are just like those around them, and antipathy toward them is for this reason an unusually illuminating instance of intolerance.

Only when social attitudes are favorable do gay people tend to form visible subcultures. In hostile societies they become invisible, a luxury afforded them by the essentially private nature of their variation from the norm, but one which greatly increases their isolation and drastically reduces their lobbying effectiveness. When good times return, there is no mechanism to encourage steps to prevent a recurrence of oppression: no gay grandparents who remember the pogroms, no gay exile literature to remind the living of the fate of the dead, no liturgical commemorations of times of crisis and suffering. Relatively few gay people today are aware of the great variety of positions in which time has placed their kind, and in previous societies almost none seem to have had such awareness.

Because of this, except in cases where they happen to wield considerable authority, gay people have been all but totally dependent on popular attitudes toward them for freedom, a sense of identity, and in many cases survival. The history of public reactions to homosexuality is thus in some measure a history of social tolerance generally.

It is only fair to point out that in addition to the advantages of using gay people to study intolerance, there are several salient disadvantages. The most fundamental of these is the fact that the longevity of prejudice against gay people and their sexuality has resulted in the deliberate falsification of historical records concerning them well into the present century, rendering accurate reconstruction of their history particularly difficult. [. . .] As in most matters, half-truths are more misleading than whole lies, and the historian's greatest difficulties are presented by slight twists of meaning in translations which appear to be complete and frank. [. . .]

It is little wonder that accurate analysis of gay people in a historical context is so rare when such formidable barriers oppose access to the sources for anyone not proficient in ancient and medieval languages. Even those who have taken the trouble to learn the requisite tongues find that most lexical aids decline to comment on the meaning of terms related to acts of which the lexicographers disapprove; only painstaking collation and very extensive reading in the sources enables the investigator to uncover with any degree of accuracy the actions and attitudes of previous cultures which have not suited the tastes of modern scholarship. Until a new generation of translators has removed the fig leaves, research on a large scale will be difficult.

A second difficulty in investigating this type of intolerance is presented by the fact that it concerns sexual and emotional matters which are essentially personal[12] and would tend not to occur in official documents except in societies characterized by hostility to such feelings, where legal measures have been taken to suppress them. Even this sort of record, however, is treacherous: it would certainly be a mistake to draw conclusions about the position of gay people in most American cities from the legal strictures theoretically affecting them, and previous studies of this subject have doubtless erred in laying too much stress on the existence of restrictive statutes. Simply noting that something is illegal may be grossly misleading if one does not also comment on the extent to which such laws are honored, supported, or generally approved.

The monuments of love are principally literary: what bills of sale and tax records are to economic history, poems and letters are to the history of personal relations and attitudes toward them. As a consequence, [a study like this relies] rather more than most historical texts on literary sources. Such works often concentrate on the unusual and may present the bizarre rather than the ordinary, but this is also true of more conventional historical sources, which usually record events of note rather than common occurrences. [. . .]

A final disadvantage, the difficulty of avoiding anachronistic stereotypes, is a much more serious scholarly problem for both the author and the readers of a study of this type. It is unlikely that at any time in Western history have gay people been the victims of more widespread and vehement intolerance than during the first half of the twentieth century, and drawing inferences about homosexuality from observations of gay people in modern Western nations cannot be expected to yield generalizations more accurate or objective than inferences made about Jews in Nazi Germany or blacks in the antebellum South. Until very recently only the tiniest percentage of gay people have been willing to identify themselves publicly, and such persons, given the reactions they could reasonably expect, must have been atypical.

As a consequence, one must be extremely cautious about projecting onto historical data ideas about gay people inferred from modern samples which may be entirely atypical. The idea that gay men are less masculine, for instance, and gay women less feminine is almost certainly the result of antipathy to homosexuality rather than empirical observation. The universal expectation in cultures intolerant of gay people that males will be erotically affected only by what the culture regards as feminine—and females only by culturally defined masculinity—leads inevitably to the anticipation that males who wish to attract other males will be 'feminine' and females erotically interested in females will be 'masculine.' Atypical conformity to gender expectations appears in fact to be randomly distributed in most populations, completely independent of sexual preference; but if even a very small percentage of gay women are more masculine or a very few gay men more feminine than their nongay counterparts, they will corroborate the stereotype in the mind of a public predisposed to believe it and usually possessed of no large sampling as a control. (Effeminate nongay men or masculine heterosexual women are ignored, if possible, or considered part of the normal range of human adaptation.)

It must not be supposed, however, that such stereotypes affected more tolerant societies, or that any connection between homosexuality and 'inappropriate' gender behavior[13] was assumed. On the contrary, among ancient peoples who acknowledged the likelihood and propriety of erotic interest between persons of the same gender it was often assumed that men who loved other men would be more masculine than their heterosexual counterparts, by the logical (if unconvincing) argument that men who loved men would emulate them and try to be like them, while men who loved women would become like women, i.e., 'effeminate.' (The obverse would presumably be true of women, but in every age anxiety about female gender roles seems to have been less acute.) Aristophanes' speech in the *Symposium* of Plato is probably the most blatant example of this counterprejudice. 'Those who love men and rejoice to lie with and be embraced by men are also the finest boys and young men, being naturally the most manly. The people who accuse them of shamelessness lie; they do this not from shamelessness but from courage, manliness, and virility, embracing what is like them. A clear proof of this is the fact that as adults they alone acquit themselves as men in public careers' (192A; cf. Phaedrus's speech. This passage may be a caricature, but it is no less revealing for that).

An equation of homosexuality with effeminacy in men would hardly have occurred to people whose history, art, popular literature, and religious myths were all filled with the homosexual exploits of such archetypally masculine figures as Zeus, Hercules, Achilles, et al. Plato argued that pairs of homosexual lovers would make the best soldiers (*Symposium* 178E–179; cf. Aristotle *Politics* 2.6.6), and the Thebans actually formed an army of such pairs in what turned out to an extraordinarily successful experiment. In Greek debates about the relative merits of homosexuality and heterosexuality for men, advocates of the latter are sometimes stigmatized as 'effeminate,' but never those who favor the former. [. . .]

Romans inherited Greek attitudes on this subject and were in any case familiar with the homosexual interests of such thoroughly masculine public figures as Sulla and Hadrian. Long after public idealization of gay males disappeared in the West, they continued to distinguish themselves in traditionally masculine enterprises. Richard Lionheart, Edward II, the Duc d'Orléans, the Prince de la Roche-sur-Yon, the Grande Condé, the Maréchal de Vendôme—all these men noted for martial skill or valor were also noted for being gay, and it would have been difficult to foment in the minds of their contemporaries any necessary association of effeminacy and homosexuality in men.

Likewise, one must avoid transposing across temporal boundaries ideas about gay relationships which are highly culture-related, such as the expectation that they must parallel or imitate heterosexual relationships (e.g., with one partner adopting a 'male' and one a 'female' role). Where gay relations are approved and open, imitations of this sort are generally neither expected nor evident. Especially where someone may be acceptably involved in gay and heterosexual relationships simultaneously, one would expect the two to be independent; overlap or imitation might occur, but there is no reason to assume a priori that it would be in one direction only. Many Greek writers use homosexual love as an ideal to which heterosexual lovers might aspire. Even in other oppressive cultures one must be cautious: gay couples may imitate nongay ones, but the nature of heterosexual marriage varies widely by the time and place, and gay unions must be studied in relation to the customs of their day, not in terms of modern expectations. [. . .]

Related to this is the question of whether gay relationships may be inherently different from heterosexual ones. Most modern Westerners, even many gay people, tend to think of gay love affairs as being more transitory and physical in nature than their (often idealized) heterosexual equivalents. Whether or not this is true, it must be viewed in conjunction with the variable of social hostility. It is obviously very much to a gay person's advantage in hostile environments not to be part of a permanent relationship: the longer lasting and more intimate a relationship between two persons of the same gender, the more likely it is to incur suspicion where homosexuality is oppressed. Canny gay people may circumvent this, but the most effective defense against oppression will lie in fleeting and clandestine relationships which do not attract attention or provoke suspicion.

Where there is public admiration for gay people and their love, on the other hand, one would not expect any such syndrome to evolve for protection, and indeed one does not find anything of the sort in more tolerant societies. Many Greeks represented gay love as the only form of eroticism which could be lasting, pure, and truly spiritual. [. . .]

If the difficulties of historical research about intolerance of gay people could be resolved by simply avoiding anachronistic projections of modern myths and stereotypes, the task would be far simpler than it is. Unfortunately, an equally distorting and even more seductive danger for the historian is posed by the tendency to exaggerate the differences between homosexuality in previous societies and modern ones. [. . .]

A tendency of humans to dislike or mistrust what is different or unusual adds a certain visceral force to this belief in the rightness of majority sentiment. Especially when difficulties beset a population already inclined to value conformity for its own sake, those who are perceived as willfully different are apt to be viewed not only as mistaken (or 'unnatural') but as potentially danger- ous. It seems to have been fatally easy throughout most of Western history to explain catastrophe as the result of the evil machinations of some group distinct from the majority; and even when no specific connection could be suggested, angry or anxious peoples have repeatedly vented their negative emotions on the odd, the idiosyncratic, and the statistically deviant. In the vibrant Rome of the first century or the bustling Paris of the twelfth, Jewish or gay nonconform- ists apparently struck their contemporaries as part of the variegated fabric of life, contributing their distinctive portions to a happy whole; but in the collaps- ing and insecure Rome of the sixth century or Paris in the later fourteenth, any deviation from the norm took on a sinister and alarming mien and was viewed as part of the constellation of evil forces bringing about the destruction of the familiar world order.

Tracing the course of intolerance reveals much about the landscape it traverses, and for this reason alone it deserves to be studied. Perhaps it is not too much to hope that its examination will yield beyond this insights of use to those who might wish to reduce or eradicate the suffering associated with it. On the other hand, the social topography of medieval Europe remains so unexplored that studies of any aspect of it are largely pioneering and hence provisional. Later generations will certainly recognize many wrong turns, false leads, and dead ends mistakenly pursued by those who had no trails to follow, whose only landmarks were those they themselves posted. Once the terrain has been better mapped, it will be possible to improve initial surveys very substantially; early studies may appear in retrospect absurdly roundabout or wholly useless. To this ineluctable hazard of early research is added the difficulty in the case at issue that a great many people believe they already know where the trails *ought* to lead, and they will blame the investigator not only for the inevitable errors of first explorations but also for the extent to which his results, however tentative and well intentioned, do not accord with their preconceptions on the subject. Of such critics the writer can ask only that before condemning too harshly the placement of his signposts they first experience for themselves the difficulty of the terrain.

Notes

1 'Social' tolerance or intolerance is used in this study to refer to public accept- ance of personal variation or idiosyncrasy in matters of appearance, lifestyle, per- sonality, or belief. [. . .] 'Social tolerance' is thus distinguished from 'approval.' A society may well 'tolerate' diversity of lifestyle or belief even when a majority of its members do not personally approve of the variant beliefs or behavior.

2 In a previous study (1977), I have addressed this issue from the perspective of Muslim communities in Christian Spain in the later Middle Ages. So little scholarly work on the subject of gay people in history is presently extant that it would be premature to attempt anything in the way of a bibliographical essay. [. . .] Almost all modern historical research on gay people in the Christian West has been depend- ent on the pioneering study of Bailey (1955). This work suffers from an emphasis on negative sanctions which gives a wholly misleading picture of medieval prac-

tice, ignores almost all positive evidence on the subject, is limited primarily to data regarding France and Britain, and has been superseded even in its major focus, biblical analysis.

3 The word 'gay' is consciously employed in this text with connotations somewhat different from 'homosexual' [see also chap. 2 of *Christianity, Social Tolerance, and Homosexuality*].

4 The order in which societies come to grips with categories of invidious discrimination may reveal much about their social structure. It is interesting that in the modern West public attention has been focused on intolerance related to sexuality only long after comparable issues involving race or religious belief have been addressed; whereas in most ancient cities gay people achieved toleration long before religious nonconformists, and race (in its modern sense) was never an issue.

5 Many European monarchies of the later Middle Ages licensed prostitutes: for England, see Bellamy (1973, 60); for Spain, see Boswell (1977, 70–1, 348ff).

6 In the late nineteenth century, when the issue of homosexuality first began to exercise the minds of scientists, most authorities assumed that homosexual inclinations were congenital, and differed only on whether they were a defect (Krafft-Ebing) or a part of the normal range of human variation (Hirschfeld). The triumph of psychoanalytical approaches to human sexual phenomena resulted in general abandonment of this approach in favor of psychological explanations, but in 1959 Hutchinson published a paper speculating on the possible genetic significance of 'nonreproductive' sexuality (which he labeled 'paraphilia'), including homosexuality (1959, 81–91). In the 1970s a great deal of speculation has followed on the issue of the evolutionary significance of homosexuality, much of it agreeing on the essential likelihood of genetic viability for homosexual feelings through one selection mechanism or another.

7 This is certainly not to suggest that there may not be groups of persons whose sexual inclinations are essentially nonreproductive or that some of these persons might not qualify as 'gay.' As noted above, the homosexual/heterosexual distinction is a crude one and may obscure more significant sexual differences. Men who primarily desire to be passive, for instance, would probably leave fewer offspring than men whose principal erotic pleasure is derived from penetration of others. The former would necessarily be chiefly aroused by other men, and persons of this sort may in fact comprise the nonreproductive 'caste' [. . .], along with women who chiefly desire to arouse women (or men) with parts of their anatomy other than those involved in reproduction. [. . .]

8 The phobic theory of the origin of homosexuality (i.e., the idea that gay people prefer sexual contact with their own gender because they are frightened of such contact with the opposite sex) has been largely discredited (at least for males) by modern research. For a particularly interesting example of such disproof, see Freund, Langevin, et al. (1974); see also Freund's earlier article (1972), using the same clinical method (penile plethysmography).

9 The sexual investment required for a male to produce offspring can hardly be imagined to be so great as to preclude other outlets; the much greater parental investment required of females has been offset reproductively in most such societies by the fact that women had less choice about their marital status and suffered a much greater loss of prestige and freedom if they did not marry and reproduce.

10 In his last work, the *Laws* (636B–C; 825E–842), Plato characterizes homosexual relations as *para physin*, a phrase traditionally rendered 'against nature.' This is extremely perplexing, since sexual desire as discussed in all Plato's earlier works

is 'almost exclusively homosexual.' [. . .] The *Laws* are atypical of Plato's thought in a great many ways, and this may simply be part of a general change in his thinking, but his comment should in any case be interpreted as accurately as possible. Probably all he meant by *para physin* was 'unrelated to birth' or 'nonprocreative,' not 'unnatural' in the sense of contravention of some overriding moral or physical law.

11 For imagery in particular, see Schachar (1974), and Blumenkranz (1966).

12 But not necessarily *private*: Athenians and Romans were quite open about homosexual feelings, and gay relationships were 'public' in the sense of being frankly acknowledged and generally accepted. They did not, however, require the supervision or regulation of the state in the same way that heterosexual relationships did, and records of their existence are therefore fewer and more personal. Aeschines vs. Timarchus, Demosthenes' *Erotikos,* and a few other public orations on the subject constitute rare exceptions to this.

13 This is particularly true of 'effeminacy' in males. The use of femininity as a measure of undesirability or weakness more properly belongs in a study of misogyny, and the other senses of 'effeminate,' e.g., 'cowardly,' 'weak,' 'morally inferior,' no more relevant to gay than to nongay males, are excluded from consideration here.

Literature

Bailey, Derrick Sherwin. 1955. *Homosexuality and the Western Christian Tradition.* London: Longmans, Green & Co.

Bellamy, John. 1973. *Crime and Public Order in England in the Later Middle Ages.* London: Routledge.

Blumenkranz, Bernhard. 1966. *Le juif medieval au miroir de l'art chretien.* Paris: Etudes Augustienne.

Boswell, John. 1977. *The Royal Treasure: Muslim Communities under the Grown of Aragon in the Fourteenth Century.* New Haven: Yale University Press.

Freund, Kurt. 1972. 'The Female Child as Surrogate Object,' *Archives of Sexual Behavior* 2:119–33.

Freund, Kurt and Ron Langevin, et al. 1974. 'The Phobic Theory of Male Homosexuality,' *Archives of Internal Medicine* 134:495–9.

Hutchinson. G. E. 1959. 'A Speculative Consideration of Certain Possible Forms of Sexual Selection in Man,' *American Naturalist* 93:81–91.

Schachar, Isaiah. 1974. *The 'Judensau': A Medieval Anti-Jewish Motif and Its History.* London: Warburg Institute.

3

The Battle for Chastity

Editor's Introduction

It is the act of Christian confession that left a lasting impact on the constitution of the self in the West. 'An imperative was established: Not only will you confess to acts contravening the law, but you will seek to transform your desire, your every desire, into discourse.' Thus writes Michel Foucault in 1976 in the French edition *La Volonté de savoir*, later translated into English as the first volume of *The History of Sexuality: An Introduction* (1990, 21).

Christianity, according to Foucault, did not so much repress sexuality as it managed to transform sexual desire into discourse through an 'endless mill of speech' (21). The way in which humans experience, channel, express, and censor sexuality was nothing natural but something historically constructed – a result of discrete 'techniques of power' and 'technologies of the self', as Foucault would call these processes of transformation. Christianity had developed a specific technology, the confession, which had left a non-erasable imprint on the evolution of the modern self. Foucault described it as the 'nearly infinite task of telling – telling oneself and another, as often as possible, everything that might concern the interplay of innumerable pleasures, sensations, and thoughts which, through the body and the soul, had some affinity with sex' (20), and he traced this confessional ambition – this technique of transforming 'sex into discourse' (21) – to the ascetic and monastic movements of early Christianity.

The *Critical Reader* introduces Foucault's ideas with a chapter in which he analyzes John Cassian, a Christian monk, who, in the beginning of the fifth century, initiated monastic institutions in the West.

Foucault, born in 1926, is not a historian of religion. His relationship to religious sentiments and the church are, at best, ambiguous. This is not too surprising given that he, as a philosopher and cultural critic, had been part of the post-1945 French intellectual environment. Throughout his writings, Foucault was concerned with various regimes of power and control as these manifest themselves in social systems, such as the prison, the asylum, medicine and knowledge itself. His ideas have inspired, and continue to inspire, scholars across the humanities and social sciences, but to religion Foucault came only during the last phase of his productive life, when he started to work on *The History of Sexuality*.

Initially projected to be a series of six volumes, *The History of Sexuality* built upon his earlier interest in questions of truth and power, in the archaeology of knowledge, and in the ways in which discourses built upon another and changed conceptualizations of the self. Foucault now expanded his reach to a more sustained analysis of religion and he began to pay particular attention to Christianity's contribution to the 'self' in the West. Returning to the formative stages of this new religion within the (waning) Roman culture, he followed Christianity's confessional impulse all the way up to modernity. Jeremy Carrette describes Foucault's relation to religion in the following words:

> Foucault's work in many ways . . . 'prowls the borderlands of Christianity.' He is a writer who engages with the historical and political formations of Western culture, of which religion is a formative stratum. Foucault's work is also informed by the residue of his French Catholic background and more importantly by the avant-garde fascination with religious ideas . . . His work, alongside many so-called post-structuralist writers, engages with many theological themes with fresh historical and analytical critique, reappraising the sources of Western culture. (Carrette 1999, 3)

Of the originally planned six volumes of *The History of Sexuality*, Foucault managed to complete only three, and those in a different order. The *Use of Pleasure* and *The Care of the Self* (both published in 1984 in French and translated into English in 1992 and 1990 respectively) dealt with the Greco-Roman world. A fourth volume, *Confessions of the Flesh*, which would have addressed Christianity, was never completed because of Foucault's untimely death in 1984. Since then, his importance for religious studies has been steadily recognized (see esp. Carrette's two volumes on Foucault and religion [1999; 2000]; also Clark 1988; Bernauer 1990; Schuld 2003; Bernauer and Carrette 2004; Voigt 2007).

'The Battle for Chastity' – reprinted below (it first appeared in French in 1982) – was, according to Carrette, meant to be part of Foucault's unpublished volume on Christianity. Here, Foucault investigates an important moment in the history of Christian confessional discourse, namely John Cassian's contribution to formalizing confessional talk about sexuality in an all-male environment, the monastery. Born in the 360s, Cassian had traveled to Africa, where he had learned first-hand about the Christian monastic movements in Egypt. He eventually settled in Gaul, southern France, and his two important works, *Institutes* and the *Conferences*, profoundly shaped 'the emerging Latin monastic rules' (Stewart 1998, 25).

Foucault has been criticized for his own gender-blindness, especially in regard to his erasure of women and women's experiences in his works on the formative stages of Christianity and late antiquity (Richlin 1998; also Carrette 1999, 7–13). Indeed, the 'Battle for Chastity', which looks at the rules that transformed celibacy into a discourse on chastity, simply presumes the male sexual experience rather than foregrounding these techniques as a gendered experience of men. Toward the end of his life Foucault got more involved in addressing issues of gay sexuality and identity (see Halperin 1995), but this nod toward an autobiographical turn does not undo the lack of critical discernment toward gender of this otherwise so astute observer and analyst of the underpinnings of Western culture. Nevertheless, a critical study of men in religion cannot get around Foucault's insights, and we see this reflected in the contributions by Schneider (chapter 7), Goss (chapter 12), Stone (chapter 16), Burrus (chapter 20), Brakke (chapter 24) and Long (chapter 28) in this volume.

Publications by the Same Author

Dates in [brackets] indicate the year of the original French publication

Foucault, Michel. [1963] 1991. *The Birth of the Clinic: An Archaeology of Medical Perception*, trans. Alan Sheridan. London: Routledge.
——. [1966] 1991. *The Order of Things: An Archaeology of the Human Sciences*, trans. Alan Sheridan. London: Routledge.
——. [1969] 1991. *The Archaeology of Knowledge*, trans. Alan Sheridan. London: Routledge.
——. [1975] 1991. *Discipline and Punish: The Birth of the Prison*, trans. Alan Sheridan. London: Penguin.
——. [1976] 1990. *The History of Sexuality, Volume 1: An Introduction*, trans. Robert Hurley. London: Penguin.
——. [1984a] 1992. *The Use of Pleasure: The History of Sexuality, Volume 2*, trans. Robert Hurley. London: Penguin.
——. [1984b] 1990. *The Care of the Self: The History of Sexuality, Volume 3*, trans. Robert Hurley. London: Penguin.

Further Reading

Bernauer, J. W. 1990. *Michel Foucault's Force of Flight: Towards an Ethics of Thought*. London: Humanities.
Bernauer, J. W. and Jeremy Carrette. 2004. *Michel Foucault's Theology: The Politics of Religious Experience*. Burlington: Ashgate.
Carrette, Jeremy R. (ed.). 1999. *Religion and Culture* (by Michel Foucault). London and New York: Routledge.
——. 2000. *Foucault and Religion: Spiritual Corporality and Political Spirituality*. London and New York: Routledge.
Clark, E. A. 1998, 'Foucault, the Fathers and Sex'. *Journal of the American Academy of Religion* 56/4:619–41.
Halperin, David. 1995. *Saint Foucault: Toward a Gay Hagiography*. Oxford: Oxford University Press.
Richlin, Amy. 1998. 'Foucault's *History of Sexuality*: A Useful Theory for Women?', in *Rethinking Sexuality: Foucault and Classical Antiquity*, eds D. H. Larmour, P. A. Miller and C. Platter. Princeton: Princeton University Press. Pp. 138–70.
Stewart, Columba. 1998. *Cassian the Monk*. Oxford: Oxford University Press.
Schuld, Joyce J. 2003. *Foucault and Augustine: Reconsidering Power and Love*. Notre Dame: University of Notre Dame Press.
Voigt, Friedemann. 2007. 'Genealogie der Lebensführung: Michel Foucaults Deutung des Christentums'. *Zeitschrift für Neuere Theologiegeschichte/Journal for the History of Modern Theology* 14/2:238–59.

The Battle for Chastity

MICHEL FOUCAULT

The battle for chastity is discussed in detail by Cassian in the sixth chapter of the *Institutiones*, 'Concerning the spirit of fornication,' and in several of his *Conferences*: the fourth on 'the lusts of the flesh and of the spirit,' the fifth on 'the eight principal vices,' the twelfth on 'chastity' and the twenty-second on 'night visions.' It ranks second in a list of eight battles,[1] in the shape of a fight against the spirit of fornication. As for fornication itself it is subdivided into three categories.[2] On the face of it a very unjuridical list if one compares it with the catalogue of sins that are to be found when the medieval church organizes the sacrament of penance on the lines of a penal code. But Cassian's specifications obviously have a different meaning.

Let us first examine the place of fornication among the other sinful tendencies. Cassian arranges his eight sins in a particular order. He sets up pairs of vices that seem linked in some specifically close way:[3] pride and vainglory, sloth and accidie, avarice and wrath. Fornication is coupled with greed, for several reasons. They are two 'natural' vices, innate and hence very difficult to cure. They are also the two vices that involve the participation of the body, not only in their growth but also in achieving their object; and finally they also have a direct causal connection—over-indulgence in food and drink fuels the urge to commit fornication.[4] In addition, the spirit of fornication occupies a position of peculiar importance among the other vices, either because it is closely bound with greed or simply by its very nature.

First the causal chain. Cassian emphasizes the fact that the vices do not exist in isolation, even though an individual may be particularly affected by one vice or another.[5] There is a causal link that binds them all together. It begins with greed, which arises in the body and inflames the spirit of fornication: these two engender avarice, understood as an attachment to worldly wealth, which in turn leads to rivalries, quarrelling, and wrath. The result is despondency and sorrow, provoking the sin of accidie and total disgust with monastic life. Such a progression implies that one will never be able to conquer a vice unless one can conquer the one on which it leans: 'The defeat of the first weakens the one that depends on it; victory over the former leads to the collapse of the latter without further effort.' Like the others, the greed–fornication pair, like 'a huge tree whose shadow stretches afar,' has to be uprooted. Hence the importance for the ascetic of fasting as a way of conquering greed and suppressing fornication. Therein lies the basis of the practice of asceticism, for it is the first link in the causal chain.

The spirit of fornication is seen as being in an odd relationship to the last vices on the list, and especially pride. In fact, for Cassian, pride and vainglory do not form part of the causal chain of other vices. Far from being generated by them they result from victory over them:[6] 'carnal pride,' i.e. flaunting one's fasts, one's chastity, one's poverty etc. before other people, and 'spiritual pride,' which makes one think that one's progress is all due to one's own merits.[7] One vice that springs from the defeat of another means a fall that is that much greater. And fornication, the most disgraceful of all the vices, the one that is most shameful, is the consequence of pride—a chastisement, but also a temptation, the proof that God sends to the presumptuous mortal to remind him that he is always threatened by the weakness of the flesh if the grace of God does not come to his help. 'Because someone has for long exulted in the pureness of his heart and his body, it naturally follows . . . that in the back of his mind he rather prides himself on it . . . so it is a good thing for the Lord to desert him, for his own good. The pureness which has been making him so self-assured begins to worry him, and in the midst of his spiritual well-being he finds himself faltering.'[8] When the soul has only itself to combat, the wheel comes full circle, the battle begins again and the prickings of the flesh are felt anew, showing the inevitable continuance of the struggle and the threat of a perpetual recurrence.

Finally, fornication has, as compared with other vices, an ontological particularity which gives it a special ascetic importance. Like greed it is rooted in the body, and impossible to beat without chastisement. While wrath or despondency can be fought only in the mind, fornication cannot be eradicated without 'mortifying the flesh, by vigils, fasts, and back-breaking labor.'[9] This still does not exclude the battle the mind has to wage against itself, since fornication may be born of thoughts, images and memories. 'When the Devil, with subtle cunning, has insinuated into our hearts the memory of a woman, beginning with our mother, our sisters, or certain pious women, we should as quickly as possible expel these memories for fear that, if we linger on them too long, the tempter may seize the opportunity to lead us unwittingly to think about other women.'[10] Nevertheless there is one fundamental difference between fornication and greed. The fight against the latter has to be carried on with a certain restraint, since one cannot give up all food: 'The requirements of life have to be provided for . . . for fear lest the body, deprived through our own error, may lose the strength to carry out the necessary spiritual exercises.'[11] This natural propensity for eating has to be kept at arm's length, treated unemotionally, but not abolished. It has its own legitimacy; to repudiate it totally, that is to say to the point of death, would be to burden one's soul with a crime. On the other hand there are no holds barred in the fight against the spirit of fornication; everything that can direct our steps to it must be eradicated and no call of nature can be allowed to justify the satisfaction of a need in his domain. This is an appetite whose suppression does not lead to our bodily death, and it has to be totally eradicated. Of the eight sins fornication is the only one which is at once innate, natural, physical in origin and needing to be as totally destroyed as the vices of the soul, such as avarice and pride. There has to be severe mortification therefore, which lets us live in our bodies while releasing us from the flesh. 'Depart from this flesh while living in the body.'[12] It is into this region beyond nature, but in our earthly lives, that the fight against fornication leads us. It 'drags us from the slough of the earth.' It causes us to live in this world a life which is not of this world. Because this mortification is the harshest, it promises the most to us in this world below: 'rooted in the flesh,' it offers 'the citizenship which the saints have the promise of possessing once they are delivered from the corruption of the flesh.'[13]

Thus one sees how fornication, although just one of the elements in the table of vices, has its own special position, heading the causal chain, and is the sin chiefly responsible for backsliding and spiritual turmoil, at one of the most difficult and decisive points in the struggle for an ascetic life.

In his fifth *Conference* Cassian divides fornication into three varieties. The first consists of the 'joining together of the two sexes' (*commixtio sexus utriusque*); the second takes place 'without contact with the woman' (*absque femineo tactu*)—the damnable sin of Onan; the third is 'conceived in the mind and the thoughts.'[14] Almost the same distinction is repeated in the twelfth *Conference*: 'carnal conjunction' (*carnalis commixtio*), which Cassian calls fornication in its restricted sense; next uncleanness, *immunditia*, which takes place without contact with a woman, while one is either sleeping or awake, and which is due to 'the negligence of an unwatchful mind'; finally there is libido, which develops in 'the dark corners of the soul' without 'physical passion' (*sine passione corporis*).[15] These distinctions are important, for they alone help one to understand what Cassian meant by the general term *fornicatio*, to which he gives no definition elsewhere. But they are particularly important for the way he uses these three categories—in a way that differs so much from what one finds in earlier texts.

There already existed a traditional trilogy of the sins of the flesh: adultery, fornication (meaning sexual relations outside marriage), and 'the corruption of children.' At least these are the three categories to be found in the *Didache*: 'Thou shalt not commit adultery; thou shalt not commit fornication; thou shalt not seduce young boys.'[16] And these are what we find in the 'Epistle of St Barnabas': 'Do not commit fornication or adultery; do not corrupt the young.'[17] We often find later that only the first two precepts are imposed, fornication covering all sexual offences, and adultery covering those which infringe the marriage vows.[18] But in any case these were habitually accompanied by precepts about covetousness in thought or sight or anything that might lead one to commit a forbidden sexual act: 'Refrain from covetousness, for it leads to fornication; abstain from obscene talk and brazen looks, for all this sort of thing leads to adultery.'[19]

Cassian's analysis has two special features: one is that he does not deal separately with adultery but places it with fornication in its limited sense, and the other is that he devotes attention mostly to the other two categories. Nowhere in the various texts in which he speaks of the battle for chastity does he refer to actual sexual relations. Nowhere are the various sins set out dependent on actual sexual relations—the partner with whom it was committed, his or her age or possible degree of consanguinity. Not one of the categories that in the Middle Ages were to be built up into a great code of sins is to be found here. Doubtless Cassian, who was addressing an audience of monks who had taken vows to renounce all sexual relations, felt he could skip these preliminaries. One notices, however, that on one very important aspect of celibacy, where Basil of Caesarea and Chrysostom had given explicit advice,[20] Cassian does make discreet allusion: 'Let no one, especially when among young folk, remain alone with another, even for a short time, or withdraw with him or take him by the hand.'[21] He carries on his discussion as if he is interested only in his last two categories (about what goes on without sexual relationship or physical passion), as if he was passing over fornication as a physical union of two individuals and devoting serious attention only to behavior which up till then had been severely censured only when leading up to real sexual acts.

But even though Cassian's analysis ignores physical sex, and its sphere of action is quite solitary and secluded, his reasoning is not purely negative. The whole essence of the fight for chastity is that it aims at a target which has nothing to do with actions or relationships; it concerns a different reality to that of a sexual connection between two individuals. A passage in the twelfth *Conference* reveals the nature of this reality. In it Cassian describes the six stages that mark the advance towards chastity. The object of the description is not to define chastity itself, but to pick out the negative signs by which one can trace progress towards it—the various signs of impurity which disappear one by one—and so get an idea of what one has to contend with in the fight for chastity.

First sign of progress: when the monk awakes he is not 'smitten by a carnal impulse'—*impugnatione carnali non eliditur*, i.e. the mind is no longer troubled by physical reactions over which the will has no control.

Second stage: if 'voluptuous thoughts' (*voluptariae cogitationes*) should arise in the monk's mind, he does not let it dwell on them. He can stop thinking about things that have arisen in his mind involuntarily and in spite of himself.[22]

Third stage: when a glimpse of the world outside can no longer arouse lustful feelings, and one can look upon a woman without any feeling of desire.

Fourth stage: one no longer on one's waking hours feels any, even the most innocent, movement of the flesh. Does Cassian mean that there is no movement of the flesh, and that therefore one has total control over one's own body? Probably not, since elsewhere he often insists on the persistence of involuntary bodily movements. The term he uses, *perferre*, signifies no doubt that such movements are not capable of affecting the mind, which thus does not suffer from them.

Fifth stage: 'If the subject of a discourse or the logical consequence of a reading involves the idea of human procreation, the mind does not allow itself to be touched by the remotest thought of sexual pleasure, but contemplates the act in a mood of calmness and purity, as a simple function, a necessary adjunct to the prolongation of the human race, and departs no more affected by the recollection of it than if it had been thinking about brickmaking or some other trade.'

Finally, the last stage is reached when our sleep is not troubled by the vision of a seductive woman. Even though we may not think it a sin to be subject to such illusions, it is however a sign that some lustful feeling still lurks in the depths of our being.[23]

Amid all this description of the different symptoms of fornication, gradually fading out as one approaches the state of chastity, there is no mention of relationships with others, no acts, not even any intention of committing one. In fact there is no fornication in the strict sense of the word. This microcosm of the solitary life lacks the two major elements on which are centred the sexual ethics not only of the philosophers of the ancient world, but also of a Christian like Clement of Alexandria (at least in Epistle II of his *Pedagogus*), namely the sexual union of two individuals (*sunousia*) and the pleasure of the act (*aphrodisia*). Cassian is interested in the movements of the body and the mind, images, feelings, memories, faces in dreams, the spontaneous movements of thoughts, the consenting (or refusing) will, waking and sleeping. Now two opposing poles appear, not, one has to realize, those of mind versus body. They are, first, the involuntary pole, which consists either of physical movements or of feelings evoked by memories and images that survive from the past and ferment in the mind, besieging and enticing the will, and, second, the pole of the will itself, which accepts or repels, averts its eyes or allows itself to be ensnared, holds back or consents. On the one side then bodily and mental reflexes that bypass the mind and, becoming infected with impurity, may proceed to corruption, and on the other side an internal play of thoughts. Here we find the two kinds of 'fornication' as broadly defined by Cassian, to which he confines the whole of his analysis, leaving aside the question of physical sex. His theme is *immunditia*, something which catches the mind, waking or sleeping, off its guard and can lead to pollution, without any contact with another; and the *libido*, which develops in the dark corners of the mind. In this connection Cassian reminds us that *libido* has the same origin as *libet* (it pleases).[24]

The spiritual battle and the advance towards chastity, whose six stages are described by Cassian, can thus be seen as a task of dissociation. We are now far away from the rationing of pleasure and its strict limitation to permissible actions; far away too from the idea of as drastic a separation as possible between mind and body. But what does concern us is a never-ending struggle over the movements of our thoughts (whether they extend or reflect those of our body, or whether they motivate them), over its simplest manifestations, over the factors that can activate it. The aim is that the subject should never be affected in his effort by the obscurest or the most seemingly 'unwilled' presence of will. The six stages that lead to chastity represent steps towards the disinvolvement of the will. The first step is to exclude its involvement in bodily reactions; then exclude it from the imagination (not to linger on what crops up in one's mind); then exclude it from the action of the senses (cease to be conscious of bodily movements); then exclude it from figurative involvement (cease to think of things as possible objects of desire); and finally from oneiric involvement (the desires that may be stirred by images that appear, albeit spontaneously, in dreams). This sort of involvement, of which the willful act or the explicit will to commit an act are the most visible form, Cassian calls *concupiscence*. This is the enemy in the spiritual battle, and this is the effort of dissociation and disinvolvement that has to be made.

Here is the reason why, all through this battle against the spirit of fornication and for chastity, the sole fundamental problem is that of pollution—whether as something that is subservient to the will and a possible form of self-indulgence or as something happening spontaneously and involuntarily in sleep or dreams. So important is this that Cassian makes the absence of erotic dreams and nocturnal pollution a sign that one has reached the pinnacle of chastity. He often returns to this topic: 'The proof that one has achieved this state of purity will be that no apparition will beguile us when resting or stretched out in sleep,'[25] or again 'This is the sum of integrity and the final proof: that we are not visited by voluptuous thoughts during sleep and that we should be unaware of the pollutions to which we are subjected by nature.'[26] The whole of the twenty-second *Conference* is devoted to the question of 'nocturnal pollutions' and 'the necessity of using all our strength to be delivered from them.' And on various occasions Cassian calls to mind holy characters like Serenus, who had attained such a high degree of virtue that they were never troubled by inconveniences of this kind.[27]

Obviously, in a rule of life where renunciation of all sexual relations was absolutely basic, it was quite logical that this topic should assume such importance. One is reminded of the importance, in groups inspired by Pythagorean ideas, accorded to the phenomena of sleep and dreams for what they reveal about the quality of existence, and to the self-purification that was supposed to guarantee its serenity. Above all one must realize that nocturnal pollution raised problems where ritual purity was concerned, and it was precisely these problems which prompted the twenty-second *Conference*: can one draw near to the 'holy altars' and partake of the bread and wine when one has suffered nocturnal defilement?[28] But even if all these reasons can explain such preoccupations among the theoreticians of monastic life, they cannot account for the absolutely central position occupied by the question of voluntary or involuntary pollution in the whole discussion of the battle for chastity. Pollution was not simply the object of a stricter ban than anything else, or harder to control. It was a yardstick of concupiscence in that it helped to decide—in the light of what formed its background, initiated it, and finally unleashed it—the part played by the will in forming these images, feelings, and memories in the mind. The monk concentrates his whole energy on never letting his will be involved in this reaction, which goes from the body to the mind and from the mind to the body, and over which the will may have a hold, either to encourage it or halt it through mental activity. The first five stages of the advance towards chastity constitute increasingly subtle disengagements of the will from the increasingly restricted reactions that may bring on this pollution.

There remains the final stage, attainable by holiness: absence of 'absolutely' involuntary pollutions during sleep. Again Cassian points out that these pollutions are not necessarily all involuntary. Over-eating and impure thoughts during the day all show that one is willing, if not intending, to have them. He makes a distinction between the type of dream that accompanies them and the degree of impurity of the images. Anyone who is taken by surprise would be wrong to blame his body or sleep: 'It is a sign of the corruption that festers within, and not just a product of the night. Buried in the depth of the soul, the corruption has come to the surface during sleep, revealing the hidden fever of passions with which we have become infected by glutting ourselves all day long on unhealthy emotions.'[29] Finally there is the pollution that is totally involuntary, devoid of the pleasure that implies consent, without even the slightest trace of a dream image. Doubtless this is the goal attainable by the ascetic who has practiced with sufficient rigor; the pollution is only a 'residue,' in which the person concerned plays no part. 'We have to repress the reactions of our minds and the emotions of our bodies until the flesh can satisfy the demands of nature without giving rise to any pleasurable feelings, getting rid of the excess of our bodily humors without any unhealthy urges and without having to plunge back into the battle for our chastity.'[30] Since this is a supra-natural phenomenon, only a supra-natural power can give us this freedom, spiritual grace. This is why non-pollution is the sign of holiness, the stamp of the highest chastity possible, a blessing one may hope for but not attain.

For his part man must do no less than keep ceaseless watch over his thoughts and bodily movements day and night—during the night for the benefit of the day and during the day in thinking of the approaching night. 'As purity and vigilance during the day dispose one to be chaste during the night, so too nocturnal vigilance replenishes the strength of the heart to observe chastity during the day.'[31] This vigilance means exerting the sort of 'discrimination' that lies at the heart of the self-analysis developed in active spirituality. The work of the miller sorting out his grain, the centurion picking his troops, the money changer who weighs coins before accepting or refusing them—this is how the monk must unceasingly treat his own thoughts, so as to identify those that may bring temptation. Such an effort will allow him to sort out his thoughts according to their origin, to distinguish them by their quality and to separate the objects they represent from the pleasure they can evoke. This is an endless task of analysis that one has to apply to oneself and, by the duty of confession, to our relations with others.[32] Neither the idea of the inseparability of chastity and 'fornication' affirmed by Cassian, nor the way in which he analyzes them, nor the different elements that, according to him, inhere in them, nor the connections he establishes between them—pollution, libido, concupiscence—can be understood without reference to the techniques of self-analysis that characterize monastic life and the spiritual battle that is fought across it.

Do we find that, between Tertullian and Cassian, prohibitions have been intensified, an even greater importance attached to absolute continence, and the sexual act increasingly stigmatized? Whatever the answer, this is not the way the question should be framed. The organization of monasticism and the dimorphism that developed between monastic and secular life brought about important changes in the problem of sexual renunciation. They brought with them the development of very complex techniques of self-analysis. So, in the very manner in which sex was renounced there appeared a rule of life and a mode of analysis which, in spite of obvious continuities, showed important differences with the past. With Tertullian the state of virginity implied the external and internal posture of one who has renounced the world and has adopted the rules governing appearance, behavior, and general conduct that this renunciation involves. In the mystique of virginity which developed after the thirteenth century the rigor of this renunciation (in line with the theme, already found in Tertullian, of union with Christ) transforms the negative aspect of continence into the promise of spiritual marriage. With Cassian, who describes rather than innovates, there occurs a sort of double action, a withdrawal that also reveals hidden depths within.

This has nothing to do with the internalization of a whole list of forbidden things, merely substituting the prohibition of the intention for that of the act itself. It is rather the opening up of an area (whose importance has already been stressed by the writings of Gregory of Nyssa and, especially, of Basil of Ancyra) which is that of thought, operating erratically and spontaneously, with its images, memories, and perceptions, with movements and impressions transmitted from the body to the mind and the mind to the body. This has nothing to do with a code of permitted or forbidden actions, but is a whole technique for analyzing and diagnosing thought, its origins, its qualities, its dangers, its potential for temptation and all the dark forces that can lurk behind the mask it may assume. Given the objective of expelling for good everything impure or conducive to impurity, this can be achieved only by eternal vigilance, a suspiciousness directed every moment against one's thought, an endless self-questioning to flush out any secret fornication lurking in the inmost recesses of the mind.

In this chastity-oriented asceticism one can see a process of 'subjectiviza-tion' which has nothing to do with a sexual ethic based on physical self-control. But two things stand out. This subjectivization is linked with a process of self-knowledge which makes the obligation to seek and state the truth about oneself an indispensable and permanent condition of this asceticism; and, if there is subjectivization, it also involves an indeterminate objectivization of the self by the self-indeterminate in the sense that one must be forever extending as far as possible the range of one's thoughts, however insignificant and innocent they may appear to be. Moreover, this subjectivization, in its quest for the truth about oneself, functions through complex relations with others, and in many ways. One has to rid oneself of the power of the Other, the Enemy, who hides behind seeming likenesses of oneself, and eternal warfare has to be waged against this Other, which one cannot win without the help of the Almighty, who is mightier than he. Finally, confession to others, submission to their advice and permanent obedience to one's superiors are essential in this battle.

These new fashions in monastic sexual mores, the build-up of a new rela-tionship between the subject and the truth and the establishment of complex relations of obedience to the other self all form part of a whole whose coher-ence is well illustrated in Cassian's text. No new point of departure is involved. Going back in time before Christianity, one may find many of these elements in embryonic form and sometimes fully shaped in ancient philosophy—Stoic or Neo-Platonic, for instance. Moreover Cassian himself presents in a systematic way (how far he makes his own contribution is another question which need not concern us here) a sum of experience which he asserts to be that of Eastern monasticism. In any case, study of a text of this kind shows that it hardly makes sense to talk about a 'Christian sexual ethic,' still less about a 'Judaeo-Christian' one. So far as consideration of sexual behavior was concerned, some fairly involved thinking went on between the Hellenistic period and St Augustine. Certain important events stand out such as the guidelines for conscience laid down by the Stoics and the Cynics, the organization of monasticism and many others. On the other hand the coming of Christianity, considered as a massive rupture with earlier moralities and the dominant introduction of a quite differ-ent one, is barely noticeable. As Peter Brown says, in speaking of Christianity as part of our reading of the giant mass of antiquity, the topography of the parting of the waters is hard to pin down.

Notes

1 The seven others are greed, avarice, wrath, sloth, accidie, vainglory, and pride.

2 See below, note 17.

3 *Conferences*, V, 10. (For this and the other texts see *A Selected Library of Nicene and Post-Nicene Fathers*, ed. Phillip Schaff. vol. II, Grand Rapids: Eerdmans, 1973.)

4 *Institutions*, V and *Conferences*, V.

5 *Conferences*, V, 13–14.

6 *Conferences*, V, 10.

7 *Institutions*, XII, 2.

8 *Conferences*, XII, 6. For examples of lapses into pride and presumptuousness, see *Conferences*, II, 13; and esp. *Institutions*, XII, 20 and 21, where offences against humility are punished by the most humiliating *temptatio*, that of a desire *contra usum naturae*.

9 *Conferences*, V, 4.

10 *Institutions*, VI, 13.

11 *Institutions*, V, 8.

12 *Institutions*, VI, 6.

13 *Institutions*, VI, 6.

14 *Conferences*, V, 11.

15 *Conferences*, XII, 2.

16 *Didache*, II, 2.

17 *Epistle of St Barnabas*, XIX, 4. Earlier on, dealing with forbidden foods, the same text interprets the ban on eating hyena flesh as forbidding adultery, of hare as forbidding the seduction of children, of weasel as forbidding oral sex.

18 For instance St Augustine, *Sermon*, 56.

19 *Didache*, III, 3.

20 Basil of Caesarea, *Exhortation to Renounce the World*, 5. 'Eschew all dealing, all relations with young men of your own age. Avoid them as you would fire. Many, alas, are those who through mixing with them, have been consigned by the Enemy to burn eternally in hell-fire.' Cf. the precautions laid down in *The Great Precepts* (34) and *The Short Precepts* (220). See also John Chrysostom, *Adversus oppugnatores vitae monasticae*.

21 *Institutions*, II, 15. Those who infringe this rule commit a grave offense and are under suspicion (*conjurationis pravique consilii*). Are these words hinting at amorous behavior, or are they simply aimed at the danger of members of the same community showing particular favor to one another? Similar recommendations are to be found in *Institutions*, IV, 16.

22 The word used by Cassian for dwelling on such thoughts is *immorari*. Later, *delectatio morose* has an important place in the medieval sexual ethic.

23 *Conferences*, XII, 7.

24 *Conferences*, V, 11, and XII. Cf. above.

25 *Institutions*, VI, 10.

26 *Institutions*, VI, 20.

27 *Conferences*, VII, 1. XII, 7. Other allusions to this theme in *Institutions*, II, 13.

28 *Conferences*, XXII, 5.

29 *Institutions*, VI, 11.

30 *Institutions*, VI, 22.

31 *Institutions*, VI, 23.

32 Cf. in the twenty-second *Conference* (6) the case of a consultation over a monk, who each time he was going to communion suffered a nocturnal visitation and dared not participate in the holy mysteries. The 'spiritual physicians' after an interrogation and discussions diagnosed that it was the Devil who sent these visitations so as to prevent the monk from attending the desired communion. To abstain was to fall into the Devil's trap; to communicate in spite of everything was to defeat him. Once this decision had been taken the Devil appeared no more.

4

New Ways in Our Sexual Spirituality

Editor's Introduction

James Nelson, professor emeritus of Christian ethics, has dedicated most of his writings to a theology of incarnation, taking seriously the idea of the human body as a gift of God. Challenging assumptions about sexuality and gender in traditional Christianity, Nelson develops a body-positive theology and sex-affirmative spirituality within a Christian ethical framework. No longer condemning the body as a source of sin and temptation, he suggests moving to a framework of receptive and responsible care-taking of the human need for intimacy and pleasure. As he writes in the chapter below, 'There is a shift from understanding sexual sin as a matter of wrong sexual acts to understanding sexual sin as alienation from our intended sexuality.' Sin is no longer located in the performance of particular sexualities or in the scrutinizing of stirrings of erotic desire but, rather, is defined as alienation from our God-given embodment.

'God saw everything that he had made, and behold, it was very good' (Gen. 1.31). The first chapter of Genesis repeatedly makes the point of the goodness of God's creation. Nelson reaffirms this goodness over against a tradition that has, over the centuries, separated the body from the spirit, with the consequence of devaluing not only carnal pleasures but also, by extension, women, who had been closely aligned with matter. Nelson also takes seriously the Christian notion of God's willed incarnation in Jesus Christ: God's voluntary gift of 'in-flesh-ness' invites men and women to embrace lovingly their own bodies. In his Preface to *Embodiment: An Approach to Sexuality and Christian Theology*, he writes:

> Christian faith ought to take embodment seriously: 'And the Word became flesh and dwelt among us, full of grace and truth . . .' (John 1:14). The embodiment of God in Jesus Christ is, in faith's perception, God's decisive and crucial self-disclosure. But for those who believe in God's continuing manifestation and presence, the incarnation is not simply past event. The Word *still* becomes flesh. We as body-selves – as sexual body-selves – are affirmed because of that. Our human sexuality is a language, and we are both called and given permission to become body-words of love. Indeed, our sexuality – in its fullest and richest sense – is both the physiological and psychological grounding of our capacity to love. (Nelson 1978, 8)

This is a project of incarnational theology. Nelson understands the Christian story of 'incarnation' as an invitation to accept our bodies in their completeness – bodies that deserve loving care, deserve to be pleasured and healed, deserve to be trusted. We need to move away from 'theologies of sexuality' to 'sexual theologies', he argues, a call that has been heeded by other body-affirmative, gay and straight theologians. Among them are three men who are also contributors to this volume: Clark (1992), Boyd (1995) and Haldeman (1996).

Having prepared the ground for religious reenvisionings of sexual theology, others have pushed Nelson's ideas further, perhaps in ways beyond what he originally had in mind. Among the more daring perspectives, we can mention the work of gay and queer theologians Robert Goss (2002) and Donald Boisvert (2000) – who are also contributors to the *Critical Reader* – and Marcella Althaus-Reid (2000; 2003), who, like Nelson, is a Christian ethicist.

Nelson belongs to the same generational cohort as the early wave of feminist theologians and he makes frequent references in his many books to the work of Rosemary Radford Ruether, Carter Heyward and Mary Daly. As a Christian man writing a sex-friendly and gender-conscious theology, he has been equally concerned about the affairs of heterosexual and homosexual men. Nelson speaks repeatedly about the lack of meaningful male friendships and the danger of homophobia. Writing about the harmful effects of men being socialized to neglect their own emotional needs and to disregard caring relationships with others, he wants men to liberate themselves from socially encoded and self-imposed roles of traditional masculinity.

Publications by the Same Author

Nelson, James B. 1978. *Embodiment: An Approach to Sexuality and Christian Theology*. Minneapolis: Augsburg.

——. 1983. *Between Two Gardens: Reflections on Sexuality and Religious Experience*. New York: Pilgrim.

——. 1988. *The Intimate Connection: Male Sexuality, Masculine Spirituality*. Philadelphia: Westminster.

——. 1992. *Body Theology*. Louisville: Westminster John Knox.

Nelson, James B. and Sandra P. Longfellow (eds). 1994. *Sexuality and the Sacred: Sources for Theological Reflection*. Louisville: Westminster John Knox.

Further Reading

Althaus-Reid, Marcella. 2000. *Indecent Theology: Theological Perversions in Sex, Gender and Politics*. London and New York: Routledge.

——. 2003. *The Queer God*. London and New York: Routledge.

Boisvert, Donald L. 2000. *Out on Holy Ground: Meditations on Gay Men's Spirituality*. Cleveland: Pilgrim.

Boyd, Stephen B. 1995. *The Men We Long to Be: Beyond Domination to a New Christian Understanding of Manhood*. San Francisco: HarperSanFrancisco.

Clark, J. Michael 1992. *Masculine Socialization & Gay Liberation: A Conversation on the Work of James Nelson & Other Wise Friends*. Arlington: The Liberal Press.

Goss, Robert E. 2002. *Queering Christ: Beyond Jesus Acted Up*. Cleveland: Pilgrim.

Haldeman, Scott. 1996. 'Bringing Good News to the Body: Masturbation and Male Identity', in *Men's Bodies, Men's Gods*, ed. Björn Krondorfer. New York: New York University Press. Pp. 111–24.

New Ways in Our Sexual Spirituality

JAMES B. NELSON

It is frequently said that beginning in the 1960s a sexual revolution happened in our society. Indeed, there are some persuasive signs of just that. Significant changes occurred in numerous cultural and religious understandings about sex-role equality, about sex outside of marriage, about homosexuality, about single-parent families, about the more open portrayal and discussion of sexual matters, and so on. The shifts were spurred by a new American affluence, by the Pill, by the flood of women into the work force, by the Vietnam period's destabilization of traditional values, and by a new cultural emphasis on self-fulfillment. If none of these changes was total or without considerable resistance, still it is evident that something of major importance happened.

And, in the Orwellian year 1984, no less an authority than a *Time* cover story declared, 'The revolution is over' (April 9, 1984). Veterans of the revolution, said *Time*, are both bored and wounded. The one-night stand has lost its sheen. 'Commitment' and 'intimacy' are in (helped by the scourges of herpes and AIDS). Celibacy is again a respectable option. The 'me generation' is beginning to give way to the 'we generation.' Religious and political reaction to feminism, gay/lesbian rights, and the plurality of family forms has set in. If some changes seem lasting, there has been a decided movement back to more traditional sexual values. So said *Time's* analysis, and it bears considerable truth.

Insofar as the 'sexual revolution' involved sex for recreation it seemed promising to many, especially when it involved caring and tenderness. But it also led many people to a frantic search for sensation, thence to the deadening of sensation, and to erotic depersonalization. It is doubtful that most persons in our society want a return to the ways of sexual repression and discrimination. But what is increasingly clear is that they want something the revolution too frequently did not provide: to know the meanings of love. In that sense, the revolution is not over. It is just beginning. If the changes of the past quarter century did not usher in the wedding of sexuality and spirituality, hunger for that union was aroused, at the very least.

Some years ago, Paul Ricoeur observed that there were three major stages in Western understandings of sexuality in relation to religion (1970, 13–24). The earliest stage closely identified the two realms, with sexuality intimately incorporated into religious myth and ritual. The second stage, coming with the rise of the great world religions, brought separation. The sacred became increasingly transcendent and separate, while sexuality was demythologized and confined to a small part of the earthly order (procreation within institutionalized marriage). Sexuality's power was feared, restrained, and disciplined.

Ricoeur noted, however, that a third period now seems to be emerging, marked by the desire to unite sexuality once more with the experience of the sacred, a period prompted by more holistic understandings of the person and of the ways in which sexuality is present, in all of human experience. If (with the second period) sexual expression is still seen as needing ordering and discipline, there is (with the first period) a renewed sense of its spiritual power.

I, too, believe that we are edging into that third period—very unevenly, yet truly. If that is accurate, the sexual revolution of the 1960s and 1970s was itself a very uneven experience. There were significant gains in releasing the constructive power of sexuality and in the call for sexual justice and equality. There were losses in the trivialization and mechanization of much sexual experience. Nevertheless, there has been an important opening to the third period.

Perhaps never before in the history of the church has there been so much open ferment about sexuality issues. The outpouring of treatises, debates, studies, and pronouncements, the formation of caucuses and movements bent upon reformation of religious-sexual attitudes or upon protecting them from unwanted change—all this has appeared to an unprecedented degree. In these developments there are signs that a paradigmatic shift in religious perceptions of human sexuality is under way. There are a number of signs of this shift that I find striking and have discussed elsewhere (Nelson 1987; 1983, 73–80). What I now realize, however, is that this shift of consciousness is of particular significance to *men*.

We who are men have been more firmly locked into the older paradigm than have women. We have had more social power, and as a result we have had greater ability to control the social definitions of sexuality. Those definitions in an earlier time seemed good and true—to many women as well as to men. Those definitions also served certain interests of men, often unrecognized by them. But those perceptions are rightly being questioned today, and radically so. In one sense, it would appear that men have most to lose from a significant shift in sexual perceptions—power and control. But that 'loss' means greater justice for all. Moreover, men have an enormous amount to gain from these shifts—gains in the reunion of our sexuality and our spirituality, gains in our fuller humanity. [. . .]

1. *There is a shift from 'theologies of sexuality' to 'sexual theologies.'* Before the past two decades, the vast preponderance of Christian writers on sexuality assumed that the question before them was simply this: What does Christianity (the Bible, the tradition, ecclesiastical authority) say about sexuality? It was a one-directional question, moving from religious faith to sexual experience. Now we are also asking: What does our experience of human sexuality say about our perceptions of faith—our experience of God, our interpretations of Scripture and tradition, our ways of living out the gospel?

The ground work for this shift was laid many years ago. One of the hallmarks of the new theological liberalism in the nineteenth century was its insistence that human experience provides vital theological data. The liberals taught us that theological formulations are not static, unchanging truths revealed from on high. Rather, they are very human attempts to capture in word and thought our human experiences of God. In recent decades, several forms of liberation theology have embraced this insight in a new way. Third world and black Christians began to see that their own distinctive experiences of oppression and their possibilities of liberation afforded crucial insights into the nature of God's activity in the world.

Regarding sexuality, the important shift came from the feminist and lesbian/gay movements. Theirs was the claim that God is experienced in the movement toward liberation from sexual oppression. We must, they told us, move from experience to fresh understandings of the gospel as well as the other way around. Men are beginning to feel that hunger for liberation too. It has been slower in coming to consciousness, but it is emerging. It has varied names: hunger for friends, for living without the constant performance demand, for intimacy with lovers, for knowing one's own feelings, for knowing one's children, for the ability to play without having to win, for the possibility of living without premature death, for release from the violence men have inflicted upon the planet, for simply feeling good once again about being men. The names of the hungers are legion—these are only a few. Because men have been more split in their spirituality and their sexuality than have women, they have more healing from which to gain. There is a growing sense that theology must be grounded in this kind of experiential stuff. If we do not know the gospel in our bodies, perhaps we do not know it.

But there is more. There is the growing realization that one important reason why there has been too little sexual healing in the hearing of the gospel is that, under the male dominance of our theological tradition, many of our alienations have been written into our very understandings of the gospel. Some careful reexamination of the sexual-experiential lenses through which we have been perceiving the faith is needed.

The term 'sexual theology,' like the term 'liberation theology,' suggests this dialogical, two-directional inquiry. The two-way conversation model reminds us that theology cannot presume to look down upon human sexuality from some unaffected Olympian vantage point. It reminds us that every theological perception contains some elements and perceptions conditioned by sexual experience, and every sexual experience is perceived and interpreted through religious lenses of some kind. The consciousness of the difference: between a unidirectional and a dialogical method is the difference between a theology of sexuality and a sexual theology.

2. *A shift is occurring, from understanding sexuality as either incidental to or detrimental to the experience of God, to understanding sexuality as intrinsic to the divine–human experience.* Sexual dualism, as we have seen, has marked much of the Christian tradition. Implicit in this dualism has been an assumption of divine impassivity, literally the *apathy* of God. If the body is marked by passion and if spirit is passionless, then bodily eros has no connection with the divine. God is without hunger, and the human hungers (of which sexuality, with its drive to connection and intimacy, is one of the most basic) seem to have no relation to our experience of God.

While the recent sexual revolution often seemed more intent upon self-fulfillment through unfettered pleasure than upon the quest for intimacy, it did prompt new theological reflection on the spiritual significance of sexual desire. If some of our Protestant forebears of three centuries ago were right in believing that companionship, not procreation, is God's central design for sexuality, then the human hunger for physical and emotional intimacy is of enormous spiritual significance. It ought not be denigrated as unbecoming to the spiritual life. Thus, theology has been giving new attention to the insight that, at its core, our sexuality is part of God's design that creatures not dwell in isolation and loneliness but in communion and community.

The integration of our sexuality into our practices of prayer and meditation is an important case in point. We are heirs of a male-dominated spirituality tradition that has deeply marked us by its dualisms and sex-negativism. Hence, insofar as our sexuality enters into our prayer at all, our first inclinations may be toward prayers of confession: for release from enslaving sexual desires; of guilt for wanting sex too much and making it the substitute for other things; of temptation or infidelity. The positive valuing of our bodies and our sexual experience may be more difficult, especially for men: thanksgiving for the tastes, sounds, and smells that come through a sensuous body; gratitude for grace known in orgasm with the lover; grateful delight in our own self-pleasuring possibilities; prayerful worries over erections, potency, pregnancies, desirability—all grounded in a sense of sex's goodness. [. . .]

Sexual prayer is but one way we can reclaim a more incarnational theology. Incarnation means that the most decisive experience of God lies not in doctrine, creed, or ideas but in Word made flesh—and in Word still becoming flesh. In all of this there is a challenge to the ancient dualism that fundamentally opposed spirituality and sexuality. There is a fresh opening to the reality that sexuality is intrinsic to the experience of God. Nikos Kazantzakis puts it this way: 'Within me even the most metaphysical problem takes on a warm physical body which smells of sea, soil, and human sweat. The Word, in order to touch me, must become warm flesh. Only then do I understand—when I can smell, see, and touch' (1965, 43).

3. *There is a shift from understanding sexual sin as a matter of wrong sexual acts to understanding sexual sin as alienation from our intended sexuality.* The Christian tradition has had a pronounced tendency to define sexual sin as specific acts. This approach gained momentum during the early Middle Ages, when penitential manuals were first written detailing specific sins and their proper penances. Greatest attention was given to sexual matters. Indeed, in our heritage, 'sin' and 'morality' have had a markedly sexual focus—a 'morals charge' never means economic injustice, one can be sure. Sexual sins thus became physiologically definable and capable of neat categorization. They were those particular acts either prohibited by scriptural texts or seen to be contrary to natural law: acts done with the wrong person, in the wrong way, or for the wrong purpose.

In most other respects, adequate Christian theology has always known that sin is not fundamentally an act but rather the condition of alienation or estrangement out of which harmful acts may arise. However, it has taken a long time to acknowledge that sexual sin is fundamentally alienation from our divinely intended sexuality. To put it overly simply but I hope accurately, sexual sin lies not in being too sexual but in being not sexual enough—in the way God has intended us to be. Such alienation, indeed, usually leads to harmful acts, but the sin is rooted in the prior condition.

Sexual sin is the dualistic alienation by which the body becomes an object, either to be constrained out of fear (the Victorian approach) or to be treated as a pleasure machine (the *Playboy* philosophy). It is the dualistic alienation in

sin = alienation / estrangement

which females are kept from claiming their assertiveness and males from claiming their vulnerability. It lies in the alienation that finds expression in sexual violence, in Rambo-like militarism, in racism, in ecological abuse.

The uncompleted sexual revolution began to see some of this. In its superficial and exploitive moments it simply wanted to wipe away the category of sexual sin. 'If it feels good, do it.' In its better moments, there were insights that sexual sin was something different from, and more than, particular acts that could be neatly defined.

Men typically experience sexual alienation in a variety of ways. We males are more alienated from our bodies than are most women. Our bodies seem instrumental to us, and their deep emotions are often strange and frightening. All too frequently, violence becomes a substitute for our tears. Sexual alienation includes the loneliness fed by the fires of sexual fears. Fear of intimacy with other males is fed by homophobia, while fear of intimacy with women is inhibited by sexist distancing and internalized performance-failure fears. [. . .]

One of the most evident forms of sexual alienation that so many males feel, however, is simply the lack of a secure and solid sense of manhood. In most so-called (and probably misnamed) 'primitive' societies, the rites of passage from boyhood into manhood were clear. Though they often involved violent feats of courage and endurance of pain, they still bonded the adolescent male to the men of the tribe and gave him a clear sense that he was now a man. In the absence of such initiations, we attempt other rituals in order to fill the void. But they do not satisfy. The driver's license and feats of automotive daring, fraternity initiations, diplomas, drinking and drug rituals, scoring on the athletic field—none of these seems to bring a lasting sense that the boy has become a man. Perhaps our closest approach to the ancient manhood-confirming ritual is the military experience, which secludes younger men with older men who thrust upon them tests of psychological and physical endurance. In the absence of such initiation rites, many young men seek their rites of passage with the opposite sex. They ask young women for something that the culture has not given them—their manhood. 'Certain of her femininity and of her pregnability, she dares to wait until the time is right. Insecure about his masculinity and obsessed with proving it—to himself and his buddies, if not to her—he needs to score in order to feel that he has made the team' (Gerzon 1982, 176). But his conquest is still private; done in the dark of night, the proof of his manly virility vanishes in the light of day, a rite of passage only in his own mind, unconfirmed by the larger society.

Sexual alienation—and its unending quest for masculine identity—is rooted for many males in the father–son experience. The search, for many men, is lifelong. Samuel Osherson observes, 'The interviews I have had with men in their thirties and forties convince me that the psychological or physical absence of fathers from their families is one of the great underestimated tragedies of our times' (1986, 4). Boys become men carrying a 'wounded father' within, their conflicted inner sense of masculinity rooted in their experience of their fathers as absent, rejecting, or incompetent. Perhaps nothing would be the same in our world—whether religion, politics, science, business, education, or art—if men spent more time in the world of the infants and toddlers they have sired.

My own childhood came during the Depression years, and like many of my generation I experienced my father as having a mysterious, remote quality. I knew little of his inner life, what he thought and felt as a man. He was a large, strong figure to me, one I could neither approach nor avoid. His expectations were high, and he held his sons to them. I felt his pride in my achievements, his judgment on my failures. Like many men, he showed his love more symbolically than through his words: working hard, providing well, being a responsible and respected community leader, occasionally showing a rough tenderness. His love was expressed from a distance. Even then, he could withdraw his love, and when it was withdrawn it sometimes felt as though he might never come back. One part of me wished desperately to be a good son, while another part deeply rebelled.

Other men report experiencing their fathers somewhat differently from the way I did. Some of these sons who grew up in the 1960s and 1970s felt the impact of both the women's movement and the Vietnam War. They were drawn to those women who expressed justice and caring, and abandoned the fathers who seemed to express masculine oppression. In any event, the search for the father is the quest for authentic masculine strength and goodness. The alienation from the father that many men feel throughout their lifetimes is one very important illustration of sexual sin.

These are some of the real issues of sexual sin. It is no small shift in consciousness to move from understanding sexual sin as essentially wrong or bad acts to the realization that alienation from our intended sexuality is the core problem. None of us escapes such woundedness, and men carry their own particular kinds.

4. *We are experiencing a shift from understanding salvation as anti-sexual to knowing that there is 'sexual salvation.'* Because spiritualistic dualism has so conditioned much of the Christian tradition, we have inherited a disembodied notion of salvation. Salvation somehow means release from the lower and fleshly life into the higher life of the spirit. Indeed, popular piety has typically viewed the saints as asexual, surely without sexual needs and desires, sometimes even without genitals.

In its better moments, the sexual revolution convinced many Christians that an incarnationalist faith embraces the redemption of our alienated sexuality as well as other estranged dimensions of our lives. Justification by grace signifies God's unconditional, unmerited, radical acceptance of the whole person. God, the Cosmic Lover, graciously embraces not just a person's disembodied spirit but the whole fleshly self—the meanings of which theology is only beginning to explore.

Sanctification, the second classical salvation term, means growth in holiness (or wholeness and health—the root word is the same). Unfortunately, much in our tradition has taught us that sanctification involves the denial of our sexuality or the escape from our bodies. We are beginning to realize, however, that increasing sexual wholeness is part of our redemption intended by God. Sexual sanctification can mean growth in bodily self-acceptance, in the capacity for sensuousness, in the capacity for play, in the diffusion of the erotic throughout the body rather than in its genitalization, and in the recovery of lost dimensions of our sexuality.

A crucial part of sexual salvation for many men lies in finding their fathers. In our church's nave are five beautiful stained-glass windows depicting Jesus' parables. During worship I find my eyes regularly drawn to one window more than to any of the others. It is the forgiving father embracing the prodigal son. While this parable as Jesus told it is immeasurably rich in meaning, its central point is quite clear: the utterly gracious, profoundly accepting, unbelievably forgiving love and presence of God freely offered to us without our earning or deserving. In the story the father doesn't even wait to hear the son's confession, so eager is he to run to meet him, embrace him, kiss him, welcome him home, and begin the reunion party. All of that is quite clear from the parable. Yet, in my Sunday morning musings I find myself yearning to have that window also signify the son embracing the prodigal father. I yearn for the two simply to find reunion. [. . .]

Healing comes in different ways. My own process has been a slow one. As I have said, I was 22 and in the army when my father suddenly died. Good soldier that I was, I didn't cry. Nor did I deal with the terrible complexity of emotions that any death brings to those in the family. I buried all that in his grave with him. It was fully 24 years later that an intense group experience at the Esalen Institute opened up the grave to expose grief, anger, resentment, sadness, tears. Nor did months of these feelings now close to the surface end the process. In therapy several years after that, I realized how much unfinished business remained. I had to confront the unfulfilled longings for words of love, for physical tenderness, for intimate companionship. I had to uncover some painful memories of abuse and of fear of my father's power, and I had to deal with my rage. A turning point came one day when the therapist challenged me: 'When will you be ready to forgive your father?'

Resurrection can begin when we who are men find ourselves willing to enter our fathers' worlds as best we can, feeling into what they might have experienced and felt with their own fathers and embracing their pain. It begins when we deal with our own uncomfortable feelings about our unmet needs to have been held by our fathers, when we deal with our own betrayals and unatoned sins toward our fathers. It begins when we let go of our harbored wishes for the perfect father who would have given us everything we needed to live our lives. This process can be harder when our fathers are dead or inaccessible to us, but the process is possible.

Reconciliation with the father may be possible, and that is what many men crave. But even when it is not, healing the wounded father within is possible, as Osherson says: 'That is, because the essential elements in healing are the internal image of the father and the sense of masculinity that the son carries in his heart. The son needs to be able to understand the always poignant reasons why the past was the way it was, thus freeing him from his sense of having been betrayed by the father or having been a betrayer of him. [The son] needs to explore satisfying ways to be male that reflect his own identity. We can recognize that we are our father's son without feeling that we have to accept and love everything about him or all that happened between us' (1986, 196). [. . .]

We might be strangely reminded of one thing: our falsely masculinized and confused God images. Our patriarchal theological tradition has led us to confusion about 'God the Father.' Granted, Jesus' use of 'Father' ('Abba') was radical in its transformation of the traditional notion of divine transcendence and distance. But our uses of the image have usually failed to capture Jesus' meanings. In practice, we create God in our own image—now in the image of the human father we have experienced—and then find 'God' too often distant, absent, demanding, and conditional in 'his' love. Such deity surely needs to be forgiven. Indeed, we are surprised when 'he' can be so gracious to the prodigal son. One can say, of course, it is still we who need forgiveness, *metanoia*, a turning around in our impoverished projections upon the divine. And that is largely true. But in a curious way [. . .] the awful transcendence of God must be forgiven if we are to be reunited with the gracious divine immanence. [. . .]

Surely there are rhythms in human father–son relationships in which now one and now the other is forgiver and forgiven, embracer and embraced. There is heroism and there is failure in our fathers' lives, and in ours. To identify with the good in our fathers, 'to feel how we are like them, as well as the ways we are different from them . . . [brings] a fuller, trustworthy sense of masculinity . . . [and] the sure, quiet knowledge that men as well as women are lifegiving forces on earth' (Osherson 1986, 198).

5. *We are seeing a shift from an act-centered sexual ethics to a relational sexual ethics.* The sexual revolution in this society coincided with some important shifts in Christian ethical thought. For all of its oversimplifications Joseph Fletcher's *Situation Ethics* in the mid-sixties aroused an extraordinary interest in ethical rethinking on the part of many people not otherwise inclined to the technicalities of professional ethics. The more sophisticated approaches to an ethics of response and contextual-relational ethics, differently expressed by such thinkers as H. Richard Niebuhr and Paul Lehmann, had a major impact on ethical thought in the same decade. In the years since that time, these ethical styles have had increasing influence in Christian thinking, including feminist ethics.

In contrast, act-oriented ethics has dominated much of the Christian tradition, particularly when applied to sexual matters. Such ethics assumed that the rightness or wrongness of a particular sexual expression could be determined by the objective moral nature of the act itself, a value intrinsic in that act, a meaning unchanged by the relational context or situation. Thus, ethicists and churchly authorities could catalog various sexual acts—masturbation, same-sex intercourse, heterosexual intercourse (premarital, marital, extramarital)—as objectively and intrinsically right or wrong. The alternative to such clarity seemed to be a normless subjectivism, particularly dangerous in sexuality issues, where passions run high.

It is significant that, over the centuries, the Christian insistence on this kind of ethical precision and control was particularly evident regarding sex. It was also present to a noticeable degree in family issues and in medical ethics. But in the spheres of human activity that seemed less 'bodily' and 'personal'—economics, politics, war and peace—Christian ethics showed more willingness to take the relativities of contexts into account. That pattern ought not surprise us. The ethical tradition has been dominated by men, and men have had less comfort with the sexual, the bodily, and the personal. Further, these are areas that a patriarchal worldview has identified with the feminine, hence they appear fraught with greater anxiety for men and more in need of being controlled.

Roman Catholic sexual ethics, with its strong natural-law tradition and clearly defined ecclesiastical teaching authority, has been somewhat more inclined toward objective sexual norms than has Protestant ethics, with its more scriptural orientation. Both, however, have been more objectivistic and act-focused in sexuality issues than in almost any other moral sphere. In recent years, however, many in both traditions have moved toward a new and creative sexual ethics. Act-oriented ethics has appeared inadequate, not only in cases with unique contexts and meanings but in light of a growing recognition that Christian sexual ethics has been inadequately integrated into a holistic spirituality. If sexuality is the physiological and psychological grounding of our capacities to love, if our destiny after the image of the Cosmic Lover is to be lovers in the richest, fullest sense of that good word, then how do our sexual ethics figure into our spiritual destiny? What are our creative and fitting sexual responses to the divine loving? What are the appropriate sexual meanings to embody the meanings of Word becoming flesh?

These are the questions that seem increasingly appropriate to many. [. . .] Yet countless Christians know that a significant ethical change is under way. Such changes in ethical style—and the resistance to them—have direct connections with issues of masculine spirituality. As one who works in academic life (a theological seminary), I have been increasingly aware in recent years how abstract and hyperrationalized is much of our theology and ethics. Imagination and feeling have been underdeveloped in this male-dominated discursive tradition, and in myself as a practitioner. As a typical young male I was conditioned to protect myself against bodily attack and defend myself against the perils of the vulnerable emotions. For many years I was largely out of touch with a whole range of bodily feelings.

But such male alienation takes a terrible toll. It leads us into abstracting ourselves from the bodily concreteness of others. To stand in the ashes of that village in Vietnam and say, 'We had to destroy this village in order to save it,' is abstractionism that lured a man into an exaggerated, violent sense of reality.

When ethics loses its attention to flesh-and-blood concreteness, then bloodless abstractions, principles, and concepts begin to take on a life of their own. They become more real than people, animals, plants, and earth. What is lost, however, is not only concreteness but also the sense of connection—the deep, bodily sense of our profound connectedness to everything else. The recovery of the body brings with it the realization that the fundamental reality our lives is not our separation but our relatedness, a surprising revelation to the male conditioned to a Lone Ranger mentality. Yet, running through almost every page of the Bible is faith's perception of the deep relationality of life. The metaphors are connectional: covenant, the people of Israel, the body of Christ, the vine and the branches. [. . .]

To know myself as profoundly relational is to know myself as body. All our relationships are mediated through our bodies. In our emotions we interact with the world. In our sexual, sensuous selves our sense of relatedness is grounded. It is our sense of bodily integrity that grounds our power with others and our capacities for vulnerability with them. When I sense the holiness of my own body, I begin to sense the holiness of every other body (see Harrison 1986; Heyward 1984).

Ethics involves critical reflection on the moral life. Ethical reflection needs concepts such as principles and rules. These are the handles we get on experience in order to talk about morality with others. They make public discourse possible. But when we treat abstractions as though they were actual existing beings, we lose contact with the richness, the variety, the connectedness, and the ambiguities of life. We become too tidy about things that are not tidy. We use our ethics to control more than to liberate persons into life-giving relationships. It is true of all areas of our ethics, but our sexual ethics are a particularly telling example. These are things that women have known better than men. But we are learning them, and our ethics are changing in the process.

6. *A shift is happening, from understanding the church as asexual to understanding it as a sexual community.* Through most of its history, the church has viewed sexuality as either incidental or inimical to its life. But the sexual revolution resulted in a growing self-consciousness and empowerment of the sexually oppressed. Religious feminism articulated the ways in which the church has *always* been a sexual community—the ways it has incorporated patriarchy into its language, worship, theological imagery, leadership patterns, and ethics. A rising gay/ lesbian consciousness performed a similar function in regard to the church's heterosexism. Gradually, other groups—singles (including the widowed and divorced), the aging, those with handicapping conditions, the ill—have begun to recognize how churchly assumptions and practices have sexually disenfranchised them. The church, indeed, has always been a sexual community, though in ways often unrecognized and oppressive.

Another impetus for claiming and reforming the church as a sexual community has come from the rising hunger to reunite sexuality and spirituality. The realization that Protestant worship has been marked by a masculinist focus on the spoken word and by a suspicion of bodily feelings has suggested the need to explore and touch the varied senses more inclusively. The fact that Christian education has seriously ignored sex education has prompted the attempt to address sexual meanings as a part of faith's journey, for young and old. The recognition that most theology has given only lip service to the incarnation, failing to take ongoing incarnationalism seriously in both method and content, has inspired an effort to explore the doing and meaning of body theology.

In one sense, we must do theology simply because we *are* body-selves. As such, we are impelled into a relational existence, and we need to ask what it is all about. Through our bodily eros we are drawn into intercourse—verbal, tactile, social, political, economic, sexual intercourse—with others. And, as beings who seek meaning, we need to ask about these occasions of human intercourse. What is their value? Are they life-denying or life-giving? Do they thwart or fulfill our deepest needs as persons and as communities? What is their ultimate meaning?

If we must do theology because we are body-selves drawn into all sorts of intercourse with other body-selves, we who are Christian also theologize in certain ways because we are part of the body of Christ. Because we are Christian we deal with the centrality of a Christic revelation of God. Traditional Christology, as we have seen, all too frequently has drawn our attention away from our own bodily life. In focusing upon the singular divinity of one person and portraying that divinity as overwhelming his humanity, something else was substituted for radical incarnation. What was substituted was the belief in an unchanging, unilateral transcendent power whose divine love was utterly different from human love, whose divine body was utterly different from our bodies. Suppressed was the compelling experience of incarnation as the meaning and reality, the healing life-giving power of our embodied relationships with others. [. . .]

When we forget that the church is a sexual community, we only allow unreflective, uncriticized, and often unjust expressions of our sexuality to shape its life. When we remember, however, we have fresh awareness of the transformative power and presence of the body of Christ.

7. *There is a shift from understanding sexuality as a private issue to understanding it as a personal and public issue.* Sexual issues will always be intensely personal, engaging some of the deepest feelings, desires, self-understandings, pleasures, and pains of each individual. However 'personal' is different from 'private.' One mark of Victorian sexuality was its privatization. Not only was sexuality not to be talked about, it was to be confined to a small portion of one's private life. Indeed, sexuality was reduced to sex—'the privates.' But this, quite literally, was idiocy. (The Greek word for *idiot* refers to the person who attempts to live the private life, ignorant of and unconcerned about the public domain.)

One of the church's recent discoveries is the public dimension of sexuality issues. On the social-action agenda of mainline denominations today are sexual-justice issues regarding gender and sexual orientation. No longer foreign to church concern are the issues of abortion, family planning and population control, sexual abuse and violence, pornography, prostitution, reproductive technologies, varied family forms, sexually transmitted diseases, teenage pregnancy, and the reassessment of men's lives. [. . .]

[T]he sex factor is deeply rooted in the race problem as well, and rooted so deeply that it is often not recognized. Historically, white males' categorization of women ('either virgins or whores') proceeded along racial lines: white women were symbols of delicacy and purity, whereas black women symbolized an animality that could be sexually and economically exploited. White men projected their guilt onto the black male, fantasizing him as a dark supersexual beast who must be punished and from whom white women must be protected. Black mothers nurtured their sons to be docile, hoping to protect them from white male wrath. That upbringing in turn complicated black marriages and led to certain destructive attempts to recover black 'manliness.' We are the heirs of a distorted racial history in which sexual dynamics have been a major force.

Sexual dynamics are pervasive in our ecological abuse. We are heirs also of a powerful and hierarchical sexual dualism that has shaped much of our understanding of nature. The hierarchy begins with God on top of the chain of being, understanding God as 'nonmaterial spirit,' and continues downward to 'nonspiritual matter' at the bottom, with the bottom believed to be inferior and of value only as it serves that which is above it. [. . .] We are just beginning to see more ecological consciousness in our society growing out of enlightened human self-interest. [. . .] But a deeply transformed ecological consciousness cannot come through self-interest alone, however enlightened that may be. It must involve a new erotic sensibility, a sensibility that is rooted in a transformed male consciousness. [. . .]

Our conversion to recognize and participate in spirit-filled nature calls for an erotic transformation of our ways of thinking. White Western male rationality has emphasized the linear and the dichotomous. [. . .] Such perceptual patterns are reinforced by every hierarchy of social oppression—white people over those of color, rich over poor, heterosexual over homosexual, and of course men over women. Linear thinking categorizes, dichotomizes, focuses on parts, and misses the patterns of relationality and interdependence. But we need a whole-brain consciousness, the connectedness of the whole person.

The ways we express ourselves sexually in the bedroom are connected with everything else. There is a difference between narrowly genital, orgasm-focused sex and making love. An erotic consciousness bears the promise of the sensuous body-self making love with the earth. The universe is a participatory universe. The Hebrew word *yada'*, 'to know,' also means 'to make love sexually.' It is mutual and participatory, neither dominant and submissive nor active and passive. It is full-bodied loving, not simply a conjunction of genitals where there is pen-etrator and penetrated. It is when two knowers and two knowns reveal their connectedness. Such loving is the stuff of a new ecological awareness. [. . .]

This will not be the first time in Christian history that a major shift has taken place in the perception of sexuality. Recall that in the seventeenth century some Protestants began to affirm that loving companionship, not procreation, is the central meaning of sexuality. This religious revolution is still unfinished. But even more far-reaching changes are now taking place.

The changes in our perception and experience of male sexuality and mascu-line spirituality are an enormously important part of this more fundamental revolution. As we who are men increasingly become part of this process, we will become better lovers. We will become better friends of God, of our world, and of ourselves. We will know in a new way that the Word continues to become flesh and dwell among and within us. And as that happens, our male energy will be more life-giving than we have yet known.

Literature

Gerzon, Mark. 1982. *A Choice of Heroes: The Changing Face of American Manhood*. Boston: Houghton Mifflin.

Harrison, Beverly Wildung. 1986. *Making the Connections: Essays in Feminist Social Ethics*, ed. Carol S. Robb. Boston: Beacon.

Heyward, Carter. 1984. *Our Passion for Justice*. New York: Pilgrim.

Kazantzakis, Nikos. 1965. *Report to Greco*, trans. P. A. Bien. New York: Simon & Schuster.

Nelson, James B. 1983. *Between Two Gardens*. New York: Pilgrim.

——. 1987. 'Reuniting Sexuality and Spirituality,' *The Christian Century* 104/6 (Feb. 25):187–90.

Osherson, Samuel. 1986. *Finding our Fathers: The Unfinished Business of Manhood*. New York: Free Press.

Ricoeur, Paul. 1970. 'Wonder, Eroticism, and Enigma,' in *Sexuality and Identity*, ed. Hendrik Ruitenbeek. New York: Dell Publishing. Pp. 13–24.

Part 2

A New Field Takes Shape

'Part of what needs to be done,' Stephen Boyd wrote in the spring of 1990, 'is to analyze carefully the religious traditions that have shaped, for better or worse, our [men's] psyches and our bodies in order to identify both what is negative, oppressive and deadening and what is positive, liberating and enlivening in those traditions. To facilitate this work, seventeen scholars from various fields in the study of religion have submitted a proposal to the American Academy of Religion [AAR] to begin an experimental session, Men's Studies and Religion' (Boyd 1990, 8). This moment formally constituted the hour of birth of men's studies in religion. The proposal, which pulled together and formalized a men's studies perspective on religion, was accepted by the AAR the same year. Since then, sessions have been held regularly at the Academy's annual meetings.

When the proposal was submitted in 1990, another group working on men's issues in religion had already been in place for two years in the same professional organization. The Gay Men's Issues in Religion group, founded in 1988, made it its mission to reflect on the gay male experiences in all forms of religious life. This group came into being in the wake of a wider social call to acknowledge the subjectivity of people who had been previously subjugated, rendered invisible, or declared deviant. Progressive theologians responded to these social changes by developing their own liberative paradigms. A number of 'theologies of particularity' appeared that affirmed the fullness and wholeness of previously ignored or marginalized groups, such as feminist theology, womanist theology, black theology, minjung theology or *mujerista* theology. No longer adopting an apologetic stance and trying to explain to the mainstream how particular people are different and why their difference is not threatening, theologians and religious scholars belonging to these communities began to articulate frameworks that would be rooted in their own experiences and do justice to their lives. It is not surprising, then, that gay men also created their own supportive environment to reflect religiously on their experiences.

Given this context, the 1990 proposal spearheaded by Stephen Boyd concerning a Men's Studies and Religion group must be seen as a response to these developments. As a new field, it recognized the widespread disengagement of heterosexual male scholars on questions concerning their own gendered roles and sexual orientation, and it aimed at redressing the 'relative lack of critical analysis of religion from a men's studies perspective' (Boyd 1990, 1). Although never explicitly stated – and, in fact, the group has been welcoming men and women of different sexual orientations – the heterosexual perspective has been operative in the men's studies group and continues to provide one of the reasons for maintaining a separate identity from the gay men's group at the AAR.

It must be noted, however, that the Men's Studies in Religion group does not see itself in competition with gay men's studies (or, for that matter, with feminist scholarship), but rather as a complementary activity. It has been conscientious about inviting gay and straight scholars alike to explore together the relationship between male experiences and religious practices in a non-sexist and non-homophobic environment. Indeed, both the AAR's Gay Men's Issues group and the Men's Studies in Religion group have co-operated at several occasions over the years. Here is how each of them describes and defines itself in 2008 on the official AAR webpage:

> The *Men's Studies in Religion group* provides a forum within which the phenomenon of masculine gendered identity is examined using the range of methodologies found in the broad fields of theology and religious studies. Men's Studies in Religion engages in the study of men's ways of being, behaving, and believing through a critical examination of both hegemonic (dominant and dominating) and non-hegemonic (marginalized) forms of masculinity. Emerging from, and pairing with, the liberative and critical gender discourses found in feminist, gay, and queer studies, this area of intellectual concentration focuses on the phenomenon of men *qua* men and its impact on the religious and theological terrain. The group calls men to greater self-awareness and critical self-reflection regarding their own identities as people and scholars.

> The *Gay Men's Issues in Religion group* seeks to understand and provide scholarly reflection and writing on the varied intersections of gay male experience and religious traditions and spiritual practices. We seek to affirm the contributions made to religious scholarship by gay male perspectives, methodologies and approaches and to challenge the privileging of those perspectives that undermine or discredit such contributions.

This section of the *Critical Reader* presents three chapters that discuss the formation and contours of the field of men's studies in religion. It begins with Stephen Boyd's reflections on the central themes of this field – nine years after he had helped to institute it at the AAR. His chapter is followed by J. Michael Clark's 'A Gay Man's Wish List for the Future of Men's Studies in Religion', which queries the potential cloistering effect of this new field. Finally, Laurel Schneider pushes the discussion further by introducing queer theory. Emphasizing that the link to feminism cannot be neglected among scholars working on men and masculinities issues, she offers helpful ways of thinking about the differences between gay theology and queer theory.

Literature

Boyd, Stephen B. 1990. 'Domination as Punishment: Men's Studies and Religion'. *Men's Studies Review* (Spring):1, 4–9.

5

Trajectories in Men's Studies in Religion: Theories, Methodologies, and Issues

Editor's Introduction

In 1995, Stephen Boyd published *The Men We Long to Be: Beyond Domination to a New Christian Understanding of Manhood*, in which he charts a new way for men. He writes:

> We men are not inherently or irreversibly violent, relationally incompetent, emotionally constipated, and sexually compulsive. To the extent that we manifest these characteristics, we do so not because we are male, but because we have experienced violent socialization and conditioning processes that have required or produced this kind of behavior and we have chosen to accept, or adopt, these ways of being, thinking, and acting. (1995, 14)

This short paragraph articulates well a concern for men from a heterosexual, Christian perspective. It is geared primarily toward men who, in principle, have been in social positions that made them the beneficiaries of traditional gender discourse but who are now searching for ways to break out of what they and others believe to be normative male behavior. Like James Nelson before him, Boyd argues that certain observable masculine characteristics (violent, compulsive, emotionally impoverished, etc.) are not innately 'male' but to a large extent learned behavioral patterns. Because they are systemically enforced and upheld by religion and society, these behaviors often appear immutable, although they can, with some effort, be unlearned. 'It is possible for us to experience transformation and to make different choices', Boyd writes, and certain 'alternative traditions' in Christianity can 'call us to personal and interpersonal reconciliation and communion with God' and thus enable men to care for 'the well-being and flourishing of all others' (Boyd 1995, 14). No doubt, such a transformation would not come easy (recall, for example, what Mary Daly had said about men looking inside: they would start 'wondering what was wrong with them'; see chapter 1). The reward, however, would be far greater than the pain experienced during this transition: Men would experience 'bliss', which Boyd defines as the 'means by which God calls us into wholeness' (1995, 14).

Boyd is committed to helping men transform themselves. His efforts in establishing a forum for the academic study of men and religion must be seen as part of his larger mission to bring about changes for heterosexual men living in a heterosexist and (post-) patriarchal culture. 'Men, individually and collectively',

Boyd writes, 'need to "lay hold of their souls," as fourth-century desert ascetics would say, or distinguish our selves from those dominative roles to which we have been gendered. To facilitate this examination we need to complement feminist scholarship with an analysis of religion from men's studies perspectives' (1990, 8).

When men's studies in religion was established at the AAR, Boyd chaired it for several years and, later, co-edited the volume *Redeeming Men: Religion and Masculinities* (1996). In 'Trajectories in Men's Studies in Religion' (1999), reprinted below, he reflects on the early results of a 'sustained inquiry into what religious beliefs and practices entail for men as men', and concludes by suggesting areas in need of further analysis.

Publications by the Same Author

Boyd, Stephen B. 1990. 'Domination as Punishment: Men's Studies and Religion'. *Men's Studies Review* (Spring):1, 4–9.

——. 1995. *The Men We Long to Be: Beyond Domination to a New Christian Understanding of Manhood.* San Francisco: HarperSanFrancisco.

——. 1999. 'Trajectories in Men's Studies in Religion: Theories, Methodologies, and Issues'. *The Journal of Men's Studies* 7/2:3–12.

Boyd, Stephen B., Merle Longwood and Mark Muesse (eds). 1996. *Redeeming Men: Religion and Masculinities.* Louisville: Westminster John Knox.

Trajectories in Men's Studies in Religion: Theories, Methodologies, and Issues

STEPHEN B. BOYD

This essay [. . .] sketches a brief history of the Men's Studies in Religion group (MSRG) of the American Academy of Religion (AAR), and describes its purposes, goals, and interdisciplinary character. In addition, I identify themes that have emerged in the group's work and areas demanding further investigations. [. . .] The Men's Studies in Religion Program Unit was organized in 1990 in order to apply the critical perspectives of the interdisciplinary area of the new, or antisexist, men's studies to the study of religion. [. . .]

Men's studies, with roots in the social sciences, developed in the late 1970s and 1980s, responding to the challenge of feminist studies to explore and seek to understand human experience as it is lived by gendered beings. By the late 1980s, scholars developed new critical theories and research strategies pursued in such bodies as the American Psychological Association, the British Sociological Association, and the Modern Languages Association. By 1991, approximately 400 courses were being taught in North American institutions of higher education that had men's studies perspectives and materials as a major component.

However, very little work was being done to apply these new perspectives to the study of religion.

The initiators of the MSRG were convinced that feminist scholarship had clearly demonstrated that an adequate understanding of religious practices and symbols must include gender (i.e., the cultural experience of being male or female) as a category of analysis. Within the AAR several groups (e.g., the Women and Religion Section, the Lesbian-Feminist Issues in Religion, and the Womanist Approaches to Religion and Society groups) had been contributing to the understanding of the ways in which religious symbols and practices shape, challenge, and transform women's roles and the ways women understand, appropriate, and change religious symbols and practices. However, while a growing number of AAR program units studied men's spiritual and religious lives, very few of these groups supported a sustained inquiry into what religious beliefs and practices entail for men *as* men. MSRG was begun to provide a forum for investigating both: how men's gender identities shape the religions men create and practice and how religions construct and shape men's gender identities.

It was the belief of many in the group that men's studies, because of its deep sympathy to the work of women's studies scholars, is also crucial to the goals of many of those scholars. Without a thorough and succinct investigation of masculinities and masculine experiences in all their complexity under patriarchy and a study of alternatives to patriarchy, many participants believed, the effort of feminist/*mujerista*/womanist scholars of religion would remain only partially successful in bringing forth a sophisticated model of the construction of gender and in understanding its impact on religion. Due to the unit's interdisciplinary outlook and its commitment to a full representation of the constituency of the AAR, the MSRG provides a vital and necessary scholarly forum toward that understanding. In fact, the MSRG is the only such forum in North America and, perhaps, the world where the formal academic study of men is focused on religious matters.

The leadership of the MSRG began with a strong commitment to interdisciplinary work and to critical theory related to issues of class, race, sexual orientation, and ecology. Included among the disciplinary areas that have been represented by participants in the unit's work are historical studies, social ethics, constructive and deconstructive theology/thealogy, psychology of religion, sociology of religion, biblical studies, and the visual arts. Consequently, the methodologies employed by presenters and respondents have been pluriform—feminist studies; ritual studies, including phenomenological description; cultural criticism; psychoanalytic theory; literary criticism; and gay studies. The steering committee and co-chairs intentionally structured calls for papers to elicit interest and engagement of scholars working from various social locations. That effort, along with formal and informal networking with other program units and the selection of respondents, has produced a fairly rich mix of female and male scholars from Euro-American, African American, gay and lesbian, Jewish, and Native American contexts. The co-chairs and committee learned that cultivating diversity among presenters takes significant intentional effort and communication about men's studies theories and research strategies, as well as careful attention to the issues and methodologies of scholars in other program units. Attention to that effort is one of the major criteria used in selecting new leadership for the unit.

Among the central themes that have emerged in the unit's work are:

1. the ways that being religious affects men's sense of masculinity, including analyses of fundamentalism, liberal Protestantism, evangelicalism, the black church, Judaism, and Goddess traditions;

2. the influence of sexist, heterosexist, racist, and classist definitions of hegemonic masculinity on religious ideas and practices, such as ritual sacrifice, sexual ethics, social ministries, and pastoral authority;

3. the effects of specifically male experiences and various constructions of masculinity on the religious and spiritual dimensions of men's relationships to women, other men, children and nature; and

4. the ways religious rhetoric and practices have shaped such prominent movements as the Million Man March, the Promise Keepers, and the Men's Mythopoetic Movement and their effects on American political and religious life.

Since the group's founding, there has been a steady increase of papers in other program units that have dealt with the cultural construction of masculinity or specifically male experiences as a central focus. [. . .] These have been presented in ten other units within the AAR and five units in the Society of Biblical Literature. In addition, the work of the MSRG has drawn increasing interest from both publishers and international scholars. Among the presses with whom our unit's participants have published are Beacon, Fortress, Harper-Collins, New York University Press, Pilgrim, and Westminster. In addition, journals such as *The Journal of Men's Studies* and *Masculinities* have sought submissions from the unit. Scholars in Great Britain, Australia, New Zealand, Canada, and Germany who are just beginning to apply men's studies research strategies to the study of religion have contacted the MSRG co-chairs for help.

After two years as an experimental consultation and a five-year stint as a group, we saw the first year of our renewed group status as an opportune moment to take stock of the group's momentum by giving more intentional theoretical attention to clarifying the goals, premises, methodologies, and commitments of men's studies in religion. We had encouraged the use of men's studies perspectives and research strategies among our colleagues in the AAR with increasing success. We believed, however, that it was time to become more self-conscious and critically sophisticated about what we do in men's studies and why. While it is valuable, even essential, to address such significant events as the Million Man March and the Promise Keepers, we felt a need simultaneously to be concerned with the ongoing development and refinement of men's studies as an academic/political endeavor.

In order to build on and expand the themes that had emerged and to deepen the critical analysis of the unit's work, we planned to address the following topics in the next few years of the group's work:

1. What is the relationship between critical theorizing and religious practices that challenge patriarchal structures and consciousness?

2. Where are the convergences and divergences among men's studies theory, feminist/*mujerista*/womanist theories, and queer theory? What are the unique contributions men's studies make to the use of gender as a category of analysis in the study of religion?

3. Which masculinities (hegemonic and subordinated), if any, should be central to theorizing about masculinity, or does all such privileging lead to distortion and unjust power relations? Should diversity of perspectives be encouraged to produce a more inclusive men's studies theory, or does the practice of inclusion require the abandonment of the search for a single, dominant theory of masculinity? How and why do some forms of masculinity (hegemonic) serve some men in the maintenance of unjust relations, and other forms (e.g., gay, Jewish, African American, Latin American) serve others, in the resistance to various forms of oppression? How do religious ideas, rituals, and institutions reflect and shape these various forms of masculinity?

4. Is the use of terms like masculinity and maleness helpful, or do these terms reify the very dynamics that men's studies scholarship criticizes? What relations do these terms have to a biological given, or is there such a thing? What role do religious discourse and practice play in these issues? [. . .]

A Gay Man's Wish List for the Future of Men's Studies in Religion

Editor's Introduction

J. Michael Clark has been an active voice in the dialogue between gay and straight men in religious studies. He has taken both groups to task and called upon them to learn from each other. In several of his writings he has addressed the importance of thinking about men's studies in religion as a shared venture between gay and straight men, and he has repeatedly warned of the detrimental effects of protecting one's turf, for it would lead to a specialized language representing the interests of an in-group only. He is especially concerned about the ghettoization of gay studies: although a protected turf would bolster particular understandings of what it means to be gay, without dialogue, gay theology might eventually lose social and political relevance.

Clark sees some of the same ghettoizing mentality at work among heterosexual scholars pursuing themes on men and religion, and he is urging both the gay and straight communities, after they have done their homework, to join hands in helping each other in 'de-ghettoizing our men's studies work in religion', as he puts it in the chapter below. Elsewhere, Clark writes:

> Failing to do our men's studies homework, failing to confront our socialization as men and its effects on our lives as men who are also gay men, not only leaves heteropatriarchy intact, but also precludes our envisioning any more liberating ways to construct our lives than the narrowly sexual models endemic to the ghetto . . . We must re-examine our relationship, paying particular attention to any dynamics that may be of liberational value for other men, gay or nongay, who are also reflecting upon struggling within their own relationships. In that process, we want to take even more seriously the ethical demand to do our men's studies homework . . . and to continue to nurture that activity among gay men, gay theologians, and men's studies scholars whereby our specifically located voices weave our partial truths into the dynamic whole of being-and-doing. (Clark 1997b, 316)

This passage echoes concerns voiced already by Mary Daly, James Nelson, and Stephen Boyd. Although Clark does not quote or credit Mary Daly directly, her language of 'being' as a way of perceiving one's life-sustaining activities in the world, which has been key to her thinking, has seeped into other discourses of liberation. Clark also builds upon James Nelson's ethical demand to nurture ourselves into 'wholeness' (1983; 1988), an idea that has guided Boyd's vision of men's transformation, too. 'My earlier effort', Clark writes, 'engaged the works of James Nelson' and, more recently, also 'Stephen Boyd's (1995) *The Men We Long to Be*'; the latter is a 'primary methodological starting point' and 'the main conversational partner for our shared reflections' (Clark 1997b, 316–17; also 1992; 1994).

Not everyone among gay scholars of religion agrees with Clark's perspective on a gay ethics of relationality, spirituality and mutuality. These critics fear that building alliances across different constituencies and continuously seeking dialogue with other groups (straight men, feminist women, etc.) might, in fact, weaken a proud discourse on gay identity and dilute the gay 'difference'. We will encounter such a voice in Ronald Long's chapter (28; also 1994).

In the chapter below, Clark addresses the urgency of becoming strong advocates of men's studies in religion and of supporting such engagement with carrying out constructive theology with respect to men's transformative work. 'If we don't advocate for our own men's studies work' and 'de-ghettoize our own', he writes, 'no one else will do it for us.'

Publications by the Same Author

Clark, J. Michael. 1989. *A Place to Start: Toward an Unapologetic Gay Liberation Theology*. Dallas: Monument Press.

——. 1992. *Masculine Socialization & Gay Liberation: A Conversation on the Work of James Nelson and Other Wise Friends*. Arlington: The Liberal Press.

——. 1993. *Beyond Our Ghettos: Gay Theology in Ecological Perspective*. Cleveland: Pilgrim.

——. 1994. 'Men's Studies, Feminist Theology, and Gay Male Spirituality', in *Sexuality and the Sacred: Sources for Theological Reflection*, eds James B. Nelson and Sandra P. Longfellow. Louisville: Westminster John Knox. Pp. 216–28.

——. 1996. 'Gay Men, Masculinity, and an Ethic of Friendship', in *Redeeming Men*, eds Stephen B. Boyd, Merle Longwood and Mark Muesse. Louisville: Westminster John Knox. Pp. 252–62.

——. 1997a. *Defying the Darkness: Gay Theology in the Shadows*. Cleveland: Pilgrim.

——. 1997b. 'Doing the Work of Love: I. Men's Studies at the Margins'. *The Journal of Men's Studies* 5/4 (May):315–31.

——. 1999. 'A Gay Man's Wish List for the Future of Men's Studies in Religion'. *The Journal of Men's Studies* 7/2 (Winter):269–73.

——. 2002. 'Faludi, *Fight Club*, and Phallic Masculinity: Exploring the Emasculating Economics of Patriarchy'. *The Journal of Men's Studies* 11/1 (Fall):65–76.

——. 2005. 'The Agrarian Male: Economic and Ecological Challenges in a New Century'. *The Journal of Men's Studies* 13/3 (Spring):369–88.

Clark, J. Michael and Tina Pippin. 2006. 'Revelation/Apocalypse,' in *The Queer Bible Commentary*, eds D. Guest et al. London: SCM Press. Pp. 753–68.

Further Reading

Boyd, Stephen B. 1995. *The Men We Long to Be: Beyond Domination to a New Christian Understanding of Manhood*. San Francisco: HarperSanFrancisco.

Long, Ronald E. 1994. 'An Affair of Men: Masculinity and the Dynamics of Gay Sex'. *The Journal of Men's Studies* 3/1 (August):21–48.

Nelson, James B. 1983. *Between Two Gardens: Reflections on Sexuality and Religious Experience.* New York: Pilgrim.

———. 1988. *The Intimate Connection: Male Sexuality, Masculine Spirituality.* Philadelphia: Westminster.

A Gay Man's Wish List for the Future of Men's Studies in Religion

J. MICHAEL CLARK

I want to take a more whole-bodied approach [to men's studies in religion], fusing theory and practice to focus on [. . .] three clusters of activities I think we need to pursue more: (1) doing constructive theology, (2) de-ghettoizing our men's studies work in religion, and (3) practicing what we preach.

Given my specific ecolocation as a gay man doing theology and ethics related to men's studies, my first impression is that the majority of our work in religion here has been *deconstructive.* As profeminist men for the most part, we have become adept at using feminist theory to analyze how men specifically, and the patriarchal universe more generally, have gotten us into the fix we're in. We've made some tentative and provisional suggestions as to how we might repair our individual lives as well as the world at large; however, because we're so afraid that systematically proscriptive or prescriptive work will be seen as reverting to authoritative male privilege, we have not engaged enough in *constructive* theology.

Although Stephen Boyd's *The Men We Long to Be* (1995) attempts to (re)construct a primarily heterosexual relational ethics and Seth Mirsky's paper (1996) [. . .] might serve as a prolegomenon for doing ecological ethics, most of our religious studies work remains piecemeal and unintegrated, as reflected in the recent anthology edited by Boyd, Longwood and Muesse (1996). While the reviewer of that anthology in *The Journal of Men's Studies* applauds its 'diversity,' its 'multiplicity of voices,' and even the success of the editors' 'non-combative and non-competitive mode' (Krondorfer 1997, 353, 355), that same reviewer bemoans the fact that the tension 'created by those voices is not put into a more fruitful debate' (355) or integrated conversation. The 'disagreements and creative tensions between these differing positions' (356) are merely juxtaposed, not engaged in dialogue as such even by the editors. Finally, when the reviewer notes with surprise 'that critical reflections on men's issues in religion are still few and far between' (354), we are again reminded that systematic and/or constructive liberation theologies and ethics, similar to those emerging from the feminist and gay/lesbian camps (e.g. Clark 1989; Comstock 1993; Hunt 1991; Ruether 1972; Welch 1990) with which profeminist men have allied themselves, have not yet emerged from this group.

Even if we grant the fact that nearly all theology has been male-written and -directed historically, I still have a number of questions for us to consider: What might the constructive work of a profeminist, gay-affirmative men's studies-based theology look like? What might be at least some of our more integrated, post-deconstructive or post-analytical visions? How does a profeminist, gay-affirmative men's studies-based theology recast the doctrine of God or name and describe the Divine? How does it engage in scriptural work, both deconstructive and reconstructive? How does it engage the figures of Abraham, Isaac, and Jacob—those formative patriarchs of Judaism—or of Jesus and Paul—the formative males of Christianity—and, likewise, how does it undertake the activity of Christology? In fact, it strikes me now that over the years we have virtually ignored the figure of Jesus altogether in men's studies in religion. How might what we are learning together reshape and reconstruct sacraments, liturgy, even religious communities (such as our churches and synagogues)? How might it reshape religious education in terms of both pedagogy and curricula? In other words, are we profeminist, gay-affirmative, presumably newly enlightened men merely going to content ourselves with giving assent to what our feminist and gay/lesbian allies have already done in these areas, or are we willing to start using what we've learned together over the last years to interact with, and undertake, work relevant to the larger theological project? Obviously, I'm inclined toward the latter.

I think part of the problem here relates to the second activity I want to advocate for us. We need to get our work outside what I would call 'the men's studies ghetto.' We need to quit simply 'preaching to the choir.' If we are only willing to present our men's studies work in religion within the safe and secure confines of the AAR [American Academy of Religion] or the AMSA meetings [American Men Studies Association], we will continue to wall ourselves off from larger audiences. We will continue to reinforce the academically patriarchal notion that our work is something merely extracurricular and therefore not 'real scholarship'—the same argument traditionally used to marginalize women's studies, gay/lesbian studies, and, at times, even various ethnic studies. To put it bluntly, giving talks at meetings alone will not do; *we must publish more.* As I understand it, within the last couple of years, one men's studies journal folded altogether, and another one almost did—in both cases due to a lack of submissions. And, I think I know why, at least in part.

We, ourselves, have too often devalued our own men's studies work, giving it a lower priority in our academic lives than the more 'acceptable' publication demands related to job-seeking and hiring, tenure and promotion, within a very patriarchal academic system. If we have had two papers sitting unrevised on our desks, one on [men's studies] and one our last talk in one of the 'mainstream' AAR sessions, and with time only to revise one of those papers for publication (given the competing demands on our time), we have *not* chosen to work on our men's studies articles or book ideas or whatever. We have capitulated to the very patriarchy we've been critiquing. To be blunt again, we've allowed ourselves to become profeminist men's studies hypocrites, *albeit by default.* My concern here is that we have to take some risks. We alone must insist that our work matters to ourselves and to others. We have to insist that it is 'real' scholarship. We have to ask ourselves: are we willing to compromise both our critical theory and our values just for the sake of a full-time academic position, or tenure, or the next promotion? Can we authentically deconstruct the systemic evils of masculine socialization and patriarchy—academia included—while nonetheless protecting male privilege within that system? I think not, and I say this as someone who knows the costs of being perennially excluded and marginalized by 'the system' since graduate school many years ago. It is only because I also know the margins as a place of theological creativity and of spiritual liberation that I can affirm that the risks of authenticity are well worth the costs. If we don't advocate for our own men's studies work, if we don't (re)prioritize our publication choices and de-ghettoize our own work, no one else will do it for us.

Such risk-taking is directly related to the third activity I'm advocating here—practicing what we preach. To put this another way, I think that as liberationist thinkers we have to insist—to enact and to embody—the conviction that theology is advocacy (Ellison 1996, 11), in our case advocacy on behalf of all those lives which have been historically marginalized by patriarchal thought and action. One way to do this might be to engage in genuinely collaborative projects across various lines of difference. My experience as a gay man in this group, for example, mirrors the criticisms of the anthology I described earlier: various perspectives are very clearly welcome here, but too often this inclusivity is merely a matter of juxtaposition—gay men and nongay men appear on the same agenda but we are not really working together. The closest we may have come has been to have a gay man serve as the respondent to a set of papers written by nongay men. While that arrangement at least creates some dialogue across our differences, what I'm advocating is real cross-pollinating, working-together collaboration in both shared activism and shared scholarship. We need more than just shared meeting spaces.

Relative to our scholarship, for example, the positive responses to my AMSA keynote (Clark, 1997) suggest that one specific area ripe for our collaboration would be to examine how our shared masculine socialization to a sense of sexual entitlement shapes how we men enact our sexuality and how that, in turn, affects our capacities (or our failures) to engage in monogamous relational commitments. In other words, how does our shared conditioning to substitute genital activity for intimacy and affection as well as our related sexual behavior as men—whether gay or nongay—affect our relationships? As another example, my engagement with the Mirsky ecology paper (1996) suggests that men of various differences—not just sexual orientation—might collaborate in doing environmental ethics and ecospirituality. We need to look more closely still at how our similarities and our differences as men shape our relationships with the nonhuman world all around us. Our differing socio-economic and ecolocations could certainly enhance that conversation. One final area also needing our collaboration concerns the pedagogical impact of our work: how might we take a more proactive role in getting our profeminist and gay-affirming ideas into the classroom conversations of colleges, seminaries, and even adult education or Sunday school programs? This is increasingly a concern among gay men in religious studies. Of course, our working together will require some genuine listening to one another and a real openness to criticism, as well as to praise, so that we may avoid creating any double standards in our work. I find the possibility of such life-affirming mutuality and shared creativity very exciting.

The issue of shared activism is the more difficult challenge here, because the onus must be upon those who currently enjoy the most privileged positions. Ethicist Marvin Ellison (1996) has suggested, for example, that nongay white men who enjoy economic, social and academic privileges 'must not only acknowledge their privileges, but also find creative'—and I would add, even subversive—'ways to use that privilege to make justice happen' (112). While I want to challenge the safety of heterosexual male privilege, I realize I cannot realistically expect my colleagues to relinquish their academic privileges. I do think, however, that I have a right to expect them to practice what they preach. I can realistically expect them to take some risks, to use their positions of tenured privilege to compel inclusivity across lines of marginality, especially in the tough area of hiring marginalized colleagues. And, I might add, it is especially offensive to standards of justice whenever someone who is safely tenured and *also gay* remains closeted and fails to use that privilege to create justice for other marginalized men, including gay men.

A striking example of efforts to create justice in hiring has recently been reported for departments of philosophy: rather than punish new Ph.D.s and junior colleagues to create proportional racial and gender equity, some departments are encouraging or even forcing early retirement for the older white male generation whose privileged rule over professional philosophy is perceived as responsible for existing inequities (McGowan 1997). This solution raises a number of thorny questions outside the scope of this discussion. However, I am aware that some of my heterosexual colleagues right here in this room enjoy not only full-time academic employment, but even tenured security, because some search committee decided in advance that they wanted person X and therefore crafted a position description so carefully that only person X could fit the requirements, thereby eluding equal opportunity or affirmative action policing. If the good ol' boy network has subverted the system in the past to hire one of its own, why not 'subvert the dominant paradigm' for liberationist purposes? I think it would be incredibly exciting to discover that a search committee or an institution somewhere decided in advance that it wanted a Ron Long, or a Gary Comstock, or even a Michael Clark, and then worked the system to hire that particular, marginalized men's studies colleague. I am not defending the good ol' boy network here, but granted that it is functionally alive and well, I am suggesting we manipulate it to 'make justice happen,' as Ellison recommends. [. . .]

I want to reiterate that our 'trajectories' for men's studies must fuse theory and praxis; our efforts must be practical as well as intellectual as we engage, however belatedly, in doing constructive theology and ethics (both individually and collaboratively), in increasing our men's studies publishing output to reach larger audiences, and in creating justice in our interpersonal relationships, in our shared social justice activism, and in our hiring and promotion activities. Through working together on these and other issues will we discover our empowerment as a liberational community of men's studies professionals.

Literature

Boyd, Stephen B. 1995. *The Men We Long to Be: Beyond Domination to a New Christian Understanding of Manhood*. San Francisco: HarperSanFrancisco.

Boyd, Stephen B., Merle Longwood and Mark W. Muesse. (eds). 1996. *Redeeming Men: Religion and Masculinities*. Louisville: Westminster John Knox.

Clark, J. Michael. 1989. *A Place to Start: Toward an Unapologetic Gay Liberation Theology*. Dallas: Monument Press.

——. 1997. 'Doing the Work of Love. I: Men's Studies at the Margins.' *The Journal of Men's Studies* 5:315–31.

Comstock, Gary D. 1993. *Gay Theology Without Apology*. Cleveland: Pilgrim.

Ellison, Marvin M. 1996. *Erotic Justice: A Liberating Ethic of Sexuality*. Louisville: Westminster John Knox.

Hunt, Mary E. 1991. *Fierce Tenderness: A Feminist Theology of Friendship*. New York: Crossroad.

Krondorfer, Björn. 1997. Book Review of *Redeeming Men: Religion and Masculinities* (eds. Stephen B. Boyd et al. Louisville: Westminster John Knox). *The Journal of Men's Studies* 5:353–6.

McGowan, Richard J. 1997. 'Preferential Programs in Academia and the Disproportionate Burden Placed on Young Male (Philosophy) Scholars.' *The Journal of Men's Studies* 5:273–83.

Mirsky, Seth. 1996. 'Green Earth, Green Men: Sources for a Feminist, Ecological Male Spirituality.' Paper presented at the meeting of the American Academy of Religion, New Orleans (November 24).

Ruether, Rosemary Radford. 1972. *Liberation Theology*. New York: Paulist.

Welch, Sharon D. 1990. *A Feminist Ethic of Risk*. Minneapolis: Augsburg Fortress.

7

Homosexuality, Queer Theory, and Christian Theology

Editor's Introduction

Queer theory 'refuses the dominant categories of discourse', Claudia Schippert writes, 'and challenges assimilationist and liberal-pluralist politics aimed at the legitimization and toleration of excluded groups . . . *Queer* is thus not defined around an identity, but as dissent from and defiance of dominant meanings of sex and gender' (Schippert 1998, 825). If queer theory neither embraces the liberal paradigm of 'tolerating' marginalized groups nor submits to the liberationist paradigm of identity politics, then it puts forth a challenge to both the heterosexual men's scholarship on religion with its professed openness to others as well as to the community of gay religious scholars with its insistence on strengthening a gay identity. Queer theory, then, might actually undermine some of the efforts of the field of critical men's studies in religion since it disavows the categories on which men's studies bases its observations, diagnosis and prescriptions for a cure.

Yet, both gay and straight scholars of men's studies in religion have included queer theory into their approaches or, in any event, claim that they are engaged in 'que(e)rying religion' (Comstock and Henking 1997). Robert Goss, for example, has recently pushed to move from 'gay theology' to 'queer sexual theologies' (Goss 2002, 239); Dale Martin wonders whether the 'historical Jesus' is 'too *queer* for good historiography' (2006, 98); and Stephen Moore's *God's Beauty Parlor: And Other Queer Spaces in and around the Bible* (2001) brings queer theory to bear upon biblical interpretation.

In this chapter, Laurel Schneider reflects on the relationship between queer theory and gender in religion, particularly as it pertains to the differences between the study of homosexualities and theories of queerness. Originally published as a review article on several books on sexuality, gender and religion (Schneider 2000), the condensed reprint below introduces the reader to helpful distinctions. Schneider, like Claudia Schippert, traces the emergence of queer thinking to Michel Foucault's work on sexuality, and suggests that 'queerness' is 'more transgressive, more productive of difference, and more disruptive of stable, normative sexual identities than what we think of when we use the terms gay, lesbian, or homosexual'. Queer theory and theology, she continues, 'take on the whole paradigmatic system of meaning that produces heterosexuality and homosexuality in the first place and tend to view religious ideas as cultural means of production for that system'. Gay and lesbian writings, on the other hand, 'concern themselves with problems of exclusion and the need to obtain justice for gay, lesbian, bisexual, and transgendered people as full persons equal to their heterosexual neighbors in religious communities'.

Historians of homosexuality tend to assess the possibilities of a sustained analysis of gay men in the history of religions differently from the somewhat more skeptical assessment of Schneider. John Boswell may have been among these historians (see also Jordan, chapter 21), but he died before queer theory fully emerged, and, hence, we cannot say for sure how his research may have developed. Another medieval historian, Allen Frantzen, however, articulates well the discomfort he feels when privileging queer theory. In his article 'Between the Lines: Queer Theory, the History of Homosexuality, and Anglo-Saxon Penitentials' he writes:

> Queer theorists are obviously political, seeking ideological confrontations and engagements with contemporary politics that traditional historians of homosexuality have shunned, at least in their scholarship. It almost seems as if queer theorists look ahead, while historians of sexuality look back . . . There is, however, some reason to believe that queer theorists are hostile to the basic premises of medieval scholarship, not only to the analysis of historical categories but even to the analysis of history itself. (Frantzen 1996, 259, 257)

The question of whether queer theory implodes systems of classification and rules of discourse to such an extent that addressing 'men' and 'religion' would be, in the eyes of queer theorists, nothing but reiterations of normative regulations, or whether, on the other hand, the critical study of men in religion can be deepened by queer stipulations must remain open. Schneider's chapter, for one, makes us aware of the significance of the debate for this field of study. After all, she says, both gay and lesbian theologies as well as queer theories are all 'concerned with gender, history, oppression, identity, and liberation'. She continues:

> But without the internal critique that queer theory offers, I am convinced that lesbian and gay liberation attempts in theology will not be able to avoid the mimesis that conditions homosexual inclusion in a heteronormative communion. They will not be able to avoid, in other words, advocating 'good' homosexuals who incidentally look and act a great deal like good heterosexuals at the expense, perhaps, of many of the rest of us.

Publications by the Same Author

Schneider, Laurel C. 1999. *Re-Imagining the Divine: Confronting the Backlash Against Feminist Theology.* Cleveland: Pilgrim.

——. 2000. 'Homosexuality, Queer Theory, and Christian Theology'. *Religious Studies Review* 26/1 (January):3–12.

——. 2007. *Beyond Monotheism: A Theology of Multiplicity.* New York: Routledge.

Further Reading

Comstock, Gary David and Susan E. Henking (eds). 1997. *Que(e)rying Religion: A Critical Anthology*. New York: Continuum.

Goss, Robert E. 2002. *Queering Christ: Beyond Jesus Acted Up*. Cleveland: Pilgrim.

Frantzen, Allen. 1996. 'Between the Lines: Queer Theory, the History of Homosexuality, and Anglo-Saxon Penitentials'. *The Journal of Medieval and Early Modern Studies* 26/2 (Spring):255–96.

Martin, Dale B. 2006. *Sex and the Single Savior: Gender and Sexuality in Biblical Interpretation*. Louisville: Westminster John Knox.

Moore, Stephen D. 2001. *God's Beauty Parlor: And Other Queer Spaces in and around the Bible*. Stanford: Stanford University Press.

Schippert, Claudia. 1998. 'Queer Theory', in *Encyclopedia of Women and World Religions* (vol. 2), ed. Serenity Young. Detroit and New York: Macmillan. Pp. 825–6.

Homosexuality, Queer Theory, and Christian Theology

LAUREL C. SCHNEIDER

A host of problems arise when the 'homosexual question' and its contemporary academic counterpart—queer theory—meet religion, theology, and the various other aspects of religious studies. One problem revolves around defining homosexual identity and queerness. Another revolves around the status of homosexuality in history, and yet another concerns the relationship of homosexualities—however defined—to religious traditions, theologies, and spirituality. What is interesting from an academic, religious studies point of view is the emergence of some key political and methodological differences between what might be called gay/lesbian liberation writings in religion and, on the other hand, queer theory and Christian theology.[1] The former concern themselves with problems of exclusion and of justice for gay, lesbian, bisexual, and transgendered people as full persons equal to their heterosexual neighbors in religious communities. The latter take on the whole paradigmatic system of meaning that produces heterosexuality and homosexuality in the first place and tends to view religious ideas as cultural means of production for that system.

Homosexuality seems, at first glance, to refer simply to people who physically love people of the same sex and identify themselves as gay or lesbian. Defined in this way, discussions of homosexuality tend to focus on issues of social, political, and cultural status, natural and political law and so forth, that have to do with the history and place of lesbian and gay persons in society and religion. Queer theory, which emerged after the 1985 English publication of Michel Foucault's first volume of the *History of Sexuality*, foregrounds the role of historical and social construction in the production of what we think of as sexual natures. Thus, queer thinking complicates simple associations of homo-sexuality with persons.

Queerness is therefore something more transgressive, more productive of difference, and more disruptive of stable, normative sexual identities than what we think of when we use the terms gay, lesbian, or homosexual. Queer theory disrupts not only homosexuality as a stable signifier for particular groups of men or women who consider themselves to be homosexual, but—and this is what really disturbs the religious right—it disrupts the stability and natural givenness of heterosexuality as well. Queer theory 'queers' our taken-for-granted cultural associations concerning sexual identity by revealing their vulnerability to history and, therefore, to change.

This means that those who argue for gay and lesbian inclusion in religious communities on the basis of a 'natural' homosexuality face challenges from two opposing directions. On the one hand, as we know from our daily news-papers, they must defend themselves against those who view sex between men or between women as sinful and abominable. Arguments for homosexuality as a natural variation in human life are a strong position against these views, thus accounting for some of the energy behind locating a 'gay gene' even as that search causes concern among others for whom eugenics looms as a tool for genetic conformity. At the same time, the liberationist strategy of positing a natural homosexuality is challenged by queer theory, which argues for radical social construction in sexual identity and a wider scope to sexual and gender possibilities. Social constructionist theories of sexuality tend to undermine the political and doctrinal value of any arguments from nature.

Although tempting, it is important to avoid too rigid a distinction between what I am calling the gay/lesbian liberationist argument that emphasizes iden-tity and queer theory that troubles identity. Both trajectories in self-proclaimed gay, lesbian, or queer scholarship oriented toward opening a hate-free zone in religion, politics, and daily life are constantly evolving and mutually informing. Nevertheless, something of a distinction is meaningful, especially in religious studies because of the particularly sharp and poignant position of religion and religious people in debates about homosexuality. Indeed, in many ways, gay and lesbian theologies and queer theories in religious studies mirror the evolution and current struggles in academic feminism. Both, after all, are con-cerned with gender, history, oppression, identity, and liberation. Like academic feminism, however, lesbian and gay studies in religion face important internal critiques from queer theory, critiques that may force even more painful divi-sions in religious communities and may spell disaster for gays and lesbians who just want to be included at church. But without the internal critique that queer theory offers, I am convinced that lesbian and gay liberation attempts in theo-logy will not be able to avoid the mimesis that conditions homosexual inclusion in a heteronormative communion. They will not be able to avoid, in other words, advocating 'good' homosexuals who incidentally look and act a great deal like good heterosexuals at the expense, perhaps, of many of the rest of us.

Homosexuality and queer theory are popular topics for study at the moment both because they are relatively new to academia and because they cause a great deal of political, religious, and social frothing at the mouth. The wide-spread participation of homosexuals in religious life makes the current debates about homosexuality in religion both more understandable and more bizarre. Reasons for hysteria can be located in various social theories that account for inchoate fears of change at symbolic levels. Certainly queer theory does threaten the whole fabric of social meaning that heteronormativity has provided to the modern world. Homosexuality's unresolved and publicly contested social status as a crime, a natural state, a sin, a choice, a psycho-medical condition, a genetic variation, an identity, a behavior, a hip fancy, a product of capitalism, a product of patriarchy, a product of feminism, a product of the Phil Donahue–Oprah competition, or a myriad of other possibilities is part of its popular appeal in public discourse. Apart from this public debate, however, the content of emerging works in lesbian and gay studies and in queer theory indicates a theoretical depth in cultural analysis that will not fade soon, particularly for scholars in religion.

In part, and similar to the explosive growth of research on women, studies of homosexuality in general are responding to a void of information. So little is known about the existence of homosexuals in Western history that the usefulness of the term itself is hotly debated. Is or was homosexuality limited to the Eurocentric cultures of the West? Apparently not, but all hinges on how homosexuality—as practice, identity, nature, or all of the above—is defined. Were there even any homosexuals before, say, the nineteenth century? Some, like classicist David Halperin (1989; 1991), follow Foucault and say no. Others, like Adrienne Rich ('Compulsory Heterosexuality,' in Abelove et al. 1993), John Winkler ('Double Consciousness in Sappho's Lyrics,' in Abelove et al. 1993), and John Boswell (in Comstock and Henking 1996), suggest otherwise. Certainly homosexuality as we understand it today (assuming that we do have an understanding of it today) did not exist *as such* throughout history. This is a vexing problem for scholars, who depend upon lineages of ideas, even as they seek new ones. Feminist historians at least do not have to make the argument that there were women throughout all of patriarchal history. It is considered reasonable to infer the presence of women (even if the meaning of the term 'woman' changes over time).

Scholars in lesbian and gay studies and queer theory are primarily interested in the differences that sexualities make in cultures that have rules about such things. Questions about the difference that homosexuality makes lie at the root of queer theory. They have enlarged and deepened an already wide-ranging debate within theology and religious studies about the sources and authority of traditions that define social norms and human identities in terms of sin, redemption, good, and evil, particularly as these categories are expressed through gender and race. Homosexuals are, in one sense, additional 'others' to add to the list of those ostracized by social norms originating in the mists of myth and codified in religious doctrines and traditions. Yet homosexuality also represents a convergence of issues and ideas troubling theology, religion, and scholarship that only now is beginning to emerge. According to Gayle Rubin's essay that introduces *The Lesbian and Gay Studies Reader*, 'Contemporary conflicts over sexual values and erotic conduct have much in common with the religious disputes of earlier centuries. They acquire immense symbolic weight. Disputes over sexual behavior often become the vehicles for displacing social anxieties, and discharging their attendant emotional intensity' (Abelove et al.

1993, 3–4). Homosexuality, or perhaps more broadly, queerness, takes shape in contemporary debates in the midst of this anxiety and is certainly fueled by it. Because the status of homosexuality itself is part of the question, its scope of study is necessarily diffuse. Homosexuality and queerness form the content, in other words, of a debate seeking a contested subject when subjects as such are not taken for granted.

This tension leaves visible traces in the literature. Queerness refers to a particular kind of difference that stands outside of and against normative sexual identity and so refers to more than homosexual pairings of men or of women. Queerness *qua* difference is a difficult target for theory and research, even though theory is its home. Can homosexualities be isolated in any meaningful ways, for example, from other categories of difference like race, ethnicity, class, and so forth? Lesbian and gay studies and queer theory are still nascent enough to have reached little clarity on this question. They tend to demonstrate even less success at theorizing such differences in any thoroughgoing way. Evelynn Hammonds, for example, points out the importance of racialized sexualities involving complexes of power that configure homophobia—and sexuality—for black lesbians in significantly different ways than for white lesbians ('Black (W)holes and the Geometry of Black Female Sexuality,' in Weed and Schor 1997). This is no mere matter of inclusion or exclusion of black experiences in writings on lesbianism; it is a matter, Hammonds claims, of the differences that race (or class, ethnicity, etc.) makes to all theorizing about sexuality. Hammonds also points out the lack of such theoretical sophistication in *The Lesbian and Gay Studies Reader.*

It appears true that most white theorists still think in terms of simple inclusion, and since most writers on sexuality are white, the bulk of queer theory continues to isolate sexuality from these other shaping considerations. Can queer thinking encompass a dynamic constellation of interrelated issues in more meaningful and, dare we say, systematic ways? When should race and ethnicity enter the discussion, and when class? When should disease politics or ecology enter, and when sex and sexism, religion, or other cultural configurations of meaning? Is there a priority of theoretical considerations that should configure gay and lesbian or queer studies? [. . .][2]

Queer theory's adaptation of feminism (the kind of feminism, that is, that argues for the differences gender makes in perspective and meaning) claims that people who do not fit the heterosexual norm do not just live differently from the norm. They *are* different, see differently, and constitute a difference that both supports and undermines the givenness of the norm. In other words, the persistent recurrence of homosexuals—literally out of the arms of heterosexuals—betrays an inessential, arbitrary, produced dimension to heterosexuality (and perhaps homosexuality) that at the same time supports the normativity of heterosexuality by providing a reminder, always, of what heterosexuality is not.

Years ago, Rosemary Radford Ruether (1975) argued that sexism is built upon a deep cultural dualism that feminizes evil and therefore requires the persistence of the subjugated female in order to retain the valorization of the masculinized good. Likewise, Eve Kosofsky Sedgwick argues that normative heterosexuality needs homosexuality in order to retain its norm-defining status. The closet therefore makes the heterosexual, not the homosexual, possible (in

Abelove et al. 1993, 45–61; also Sedgwick 1990). Queer theory enlarges and critically sharpens feminism; together they constitute a deep challenge to religion
precisely because they turn attention to the very exclusions that define religious
ideas upon which those ideas are contingent. [This debate . . .] provides an intellectual framework for treating homosexuality as a meaningful site of difference that could illuminate religion and religious ideas in helpful, if sometimes
unsettling, ways. This is perhaps the point of greatest tension between queer
theory that destabilizes homosexual identities and lesbian/gay theologies that
seek to make a space for them. At the same time, this tension also offers a point
of possibility for deeper critical thought in religious studies.

Queering Religion?

[. . .] Queer theorists in general, concerned with the cultural production
of normative heterosexualities and thereby the cultural production—and
repression—of homosexualities, illuminate the accidental quality (speaking
philosophically) of all social formation, meaning, and identity. This creates and
recreates the tension between queer theory's questions and gay and lesbian
liberationist attempts at answers in religious scholarship. Writers and scholars
in the area of homosexuality and religion still edge warily around queer questions of social historicity and performativity in order to support those gay and
lesbian Christians battling for a place at the communion table on the basis of a
stable homosexual identification.

When queer thinking meets religion, as it begins to do in the *Que(e)rying
Religion* anthology, the result is uneven. Not all of gay and lesbian religious
scholarship is dedicated to more or less stable assertions of homosexual identity
in what Mary McClintock Fulkerson calls 'the therapeutic and scientific discourses of modernity' (in Comstock and Henking 1997, 189), but few of the contributors to *Que(e)rying Religion* take such a critical or historicist position. Some,
like Boswell, indicate an understanding and appreciation of historicism and the
social production of homosexuality, even as he dismisses its more radical implications for claims about homosexuality in history (in Comstock and Henking
1997, 116–29). On the whole, however, this is not an anthology of writers engaging queer theory with religious studies. Instead, it is a loose organization of
voices that are for the most part documenting a kind of homosexual history in
religion, describing homosexual presences in religious communities, or advocating for homosexual inclusion in those communities.

Perhaps because contemporary Western religious institutions are currently
embroiled in so much hysteria about homosexuality, it is difficult to develop
and maintain a theoretical discussion about the niceties of queer theory in
relation to religion. To be sure, when homosexuality is introduced, arguments
about good and evil, sin and redemption, and the nature of being Christian
metamorphose from fairly sedate, sometimes clubbish, and often anachronistic meditations into high-pitched, public tantrums. Uncounted gay and lesbian
clergy and lay people continue to suffer seemingly endless violent exclusions in
their own denominations and congregations, even as high-profile church trials
of heterosexual pastors receive more publicity. [. . .]

So where do things queer and things Christian meet? The current small explosion of sorts going on in monograph publishing about religion and homosexuality indicates that religion is ripe for queer analyses. [. . .] Mark Jordan's careful work on the history of the idea of sodomy in *The Invention of Sodomy in Christian Theology* (1997) is a good example. It traces the invention and development of the idea of the sodomite in Christian theology from Peter Damian's virulent polemics to Thomas Aquinas's systematic assumption of sodomy as the 'vice which cannot be named' (1997, 150). Jordan's work reveals the profoundly constructed quality of homosexuality in the evolution of Christian heteronormative ethics. What is fascinating in this project is its queerness. Jordan uncovers Peter Damian's medieval invention of the terms sodomy and sodomite and his consequent attachment of a relatively stable, criminal identity to men who perform homosexual acts. These are sodomites who are fundamentally deformed in their persons by both their homosexual desire and behavior. Jordan argues persuasively that Damian forges a link between act and essence that creates, for the first time, a homosexual identity in the lexicon of beasts and demons. 'That transition from acts to persons,' he suggests, 'is perhaps what an essence does best. By coining an abstract term [sodomy] to group together a series of acts, Peter Damian has made the inference from acts to agent almost automatic. The acts display an essence, the essence of Sodomy' (1997, 44).

Jordan's history of sodomy is provocative for queer theory and for religious studies in that it explores invented identities through negation. Unlike Boswell in *Christianity, Social Tolerance, and Homosexuality* (1981) or *Same-Sex Unions in Premodern Europe* (1994), Jordan views homosexuality in relief through the polemical invention of the sodomite. He does not attempt to argue for the existence of homosexuals who would have understood themselves as such in medieval Europe; rather he documents the development of a logic of identity and essence in the polemics of prohibition and the systematics of theological construction. What a provocative end run this becomes around current debates about the history of homosexual identity assertion!

Jordan's conclusion that sodomy is a medieval invention does not surprise queer theorists nor does it change the conclusions of any authors working on reformulating traditional Christian prohibitions against homosexuality. His critical analysis of this particular historical development in Christian thought supports that work through specific documentation and inference, but the possibility that a premodern presumption of essence to homosexuality can be inferred from the development of an essential sodomitic identity (although Jordan is careful to point out that Peter Damian's and our concepts of identity do not coincide) provides an interesting twist in the social construction of homosexuality. [. . .]

Intrepid queers who seek to root out homophobia at its deepest levels must at some point turn to religion to do so, but because of the depth of religious polemics against homosexuality, they must choose their political tools carefully. Homosexuals who want to claim religious traditions and existing Christian communities as their own have to make the case that lesbianism and gay experiences are themselves legitimate in Christian or religious terms. This tends to mean a reformulation of human nature to include homosexual desire in order to place homosexuality under the aegis of divine good will. This task by itself establishes a methodological tension with queer theory's suspicion of 'natural' identity claims of any kind. [. . .]

Scholars and writers concerned with formulating theologies and ethics that start from the assumption that homosexuality is good still have the task of constructing a rationale for that assumption against textual and performed traditions. Lesbian theologians like Carter Heyward (1984; 1989), Mary Hunt (1992), and Virginia Ramey Mollenkott (1992) and gay theologians such as Gary Comstock (1996), J. Michael Clark (1996; 1997), and John McNeill (1988; 1993; 1995) have worked on this task for over a decade. Their efforts were fueled in no small part by the AIDS epidemic that provoked comparisons to biblical leprosy, whose outcasts were most notoriously embraced by Jesus. Given the history of homosexual prohibition and demonization at least since early modernity, the task of creating a theological space for homosexuality in Christian thinking has been no small one.

In fact, the range of scholarship in gay and lesbian or in queer theology remains very small. It is predominantly, as L. J. Tessier points out, apologetic (1997, 165). Most argue for a reformed view of gay and lesbian identities as natural and divinely given. Certainly John McNeill's gay theological trilogy, concluding with *Freedom, Glorious Freedom* (1995), is an apology for gay and lesbian inclusion in Christian spiritual community based on the argument that church (and specifically Catholic) doctrine is in error regarding modern homosexuals. His is a therapeutic approach, seeing the habilitation and incorporation of lesbians and gays into Christian communion as a rehabilitation of Christianity into a more life-giving, and ultimately more Christian religion. Gay and lesbian Christians are therefore not disruptive of the logic of Christianity but inherent to it.

In McNeill's view, homosexuality is a productive but not a culturally produced identity. In fact, he argues that 'God, from the beginning of time, saw that our lesbian or gay reality is good and through a unique act of love willed us into being' (1995, 147). Homosexuality is not queer or even historically produced here. It does not disrupt natural law because it is a part of divinely ordained natural law (perhaps McNeill is the essentialist exception that proves Boswell's point). As such, the theological task for McNeill remains what it has been since Thomas Aquinas: to discern from the natural order the ways of God and the normative requirements for human beings who seek to live and act in obedience to God's will for them. Homosexuality is one of the forms of God's will and so falls within normative reach. Like Robert Goss's (1993) positioning of queers around Jesus' radical ministry in *Jesus Acted Up*, McNeill establishes homosexuals as the true subjects of Christian theology precisely because of their outsider but fundamentally love-oriented status. How to *be* a good gay or lesbian Christian is, presumably, very similar to or even the same as being a good heterosexual. There is nothing disruptively queer here, unless the heart of Christian theology is queer—a possibility that is becoming ever more distinct.

This rehabilitative approach to arguments for the inclusion of gay and lesbian identities in church communities also forms the interpretive intent of *Unrepentant, Self-Affirming, Practicing* (Comstock 1996). Gary Comstock's broad sociological study of homosexual people in organized religious communities in the United States documents their presence, activity, and contributions to American religious life. Given the overt hostility of so many modern religious traditions to homosexual practice and life, it is astounding that so many members of so many religious communities are gay, lesbian, or bisexual. Comstock's survey offers data to support the old closet phrase that gay and lesbian people are members of the choir. They often literally are the choir, as well as members of the nominating committees, the stewardship boards, the diaconate, and every other arm (yes, even the clergy) of organized religious life. 'That gay people participate extensively within their religious bodies and serve the needs of people in their wider communities is apparent. But . . . their participation and service are often unrecognized and rejected' (1995, 95).

Comstock's findings still suggest that the majority of gay, lesbian and bisexual Americans have left religious organizations in the dust. The intense leadership involvement of those who remain may be the result of a natural winnowing process. For remaining in such a contested environment to make any sense at all to a queer person, there must be a high level of investment in the community. Not surprisingly, the highest numbers of out gay and lesbian members of church congregations are found in those denominations (like the United Church of Christ and Metropolitan Community Church) that fully accept homosexuality as an acceptable Christian identity. For those who are members of more conflicted religious bodies (like the United Methodist Church or Presbyterian Church) and whose investment in the community is less, the incentive to leave is far greater. [. . .]

Daniel Spencer constructs an ethical basis for gay and lesbian spirituality in *Gay and Gaia* (1996; also Say and Kowalewski 1998) that is predicated on assumptions of gay and lesbian identification and religious arguments for ecological reform. Spiritual health, he argues, must be global and not merely anthropocentric. Based on primarily lesbian writings (Carter Heyward, Mary Hunt), Spencer adopts arguments for relationality in order to refigure embodiment and eroticism as ecological and liberative. The habilitation of homosexuality can only occur, he argues, in terms of a much larger vision of ecological, erotic, embodied wholeness. The focus cannot be on how to fit gays and lesbians into existing structures of thought but on how to change the structures of thought (what he calls the grounding) to encompass gay, lesbian, and bisexual experiences of life.

Spencer is quite conscious of feminist and queer theory's arguments for gender construction and so does not suggest with McNeill's confidence that God established homosexuality as we know it today from the beginning of time. Instead he argues for a process-based relationality that allows for historical change and social construction in all forms of identity, from binary homosexual and heterosexual oppositions, to queer multiplicities, to animal, human, and planetary relations. His point is that homosexuality is not an add-on identity to a list of outsider identities protesting the status quo. Instead he wants to establish sexualities of all kinds as integral expressions of the wholeness evident in all of life, a wholeness that in its fecundity does not exclude any particularity of bodily intensity. Homosexuality or queerness will always remain oppressed and outside of the dominant norm unless queer sensibility becomes a larger ecological sensibility. [. . .] Spencer challenges homosexualities that serve to reinforce heteronormative assumptions—stable homosexualities that, in other words, oppositionally mirror heterosexuality and provide the rationale for its dominance. Spencer's distinctly queer shift away from identities and onto ecological processes could create a more liveable space for gay, lesbian, bisexual, transgendered, and straight people and thus a more challenging, if more viable, space for queer religion.

A Space for Queer Theology?

In a sense, whether intentional or not, all these theologies and theories together could be labeled queer. That is, the relationship between homosexualities that are construed as act, as identity, as public forum, as dissent, and as difference remain unclear and in many ways unresolvable. The notorious instability of sexual identities becomes a problem only when there is something at stake in fixing them. What could be at stake? The stability of heterosexuality, for one. And of course the stability of homosexuality. The place of bisexuality is also at stake, and the relationship of bodies to sex and gender. From these follow investments in notions of creation and divine will. There are other more intimate things at stake as well, such as expectations for love and erotic companionship, for friendships, and for politics.

The tension that underlies all of this discussion is one we cannot avoid. In an academic sense it is, as I have suggested, the tension between strategies of lesbian and gay liberation on the one hand and queer reimagining of the world on the other. On an entirely more raw and close level, lesbian and gay liberation may be about intense and intimate needs for inclusion, recognition, and identity that are worth the cost of some heteronormativity. Queer theology may be about creative reimagining of possibilities in which we are no longer recognizable, but in which we no longer beg for recognition either. The cost of freedom and integrity seems so great on the one side and the risk of loss so real and impossible on the other.

This tension is powerful, creative, and dynamic, but it is powerfully devastating as well. Our need to be human in the grandest and most intimately social senses of that term implicates us in conservative strategies that would reduce the threat to heteronormativity (reassuring our families, neighbors, employers, students, and potential bashers) by establishing a normative identity to homosexuality. Which side is the more correct? There is so little information about us and so much speculation that the real queerness here may be only just beginning. [. . .]

Gay and lesbian liberationist attempts to challenge, reform, and reframe Christian faith to value, bless, and incorporate queer experiences are, in the perspective of more radical queer theory, simply ludicrous. But the gay/lesbian liberationist and the queer theorist positions both rest on very different key assumptions about Christian faith and its contents. For the liberationists, Christian faith is fundamentally about something true and real, although it can be (and has been) distorted. The object of gay liberationist faith is an 'Act-Up' kind of Jesus who preached appallingly radical kindness and who transgressed all sorts of rules about who should be in or out. In the context of this type of assumption, religious reform makes a particular kind of sense. From this viewpoint, the God-man of Christian faith would most certainly associate with fags and dykes. He might even call them his own 'family' (what was that about the beloved disciple?). This view grants to the object of Christian faith a position of truth that demands reinterpretation in contemporary terms.

But in much of queer theory, indebted as it is to postmodern literary criticism, the objects of religious faith can never be resolved enough to matter in the ways that the subjects of faith can. Religion and its contents illuminate the workings of cultural formation and of compulsory heterosexuality because religion is the locus of that compulsion. To develop new theologies that include and even affirm homosexuality may make some gay Christians feel better, but the compulsory aspect of religion remains the same, therefore always excluding queerness even after homosexuals are admitted. [. . .]

The battles over homosexuality today are most bitterly and publicly waged in religious venues, although the battlegrounds are also in college dormitories, on lonely Wyoming fences, in small Alabama towns, and in some legislatures. Christian denominations and communities are politically polarized, enacting a drama in relief for the entertainment of the larger culture. Ironically, state and federal attempts at nondiscrimination legislation exempt religious institutions. Laws that protect gay and lesbian persons from discrimination in the public sphere do not apply to ordaining bodies, church colleges, or parochial institutions. The gay and lesbian liberationist literature is crucial in the fray of these battles because the battles are primarily about rights and privileges predicated on the modernist logic of identity and community. If gay and lesbian scholars in religion can demonstrate clear moral grounds for homosexuality as a good, they have gone a long way to dismantle the grounds of the opposition.

Gay and lesbian theologies, linked to the prophetic outsider ministry of Jesus, argue for the legitimacy of homosexuality within Christian teaching, but they also argue for a particular kind of Christian theology that de-emphasizes tradition and commandment and emphasizes justice and inclusion. They de-emphasize purity as a basis for Christian life and emphasize relationality and mercy. This is not just queer theology; it is a particular kind of ethical theology. Queer theory as intellectual acrobatics of difference and performance cannot encompass this move or even begin to approach it, but theology that shifts its locus to the Act-Up, dangerously kind Jesus is certainly queer and cannot be fixed (in any sense of that word).

Queer theology is still, therefore, waiting to be written. [. . .] To the extent that religion produces and legitimizes coercive norms, queer theology must critique it and stand outside of it. To the extent that religion transforms fear into life and denial into risk, queer theology should articulate it and support it. As critical and engaged theory and prophecy, queer theology will have to wager on surrender and redemption but not assume too quickly or easily that a place for queer thinking will open up. Homosexuals engaged in religious communities are warring over a place at the table and so cannot devote much energy to anything beyond the polarizations and solidifications of identity that come in times of war. Queer theorists in religion have the task of complicating the warring positions without losing sight of the stakes that remain for those they would help. To employ the bread metaphor again, preaching and baking may be the same thing when people are starving. Queer theology needs both the critical edge that queer theory offers and the prophetic inclusion that liberationists demand. In the end, full inclusion may mean that neither homosexuality nor the heterosexual norm will be left intact. Indeed, there may be no Christianity for queers, although there may be a queer Jesus. Surrender, Tessier suggests, come apart, and dance.

Notes

1 In its theological aspects, this essay focuses on Christian writings. This does not mean that other projects addressing homosexuality, queer theory and theology are not underway by religious scholars dealing with other traditions. However, the majority of writings to date deal with Christian theology and so form the subject of this study.

2 Editor's note: For a fuller discussion of the essential link between feminism and queer theory, see Laurel C. Schneider's original article in the *Religious Studies Review* 26/1 (January 2000):5–6. For Schneider, it is important that the link to feminism is not neglected among scholars working on men and masculinities issues, especially in terms of queer theory. See Fulkerson (1994).

Literature

Abelove, Henry, Michèle Aina Barale and David M. Halperin (eds). 1993. *The Lesbian and Gay Studies Reader.* New York: Routledge.

Boswell, John. 1981. *Christianity, Social Tolerance, and Homosexuality: Gay People in Western Europe from the Beginning of the Christian Era to the Fourteenth Century.* Chicago: University of Chicago Press.

——. 1994. *Same-Sex Unions in Premodern Europe.* New York: Vintage.

Clark, J. Michael. 1996. *Beyond Our Ghettos: Gay Theology in Ecological Perspective.* Cleveland: Pilgrim.

——. 1997. *Defying the Darkness: Gay Theology in the Shadows.* Cleveland: Pilgrim.

Comstock, Gary David. 1996. *Unrepentant, Self-Affirming, Practicing: Lesbian/Bisexual/ Gay People Within Organized Religion.* New York: Continuum.

Comstock, Gary D. and Susan Henking (eds). 1997. *Que(e)rying Religion: A Critical Anthology.* New York: Continuum.

Foucault, Michel. 1985. *The History of Sexuality: An Introduction.* New York: Vintage.

Fulkerson, Mary McClintock. 1994. *Changing the Subject: Women's Discourses and Feminist Theology.* Minneapolis: Fortress.

Goss, Robert. 1993. *Jesus Acted Up: A Gay and Lesbian Manifesto.* San Francisco: HarperSanFrancisco.

Halperin, David M. 1989. *One Hundred Years of Homosexuality: And Other Essays on Greek Love* (The New Ancient World Series). New York: Routledge.

——. 1991. *Before Sexuality: The Construction of Erotic Experience in the Ancient Greek World.* Princeton: Princeton University Press.

Heyward, Carter. 1984. *Our Passion for Justice: Images of Power, Sexuality, and Liberation.* Cleveland: Pilgrim.

——. 1989. *Speaking of Christ: A Lesbian Feminist Voice.* Cleveland: Pilgrim.

Hunt, Mary E. 1991. *Fierce Tenderness: A Feminist Theology of Friendship.* New York: Crossroad.

Jordan, Mark D. 1997. *The Invention of Sodomy in Christian Theology*. Chicago: University of Chicago Press.

McNeill, John J. 1988. *Taking a Chance on God: Liberating Theology for Gays, Lesbians, and Their Lovers, Families, and Friends*. Boston: Beacon.

——. 1993. *The Church and the Homosexual*. Boston: Beacon.

——. 1995. *Freedom, Glorious Freedom: The Spiritual Journey to the Fullness of Life for Gays, Lesbians, and Everybody Else*. Boston: Beacon.

Mollenkot, Virginia Ramey. 1992. *Sensuous Spirituality: Out from Fundamentalism*. New York: Crossroad.

Ruether, Rosemary Radford. 1975. *New Woman/New Earth: Sexist Ideologies and Human Liberation*. Boston: Beacon.

Say, Elizabeth A. and Mark R. Kowalewski. 1998. *Gay, Lesbian, and Family Values*. Cleveland: Pilgrim.

Sedgwick, Eve Kosofsky. 1990. *Epistemology of the Closet*. Berkeley: University of California Press.

Spencer, Daniel. 1996. *Gay and Gaia: Ethics, Ecology, and the Erotic*. Cleveland: Pilgrim.

Stuart, Elizabeth, with Andy Braunston, Malcolm Edwards, John McMahon and Tim Morrison. 1997. *Religion is a Queer Thing: A Guide to the Christian Faith for Lesbian, Gay, Bisexual and Transgendered People*. Cleveland: Pilgrim.

Tessier, L. J. 1997. *Dancing after the Whirlwind: Feminist Reflections on Sex, Denial, and Spiritual Transformation*. Boston: Beacon.

Weed, Elizabeth and Naomi Schor (eds). 1997. *Feminism Meets Queer Theory*. Bloomington: University of Indiana Press.

Part 3

Theorizing and Theologizing
Alternative Masculinities

Available books on men and religion, especially from popular presses, have often stressed spiritual and practical concerns of men. If not that, some have limited themselves to describing historical manifestations of masculinity without seriously probing the underlying paradigms, thus often reiterating rather than challenging versions of patriarchal modes of thinking. Theoretical sophistication, a common lament among scholars of gender, is still missing in the study of masculinities in general, and in the study of religion and masculinities in particular. 'If masculinity is to be a viable methodological compass, scholars must seriously pursue the complex theoretical and historical quagmires such a concept poses', writes Kathryn Lofton in her review of works in religion and masculinity (2004).

This section takes up the challenge. The following six chapters represent a diverse set of theoretical and theological investigations revealing some of the complexities of a critical men's studies approach. With Daniel Boyarin, we encounter a Jewish intellectual maverick who embraces Jewish orthodoxy as an alternative masculine ideal of queerness. Graham Ward, a Christian theologian belonging to the British-based school of radical orthodoxy, engages postmodern discourse on desire (especially the French deconstructionist thinkers like Luce Irigaray, Julia Kristeva and Jacques Lacan) for his theological project of understanding the 'male' body of Christ. Philip Culbertson, another Christian theologian, wonders what would happen when the heterosexual male gaze does not rest on the bodies of Others but turns against itself: would the heterosexual body disappear? Looking for answers, Culbertson turns to Eve Kosofsky Sedgwick's concept of homosociality. Jay Johnson's theological probing of the contributions of gay theology leads him, with the help of American pragmatism, towards an epistemology of the 'gay experience'. Robert Goss applies queer theory to the task of queer theologizing, aiming at shaking up self-imposed templates of gay normativity. Stephen Moore, finally, muses on the impact of the autobiographical turn in literary criticism on biblical studies, assessing the efforts of male biblical scholars to insert autobiographical disclosures into their own texts.

Literature

Lofton, Kathryn. 2004. 'The Man Stays in the Picture: Recent Works in Religion and Masculinity'. *Religious Studies Review* 30/1 (January):23–8.

8

Unheroic Conduct: The Rise of Heterosexuality and Jewish Masculinity

Editor's Introduction

Who are Jewish men? What are Jewish ideals of masculinity? Stereotypes abound about Jewish men, frequently nourished by the Christian imagination that either looks at Judaism benignly as its brother/sibling religion or maliciously as a people who refuse to accept Jesus Christ as messiah. In modernity, the antisemitic imagination wrought further havoc, adding to the long list of Christian portrayals of Jewish men (such as wise, gentle, stubborn, hypocritical) the damaging attributes of dangerous, power-hungry, greedy, degenerate or polluting. Although some of these images can be quickly discarded as the political fantasies of proponents of racial hatreds (as most viciously manifested in the antisemitic propaganda of Nazism), other images have a much longer history and are deeply ingrained in both the self-perceptions of Jews as well the external perceptions of Jews by others. Jewish men, ancient and modern, have been pressed into limiting, often diminutive roles. When asking, for example, her students to imagine the ancient rabbis, Miriam Peskowitz reports:

> In the imagination of my students, [they] are 'little old Jewish guys,' 'nice, sweet,' 'kind of grandfatherly.' They are 'bearded' and 'balding' [and they are] 'sitting, studying,' 'hunched over,' and 'slight of frame.' They 'would have worn glasses, had they been invented' . . . [They do not] contemplate sexual desires . . . or hide beneath their teacher's bed to listen to and analyze the sounds of sexual intercourse. Invariably, my students think ancient 'Rabbis' are 'very unattractive,' if their bodies can be imagined at all. (Peskowitz 1995, 288)

We find a modern counterpart in Paul Breines's study on the transformation of moral identity in American Judaism. He observes that 'two longstanding, deeply ingrained stereotypes of the Jew – the Jewish weakling and the gentle Jew', are currently replaced by the new image of the 'tough Jew'.

There is, on one side, the waning of what could be called the Woody Allen figure, that is, the schlemiel: the pale, bespectacled, diminutive vessel of Jewish anxieties who cannot, indeed, must not, hurt a flea and whose European forebears fell by the millions of Jew-hating savagery. And there is, on the other side, the emergence in *American* culture of less whiny, more manly and muscular types . . . [I]mages of Jewish wimps and nerds are being supplanted by those of the hardy, bronzed kibbutznik, the Israeli para-trooper, and the Mossad (Israeli intelligence) agent. (Breines 1990, 3; also Rosenberg 2001)

From these descriptions, we do not learn, of course, who Jewish men really are, but we do learn how cultural surroundings and political circumstances have shaped the portrayal of Jewish men. Given the almost 2,000-year history of Jews living in exile, in which Jewish men were bereft of political, military and national autonomy and, in its stead, found themselves beleaguered as a religious minority, it is a difficult task to untangle the lived experiences of men from the stereotypes that surround them. Jewish masculine ideals were shaped not only by the intrinsic religious logic of Judaism itself (based on its stories, practices and way of life) but also in response to the religious discourse of the majority culture (Christianity; Islam; modernity) to which Jews in the Diaspora had to accommodate. Scholarship that explores Jewish ideals of masculinity, then, must be mindful about the dynamics of the formation of religious and gender identity as a minority community, and must carefully distill what might be called a genuine Jewish male identity within local contexts from the imposition of external images and enduring stereotypes.

Daniel Boyarin, professor of Talmudic culture, has been at the forefront of pushing the scholarly community to recognize the complexity of the formation of Christian and Jewish communal identities. In his many books, he continuously and insightfully has challenged old metaphors and paradigms that are employed in describing the differences of Judaism and Christianity, arguing both for a Jewish *difference* in how Christians tend to see Judaism, and for a Jewish *internal* difference in reinterpreting sources. In other words, much of Boyarin's work is dedicated to exploring ways of understanding Judaism that is new to both traditional Jewish historiography as well as to Christian supercessionist and colonialist readings of Judaism. At the same time, he remains cognizant of the continuous historical interactions between Judaism and Christianity.

Boyarin's overall theoretical ambition impacts his understanding of Jewish masculinities in beneficial terms. In his 1997 work, *Unheroic Conduct: The Rise of Heterosexuality and the Invention of the Jewish Man*, he presents an argument for the Jewish 'difference' of Jewish masculinities to Christian conceptions of masculinities as he challenges, at the same time, Jewish orthodox notions of masculinity. Creatively and daringly, he reappropriates potentially derogatory images of Jewish men as counter-cultural models. Rather than simply discarding the supposedly weak and effeminized Jewish man as a figment of the anti-Jewish Christian imagination, Boyarin embraces the effeminized Jewish man as an alternative trajectory of manliness. He is not interested in an apologetic discourse that tries to disprove external misunderstandings and colonial misreadings of male gender in Judaism, nor is he interested in replacing the supposedly effeminate Jewish man with a 'tough Jew' (for the latter, see, for example, Klein Halevi 1995). Boyarin refuses to assimilate into the normative gender discourse of the majority culture.

For Peskowitz's American students, even American Jews, the gentleness of the rabbinic male can only be imagined as sexlessness, encoded as unattractiveness, because the students (like most of us) have been molded so thoroughly by the 'dominant fiction' of gender that our culture maintains. A gentle, studious, sweet man can only be imagined as old and nearsighted (i.e. castrated?) and could not possibly be attractive sexually. In the readings that follow, we will see that such a man is interpreted as anything but sexless within rabbinic texts; indeed, he is represented as the paramount desiring male subject and object of female desire. (Boyarin 1997, 2)

The chapter below is based on excerpts from the 'Prologue' and 'Introduction' to Boyarin's *Unheroic Conduct*. Readers interested in picking up the thread of Jewish masculinities should compare Boyarin's reflections with the chapters by Howard Eilberg-Schwartz (on Israelite men), Michael Satlow (on rabbinic men), and Harry Brod (on circumcision).

Publications by the Same Author

Boyarin, Daniel. 1993. *Carnal Israel: Reading Sex in Talmudic Culture*. Berkeley: University of California Press.

——. 1994. *A Radical Jew: Paul and the Politics of Identity*. Berkeley: University of California Press.

——. 1997. *Unheroic Conduct: The Rise of Heterosexuality and the Invention of the Jewish Man*. Berkeley: University of California Press.

——. 1999. *Dying for God: Martyrdom and the Making of Christianity and Judaism*. Stanford: Stanford University Press.

——. 2004. *Border Lines: The Partition of Judaeo-Christianity*. Philadelphia: University of Pennsylvania Press.

Boyarin, Daniel, Daniel Itzgovitz and Ann Pellegrini (eds). 2003. *Queer Theory and the Jewish Question*. New York: Columbia University Press.

Further Reading

Biale, David. 1992. *Eros and the Jews: From Biblical Israel to Contemporary America*. New York: Basic Books.

Breines, Paul. 1990. *Tough Jews: Political Fantasies and the Moral Dilemma of American Jewry*. New York: Basic Books.

Gilman, Sander L. 1991. *The Jew's Body*. New York and London: Routledge.

Klein Halevi, Yossi. 1995. *Memoirs of a Jewish Extremist*. Boston: Little, Brown and Company.

Peskowitz, Miriam. 1995. 'Imagining the Rabbis: Daniel Boyarin and "Israel's" Carnality'. *Religious Studies Review* 21/4:285–90.

Rosenberg, Warren. 2001. *Legacy of Rage: Jewish Masculinity, Violence, and Culture*. Amherst: University of Massachusetts Press.

Rudavsky, Tamar M. (ed.). 1995. *Gender and Judaism: The Transformation of Tradition*. New York: New York University Press.

Unheroic Conduct: The Rise of Heterosexuality and Jewish Masculinity

DANIEL BOYARIN

As I reflect on my coming of age in New Jersey, I realize that I had always been in some sense more of a 'girl' than a 'boy.' A sissy who did not like sports, whose mother used to urge me, stop reading and go out and play, in fifth grade I went out for—ballet. (Of course I explained to the guys that it was a kind of sophisticated bodybuilding.) This in itself is rather a familiar story, a story of inexplicable gender dysphoria, but one that had for me, even then, a rather happy ending. I didn't think of myself so much as girlish but rather as Jewish.

I start with what I think is a widespread sensibility that being Jewish in our culture renders a boy effeminate. Rather than producing in me a desire to 'pass' and to become a 'man,' this sensibility resulted in my desire to remain a Jew, where being a sissy was all right. To be sure, this meant being marginal, and it has left me with a persistent sense of being on the outside of something, with my nose pressed to the glass looking in, but the cultural and communal place that a sissy occupied in my social world was not one that enforced rage and self-contempt. In a quite similar account another male American Jew of my generation, Harry Brod, writes:

> I found the feminist critique of mainstream masculinity personally empowering rather than threatening. As a child and adolescent, I did not fit the mainstream male image. I was an outsider, not an athlete but an intellectual, fat, shy and with a stutter for many years. The feminist critique of mainstream masculinity allowed me to convert my envy of those who fit the approved model to contempt. It converted males previously my superiors on the traditional scale to males below me on the new scale, for I had obviously shown premature insight and sensitivity in rejecting the old male mode. I could pretend that others' rejection of me had really been my rejection of them. Of course, I could not have admitted this at the time. To do so would have seemed effeminate, and confirming of my fears of others' worst judgments of me. (Brod 1988, 7)

Brod moves on to a critique of this sensibility, referring to it as a 'shield against other men.' While I share his concern about the self-serving (and triumphant) countenance of the 'use of my Jewishness to avoid being categorized as a "real" man, "real" understood as a term of critique rather than praise' (Brod 1988, 8), I want to use the sissy, the Jewish male femme as a location and a critical practice.

I am interested right now in investigating what critical force might still be left in a culture and a cultural memory within which 'real men' were sissies. The vector of my theoretical-political work, accordingly, is not to deny as antisemitic fantasy but to reclaim the nineteenth-century notion of the feminized Jewish male, to argue for his reality as one Jewish ideal going back to the Babylonian Talmud. I desire also to find a model for a gentle, nurturing masculinity in the traditional Jewish male ideal—without making claims as to how often realized this ideal was—a male who could be so comfortable with his little, fleshy penis that he would not have to grow it into 'The Phallus,' a sort of Velvet John. He whom a past dominant culture (as well as those Jews who internalized its values) considers contemptible, the feminized Jewish (colonized) male, may be useful today, for 'he' may help us precisely today in our attempts to construct an alternative masculine subjectivity, one that will not have to rediscover such cultural archetypes as Iron Johns, knights, hairy men, and warriors within.

I am increasingly called upon to clarify something that I have never quite been able to explain until now, namely, the grounds for, and possibility of, a dual commitment to radical reclamation of traditional Jewish cultural life/practice/ study and to radical reconstruction of the organization of gendered and sexual practices within our society (including necessarily the Jewish subculture). The first commitment is generated out of a sense of cultural/religious continuity as a value in itself and of Judaism as a rich, sustaining, and fulfilling way of life; the second derives from a deeply held conviction (and the affective stance) that Jewish practices have been oppressive to people in ways that I cannot stomach.

I have learned these dual commitments through living experience. Growing up in a way typical of most American Jews of my generation (the 1960s), I experienced Judaism as a vaguely attractive, sometimes silly, sometimes obnoxious set of occasional instructions in my life, called Rosh Hashana, Yom Kippur, and Pesah. On the positive side, it represented for me a compelling passion for social justice which led me in high school to (almost) join the Communist Party of America. I finally turned, again like many American Jews of my time to Far Eastern mysticism as a mode of escape from the arid, nonspiritual microclimate that the synagogue had become and the equally arid possibilities and promises of a life without spirit at all.

Chance encounters—with a lulav-wielding Lubavitcher, with a therapist who gave me an English translation of the Zohar, with a young disciple of Zalman Schachter—began to hint that there might be more to Judaism than I had been misled to believe by American liberal Judaism. One night, in my second year in college, I dreamed that I was in Israel, and so came to spend my third year of college in Israel thinking that I was destined for a life as a kabbalist. I wasn't.

The Talmud tempted me away from kabbala. Most American Jews don't have an inkling even of what the Talmud is. I certainly didn't. Sometimes I think I imagined it as a sort of commentary on the Torah (confusing it, I suppose, with midrash); sometimes as something like Euclid's geometry applied to precisely what I couldn't imagine, since my image of Jewish 'Law' was that it was something unambiguous and found in a book called the *Shulkhan Arukh*. I had never seen even the outside binding of the Talmud, let alone the *Shulkhan Arukh*.

My friend, the aforementioned disciple of Schachter, had said to me: 'Before you can understand Zohar, you have to know Talmud,' so at the Hebrew University I signed up for the preparatory course in reading the Talmud and was charmed—in the full antique sense of the word—from almost the first sentence we read. Here was a world so strange and rich, so colorful and exciting, with myths and legends, challenges to the intellect, and, most of all, personalities rendered so vital that they seemed living men, men, moreover, who devoted their lives to the elaboration of what it means to live correctly, as a Jew. And this was all 'mine.' I became Orthodox for love of the Talmud. I admit freely, if ruefully, that it was so absorbing that I hardly noticed they *were* all men, or that the text was primarily addressed to me just because I was a Jewish *man*—I didn't recognize the exclusions and oppressions that those facts encode and mystify.

I believe there is no textual product of human culture that is quite like the jumbled, carnivalesque, raucous, bawdy, vital, exciting Talmud, nor is there anything quite like the practices of study that characterize it and the whole way of life that it subtends.[1] These are not, of course, the adjectives that have been traditionally used, either from within or from without, to describe the talmudic life. I make it sound, and indeed I experience it, as if it were almost Rabelaisian. When after a year and a half of study I came upon a text that described the death of Rav, I underwent an emotional experience akin to hearing of the death of a beloved teacher. It had become, I realized, almost unimaginable to me that Rav was not alive, because he was so alive in the text—alive I would add because not idealized, because the Talmud was as open to the flawed humanity of its heroes as the Bible had been to its. I have discovered that I am not alone: there are many people, including many women and lesbigay people, who are just as entranced by the Talmud as I have been and just as passionate about devoting their lives to it.

I deeply love and feel connected to rabbinic texts and culture, and even more to the Rabbis themselves, but there is much within them that I find deeply disturbing as well, and much of that has to do with the oppression of women. [. . .] My endeavor is to justify my love, that is, both to explain it and to make it just. I explain my devotion in part by showing that Judaism provides exempla for another kind of masculinity, one in which men do not manifest 'a deeply rooted concern about the possible meanings of dependence on other males' (Edelman 1990, 50) and thus one within which 'feminization' is not experienced as a threat or a danger. I cannot, however, paper over, ignore, explain away, or apologize for the oppressions of women and lesbigay people that this culture has practiced, and therefore I endeavor as well to render it just by presenting a way of reading the tradition that may help it surmount or expunge—in time—that which I and many others can no longer live with.

In this dual aspect of resistance to pressure from without and critique from within, my project is homologous to other political, cultural acts of resistance in the face of colonialisms. For some 300 years now, Jews have been the target of the civilizing mission in Europe. [. . .] Laura Levitt makes palpably clear the homologies between the 'liberal' colonizing impulse directed toward those Others within Europe and toward the colonized outside of Europe insofar as for both it is constituted by a demand that their sexual practices be 'reformed' to conform to the liberal bourgeois regime (Levitt 1993, 152–73). One of the most common of liberal justifications for the extension of colonial control over a given people and for the maintenance of the civilizing mission is the imputed barbarity of the treatment of women within the culture under attack (Butler 1990; Geller 1994; Hyams 1995; Sharpe 1991). The civilizing mission, and its Jewish agents among 'the Enlighteners,' considered the fact that Jewish women behaved in ways interpreted as masculine by European bourgeois society to be simply monstrous.[2] Modern Jewish culture, liberal and bourgeois in its aspirations and its preferred patterns of gendered life, has been the result of this civilizing mission. As Paula Hyman has recently demonstrated, the very Jewish religiosity of the modern bourgeois Jewish family is an assimilating mimicry of Protestant middle-class piety, not least in its portrayal of proper womanhood (Hyman 1995, 26–7). The richness of Jewish life and difference has been largely lost, and the gains for Jewish women were largely illusory (Magnus 1995). This having been said, however, the Jewish anticolonial project—like any other—cannot refrain from a trenchant, unflinching, and unapologetic internal critique of the harsh oppressions within the very traditional culture that it seeks to protect from destruction from without, namely, the structure of systematic exclusion of women from the practices that the culture most highly regards and especially the study of Torah. This exclusion has been a breeding ground of contempt—sometimes quite extreme—for women and a perpetrator of second-class status within Jewish law. [. . .]

Male self-fashioning has consequences for women. I feel an inner mandate to see to it that a project of reclamation of Judaic culture from the depredations of civilizing, colonializing onslaught to which it has been subject does not interfere with (even perhaps contributes something to) the ongoing project of feminist critique of that same traditional culture from within—to see to it, as best I can, that is, that my practice, whether or not it is part of the solution, is not part of the problem. I thus try to meet the challenge implicit in Tania Modleski's observation that male critique of masculinity is feminist when 'it analyzes male power, male hegemony, with a concern for the effects of this power *on the female subject* and with an awareness of how frequently male subjectivity works to appropriate "femininity" while oppressing women' (Modleski 1991, 7). The dual movement of the political project, to resist the delegitimization of Judaic culture from without, while supporting the feminist critique from within, dictates the structure of my work.

Thinking about the sissy body of the 'Jewish man,' I think simultaneously about another discourse and practice—possibly but not necessarily liberatory—that constructs the male body in a very different way. The 'gay male gym body' is an example of another male body constructed as an alternative to the heterosexual male body. David Halperin (following in part D. A. Miller) has recently given us a brilliant and moving rejoinder to 'straight, liberal' attacks on gay male bodybuilding by arguing for an absolute, total differentiation between the 'macho straight male body' and 'the gay male gym body': 'What distinguishes the gay male gym body, then, in addition to its spectacular beauty, is the way it advertises itself as an object of desire. Gay muscles do not signify power.' He further makes the impeccable point that the (ideal) gay male body does not look at all like the straight macho body (Halperin 1995, 117). [. . .]

This is inarguable—and I am hardly insensible to the attraction of that 'spectacular beauty'—but it nevertheless remains the case that the very standard for male beauty that is being prescribed is one of a certain form of muscular development that emphasized the dimorphism of the gendered body and thus participates, to this extent, in the general cultural standards of masculinity rather than resisting it. The pale, limp, and semiotically unaggressive 'nelly' or sissy male body is not seen within this construct as beautiful or erotic at all, but this exclusion as well can be shown to be culturally specific and limited. [. . .]

The politics of my project to reclaim the eroticized Jewish male sissy has, however, two faces. The traditional valorization of 'effeminism' for Jewish men hardly secured good news for Jewish women. There is no question that women were disenfranchised in many ways in traditional Jewish culture. The culture authorized, even if it did not mandate, efflorescences of misogyny. If the ideal Jewish male femme has some critical force vis-à-vis general European models of manliness, at the same time a critique must be mounted against 'him' for his oppression of Jewish women—and indeed, frequently enough, for his class-based oppression of other Jewish men as well, namely, the ignorant who were sometimes characterized as being 'like women' (Weissler 1989). Any attempt at a feminist rereading of Jewish tradition must come to terms with this material fact and the legacies of pain that it has left behind. My goal is not to preserve rabbinic Judaism 'as we know it,' but to reconstruct a rabbinic Judaism that will be quite different in some ways from the one we know and yet be and feel credibly grounded in the tradition of the Rabbis. My work is one of changing ethos and culture and I hope it joins with a stream of feminist work on rabbinic Judaism that includes the research of Judith Baskin, Judith Hauptman, Miriam Peskowitz, Laura Levitt, Susan Shapiro, and others. [. . .]

What I want is to produce a discursive catachresis, not a quick fix by a halakhic committee but a new thing in the world, the horizon of possibility for a militant, feminist, nonhomophobic, traditionalist—Orthodox—Judaism. The reasons for Jewish conservatism are not essential but accidental. The force of my writing is to avow not that traditional Judaism does not need radical change but rather that it can accommodate radical change and still remain viable if the terms of the change themselves can be seen as rooted in the documents, traditions, texts of the Rabbis. The only reason—other than divine mandate— for seeking this accommodation is that such practice brings to many men and women an extraordinary richness of experience and a powerful sense of being rooted somewhere in the world, in a world of memory, intimacy, and connectedness, a pleasure that I call *Jewissance*. Note that I am *not* arguing for a continuation of Judaism on the grounds that it makes people better, although in some sense my justification for indulging in the extreme pleasures of Jewishness is the assumption that it does have something to contribute to the world as well. I treasure in principle and with deep emotion cultural difference per se—not only my own—and for me the disappearance of a cultural form is attended with a pathos and pain not unlike that experienced by many people when a species of bird goes out of the world. The demand for cultural sameness, universalism, has done much harm and violence in the world, but cultural difference as well has to work hard to do no harm; to participate in this work is the calling of the scholar. [. . .]

Embodying Rabbis

The dominant strain within European culture [. . .] continues to this day to interpret activity, domination, and aggressiveness as 'manly' and gentleness and passivity as emasculate or effeminate. I will argue that the early modern Ashkenazic traditional ideal Jewish male, 'unmanned' but not desexualized, has something compelling to offer us in our current moment of search for a feminist reconstruction of male subjectivity (while being ever mindful, at the very same time, of the absolute necessity for an equally trenchant critique of that very culture for its *own* systems of oppression of women). [. . .]

[T]here is something correct—although seriously misvalued—in the persistent European representation of the Jewish man as a sort of woman. More than just an antisemitic stereotype, the Jewish ideal male as countertype to 'manliness' is an assertive historical product of Jewish culture. This assertion constitutes the central new point [. . .], in contrast to the consensus, according to which the 'ideal of masculinity, indeed modern society as a whole, needed an image against which it could define itself. Those who stood outside or were marginalized by society provided a countertype that reflected, as in a convex mirror, the reverse of the social norm. Such outsiders were either those whose origins, religion, or language were different from the rest of the population or those who were perceived as asocial because they failed to conform to the social norms. For those so marginalized, the search for an identity proved difficult and painful. However, not all outsiders faced the same problems, though basically their options were limited to a denial of their identity or its co-optation by the acceptable norm, until—in the last decades of the nineteenth century—these choices were increased by acts of self-emancipation' (Mosse 1996, 56).

For Jews, male Jews at any rate, one can neatly reverse this picture. Jewish society needed an image against which to define itself and produced the 'goy'— the hypermale—as its countertype, as a reverse of its social norm, and its self-identity was hardly difficult or painful (except, of course, for the pain of being mistreated physically). This form of Jewish stereotyping of the gentile Other had enormous historical tenacity. Emblematic, perhaps, of this relationship is the fact that in early modern Europe, the little finger was referred to by gentiles in certain place as 'the Jew,' while the thumb is called in Yiddish 'the goy!' In other words, rather than thinking of the stereotype as a one-way process of domination, we must begin to consider processes of complex mutual specular relations. Premodern Jewish culture, I will argue, frequently represented ideal Jewish men as femminized[3] through various discursive means. This is not, moreover, a representation that carries with it any hint of internalized contempt or self-hatred. Quite the opposite; it was through this mode of conscious alternative gendering that Jewish culture frequently asserted its identity overagainst its surroundings. If anything, [. . .] it was the process of 'Emancipation' of the late nineteenth century that produced both the pain and the difficulty of Jewish (male) identity.

By suggesting that the Jewish man was in Europe a sort of 'woman,' I am thus not claiming a set of characteristics, traits, behaviors that are essentially female but a set of performances that are read as nonmale within a given historical culture.[4] This culture can be very broadly described as Roman in its origins and as European in its scope and later history (Veyne 1985). It is the culture of romance that, while always contested—in large part precisely by 'feminized' Christian religious men—maintained hegemony as a male ideal, ever gaining intensity through the nineteenth century and beyond.[5] [. . .]

However, and quite paradoxically, it is also this very insistence on embod-iedness that marks the male Jew as being female, for maleness in European culture has frequently carried a sense of not-being-a-body also, while the body has been inscribed as feminine. A medievalist, Clare Kinney, has recently writ-ten of another definitive moment in European cultural history: 'Real men—that is, representative Arthurian heroes—don't have bodies' (Kinney 1994, 49).[6] If this 'not-having-a-body' is defined as manliness, then Jewish men were not 'real men' at all, for they quite decisively were bodies, were defined by their bodies. This idealization of the male body and its reinscription as spirit with no body reached its apotheosis in the nineteenth century. As George Mosse has observed, 'Above all, in the first decades of the nineteenth century, male beauty symbolized timeless order' (1985, 31). The Lacanian distinction between the phallus and the penis reinscribes precisely the identical dualism that privileges 'male' incorporeality over 'female' embodiedness. This cultural motive, which goes back at least to the pre-Socratics in Greek culture, privileges the ideal over the real, the homogeneous over the heterogeneous, and thence the phallus (as an ideal abstraction from the penis) over the female body, the sex that is not one.[7] Insofar as the penis of flesh—as opposed to the phallus, which is a platonic idea of the penis—is paradoxically feminine in the European Imaginary because it is body (Montrelay 1994), it is this insistence precisely on the penis that inscribes the Jewish male as forever carnal and thus female. Another way of making the same point would be to avow that for rabbinic culture, femminization is not equivalent to castration precisely because masculinity was not defined by pos-session of the phallus. To resist this sort of patterning, rabbinic thought must be anti-dualistic.

It seems highly significant that nowhere in rabbinic literature is there a repre-sentation, for instance, that would have the body of the embryo supplied by the mother, while the spirit is provided by the father, nor, a fortiori, one in which the father supplies the form and the mother the raw matter. Indeed, the standard and explicit myth of conception in rabbinic texts is a partnership of three in that the father supplies the white parts of the body: bones, teeth, the white of the eye, brain matter; the mother the red parts: blood, muscle, hair, the pupil of the eye; and God supplies the intelligence, the spirit, the soul, eyesight, motion of the limbs, and the radiance of the face (Nidda 31a).[8] In other words that which in many of the surrounding Greco-Roman cultures was bestowed by the father is provided here by God. For rabbinic Judaism, the father and mother provide the matter—the white and the pupil—of the eye, and only God provides spirit, the capacity of the eye to see. The father and the mother provide the muscle and sinew; only God provides the spirit, the active motor capacity. [. . .]

Hardly feminist, rabbinic Jewish culture thus refuses prevailing modes through which the surrounding cultures represent maleness as active spirit, femaleness as passive matter, a representation that has dominated much (if certainly not all) of European cultural imagination and practice. Maleness is every bit as corporeal as femaleness in this patriarchal culture. This refusal provides a partial explanation for how Jewish cultural imaginings could con-ceive of a valued masculinity as being femminized in the terms of the dominant Roman culture. When Europe has sought female equality and autonomy, this has been achieved through dis-embodying the female (Boyarin 1993); we have, rather, to embody men, to take away the phallus and leave only the penis behind. Only a new cultural theme—not a mere transformation of the old one—could re-embody the male. [. . .]

In the antisemitic imaginary of Christian Europe (and perhaps Muslim Africa and Asia as well), male Jews have been represented traditionally as female (Mirrer 1994), but as Sheila Briggs points out with reference to the latest forms of this representation, this obtained only with respect to 'the negative sense of the feminine' (1985, 256). There is, however, a positive signification to 'feminization' as well. In a cultural system within which there are only two genders, the only way to symbolize 'refusing to be a man' (Stoltenberg 1989) may be an assertion that one is, in some sense, a woman. This represents then, at least potentially, a positive oppositional identity to 'manliness' that is neither 'castrated' nor emasculate, because it does not read femininity as lack. [. . .] It is not the identification with women that bears here the 'feminist' potential but precisely the 'refusal to be a man.' The identification with women is an epiphenomenon of resisting manliness, but not one that implies 'castrated' status for either the unmanly man or the woman.[9] Traditionally many Jewish men identified *themselves* as femminized, beginning with the Talmud and through an opposition to 'Roman' ideals of the male, and understood that femminization as a positive aspect of their cultural identity. Accordingly, while not feminist, rabbinic culture might yet prove a resource in the radical reconstruction of male subjectivities that feminism calls for.

Lest this appear an idyllic picture, I must introduce at this juncture some less than idyllic images, powerful moments within which early rabbinic discourse is not resistant to Roman representations of masculinity and violent exercise of sexual power but fully complicit with them. Michael Satlow has demonstrated that Palestinian rabbinic culture in the Roman period did not eschew representations of penetration as marking status (Satlow 1994a). [. . .] It hardly needs saying yet again that the official discourse of this culture was certainly sympathetic neither to women nor to homoeroticism, and yet it is important that I say it here lest I be perceived (once more) as denying these nearly self-evident facts. Modern Jewish 'Orthodoxy' is marked by pervasive (though not ubiquitous) misogyny and by nearly ubiquitous homophobia. Clearly the seedbed for extremely violent discourses of gender and sexuality is well prepared within rabbinic textuality; my task here is not to deny the existence of these seedbeds but to cultivate other ones that are equally 'there' in the texts, even if not highly regarded or even noted by the current social institutions within which rabbinic Judaism is (mostly) lived.

Jewish Culture and the 'Rise of Heterosexuality'

[. . .] Queer theory is theory that recognizes that human desire—that is, even desire for 'straight sex'—is queer, excessive, not teleological or natural and for which the refusal of heteronormativity on the part of gays, lesbians, bisexuals, and others provides a privileged but not exclusive model. The conformations of desire are a cultural construction, and traditional Judaic culture, for all its well-known abhorrence of a certain homosexual act, male anal intercourse, and its near-universal inducement of marriage and procreation (Boyarin 1995), was *not* a 'heterosexual' culture—because 'heterosexuality' had not yet been 'invented.' As Michael Satlow has recently pointed out, 'The rabbis [of the talmudic period] considered male sexual attraction to other males to be unexceptional,' and 'no evidence suggests that the rabbis defined people by the gender of the object of their sexual desire' (1994a, 18, 24).

'Heterosexuality' is a peculiar institution of contemporary Euro-American culture. It has been best defined by David M. Halperin as 'the production of a population of human males who are (supposedly) incapable of being sexually excited by a person of their own sex *under any circumstances*,' and has been referred to by him as 'a cultural event without, so far as I know, either precedent or parallel' (1990, 44). Neither the assumption that some (even most) people prefer to have sex with people who have different genitals than they do, nor even the tabooing of certain or all same-sex genital acts constitutes heterosexuality (see Halperin 1995, 44). Only the premise that same-sex desire is *abnormal*, that it constitutes, in Foucault's words, a separate species of human being, creates this category. There is an enormous gap between the earlier condemnation of one who pursues certain forms of pleasure as a sinner, on the same order as one who eats forbidden foods, for instance, and the modern placing of that person into a special taxon as an abnormal human being. This is not to say, of course, that the earlier formation was more benign to those who engaged in same-sex practices than the latter; but the production of the heterosexual, as the normal type of human being, has powerful effects that ripple throughout the projects of constructing gender within a social formation such as our modern one. And as Satlow has concluded, 'Penetration, not same-sex desire was problematic for the rabbis' (1994a, 24). [. . .]

Homophobia in this exact sense is a product of the modern culture of heterosexuality,[10] in which male sexual desire for men or any effeminate behavior threatens to reveal and expose that the man is essentially not straight but queer.[11] Without a doubt, and to somewhat understate the case, male–female sexual relationships were nearly exclusively prized within traditional Jewish culture. In that sense, one could surely claim that rabbinic Jewish culture has always been heteronormative, even if not heterosexual, that is, homophobic. The absence of heterosexuality permits a much greater scope for forms of male intimacy, eroticized and otherwise: 'Who is a friend?,' a midrash asks, 'He that one eats with, drinks with, reads with, studies with, sleeps with, and reveals to him all of his secrets—the secrets of Torah and the secrets of the way of the world' (Shechter Aboth, ch. 10). 'Sleeps with' does *not* have the metaphorical value that it has in English or German, but the text is certainly reaching for a very intense and passionate level of male–male physical intimacy here. The 'way of the world' is a somewhat ambiguous metaphorical term that can refer to several areas of worldly life, including business, but especially sex.[12] Male intimacy, it seems, for the talmudic culture includes the physical contact of being in bed together while sharing verbally the most intimate of experiences, a pattern not unknown in other cultures. The image of two men in bed together talking of their sexual experiences with women is reminiscent of ethnographic descriptions of Barasana (Columbian) tribesmen, lying in hammocks, fondling each other and talking about sex with women (Greenberg 1988, 71). Thus, while we cannot draw conclusions about the sexual practices of rabbinic men from such a passage, we can certainly, it seems to me, argue that it bespeaks a lack of 'homosexual panic' such as that necessitated by the modern formation known as 'heterosexuality.' The absence of homosexual panic in premodern Jewish culture permitted a much greater scope of behavior coded as 'feminine' within the larger cultural context to be normative in male performance in general and in affective relations between men. [. . .] [T]his very structure for the production of gentler, antimacho men was not thereby rendered empowering for women. If anything, this 'kinder, gentler' form of patriarchy may have solidified certain forms of male power. [. . .]

[I do not] say then, nor even suggest or hint—in fact I wish to expressly deny—that we find some sort of nonpatriarchal paradise in Jewish or any other colonized society. Gender and hierarchies do not cease to be a problem in these subaltern formations—indeed they may be exacerbated—but we do end up with a very different sense of how gender and the symbolization of the sexed body function within these subcultures. [. . .] [One of these subcultures], traditional Ashkenazi Jewish culture, produced a model of masculinity that was openly resistant to and critical of the prevailing ideology of 'manliness' that was dominant in Europe. The alternative Jewish form of maleness was known as *Edelkayt* (literally, 'nobility,' but in Yiddish: 'gentleness and delicacy'!); its ideal subject was the *Yeshiva-Bokhur* (the man devoting his life to the study of Torah) and his secularized younger brother, the *Mentsh*. [. . .]

Talmudic culture is the culture that is crucially informed by a pivotal practice of reading the Talmud as its most valued book. Actual cultural forms are mediated through a complex set of social, economic, historical, and cultural conditions, which frequently include the nature of the cultural practice of the societies within which Jews found themselves in different times and climes. Not a history, my book attempts to understand one Jewish social formation, Ashkenaz on the cusp of modernity, as one such a realization of the cultural possibilities that a certain strain of talmudic discourse made possible. Another way to describe the difference of this text from a history would be to say that I am not trying to recover the 'truth' of Jewish culture but rather the 'best' of what Jewish culture has offered in the past, and I want to suggest what it can be in the future. This 'best' is, of course, a value judgment, one that many will not share, and the judgment grows out of who I am, where I come from, and where I have been in my life. *Unheroic Conduct* also constitutes a narrative of how I take myself to be a Jew and to be a product of my love for the Talmud and my feelings of commitment to its authority, as well as my commitments to certain ethical norms, including most prominently my feminism and my identification with gay, lesbian, and bisexual Jews (and the Queer Nation as a whole).[13]

Notes

1 Astonishingly to me, I know not why, Eve Kosofsky Sedgwick has captured perfectly my sensibility when she writes of 'Talmudic desires, to reproduce or unfold the text and to giggle' (1990, 240). I am grateful for that sentence, as for much

else in her work. In contrast to this, I wonder at Christine Delphy's (1991) repeated use of 'Talmudic' as a pejorative for the discourse of false feminists. This remains a stumbling block for me in my appreciation of her otherwise quite wonderful work.

2 In an earlier version I had written: 'its Jewish agents, the "Enlighteners,"' but as Naomi Seidman has correctly admonished me, this was not entirely fair, since there was a genuine feminist impulse animating a not insignificant component of the Jewish Enlightenment as well. Nor am I prepared, of course, to entirely disavow the Enlightenment project as part of who I am. Nevertheless, the insistence of the Jewish Enlightenment that only an eradication of the 'talmudic spirit' could fit the Jews for civilization is an unremittingly colonialist project. As my student Abe Socher has pointed out: 'Jewish Enlighteners (*Maskilim*) even identified the mortifying "jargon" of Yiddish with the Aramaic of the Talmud. Just as Yiddish was a corruption of the pure language of German and, as such, an impossible vehicle for anything but *Unbildung*, so too was Aramaic a corruption of the pure Hebrew of the Bible. This equation between the two pure languages of biblical Hebrew and eighteenth-century German was epitomized in Mendelssohn's *Biur*, a Hebrew Bible with a running translation into High German, rendered in Hebrew letters. Almost a century later, the great nineteenth-century historian Heinrich Graetz summed up the *Maskilic* attitude when he wrote of the eastern European Talmudists' love of "twisting, distorting, ingenious quibbling," which has "reduced the language of German Jews to a repulsive stammer"' (Socher 1995; see also Aschheim 1982, 14–15).

3 I write this way to indicate clearly that I am not ascribing some form of actual or essential femininity to certain behaviors or practices, as to a Jungian *anima*. For the toxic effects of that ideology, see Connell (1995, 12–15); and cf. now especially Garber (1995, 211–14). I am rather marking these performances as 'femme' within the context of a particular culture's performatives, and particularly as it intersects with other cultural formations. The point is then not to reify and celebrate the 'feminine' but to dislodge the term. 'Phallus' and the 'feminine' (and in only a slightly different register 'Jew') are fatally equivocal terms in Western discourse, insisting on their disconnection from real human beings of particular groups—men, women, Jews—at the same time that they inescapably declare their connection with these groups. Weininger goes through contortions to insist that everyone is 'Jewish' but Jews only more so, and that there can be Jews (such as Weininger) who escape being Jewish; by doing so he provides only one dramatic example of this aporia. For the coinage itself, compare Ed Cohen's '"fem"-men-ists' (1993, 174). I had, in fact, for a long time considered 'femmenize' but worried that it would be read as a pun on 'men' and not on 'femme.' My usage further distinguishes the cultural processes that I am describing from those referred to when one speaks of the 'feminization of the synagogue,' by which is meant the fact that in certain 'assimilating' communities only women typically attended the synagogues (at the same time that Protestant churches were being feminized in the same sense). This phenomenon, discussed most recently and cogently by Paula Hyman (1995, 24–5), is not what I am talking about here.

4 The project has nothing to do with men 'getting in touch with their feminine sides' or the anima or 'androgynous Judaism' but rather with unsettling and destabilizing the cultural model(s) of gender that such formulations and movements underwrite and reinforce for our culture (Garber 1995, 223–6).

5 More accurately, as pointed out by George Mosse, the romanticism of the nineteenth century involved a fantasized revival of medieval romance (1985, 8). Mosse provides a much more detailed and nuanced account of both what is retained or

reappropriated from early ideals—Roman martial ones or medieval chivalrous ones—and what is wholly transformed from them in the production of modern manliness (Mosse 1996).

6 For quite a different—but not entirely irreconcilable—reading of the same text, see Dinshaw (1994).

7 This sort of patterning presumes an allegorical metaphysics, and in its crudest naturalizations, an allegorical physics, as well. Woman is man's signifier. As such, she may never be the thing signified but allegorical discourse allows her to be *taken for* the signified as a kind of reading procedure. And man is God's signifier in much the same way.

8 This is based, of course, on a notion of menstrual blood as being the female equivalent of semen (Satlow 1994b, 158–62). Here again, as Satlow points out, rabbinic conception(s) are quite different from the ones of the more Hellenized Greek-writing Jews, whose views were Aristotelian.

9 See the very interesting discussion in Dellamora (1990, 141–6).

10 Jonathan Ned Katz (1995, 33–55). This chapter of Katz's is one of the most convincing demonstrations and exemplifications of Foucault's hypothesis about the invention of sexuality that I have yet seen. Unfortunately this fine book is marred by a cynical and vicious foreword by Gore Vidal which demonstrates only that he had not even read the book when he wrote the foreword.

11 Note the difference between this account and a superficially similar one that treats the man policing 'himself for traces of femininity' as thereby victimized (Lentricchia 1987, 743) or that elides the difference between 'teaching men who will not conform how to alienate and despise themselves'—and 'even men who do conform' (774–5)! For discussion, see Edelman (1990). I am not commiserating here with the 'poor' male who 'submits' to heterosexuality by dominating others but with the victims of this practice. Lentricchia's discourse is reminiscent of those Israeli liberals, like Golda Meir, who are most angry at the Palestinians because the latter have 'forced them to be oppressors.'

12 As indicated by the following text among others: 'When his wife died, Rabbi Tarfon said to her sister during the mourning period: Marry me and raise your sister's children. And even though he married her, he did not behave with her according to the way of the world until after thirty days.' (Kohellet Rabba, 9. See also Bereshit Rabba, 22). Now although the sexual meaning is not the most frequent one for this collocation, it is certainly a readily available one. Thus while it is a meaningless claim (because unfalsifiable) that this is what the author of this text 'intended,' it is hard to escape concluding that the sexual connotation would have been present for any recipient of this text.

13 I would like to express here my feeling that the spaces in which I have felt most accepted and validated as an 'out' Orthodox Jew in America, yarmulke, beard and all, have been such queer environments as Pride parades and gay, lesbian, and bisexual studies conferences.

Literature

Aschheim, Steven E. 1982. *Brothers and Strangers: The East European Jew in German and German Jewish Consciousness, 1800–1923*. Madison: University of Wisconsin Press.

Boyarin, Daniel. 1993. *Carnal Israel: Reading Sex in Talmudic Culture*. Berkeley: University of California Press.

——. 1995. 'Are There Any Jews in the "History of Sexuality"?' *Journal of the History of Sexuality* 5/3:333–55.

Briggs, Sheila. 1985. 'Images of Women and Jews in Nineteenth- and Twentieth-Century German Theology,' in *Immaculate and Powerful: The Female in Sacred Image and Reality*, eds Clarissa W. Atkinson, Constance H. Buchanan and Margaret R. Miles. Boston: Beacon. Pp. 226–59.

Brod, Harry (ed.). 1988. *A Mensch among Men: Explorations in Jewish Masculinity*. Freedom: Crossing.

Butler, Judith. 1990. *Gender Trouble: Feminism and the Subversion of Identity*. London: Routledge.

Cohen, Ed. 1993. *Talk on the Wilde Side: Towards a Genealogy of Male Sexualities*. New York: Routledge.

Connell, Robert W. 1995. *Masculinities*. Berkeley and New York: University of California Press.

Dellamora, Richard. 1990. *Masculine Desire: The Sexual Politics of Victorian Aestheticism*. Chapel Hill: University of North Carolina Press.

Delphy, Christine. 1984. *Close to Home: A Materialistic Analysis of Women's Oppression*, trans. and ed. Diane Leonard. Amherst: University of Massachusetts Press.

Dinshaw, Carolyn. 1994. 'A Kiss is Just a Kiss: Heterosexuality and Its Consolations in *Sir Gawain and the Green Knight*,' *diacritics* 24/2–3:205–26.

Edelman, Lee. 1990. 'Redeeming the Phallus: Wallace Stevens, Frank Lentricchia, and the Politics of (Hetero)sexuality,' in *Engendering Men*, eds Joseph A. Boone and Michael Cadden. New York: Routledge. Pp. 36–52.

Garber, Marjorie. 1995. *Vice-versa: Bisexuality and the Eroticism of Everyday Life*. New York: Simon & Schuster.

Geller, Jay. 1994. 'Of Mice and Mensa: Anti-Semitism and the Jewish Genius,' *Centennial Review* 38:361–85.

Greenberg, David F. 1988. *The Construction of Homosexuality*. Chicago: University of Chicago Press.

Halperin, David M. 1990. *One Hundred Years of Homosexuality, and Other Essay on Greek Love*. New York: Routledge.

——. 1995. *Saint Foucault: Towards a Gay Hagiography*. Oxford: Oxford University Press.

Hyams, Barbara. 1995. 'Weininger and Nazi Ideology,' in *Jews & Gender: Responses to Otto Weininger*, eds Nancy A. Harrowitz and B. Hyams. Philadelphia: Temple University Press. Pp. 155–68.

Hyman, Paula E. 1995. *Gender and Assimilation in Modern Jewish History: The Roles and Representation of Women*. Seattle: University of Washington Press.

Katz, Jonathan Ned. 1995. *The Invention of Heterosexuality*. New York: Dutton.

Kinney, Clare R. 1994. 'The (Dis)embodied Hero and the Signs of Manhood in *Sir Gawain and the Green Knight*,' in *Medieval Masculinities*, ed. Clare A. Lees (Medieval Cultures 7). Minneapolis: University of Minneapolis Press. Pp. 47–57.

Lentricchia, Frank. 1987. 'Patriarchy against Itself: The Young Manhood of Wallace Stevens,' *Critical Inquiry* 13/4:742–86.

Levitt, Laura S. 1993. *Reconfiguring Home: Jewish Feminist Identity/ies*. Ph.D. Diss. Emory University. Microfilm.

Magnus, Shulamit S. 1995. 'Pauline Wengeroff and the Voice of Jewish Modernity,' in *Gender and Judaism: The Transformation of Tradition*, ed. Tamar M. Rudavsky. New York: International University Press. Pp. 181–90.

Mirrer, Louis. 1994. 'Representing "Other" Men: Muslims, Jews, and Masculine

Ideals in Medieval Castilian Epic and Ballad,' in *Medieval Masculinities*, ed. Clare A. Lees (Medieval Cultures 7). Minneapolis: University of Minneapolis Press. Pp. 169–86.

Modleski, Tania. 1991. *Feminism without Women: Culture and Criticism in a 'Post-feminist' Age*. New York: Routledge.

Montrelay, Michèle. 1994. 'Why Did You Tell Me I Love Mommy and That's Why I'm Frightened When I Love You,' *American Imago* 51/2:395–429.

Mosse, George L. 1985. *Nationalism and Sexuality: Middle-Class Morality and Sexual Norms in Modern Europe*. Madison: University of Wisconsin Press.

——. 1996. *The Image of Man: The Creation of Modern Masculinity*. New York: Oxford University Press.

Satlow, Michael L. 1994a. '"They Abused Him Like a Woman": Homoeroticism, Gender Blurring, and the Rabbis in Late Antiquity,' *Journal of the History of Sexuality* 5:1–25.

——. 1994b. '"Wasted Seed," the History of a Rabbinic Idea,' *Hebrew Union College Annual* LXV:137–75.

Sharpe, Jenny. 1991. 'Unspeakable Limits of Rape: Colonial Violence and Counter-Insurgency,' *Genders* 10 (Spring): 25–46.

Sedgwick, Eve Kosofsky. 1990. *Epistemology of the Closet*. Berkeley and Los Angeles: University of California Press.

Socher, Abe. 1995. 'A Magus from the East; or, Maimon at the Margins of the Public Sphere.' Unpublished Paper. Berkeley. Photocopy.

Stoltenberg, John. 1989. *Refusing to Be a Man: Essays on Sex and Justice*. New York: Meridian Books.

Veyne, Paul. 1985. 'Homosexuality in Ancient Rome,' in *Western Sexuality: Practice and Precept in Past and Present Times*, eds Philippe Ariès and Andrè Béjin. Oxford: Oxford University Press. Pp. 26–35.

Weissler, Chava. 1989. 'For Women and for Men Who are like Women,' *Journal of Feminist Studies in Religion* 5:7–24.

9

Bodies: The Displaced Body of Jesus Christ

Editor's Introduction

Can a messianic savior figure (that has appeared in a male body) redeem men and women alike? Is it significant that, according to the Christian story, the incarnation of the Divine took place in male flesh? Is it important that Jesus Christ was a man – and, if so, for whom and under what circumstances?

> For Christians, incarnational faith opens the possibility of experiencing the divine presence at work in the human body. For Christian men, the fact that God became incarnate in a male saviour figure (rather than a female body) had two lasting consequences: first, men could argue theologically for their privileged position within the emerging church, rationalising the exclusivity of the male clergy and papacy on the grounds of Christ's maleness. Second, they disciplined their male bodies and passions through asceticism, monasticism and an ethics of chastity in the hope of imitating the sinless Christ, who was seen as the embodiment of an ideal masculinity. (Krondorfer 2007, 658)

If this description of the effects of the incarnation is true for Christian men, how about women? Rosemary Radford Ruether, like other feminist theologians, wonders correctly whether 'a male Savior [can] save women' (1983, esp. 116–38). Does the maleness of Christ carry an exclusiveness that is either implicitly conveyed or, at other times, explicitly stated? We can think here of the arguments barring women from the position of clergy in the Catholic and Orthodox traditions, or of Thomas Aquinas arguing for women's lesser quality of reason and soul, or the Gnostic saying in the *Gospel of Thomas* that a woman has first to 'make herself male' in order to enter the kingdom of heaven.

Graham Ward addresses the issue of the male body of Jesus Christ in the chapter below. He presents an argument that disclaims any partial or privileged access to the body of Christ through a specific group of people, whether they are male or female, straight or gay, black or white. The body of Jesus Christ, Ward argues, has been a particular body only during his lifetime; yet, already during his lifetime, his Jewish, male body undergoes a series of transformations that renders it inaccessible to the desires we bring to this body as members of particular communities. After these transformations, 'the body of Jesus Christ' is a 'multigendered body', whose historical particularity has disappeared and is no longer accessible to us. 'Theologians framing questions such as "Can a male savior save women?", or engaged in investigating the sexuality of Jesus,' Ward concludes, 'fail to discern the nature of the body of Christ.'

Ward's position may not be shared by other scholars in the field of the critical study of Christian masculinities, but his dense theological musings, consistent with a more orthodox understanding of the universality of the Christian message, offer a challenging counterpoint to theologies of particularity, as they are expressed, for example, in gay theology. Ward's chapter may be fruitfully read in tandem with the chapters by Dale Martin ('Sex and the Single Savior') and Donald Boisvert ('Sanctity and Male Desire').

Ward belongs to a school of thought that named itself 'radical orthodoxy'. It is a fairly recent theological movement that might be depicted as a crossing of Augustine, Karl Barth and Jacques Lacan. It describes itself as a 'theological project made possible by the self-conscious superficiality of today's secularism' that wants to 'visit sites in which secularism has heavily invested – aesthetics, politics, sex, the body, personhood, visibility, space':

> And just how is it *radical*? Radical, first of all, in the sense of a return to patristic and medieval roots, and especially to the Augustinian vision of all knowledge as divine illumination . . . Radical, second, in the sense of seeking to deploy this recovered vision systematically to criticize modern society, culture, politics, art, science and philosophy with an unprecedented boldness . . . Underpinning [radical orthodoxy], therefore, is the idea that every discipline must be framed by a theological perspective; otherwise these disciplines will define a zone apart from God, grounded literally in nothing. (Milbank, Pickstock, and Ward 1999, 1–3)

Radical orthodoxy is strongly philosophical in outlook: 'Where Barthianism can tend to the ploddingly exegetical, radical orthodoxy mingles exegesis, cultural reflection and philosophy in a complex but coherently executed *collage*' (Milbank, Pickstock, and Ward 1999, 2). Select titles of a whole series published on radical orthodoxy demonstrate the scope and depth of this intellectual movement (see, for example, Long 2000; Ward 2000; Bell 2001; Hanby 2003; Milbank 2003), and a critical rejoinder to this movement has already been published by Hankey and Hedley (2005).

Ward's own perspective is 'radical' insofar as it does not shy away from a theological encounter with contemporary discourse on desire – from Sigmund Freud to Luce Irigaray and Judith Butler. And it is radically 'orthodox' insofar as it relies on a neo-Barthian vision of a Christianity that is the ground of all knowing and being, and hence always larger than any particular human expression. For Ward, the 'good news' of the Gospel narratives does not occur outside of human erotic desire but is always larger than the sexual and spiritual imagination of the contingent subject. As he writes in the chapter below:

> We have no access to the body of the gendered Jew. So all those attempts to determine the sexuality of Jesus are simply more recent symptoms of the search for the historical Christ – which Schweitzer demonstrated was pointless at the beginning of this century. It is pointless not only because it is a human attempt to give Christianity an empirically verifiable foundation . . . [but also] because the church is now the body of Christ, so to understand the body of Jesus we can only examine what the church is and what it has to say concerning the nature of that body.

Publications by the Same Author

Ward, Graham G. 1995. *Barth, Derrida and the Language of Theology*. Cambridge: Cambridge University Press.

——. 1996. 'Divinity and Sexuality: Luce Irigaray and Christology'. *Modern Theology* 12/2:221–37.

—— (ed.). 1997. *The Postmodern God: A Theological Reader*. Oxford: Blackwell

——. 1998. 'Karl Barth and the Erotics of Redemption'. *Theology and Sexuality* 8: 52–72.

——. 1999. 'Theology and Masculinity'. *The Journal of Men's Studies* 7/2 (Winter): 281–6.

——. 2000. *Cities of God*. London: Routledge.

—— (ed.). 2000. *The De Certeau Reader*. Oxford: Blackwell.

——. 2003. *True Religion*. Oxford: Blackwell.

——. 2005. *Christ and Culture*. Oxford: Blackwell.

Ward, Graham G. and Michael Hoelzl (eds). 2006. *Religion and Political Thought*. New York: Continuum.

—— (eds). 2008. *The New Visibility of Religion*. New York: Continuum.

Further Reading

Bell, Daniel. 2001. *Liberation Theology after the End of History: The Refusal to Cease Suffering*. London: Routledge.

Hanby, Michael. 2003. *Augustine and Modernity*. London: Routledge.

Hankey, Wayne J. and Douglas Hedley (eds). 2005. *Deconstructing Radical Orthodoxy: Postmodern Theology, Rhetoric and Truth*. Aldershot, UK, and Burlington: Ashgate.

Krondorfer, Björn. 2007. 'World Religions, Christianity', in *International Encyclopedia of Men and Masculinities*, eds M. Flood, J. K. Gardiner, B. Pease and K. Pringle. London, New York: Routledge. Pp. 658–60.

Long, Stephen. 2000. *Divine Economy: Theology and the Market*. London: Routledge.

Milbank, John. 2003. *Being Reconciled: Ontology and Pardon*. London: Routledge.

Milbank, John, Catherine Pickstock and Graham Ward (eds). 1999. *Radical Orthodoxy: A New Theology*. London: Routledge.

Ruether, Rosemary R. 1983. *Sexism and God-Talk: Toward a Feminist Theology*. Boston: Beacon.

Bodies: The Displaced Body of Jesus Christ

GRAHAM WARD

Karl Barth announced that theology is always a post-resurrection phenomenon working within an eschatological horizon. Theology reads Scripture, the traditions of the church and the world in the light of the glory of the Risen Christ in the space opened between that resurrection and our own. While not wishing to contradict that, I want to argue for the place of the ascension in Christianity, its practices, its Scriptures and its theological task. This nascent theology of the ascension will begin by investigating the gendered body of that Jewish man, Jesus the Christ. It will begin, therefore, not with those concepts philosophically and theologically honed by the ante- and post-Nicene Fathers, but with the gendered body as Scripture presents it to us and as the church has reflected upon it. It will attempt to demonstrate, through this approach, how questions such as 'Can a male Savior save women?'[1] and modern investigations into the sexuality of Jesus,[2] which simply continue the nineteenth-century rational search for the historical Jesus, fail to discern the nature of corporeality in Christ. For these approaches take the human to be a measure of the Christic. What happens at the ascension, theologically, constitutes a critical moment in a series of displacements or assumptions[3] of the male body of Jesus Christ such that the body of Christ, and the salvation it both seeks and works out (Paul's *katergomai*), become multigendered. I wish to argue that, since none of us has access to bodies *as* such, only to bodies that are mediated through the giving and receiving of signs, the series of displacements or assumptions of Jesus' body continually refigures a masculine symbolics until the particularities of one sex give way to the particularities of bodies which are male and female. To that end, this essay examines the presentation of the male Jesus in the Gospels and its representation in the life of the church. It examines both the performance of Jesus the gendered Jew and the way that performance has been scripted, reperformed, and ventriloquized by the community he brought to birth. It traces the economy of the deferred identity of the body of the Messiah;[4] an economy which becomes visible in a series of displacements. The ascension marks the final stage in the destabilized identity of the body of the Messiah.

Incarnation and Circumcision

In a recent book on the sexed body of Jesus, Leo Steinberg writes: 'from Hilary and Augustine to Michelangelo, the humanity of the Incarnate is perceived as volitional condescension,' and in this condescension Christ straddles 'humanness in pre- and in post-lapsarian modality' (1996, 296). In what follows, then, I am not denying the creedal statement that Christ is both fully God and fully man, but pointing up this pre- and post-lapsarian corporeal ambiguity. Tertullian, writing one of the earliest treatises on the body of Jesus Christ, *De Carne Christi*, situates the very ambiguity of Christ's flesh (as opposed to other forms of flesh, including spiritual flesh and the flesh assumed by angels) in the fact that it is flesh like ours, and yet: 'As, then, the first Adam is thus introduced to us, it is a just inference that the second Adam likewise . . . was formed by God into a quickening spirit out of the ground—in other words, out of the flesh which was unstained as yet by any human generation.'[5] This is 'the flesh which was made of a virgin'—a flesh of complex theological designation.[6] It is interesting that, later, theological figures like Augustine and Athanasius, who also embraced the full humanity of Christ, found, when describing that full humanity which Christ possessed, pre-lapsarian faculties beyond those available to human creatures in the post-lapsarian world.

From the moment of the incarnation, this body then is physically human and subject to all the infirmities of being such, and yet is also a body looking backward to the perfect Adamic corporeality and forward to the corporeality of resurrection. The materiality of this human body is eschatologically informed. We will be examining such materiality in more detail later. For the moment, it is sufficient to emphasize how the specificity of Jesus' male body is made unstable from the beginning. This is made manifest by the absence (in Matthew and Luke) of a male progenitor; by the way that, in Mark, Jesus issues without a past into the emptiness of the wilderness (like John before him), and by the manner in which John's Gospel relates how the Word became flesh and dwelt (*Eskēnōsen*—tabernacled) among us. The paternity of God is formal, rather than material. But this formality informs substance, such that our notions of 'materiality' itself become unstable. The nature of paternity is redefined—Ephesians 3.14–15[7]—in a way which points up the inseparability of what Judith Butler calls 'bodies that matter' (1993)[8] from a doctrine of creation. The XY chromosomal maleness of Jesus Christ issues from the XX chromosomal femaleness of his mother as miracle, and so this male body is unlike any other male body to date. Its materiality is, from its conception, unstable; though, with the circumcision, its specifically sexed nature is affirmed.

Patristic theologies of both the incarnation and the circumcision emphasize the instability of Jesus' gendered corporeality. Augustine's description of the baby Jesus—'His appearance as an Infant Spouse, from his bridal chamber, that is, from the womb of a virgin'[9]—demonstrates this. The baby boy is husband and bridegroom, spouse and prefigured lover of the mother who gives him birth, whose own body swells to contain the future church. The bridal chamber is the womb which the bridegroom will impregnate with his seed while also being the womb from which he emerges. The material orders are inseparable from the symbolic and transcendent orders, the orders of mystery. The material orders are caught up and become significant only within the analogical orders. And so here Jesus' body is brought within a complex network of sexualized symbolic relations that confound incest and the sacred. Augustine further makes plain that the infant Jesus was not born helpless and ignorant like other children: 'that such entire ignorance existed in the infant in whom the Word was made flesh, I cannot suppose . . . nor can I imagine that such weakness of mental faculty ever existed in the infant Christ which we see in infants generally.'[10] Again, the logic here is theological—Augustine makes these suggestions on the basis of a doctrine of creation revealed through the incarnation in which materiality participates in God. Matter itself is rendered metaphorical within the construal of such a logic. Since creation issued from the Word of God, then, seen from the perspective of God's glory, all creation bears the watermark of Christ.[11] The material orders participate in theological orders such that they are rendered both physical and symbolic.

And so one finds that the theology of circumcision—developed from the early Fathers through to the sermons preached in Rome on the Feast of the Circumcision (January 1) in the fifteenth century—interpreted this one action upon the body of Jesus as prefiguring the final action in the crucifixion: the first bloodletting becoming the down-payment on the redemption to come. The circumcision takes place on the eighth day, and so it is linked also to resurrection, the perfection of creation and of corporeality. The body of Jesus is, once more, stretched temporally, the baby body prefiguring the adult body, the adult body figuring the ecclesial body, in its march to its resurrection. The physicality of the body, its significance as a body, and the acts with which it is involved, are figured within an allegorical displacement.

Transfiguration

Throughout the Gospel narratives Jesus the man is viewed as a man unlike other men (or women). This man can walk on water. This man can sweat blood. This man can bring to life. This man can multiply material so that 5,000 are fed from a few loaves and fish. This man can heal by touch; and not just heal but create wine from water, the eyes of the man born blind, the ear of the Temple guard. But it is the explicit displacements of his own physical body which interest me, the various assumptions or trans-figurations that occur in which the divine is manifested in the sexed and corporeal, and the implications of these trans-figurations. In these assumptions Jesus is not alone. Tertullian [. . .] points out that angels frequently 'changed into human form' and the Holy Spirit 'descended in the body of a dove.'[12] The displacements of Jesus' body simply give Christological significance to the nature of embodiment. John's Gospel is emphatic about these assumptions, with its repetitions of ontological scandal— I am the way, the life, the truth, the Temple, the bread, the light, the vine and the gate into the sheepfold. But in the Gospels generally, in those stories which focus on the body of Jesus, there are five scenes where these displacements are dramatically performed: the transfiguration itself; the eucharistic supper; the crucifixion; the resurrection; and, finally, the ascension. Each of these scenes, in an ever-deepening way, problematize the sexed nature of Jesus' body and point towards an erotics far more comprehensive and yet informing the sexed and the sexual.

The pre-lapsarian body of Adam (and Eve) is erotically charged—perfect in its form, its goodness, and its beauty—and naked. Fashions in the figuration of that form change. Today's cult of the firm, hard, male physique, like the various cultural pursuits it has fostered (body-building and dieting), is the result of certain conventions of masculinity which arose in Germany in the late eighteenth century—a masculinization modeled on classical sculpture (see Mosse 1996, 17–39). But whatever the fashion of our representations, something Promethean, powerful and vulnerable, sticks close to the image of Adam in Paradise. What is glimpsed in and through his magnificence is the image of God—the trace of the uncreated in the created. Insofar as in Christ human beings are restored to their pre-fallen splendor, the transfiguration scene on the Mount of Olives presents us with Jesus as the Second Adam. Not naked in any obvious sense, but nevertheless bathed in a certain translucence. What I am describing here as erotically charged is the way these manifestations of humankind glorified by God are attractive. They are incarnations of divine beauty and goodness, and as such they possess the power to attract, to draw us towards an embrace, a promise of grace. These disclosures establish economies of desire within which we are invited, if not incited, to participate. The transformation does not simply portray a resurrection hope, it performs it, solicits it. [. . .] The physical body of Jesus is displaced—for it is not the physical body as such which is the source of the attraction but the glorification of the physical body made possible by viewing him through God as God. We are attracted to the man and beyond him, so that the erotic economy does not flounder on questions of sexuality (i.e. is my attraction to this man as a man homoerotic, is my attraction to this man as a woman heterosexual?). The erotic economy propels our desire towards what lies beyond and yet does so in and through this man's particular body. This economy of desire does not deny the possibility of a sexual element; it does not prevent or stand in critical judgment of a sexual element. It simply overflows the sexual such that we cannot, without creating a false and idolatrous picture of Christ, turn this man into an object for our sexual gratification. This man cannot be fetishized, because he exceeds appropriation. Desire is not caught up here in an endless game of producing substitutes for a demand that can never be satisfied. [. . .]

Notice how, in both Matthew's account (17.1–13) and that of Luke (9.28–36), we focus upon the face of Christ. It is a face full of light and energy, and the descriptions no doubt allude to the shining face of Moses as he came down from the mountain, having spoken with God. But Matthew's description exceeds any allusion to the lawgiver. He writes of Jesus' face 'shining like the sun.' We are drawn to love the beautiful and the good in Him. His corporeality becomes iconic.[13] We are silenced, like James and John, before this Christic sublime.[14] In the presence (where 'in' is strongly locational) of the holy, we listen, we receive, we worship, we give thanks.

Eucharist

The displacement of the physical body becomes more abrupt in the eucharistic supper. The body begins its withdrawal from the narrative. Transfiguration turns into transposition: 'He took bread, and blessed and broke it, and gave it to them, and said "Take; this is my body."' Matthew adds 'eat.' Neither Luke nor Mark mentions the consumption, only the giving and receiving of the bread-as-his-body. It is the handing-over of himself that is paramount. He places himself in the hands of the disciples who then hand him over to the authorities. It is the surrendering that is important. It is effected by that demonstrative indicative—'*this* is my body.' These words perform the transposition. They set up a logic of radical re-identification. What had throughout the Gospel story been an unstable body is now to be understood as an extendable body. For it is not that Jesus, at this point, stops being a physical presence. It is more that his physical presence can extend itself to incorporate other bodies, like bread, and make them extensions of his own (see also Ward 1998). A certain metonymic substitution is enacted, resituating Jesus' male physique within the neuter materiality of bread (*to arton*). The 'body' now is both sexed and not sexed. [. . .]

With the eucharistic displacement of the physical body, a new understanding of embodiment is announced. Bodies in Greco-Roman culture, according to Dale Martin, were not viewed as discrete auto-defining entities. They were malleable; and because they are made of the same stuff as the world around them, 'the differentiation between the inner and outer body was fluid and perme-able' (Martin 1995, 20). Physical bodies were mapped onto other bodies—social, political, cosmic. Hence

> for most people of Greco-Roman culture the human body was of a piece with its environment. The self was a precarious, temporary state of affairs, consti-tuted by forces surrounding and pervading the body, like the radio waves that bounce around and through the bodies of modern urbanities . . . the body is perceived as a location in a continuum of cosmic movement. (Martin 1995, 25)

Even so, the displacement of Jesus' body at this point is somewhat different, more radical. It begins with a breaking. It is not just a blurring of the boundaries between one person and another—though it effects that through the handing over and the eating of the 'body.' The bread here does mediate the crossing of frontiers. But more is involved in what Jesus does and says in that upper room. For 'This is my body' is not a symbolic utterance. It is not a metaphorical utterance. The bread is not the vehicle for significance, for anthropomorphic projections. The bread *is* also the body of Jesus. That ontological scandal is the epicenter for the shock-waves which follow. For it is actually the translocational-ity that is surprising—as if place and space itself are being redefined such that one can be a body here and also there, one can be this kind of body here and that kind of body there. Just as with the transfiguration, the translucency of one body makes visible another hidden body, so too with the Eucharist, although in a different way, the hidden nature of being embodied is made manifest. Bodies are not only transfigurable, they are transposable. In being transposable, while always being singular and specific, the body of Christ can cross boundaries—gender boundaries, for example. Jesus' body as bread is no longer Christ as simply and biologically male.

Crucifixion

The crucifixion develops the radical form of displacement announced in the eucharistic supper. The breaking of the bread is now relocated in the break-ing of the physical body of Jesus. The handing over is taken one step further. The male body of Christ is handed over to death. The passivity of Jesus before Jewish and Roman authorities, and the two scenes of his nakedness (stripped by the Roman guards, according to Matthew and implied by Luke, then reclothed to be stripped again for his crucifixion), set this vulnerable body to play in a field of violent power games. The sexual charge is evident in the delight taken by the soldiers in abusing his body and in the palpable sense of power created through the contrast between Pilate's towering authority and Jesus' submissiveness. The quickening pace of the narrative, the breathless surge of activity which propels the body of Christ towards the resting-place of the cross, bears witness to the energetic force-field within which this body is placed and its power to effect, to draw in. The violent acts by which bodies touch other bodies—beginning with the kiss by Judas, moving through the slapping 'with the palm of his hand'

by the Temple guard in the house of Caiaphas, to the scourging by the Roman
soldiers and the nailing on the cross, and on finally to the piercing of the side
with the lance—are all sexually charged manifestations of desire in conflict.[15]
The whipped-up hysteria of the crowd shouting 'crucify' reveals the generative
power of such violence—what Girard has analyzed as the 'mimetic nature of
desire' which seeks out a surrogate victim and marks the approach of sacrificial
crisis (Girard 1977, 169). It climaxes with the strung-up nakedness of Christ on
the cross.

Throughout the play of these erotic and political power games the actual
maleness of the body of Jesus is forgotten. This is a man among men; no sexual differentiation is taken account of. It is no longer 'this' body or 'my' body,
but 'that' undifferentiated body. The body becomes an object acted upon at the
point when the dynamic for the narrative is wrenched from Jesus' grasp and
put into the hands of the Jewish and the Roman authorities. The displacement
of Jesus' body is accentuated through the displacement in the direction of the
storytelling, the displacement in the responsibility for the unfolding of events.
The body as object is already being treated as mere flesh, a consumable, a dead,
unwanted, discardable thing, before Jesus breathes his last.

There is a hiatus at this point. The orgiastic frenzy abates and there is the
shaping of a new desire. Each Gospel writer shapes this new desire by relocat-
ing Christian witness within a scene that, since Peter's betrayal, has lacked it.
Matthew reintroduces the women who had followed Jesus from Galilee; Luke,
who also frames this scene with the women, first effects the shaping of a new
desire through the thief on the cross; Mark introduces his famous centurion;
and John inserts into the Passion narrative a conversation between Jesus and
John concerning Mary. John's Gospel testifies, proleptically, to the nature of this
reorientation of desire when he has Jesus state: 'And I, if I be lifted up from the
earth, will draw all men unto me' (12.32). The desire is no longer libidinal, but
issues from a certain pathos. The iconic status of the body of Jesus re-emerges,
but the manner in which it draws us is configured through an identification with
the suffering of the body, rather than earlier, at the Eucharist, through the feeding and the sharing, and the being nurtured by the body of Christ. The displacement of the body at the Eucharist effects a sharing, a participation. We belong
to Jesus and Jesus to others through partaking of his given body. We exist in
and through relation. The displacement of the body here effects a detachment,
a breaking of that relation. Displacement is becoming loss, and with the loss a
new space opens for an economy of desire experienced as mourning. The affectivity of the one displacement can come about only through the other—without
the sharing and participation there cannot arise the sense of a coming separation and loss. With the sense of loss comes also, paradoxically, the recognition
of an identification, but an identification now passing. The space of this pathos
heightens the iconicity of the crucified one. It emotionally colors a certain
liminality within which the affectivity of this object is offered to us—the *inter
alia* between dying and death, presence and departure; and between death and
burial, departure and removal of the departed one. The liminality reinforces the
sacredness of the space. Through it the crucifixion is already ritualized. [. . .]

Iconicity transcends physicality. It does not erase the physical but overwhelms
it, drenching it with significance. The maleness of Christ is made complex and

ambivalent, in the way that all things are made ambivalent as their symbolic possibilities are opened up by their liminality. Victor Turner remarks about liminal *personae* that they become 'structurally, if not physically, "invisible"' . . . They are at once no longer classified and not yet classified' (1967, 95–6). [. . .] Such bodies become floating signifiers. The medieval church bears witness to this ambivalence in finding it appropriate to gender Jesus as a mother at this point, with the wounded side as both a lactating breast and a womb from which the church is removed (see Bynum 1992). The pain and suffering of crucifixion is gendered in terms of the labor pains of birthing. There is a logic to the mother-ing symbolism, at this point where the economy of desire is triggered by the withdrawing of the body. A logic, that is, if Freud et al. are right is that all with-drawal and subsequent mourning is a reminder of the primary break from, and the libidinal desire to return to, self-unity established in and through that pri-mary separation from the body of the mother. The symbolic template of Jesus' crucified body, and the empathy with human suffering which it invokes, draws forth deeper awarenesses of our human condition and of the primary levels of desire which constitute it. His body becomes the symbolic focus for all bodies loved and now departed: real, imaginary, and symbolic mothers; real, imagi-nary, and symbolic fathers.[16] His body calls forth all the cathectic objects of our past desires which have been abjected to facilitate our illusory self-unity.[17]

The allure of the abject, and the mourning which now will always accom-pany Christian desire, manifests an internalization of displacement itself. That is: the lack will now foster an eternal longing and will structure our desire for God. The economy of our salvation is triggered by this event, for, as Augustine understood, we reach 'our bliss in the contemplation of the immaterial light through participation in his changeless immortality, which we long to attain, with burning desire.'[18] It is not simply that the physical body of Jesus is dis-placed in the Christian story; our bodies, too, participate in that displacement in and through the crucifixion. At the Eucharist we receive and we are acted upon: now, having been brought into relation and facing the acknowledgment of the breaking of that relation we recognize displacement of the body as part of Christian living. Our bodies too, sexually specific, will perform in ways that transgress the gendered boundaries of established codes. Men will become mothers—witness the writings of Bernard of Clairvaux and Aelred of Rievaulx (see Bynum 1992, 158–60); women will become virile—witness the writings of Mechthild of Magdeburg and Hadewijch.[19] The eucharistic fracture, repeating differently the crucifixion, disseminates the body—of Christ and the church as the body of Christ. The dissemination sets each body free to follow (and both be transposed and transfigured) within the plenitude of the Word which passes by and passes on. What initiates the following after is the awareness of our being involved, of our having been drawn into the ongoing divine activity. Our being involved is a tasting of that which we know we long for; we drink of eternal life in that participation. [. . .]

The structure of Christian desire is, significantly, twofold—not only my desire but God's desire for me. It is this twofoldedness which characterizes participation. The self is fissured in such participation, and fissured endlessly. [. . .] The theological implication of this is that the displacement of the body in the crucifixion is not cancelled out by the resurrection, as if the tragic moment of

the broken is swept into a comic finale of triumphant reconciliation. The resurrection only expands the kenotic movement of displacement effected through
the crucifixion. It does not reverse it and yet neither does it constitute, by its equi-
primordiality, the paradox of crucifixion–resurrection. The death of the physical body is not the end of, but rather the opening for further displacements—the
eucharistic fracturing promoted through the church. It makes brokenness and
lack a *sine qua non* of redemption. This redemption is not an emptying of oneself
into nothingness (*à la* Lacan); but a recognition of the lack of foundations within
oneself which requires and enables the reception of divine plenitude. Lacan
returns the subject to the *nihilo* and denies that God made anything out of it. The
Christian awareness of the absent body of Christ, and of death itself, returns us
to our createdness—to the giftedness of creation out of nothing.

Resurrection

The resurrected body of Jesus sums up all the modes of displacement that were
seen in evidence before his death. The life of Christ continues, playing out the
glorified body of the transfiguration, the broken body of the Eucharist, and the
unstable physicality of the body that walked on water. The ability to disappear,
walk through walls, occupy other bodies (which causes so many misidentifications of who he is) is countered by a corporeality which is tangible and able to
eat. Displacement opens up a spiritual *topos* within the physical, historical, and
geographical orders. Displacement is figured in the narrative, first, through the
empty tomb. This emptiness is emphasized in John's Gospel by the presence of
two angels at either end of where the body had been (20.12). It is not emptiness
as such; rather it is akin to that space opened by the two angels on either side
of the ark of the covenant in the Holy of Holies: the emptiness announces the
plenitude of God's presence.[20]

The displacement is figured, second, in the actual body of Christ. It is no
longer recognizable. The two on the road to Emmaus talk to him for hours, but
it is only when he breaks the bread they will eat for supper that they recognize
him. John records Mary at the tomb turning from the angels, seeing Jesus and
not knowing that it was Jesus, supposing him to be a gardener even when he
had spoken to her. She recognizes him only when he calls her by her name. Later
in the same Gospel the disciples, out fishing, saw Jesus walking on the shore
and they did not know it was Jesus, even though he spoke to them. It was only
after they had obeyed the instruction to fish on the other side of the boat and
the nets were drawing in the heavy load that Peter said: 'It is the Lord.' These
narrative details cannot be taken, as they have been by some, as disfigurations
which follow the almost atomic power of the resurrection. Such an explanation assumes what Mary Douglas calls a 'medical materialism' (1966, 37). The
misidentifications are part of the unfolding logic of displaced bodies, bodies
which defer or conceal their final identity; bodies which maintain their mystery.
In each case, from the hiddenness comes the revelation, the realization which
has the structure of an initiation—the move from what is familiar to what is
strange, to what is once again familiar albeit in another guise. These bodies of
Jesus bear analogical resemblance to each other, but they are not literally identi-

cal. The body is analogical by nature—it moves through time and constantly changes, and yet all these changes are analogically related to each other.[21] With the new identifications ('It is the Lord'; 'Their eyes were opened'; 'Rabboni') a new relationship and understanding are opened up. The logic of the displacement-deferral of the Word is a pedagogical logic.

The third figuration of displacement, opening a spiritual *topos*, is the structure of the narrative itself. The Gospel narrative, which had previously followed Jesus Christ wherever he went until his disappearance into the tomb, now can follow him no longer. A series of appearances, visitations, or epiphanies occur. The body of Christ keeps absenting itself from the text. Where does it go to? What the body is replaced by is the witness of the church. First the angels pass on the news that he is risen, and then Mary bears witness. Finally, several other disciples narrate their experiences (those on the road to Emmaus, the disciples in the upper room to Thomas). Jesus' presence is mediated through the discourses of those who will comprise the early church.

Patristic and medieval theology announced this creation of a new body, through the displacement of Christ's physical body, in gendered language: through the wound in Jesus' side the church is brought to birth. Jesus makes manifest the motherhood of the divine. Caroline Walker Bynum has exhaustively researched this material. In her *Speculum of the Other Woman*, Irigaray too alludes to the wounding of Christ that marks a femininity within him (1985, 199–200). There is much more material, and much less explored material, in the writings of the Syrian Fathers, like Ephraim: material which speaks profoundly of the wombs from which creation and the church issue. The water and the blood which flow from the side of Christ are the sacramental fluids which nurture and nourish his child-bride, the church. What I wish to emphasize—and to some extent Michel de Certeau (1997, 146–7) has emphasized it before me—is the textuality of these bodies. The body of Christ crucified and risen, giving birth to the ecclesial *corpus*, the history and transformations of that ecclesial body—each of these bodies can materialize only in, through and with language. [. . .] Thus, the absenting body of Christ gives place to (is supplemented by) a body of confessional and doxological discourse in which the church announces, in a past tense which can never make its presence felt immediately: 'We have seen him. He is risen.' The testimonials cited in the Gospels provide a self-conscious trope for the writing of the Gospel narratives themselves. For we had only the mediated body of Jesus Christ throughout. We have been reading and absorbing and performing an ecclesial testimony in the fact that we have the Gospel narratives (and Pauline Epistles) at all. The confessions and doxologies staged within the narratives are self-reflexive moments when the narratives examine that which makes the Gospels possible: the giving and receiving of signs.

The appearance–disappearance structure of Christ's resurrected body serves to emphasize the mediation of that body—its inability fully to be present; to be an object to be grasped, catalogued, atomized, comprehended. The appearance–disappearance serves as a focus for what has been evident throughout—the body as a mystery, as a materiality which can never fully reveal, must always conceal, something of the profundity of its existence. In Mark's Gospel a young man sits astride the head of the empty tomb and tells the women: 'He is risen. He is not here. He goes before you to Galilee.' Galilee was where the story began and will begin, when the story is retold (at least by Mark). The young man points them back to the beginning of their discipleship. The beginning is doubled. In Matthew's Gospel the young man is an angel (*aggelos*, a messenger *par excellence*). In Luke's Gospel there are two angels, and the story proceeds to narrate the testimonies of the disciples who saw the Risen Christ appear on the road to Emmaus, noting also the testimony of Simon Peter (whose story of Christ's visitation does not appear in the text). In John's Gospel it is Mary Magdalene who communicates the news, who becomes an angel (and envoy); Jesus subsequently appearing to confirm the news. Meditation, the dissemination of messages, the narration of stories, the communication in one context being transposed and reported in another—these constitute the poetics of the New Testament itself, the letteral Word of God which supplements the incarnate Word of God. The practices of Christian living parse the divine grammar: in our words and our worlding we are adverbial in the sense Eckhart gives that part of speech when he prays: 'may the Father, the Verbum, and the Holy Spirit help us to remain adverbs of this Verbum.'[22]

Communication confers communion and creates community. From the dispersal of the disciples on the point of Christ's crucifixion, a new collectivity of relations begins to form following the resurrection. People are sent to each other—by the young man, by the angels, and by Jesus. [. . .] Relationality and spatiality, the new collectivity born within and borne across the distensive absence, a new collectivity issuing from the divinely driven imperative to bear witness to the appearance and disappearance of Jesus Christ—all come to an apex in the scene of the ascension.

Ascension

The ascension is the final displacement of the body of the gendered Jew. The final displacement rehearses the logic of the eucharist: the body itself is transposed. A verse from Colossians elucidates this: 'The church is his body, the fullness of him who fills all in all.' [. . .] The final displacement of the gendered body of Jesus Christ, always aporetic, is the multi-gendered body of the church. A new spatial distance opens up with the ascension—a vertical, transcending spatiality such as divides the uncreated God from creation. There will be no more resurrection appearances. The withdrawal of the body is graphically described. The emptiness is emphasized by the angels: 'Why stand ye gazing up into heaven?' It is a moment of both exaltation and bereavement. [. . .]

The disciples are caught between memory and anticipation. But the absenting is not a decisive break. I have argued throughout that the body of Jesus Christ is continually being displaced so that the figuration of the body is always transposing and expanding its identity. That logic of displacement is now taken up in the limbs and tissue of his body as the church. Poised between memory and anticipation, driven by a desire which enfolds it and which it cannot master, the history of the church's body is a history of transposed and deferred identities: it is not yet, it never was, and still it will be. Furthermore, the absenting does not culminate in bereavement. The new body of Christ will not promulgate and live out endless simulacra for fulfillment. The loss of the body of Jesus Christ cannot be read that way. The logic of the ascension is the logic of birthing, not dying. The withdrawal of the body of Jesus must be understood in terms of the Logos creating a space within himself, a womb, within which (*en Christoi*) the church will expand and creation be recreated. In this way, the body of the church and the body of the world are enfolded through resurrection within the Godhead. The body of Jesus Christ is not lost, nor does it reside now in heaven as a discrete object for veneration (as Calvin thought and certain Gnostics before him).[23] The body of Jesus Christ, the body of God, is permeable, transcorporeal, transpositional. Within it all other bodies are situated and given their significance. We are all permeable, transcorporeal, and transpositional. 'There is neither Jew nor Greek, there is neither bond nor free, there is neither male nor female, for ye are all one in Christ (*eis este en Christoi*)' (Philippians 2.12). This theo-logic makes possible, as I mentioned at the beginning of this essay, an understanding of the omnipresence or ubiquity of God.

We have no access to the body of the gendered Jew. So all those attempts to determine the sexuality of Jesus are simply more recent symptoms of the search for the historical Christ—which Schweitzer (1922) demonstrated was pointless at the beginning of this century. It is pointless not only because it is a human attempt to give Christianity an empirically verifiable foundation and because the metaphysics implied in believing that project to be possible are profoundly anti-Christian (atomism, positivism, atemporality, immanentalism, access to the immediate and subjectivism). It is pointless because the church is now the body of Christ, so to understand the body of Jesus we can only examine what the church is and what it has to say concerning the nature of that body. The church dwells in Christ and in Christ works out its salvation and the salvation of the world. The body of Christ is a multigendered body. Its relation to the body of the gendered Jew does not have the logic of cause and effect. This is the logic that lies behind such questions as 'Can a male savior save women?' [. . .] God in Christ dies and the church is born. One gives way to the other, without remainder: the relationship between Jesus and the church is processional, as the relationship between the trinitarian persons is processional. One abides in and through the other. The body of the gendered Jew expands to embrace the whole of creation. That body continues to expand by our continual giving and receiving of signs. This is the textuality of Christian time, made up, as it is, of doxological words and liturgical practices. The expansive bloom of the flower is not the effect of the bud, but its fulfillment.

Those theologians framing questions such as 'Can a male savior save women?', or engaged in investigating the sexuality of Jesus, fail to discern the nature of the body of Christ; fail to understand the nature of bodies and sex in Christ. As Gregory of Nyssa points out in his thirteenth sermon, on *Song of Songs*: 'he who sees the church looks directly at Christ . . . The establishment of the church is recreation of the world . . . A new earth is formed, and it drinks up the rains that pour down upon it . . . [B]ut it is only in the union of all the particular members that the beauty of [Christ's] Body is complete.'[24] The next step in understanding the body of Christ is to investigate the church, that Spouse 'wounded by a spiritual and fiery dart of desire (*eros*). For love (*agape*) that is strained to intensity is called desire (*eros*).'[25] To continue would be to detail and discuss the body of the church as the erotic community.

Notes

1 I am quoting a question that forms the subtitle of a chapter in Ruether (1983, 116–38). I do not intend this essay to be an attack on Ruether herself. Rather I am attacking the biological essentialism which lies behind many of the recent moves by feminists towards a post-Christian perspective, and attempting to show how a masculinist symbolics can be refigured in a way which opens salvation through Christ to both (if there are only two, which I doubt) sexes.

2 The question was opened, and the investigations undertaken, because sexuality and Christianity had become so divorced from one another. The topic had become taboo, as Tom Driver suggested at the outset of his article 'Sexuality and Jesus' (1965, 235–46). Stephen Sapp, in a chapter of his book *Sexuality, the Bible, and Science* (1977) entitled 'The Sexuality of Jesus,' developed the discussion. Driver and Sapp, in their attention to this sexuality—and by calling into question dogmas such as the virgin conception and birth—employ medical materialism to offset a potential docetism. Both of them needed to go back to Tertullian and a cultural epoch when *eros* could still be theologically valued beyond its implications for sexuality. Ruether joined in with her own note 'The Sexuality of Jesus' (1978).

3 I employ this word because of its associations with patristic theologies of Christ's flesh. These patristic theologies understood bodies more fluidly than we who have inherited notions of 'body' following the nominalist (and atomistic) debates of the late Middle Ages, the Cartesian definition of bodies as extended things (*res extensae*), the seventeenth-century move towards unequivocation, and Leibniz's understanding of the individuation of matter. See Funkenstein (1986, 23–116).

4 The deferral of this corporeal identity can be related to the diverse names and tides given to Jesus, most particularly in John's Gospel. For an examination of these titles in relation to the early formation of doctrine, see Dunn (1989).

5 *De Carne*, xvii. Tertullian, polemically engaging with various Gnostic heresies—the Ebionites, Valentinians, and Marcionites—suggests that copulation changes corporeality. He speaks of sinful flesh, angelic flesh and virginal flesh, besides spiritual flesh (or 'flesh from the stars').

6 Tertullian notes that Mary is both virgin and not a virgin, a virgin and yet mother, a virgin and yet a wife, married and yet not married (*De Carne*, xxxiii).

7 '[T]he Father from whom [out of whom, *ex ou*] every fatherhood in the heavens and upon the earth is named.'

8 While Butler sees how the material is informed by the way in which we represent it, she does not take this further to ask: What then is the nature of materiality itself? She does not date it to a wider genealogy to show the way in which representations of the corporeal, the philosophical notion of substance itself, are historically situated and theologically indebted.

9 *Sermons*, IX. 7.

10 *On the Merits and Remission of Sins and on the Baptism of Infants*.

11 The doctrine of the ubiquity of omnipresence of God starts here. For the way in which these theological notions change and become secularized (becoming the feared omnipotent God of the nominalists), see Funkenstein and Gillespie (1996, 1–32).

12 *De Carne*, iii.

13 For a phenomenology of the invisible within the visible, the iconic beyond the idolized, see Jean-Luc Marion (1991, 11–46).

14 The sublime here follows Longinus' sublime: it elevates, it ennobles the soul,

it leads to reflection and examination, it 'exerts an irresistible force and mastery' (1965, 99–113).

15 Cinematographic accounts of the crucifixion scene enable us to appreciate the erotic charge of the action, because they place us (as none of the disciples were placed) as voyeurs, observing the playful abuse perpetrated. See Franco Zeffirelli's *Jesus of Nazareth*.

16 The terms real, imaginary and symbolic are Jacques Lacan's. I am not using them in his technical sense (particularly his understanding of *réel*), but more in the looser manner of Gatens (1996). The real bodies are the empirical and historical, medical and material ones to which we have no access other than through the 'images, symbols, metaphors and representations . . . the (often unconscious) imaginaries of a specific culture: those ready-made images and symbols through which we make sense of social bodies and which determine, in part, their value, their status and what will be deemed their appropriate treatment' (1996, viii).

17 See Kristeva (1982); and specifically on the relation of abjection to Christ's death and resurrection, Kristeva (1988).

18 *City of God* (Augustine 1972), XII. 21.

19 See Newman (1995) and Castelli (1991, 49–69). Of course this trans-gendering or making women virile—which goes back to the Gnostic *Gospel of St Thomas*—is part of a masculine ideology. I do not wish to suggest that in late antiquity or the medieval period there was a cultural openness such that men being figured as women and women being figured as men were equally valued.

20 Irigaray refers to the holiness of this spacing, which she likens to the sacred hiatus which is constituted by sexual difference, in her essay 'Belief Itself' (1993, 25–53). 'Those angels . . . guard and await the mystery of the divine presence that has yet to be made flesh' (45).

21 Gregory of Nyssa uses the Greek term *scopos* to describe the growth here through all its stages. See also Jean Danielou's 'Introduction' to Herbert Musurillo (1961, 56–71).

22 Quoted by Derrida (1987, 578).

23 Calvin, *Institutio* IV:17, 'The Sacred Supper of Christ and What it Brings to Us.'

24 *Comm. on the Cant.*, 13, 1049B-1052A.

25 Ibid. 13, 1048A.

Literature

Augustine, 1972. *City of God*, trans. Henry Bettenson. Harmondsworth: Penguin Books.

Butler, Judith. 1993. *Bodies that Matter: On the Discursive Limits of 'Sex'*. London: Routledge.

Bynum, Caroline Walker. 1992. *Fragmentation and Redemption: Essays on Gender and the Human Body in Medieval Religion*. New York: Zone Books.

Castelli, Elizabeth. 1991. "'I Will Make Mary Male": Pieties of the Body and Gender Transformation of Christian Women in Late Antiquity,' in *Body Guards: The Cultural Politics of Gender Ambiguity*, eds Julia Epstein and Kristina Straub. London: Routledge. Pp. 49–69.

Certeau, Michel de. 1997. 'How Is Christianity Thinkable Today?', in *The Postmodern God*, ed. Graham Ward. Oxford: Blackwell. Pp. 142–58.

Derrida, Jacques. 1987. 'Comment ne pas parler: dénegations,' in *Psyche*. Paris: Galilee.

Douglas, Mary. 1966. *Purity and Danger*. London: Routledge.

Driver, Tom. 1965. 'Sexuality and Jesus,' *Union Seminary Quarterly Review* 20 (March): 235–46.

Dunn, James D. G. 1989. *Christology in the Making: An Inquiry into the Origins of the Doctrine of the Incarnation*. London: SCM Press.

Funkenstein, Amos. 1986. *Theology and the Scientific Imagination*. Princeton: Princeton University Press.

Funkenstein, Amos and Michael Allen Gillespie. 1996. *Nihilism Before Nietzsche*. Chicago: University of Chicago Press.

Gatens, Moira. 1996. *Imaginary Bodies: Ethics, Power and Corporeality*. London: Routledge.

Girard, Rene. 1977. *Violence and the Sacred*, trans. Patrick Gregory. Baltimore: The Johns Hopkins University Press.

Irigaray, Luce. 1985. *Speculum of the Other Woman*, trans. Gillian C. Gill. New York: Cornell University Press.

——. 1993. 'Belief Itself,' in *Sexes and Genealogies*, trans. Gillian C. Gill. New York: Columbia University Press. Pp. 25–53.

Kristeva, Julia. 1982. *Power of Horror: An Essay on Abjection*, trans. Leon Roudiez. New York: Columbia University Press.

——. 1988. *In the Beginning Was Love: Psychoanalysis and Faith*, trans. Arthur Goldhammer. New York: Columbia University Press.

Longinus. 1965. *On the Sublime*, trans. T. S. Dorseh. London: Penguin Books.

Marion, Jean-Luc. 1991. *La Croisee de visible*. Paris: La Difference.

Martin, Dale. 1995. *The Corinthian Body*. New Haven: Yale University Press.

Mosse, George. 1996. *The Image of Man: The Creation of Modern Masculinity*. Oxford: Oxford University Press.

Musurillo, Herbert. 1961. *From Glory to Glory: Texts from Gregory of Nyssa's Mystical Writings*. London: John Murray.

Newman, Barbara. 1995. *From Virile Woman to Woman Christ: Studies in Medieval Religion and Literature*. Philadelphia: University of Pennsylvania Press.

Ruether, Rosemary Radford. 1978. 'The Sexuality of Jesus,' in *Christianity and Crisis* 38 (29 May):134–7.

——. 1983. *Sexism and God-Talk: Towards a Feminist Theology*. London: SCM Press.

Sapp, Stephen. 1977. *Sexuality, the Bible, and Science*. Philadelphia: Fortress.

Schweitzer, Albert. 1922. *The Quest for the Historical Jesus*, trans. W. Montgomery. London: A. & C. Black.

Steinberg, Leo. 1996. *The Sexuality of Christ in Renaissance Art and Modern Oblivion*. Chicago: University of Chicago Press.

Turner, Victor. 1967. *The Forest of Symbols*. Ithaca: Cornell University Press.

Ward, Graham. 1998. 'Transcorporeality: The Ontological Scandal,' in *Representation, Gender and Experience*, ed. Grace Jantzen. Special issue of *The John Rylands Bulletin* 80 (June): 235–52.

Designing Men: Reading the Male Body as Text

Editor's Introduction

'Why is it so difficult for men,' Philip Culbertson asks in the chapter below, 'to direct their heterosexual male gaze toward another man?' Gazing at a person means to objectify a person, to turn a person into an object of sexual desire. *Gazing* implies an activity that denotes power, while being *gazed at* inscribes a position of subjection. In a patriarchal, heterosexual society it is the man who gazes at the objects he desires. This gaze, Culbertson states, 'desires' when it is 'turned toward a woman'. When 'turned toward a gay man, it often despises', and when turned toward the heterosexual body itself, the body disappears from sight. As a 'textless text', the heterosexual male body remains elusive and resists being read.

The 'male gaze' – one of two important concepts Culbertson's chapter adds to a gendered analysis of masculinity and religion – addresses issues of desire and power between men and women, men and men, and men and the divine. If being 'gazed at' is understood as a position of passivity and of potential violation and vulnerability, the divine gaze might render men effeminate in relation to God. This is a topic that Howard Eilberg-Schwartz has pursued in his analysis of Israelite and rabbinic men in *God's Phallus* (1994). Culbertson mentions Eilberg-Schwartz's study in the chapter below, and the *Critical Reader* follows up on it in chapter 14.

The male gaze is also addressed by Ward (chapter 9), Boisvert (chapter 29) and De La Torre (chapter 32). For Ward, a desiring and sexual gazing at the body of Jesus Christ does not tell us anything about the sexuality of Christ. To him, a sexual gazing would actually constitute a misplaced desire, since it misreads the theological significance of Christ's body, which is available to the believer only in the form of the church (for Culbertson, on the contrary, de-sexualizing the gaze of the believer would merely indicate another way of heterosexual men to evade looking passionately at a male body). For Boisvert, the devotional gaze at the body of Christ positively affirms a gay spirituality; and for De La Torre, it is the colonial gaze that complicates Latino masculinity.

The second theoretical concept Culbertson inserts is 'homosociality', a neologism first used by queer theorist and literary critic Eve Kosofsky Sedgwick. Homosociality refers to 'the social bonds between persons of the same sex' (Sedgwick 1985, 1; cf. Van Leer 1989), creating a space for men in which they can operate in close proximity without homosexual desire manifesting itself. Through a series of subtle and preconscious social agreements and transferences, homosocial bonds allow heterosexual men to interact with each other in all-male spaces that require close social or physical contact. Homosocial relationships, then, are same-sex social interactions not defined by sexual relations. We can think here of the military, sports clubs, the male-dominated work sphere or of various *Männerbünde* (voluntary associations of men; see Mosse 1996). Concerning religions, the concept of homosociality helps to analyze forms of religious organizations that are based on gender exclusivity, such as monastic movements, the priesthood or other realms of sacred authority available only to men. The contributions of Mathew Kuefler and Michael Satlow about Jewish and Christian men in late antiquity (chapters 18 and 19) as well as of Sean Gill and Charles Lippy on modern Christian men's movements (chapters 22 and 23) are particularly relevant in this regard.

Philip Culbertson, professor of pastoral theology, has contributed for many years to the field of men's studies in religion. Several of his publications are geared toward the spiritual needs of men (1992; 1994; 1996; 2002), while others have deepened the field's theoretical and definitional frameworks (2004; 2006; 2007). The chapter reprinted below (first published in 1998) belongs to the latter category. In it, Culbertson argues that the absence of the heterosexual male gaze at the heterosexual male body is deeply rooted in the histories of Judaism and Christianity. For Culbertson, this avoidance is not just a historical problem but of contemporary relevance, since it impedes men's spiritual vitality.

Publications by the Same Author

Culbertson, Philip L. 1992. *New Adam: The Future of Male Spirituality*. Minneapolis: Fortress.

——. 1994. *Counseling Men*. Minneapolis: Fortress.

——. 1996. 'Men and Christian Friendship', in *Men's Bodies, Men's Gods*, ed. Björn Krondorfer. New York: New York University Press. Pp. 149–80.

——. 2002. *The Spirituality of Men: Sixteen Christians Write about their Faith*. Minneapolis: Fortress.

——. 2006. 'Mothers and Their Golden Sons: Exploring a Theology of Narcissism', in *Religion and Sexuality: Passionate Debates*, ed. C. K. Robertson. New York: Peter Lang. Pp. 205–34.

——. 2007. 'Christian Men's Movements', in *International Encyclopedia of Men and Masculinities*, eds M. Flood, J. K. Gardiner, B. Pease and K. Pringle. London and New York: Routledge. Pp. 65–7.

Culbertson, Philip and Björn Krondorfer. 2004. 'Men Studies in Religion', in *Encyclopedia of Religion*, 2nd edition (vol. 9), ed.-in-chief Lindsay Jones. Detroit and New York: Macmillan. Pp. 5861–5.

Further Reading

Eilberg-Schwartz, Howard. 1994. *God's Phallus: And Other Problems for Men and Monotheism*. Boston: Beacon.

Mosse, George L. 1996. *The Image of Man: The Creation of Modern Masculinity*. New York: Oxford University Press.

Sedgwick, Eve Kosofsky. 1985. *Between Men: English Literature and Male Homosocial Desire*. New York: Columbia University Press.

Van Leer, David. 1989. 'The Beast of the Closet: Homosociality and the Pathology of Manhood'. *Critical Inquiry* 15 (Spring):587–605.

Designing Men: Reading the Male Body as Text

PHILIP L. CULBERTSON

'Why does it always have to be the *female* body that's presented as exotic, other, fascinating to scrutinize and imagine?' one woman asked me. 'Why is it never the *male* body?' (Goldstein 1997, vii)

An essay of this type must begin with definitions, in order that the author and the reader may construct together a line of reasoning. Of particular consequence between author and reader is a mutual agreement within the definitional fields of Social Construction and Reader Response. Once these two fields have been defined and wed, the author will proceed to his central argument: that there exists no such reality as a heterosexual male body, for it is a socially constructed textless text[1] which blocks all attempts to read meaning into it.

We know a fair amount about what happens when the heterosexual male gaze is turned upon women. The victims of that gaze are increasingly finding their own voices and refusing to submit to objectification. But what happens when the heterosexual male gaze is turned upon another heterosexual male? What happens when a heterosexual male turns his own gaze upon himself? Writers such as Rosalind Coward (1985, 227) and Maxine Sheets-Johnstone (1992, 69) have complained about the absence of study and analysis, and indeed it would seem the male body, already a textless text, has absented itself completely within the past two decades. I recently suggested that a student do some work on the same materials this essay addresses, and suggested that he begin by stripping off and studying himself naked in the mirror. So far two weeks have gone by, and he's still trying to get up the nerve to look.[2]

Social constructionism argues that human identity, both individual and interpersonal, is the product of the social contexts within which we have spent our lives. A social context teaches us what we are allowed to feel or not feel and how to express our feelings; which relationships are mandatory, preferred, obligatory, optional, or undesirable; what we can dream and what we must never dream; which wishes are within the realm of possibility and which are not; and the common standards of aesthetics, virtue, and common good. Social constructionism creates each of us, in this sense, by teaching us how to see; what to value; and how to respond once we have seen and valued.

The foundational assumption of Reader Response is that a text does not have a sole inherent meaning, but has as many possible meanings as its readers bring to it.[3] The idea is long familiar in both Christian and Jewish traditions. Early Judaism spoke of the 'seventy faces of the Torah,' a metaphor for multiplex meanings.[4] St Augustine (1982) sought out nine separate meanings for each of the opening verses of Scripture, and medieval Christianity asserted that every verse of the Bible has at least four meanings: the literal, the allegorical, the tropological, and the anagogical (see Culbertson 1991a). While the early writers in both traditions understood the meanings as inherent in the text, today we understand that they are created by the interaction between a text and a reader, placing as much responsibility for meaning-making upon the reader as upon the text itself.

Social constructionism and reader response theory, then, help us understand that we read meaning into many things other than the printed page. What we are able to see, value, and respond to in a text is socially constructed, and the meaning we draw from whatever we encounter is a priori resident within—generated by—ourselves, and shaped by the complex interaction of culture, life experience, and individual need.

We can now understand bodies as a textless text into which outside meanings are read. The study of the human body as a metaphorical vehicle is sometimes called 'Human Social Anatomy.' Dutton describes it as follows:

> The human body, in this view, can be understood only in the context of the social construction of reality; indeed, the body itself is seen as a social construct, a means of social expression or performance by which our identity and value—for ourselves and others—are created, tested, and validated. (Dutton 1995, 13)

The human body is not simply a blank page upon which words have not yet been written. It is, more aptly, a textless text whose meaning is read by many readers, whether they are invited to read or not. It is a text which is almost always read from the outside (the reader introjecting meaning), but which always has the potential to be read from the inside, in that the body-bearer may at any point choose to wrest control over the text to interpret it as his or her own, making unique meanings and giving them primacy of place.

Objectification, the Male Gaze, and Homosociality

To read indicates 'to objectify.' We maintain the comfortable fiction that encountering a text is an I–Thou relationship, though the history of religious literalism and fundamentalism indicates it is mostly an I–It relationship. In fact, we can't read into a subject because it won't sit still for us to do that. We have to objectify in order to interpret and then meaning-make.[5] In the same way, we objectify the body texts around us. At present, the way that men look at women is the most commonly studied form of objectification with the field of gender studies.

The term 'the male gaze' seems to have been first used by Laura Mulvey (1975; also Lehman 1993, 2–3), who argued that within the classical structure of cinema, men possess the gaze and women are its object. As Schehr explains:

> it is the gaze, the defining mode of operation of masculinist discourse, that constructs the 'woman' as textual object, prevents the woman from being

herself—from 'being,' from 'Being,' from having a 'self' separate from or prior to the sociovisual construct imposed by the male gaze and its/his discourse. (Schehr 1997, 82–3)

A gaze turns a subject into an object. The male gaze values—when turned toward a woman, it desires; when turned toward a gay man, it often despises. In either case, it seizes control from the other. The other may experience the male gaze as a violation, a rape; the object of the gaze is no longer another person, but someone to be possessed or disposed of. Within the world of texts, the male gaze might be described as 'one-handed reading,' in that its purpose is clearly one of self-stimulation and erotic satisfaction.[6]

Homosociality is a term coined by Eve Kosofsky Sedgwick (1985) to describe the basic structure of patriarchy: men pleasing other men via the medium of women.[7] Sedgwick describes the process whereby men attempt to establish some intimacy with each other, usually in a triangulated relationship with a woman who functions to disguise the gestures between the men, as 'homosociality':

'Homosocial' is a word occasionally used in history and the social sciences, where it describes social bonds between persons of the same sex; it is a neologism, obviously formed by analogy with 'homosexual,' and just as obviously meant to be distinguished from 'homosexual.' (Sedgwick 1985, 1)

Sedgwick's theory is directly related to family systems theory, presuming that human beings relate to each other within triangular structures.[8] In the triangle of two men and a woman, the attraction between the two men must be taken at least as seriously as the attraction between each man and the woman. The attraction is heightened when either man realizes that he can accumulate further power and influence by forming an alliance with another of the two members of the triangle. Since women rarely have power, the obvious choice with whom to form the alliance is the other man. The alliance may take the form of co-operation or competition or even aggression. Whatever its form, the alliance as power-brokering cannot be denied. This desire to unite powers with another man is one possible non-genital form of Eros, this desire and attraction creating the exaggerated impulse to homosociality. Sedgwick even describes the attraction as 'intense and potent.' Most men operate this way on occasion, though few are aware of it.

The male gaze not only objectifies, but *must* objectify for homosociality to work. Ironically, the homosocial system can be maintained only when men avert their gaze from each other; the gaze, however figuratively, must remain focused on a woman. When the male gaze turns toward another man, homosociality threatens to disintegrate into homoeroticism, as the novels of D. H. Lawrence illustrate.[9] Thus patriarchy is built upon the assumption that a male body is a text which will reject all attempts by other men to read it. To accept such an attempt would be to destroy the basis of power and control.

Thinking about writing this essay, I decided to poll a group of men I spend a lot of time with. Sitting in a corner at a party, I asked them 'When a woman walks into the room, what's the first thing you notice about her?' They answered variously 'Her breasts; I'm a tit man.' 'Her legs.' 'Her hair.' 'Her ass.' Each man had a quick and clear answer. I continued: 'So when a man walks into the room, what's the first thing you notice about him.' 'The whole package,' they seemed to answer in one voice. Not satisfied, I asked my question about men again, and got the same univocal answer again. In fact, the guys wouldn't budge. They would not name a male body part that attracted their attention, would not name any aspect of a male that they read first as an entry point into the larger text. They were willing to engage the text as a whole, but not to do the sort of close reading that is now assumed within the field of textual criticism.

Averting the Gaze, Refusing to Read

Why is it so difficult for men to direct their heterosexual male gaze toward another man? Why is it apparently even more difficult for them to turn the gaze upon their own male bodies? The complexity of the answer may help explain why the subject is almost completely ignored in the exploding literature on masculinity. Let me explore five different reasons.

Reading is Dangerous: To read is to risk making one's self vulnerable, to risk encountering what Wayne Booth has called 'the otherness that bites.'[10] Most people are highly selective about what they read, and will avoid texts which threaten their comfortability or security. A man may not be consciously aware that to read another man's body is dangerous, but subconsciously he is aware. He is also aware that to read another man's body raises the possibility that another man may attempt to read his, and perhaps in the reading find him wanting.

Reading Re-Positions the Reader: As I have claimed elsewhere, masculinity as a gender construction in virtually every society is fragile and must be constantly defended (Culbertson 1992; 1994; 2006). Michael Satlow makes the same claim in relation to the rabbinic understanding of masculinity: 'For the rabbis, therefore, manliness is never secure; it is achieved through the constant exercise of discipline in pursuit of virtue, and vanishes the moment a male ceases to exercise that discipline' (Satlow 1996, 27). To gaze at another man re-positions a straight man as a gay man, thereby shattering his fragile masculinity. Reading affects the reader much more deeply than it affects the text; gazing affects the gazer much more deeply than the one toward whom the gaze is directed. Susan Bordo points out that the male gaze has the power not only to objectify, but to feminize:

> What exposure is most feared in the shower? Not the scrutiny of the penis (although this prospect may indeed make a heterosexual men uncomfort-able), but the moment when one bends down to pick up the soap which has slipped from one's hands. It is in the imagination of this moment that the orthodox male is most undone by the consciousness that there may be homo-sexuals in the shower, whose gaze will define him as a passive receptacle of *their* sexuality, and thus as 'woman.' There is a certain paradox here. For although it is the imagined effeminacy of homosexual men that makes them objects of heterosexual derision, here it is their imagined *masculinity* (that is,

the consciousness of them as active, evaluating sexual subjects, with a defining and 'penetrating' sexual gaze) that makes them the objects of heterosexual fear. (Bordo 1997, 287)

Men's fear of the male gaze, ultimately, is the fear of becoming, feeling, or
representing female desire within the phallocentric order. In the shower, the
homosexual body is the same as the heterosexual body, the only difference
being in the desirer. (Schehr 1997, 151)

Reading a Text Which Won't Focus: As if the male body were not already a difficult
enough text to read, it seems to disappear altogether when a man is unclothed. In
a patriarchal system, the penis cues masculinity, and once that occurs, the body,
'the being' disappears and the person becomes a function, the form becomes the
essence, the masculinity, the 'doing.' The part overwhelms the whole, so that the
whole fades into insignificance, leaving us to attempt to read a part or 'member'
which is, at best, dissociative. Phillip Lopate writes:

This part of me, which is so synecdochically identified with the male body (as
the term 'male member' indicates) has given me both too little, and too much,
information about what it means to be a man. It has a personality like a cat.
I have prayed to it to behave better, to be less frisky, or more; I have followed
its nose in matters of love, ignoring good sense, and paid the price; but I have
also come to appreciate that it has its own specialized form of intelligence
which must be listened to, or another price will be extracted. (Lopate 1997,
211)

The penis will not behave: now a penis, now a phallus, the one when we wish
the other, it is itself a text that we can barely read, even with double vision.
It seems not one thing but two. The phallus is haunted by the penis and vice
versa. It has no unified social identity, but is fragmented by ideologies of race
and ethnicity. 'Rather than exhibiting constancy of form, it is perhaps the most
visibly mutable of bodily parts; it evokes the temporal not the eternal. And far
from maintaining a steady will and purpose, it is mercurial, temperamental,
unpredictable' (Bordo 1997, 265–6). It is this unpredictability which fascinates,
frustrates, and ultimately offends many readers of male bodies.

Because it is two and not one, we do not even know how to count the male
body parts. Girls are made of indiscrete amounts of stuff: 'sugar and spice and
everything nice.' No quantities are given, nor do they need to be. But boys are
made of countable things: 'snips and snails and puppy dog tails . . . Countable,
if not to say detachable, things, metonymies of their always castrated penises'
(Schehr 1997, 80). But do we count the penis as one and the phallus as another?
Or is the penis simply a potential text, a text which seems to self-create at will?
St Augustine claimed it was two: the penis, which is the 'logical extension' of all
rational men, created in the image of the divine logos, and the phallus, which as
rationally uncontrollable, must simply be the handiwork of the Not-God, Satan.
The phallus for Augustine is the wily serpent in the garden[11] and, as the only
body part which refuses to submit to the brain, the constant reminder of our
fallenness. Augustine despised the phallus, the conveyer of original sin. And
yet even so great a saint could be overcome by his phallicly inflated male ego,

declaring that in heaven, women will receive their penises back. Perhaps he would have been happier if the penis really had been detachable, to be awarded, or not, like a prize for good behavior.

In a 1986 movie called *Dick Talk*, a group of women are filmed discussing their responses to the male body, and to male genitals in particular. In the opening section, 'The First,' the moderator asks women about the first time they thought about a penis and what they thought about it. One relates how she thought penises were like rockets that detached themselves from men, entered women's bodies, and transformed themselves into babies. She had seen diagrams in a book, and since she had seen her father walking around the house in his shorts without a visible erection like that in the diagram, she assumed that his had become detached. She then relates a dream about men in suits with attaché cases in which they keep their penises.[12]

A detachable phallus, in the above fantasy, must leave behind only its shadow, the penis. Schehr argues that this is why the penis is hidden so often: 'It is my contention that the penis has been the most hidden of male body parts because of the ideological as well as the psychoanalytical temptation to turn the penis into its evil twin brother, the phallus' (Schehr 1997, 16). Note the genitals in the ceiling paintings in the Sistine Chapel: they are all disproportionately small. This makes them safe and aesthetic, an extension of ancient Greek ideals of desirable male nudity. K. J. Dover analyzed the representation of penises on Greek vases within the context of his study of homosexuality in ancient Greece. Attractive penises were particularly small, with no pubic hair: the penis of a pre-adolescent. Unattractive penises were exaggeratedly large, threatening, and attached to hairy bodies. The cultural index of penile beauty, then, in Dover's reading of vases, is that of modesty and subordination, an abjuration of sexual initiative or sexual rivalry (Dover 1978, 125). Source of pride, seat of shame, many men cannot figure out how to read their own penises realistically, and refuse to read the penises of others. Judaism attempted to resolve the textual dilemma with the cry 'Off with its hat!' Christianity responded more adamantly: 'Off with its head,' creating a culture of either symbolic or literal castration. The Christian male body was symbolically castrated through body-denial, the circumscription of sexual activity to heterosexual intercourse within marriage for the sole purpose of procreation, and the forbidding of *jouissance*.[13] For some of the saints, this was not enough. Origen in the third century and Peter Abelard in the twelfth century are two who excised altogether any genital text from their body.[14]

Reading a Text Which Does Not Belong To Us: Those who have the greatest investment in reading interpretive meanings into textless texts are those whose power is most easily promoted by the interpretation. The entire subject of identifying readings, of deconstructing the construction of the heterosexual male body, is so inherently elusive that I had repeatedly to struggle to keep any sense of objectivity while writing this essay.

Those with the greatest investment in reading meaning into the male body are governments and politico-military authorities, which need men to conceive themselves in certain ways in order to retain their present positions of power. In other words, the primary reader who inserts meaning into the male textless text is the government structure of the society in which these men live. In his essay 'Consuming Manhood,' Michael Kimmel points out that in order for a man in nineteenth-century puritanical America to become a real man, a 'Marketplace Man,' governments realized it would be necessary to control the flows of desire and of fluids filling his body (Kimmel 1997). Certain flows of desire would need to be deemed morally repugnant because they were economically counterproductive; undesirable or counterproductive flows of desire would henceforth be deemed pathological. In *The History of Sexuality*, Michel Foucault stresses the development of such discourses of biopolitics, those official discourses that seek to regulate the individual through a series of proscriptions, admonitions, and recommendations. The discourses of biopolitics involve the identification of the individual with his (and not 'his or her') political self as a citizen. The individual was to act so as best to fulfill the functions of a member of society. In order to produce Marketplace Men, bodies would need to be owned, men would have to be read as both heterosexual and 'manly,' and the siring of children would be understood as mandatory. These were the responsibility of every good citizen.[15]

Male bodies are textless texts into which governments read self-securing values and expectations, giving lie to the myth of genuine concern or human rights. Heterosexuality is read onto men's bodies, which is why, in the present debate on the genesis of sexual orientation, gay men can usually chart the development of their sexual self-awareness, while straight men believe they have 'always been that way.' Heterosexuality is a government-designed and -controlled process of breeding, of animal husbandry. Masturbation, voluntary celibacy, homosexuality, and any other alternative sexual expression has to be controlled and even anathematized, for only through heterosexual marriage and the procreation of children can a phallic political power assure its own authority into the future.[16] The heterosexual male gaze is the ultimate sign of capitulation to an imposed external meaning, an abandonment of human *jouissance*.

Reading Unmasks the Divine Ambiguity: An additional difficulty in reading men's bodies confronts Jewish and Christian men, whether gay or straight. Danna Nolan Fewell and David Gunn (1996) and Howard Eilberg-Schwartz (1994; 1996) have explored extensively the central gender problem of Scripture: how can men and women understand themselves as created in God's image when God apparently has no body? Eilberg-Schwartz writes:

> Does God have genitals and, if so, of which sex? It is interesting that interpreters have generally avoided this question. This seems a particularly important lacuna for interpreters who understand Genesis 1.26–27 to mean that the human body is made in the image of the deity. By avoiding the question of God's sex, they skirt a fundamental question: how can male and female bodies both resemble the divine form? Since God's sex is veiled, however, any conclusions have to be inferred indirectly from statements about God's gender. But however this question is answered poses a problem for human embodiment generally and sexuality in particular. If God is asexual, as many interpreters would have it, then only part of the human body is made in the image of God. (Eilberg-Schwartz 1996, 47)

The part of a man's body which is obviously not made in God's image is the penis. To read another man's body is to read the Divine Ambiguity. And this ambiguity, too, is read into men's penises—into the penises of others, and into one's own.

Given how daunting all this is, no wonder that the heterosexual male gaze is never directed toward other heterosexual men. No wonder 'the guys' only wanted to look at the whole package, if even that! If a man cannot read the body of another, what then is the effect when he turns his male gaze upon himself, upon his own body with all its strengths and weaknesses?

Notes

1 I first encountered the term 'textless text' in Dane (1991). Dane uses the term to describe Oral Torah, but I find its usefulness much wider.

2 This is not, however, R. Judah the Patriarch, who was referred to as 'our holy rabbi' because he never looked at his own penis, or even touched it (b. Shabbat 118b). Nor is it George Eliot's Daniel Deronda, who seems to take three-quarters of this 800-plus-page novel before he ever notices that he is circumcised. Both serve as examples of men's enormous investment in dissociating from their penises, while simultaneously making them synecdoches of masculine identity.

3 Such a claim is, of course, simplistic, for however passive a text may be, it still has its own syntax, rhetorical structures, and genres. See Gadamer (1982).

4 See Culbertson (1996, 25–52; 1991b).

5 Many authors develop this idea. Among the foundational texts are Austin (1975); Fish (1980); and Bakhtin (1981).

6 See also Schehr (1997, 113).

7 See also Rubin (1975). Ortner (1996) describes Polynesian cultures as homosocial, in that powerful men retain their position by bartering young virgins in order to form political alliances. Such a social structure appears to make women important, but in fact their value is only in their agency as 'negotiable tender.' George (1996) describes the relation between David and Jonathan as sitting at the homosexual end of the homosocial spectrum.

8 See Bowen (1985) and Guerin et al. (1996) for cogent explanations of this theory.

9 See, for example, the relationship between Maurice and Bertie in his short story 'The Blind Man,' or between Gerald Crich and Rupert Birkin in Women in Love.

10 'I embrace the pursuit of the Other as among the grandest of hunts we are invited to . . . But surely no beast that will prove genuinely other will fail to bite, and the otherness that bites, the otherness that changes us, must have sufficient definition, sufficient identity, to threaten us where we live' (Booth 1990, 70).

11 See the excellent comments by Rashkow (1994, 32 n.32). For a vivid picture of adolescent revulsion at phallic erection, see Stephen Fry's novel The Hippopotamus (1994, 88–9).

12 See Lehman (1993, 148–9).

13 See, among various sources, Ranke-Heinemann (1990).

14 See Brown (1988, 117, 168–9). I believe there are deeper psychological implications of male castration which are not yet adequately explored. For example, is Christian castration a form of despair masquerading as discipline? Is it an early form

of mental illness like the forms of self-mutilation we know today, where a patient will bang her head against a wall repeatedly, creating a controlled external pain which distracts from the uncontrollable internal psychiatric pain? Unfortunately, the subject of voluntary castration in Christian tradition is little written-about; one of the few texts is Browe's, *Zur Geschichte der Entmannung* (1936).

15 In Jim Thompson's novel *The Nothing Man*, protagonist Clint Brown returns from World War Two having had his genitals blown off by a landmine. He describes himself as having 'given his penis for his country' (1988, 3).

16 The *Hite Report on Male Sexuality* (1981) concluded that sexual intercourse for men was satisfying not only because of their attraction to their sexual partner 'but also from the deeply engraved cultural meaning of the act. Through intercourse a man participates in the cultural symbolism of patriarchy and gains a sense of belonging to society with status/identity of "male."' See Walters et al. (1988, 215).

Literature

Augustine. 1982. *The Literal Meaning of Genesis*, trans. John Hammond Taylor, S. J., 2 vols (Vols 41–42 in the Ancient Christian Writers Series). New York: Newman Press.

Austin, J. L. 1975. *How To Do Things With Words* (2nd edition), eds J. O. Urmson and Marina Sbisa. Cambridge: Harvard University Press.

Bakthin, Mikhail Mikhailovich. 1981. *The Dialogic Imagination: Four Essays*, ed. Michael Holquist, trans. Caryl Emerson and Michael Holquist. Austin: University of Texas Press.

Beal, Timothy and David Gunn (eds) 1996. *Reading Bibles, Writing Bodies: Identity and the Book*. London: Routledge.

Booth, Wayne C. 1990. *The Company We Keep: An Ethics of Fiction*. Berkeley: University of California Press.

Bordo, Susan. 1997. 'Reading the Male Body,' in Goldstein, pp. 265–306.

Bowen, Murray. 1985. *Family Therapy in Clinical Practice*. Northvale: Jason Aronson.

Browe, Peter. 1936. *Zur Geschichte der Entmannung: Eine religions- und rechtsgeschichtliche Studie*. Breslau: Muller.

Brown, Peter. 1988. *The Body and Society: Men, Women, and Sexual Renunciation in Early Christianity*. New York: Columbia University Press.

Coward, Rosalind. 1985. *Female Desires: How They Are Sought, Bought, and Packaged*. New York: Grove Press.

Culbertson, Philip. 1991a. 'Known, Knower, Knowing: The Authority of Scripture in the Anglican Tradition,' *Anglican Theological Review* 74/2 (Autumn):144–74.

——. 1991b. 'Multiplexity in Biblical Exegesis: The Introduction to Megillat Qohelet by Moses Mendelssohn,' *Cincinnati Journal of Judaica* 2 (Spring):10–18.

——. 1992. *New Adam: The Future of Male Spirituality*. Minneapolis: Fortress.

——. 1994. *Counseling Men*. Minneapolis: Fortress.

——. 1996. *A Word Fitly Spoken: Context, Transmission, and Adoption of the Parables of Jesus*. Albany: SUNY Press.

——. 2006. 'Men's Quest for Wholeness: The Changing Counseling Needs of Pakeha Males,' *UNIversitas: The Journal of the University of Northern Iowa*, 3(1):1–19; http://www.uni.edu/universitas/.

Dane, Perry. 1991. 'The Oral Law and the Jurisprudence of a Textless Text,' *S'vara* 2/2:11–24.

Dover, K. J. 1978. *Greek Homosexuality*. Cambridge: Harvard University Press.

Dutton, Kenneth. 1995. *The Perfectible Body: The Western Ideal of Male Physical Development*. New York: Continuum.

Eilberg-Schwartz, Howard, 1994. *God's Phallus, and Other Problems for Men and Monotheism*. Boston: Beacon.

——. 1996. 'The Problem of the Body for the People of the Book,' in Beal and Gunn, pp. 34–55.

Fewell, Danna Nolan and David Gunn. 1996. 'Shifting the Blame: God in the Garden,' in Beal and Gunn, pp. 16–33.

Fish, Stanley. 1980. *Is There a Text in This Class? The Authority of Interpretive Communities*. Cambridge: Harvard University Press.

Fry, Stephen. 1994. *The Hippopotamus*. London: Arrow Books.

Gadamer, Hans-Georg. 1982. *Truth and Method*. New York: Crossroad.

George, Mark. 1996. 'Assuming the Body of the Heir Apparent: David's Lament,' in Beal and Gunn, pp. 164–74.

Goldstein, Laurence (ed.). 1997. *The Male Body: Features, Destinies, Exposures*. Ann Arbor: University of Michigan.

Guerin, Philip, Thomas Fogarty, Leo Fay and Judith Gilbert Kautto. 1996. *Working with Relationship Triangles: The One-Two-Three of Psychotherapy*. New York: Guilford.

Kimmel, Michael. 1997. 'Consuming Manhood: The Feminization of American Culture and the Recreation of the Male Body, 1832–1920,' in Goldstein, pp. 12–41.

Lehman, Peter. 1993. *Running Scared: Masculinity and the Representation of the Male Body*. Philadelphia: Temple University Press.

Lopate, Phillip. 1997. 'Portrait of My Body,' in Goldstein, pp. 204–13.

Mulvey, Laura. 1975. 'Visual Pleasure and the Narrative Cinema,' *Screen* 16/3:6–18.

Ortner, Sherry. 1996. *Making Gender: The Politics and Erotics of Culture*. Boston: Beacon.

Ranke-Heinemann, Uta. 1990. *Eunuchs for the Kingdom of Heaven: Women, Sexuality, and the Catholic Church*. New York: Penguin.

Rashkow, Ilona. 1994. 'Daughters and Fathers in Genesis . . . Or, What is Wrong with this Picture,' in *A Feminist Companion to Exodus to Deuteronomy*, ed. Athalya Brenner. Sheffield: Sheffield Academic Press. Pp. 22–36.

Rubin, Gayle. 1975. 'The Traffic in Women: Notes on the "Political Economy" of Sex,' in *Toward an Anthropology of Women*, ed. Rayna Reiter. New York: Monthly Review Press. Pp. 157–210.

Satlow, Michael. 1996. '"Try to Be a Man": The Rabbinic Construction of Masculinity,' *Harvard Theological Review* 89/1:19–40.

Schehr, Lawrence. 1997. *Parts of an Andrology: On Representations of Men's Bodies*. Stanford: Stanford University Press.

Sedgwick, Eve Kosofsky. 1985. *Between Men: English Literature and Male Homosocial Desire*. New York: Columbia University Press.

Sheets-Johnstone, Maxine. 1992. 'Corporeal archetypes and Power,' *Hypatia* 7/3 (Summer):39–76.

Thompson, Jim. [1954], 1988. *The Nothing Man*. New York: Mysterious Press.

Walters, Marianne, Betty Carter, Peggy Papp and Olga Silverstein. 1988. *The Invisible Web: Gender Patterns in Family Relationships*. New York: Guilford.

Constructing Common Ground: Mapping the Contributions of Gay People to Christian Theology

Editor's Introduction

Jay Johnson's 'Constructing Common Ground', first published in 1996, presents a gay theological voice that has moved far away from the early beginnings of gay theology. In the 1950s and 1960s, gay theologians, together with lesbian activists, argued for the compatibility of homosexuality and the Christian church, hoping to convince the churches to fully accept the homosexual person into their community (see, for example, McNeill 1976).

Encountering continued homophobia in the churches, gay and lesbian theologians later adopted a non-apologetic stance (Clark 1989; Hunt 1991; Comstock 1993; Mollenkott 1996; Alpert 1998) that worked with a liberationist hermeneutics shared by other liberation theologies and the LGBT communities (lesbian-gay-bisexual-transgender). This prepared the way for the eventual shift of focus from religious activism to scholarly writings within an academic setting. Though the activist dimension rarely disappears fully from sight, scholarly writings have, since the late 1980s, diversified gay perspectives in religious studies (for a brief history, see Spencer 2004). From now on, the sought-after conversation partners were no longer mainstream Bible scholars and theologians, church officials and parishioners but other gay scholars and theologians. In internal debates, they refined their arguments and sought clarity about the kind of theologies appropriate for a gay identity. Would one begin the exploration as a Christian theologian who would draw insights from the theological traditions applicable to the gay experience? Or would one begin as a gay man who would seek theological frameworks that would best serve the spiritual needs of the gay community? In other words, would the prime reference point be either the 'gay experience' or 'Christian theology'? 'The difference,' Johnson suggests, 'surfaces in the respective methods employed for the projects. The first seeks to construct a theology on gay experience, the second seeks to speak theologically with a gay voice.'

Johnson locates his reflections within academic discourse as he attempts to bridge the gap between those gay theologies that take on a more social constructionist view on gender (like J. Michael Clark) and those with an essentialist view on identity (like Ronald Long). Johnson argues that neither is sufficient in itself. 'For those who remain convinced of an essential reality behind our cultural categories and those who remain content with examining their social construction, co-operation rather than polarization will bring common ground.'

Publications by the Same Author

Johnson, Jay E. 2005. *Dancing with God: Anglican Christianity and the Practice of Hope.* Harrisburg: Morehouse.

Further Reading

Alpert, Rebecca T. 1998. *Like Bread on the Seder Plate.* New York: Columbia University Press.

Alpert, Rebecca T., Sue Levi Elwell and Shirley Idelson (eds). 2001. *Lesbian Rabbis: The First Generation.* New Brunswick: Rutgers University Press.

Clark, J. Michael. 1989. *A Place to Start: Toward an Unapologetic Gay Liberation Theology.* Dallas: Monument Press.

Comstock, Gary David. 1993. *Gay Theology Without Apology.* Cleveland: Pilgrim.

Hunt, Mary. 1991. *Fierce Tenderness: A Feminist Theology of Friendship.* New York: Crossroad.

McNeill, John J. 1976. *The Church and the Homosexual.* Kansas City: Sheed Andrews and McMeel.

Mollenkott, Virginia R. 1996. 'Lesbian', in *Dictionary of Feminist Theologies*, eds Letty M. Russell and J. Shannon Clarkson. Louisville: Westminster John Knox. Pp. 166–8.

Spencer, Daniel T. 2004. 'Lesbian and Gay Theologies', in *Handbook of U.S. Theologies of Liberation*, ed. Miguel De La Torre. St. Louis: Chalice Press. Pp. 264–73.

Constructing Common Ground: Mapping the Contributions of Gay People to Christian Theology

JAY EMERSON JOHNSON

Recent moves toward developing a 'gay theology' have highlighted a subtle but growing divide between theologians who understand their primary point of reference to be the experience of gay people and those who work within the Christian tradition but from a gay perspective. Both claim significance for the social location of gay and lesbian people in theology. The difference surfaces in the respective methods employed for the projects. The first seeks to construct a theology on gay experience, the second seeks to speak theologically with a gay voice.[1]

With this essay I propose another way to map the theological contributions of gay people with the hope of constructing some common ground from which to move into the future. [. . .] I propose three related theses for mapping those trails to common ground, to the possibility for a foundational Christian theology from within gay experience.

Thesis 1: To theological discourse gay and lesbian experience contributes epistemological insights (how we know and how we appropriate what we know).

Recent work in the Gay Men's Issues in Religion group on family, sex, and church will illustrate the potential of that contribution. I shall argue for what remains 'essential' (epistemologically) in those three categories even as they are reconstructed by gay experience.

Thesis 2: The frequently overlooked resource of American pragmatism provides conceptual shape to gay and lesbian experience. A sketch of two American figures in particular (Orestes Augustus Brownson and Charles Sanders Peirce) will suggest ways in which both strict essentialists and excessive social constructionists can 'break camp' and move toward common ground.

Thesis 3: Gay and lesbian experience manifests and insists on hope as an indispensable theological category. For Christian theologians, hope means engaging eschatology, a doctrinal discourse about which many feminist and gay theorists have considerable reservations. A review of J. Michael Clark's critique of Christian eschatology will provide a test for the common ground I am proposing.

To conclude, I will suggest the contours of the work ahead if these three theses prove useful for mapping gay contributions to Christian theology. In brief, the Holy Spirit would seem to fill the horizon we glimpse from that plateau and which may provide the theological language we need for describing the oft contested and variously defined 'gay sensibility.'

Family, Sex, and Church

Projects in the Gay Men's Issues in Religion group often postulate, to varying degrees, certain unique perspectives which gay men bring to religious and cultural discourse. Recent work has addressed family, sex, and church. The work of reconstructing these 'categories' based on gay experience reveals a tension similar to that found in the relationship between essentialist and social constructionist categories for gender and sexual orientation. It reveals as well the importance of resisting the temptation to make either the 'essential' element of the category or its reconstruction the exhaustive locus for meaning.

Family: Mark Kowalewski and Elizabeth Say (1994) have engaged the task of reclaiming 'family values' through an exploration of the new patterns of community created by lesbians and gay men. Clearly, 'family' is a socially constructed category. The complex of social relations to which the category 'family' refers has changed significantly over time and remains mobile even within a given culture. Yet the word itself persists, and those engaged in a host of relational configurations continue to insist on appropriating the category to describe those configurations.

Might the persistence of the word itself, despite the vast diversity of the configurations to which it refers, point to something *essential*, a relational quality that contributes to what it means to be human? Despite the cultural baggage attached to the category, lesbian women and gay men have been loathe to relinquish their claim on it. Granting the political expediency it offers in a hostile cultural climate, the urgency with which some engage its appropriation still seems to point to a reality 'behind' the inadequate models delivered by a dominant discourse. It would seem to indicate a reality in which lesbian women and gay men are not only claiming their rightful place but their own contribution to its reconstruction. Although few would argue for an ideal form of 'family,' the category itself may still refer to a quality of relation that, in part, is constitutive of being human.

A gay and lesbian contribution to the family might mean articulating, however imperfectly, why the category itself (even the language for it) persists. It would surely mean continuing Carter Heyward's (1982) trail-blazing work on the theological significance of relation itself and thereby insisting that the value of 'family' cannot be contained within a static category in perpetual need of reconstruction. It might mean arguing that the attraction to this category comes from its ability to open at least one doorway to *transcendence*. Here I would argue for at least a minimal definition of transcendence as that quality of relation which is more than the sum of the parts being considered.

The experience of such transcendence presents an epistemological opportunity: Relation and knowledge are linked. What we know and value about families comes from what we learn in our relationships with one another and which we could not have learned on our own. The gay experience of relationships offers an epistemological insight that goes beyond apologetics (*but we are also a family*); it contributes to the ongoing quest for understanding how human beings know anything at all.

Sex: The link between relation and knowledge appears in a more particularized form regarding sex. Ron Long has attempted a long overdue phenomenology of gay sex in which he proposes an inextricable link between sex and religious epiphany. Long offers a critique of the Western tradition generally as offering precious little for analyzing the 'common association' between God and sex among gay men (1995, 70). The key move here is Long's insistence that sex is irreducible to an expression of intimacy among couples; sex itself is his subject. Long prefers, in other words, to disengage from the question of what constitutes 'legitimate' intimate relations and focuses on the 'spiritual dimensions' of sex *qua* sex. As such, Long's phenomenology removes sex from formal ethical considerations and provides an important locus for examining the dynamics of physical relation as such.

In his analysis Long might have countered the traditional restrictions for sexual expression by arguing that sex opens yet another avenue for the experience and even appropriation of transcendence. Instead (and unfortunately in my view), Long reduces transcendence to sex itself.[2] This move is a rather odd twist as Long appears to reproduce the view of sex he had hoped to deconstruct. In his critique of the Christian tradition, and Augustine in particular, he rejects the understanding of 'appropriate' sex as simply licit lust for the sake of procreation (or more recently, for the sake of expressing intimacy in a committed relationship). Long rejects, in other words, restricting sex a priori to predetermined or essential ends. But to suggest that relation itself *is* transcendence, *is* divine, *is* God begins to strike an even more virulently essentialist chord than the view he had hoped to enhance or perhaps even subvert.[3]

Our reflection on sex could lead in another direction. If sex seems inescapably tied to biology, it is clearly not tied to procreation. As gay men and lesbians have learned, if sex is not *pro*creative it is certainly a creative, even *imaginative* activity. Human beings are not necessarily determined by biology in our sexual expressions and sexual affections, even if biology assigns certain physical limitations to the activity itself. Imaginative physical configurations for sex are not, furthermore, a stop-gap measure for gay people who cannot achieve the 'fuller' expression of human sexuality by conceiving a child. As Long's phenomenology rightly suggests, a great deal of what is otherwise not considered sex contributes to sex, including posturing, cruising, fantasizing, and the imaginative appropriations of gender displays.

To the epistemological contribution made by gay experience we might then add the human imagination, or how we appropriate what we know. A phenomenology of sex, in other words, might present an opportunity to take seriously the role of the imagination in the ongoing task of understanding and appropriating human experience: the capacity to transcend simple biological categories; the vision to see beyond the limits of otherwise fixed patterns of relating; the recognition and imaginative appropriation of possibilities for human relating and knowing which are not self-evident from either immutable biological essences or constructed cultural configurations. This is an epistemological imagination which ought to lead us beyond a simple one-to-one identification between God and the sex-act and toward the doorway of transcendence presented to us by every intimate act of relating (including so-called 'casual' sex).

Church: These fundamental contributions to theological reflection from gay experience begin to coalesce in relation to the work on ecclesiology offered by Daniel Spencer. 'Church' as a category in theological discourse reflects the same inseparability of what I have been calling more generally essentialist and social constructionist positions. As ecclesiological reconstructions proceed along the lines proposed by liberation and feminist theologies, 'Church' retains its status as an essential category for theological discourse. Rather than abandoning the category, the reconstructions broaden and eventually reconceive it on the terms proposed by the experience of those at the category's margins.

'Once you were no people,' Spencer suggests, quoting from the biblical First Letter of Peter. The foundational experience for a gay and lesbian ecclesiology, located on cultural margins, is marked by Diaspora. 'But now you are God's people.'[4] Families expand for gay and lesbian Christians in communities bound together not through biology or even shared oppression, but from a common vision which transcends expected cultural constructs.

Theologically, the category 'Church' brings together the imaginative epistemological contributions offered by gay experience. As L. William Countryman has suggested, gay people of faith discover their own unique 'priesthood,' whether institutionally sanctioned or not. This priesthood springs directly from our shared humanity in which each offers the insights gained from his or her own unique access to the mystery of God hidden beneath the routine of everyday life. This priesthood, Countryman suggests, is one of 'hidden things, or secrets ... because they have to do with dimensions of human experience where language fails.' The experience of coming out, for example, releases the power to 'defy cultural constructs' and offers a different vision of humanity's relation to the holy.[5]

Knowledge from relation, a creative imagination, reconstructions and hidden things revealed: The contribution to theology made by gay experience can be described, however inchoately or dimly, with words such as these.

Breaking Camp for Common Ground

If family, sex, and church can be conceived as *essential* categories *reconstructed* by gay experience, some common ground begins to emerge for both strict essentialists and excessive social constructionists. The early development of American pragmatism may provide some help for giving conceptual shape to that experience and for negotiating the trails to that common ground.

Communal Knowing—Strict Essentialists Breaking Camp: John Boswell (1989, 19) insists that few, if any, hold to a truly essentialist position. However true that may be, many theorists in both gender and gay studies continue to battle essentialist positions or simply acquiesce to their inevitable, albeit hidden, presence. The question at hand may reduce to the quest for knowledge itself, including rather traditional epistemological problems: How do human beings know anything at all?

An early pioneer in the North American tradition is the often misunderstood, even maligned figure of Orestes Augustus Brownson. His work reoriented the epistemological question by planting the seeds of what would later be called American pragmatism. He provides as well the first signpost on the trail away from the strict essentialist camp by insisting on the fundamentally *communal* nature of knowledge.

Within the complex interaction of Lockean empiricism, revivalist religion and New England Transcendentalism—all of which gave birth to early American intellectual history—Brownson embarked on a quest for truth. [. . .] [He insist[ed] that knowledge is not reducible to either rationalist subjectivity nor the distanced objectivity of the empiricists, but emerges from a complex interaction of both subject and object. Rather than the philosophy of *being* (essentialism), Brownson argued for the science of *life*:

> Here in the phenomenal, the fact of Life, where only we are able to seize either the subjective world or the objective world, the subjective and objective are given not as separate, not one to be obtained from the other, but in an *indissoluble synthesis*. This is wherefore I call philosophy not the science of *Being*, but the science of Life; and also where I add to it the epithet, *synthetic*.[6]

Communal knowledge means for Brownson the dependence of each individual on both nature and society, a dependence which is not accidental to, but constitutive of being human. [. . .] Gay and lesbian experience not only confirms Brownson's epistemological insight in principle, gay people rely on such insights in practice. 'Reality' does not speak for itself, as any gay or lesbian person readily admits with reference to 'coming out.' Coming out, while intensely personal, nevertheless relies on the language for doing so as it is articulated by the communal experience of other gay people who have blazed the trail.[7]

The Imagination—Excessive Social Constructionists Breaking Camp: If strict essentialists can break camp by acknowledging that human knowing depends on, to a certain degree, the constructs created by a community of knowers, social constructionists might begin to break camp by addressing the human imagination. The contextual boundaries set by excessive social constructionists provide little explanatory help for understanding particularly creative projects which appear to transcend the limits of a given cultural context. Indeed, without such moments of transcendent imagination, revolutionary social change seems inconceivable. From whence did such an imagination come? [. . .]

Charles Sanders Peirce may prove useful here. Following on the heels of Brownson, Peirce engaged the polarization of the substance and process models of the human self. Human experience relies not merely on facts and sensations (as in the Whiteheadian view) but on the laws discovered in their effects. For Peirce, these laws are real, but they are perceived inferentially and through the appropriation of a creative imagination. As such, these 'laws' imply not only continuity with the past but the condition for the possibility of growth and development. 'Self-transcendence,' the basis for any growth and development, depends on the reality of such laws, or 'tendencies,' as they enable an intentional, self-directed movement into a novel future.[8]

For all his insistence on laws, Peirce is not a simple essentialist. Foundations of absolute certainty in knowledge are neither possible nor even desirable. Instead, Peirce argues for the 'accumulation of probabilities' developed from the inferential perception of real laws and tendencies as the basis for any adequate explanation of human experience. It means a creative, imaginative appropriation of those tendencies, the results of which the brute facts and sensations of any given moment could have neither predicted nor provided.[9]

To break camp as an excessive social constructionist means expanding the raw material from which the human self is explained. For Peirce it means the 'entire mental product,' and not merely sense-perceptions, rational discourse, or the constructs provided by cultural configurations. Again, the experience among gay people of creative, imaginative appropriations of novel possibilities—possibilities not previously given room or even considered within a given social construct—provides an important locus for reconsidering the claims of excessive social constructionism.

In short, Brownson's description of knowledge as communion between subject and object and Peirce's realist construct of human experience offer some conceptual help for explaining the unique contributions to theology made by gay and lesbian people. Taken together, Brownson and Peirce also provide the contours of that common ground from which those gay contributions can be made. [. . .]

The Experience of Hope and Christian Eschatology: [. . .] Can we find a way to speak theologically of the hope gay and lesbian people experience? In other words, can gay experience, a truly embodied experience rooted in concrete historical realities, contribute to a theological tradition which has so often fallen prey to 'other-worldly' discourse?[10]

Christian eschatological speculation has never felt completely comfortable in the concrete realities of human history. The uneasy relationship between the two has led many of those engaged in recent reconstructions of theology to abandon eschatology altogether, or at least to dismantle the category beyond recognition. I would argue that such reconstructions can be understood as operating from within a false dichotomy between two *essentialist* categories. The first is often characterized as a 'sweet by-and-by, pie-in-the-sky' hope without reference to a concrete history. The second could be characterized as the more realistic ('down to earth') cycles of nature in which the self-evident rhythms of life and death perfectly and completely circumscribe human destiny. [. . .] Rosemary Radford Ruether (1983; esp. ch. 10) and more recently, but to a lesser degree, Catherine Keller (1994) represent this move from the feminist perspective. J. Michael Clark (1993) repeats the move through a gay lens which merits several, necessarily brief observations.

By taking seriously the ecological crisis we now face, Clark (1993) proposes that a gay ecotheology enhances ecofeminism by extending its critique of patriarchy's 'devaluation' of the earth to its utter 'disvaluation.' By adding the qualifier 'hetero' to 'patriarchy' Clark hopes to clarify even more forcefully the reality of our present cultural morass. While the extended critique offers a gay voice to the conversation, his argument receives much of its strength from conflating 'eschatology' and 'apocalypticism.' By conflating the two, Clark is able to dismiss the category altogether as harmful to the ecologically sensitive vision he proposes. However, if the facile identification of 'eschatological otherworldliness' and the 'apocalyptically minded' can be avoided, it is not at all self-evident that eschatology as such leads inexorably to a disvaluation of the earth or even our bodies. [. . .] But the essence of eschatology as such is *transcendentality*, which is meant to describe (as even Kant argued) that quality of thinking which a particular context could not have supplied on its own. In short, given the continued and horrifying specter of violence and oppression worldwide, the project of envisioning a more just and hopeful future demands transcendental thinking and dreaming.

Much remains in Clark's work to which theologians ought to give serious attention. For example, 'transcendental escapism' can and sometimes does provoke an abdication of earthly responsibility. Nevertheless, its correction cannot spring from what I would call a 'contextual escapism' without also depriving the means by which action remains hopeful. Without eschatological, transcendental thinking and hoping, I would argue that a global narcissism emerges, a narcissism just as plausible and rationally defensible as any program of social and ecological justice (see also Griffin 1989). Further, any claim against rampant, global narcissism within the kind of socially constructed model Clark proposes requires a greater leap of faith than any traditional theological model.

Visions of justice are powered by the engine of an imaginative hope. I have tried to argue here that an exclusively 'contextualized' or 'socially constructed' vision of the sort Clark proposes lacks the fuel to power the engine. The fuel we require is nothing less than transcendentality. It requires a leap; a leap which finds help from the communal knowledge and creative imagination with which gay people are already quite familiar.

On the other hand, as Clark eschews 'wishful thinking' for a future free of sexism, homophobia, and planetary degradation, he has effectively removed the motivation for social change under the guise of rejecting 'escapism' (Clark 1993, 87). Further, Clark envisions the process as beginning in our 'own backyards' where 'local crises facilitate consciousness-raising' through which we are 'compelled to exchange egocentrism for ecocentrism' (88). Local crises may indeed prompt immediate action; how such action extends beyond immediate self-interest remains unanswered. Clark proposes a self-evident connection between local crises and global degradation, a connection which will emerge from sustained consciousness-raising. Such a proposal simply begs the question: How? It demands making connections which in fact are not immediately self-evident from the toxic waste dump across the street or the belching factory towers down the block. Clark's argument depends upon making the kind of leap which his own contextual restrictions render both impossible and undesirable.

The question here is whether and to what extent human beings live in hope, not just hope for clearer water or the spotted owl's survivability, but the kind of imaginative hope which can dream of a future unlike any for which the present context would offer a warrant. [. . .]

Such claims will not seem foreign to gay people who already rely on hope for their own survival. Coming out is more than a crude necessity; it represents one of the most hopeful decisions one might undertake in a hostile culture. The reconstruction of that which remains essential to Christian eschatology may be helped not only by the communal knowing of gay men and lesbian women, but by their 'communal hoping.' What Christians hope for, gay or straight, does not emerge from the arguments of rational discourse, nor the prompting toward consciousness-raising provoked by local environmental crises, although these surely make a contribution. Rather, communal hoping finds its best expression in the utterances urged by an otherwise inexplicable imagination and the actions taken from otherwise inexplicable life-decisions. Such would be a minimal description, it seems to me, of what it means to 'come out.'

I would argue further that the strength of such an imaginative, communal hoping cannot reside in definitive (whether essentialist or social constructed) claims, but the evocative power of the *poetic*. Walter Brueggemann argues that only the poetic can shatter a world in which truth has been flattened, trivialized, and rendered inane. 'To address the issue of a truth greatly reduced,' Brueggemann writes, 'requires us to be poets that speak against a prose world' (1989, 3). By a 'prose world' Brueggemann means a world that is organized in settled formulae and which is thereby incapable of being moved by even the most forceful rational argument. Gay men and lesbians already know well the destructive force behind such rational discourse, countered only by the creative, even poetic experience of transcending the limits of that discourse in imaginative patterns of relating.

If Christian eschatology retains any of its evocative power as we approach a new millennium, gay people of faith can contribute their experience to the project of proclaiming the kind of hope a 'world of prose' longs to hear. That hope cannot remain a universal category abstracted from the concrete historical context in which it is proclaimed. But neither can it reduce to a reality created in our own image without reducing to a solipsism. Rather, hope conceived in eschatological terms and grounded in gay experience can transcend the 'what-you-see-is-what-you-get' versions of the most excessive social constructions while evoking the (necessary) vision of the 'sweet-by-and-by' which is not disconnected from the wreckage of the painful history it was meant to redeem.

Conclusion: A Glimpse of the Horizon

In this essay I have not addressed the *content* of a Christian theology to which gay experience might make a contribution. Instead, I have tried to address the conditions for the possibility of common ground, that is, the beginning of what might constitute a foundational theology for gay Christians—a theology which need not abandon 'essential' Christian categories nor acquiesce to a construction of those categories which excludes a priori gay experience. [. . .] Where might a 'foundational' Christian theology based on gay experience take us?

In his recent work on Christology, Robert Goss adds an important gay voice to the ongoing construction of a traditional (essential) theological category in the Christian tradition. Imaging a queer Christ who 'acted up' along the lines proposed by Michel Foucault, Goss finds conceptual help for articulating the liberating discursive practices of gay and lesbian Christians (Goss 1993, 59). I would propose that the importance of desire, pleasure, and the erotic generally, which Goss assigns to such practices, suggests a horizon for gay theological reflection marked by the Holy Spirit.

Popular discourse devotes a great deal of attention to what we mean by a 'queer sensibility' or the 'gay spirit.' The articulation of that sensibility would surely include the elements of gay experience I have outlined above. Perhaps the time has come to name those elements theologically with renewed attention to pneumatology. [. . .] 'Spirit-talk' may in fact energize the work before us should the three theses I have proposed in this essay contribute to the construction of some common ground. [. . .]

Transcendence reveals the fecundity of the human spirit which seems perpetually to transcend its own limitations and boundaries (even if only briefly) to catch a glimpse over the horizon. In that transcendence resides the hope we need to inspire our journey into the future, and which can be appropriated best by the work of a poetic imagination. Such can be the experience of that community of faith called church in which Christians often turn to spirit-language for expressing their experience of (erotic) familial bonds.[11] In short, gay theologians may profit from identifying *eros* as none other than the Holy (gay) Spirit itself.[12]

Further, to engage in 'spirit(ed) language' may be the only way to describe the common ground that emerges when neither essential nor socially constructed categories suffice for describing human sexuality, let alone those experiences to which theological language can only point. Spirit-language may yet free us, in other words, from understanding the 'truth' about ourselves as something we now, or might soon *possess*, and instead lead us to embrace the search itself. For strict essentialists, the search concludes with reified, even simple biological categories. For excessive social constructionists, the search yields only the prospect of adjudicating conflicting claims and rights. In both cases, the nature of the quest itself is lost and the search stalls.

For those who remain convinced of an essential reality behind our cultural categories and those who remain content with examining their social construction, cooperation rather than polarization will bring common ground—the 'plateau'—into view. From that vantage point, the quest for truth is nothing new; it is the ancient quest for the truth about ourselves in relation to each other and to God as we narrate the ongoing story of our identities. I have tried to argue that those identities are *both* culturally determined *and* at the same time irreducible to cultural determinants. Further, the theological language for that 'both/and' formation of our subjectivity may well come from equally ancient reflections on the Holy Spirit. [. . .]

As the horizon of our quest stretches before us, a horizon which is marked by that Spirit we may call both holy and erotic, it may yet lead us into that truth which, we are told, Jesus said would make us free.

Notes

1 This distinction, rather than semantic hair-splitting, is meant to describe what seems to me to be a fundamental methodological difference. Representative works in the first case would include Comstock (1993) and Clark (1993), and, in the second case, Goss (1993) and McNeill (1995).

2 Long relates the anecdotal comparison between fellatio and Holy Communion and suggests as well that for many gay men 'sex *constitutes* for them a religious experience' (1995, 72; emphasis added).

3 Long's claim resembles those made by both Heyward (1982) and Comstock (1993). Long's attempt, however, to avoid any necessary link to intimacy between committed couples or friends marks a rather novel approach. Or rather, Long's reassessment of what counts as 'intimacy' (which for him can include so-called anonymous 'tricking') charts some bold territory here (1995, 103).

4 Daniel Spencer, 'Shattering the Image, Reshaping the Body: Toward Constructing a Liberating Gay and Lesbian Ecclesiology' (paper presented at the annual meeting of the American Academy of Religion, Washington, DC, 1992).

5 L. William Countryman, 'The Priesthood of Being Lesbian/Gay' (paper presented to the LGCM Annual Meeting, London, 1994). Among the ministrations offered by a gay and lesbian priesthood, Countryman includes the opportunity to assist the church as a whole to deal with its betrayal of God's created gift of sex. The lesbian/gay priesthood may also minister to heterosexual men and women who may not have reflected on their own identity formation to the same degree, and who seek creative appropriations of human relation similar to those found in gay experience.

6 Brownson, vol. 1 (1882–1908, 60). Brownson also may be read as bolstering the essentialist position in terms of 'objective' knowledge. That he can be read either way is precisely the point: Knowledge, though objective, is nevertheless a product of the 'communion' between subject and object; but the results are still the product of communal knowing and therefore a construct.

7 This is not to say that all 'coming out' experiences are the same or described with precisely the same language. Still, the language provided by a community of knowers to the person in the process of coming out would seem to offer what the otherwise 'essential' identity lacked in order to be appropriated. Clearly, the essentialist argument remains in tact here. That too is the point: An inextricable relation between the two positions.

8 Much like Brownson, Peirce can be read in favor of either the social constructionist or essentialist position. Again, this is precisely the point. The *polarization* of immutable essences (in a substance, or essentialist position) and perpetually constructed subjects (in a process, or social constructionist position) does not suffice for an adequate account of human experience. In that sense, Peirce is a *realist*, but a 'critical realist' whose pragmatic principle mutes an otherwise overt essentialism.

9 Though not primarily a theologian, Peirce nevertheless applied his insights to religious questions. Regarding ecclesiology, the 'essentialist,' or more aptly the 'realist' conclusion is hard to miss: 'The *raison d'être* of the church is to confer upon [human beings] a life broader than their narrow personalities, a life rooted in the very truth of being' (Peirce 1960–66, 6:451).

10 This is, of course, the same question posed by, among others, Latin American liberation theologians and feminists. The point here is to engage what has been an ongoing (and until recently unspoken) problem for Christian theology from a gay perspective.

11 This argument comes close to Comstock's treatment of the Holy Spirit as the spirit of the community (1993, 138–40), but it is not identical to my overall argument for that quality of relation which transcends the particular context considered. I would argue that spirit-experience implies something more than what can be self-generated by any given community.

12 A 'gay spirituality' to which I have alluded here finds fuller expression in recent work by Ritley in which she identifies the root tasks for gay spiritual ministry as 'the reclaiming of our communal memory, the articulation of communal wisdom, and the affirmation of communal destiny' (1994, 23).

Literature

Boswell, John. 1989. 'Revolutions, Universals, and Sexual Categories,' in *Hidden From History: Reclaiming the Gay and Lesbian Past*, eds Martin Bauml Duberman, Martha Vicinus and George Chauncey, Jr. New York: Penguin. Pp. 17–36.

Brownson, Orestes Augustus. 1882–1908. 'Synthetic Philosophy,' in *The Works of Orestes Augustus Brownson*, 20 vols, collected and arranged by Henry F. Brownson. Detroit: Nourse. Vol. 1, pp. 58–129.

Brueggemann, Walter. 1989. *Finally Comes the Poet: Daring Speech for Proclamation.* Minneapolis: Augsburg Fortress.

Clark, J. Michael. 1993. *Beyond our Ghettos: Gay Theology in Ecological Perspective.* Cleveland: Pilgrim.

Comstock, David Gary. 1993. *Gay Theology Without Apology.* Cleveland: Pilgrim.

Goss, Robert. 1993. *Jesus Acted Up: A Gay and Lesbian Manifesto.* San Francisco: HarperSanFrancisco.

Griffin, David Ray. 1989. *God and Religion in the Postmodern World.* Albany: SUNY Press.

Heyward, Carter. 1982. *The Redemption of God: A Theology of Mutual Relation.* Washington, DC: University Press of America.

Keller, Catherine. 1994. 'Eschatology, Ecology, and a Green Ecumenacy,' in *Reconstructing Christian Theology*, eds Rebecca S. Chop and Mark Lewis Taylor. Minneapolis: Fortress. Pp. 326–45.

Kowalewski, Mark and Elizabeth Say. 1994. 'Lesbian and Gay Family: Iconoclasm and Reconstruction,' in *Spirituality and Community: Diversity in Gay and Lesbian Experience.* Las Colinas, Texas: Monument. Pp. 185–217.

Long, Ron. 1995. 'Toward a Phenomenology of Gay Sex: Groundwork for a Contemporary Sexual Ethic,' in *Embodying Diversity: Identity, (Bio)Diversity, & Sexuality.* Las Colinas, Texas: Monument. Pp. 69–112.

McNeill, John J. 1995. *Freedom, Glorious Freedom: The Spiritual Journey to the Fullness of Life for Gay, Lesbians, and Everybody Else.* Boston: Beacon.

Peirce, Charles. 1960–66. *Collected Papers*, eds Charles Hartshorne and Paul Weiss. Cambridge: Harvard University Press.

Ritley, M. R. 1994. *God's Gay Tribe: Laying the Foundations of Communal Memory.* New Haven: Gay Christians Readings Group.

Ruether, Rosemary Radford. 1983. *Sexism and God-Talk: Toward a Feminist Theology.* Boston: Beacon.

Transgression as a Metaphor for Queer Theologies

Editor's Introduction

In the previous chapter, Jay Johnson promotes a deepening of the internal debate among gay theologians, using a theological idea, namely the Holy Spirit, to reconcile differences. Robert Goss, who, in his own words, 'lived Jesuit spirituality for more than thirty years, most in a queer, unorthodox fashion' (2002, xv; also 2005), moves the discussion in a new direction, abandoning traditional theological categories and paving the way for a 'queer sexual theology' (2002, 239–58; also 2003). In his assessment, gay theology in the 1980s 'found itself in an apologetic mode,' focusing, on the one hand, on 'biblical texts that were used to justify homosexuality as sin' and, on the other, on 'psychological issues of sexual orientation to deconstruct moral theologies based on natural law' (2002, 241). Developments in the 1990s, he writes, eventually 'transformed gay theology into queer theology' (242), and Goss himself was one of the motors of this change, particularly his publication of *Jesus Acted Up* (1993; also Goss and West 2000; Goss et al. 2006).

In chapter 7, Laurel Schneider argues that gay theology differs from queer theology in that the former is more concerned about problems of exclusion while the latter is more transgressive. The chapter below, reprinted from Goss's *Queering Christ* (2002), centers on 'transgression' as a positive paradigm that erases restrictive boundaries and creates spaces for imagining alternatives to normative behavior. What must be challenged and transgressed is 'heteronormativity', a significant term introduced by queer studies. Like homosociality, it is a neologism:

> By heteronormativity, [queer scholars] mean the set of norms that make heterosexuality seem natural and right and that organize homosexuality as its binary opposite . . . As a result, the dominance of heterosexuality often operates unconsciously or in unmarked ways that make it particularly difficult to expose and dislodge. (Corber and Valocchi 2003, 4)

Goss takes it one step further: He understands the task of queer sexual theologies to critically investigate *all* normativities, straight and gay. 'Queer,' he writes, 'defies heteronormative and homonormative theologies.'

Publications by the Same Author

Goss, Robert E. 1993. *Jesus Acted Up: A Gay and Lesbian Manifesto*. San Francisco: HarperSanFrancisco.

——. 2002. *Queering Christ: Beyond Jesus Acted Up*. Cleveland: Pilgrim.

——. 2003. 'Gay Erotic Spirituality and the Recovery of Sexual Pleasure', in *Body and Soul: Rethinking Sexuality and Justice-Love*, eds Marvin M. Ellison and Sylvia Thorson-Smith. Cleveland: Pilgrim. Pp. 201–217.

Goss, Robert E. and Amy Adams Squire Strongheart (eds). 1997. *Our Families, Our Values: Snapshots of Queer Kinship*. New York: Haworth Press.

Goss, Robert E. and Mona West (eds). 2000. *Take Back the Word: A Queer Reading of the Bible*. Cleveland: Pilgrim.

Goss, Robert E. and Donald L. Boisvert (eds). 2005. *Gay Catholic Priests and Clerical Sexual Misconduct: Breaking the Silence*. New York: Haworth Press.

Goss, Robert E., Deryn Guest, Mona West and Thomas Bohache (eds). 2006. *The Queer Bible Commentary*. London: SCM Press.

Further Reading

Althaus-Reid, Marcella. 2000. *Indecent Theology: Theological Perversions in Sex, Gender and Politics*. London and New York: Routledge.

Corber, Robert and Stephen Valocchi (eds). 2003. *Queer Studies: An Interdisciplinary Reader*. Malden, Oxford: Blackwell.

Wilson, Nancy. 1995. *Our Tribe: Queer Folks, God, Jesus, and the Bible*. San Francisco: HarperSanFrancisco.

Transgression as a Metaphor for Queer Theologies

ROBERT E. GOSS

Queer theory emerged in the 1980s from AIDS activism and a new wave of political activism to counter the backlash of the new right under the Reagan and Bush presidencies. The radical polities of difference—influenced by the French postmodernists such as Lacan, Derrida, and Foucault—challenged the polities of gay and lesbian identities. A gay/lesbian academic conference, the Politics of Pleasure, held at Harvard University in 1990, brought AIDS activists and gay/lesbian academics together. The debate over whether gay and lesbian identities were essential or socially constructed was nearing its conclusion, and the social constructionists gained prominence as the popularity of Michel Foucault was on the rise. There was a synergy at the conference between street activists and academics, for queer theory was undergoing its birth pangs. The deans of queer theory—Eve Sedgwick, David Halperin, and Judith Butler—shaped its birth, giving it a contentious edge in deconstructing the ethnic model of identity politics that was shaped by Stonewall and that continued into gay/lesbian activism in the 1980s. Queer theory was an academic and political Stonewall whose significance continues to impact translesbigay academics and politics. It also challenges and will change theology.

Heteronormativity, a neologism, was coined as a new category when queer theory defined itself as an academic-cultural movement. It became a term to describe the dominant sex/gender system that privileges heterosexual males while it subordinates women and disprivileges gender/sexual transgressors. For many people, gender and sexuality are only intelligible within a heterosexual matrix. This heteronormative understanding creates a gender/sexual fundamentalism that pathologizes gender and sexual differences and fails to accept the fluidity of gender and sexual identity. [. . .]

Heteronormative theology is not the only orthodoxy. Lesbian and gay theologies a decade ago seldom mentioned bisexuals and never even addressed the transgendered. In the American Academy of Religion, the largest professional association of religious scholars, the Lesbian Feminist Issues Group in Religion and the Gay Men's Issues Group in Religion were formed to promote gay and lesbian voices in religion. During the last ten years, many of the major lesbian and gay theological books arose from papers delivered at the annual conferences each November. These lesbian and gay theologies have underscored their struggles against the hetero/homosexual categories, making significant scholarly contributions and critiques based upon affirmative lesbian and gay identities.

Many gay and lesbian theologians have, however, fallen into a trap that makes hetero/homosexual preferences the exclusive metacategories of sexual identity. There are other homosexuals who do not fit into the categories of heterosexual, lesbian, and gay. The idea of a unitary gay or lesbian identity has been fundamental to the formation of gay/lesbian theologies. But these theologies have framed identity on the assumption that gays are like an ethnic group; we have minoritized our identity based on our homoerotic desires and attractions. But do our sexual attractions to men unite us like an ethnic group? Or as we probe beyond this surface of ethnicization of sexual desire, do we find a great deal of difference and hybridity?

Cultural critic Steven Seidman notes recent critique of the ethnic model: 'The dominant ethnic model of identity and community was accused of reflecting a narrow white middle-class, Eurocentric experience. The very discourse of liberation, with its very notion of a gay subject unified by common interests, was viewed as a disciplining social force oppressive to large segments of the community in whose name it spoke' (1993, 125). The minoritization of male sexual identity does not neatly fold into the categories of gay normativity. Neither bisexual men nor female-to-male transsexuals nor the intersexed fit neatly into our gay template. Elias Farajaje-Jones speaks of an 'in-the-life' identity for a range of African American males attracted to the same gender or both genders (1993). Hispanic American, Asian American, and Native American men have social constructions of identity that may not easily be subsumed under the category of gay since it is frequently constructed as white, middle-class male. Gay identity can be as confining as 'closetedness' in its minoritization and elision of the social-cultural differences of same-sex desire while privileging white gay males.

While gay/lesbian theological works have concentrated mainly on questions of homosexuality, queer theory has expanded its realm of investigation to sexual desire, paying close attention to cultural construction of categories of normative and deviant sexual behavior. Queer theory expanded the scope of its queries to all kinds of behaviors linked to sexuality, including gender-bending and nonconventional sexualities. It analyzed sexual behaviors, all concepts of sexual identity, and categories of normative and deviant. These formed sets of signifiers, which created constructed social and cultural meanings. Queer theory is a set of ideas based around the notion that identities are not fixed and do not entirely determine who we are. As a field of inquiry, queer theory shifts the emphasis away from specific acts and identities to the myriad ways in which gender and sexualities organize and even destabilize society. [. . .]

Queer studies

Queer studies thus represent a paradigm or discursive shift in the way some scholars view sexual identity. Queer studies attempt not to abandon identity as a site for knowledge and politics but to problematize fixed and hegemonic notions of identity:

> Queer theory is suggesting that the study of homosexuality should not be a study of a minority—the making of the lesbian/gay/bisexual subject—but a study of those knowledges and social practices that organize 'society' as a whole by sexualizing—heterosexualizing or homosexualizing—bodies, desires, acts, identities, social relations, knowledges, culture, and social institutions. (Seidman 1996, 12)

Queer theorists argue that identities are always multiple, hybrid, provisional, or composite and that an infinite number of identity markers can combine to form new sites of knowledge. For queer theorist Michael Warner queer is a transgressive paradigm, representing 'a more thorough resistance to the regimes of the normal' (1993, xxvi). Likewise, David Halperin states, 'Queer, then, demarcates not a positivity but a positionality vis-à-vis the normative—a positionality that is not restricted to lesbians and gay men but is in fact available to anyone who is or who feels marginalized because of her or his sexual practices' (1995, 62). Michael Warner, David Halperin, Judith Butler, Eve Kosofsky Sedgwick, and other theorists perceive the queer paradigm as resistance to normativity, including heteronormativity and gay and lesbian normativities (see Warner 1993; Seidman 1996; Butler 1993).

Queer is often understood as critically nonheterosexual, transgressive of all heteronormativities and, I would add, homonormativities. 'Queer' turns upside down, inside out, and defies heteronormative and homonormative theologies.[1] I use 'queer' theologically, not only as an identity category but also as a tool of theological deconstruction, for 'queer' as a verb means 'to spoil or to interfere.' Heteronormative theologies exclude me except in their hermeneutics of abomination while gay/lesbian normative theologies exclude those who do not neatly fit into the categories. When I queer or spoil an already spoiled hetero- or gay-

normative theological discourse, I have transgressed the boundaries of normativity that are embedded in particular discourses and practices. In traditional
theological language, queering has a prophetic edge in its critiques.

I want to address the hermeneutical role of normative transgression in emerging queer theologies and for the future development of hybrid queer theologies. In other words, I want to queer the template of gay normativity. In *The
Mythology of Transgression*, cultural critic Jamake Highwater describes several
negative metaphors for transgression: as abomination, deformity, and science.
He perceives some positive metaphors of transgression, such as sensibility,
culture, and revelation. The commonplace understanding of transgression is a
violation of morality. Highwater asserts:

> [T]he word 'transgression' is generally understood to mean an action that is
> morally subversive. A transgression is closely associated with the religious
> idea of damnation. Therefore, we do not admire those who transgress. We
> reproach them as sinners. And the more 'terrible' the transgression, the more
> we reproach them. We may ridicule them, disdain them, beat them, imprison
> them, or we may even kill them. But the worst of all punishments is doubt-
> lessly our attempts to redeem them, to change them from their sinful ways to
> our blessed ways. (1997, 42)

The Latin *transgredior* means 'to pass over, to go beyond, or to advance.' *Transgredior* is an action that carries a person across fixed boundaries or beyond
borders. Transgression destroys traditional boundaries or undermines established paradigms by revealing their fragility and instability. It challenges modes
of regulating discourse: Who is canonically allowed to speak? Who is allowed
entry? Who is denied access? Who can speak for me?

Michel Foucault understood transgression as resistance to normalizing practices of master narratives. Foucault said in an interview, 'To resist is not simply
a negation but a creative process' (quoted in Halperin 1995, 60). Transgression
is not merely a rebellious act but a Foucaultian liberative action driven by the
imagination of alternative possibilities and hopes. Along with Highwater,
I comprehend transgression primarily as 'an act that brings about transformation' (Highwater 1997, 43). Transgression is essential to the hermeneutical
development of queer theologies and queer hybrid theologies. [. . .]

For theology, queering becomes a productive style of theological practice and
discourse that can disorganize our normative categories. Queer desire crosses
all identity and gender boundaries; it is ineffable, an ever shifting transgres-
siveness that uncovers ever-new hybrid identities. For example, asserting an
African American 'in-the-life' or Native American 'two-spirited' identity does
not adequately articulate the differences that have to do with religion, geography, relation to gay, white males, gender, class, age, ability, education, and so on.
Frank Browning's latest book, *A Queer Geography*, investigates how geography
shapes homoerotic desires and identities, demonstrating what anthropologists
and cultural historians have argued for some time how cultures organize structures of sexual identity (Browning 1996; also Blyes 1995; Murray and Roscoe
1997; Schmitt and Sofer 1992; Greenberg 1988).

Queer theory has deconstructed the colonial category of 'gay' as white, North

American, middle-class, late-capitalist, and even middle aged. Gay identity seems too hardened, too mainstream a category for adequate queer theological reflection, and too inflexible for developing a full queer politics of difference. It is the same critique that I would make of heteronormative theologies and postmodern theologies. Queer has widened my self-definitions by navigating me into uncharted waters where I engage in conversations with people whose identities are shaped by particular markers and personal experiences quite different from my own. These experiences are challenging, engaging, and ever-widening. I find myself theologically committed to engage and learn from different worlds, cultures, histories, and communities. Queering is ultimately opening space to new immigrant identities to articulate their own perspectives, quite radical and even challenging to my own.

I am prepared to argue that my own theological positions, like identity categories, are only tentative and that they need to be subverted from a gay/lesbian paradigm into uncharted territories and geographies of diverse sexual and gender hybridities. If I am to take 'queer' as a serious paradigm for theological discourse and practice, I need to engage not only bisexual and transgendered voices but also the voices of the intersexed and of men and women of color who share homoerotic desires. In *Jesus Acted Up*, I wrote from a queer perspective that was limited to gay and lesbian voices. I remember a bisexual student from Eden Seminary who challenged me, 'Where is my bisexual voice?' That comment greatly troubled me while I fumbled for an explanation of my postmodern commitments to particularity and apologetically pointed to the voices that have shaped my queer theological practice. At the 1994 Freedom Celebration in San Francisco, I encountered a transsexual, Victoria Kolakowski, who challenged my gendered categories and ever since has mentored me to an awareness of transsexualism and theological discourse (see Kolakowski 1997a; 1997b). How many others could raise the same question from social locations of the ethnic, the underclass, the illegal immigrant, or other communities? [. . .]

Critiques: New Transgressions and Hybridity

There is much current debate in and around queer studies; much of the debate revolves around the assimilation of tendencies of segments of the gay community into mainstream culture. Sociologist Steven Seidman, however, criticizes queer theory for 'denying the differences by either submerging them in an undifferentiated oppositional mass or by blocking the development of individual and social differences through the disciplining compulsory imperative to remain undifferentiated' (1993, 133; also 1996, 1–29). Seidman and other critics have raised vital questions whether a liberation movement can build political cohesion based on the violations of normative structures. On the other hand, queer raises questions about the nature of our social identities as multicultural, multigendered, and multisexual. Its critics like Seidman and others fear that queer will elide hard-fought differences. Objections to queer theology find similar criticisms from some lesbian and gay theologians in their failure to engage different notions of postmodern sexualities and genders. While admittedly queer does muddy the distinctions among sexual-identity categories and the differences between men and women, it also raises epistemological questions about the stability of these templates of sexual and gendered identity. It subverts our normative assumptions about identity and gender while articulating the varied particularities of emerging hybrid voices. In its transgressions, queer discursive practice may decolonize our identity and gendered templates because multigendered and multicultural sexual identities navigate us into a radical inclusion of voices that trouble heteronormative- and gay-normative theological discourse. Engaging in what appears to be 'Balkan-style,' carnivalesque dialogues of diversity subverts our attempts at universal but exclusionary theological discourse. They force us to deal with the plurality of social context and personal narrative histories about sexual desire.

Will queer theologies remain queer, or will queer theologies ultimately transgressively reinscribe themselves into some new hybrids? If queer theologies remain open-ended theological discourses that participate in a creative dialogue with the various hybrid subcultures of desire and gender, of outsiders and insiders, of diverse social locations, then new sexual and gendered hybrid theologies will emerge. Let me speculate on some new transgressions. Bisexual theologies will certainly undermine gay/lesbian and heterosexual theological discourse. Both gay/lesbian and heterosexual theologies subscribe to the politics of otherness with an either/or paradigm while bisexual theologies represent a subversive alternative to either/or thinking. They stress a both/and method that undermines either straight or gay methods of theological reflection and promote mediating methods to bridge hetero and gay theological discourses. Veteran gay/lesbian theologians have a difficult time disprivileging their own discourse and allowing the multiple voices to disrupt their discourse.

As we immerse ourselves in the narrative histories and theological discourses of Asian American homosexual men, bisexual womanists, or biracial female-to-male transsexuals, we may learn about sexualities in the plural, their instabilities, and the different social/cultural constructions of hybrid sexual identities. We may also learn about the multidimensional and multicultural perspectives of sexual identity. Hopefully we may expose all traces of privilege within our own theological discourse, any traces of American white supremacism, centrism, sexism, classism, or biphobia. Thus we may become more responsible in making new hybrid voices accessible.

Transgendered theologies, likewise, raise some profound questions and presumptions about gender. Gender-bending and intersexuality threaten a society that maintains gender rigidity. Transgendered and intersexual activists are only recently raising their voices to further widen the sex and gender liberation movement. While transgendered theology is only in its infancy, we can expect it to undermine heteronormative and gay/lesbian normative constructions of maleness and femaleness with new interstitional gender spaces.

The development of bisexual and transgendered theologies will offend some by their inclusiveness, moving beyond binary thinking of hetero/homo and deconstructing rigid gender boundaries. Bisexual and transgendered theologies will threaten far more those gays who want to assimilate into mainstream society. There are many ways to be queer, and future queer theologians will connect those ways with the networks of power relationships that shape race, gender, sexuality, ethnicity, religion, class, physical conditions, age, and our relationships to the earth. Rather than assimilate, future queer theologies will mainstream and celebrate sexual/gender diversities, shifting theological practice into uncharted intersections of sexual, gendered identities. During the twenty-first century, queer theologies will undergo profound changes as the contextual translesbigay theologies emerge from postcolonial Asia, Latin America, and Africa, critiquing and disorganizing our queer categories.

Queer theologies, I may conclude, will not ever abandon identity and gender as categories of knowledge or liberative practice but will render them open and contestable to various meanings that promote coalitional politics. Queer discursive practice will challenge our theological discourse based on a narrow regime of sexual and gendered truth by undermining our identity templates of heterosexual/homosexual and gender categories of male/female. Can we meet the challenge of being mentored by new queer voices? The challenge is unsettling, but I find it also thoroughly queer. [. . .]

Note

1 For a sampling, see the following authors' discussion of queer: Clark (1997, 6); Goss (1993, xix, 55–7; 1996, 16–19); Warner (1993, xxvi); Halperin (1995, 60–6).

Literature

Blyes, Rudi C. 1995. *The Geography of Perversion*. New York: New York University Press.

Browning, Frank. 1996. *A Queer Geography: Journeys Towards a Sexual Self*. New York: Crown Publishers.

Butler, Judith. 1993. *Bodies That Matter*. New York: Routledge.

Clark, J. Michael. 1997. *Defying the Darkness: Gay Theology in the Shadows*. Cleveland: Pilgrim.

Farajaje-Jones, Elias. 1993. 'Breaking Silence: Toward an In-the-Life Theology,' in *Black Theology* (vol. 2), eds James H. Cone and Gayraud S. Wilmore. Maryknoll: Orbis. Pp. 2:139–59.

Goss, Robert E. 1993. *Jesus Acted Up*. San Francisco: HarperSanFrancisco.

——. 1996. 'Insurrection of the Polymorphously Perverse: Queer Hermeneutics,' in *A Rainbow of Religious Studies*, eds J. Michael Clark and Robert E. Goss. Las Colinas: Monument Press. Pp. 9–31.

Greenberg, David E. 1988. *The Construction of Homosexuality*. Chicago: University of Chicago Press.

Halperin, David M. 1995. *Saint Foucault: Towards a Gay Hagiography*. New York: Oxford University Press.

Highwater, Jamake. 1997. *The Mythology of Transgression: Homosexuality as Metaphor*. New York: Oxford University Press.

Kolakowski, Victoria S. 1997a. 'Toward a Christian Ethical Response to Transsexual Persons,' *Theology and Sexuality* 6 (March):10–31.

——. 1997b. 'Eunuchs and Barren Women: Queering the Breeder's Bible,' in *Our Families, Our Values: Snapshots of Queer Kinship*, eds Robert E. Goss and Amy Adams Squires Strongheart. New York: Harrington Park Press. Pp. 35–50.

Murray, Stephen O. and Will Roscoe (eds). 1997. *Islamic Homosexualities: Culture, History, and Literature*. New York: New York University Press.

Seidman, Steven. 1993. 'Identity and Politics in a Postmodern Gay Culture: Some Conceptual and Historical Notes,' in *Fear of a Queer Planet*, ed. Michael Warner. Minneapolis: University of Minnesota Press. Pp. 105–42.

——. (ed.). 1996. *Queer Theory/Sociology*. Cambridge: Blackwell.

Schmitt, Arno and Jehoeda Sofer. 1992. *Sexuality and Eroticism among Males in Moslem Societies*. New York: Harrington Park Press.

Warner, Michael (ed.). 1993. *Fear of a Queer Planet*. Minneapolis: University of Minnesota Press.

13

True Confessions and Weird Obsessions:
Autobiographical Interventions in Literary
and Biblical Studies

Editor's Introduction

Among male scholars writing on men and religion, one can observe a trend toward inserting autobiographical segments and confessional fragments into their scholarly texts. Doing so, these authors counteract the seeming neutrality and objectivity of their authorial voice. Positioning themselves as individuals and as members of particular communities, they seek to reveal how their perspectives are influenced and limited by their social and cultural backgrounds. On one level, these autobiographical insertions are a response to the feminist challenge of abandoning the supposed objectivity of (male) scholarship. On another level, such acts of self-disclosure must be seen as part of a longer trend in Christian history: they constitute a return of the confessional mode (see Brooks 2000; Krondorfer 1996; 2002; 2008).

Largely due to the lasting influence of Augustine's *Confessions* and the monastic model of confessional discourse, 'very complex techniques of self-analysis' (Foucault 1999, 195) developed in Western Christianity that concerned themselves with sexual practices, desires and politics (see chapter 3). Scholars working on confessional modes of male religious discourse have recently applied Foucault's influential theory about the Christian monastic roots of the modern ambition of self-disclosure (see Coles 1992; Schuld 2003; Krondorfer and Culbertson 2004).

Stephen Moore, professor of New Testament at Drew University, is certainly aware of the confessional impulse in Christianity, but in the chapter below he traces the recent autobiographical turn in biblical studies to the influence of literary criticism. Citing instances of confessional statements by female literary critics, he eventually turns his attention to evaluating the attempts of male biblical scholars who insert their own personal fragments. Though he remains somewhat skeptical of their efforts, he commends Jeffrey Staley's postcolonial analysis that blends biblical interpretation and autobiographical reflection (see also chapter 17).

Moore himself does not shy away from autobiographical insertions, as he has demonstrated in his book *God's Gym* (1996). There he discloses, for example, that he 'quit bodybuilding ... at age thirty-two because it was cutting too deeply into my research time. I set about building up my bibliography instead. The flesh began to peel away from my bones. I cut it into squares, stacked it in piles, and traded it for an assistant professorship' (1996, 75). In the chapter below, he confesses to a drug-induced religious conversion experience, which resulted in 'involuntary confinement . . . complete with electric shock therapy. Yes. I had to be crazy to become a biblical scholar (for that's how it all began).' Today, Moore is a leading voice in the intersection of biblical studies, masculinity studies, and queer theory (1996; 2001; 2003), and Foucault certainly had a strong influence on his work (Moore 1994).

The autobiographical and confessional impulse can be traced in several parts of the *Critical Reader*, and particularly relevant are the contributions by Jeffrey Staley (chapter 17), Harry Brod (chapter 25), Scott Haldeman (chapter 27), and Björn Krondorfer (30).

Publications by the Same Author

Moore, Stephen D. 1994. *Post-Structuralism and the New Testament: Derrida and Foucault at the Foot of the Cross*. Minneapolis: Fortress.

——. 1996. *God's Gym: Divine Male Bodies of the Bible*. New York: Routledge.

—— (ed.). 1998. *In Search of the Present: The Bible through Cultural Studies*. Semeia 82. Atlanta: Scholars Press.

——. 2001. *God's Beauty Parlor: And Other Queer Spaces in and around the Bible*. Stanford: Stanford University Press.

Moore, Stephen D. and Janice Capel Anderson (eds). 2003. *New Testament Masculinities*. Atlanta: Society of Biblical Literature.

Further Reading

Brooks, Peter. 2000. *Troubling Confessions: Speaking Guilt in Law and Literature*. Chicago: Chicago University Press.

Coles, Romand. 1992. *Self/Power/Other: Political Theory and Dialogical Ethics*. Ithaca: Cornell University Press (esp. chapters 2 and 3 on Augustine and Foucault).

Foucault, Michel. 1999. 'The Battle for Chastity', in *Religion and Culture: Michel Foucault* (selected and ed. by Jeremy R. Carrette). Routledge: New York. Pp. 188–97. First published 1982.

Krondorfer, Björn. 1996. 'The Confines of Male Confessions: On Religion, Bodies, and Mirrors', in *Men's Bodies, Men's Gods*, ed. Björn Krondorfer. New York: New York University Press. Pp. 205–34.

——. 2002. 'Revealing the Non-Absent Male Body: Confessions of an African Bishop and a Jewish Ghetto Policeman,' in *Revealing Male Bodies*, eds Nancy Tuana et al. Bloomington: Indiana University Press. Pp. 247–68.

——. 2008. 'Textual Male Intimacy and the Religious Imagination: Men Giving Testimony to Themselves'. *Literature and Theology* 22/3 (September):265–79.

Krondorfer, Björn and Philip Culbertson. 2004. 'Men Studies in Religion,' in *Encyclopedia of Religion*, 2nd edition (vol. 9), ed.-in-chief Lindsay Jones. Detroit and New York: Macmillan. Pp. 5861–5.

Schuld, Joyce J. 2003. *Foucault and Augustine: Reconsidering Power and Love*. Notre Dame: University of Notre Dame Press.

True Confessions and Weird Obsessions: Autobiographical Interventions in Literary and Biblical Studies

STEPHEN D. MOORE

[. . .] 'There is no theory that is not a fragment, carefully preserved, of some autobiography,' claimed Paul Valery.[1] If so, the recent irruption of autobiographical criticism in literary studies would simply represent—once again, in yet another guise—the return of the repressed. But because similar autobiographical interventions have recently been recorded in biblical studies,[2] autobiographical literary criticism may provide a yardstick with which to measure the (slighter) autobiographical swerve in biblical studies, and to assess the collision of the personal and the professional that has resulted from that swerve, along with its consequences or lack thereof.

I see a confessional flanked by a pew. The pew contains a queue of literary and cultural critics, mostly women. A few still sport the latest Parisian fashions, although most affect a more indigenous look. As I look on, a small group of biblical scholars, mostly men, several draped in the fashions of yesteryear (wide collared disco shirts open to the navel, exposing hirsute chests adorned with faux gold chains) slink in and shyly take their places at the end of the row. One by one, the critics enter the confessional . . . [. . .]

Me and My Bladder

What, precisely, is personal (confessional, autobiographical) criticism? Let a minimalist definition suffice for now. 'Personal criticism, as I mean the term in this book,' explains Miller in *Getting Personal*, 'entails an explicitly autobiographical performance within the act of criticism' (1991, 1; cf. Brownstein 1996, 31).

Miller's use of the term 'performance' is interesting here. Veeser, wrestling with the question, 'What does the confessional critic want?' (the very question that, 'mutatis mutandis, stumped Freud'), hazards three answers, the first of which is, simply, that the confessional critic wants to perform *(1996a, xiii). Personally, I want them to perform, and to perform well. Perhaps I have contracted a deadly disease from my undergraduates, but increasingly I want to be entertained even as I am being informed. I want to be moved, amused, aroused, absorbed. Admittedly, these are the very things that* literature *is supposed to do to one, but the literary criticism I feel most drawn to is criticism that happens to be literary as well as critical.*

Personal criticism is a form of self-disclosure, but needless to say the degree of self-disclosure, of self-exposure, varies wildly. What is 'personal,' anyway?

'Is it personal only if it's embarrassing?' muses Miller (1991, 19). At the 'degree-zero' end of the scale of self-exposure, Miller places the 'academic anecdote' (1), an autobiographical vignette set in the hallowed groves of academe, in which the professor plays, well, a professor: 'As a young visiting instructor at DePauw University in 1954, I recall vividly the experience of standing before a black-board with my back to a class of college students. I was lecturing on the synoptic problem . . .' (Farmer 1994, ix). What might we expect to encounter at the other end of the scale? Miller herself provides a memorable example. Her concluding chapter, 'My Father's Penis,' is a well-wrought rumination on patriarchy, the phallus, and, yes, her father's penis ('I have seen his penis. I have even touched it . . . [I]t felt soft and a little clammy' [144]). And Miller's central example in her opening chapter concerns Jane P. Tompkins's bladder.

Tompkins is perhaps better known to biblical scholars as the enterprising editor and agile theorist of *Reader-Response Criticism: From Formalism to Post-Structuralism* (Tompkins 1980).[3] In 1987, however, she published a daringly unorthodox article entitled 'Me and My Shadow,' which, in hindsight, readily assumes the appearance of a pioneering work of personal criticism, and is cel-ebrated as such in *The Intimate Critique*, where it is reprinted (Tompkins 1993). A certain scene from 'Me and My Shadow' has imprinted itself in my mind. And not just in mine, apparently. Miller (1991, 5–7) reports that hostile readers of the article (most of her own students included) have been unable to get past this scene, in which Tompkins, seated in her study, protests that she does not know how to enter the sterile academic debate that she is called upon to enter (she has a response article to write) 'without leaving everything else behind—the birds outside my window, my grief over Janice [a friend who recently committed suicide], just myself as a person sitting here in stockinged feet, a little bit chilly because the windows are open, and thinking about going to the bathroom. But not going yet' (Tompkins 1993, 28).[4]

In our residually prudish culture, explicit toilet-talk is the last bastion of inti-macy (when it is not the first recourse of crudity), one that many lifelong couples never care to conquer. And in 'polite society,' whether in a formal or semi-formal setting, and above all in mixed company, any volunteering of information con-cerning the status of one's bladder or bowel, beyond the exquisite euphemism 'I need to use the bathroom' (if one is American), is taboo. A statement such as 'I need to go, but I think I can hold out for another few minutes' would invite the putdown, 'Thanks, but that's more than I need to know right now,' unless the sufferer is four or under, in which case the putdown may be substituted with the beaming rejoinder, 'My, but you're getting to be *such* a big girl!' Do such considerations account entirely for the derision, discomfort, and downright dis-gust that Tompkins's realist self-portrait (legs tightly crossed) has elicited, or is there more? Miller thinks there is. She reports that her students, 'especially the women . . . felt confused and put off' by the author's abdication throughout the article of 'the very positions of academic authority' that they themselves 'were struggling hard to mime, if not acquire' (1991, 6), an abdication that achieves its perigee, or perhaps its apogee, in the potty passage. Miller concludes: 'To the extent that as academics we worry about our own ability to produce the authority effect, we're not sure we want ourselves going to the bathroom in pub-lic—especially as women and feminists—our credibility is low enough as it is'

(8). Frank Lentricchia, in contrast, can go the bathroom in public with impunity in his autocritographical experiment, *The Edge of Night:* 'Halfway there I have to take a leak . . . I can't hold it in for another three hours and twenty-eight minutes . . . Dick in hand, I worry about my writing' (1994, 70). The moral of the tale, it would seem, is that personal criticism is more risky for women than for men.

Tompkins herself is not unaware of the danger. 'Me and My Shadow' originated as a response to another article in the same issue of *New Literary History*, one by Ellen Messer-Davidow that inquired what the position of feminists should be toward the dominant male intellectual traditions. Tompkins began:[5]

> There are two voices inside me answering, answering to, Ellen's essay. One is the voice of a critic who wants to correct a mistake in the essay's view of epistemology. The other is the voice of a person who wants to write about her feelings (I have wanted to do this for a long time but have felt too embarrassed). This person feels it is wrong to criticize the essay philosophically and even beside the point: because a critique of the kind the critic has in mind only insulates academic discourse further from the issues that make feminism matter. That make *her* matter. The critic, meanwhile, believes such feelings, and the attitudes that inform them, are soft-minded, self-indulgent, and unprofessional.
>
> These beings exist separately but not apart. One writes for professional journals, the other in diaries, late at night. One uses words like 'context' and 'intelligibility,' likes to win arguments, see her name in print, and give graduate students hardheaded advice. The other has hardly ever been heard from. She had a short story published once in a university library magazine, but her works exist chiefly in notebooks and manila folders labeled 'Journal' and 'Private' [. . .]. (1993, 24)

A lively argument then ensues between the journal writer and the writer for journals. Of course, the former is given the last word: 'So for a while I can't talk about epistemology. I can't deal with the philosophical bases of feminist literary criticism. I can't strap myself psychically into an apparatus that will produce the right gestures when I begin to move. I have to deal with the trashing of emotion [by male academics] and with my anger against it. This one time I've taken off the straitjacket, and it feels so good' (1993, 40).

'I was electrified by this piece when it first appeared,' writes Miller (1991, 4). Well, so was I, all the more so since Tompkins the theorist, author of the audaciously clever introduction to Reader-Response Criticism, *had been something of a role model for me as a graduate student vainly attempting to track the 'implied reader' through some of the thornier thickets of Luke-Acts (she helped me to see that the tracks were mainly my own). Riveted, I didn't want the piece to end, and I remember realizing that this was the first time in ages that I had had that reaction to an academic article, so many of which I begin enthusiastically and end hurriedly, if at all. 'Sometimes, when a writer introduces some bit of story into an essay, I can hardly contain my pleasure,' admits Tompkins. 'I love writers who write about their own experience. I feel I'm being nourished by them, that I'm being allowed to enter into a personal relationship with them' (1993, 25). And that, of course, was exactly how I felt reading 'Me and My Shadow,' although according to the argument mounted therein, I shouldn't have felt that way at all, being a man.*

The soft underbelly of the piece, an irresistible target for the cruel barbs of the critics (cf. Miller 1991, 7; Brownstein 1996, 35; Lang 1996, 52), is its stereotyping of gender roles, its essentialism. Tompkins has been nibbling on an assorted bunch of academic books plucked at random from her bookshelf. [. . .] She eventually decides that 'what is gripping, significant, "juicy"' for men 'is different from what is felt to be that way by women.' It is a question of 'what is important, answers one's needs, strikes one as immediately *interesting*. For women, the personal is such a category' (1993, 36; her emphasis).[6]

Essentialism aside, it is of course statistically the case that, to date (and notwithstanding the risk noted earlier), very many more women than men have felt compelled to write personal criticism, at any rate in literary studies. 'Maybe personal criticism is for women only,' Miller surmised in her 1991 book (prematurely, as it turned out, for the next few years would see the appearance of Henry Louis Gates's *Colored People* [1994]; Lentricchia's *The Edge of Night* [1994]; *The Intimate Critique* [Freedman et. al 1993] with its three male contributors—only three out of twenty-five, admittedly; *The Confessions of the Critics* [Veeser 1996b] with its twelve male contributors—although four of them refuse to confess; and Staley's *Reading with a Passion* [1995]). 'Or do women seem better at it because they've been awash in the personal for so long?' continued Miller (1991, 19). Or is it simply that some men are so bad at it? This brings me to the recently released first volume of *Reading from this Place*, edited by Fernando F. Segovia and Mary Ann Tolbert (1995).

Impersonal Criticism

A projected three-volume work, *Reading from this Place* is designed to explore the intricate interface between social location and biblical interpretation. How does the former impinge upon the latter? How does one's gender, race, ethnicity, nationality, class, sexual orientation, or religious affiliation affect one's exegesis? Of course, *Reading from this Place* does not purport to be personal criticism; *positional* criticism might be a better term for the offerings assembled between its covers. Several of the essays in the inaugural volume, however [. . .], also happen to be examples of personal criticism,[7] while several others manage to be autobiographical and impersonal at once. I shall review the latter first.

Daniel Patte's 'Acknowledging the Contextual Character of Male, European-American Critical Exegeses: An Androcritical Perspective' (1995a) is a spin-off from his latest book, *Ethics of Biblical Interpretation* (1995b). I am in fundamental agreement with Patte's basic thesis, which is that the work of male European and North American biblical scholars, notwithstanding traditional claims for objectivity, neutrality, and universality, is every bit as interested, ideological, and contextual as that of any other group of scholars; and I admire the earnest passion with which he argues his thesis. [. . .] Reading Patte's essay, however, I was struck by its strange avoidance of autobiographical detail. Three pages into the piece we read:

Though dispersed throughout the world and thus very different from each other, androcritical biblical scholars[8] share a common twofold experience:

that of *having been fundamentally challenged in our interpretive and pedagogical practices* by feminist, womanist, *mujerista,* African-American, Hispanic-American, Native-American, and/or Third World liberation theologians and biblical scholars, among others; and that of striving to respond constructively to this challenge by radically transforming our practices as critical exegetes and teachers. (Patte 1995a, 37; emphasis added)

I'm intrigued; this has happened to me too; although I sense that Patte's experience has been more devastating than mine. But I want to hear the particulars. A further three pages into the essay, buried in a footnote, I come upon a cryptic reference to a certain conference, a 'watershed event' for Patte and his confrere Gary Phillips, at which the failure of Patte, Phillips, and other unnamed 'male European Americans' 'to acknowledge and affirm [their] otherness was confronted by feminist, womanist, *mujerista,* African-American, Hispanic-American, and Jewish scholars in biblical criticism and ethics' (1995a, 40, n. 17). But what precisely was said? What did Patte and his white male colleagues say or do to anger or alienate this formidable phalanx of women and minority scholars? And what did the latter say or do in return? We are never told. The scene in question is implicitly presented as the essay's *raison d'être* (see also 1995a, 44, n. 25).[9] As such, it is potentially the essay's most powerful rhetorical resource, and begs to be shown. What we have here is a failure, or inability, to stage an autobiographical 'performance,' and the essay's efficacy is diminished as a result.

Patte's essay is followed by Fernando F. Segovia's 'Toward a Hermeneutics of the Diaspora: A Hermeneutics of Otherness and Engagement.' It begins: 'As the title of the present essay indicates, I believe that the time has come to introduce the real reader, the flesh-and-blood reader, fully and explicitly, into the theory and practice of biblical criticism; to acknowledge that no reading, informed or uninformed, takes place in a social vacuum or desert; to allow fully for contextualization, for culture and experience . . .' (1995b, 57). This sounds promising. But on the very next page, a caveat is introduced: 'In this essay I should like to propose, therefore, the beginnings of a hermeneutical framework for taking the flesh-and-blood reader seriously in biblical criticism, *not so much as a unique and independent individual but rather as a member of distinct and identifiable social configurations,* as a reader from and within a social location' (58, emphasis added). A footnote qualifies the caveat: 'I certainly do not mean to deny the presence of independence and uniqueness to individuals within such social groupings, but rather to focus on those aspects that characterize individuals as members of special social groupings' (58, n. 3). Segovia then proceeds to outline his own position 'as a Hispanic American, with an emphasis on the general characteristics and similarities of this reality rather than on its distinguishing features or characteristics' (61). What follows is instructive and illuminating, yet not as effective as it might have been. More even than Patte's, Segovia's self-portrait is a study in abstract minimalism; nothing approaching an autobiographical anecdote is allowed to mar its spare lines and muted tones.[10] [. . .]

Personalism, however, particularly in biblical studies, carries a risk of another sort, namely, the suspension of criticism. The seventh essay in *Reading from this Place* is the first that is truly autobiographical. Justo L. González opens his 'Reading from My Bicultural Place: Acts 6:1–7' with a reminiscence:

I must have been six or seven years old. In a large Methodist church in Cuba, in rather broken Spanish, our missionary pastor was speaking of Peter's denial. 'How was it that people knew that Peter was one of Jesus' followers?' he asked. And his answer was quite simple: 'When you have been with Jesus, it shows on your face.' It was a rather inspiring sermon, calling us all to closer fellowship with Jesus. The problem came later. After the service ended, I sat on a wall by the door, carefully looking at each parishioner as they filed out of the church, and deciding that not one of them had been with Jesus! (González 1995, 139)

A page or two later I abruptly realize that what I am reading is itself a sermon. This is confessional criticism of an entirely different kind.

'Why is it sexy when literary critics do it, but not when biblical critics do it?' a frivolous little voice inside me wants to know. More substantially, I experience the same problem reading González's essay, and even the haunting essay by Ada María Isasi-Díaz that follows it ('It was the summer of 1961, in Santa Rosa, California, when I first read Psalm 137. I remember resonating with most of what the psalm says; I remember feeling it could appropriately voice the pain I was experiencing being away from my country against my will . . .' [1995, 149]), that I've experienced with so much liberation exegesis: it's confessional exegesis, written from faith to faith, written about a 'we' that doesn't include me. ('The problem is that as a church we . . .' [González 1995, 146]). Of course, there's absolutely no reason why it should include me. But it does tend to aggravate a persistent little problem of my own, an itch I can't seem to scratch: Why am I still in biblical studies?

[. . .] Is it possible for a biblical scholar, committed to writing self-consciously out of his or her social location, to navigate successfully between the Scylla of insufficient personalism, on the one hand, and the Charybdis of insufficient criticism, on the other? I believe it is. I see it happening in Amy-Jill Levine's '"Hemmed in on Every Side": Jews and Women in the Book of Susanna,' for example, which begins so compellingly ('I am a Jew. My interest in the origins of Christianity began when a neighbor accused me of 'killing the Lord' . . .' [1995, 175]), and continues as critically as the subject matter demands; or in Regina M. Schwartz's 'Nations and Nationalism: Adultery in the House of David' (1992), in which the author's reflections on early Israelite monarchy are skillfully refracted through her first-hand impressions of modern Israeli militarism; or in Robert Allen Warrior's 'Canaanites, Cowboys, and Indians: Deliverance Conquest, and Liberation Theology Today' (1989), an eye-opening reading of the biblical conquest narratives by a Native American; [. . .] or in Staley's *Reading with a Passion*, about which I shall have much to say below. [. . .]

Shortly after beginning this section, right after I had quoted Tompkins on the stab in the entrails, I myself was disemboweled. The heavens opened and a great sword descended, or at any rate the doorbell rang. It was the mail, including a mystery envelope from Fortress Press, which turned out to contain, not a check, to my disappointment, but a copy of a review of my last book by somebody whose own work I've read and whom I once ran into at a conference (where else?). Anyway, he has some very nice things to say about the book initially, but I won't bore you with those. The part of the book that least impressed him, however, is the part that most impressed me (is it ever otherwise?), my first foray into autobiographical criticism, which begins 'My father was a butcher' (which he was), goes on in that (opened) vein for a paragraph or two, and then cuts to an extended meditation on Paul's fixation with Jesus' gruesome demise in light of Foucault's Discipline and Punish, particularly its grisly opening scene. By way of inclusio, I wax autobiographical again at the end, although briefly. Well, the reviewer was entirely unconvinced that 'the story of a sensitive young Irish boy . . . who witnessed the slaughter of animals by his butcher father, but who did not collapse until a priest preached of the dreadful slaying of Jesus at a Good Friday service,' could have anything to do with Paul's contagious cruci-fixation. He concludes: 'It appears to me that there are sounder ways of making sense of Pauline Christology (especially via the apocalyptic paradigm advocated by J. C. Beker).' Yes, but a dutiful display of sound sense could have been enacted in this case only at the cost of a certain repression, a strong, silent misrepresentation of what the crucifixion has really meant in my life, and at the time I wasn't willing to pay the price.

Anyway, what I want to mull on here is my sense, undoubtedly exaggerated, that this reviewer and I hail from different dimensions. Because if Patte is correct, the reviewer and I should be shoulder to shoulder on the same team, covertly pursuing our group's common interests and concerns. I'm white, male, and of Irish Roman Catholic stock, and so is he. We should be golf buddies, surely. And perhaps to a casual observer, a third biblical scholar from the Third World, say, this individual and I might indeed appear as alike in our exegetical strategies as two peas in the proverbial pod, although I doubt it. You see, this person happens to be a Roman Catholic priest, whereas I, on a good day, am an agnostic. Yes, we do have a common set of professional interests to promote—the per-petuation of an expert discourse on the Bible, something that is essential to our material survival (mine more than his, perhaps)—but I assume that's true of everyone, anywhere, who makes, or ekes, a living from teaching and writing on this perennial best seller. I don't know for certain, of course, but I strongly suspect that this person's scholarly research has the overall effect of validating his original decision to become, his daily deci-sion to remain, a priest. I do know for certain that my own scholarly research has had the (no less convenient) effect of validating, indeed precipitating, my own unbelief. And I further suspect that that is the real reason why he and I can have so much, and yet so little, in common.

Why am I still in biblical studies? Simple: because I'm stuck here. I do still love the Bible, but I'm no longer in love with it (much less with Him), and I haven't been for a very long time. There are many other things—literature, popular culture, art . . .—that I could imagine teaching or researching instead, and with a passion. Still, I plan to remain faithful to the Bible till retirement do us part. Of course, the temptation to squeeze all my other interests into my biblical work has long proved irresistible. ('What are you work-ing on?' a colleague from English politely inquires. 'The muscular male body,' I reply. [Pause.] 'And the Bible?' she prompts dubiously. With minor variations, this scene has been played again and again over the years; only the inquirer and my reply change.) I've just completed a manuscript (on the Bible—what else?) that begins: 'This is an intensely personal book. Its three parts spring from a phobia and two fascinations, each of which has shadowed me since childhood . . .' Autobiography by any other name? Assuredly. Self-indulgent? Perhaps. But whom should I indulge instead? The stern fathers of our discipline (as it is so aptly named)?

[. . .]

Scrambled Selves

[W]hat else might be impelling the autobiographical turn in literary studies? The latter cannot be unrelated to the upsurge of interest in the *study* of autobiography that the profession has witnessed in recent years (e.g., Ashley, Gilmore, and Peters 1994; Bruss 1976; Eakin 1985; Folkenflik 1993; Gunn 1982; Lejeune 1989; Olney 1972, 1980; Marcus 1994; Pascal 1960; Spengemann 1980). Suddenly 'everyone' in literary studies 'seems to be talking about autobiography,' Sidonie Smith could write (1987, 3), and the fascination has waxed rather than waned in the interim, as even a cursory glance at recent programs of the annual MLA convention reveals. This interest is not itself unrelated to feminism, since much of it has focused on women's autobiographies (e.g., Benstock 1988; Brodski and Schenck 1984; Gilmore 1994; Jelinek 1980, 1986; Kosta 1994; Perreault 1995; Personal Narratives Group 1989; Smith 1987; Stanley 1992; Stanton 1987). 'During the past five hundred years, autobiography has assumed a central position in the personal and literary life of the West precisely because it serves as one of those generic contracts that reproduces the patrilineage and its ideologies of gender,' argues Smith (1987, 44). For most of this period, women have been consigned to the margins of the dominant autobiographical tradition; with few exceptions, the letter, the diary, the journal, and other 'culturally muted' media of self-representation have been their assigned province (44). The issue assumes a particular intensity and importance in the colonial context. Traditionally, as Smith and Julie Watson explain elsewhere, the subject of autobiography has been conceived of, quintessentially, as a man, or even as 'Man,' the universal human subject, alias the 'straight white Christian man of property' (Smith and Watson 1992, xvii). Over against this representative Man, Western thought, at least since the 'age of discovery,' has tended to set the colonized, an anonymous, amorphous, 'opaque collectivity of undifferentiated bodies' (xvii). It is the self-representation, oral or written, of the colonized subject, above all the female subject, that is the focus of much of the most provocative recent work on autobiography (see esp. Lionnet 1989; Smith and Watson 1992). [. . .]

The postcolonial condition receives a rather different, and rather risky, treatment in Jeff Staley's *Reading with a Passion* (1995). The book is divided into two parts. Part One is entitled 'Reading the Text,' the text in question being the Fourth Gospel, and Part Two is entitled 'Reading the Reader,' the reader being the author himself. 'The arguments raised against formalist reader-response criticism have finally worked their way under my thick skin,' the second part begins (113). Staley is now ready to come clean and confess that the 'implied reader' of the Fourth Gospel, the protagonist of his published doctoral dissertation (Staley 1988), was really Staley himself all along. But Staley is going to need some time to slip into a new persona. 'When you've been hiding behind implied and encoded readers as long as I have, it's not easy to slip into something more comfortable, curl up in a chair, and tell a stranger who you are' (1995, 114). And Staley insists that he doesn't know who he is in any case, as we shall see.

When Staley was seven years old, his missionary parents moved the family to the Navajo Indian reservation in northeastern Arizona. Staley's strange sojourn on the Navajo reservation is the subject of 'Not Yet Fifty: Postcolonial Confessions from an Outpost in the San Juan Basin,' the autobiographical, and pivotal, chapter of *Reading with a Passion*. As literature, the chapter beggars summary, except of the most banal sort. For present purposes, I shall restrict myself to those passages in which Staley reflects on the roles that the Gospel of John has played in his life and the roles that *he* has played in *John's* life. 'I have uncovered St John every time that I have peered into my past,' he writes. 'In my childhood years on the Navajo reservation it flowed with the muddied waters of the San Juan River of northern New Mexico and southern Utah. It lay deep beneath the snowcapped San Juan Mountains of southern Colorado' (197). On the banks of the San Juan, Staley learned that

> the word *john* was pejorative reservation slang derisively used by Anglos and 'town Navajos' for any Navajo who had not made the transition from tradi-tional Indian culture to the dominant Caucasian culture and its values. Like a chapter from my childhood (like the red-letter text of John in my missionary parents' home or the two-dimensional topographical map on our schoolroom wall), John seems to me to be a Gospel that outwardly has a simple message, clearly stated and transparent. But underneath that message there is another which—like the john world outside my childhood front door, or the three-dimensional desert floor—often seems to subvert and controvert the previ-ously established norm. As I approach the end of my fifth decade of life, I am beginning to think that I have long been the unsuspecting victim of two johns, two geographies, and two existential ironies. (195)

The john world was a harsh one, in many ways, for the gestating Johannine scholar. 'Outside our childhood home, white-skinned people were dirty, smelly, and stupid,' he recalls. 'To most of the Navajo children we played with, our heads were strangely shaped, protruding out from the backsides of our necks like grossly overgrown tumors; likewise our genitals were curiosity pieces, a topic of frequent speculative conversations. We transmitted ghost-sicknesses, and a strange cow-like odor followed us wherever we went' (170). He recalls how he and his brother once incurred the wrath of four Navajo men, one brandishing a shotgun, by swimming in a small irrigation reservoir near the mission. 'As it turned out, the Navajos were afraid that our pallid skin would somehow wash off in the coffee-colored water, spreading deadly diseases to their sheep that drank from the reservoir' (171). Through this and other trials, the misplaced missionaries' son soon learned 'that brown skin denoted intelligence, along with beauty, cleanliness, and everything that was good in the world' (172).[11]

What conclusions does the elder Staley, explorer of St John's Gospel, draw from the cultural misadventures of the younger Staley, explorer of the john world of the San Juan basin? In the preceding chapter he speculates that the theory of 'Johannine reader victimization,' which he first conceived in *The Print's First Kiss* (1988, 95–118), and further fleshed out in *Reading with a Passion* (1995, 85–109)—the notion that the implied reader of the Fourth Gospel is the foremost victim of its ironies—'was rooted in [his] own childhood experience of being a victim of ethnic and racial discrimination as much as it was rooted in [his] professional reading of literary criticism' (115). If this is indeed the case, the critics of biblical reader-response criticism would be proved right ('What Staley's generalized reader masks is the critic himself: Staley's reader reads the way Staley does,' etc.), Staley's scholarship being shown to be unconscious, unacknowledged autobiography.

As will by now be apparent, Staley treads a fine line in his autobiographical reminiscences and reflections. The risk he ran was that of writing something that would be read as a resentful tale of reverse discrimination. It seems to me that he has successfully circumvented that danger. There is not a trace of bitterness in his tone. He shows himself to be well aware both of the horrific history of exploitation and oppression that made the reservations 'necessary' in the first place, and of the fact that his Caucasian features and complexion sufficed to open up innumerable doors for him in the world outside the reservation that would forever be closed to his Navajo friends (see esp. 1995, 184–5).

Staley's book constitutes a double challenge to biblical scholars. First, he challenges us to come out from behind the assorted ceremonial masks that we don whenever we exegete the biblical texts, whether those masks bear the blurred features of a hypothetical 'original' reader or hearer of the texts (what historical critics like to hide behind), or the highly stylized, heavily made up features of an 'implied' reader of the texts (what most literary critics like to hide behind), or, more generally, the cold, withdrawn, impassive features of a strenuously impersonal style of writing (what most of us like to hide behind most of the time). But this is a challenge that has already been voiced by others. What sets Staley's book apart is his determination to press beyond the now facile formula, 'I am a white, male, middle-class, heterosexual, Protestant biblical scholar,' and expend the same amount of energy exegeting his own investments, biases, and neuroses as an interpreter as he expends in exegeting the biblical text.

This is commendable, but uncommonly difficult. For what Staley discovers, as we shall see, is that the self is no less slippery than the text, and never more so than when the interpreter is reaching out, hammer in hand, to grasp it and nail it down. Then it begins to thrash uncontrollably. And even should the interpreter succeed in gripping it, he or she might find that it is not a single self after all, but a fistful of selves, which slither surreptitiously between the fingers and slip away. [. . .]

In recent years it has become commonplace, particularly in feminist circles, to point out how, coincidentally, or perhaps conveniently, the dramatic 'disappearance' of the subject staged by structuralist and poststructuralist theorists in the 1960s and 1970s—white male theorists, almost without exception—occurred just as women and ethnic minorities, in precisely those parts of the world where structuralism and poststructuralism were flourishing (Western Europe and North America), were, after many centuries of marginalization and invisibility, finally themselves achieving unprecedented status as full subjects and free agents. [. . .] In still other circles, however, including those from which personal criticism has begun to emerge, the poststructuralist erasure of the subject is dismissed with a casual shrug. More precisely, it is read in hindsight as a rhetoric of hyperbole, useful, even necessary, in its day, but not any longer. [. . .]

Nevertheless, the specter of the insubstantial self continues to be conjured up to unnerve the personal critics. David Simpson invokes it, for example, in 'Speaking Personally' (1996), his contribution to *Confessions of the Critics*. Countering Tompkins's allegation in 'Me and My Shadow' that academics 'are scared to talk about themselves, that they haven't got the guts to do it' (1993,

25), Simpson remarks that talking about oneself 'bears not at all upon whether there is a significant "self" to contain those guts' (1996, 85). Simpson then turns his attention to Tompkins's bathroom passage, 'the now best known item of personal situatedness in her narrative,' arguing that Tompkins's evocation of her full bladder is best understood 'as a conventional instance of the *vraisemblable*,' its sole purpose being to inscribe the reality of the scene in which it occurs (86; cf. Lang 1996, 52). 'And so, by contagion, we are talking about a real person, with a real self' (Simpson 1996, 86). And what sort of self is it? [. . .] 'After Foucault and many other critics and philosophers . . . the private voice of Jane Tompkins or anyone else' can no longer bear any necessary correlation to a self, such selves having once and for all been exposed 'as nothing more than a string of attributes and contingent connections masquerading as an entity' (1996, 86).

Even Staley, feminized man though he must be, on Simpson's reading, is similarly dismissive of the solid-seeming self whose interpretive misadventures, first in St John's Gospel, then in the San Juan Basin, he has been narrating in *Reading with a Passion*:

> I have discovered nothing from reading myself as a reader. Nothing except that I can as easily hide and lie about myself as I can about the Gospel of John. And if the critics of reader-response criticism tell me my Johannine 'reader' is a fiction, critics of autobiography tell me that the 'self' I have read reading the Gospel of John is no less a fiction. The 'I' of this chapter is nothing more than print and paper conceived from the unholy trinity of Tony Hillerman's popular, quasi-anthropological detective novels, my own piecemeal memory, and sacred Scripture. But then, the same can be said of Jesus' self-disclosing 'I Am' in John's Gospel. It is not his own either. It is merely the text of Exodus 3.14 pinned precariously to his lips by some nameless author. All our reconstructed personae are intertextual and linguistic fictions, whether the referent (or 'deferent') is 'Jesus,' 'Jeffrey,' or the 'Johannine encoded reader.' (Staley 1995, 198)

Yes, but so what? The notion of an undivided self, an ontologically prior essence, an internal fountain of truth capable of expressing itself without misrepresenting itself is certainly a fiction. But this fiction is by no means necessary in order for selves to communicate, imperfectly but adequately, with other selves, and thereby effect change in the material conditions of their existence. Yet even that is not the bottom line. Theory may indeed cause the unproblematized self to shimmer, flicker, and finally vanish. But the fictional, unfragmented self reappears, or had better reappear, the moment one begins to interact again with other selves, or else one risks confinement in one of those highly unpleasant holding places that our society reserves for ill-formed selves.[12]

Does such an uncontroversial assertion need substantiation? I speak from experience, in case it does, although it was not megadoses of Lacan, Foucault, or Barthes (LFB?) that caused it; rather, it was megadoses of LSD. I was through with acid by 1972, but it wasn't through with me. Two years later I experienced a religious conversion that took the form of a six-week LSD flashback, at the height of which I became convinced that I was God bringing Myself into existence (I'm nothing if not modest), and that resulted in an involuntary confinement (my second), complete with electric shock therapy. Yes. I had to be crazy to become a biblical scholar (for that's how it all began). Best leave the last word to Tompkins, then: 'This one time I've taken off the straitjacket, and it feels so good' (1993, 40).

Notes

1 The statement appeared as an epigraph to James Olney's influential anthology, *Autobiography* (1980), and has reappeared regularly in subsequent work on autobiography and autobiographical criticism. Nobody (except Olney?) seems to know its exact source, however.

2 See Staley (1995, 118, n. 13; 122–36) for bibliography and analysis. Specific examples will be discussed below. Interest in autobiography among religion scholars, however, has by no means been confined to biblical specialists; see, in addition, Comstock 1995; Barbour 1987; Henking 1991; Mueller 1987; Ross 1991; also Gilmore 1994, 131–48; Lionnet 1989, 35–66; Smith 1987, 64–83.

3 Although in literary studies, Tompkins's reputation rests primarily on her New Historicist monograph, *Sensational Designs* (Tompkins, 1985), a book whose influence on biblical studies can hardly be underestimated.

4 See also Tompkins (1993, 30). Compare law professor Patricia J. Williams's self-portrait in her *Alchemy of Race and Rights:* '[Y]ou should know that you are dealing with someone who is writing this in an old terry bathrobe with a little fringe of blue and white tassles dangling from the hem, trying to decide if she is stupid or crazy' (1991, 4).

5 Subsequently Tompkins prefaced the passage that follows with a rejoinder to a critique of her article by Gerald MacLean. It is the longer version that appears in *The Intimate Critique* (reprinted from yet another collection, *Gender and Theory*).

6 Related to this argument is a second one about emotion. 'The public-private dichotomy, which is to say, the public-private *hierarchy*, is a founding condition of female oppression,' she contends (1993, 25, her emphasis). Why? Because Western epistemology 'is shaped by the belief that emotion should be excluded from the process of attaining knowledge,' and because 'women in our culture are not simply encouraged but *required* to be the bearers of emotion,' so that 'an epistemology which excludes emotions from the process of attaining knowledge radically undercuts women's epistemic authority' (25–6, her emphasis; cf. 39–40). In part she is appealing here to an unnamed lecture by Alison Jaggar.

7 Just as several of the essays in *The Intimate Critique* happen to be explorations of social location. 'While not essentializing, the writers in this volume assume the categories of gender, race, class, and ability are among matrices that influence their reading, knowing, and writing' (Freedman, Frey, and Zauhar 1993, 10).

8 Patte's term for white male biblical scholars who are critical of androcentrism.

9 So it seemed to me, at any rate. Upon reading Patte's *Ethics of Biblical Interpretation* (1995b), however, I learned that the idea for the book (of which the essay is a by-product) predated the conference, which was held in March 1991 at Vanderbilt University and entitled 'Ethical Responsibilities and Practices in Biblical Criticism.' Nevertheless, the criticism Patte received at the conference was responsible for the present form of the book (and the essay, too, by extension): he reports that after the conference he had to toss away the current draft of the book (1995b, x). The book is as

thin on anecdotal detail as the essay. The fatal conference is mentioned three times, but always in passing (x; 33, n. 21; 71, n. 66). There are also a few hurriedly sketched passages on Patte's classroom experiences (23, 41–2). Months after the present article was completed, I finally received a copy of Patte and Phillips' 'A Fundamental Condition for Ethical Accountability in the Teaching of the Bible by White Male Exegetes' (1991) in which the conference also looms large. Moreover, a more detailed account of the confrontation that so affected Patte and Phillips appears to be included in it (9–10). I say 'appears' because, as though to chide me for my curiosity, my copy of the article lacked p. 9!

10 Paradoxically, Segovia's general introduction to the volume contains a little more in the way of explicit autobiographical information (1995a, 1–3 passim).

11 And he learned well. Later he would fall in love with a dark-skinned woman, who, although not herself a Navajo, conformed perfectly to Navajo ideals of physical beauty. 'On Barbara's first visit to the mission, her waist-length, raven-black hair immediately hypnotized the young Navajo girls. They followed her wherever she walked, crowded around her, and ran their fingers through it, whispering, "Nízhóní, nízhóní" ("beautiful, beautiful"). I noted their spontaneous reactions with deep interest and knew that I had found the woman I would marry' (172).

12 In fairness to Staley it should be noted that he too raises, and wrestles with, the 'so what?' question, although from a different angle (see esp. 19–20, 199, 236ff).

Literature

Ashley, Kathleen, Leigh Gilmore and Gerald Peters (eds). 1994. *Autobiography and Postmodernism*. Amherst: University of Massachusetts Press.

Barbour, John D. 1987. 'Character and Characterization in Religious Autobiography,' *JAAR* 55:307–27.

Benstock, Shari (ed.). 1988. *The Private Self: Theory and Practice of Women's Autobiographical Writing*. Chapel Hill: University of North Carolina Press.

Brodski, Bella and Celeste Schenck (eds). 1984. *Life/Lines: Theorizing Women's Autobiography*. Ithaca: Cornell University Press.

Brownstein, Rachel M. 1996. 'Interrupted Reading: Personal Criticism in the Present Time,' in Veeser, 1996b. Pp. 29–39.

Bruss, Elizabeth W. 1976. *Autographical Acts: The Changing Situation of a Literary Genre*. Baltimore: The Johns Hopkins University Press.

Comstock, Gary L. 1995. *Religious Autobiographies*. Belmont: Wadsworth.

Eakin, Paul John. 1985. *Fictions in Autobiography: Studies in the Art of Self-Invention*. Princeton: Princeton University Press.

Farmer, William R. 1994. *The Gospel of Jesus: The Pastoral Relevance of the Synoptic Problem*. Louisville: Westminster John Knox.

Folkenflik, Robert (ed.). 1993. *The Culture of Autobiography: Constructions of Self-Representation*. Stanford: Stanford University Press.

Freedman, Diane P., Olivia Frey and Frances Murphy Zauhar (eds). 1993. *The Intimate Critique: Autobiographical Literary Criticism*. Durham: Duke University Press.

Gates, Henry Louis, Jr. 1994. *Colored People: A Memoir*. New York: Alfred A. Knopf.

Gilmore, Leigh. 1994. *Autobiographics: A Feminist Theory of Women's Self-Representation*. Ithaca: Cornell University Press.

González, Justo L. 1995. 'Reading from My Bicultural Place: Acts 6:1–7,' in Segovia and Tolbert 1995. Pp. 139–47.

Gunn, Janet Varner. 1982. *Autobiography: Toward a Poetics of Experience*. Philadelphia: University of Pennsylvania Press.

Henking, Susan E. 1991. 'The Personal Is the Theological: Autobiographical Acts in Contemporary Feminist Theology,' *JAAR* 59:511–26.

Isasi-Díaz, Ada María. 1995. '"By the Rivers of Babylon": Exile as a Way of Life,' in Segovia and Tolbert 1995. Pp. 149–63.

Jelinek, Estelle C. 1986. *The Tradition of Women's Autobiography: From Antiquity to the Present*. Boston: Twayne.

—— (ed.). 1980. *Women's Autobiography: Essays in Criticism*. Bloomington: Indiana University Press.

Kosta, Barbara. 1994. *Recasting Autobiography: Women's Counterfictions in Contemporary German Literature and Film*. Ithaca: Cornell University Press.

Lang, Candace. 1996. 'Autocritique,' in Veeser 1996b. Pp. 40–54.

Lejeune, Philippe. 1989. *On Autobiography*, ed. Paul John Eakin, trans. Katherine Leary. Minneapolis: University of Minnesota Press.

Lentricchia, Frank. 1994. *The Edge of Night*. New York: Random House.

Levine, Amy-Jill. 1995. '"Hemmed in on Every Side": Jews and Women in the Book of Susanna,' in Segovia and Tolbert 1995. Pp. 175–90.

Lionnet, Francoise. 1989. *Autobiographical Voices: Race, Gender, Self-Portraiture*. Ithaca: Cornell University Press.

Marcus, Laura. 1994. *Auto/Biographical Discourses: Theory, Criticism, Practice*. New York: St. Martin's Press.

Miller, Nancy K. 1991. *Getting Personal: Feminist Occasions and Other Autobiographical Acts*. New York: Routledge.

Mueller, Janel M. 1987. 'Autobiography of a New "Creatur": Female Spirituality, Selfhood, and Authorship in "The Book of Margery Kempe,"' in Stanton 1987. Pp. 63–75.

Olney, James. 1972. *Metaphors of Self: Meaning in Autobiography*. Princeton: Princeton University Press.

—— (ed.). 1980. *Autobiography: Essays Theoretical and Critical*. Princeton: Princeton University Press.

Pascal, Roy. 1960. *Design and Truth in Autobiography*. Cambridge: Harvard University Press.

Patte, Daniel. 1995a. 'Acknowledging the Contextual Character of Male, European-American Critical Exegeses: An Androcritical Perspective,' in Segovia and Tolbert 1995. Pp. 35–55.

—— 1995b. *Ethics of Biblical Interpretation: A Reevaluation*. Louisville: Westminster John Knox.

Patte, Daniel and Gary A. Phillips. 1991. 'A Fundamental Condition for Ethical Accountability in the Teaching of the Bible by White Male Exegetes: Recovering and Claiming the Specificity of Our Perspective,' *Scriptura* 9:7–28.

Perreault, Jeanne. 1995. *Writing Selves: Contemporary Feminist Autobiography*. Minneapolis: University of Minnesota Press.

The Personal Narratives Group (eds). 1989. *Interpreting Women's Lives: Feminist Theory and Personal Narratives*. Bloomington: Indiana University Press.

Ross, Ellen M. 1991. 'Spiritual Experience and Women's Autobiography: The Rhetoric of Selfhood in *The Book of Margery Kempe*,' *JAAR* 59:527–46.

Schwartz, Regina M. 1992. 'Nations and Nationalism: Adultery in the House of David,' *Critical Inquiry* 19:131–50.

Segovia, Fernando F. 1995a. '"And They Began to Speak in Other Tongues":

Competing Modes of Discourse in Contemporary Biblical Criticism,' in Segovia and Tolbert 1995. Pp. 1–32.

——. 1995b. 'Toward a Hermeneutics of the Diaspora: A Hermeneutics of Otherness and Engagement,' in Segovia and Tolbert 1995. Pp. 57–73.

Segovia, Fernando F. and Mary Ann Tolbert (eds). 1995. *Reading from this Place*. Vol. 1. *Social Location and Biblical Interpretation in the United States*. Minneapolis: Fortress.

Simpson, David. 1996. 'Speaking Personally: The Culture of Autobiographical Criticism,' in Veeser 1996b. Pp. 82–94.

Smith, Sidonie 1987. *The Poetics of Women's Autobiography: Marginality and the Fictions of Self-Representation*. Bloomington: Indiana University Press.

Smith, Sidonie and Julia Watson (eds). 1992. *De/Colonizing the Subject: The Politics of Gender in Women's Autobiography*. Minneapolis: University of Minnesota Press.

Spengemann, William. 1980. *The Forms of Autobiography: Episodes in the History of a Literary Genre*. New Haven: Yale University Press.

Staley, Jeffrey L. 1988. *The Print's First Kiss: A Rhetorical Investigation of the Implied Reader in the Fourth Gospel*. SBLDS 82. Atlanta: Scholars.

——. 1995. *Reading with a Passion: Rhetoric, Autobiography, and the American West in the Gospel of John*. New York: Continuum.

Stanley, Liz. 1992. *The Auto/Biographical I: The Theory and Practice of Feminist Auto/Biography*. New York: St. Martin's Press.

Stanton, Domna (ed.). 1987. *The Female Autograph*. Chicago: University of Chicago Press.

Tompkins, Jane P. 1985. *Sensational Designs: The Cultural Work of American Fiction, 1790–1860*. Oxford: Oxford University Press.

——. 1993. 'Me and My Shadow,' in Freedman, Frey and Zauhar 1993. Pp. 23–40.

Tompkins, Jane P. (ed.). 1980. *Reader-Response Criticism: From Formalism to Post-Structuralism*. Baltimore: The Johns Hopkins University Press.

Veeser, H. Aram. 1996a. 'Introduction: The Case for Confessional Critics,' in Veeser 1996b. Pp. ix–xxvii.

—— (ed.). 1996b. *Confessions of the Critics*. New York: Routledge.

Warrior, Robert Allen. 1989. 'Canaanites, Cowboys, and Indians: Deliverance, Conquest, and Liberation Theology Today,' *Christianity and Crisis* 29:261–5.

Williams, Patricia J. 1991. *The Alchemy of Race and Rights: Diary of a Law Professor*. Cambridge: Harvard University Press.

Part 4

Biblical Musings

'What does masculinity have to do with biblical studies?' Stephen Moore asks in his introduction to the volume on *New Testament Masculinities*.

> Almost nothing – and nearly everything: *almost nothing* until relatively recently, when studies specifically analyzing the construction of masculinity in biblical and cognate texts began to appear [. . .]; but *nearly everything* throughout most of the history of critical biblical scholarship, when men, and men alone, almost without exception, constituted the rank and file of the discipline. Masculinity was, at once, everywhere and nowhere in the discipline, so ubiquitous as to be ordinarily invisible, and possessed, too, of the omnipotence that omnipresence confers. (Moore 2003, 1)

In this part, four biblical scholars render visible the invisible omnipresence of male gender in biblical texts and scholarship. We are starting with Howard Eilberg-Schwartz's reflections on the unstable masculinity of Israelite men: Why did their relationship with God threaten their masculinity? Through close readings of Torah, Eilberg-Schwartz follows some biblical threads of the feared effeminization of Israelite men and reconstructs the symbolizations and ritualizations that helped them to avert the risk of being emasculated.

Whereas Eilberg-Schwartz's chapter pivots around the figure of Moses, Dale Martin's 'Sex and the Single Savior' focuses on the central male figure of the New Testament, Jesus Christ. Was Jesus single? Was he sexual? Was he singularly sexual? Dale asks these questions not so much because he assumes that we can find definitive historical answers but because he wonders about the legitimacy of the religious imagination that fuels the curiosity about Jesus' sexuality.

Ken Stone investigates biblical texts through the lens of gay male readers. Rather than rehearsing again the worn question on how the Bible views homosexuality – the question that has occupied gay and straight biblical scholars since the 1950s – Stone presents a complex argument about the interrelation between biblical scholarship and the reading subject. How do marginalized people read biblical text? Are their identities shaped and formed by these readings, or do they resist them?

We conclude this part with Staley's 'autobiographical midrash on the gospel of John', which pushes the boundaries of what can be considered biblical scholarship. Employing a Jewish form of interpretation (*midrash*) to a New Testament text, his writings deliberately obfuscate genre and method. Is it biblical exegesis or a personal diary? Is it academic prose or poetry?

Together, these four chapters constitute only a snapshot in a broad field, and they are chosen mainly for their hermeneutical value rather than their exegetical findings. Hermeneutics are generally understood to address the theoretical underpinnings of the interpretation of Scripture, while exegesis is the detailed analysis of particular biblical passages. Since one can easily drown in the flood of exegetical detail, hermeneutics (as the more comprehensive category) provides a more broadly relevant entry into issues of masculinity and biblical scholarship. But for those interested in exegesis, Moore's and Anderson's *New Testament Masculinities* offers 13 contributions rich in exegetical insights, and it also contains an excellent bibliography of hundreds of titles on the intersection of Bible and masculinity studies. Further reading suggestions are indicated at the end of each chapter's introduction.

Literature

Anderson, Janice Capel (with Stephen Moore and Seon Hee Kim). 2003. 'Masculinity Studies: A Classified Bibliography', in Moore and Anderson. Pp. 23–42.
Moore, Stephen D. 2003. '"O Man, Who Art Thou . . .?" Masculinity Studies and New Testament Studies', in Moore and Anderson. Pp. 1–22.
Moore, Stephen D. and Janice Capel Anderson (eds). 2003. *New Testament Masculinities*. Atlanta: Society of Biblical Literature.

14

Unmanning Israel

Editor's Introduction

In the early 1990s, Howard Eilberg-Schwartz burst on the academic scene with the publication of four books (1990; 1992; 1994; 1995), making himself a name in the comparative study of Judaism and Jewish gender studies. But as quickly as he rose to prominence as a leading voice in Jewish studies (his first book received the Award of Academic Excellence of the AAR), he disappeared. In 1995, at the age of 41, he abruptly departed from his university position as head of a Jewish studies program and abandoned his academic career.

His case illustrates well the risk of taking up positions that are the result of one's scholarly inquiry but that sit uncomfortably with one's own community. Openly gay scholars have long lamented the fact that their research has been met with overt or covert job discrimination. In Eilberg-Schwartz's case, a conflict arose between a Jewish heterosexual man and his community. Though mostly a political conflict, which had much to do with the uneasy relationship between academic freedom and the implicit mission of Jewish studies programs (Mahler 1997), simmering tensions about his probing questions concerning the foundations of ancient Judaism and modern Jewish gender identity had been slowly building up. In *God's Phallus* (1994), from which the chapter below is excerpted, Eilberg-Schwartz argues that the various rituals and myths of ancient Judaism as preserved in Hebrew Scriptures tell us about the efforts of Israelite men (and, later, rabbinic men) 'to suppress the homoerotic impulse implicit in the male relationships with God' (1994, 3). Later, when praise and criticism bubbled up, Eilberg-Schwartz remained unapologetically critical of certain gendered rituals in Judaism. Elsewhere, he argued, for example, that circumcision is the inflicting of a wound on boys and that the central 'covenant between man and God' might be more 'constructively symbolized by a "nurturing act," such as feeding' (reported in Mahler 1997, 53; on circumcision, also Brod, chapter 25).

Other Jewish studies scholars working on issues of gender and sexuality cautiously empathized at the time with Eilberg-Schwartz's case. David Biale, author of *Eros and the Jews* (1992), commented, for example, that Eilberg-Schwartz's work 'has a combative quality vis-à-vis conventional opinion . . . It is no surprise that a person who takes those kinds of views might find himself in an untenable situation when he has to defend the Jewish community' (quoted in Mahler 1997, 53). The larger question that his case illuminates, though, is about conflicting loyalties. 'What does loyalty to Judaism demand? What does loyalty to women demand? What does loyalty to scholarship demand?' asks Chava Weissler. 'I too may reach the point at which the conflicting loyalties block any response but silence' (quoted in Peskowitz and Levitt 1997, 2). Her words can equally be applied to a critical study of Jewish men and masculinity.

A few words are in order to introduce the overall argument of *God's Phallus*, where Eilberg-Schwartz investigates conflicting images of masculinity within monotheism. 'It may seem paradoxical,' he writes, 'to consider that the symbol of a male God generates dilemmas for the conception of masculinity':

> Nevertheless, I would argue that at the same time that such symbol works to legitimate masculinity, which may in fact be its primary and even original function, it also renders the meaning of masculinity unstable . . . Israel's relationship with God is conceptualized as a monogamous sexual relation, and idolatry as adultery. But the heterosexual metaphors in the ancient texts belie the nature of the relationship in question: it is human males, not females, who are imagined to have the primary intimate relations with the deity. The Israel that is collectively imagined as a woman is actually constituted by men – men like Moses and the patriarchs. And these men love, in ways that are imagined erotically and sensually, a male deity. (Eilberg-Schwartz 1994, 2–3)

Publications by the Same Author

Eilberg-Schwartz, Howard. 1990. *The Savage in Judaism: An Anthropology of Israelite Religion and Ancient Judaism*. Bloomington: Indiana University Press.
—— (ed.). 1992. *People of the Body: Jews and Judaism from an Embodied Perspective*. Albany: SUNY Press.
——. 1994. *God's Phallus: And Other Problems for Men and Monotheism*. Boston: Beacon.
Eilberg-Schwartz, Howard and Wendy Doniger (eds). 1995. *Off with her Head! The Denial of Women's Identity in Myth, Religion, and Culture*. Berkeley: University of California Press.

Further Reading

Biale, David. 1992. *Eros and the Jews: From Biblical Israel to Contemporary America*. New York: Basic Books.
Mahler, Jonathan. 1997. 'Howard's End: Why a Leading Jewish Studies Scholar gave up his Academic Career'. *Lingua Franca* (March):51–57.
Peskowitz, Miriam and Laura Levitt (eds). 1997. *Judaism Since Gender*. New York and London: Routledge.

Unmanning Israel

HOWARD EILBERG-SCHWARTZ

[. . .] When a man confronts a male God, he is put into the female position so as to be intimate with God.[1] The masculinity of Israelite men was thus most secure when God turned his back, hid his face, or kept himself covered in a cloud or in the heavens. But when Israelite men had to face God, their masculinity was made uncertain. The defining traits of what it meant to be a man were called into question. In the literature of ancient Judaism, this threat to masculinity proceeds [. . .] sometimes through violence that threatens castration, even death, at other times in more subtle forms of gender reversal.

The threat to Israelite masculinity was part of a complicated process in which a complementary model of two genders or sexes (male/female) was imposed on a *ménage à trois*: God/Israelite man/Israelite woman. Because the desire of heaven was nearly always imagined as male and heterosexual, Israelite women theoretically should have been the appropriate objects of divine desire. The insertion of Israelite men into this equation required their unmanning. This chapter explores threatened masculinity in various intimate contexts of ancient Judaism: in the relationship between God and certain Israelite men, in the intrusion of God into the relations between husband and wife, and in the stories of divine attacks upon Israelite men. [. . .]

Exclusion of Women

The dilemma of intimacy between the father God and the human male offers us a new way to account for the denigration of women in Israel's religious system. According to the conventional argument, God is male because the male is the norm. Women are by definition different. The otherness of women is recognized and reinforced through rituals that associate impurity with menstruation and childbirth and that bar women from contact with the sacred. Men alone have access to the sacred and to God and find in the Temple and its cultic activity a mirror that validates the male self. This explanation of women's place in the Israelite religious system presupposes that the primary function of religious symbols is to reflect and legitimize the social order. But religious symbols are born through complex processes whose origins are often lost. Once established, they have lives of their own with unpredictable effects on the moral, imaginative, and intellectual lives of religious actors. Symbolic processes, in other words, cannot be reduced to social functions.

Thus, once God was imagined as male, he assumed male qualities, including sexual qualities. In ancient Judaic culture, as we have seen, this implied heterosexual desire, which seemed to deny men a place as God's intimates. The maleness of God therefore had two simultaneous effects: On the one hand, it established male authority. On the other, it threatened to make human masculinity redundant. The religious system of ancient Israel dealt with this dilemma of men's potential exclusion and partial redundancy by shifting it onto women. The insistence on female impurity excluded women from competition with men for divine affections. Women's impurity, in other words, arose in part from attempts to shore up men's access to the sacred. If the conventional theory explains women's cultic impurity as a result of her otherness from God, we can also see it as motivated in part by her natural complementarity to a male deity and her symbolic threat to men's place in the religious system. Women's otherness from God is precisely what made them his expected partners. They had to be excluded from the cult because they challenged the male connection with God.

Moses, Masculinity, and Monotheism

The story of Moses and God is in many ways a description of the closest male–male relationship in Israelite religion. Although it is difficult to completely disentangle the earliest mythic accounts of Moses' encounters with God, they depict a relationship of deepening intimacy. Because of his intimacy with God, Moses' masculinity is called into question. The feminization of Moses is only partially articulate, but various details in the myths suggest that a gender reversal is in process.[2]

Moses, indeed, is described on one occasion as having to deny his femininity (Num. 11.4–15 E). This denial occurs when the Israelites complain that mana does not satisfy their craving for meat, a complaint that angers God and distresses Moses. 'And Moses said to the Lord, "Why have You dealt ill with Your servant, and why have I not enjoyed Your favor, that You have laid the burden of all this people upon me? Did I conceive all this people, did I bear them, that You should say to me, 'Carry them in your bosom as a nurse carries an infant,' to the land that You have promised on oath to their fathers?"'[3] The use of maternal imagery here is important. Moses is denying that he conceived and bore Israel and by implication is saying, 'You, God, are the one who mothered Israel and hence you should nurse Your child.' This passage is sometimes cited to illustrate how feminine or female imagery is used to describe God (Trible 1983, 69; Mollenkott 1986, 20–1). But Moses' protest may actually reveal more about how the narrator imagines Moses than God. Moses has to deny his femininity because his masculinity is at risk. As God's intimate, he is in the position of God's wife and consequently is supposed to mother God's children. Like Hagar, banished to the wilderness with her child, he fears for the survival of the children of Israel (Gen. 21.14–15).[4] Moses' protest is to the point. God has in effect made him a mother of Israel.

A second suggestion of Moses' feminization can be found in the story of his encounter with God on the mountain. When Moses comes down off the mountain, the skin of his face has been transfigured and frightens the people (Exod. 34.29–35). This story has priestly elements in it, but it may also reflect a much earlier myth. The precise meaning of the transfiguration is unclear because of the use of an unusual Hebrew verb, *qāran*.[5] This verb appears to be related to the noun for horns (*qeren*). It is for this reason that the tradition of ascribing horns to Moses developed, a tradition that lies behind Michelangelo's sculpture and other artistic depictions of Moses (Mellinkoff 1970). Some modern interpreters see here allusions to a mask that priests wore, perhaps even a mask with horns, even though there is no evidence for the existence of such masks in ancient Israel. Another longstanding tradition understands *qāran* as referring to beams of light.[6] A recent philological study based on Semitic etymologies suggests that *qrn* refers to a disfiguration of Moses' skin (Propp 1987, 384–6). In any case, something is frighteningly different about Moses that requires him to veil his face. But the purpose of the veil cannot simply be to hide what is fearful, for Moses removes it when he is communicating with the people.[7]

Veils do carry associations of femininity. Although the veil was not standard attire of women in ancient Israel, it is viewed as feminine attire. Out of modesty, Rebekkah veils her face when she first sets eyes on Isaac (Gen. 24.65 J). And Tamar veils her face so that Judah will not recognize her, enabling her to seduce him (Gen. 38.14). Moses is the only Israelite male to be described as covering his face. It is true that the term for this covering (*maseweh*) is never used to describe the veils of women.[8] Still, it is likely that a covering of the face would evoke associations of feminine veiling. Cassuto intuitively makes this connection but does not see the implications for gender imagery. He writes that Moses 'put over his face, out of a sense of humility and modesty, a kind of veil, like the veil or head-scarf that women in Israel usually wear over their faces during summer to protect themselves from the sun's glare' (1967, 450). In addition to hiding his transfiguration, the veiling of Moses partially feminizes him. It points to his transformation into the intimate of God.

We may be in a position now to understand why the narrator of this story chose *qāran* to describe Moses' transfiguration. The verb's association with 'horns' could have been present even if etymologically it originally meant 'to disfigure the skin.' The mistake of understanding a word exclusively in terms of its etymological origins still tends to dominate biblical scholarship. The etymological origins of a word are forgotten by language users. And even when the original meanings of a word are still in currency, words convey additional meanings based on the synchronic relations of the linguistic system, what linguists call 'syntagmatic' similarities.[9] For example, etymologically the word 'whole' and 'hole' have no relationship. But one can imagine a context in which one of the terms draws on meanings from the other: 'There is a huge emptiness, a bottomless pit in my heart. I shall never be whole.' Puns, jokes, advertisements, dreams, and good literature depend on such linguistic associations. The same process is at work in myth. Associations to words that are etymologically unrelated convey meaning. This process need not have been conscious. The choice of words in a myth or story is perceived as just right because they build up layers of meaning that speak to people on many levels.

It therefore may have been no accident that Moses' disfiguration is described with a word that also conjures up the image of horns. The hint of a horned Moses may have partly inspired the narrator to choose this odd word. Horns, after all, are important symbols in Israel. The metaphor of Israel standing with horns held high presupposes the metaphor of Israel as bull or ram.[10] The Psalmists pray that God lift the horn of his people (Ps. 148.14) and not the horns of the wicked (Ps. 75.5). Joseph is described in Moses' final blessing in Deuteronomy as 'like a firstling bull in his majesty. He has horns like the horns of the wild-ox; with them he gores the peoples' (33.17). Interestingly, the Blessing of Joseph alludes to 'the favor of the Presence in the Bush,' the only biblical reference to the story of Moses' encounter with God at the burning bush. Here, then, is another representation of an Israelite leader who has been metaphorically horned as a result of contact with God.

Whether or not the horned Moses and Joseph are related, the metaphor is clearly masculine; it calls to mind the prowess and might of bulls and rams, as well as an image of virility. At the very moment of Moses' feminization, then, a word is chosen that reasserts his masculinity. Moses is imagined with his face covered like a woman, but with horns like a proud bull. He is caught between genders—a man as a leader of Israel, a woman as the wife of God.

The need to reestablish Moses' masculinity may explain two other perplexing statements about him. First, the priestly material which refers to Moses' 'horns' also describes him as having 'uncircumcised lips' (Exod. 6.12, 30), a curious way of explaining his speech impediment. This impediment had been described in an earlier myth as a 'heaviness of lips' (Exod. 3.10 J). Why did the priestly nar-rator feel compelled to find another metaphor? The allusion to circumcision has a very powerful association with the domain of masculinity. Moses' mouth is linked via the metaphor of circumcision to the penis. Through this 'phalliciza-tion' of Moses' mouth, his masculinity is reasserted.

Second, just after learning that Moses dies in the land of Moab before he can enter the promised land, we are told that 'Moses was a hundred and twenty years old when he died; his eyes were undimmed and his freshness unabated' (Deut. 34.7). It is not entirely certain to what this 'freshness' (*leh*) refers, but it may be a reference to his virility (Albright 1944, 32–5). Why should it be neces-sary to assert his virility at the time of his death? In part, the narrator is indicat-ing that Moses died in his prime. Despite his age, he was not an old man, and his eyes had not dimmed. But why should Moses' freshness be mentioned? Perhaps Moses' intimacy with God and his subsequent feminization raised the ques-tion of his masculinity, and it was only with his death that his manhood could be reasserted. The story suggests that one cannot be both a man and a lover of God. This line of analysis is confirmed in the story of God's attack on Moses discussed below.

As we have discussed, on a heterosexual model of desire, an intimate of a male God should be female, so Moses can only insert himself into this equation through his own partial feminization and the exclusion of women. A hint of these tensions is evident in the myth of the Sinai revelation, the first revelation to the children of Israel after their departure from Egypt. This is the first time the impurity of women is referred to in the Hebrew Bible, and this myth may be one of the oldest sources of Israelite religion to refer to women's impurity.

God says to Moses, 'Go to the people and warn them to stay pure today and tomorrow. Let them wash their clothes. Let them be ready for the third day; for on the third day the Lord will come down in the sight of all the people, on Mount Sinai' (Exod. 19.10–13 J).[11] Note, however, what happens when Moses carries out God's instruction. Moses 'warned the people to stay pure, and they washed their clothes. And he said to the people, "Be ready for the third day: do not go near a woman"' (Exod. 19.15). There is a significant discrepancy between

God's instruction to Moses and Moses' charge to the people. It is Moses and not God who insists that men stay clear of women. Most interpreters ignore or minimize the significance of this discrepancy. It seems self-evident to them that women must be avoided before an impending encounter with the sacred. But Moses' elaboration of God's instruction is ambiguous. Does the narrator wish the reader or listener to assume that Moses interpreted God's words properly? Or are we to understand that Moses' words reflect his own understanding of what it means to stay pure? Moreover, precisely why women should be avoided is not spelled out. Is it because men will spill semen and become impure? Is it because of potential contamination of menstrual blood? Or is sexual intercourse itself treated here as antithetical to the encounter with the divine?

Most interpreters sidestep these issues. They generally presume that Moses is simply making explicit what God intended. Cassuto writes that 'in the account of the implementation of the command, the words of the injunction are reiterated as usual. But Moses further adds, not as a thematic supplement of his own, but as a detailed instruction in elucidation of the concept of sanctification: *do not go near a woman*' (1967, 230). Similarly, Childs writes that Moses 'initiates the required sanctification, summarizing the commands with a specific, concrete injunction. "Do not go near a woman!"' Childs continues: 'The holy God of the covenant demands as preparation a separation from those things which are normally permitted and good in themselves. The giving of the covenant is different from an ordinary event of everyday life. Israel is, therefore, to be prepared by a special act of separation' (1974, 268–9). Why the special act of separation is the avoidance of women, neither Cassuto nor Childs speculates. None of these interpreters see any need to explain women's impurity in this context. They assume it makes sense and hence does not call for any explanation.[12]

These interpretations miss the significant fact that the avoidance of women is ascribed to Moses and not God. It seems plausible to assume that the narrator on some level wishes the reader to view this as Moses' interpretation of God's word. It is striking that when Eve adds something to God's command in the garden (Gen. 3.3), interpreters routinely assume that the narrator wishes to indicate something about her state of mind, but they have nothing to say about Moses adding to God's words in Exodus 19.15.[13] The narrator may very well have wanted to ascribe to Moses this prohibition against coming near women. After all, God's instruction seems addressed to the Israelite people as a whole, including the women; Moses is obviously directing his comments to the men alone. In this myth, the notion of women's impurity thus originates with human men and not with God, and it originates at the very moment when God calls men to face him. It is through Moses that the narrator expresses male anxieties about the promise of a God sighting. If Moses does not hide his face (Exod. 3.6), or if God does not turn his back (Exod. 33.20–23), then Moses will have to confront the full significance of a male God. To come face to face with God is to see oneself in the position of wife. 'Do not come near a woman' addresses the problem. When God approaches, men avoid women and cease temporarily to act as husbands. In this way, men collectively prepare themselves to be a feminine Israel. And by linking women and impurity, the natural complementarity between God and women is broken.

The same tensions may explain why Miriam is punished with leprosy after her attack on Moses' authority (Num. 12).[14] This is the story in which Miriam and Aaron protest Moses' role as God's only spokesman. God answers by telling them that Moses alone sees God's form and speaks to God 'mouth to mouth.' Although the challenge comes from both Miriam and Aaron, Miriam alone is stricken with snow-white scales. It may be that the author of this source was a priest who viewed himself as a descendant of Moses and wished to glorify Moses and belittle Aaron (Friedman 1987, 78). But this explanation does not exhaust the meanings of the story. In particular, it does not explain why Aaron, who is equally involved in the challenge to Moses' authority, is not punished. The imbalance is intriguing. It is as if Miriam has committed a sin that Aaron has not. The emphasis on Miriam's role makes sense given the threat posed by her gender. As a woman, Miriam is a more 'natural' intimate of God than Moses. Her challenge to Moses is thus more of a threat than Aaron's. Miriam's affliction with leprosy thus shores up Moses' relationship with God. Indeed, in the previous chapter of Numbers, the same narrator recounts the story of how the spirit of God comes upon two lads, Eldad and Medad. In this case, Moses receives the news joyfully (Num. 11.26–29). The narrator does not imagine the boys as a threat to Moses. Not so with Miriam.

There may be other indications of the competing expectations of Moses as both husband and wife of God. The narrative of Miriam and Aaron's protest begins with what seems to be an irrelevant complaint: 'Miriam and Aaron spoke against Moses on account of the Cushite woman he had married, "He married a Cushite woman!"' (Num. 12.1). The reference is odd. Some take it to mean that Moses has married a black woman, since Cush refers in the Bible to Ethiopia. But there is no report of Moses having married anyone other than Zipporah, who is a Midianite.[15] The protest against the mysterious Cushite woman is never developed and therefore is often taken to be a pretext for the real complaint about Moses' claims to an exclusive relationship with God. Although substantively the two protests seem unconnected, they may be more closely related than initially appears. Just as Moses' relationship with the Cushite woman is called into question, God's relationship with Moses is challenged. The first protest, which otherwise seems to have no relevance to the story that follows, allows the parallelism to emerge and puts Moses in the structural position of wife. Moses' feminine positioning is underscored by an abrupt aside in the narrative. After Miriam and Aaron's protest, the narrator suddenly reminds us that 'Moses was a very humble (ānāw) man, more so than any other man on earth.' The word 'humble' is used in this singular form in no other context. Why would the narrator want to mention Moses' humility at this point? Perhaps to reiterate his uniqueness among the prophets. But it is interesting to note that the word the narrator chooses is derived from a verb that is used to refer to rape, that is, to the humbling of a woman through forced intercourse (Gen. 34.2; Deut. 21.14, 22.24, 29; Judg. 19.24, 20.5; 2 Sam. 13.12, 14, 22, 32; Ezek. 22.10, 11; Lam. 5.11) (Brown, Driver, and Briggs 1975, 776). Moses is the humblest of all men because he submits completely to God.

This understanding of Moses as occupying a feminine position with respect to God suggests another way of viewing the complaint regarding the Cushite woman. There is actually an ambiguity in the Hebrew text that is glossed over in most translations. Miriam and Aaron speak against Moses 'on account of the

Cushite woman he had married.' The word ôdōt, like the English 'on account of,' has two meanings: 'because' or 'on behalf of,' as rabbinic commentators to this passage realize.[16] Miriam and Aaron thus can also be seen as speaking against Moses 'on behalf of the Cushite woman he had married.' That is, they are concerned that Moses' intimacy with God competes with his obligations to his Cushite wife. 'He married a Cushite woman and not you, God!' They are protesting on her behalf. And they do so by pointing out that God has spoken through other people and therefore need not retain the exclusive relationship with Moses. But God refuses their claim. While he does speak through other prophets, he is intimate with Moses alone. Moses alone sees his form and speaks to him 'mouth to mouth.'

The narrator of the myth was probably not conscious of these associations. But on some intuitive level, these two protests must have seemed just right. And part of what made them 'just right' was the structural parallel they established and the recognition they made of Moses' role as wife of God. Moses is cast here as having conflicting obligations, as husband to his wife, and as wife to God.

One need not fully accept this deep reading to agree with the overall point. It is significant that two of the earliest Israelite myths to reflect on women's impurity both involve contexts in which the subject is men's relationship with God. The fear here was not of woman's natural otherness, nor of her menstrual pollution. She was feared because she posed a threat to men's intimacy with the divine. Her punishment and removal opened a position for men to occupy. This explanation, of course, cannot account for the Israelite rules of impurity as a whole. Men were also deemed impure under certain conditions, and a variety of other symbolisms entered into the meaning of impurity (Eilberg-Schwartz 1990, 141–76). But this analysis suggests an additional reason for the development of laws regarding women's impurity. By removing women, Israelite men were able to come closer to God. But that intimacy involved risks: feminization, loss of manhood, and perhaps even death.

Death, Emasculation, and Circumcision

Israelite religion imagined contact with the deity as a terrifying experience. The incursion of the sacred into the realm of the profane was perceived to be devastating, resulting in death and disorder. This explains why boundaries are set around the mountain for God's appearance, why God hides in a cloud, is protected in a Temple behind veils, and why Moses is permitted to see only the divine back. The sacred operates in similar ways in other religious traditions. Indeed, the word 'sacred' is used precisely because it attempts to designate a phenomenon that occurs in many religious traditions. But this vague appeal to the dangers of the sacred ignores the fact that in this case, the sacred was a male God. The danger of contact with 'the sacred' was a particular one. It was the danger of intimacy with a male God, a threat that could be diminished only by a partial unmanning of the Israelite man.

This way of looking at Israel's conception of the sacred helps explain two early Israelite myths which have proved somewhat mysterious. The first involves Jacob's struggle with the angel as he journeys back to his homeland

and prepares to face his brother Esau (Gen. 32.23–33); the second tells of God's attempt on Moses' life, as Moses and his family journey back to Egypt to help free the Israelites. These two narratives bear remarkable similarities to each other (Westermann 1984, 517). Each involves an attack by a superhuman being during the night as the hero returns to the land of his birth and prepares to face his destiny. Each attack, as we shall see, ends with a mark on the male genitals: in the first case those of Jacob, in the second, those of Moses' son. [. . .]

It is no longer tenable to assume that these myths originated in non-Israelite contexts[17] and reflect primitive religious notions simply because they do not fit preconceived images of monotheism (Eilberg-Schwartz 1990; 1991). Moreover, even if these stories could have derived from pre-Israelite traditions, it is striking that two such similar stories have been preserved and that the attack in question was ascribed to God or to a divine being. Something about these stories struck a chord in the religious culture of Israel and led Israelite narrators to attribute the attacks to God

Israel's Unmanning

Recall the story of Jacob wrestling with the divine being on his return to Canaan (Gen. 34.23–33). When dawn began to break and the being 'saw that he had not prevailed against him, he wrenched Jacob's hip at the socket (kap-yĕrēkô), so that the socket of his hip was strained as he wrestled with him.' The narrator tells us that this is why the children of Israel do not eat the 'thigh muscle (gîd hannāšeh) that is on the socket of the hip (kap yĕrēkô).'

It is confusing as to who prevails in this contest.[18] The struggle obviously goes on all night. While the angel is able to injure Jacob, Jacob is still able to wrest a blessing from his opponent. Moreover, the angel recognizes Jacob's success in the name Israel, which is interpreted in this narrative at least to mean 'He has prevailed against beings divine and human.' But Jacob leaves the struggle with a limp and is unable to discover the being's name, and he himself does not say he prevailed, but that his life was preserved, describing it as a stand-off rather than a victory. In fact, the name Israel may originally have meant 'and God prevailed' (Sarna 1989).

Most interpreters understand the injury to Jacob to refer to some part of his leg, the thigh muscle or sciatic nerve. But there are several indications that Jacob was actually struck on the genitals, as S. H. Smith (1990) has now argued quite convincingly.[19] The divine being touched 'the hollow of the loins' (kap yĕrēkô). The thigh or loins is frequently a euphemism for the penis. Jacob's offspring, for example, are said to spring from his thigh (Gen. 46.26; Exod. 1.5). Recall also the oaths taken by placing the hand 'under the loins' (Gen. 24.2, 9; 47.29). The reference to the thigh muscle (gîd hannāšeh) in the Jacob story may be a reference to the penis. Smith also suggests that the word 'heel' with which Jacob's name is associated is sometimes a euphemism for the genitals, as it is in Jeremiah 13.22: 'It is because of your great iniquity that your skirts are lifted up, your heels exposed.' Here 'heels' is an obvious reference to genitals, consistent with the use of the foot more generally as a euphemism (Judg. 3.24; 1 Sam. 24.4; Isa. 6.2, 7.20, 47.2). Smith suggests that when Jacob is imagined as grabbing the heel of

Esau in the womb, a pun may be involved. In grabbing Esau's genitals, the story signals Jacob's future usurpation of Esau's birthright, that is, the right to be the genealogical father of Israel.

What could be the significance of this genital injury? Smith argues that 'by striking Jacob on the *kap hyerek* (inside of the thigh) God was asserting his sovereign power over Jezreel's (Israel's) procreative power. But once Jacob had acknowledged God's strength as supreme, God allowed him to inherit the Abrahamic promise, so that children sprang freely from the very loins over which God had asserted his dominance' (1990, 469).[20] Smith also notes that this injury to Jacob's genitals occurs just as he sets off to claim what by rights belongs to Esau. 'It is only by recognizing the carnal limitation of his own procreative power that Jacob, as heir apparent to the covenantal promise, is allowed to inherit the promise in reality. By striking Jacob, symbolically, upon his genitals God demonstrates that only he has the power to bring Jacob's aspiration to fruition' (472).

Smith's analysis is compelling, but there is more to be said about the symbolism of Jacob's injury. It is important to realize that Jacob has already fathered 11 of his 12 children before he is struck on the genitals. The mark on the genitals therefore cannot refer to his future virility. If it symbolizes potency at all, it is an acknowledgment that God was responsible for Jacob's past fatherhood, that he controls the continuation of Jacob's line. More significant, then, is the submission marked by this genital injury.

It is critical to note that the injury coincides with Jacob's assertion of his masculinity. Jacob begins his life as a 'mama's boy.' Unlike his brother Esau, who is born hairy and who is a hunter of game, Jacob is smooth skinned and stays at home (Gen. 25.27). Indeed, Jacob's femininity is underscored by his fleeing to Haran and marrying his matrilineal cousins, Leah and Rachel, the daughters of his mother's brother. Actually, Rachel and Leah are not only Jacob's maternal cousins but also distantly related patrilineal cousins, a point of significance, as we shall see. Initially, however, the narrative mentions only his maternal connection to these women, underscoring his association with his mother. Eventually, Jacob realizes that his uncle is taking advantage of him and he decides to return to his homeland. Jacob's break with Laban is the beginning of his self-assertion and reclamation of his own identity. Laban overtakes him. They build a mound and pillar to mark their treaty with one another. Laban swears that if either of them violates the treaty 'may the God of Abraham and the God of Nahor . . . judge between us' (Gen. 31.53). Nahor was the brother of Abraham, Jacob's paternal grandfather, so when Laban swears in the name of Abraham and Nahor, he is singling out the two men who link him to his nephew patrilineally (Jay 1988; 1992, 94–111). In this way, he marks his male connection with Jacob and ceases to consider him merely as his sister's son. Thus, as Jacob starts to reclaim his masculinity, as he takes control of his future and heads back to face Esau, perhaps risking his life, his matrilineal connection is abandoned and his patrilineal descent recognized. He is ready to become father of Israel.

Jacob for his part swears an oath by 'The *Pahad* of Isaac.' This cryptic expression is generally interpreted to be a name for God, and *pahad* is normally translated as 'fear.' But there is evidence that *pahad* may very well be an Aramaic word meaning 'thigh, hip, and loins.' Jacob thus swears by the 'Thigh of Isaac.'

As several interpreters have suggested, this represents another allusion to the oaths which are taken by grabbing a patriarch's genitals.[21] Although Jacob cannot literally grab Isaac's genitals, since his father is not present, he swears by them, indicating his own willingness to assume the obligations of the patrilineage (Eilberg-Schwartz 1990, 169–70). Jacob will later ask his son Joseph to take an oath in the same way (Gen. 47.29). By figuratively grabbing the genitals of the father, the son takes on the responsibility of the father's genealogy.

In short, Jacob has become an independent young man, no longer controlled by his uncle or afraid of his brother. He is ready to take up the obligations of manhood, and it is only after this decision that he is attacked by the angel. Significantly, he has already had one encounter with the divine that has left him unscathed. In the story of Jacob's dream, Jacob simply sees God at the top of the ladder with angels ascending and descending. But as soon as he is recognized as a man, he must be marked on the genitals, signifying his submission to God. Jacob only becomes Israel through an act of partial emasculation. Or to put it another way, the entity 'Israel' only comes into being at the moment of emasculation. The story of Jacob's wrestling match thus contains within it an inchoate representation of Israel, the collective entity who is to be imagined as God's wife. The narrative ends with the observation that this collective Israel does not eat the 'thigh muscle.'[22] [. . .]

The idea that a man's inability to protect his genitals is a sign of his domination is not limited to the myth of Jacob's wrestling. As we have seen, this is one of the reasons that sons should not see their fathers naked. It is one thing when the father chooses to expose himself for the purpose of making his sons take an oath, quite another when he does not choose. His unwilling exposure is shameful and humbling. The prophets speak metaphorically as well of God exposing Israel's nakedness, which shames 'her' and signifies her domination by other nations (Ezek. 16.37; Hos. 3.11–12; Isa. 3.17). If exposure of the genitals is shameful, the touching or injury of the genitals is that much more humiliating. This explains why a woman is expressly forbidden to grab the genitals of a man who is wrestling with her husband (Deut. 25.11–12). To do so puts her in a position of dominance over her husband's opponent. Even at the moment when her husband may need help, she may not grab the manhood of his opponent. Her husband's safety is less important than his opponent's honor. Significantly, the law does not prohibit her from assisting in some other fashion. If she bangs him over the head, he is not considered dishonored in the same way. The association of domination and circumcision is also present in the story of David's bringing back foreskins of 200 Philistine warriors as payment of a bride price for King Saul's daughter Michal (1 Sam. 18.17–29; 2 Sam. 3.14). David's military prowess alone is not sufficient. He must bring back a piece of his opponents' genitals, signifying their emasculation.

Circumcision itself conveys similar meanings.[23] It is ideally an injury inflicted by the father on the son to signify their submission to God. That circumcision carries such associations is assumed in the story of Dinah's rape in Genesis 34, which follows shortly after the story of Jacob's struggle with the angel.[24] Dinah, the daughter of Leah and Jacob, is raped by Shechem the son of Hamor, the Hivite. Shechem asks Jacob to give Dinah to Hamor in marriage. He suggests that the Hivites and the 'sons of Israel' become one people. But Jacob's sons reply that they cannot do so unless the Hivites circumcise themselves. The Hivites acquiesce to the request, and while they are incapacitated from the operation, Simon and Levi kill them. Interpreters have generally emphasized the ethnic significance of circumcision in this story. The narrative presupposes that belonging to Israel requires circumcision. While that may be true, much more is going on here. Circumcision is also part of the Israelite stratagem here. It is a vehicle for the domination of the Hivites and serves as revenge for the rape and humiliation of Dinah. Where Hamor did violence to Dinah's genitals, Jacob's sons do violence to the Hivites by getting them to injure their own genitals. The rape has been reversed.[25] In other words, circumcision is an eminently appropriate way of unmanning the Hivites and preparing to murder them. What Jacob's sons do to the Hivites, God has done in part to their father, Jacob. Indeed, read as a narrative, one could infer that Jacob's sons got the idea from their father's own injury.

Unmanning Moses

The understanding of circumcision and genital injury prepares us for the story of God's attack on Moses.

> And the Lord said to Moses, 'When you return to Egypt, see that you perform before Pharaoh all the marvels that I have put within your power . . . Then you shall say to Pharaoh, "Thus says the Lord: Israel is My first-born son. I have said to you, 'Let My son go, that he may worship Me,' yet you refuse to let him go. Now I will slay your first-born sons."'
>   At a night encampment on the way, the Lord encountered him and sought to kill him. So Zipporah took a flint and cut off her son's foreskin, and touched his feet with it, saying, 'You are truly a bridegroom of blood to me!' And when he let him alone, she added, 'A bridegroom of blood because of the circumcision.' (Exod. 4.21–26)[26]

There are dozens of ambiguities in this story. Whom precisely is God attacking? Whose feet does Zipporah touch with the foreskin? Is Zipporah touching the feet or the genitals? And what does 'bridegroom of blood' mean?

When this story is read in context, it seems that Moses must be the object of the attack.[27] Moses, after all, is being addressed by God in the preceding verses. There is also an implied parallel between God's threat to slay Pharaoh's first-born and God's attack on Moses. Interpreters have been perplexed as to why God should want to kill the messenger he has just commissioned. And why does circumcision stay in God's hand? Childs (1974, 101), following rabbinic readings, believes the circumcision corrects the fact that Moses never circumcised his son. It was this failure for which Moses was attacked. Robinson (1986, 456) assumes that Moses himself was uncircumcised and what takes place here is his vicarious circumcision. [. . .] God's attack [could also be seen] as an act of retribution against Moses for the manslaughter of the Egyptian taskmaster. The circumcision is an act of propitiation that saves his life.

But another solution to some of these questions emerges by taking seriously the similarity of this story to the attack on Jacob as he is homeward bound.[28] That story involved a threat to the man for whom all Israel would be named. Moses, too, is returning to his homeland to take up his obligations to God's people. He is reluctant to do so, protesting that he has a heaviness of lips that makes him an inappropriate spokesman. Rhetorically, the threat to Moses' life serves the same function as Jacob's wrestling with the divine being. It establishes Moses' submission to the deity, that Moses is now at the deity's mercy. God 'sets about showing Moses that although he is safe from other men (Exod. iv 19) he faces a much greater danger to his life in the wrath of the God whom he is so reluctant to serve (iv 14). Like Jacob before him, Moses must undergo a night struggle with his mysterious God before he can become a worthy instrument of YHWH' (Robinson 1986, 459–60).

A genital injury occurs at the end of each of these divine attacks. Jacob's genital injury establishes his submission to God and occurs at dawn just before the struggle is over. In the case of Moses, it is the genital disfigurement of his son that saves his life. Moreover, it is a woman and not a divine being who is the agent of the injury. Moses' wife Zipporah somehow knows that this is the way to ward off the attack on her husband. Indeed, according to one probable reading of this story, Zipporah takes the foreskin of her son and touches Moses either on the feet or, if feet is a euphemism, on the genitals.[29] Some interpreters see evidence here that Zipporah is performing a Midianite magical practice. Others see the remnant of an Egyptian myth in which the goddess Osiris hovers protectively over the genitals of her dead husband.[30] But what is this story saying about Israel's religious imagination? Certainly, as Robinson suggests (1986, 453), Zipporah's act anticipates the blood that Israelites will later put on the lintels of their house so God will not slay the Israelite firstborn (Exod. 12.23). But it also shows what is symbolically at stake in this attack. If it is Moses' genitals that she touches, then Moses' manhood must already be exposed. God's attack on Moses is in part an attack on his masculinity. This is why circumcision appeases God. The blood of circumcision is a symbolic acknowledgment that a man's masculinity belongs to God. Submitting to God and surrendering one's masculinity amounts to the same thing. The blood of circumcision, like the blood on the doorposts, is a sign to God that he should pass over Israelite men and not take their lives. In turn, it is a reminder to Israelite men that as men of God they belong to their father in heaven.[31]

Zipporah's prominence in performing the act of circumcision is striking, especially when viewed against the backdrop of ethnographic studies of circumcision. Typically, circumcision is a male bonding ceremony in which fathers or uncles are responsible for initiating men into adulthood. Furthermore, circumcision is often a rite that symbolically rips a boy out of the world of the mother and brings him into the world of men. The same themes are present in the practice of Israelite circumcision as it is articulated in later sources in the Hebrew Bible (Eilberg-Schwartz 1990, 141–76). One need not see Zipporah's centrality here as a survival of a goddess myth from Egypt. Her importance underscores the way in which women's power always potentially threatens to erupt when men encounter a male God. If that encounter is not handled properly, through a sacrifice of human masculinity and a symbolic submission to a dominating male God, then the human male is eliminated. Into the space vacated by her husband, the wife steps to assert her role as a legitimate ritual actor. If men do not submit to God, if they do not take their proper role as God's wives, then the human women are always ready to assume that role.

Zipporah's words underscore the issue of masculinity. 'You are a bridegroom (*ḥātān*) of blood to me.' The term *ḥātān* is sometimes used to mean 'father-in-law,' 'bridegroom,' and 'son-in-law.' In other words, it refers to a relationship that is created through marriage. It is not a genealogical bond. [. . .] One thing, however, is certain. In the attack, Zipporah is in danger of losing Moses to God. 'You are a bridegroom of blood *to me!*' she says. You belong to me, not God. The threat to his life and masculinity is associated with Moses' becoming a man of God. You are not God's wife, you are my bridegroom. This story thus anticipates the tensions that later develop. For Moses does become the wife of God, and his siblings end up protesting 'on behalf of the Cushite woman.'

The ambiguities of this story permit still another reading that has relevance to our analysis. When the myth says that Zipporah touched 'his feet/genitals,' it is possible that this refers to the deity. Touching God with the circumcised flesh of her son's foreskin, she declares, 'You are a bridegroom of blood to me.' On this interpretation, she is telling him to lay off Moses. He is not your wife. I am.[32] And by touching her son's foreskin to God's 'feet,' she identifies God as the father. This myth of God's attack on Moses is thus not altogether dissimilar to the story of the sons of God who have intercourse with the daughters of man. Here, too, the redundancy of the human male is implied and the natural complementarity between divine male and human female is asserted.

The image of Zipporah thus serves two contradictory functions. It indicates the threat men perceive of women stepping into the place they have created. But at the same time, it is an ideal image of an Israelite woman. Israelite women are in danger of losing their men to God. But God will leave their husbands intact if as mothers they condone the genital disfiguration of their sons and acknowledge that Israelite masculinity has been sacrificed to God.

What this analysis suggests is that circumcision was for the ancient Israelites a symbol of male submission. Because it is partially emasculating, it was a recognition of a power greater than man. The symbolism of submission to God is obviously related to the images of the feminization of Israelite men in the Hebrew Bible. Both were symptoms of the same phenomenon. God was acknowledged as the ultimate male and in his presence human masculinity was seen to be compromised and put at risk.

These symbolic associations were never fully articulated in the ancient texts. But what was not fully comprehended in the ancient Israelite religion would become explicit in certain forms of late antique Judaism.

Notes

1 This is in some sense the reverse of the process described by Castelli, who explores the masculinization of women in late antique Christianity. Christian thinkers of that period argued that the female should strive to be more like the male because 'the male embodies the generic human and therefore the potential for human existence to transcend differences and return to the same.' Castelli writes

that 'in the Christian tradition, there is virtually no evidence for the movement across conventional gender boundaries by the "male" toward the "female," except when negatively constructed, as in polemics against homosexuality' (1991, 33).

2 See W. Williams (1986, 144) for more explicit examples of the feminization of the subordinate partner in intimate male relationships defined by heterosexual representations. Bakan (1979, 143, 28) anticipates me in seeing the feminization of Moses. But he understands the mechanism and motivation very differently. In his view, the discovery of paternity led to an association of the father with procreation, making the father into a 'mother.'

3 Milgrom (1990, 89) notes that the term translated as 'nurse' may simply be 'guardian,' since it sometimes is used to refer to a male taking care of children (2 Kings 10.1, 5; Isa. 49.23). Trible (1983, 69), however, suggests that despite the masculine noun the image is of a nurse carrying a suckling child. Milgrom also notes that it is unclear whether Moses is angry with the people or with God or both.

4 The story of Hagar may come from the same E source (Friedman 1987, 247).

5 Noth (1962, 267) and Clements (1972, 225) suggest the priestly elements are later additions and the original is much older. Friedman (1987, 252) attributes the passage to P and thus understands it as serving priestly functions. For discussion of this term and its meaning, see Albright (1944), Morgenstern (1925), and Propp (1987).

6 Gressmann, Jirku, and Auerbach regard the passage as an etiology for the custom of wearing horned ritual masks in ancient Israel (cited in Propp 1987, 382). Similarly, Noth argues, 'the present passage, which says nothing at all about the appearance of this mask, shows that the priest's mask (for Moses here appears in a priestly function) was not totally lacking in Israel even though we can discover no more about the time and place at which it was used' (1962, 267). As is obvious, the historical basis for the existence of such masks is pure speculation. In Hab. 3.4, the description of God seems to use the stem qrn in association with light. Cassuto (1967, 448), Noth (1962, 267), and Clements (1972, 225) favor this translation because it makes no sense to say the skin of the face is horned.

7 One interpreter sees here an attempt to tarnish the image of Moses by priests who trace their line to Aaron (Friedman 1987, 202). But there is no indication that the disfiguration of Moses' face is intended to undermine his status. On the contrary, the narrative presents it as a sign of his intimacy with God.

8 In fact, it derives from a stem that is used only on one other occasion, in an early poem in which it is placed in parallel to the word for clothing (Gen. 49.11) (Brown, Driver, and Briggs 1975, 691).

9 This was one of the most basic insights of structural linguistics (Saussure 1966) and social and structural anthropology (Radcliffe-Brown [1952] 1962; Lévi-Strauss 1963; 1973; 1978) and is widely accepted as a principle of literary and cultural interpretation.

10 After developing this argument, I discovered I had been anticipated by J. Sasson (1968). See also Eilberg-Schwartz (1990, 115–40), on the use of bovine images as foundational metaphors for Israelite ritual.

11 Friedman (1987, 251) assigns this passage to J.

12 Milgrom (1990, 394–5) notes that sexual intercourse is forbidden in the war camp, which is also a place of God's presence. Clements gets closer to the issue: 'The period of hallowing before God appeared required abstinence from normal sexual relationships. This was to preclude any weakening of the vitality which holiness required, and did not imply that such relationships were regarded as opposed to God' (1972, 117).

13 For example, Sarna (1989, 24) views Eve as exaggerating God's prohibition, but does not come to the same conclusion with regard to Moses (Sarna 1991, 106).

14 Friedman (1987, 252) assigns this source to E.

15 There is also a place called Cushan in the Bible, which is a region in Median. The Cushite woman may thus refer to Zipporah's ethic origins (Friedman 1987, 78). But this explanation is problematic too. Moses' marriage to Zipporah occurred much earlier. Why would Aaron and Miriam suddenly protest the marriage now? It hardly solves the problem to assume that Moses left her behind (Milgrom 1990, 93) when he went to Egypt, since we are told she accompanied him back to Egypt.

16 See, for example, Gen. 21.11, which refers to the matter which distressed Abraham greatly 'on account of his son.' See also Biale's (1992, 33–4) and Boyarin's (1994) discussion of the rabbinic interpretation of this passage.

17 See Gunkel, cited in Westermann (1984, 519, 521), and Noth (1962, 49).

18 See, for example, Andersen and Freedman (1980, 607), and Mays (1969, 163).

19 See also Gevirtz (1975, 52–3). Sarna (1989, 162; 1970, 170–1), who notes the euphemism elsewhere, does not draw the conclusion that Jacob was struck on the genitals.

20 Smith's argument dovetails with my own analysis of circumcision (Eilberg-Schwartz 1990, 141–76), in which I explore how circumcision is a symbol of God's promise to Abraham of fertility.

21 Malul (1985) reviews the various interpreters who support this reading and, developing Albright's original proposal, discusses the technical etymological issues involved in interpreting this world. He points out that the whole passage has an Aramaic tinge to it. It should be noted that *pahad* is used to mean 'thigh' in Job 40.17.

22 Nanette Stahl and I, working independently of each other, found that we were arriving at very similar conclusions. Stahl also notes that the term 'thigh muscle' (*gid hannaseh*) derives from a stem (*nsh*) that sometimes means forgetting or oblivion. She observes importance of this allusion to forgetfulness 'given the strong lexical link Hebrew establishes between masculinity and memory in the root z. k. r.' She concludes that the term *gid hannaseh* serves both as a mechanism for 'memorializing Jacob's struggle and creating distance from it. It also hints at the biblical ambivalence towards the relationship between God and Israel that is being inaugurated with that very encounter' (1993, 124).

23 Bakan (1979, 140–4) also notes the connection between circumcision and feminization but understands this as a way of signifying the appropriation by men of women's procreative abilities. Circumcision is one consequence of the discovery of paternity. See also Bettelheim (1962). Bettelheim explores the feminization of circumcision among Australian Aborigines, and views the association of circumcision and menstruation as a symbolic attempt by men to appropriate women's reproductive powers.

24 Friedman (1987, 248) assigns the story to J.

25 Sarna makes a similar point: 'The part of the body used by Shechem in his violent passion will itself become the source of his own punishment!' (1989, 236).

26 Friedman (1987, 250) assigns the story to J.

27 Following Robinson (1986, 455); Childs (1974, 103). Childs also notes that Zipporah's central role implies Moses' incapacitation. Propp (forthcoming) arrives at the same conclusion when viewing this story as part of the J source.

28 As Robinson points out (1986, 451), a number of interpreters have drawn attention to the connection of these stories, including Buber, Fohrer, Hyatt, Kosmala, and

Reinarch. Propp's (forthcoming) claim that Moses is being attacked for his earlier manslaughter does not account for the similarity of this story to the attack on Jacob. Nor does the interpretation that Moses had failed to circumcise himself or his son.

29 See, for example, Robinson (1986, 447); Childs (1974, 103); and Propp (forthcoming).

30 Kosmala (1962). See Pardes's (1992, 91) intriguing comparison to Egyptian myths of Osiris.

31 Pardes, then, is mistaken when she writes that 'it is not a covenant between Yahweh and Moses. If it were, Moses would have had to be defined as Yahweh's bride, given that it is God who traditionally plays the role of bridegroom in the Bible' (1992, 87).

32 This image of Yahweh as a bridegroom of blood has interesting similarities to the image of God adopting the foundling Israel and telling her 'in your blood live' (Ezek. 16.6).

Literature

Albright, W. F. 1944. 'The "Natural Face" of Moses in the light of Ugaritic,' *Bulletin for the American School of Oriental Research* 94:32–5.

Andersen, Francis I. and David Noel Freedman. 1980, *Hosea*. The Anchor Bible Series. Garden City: Doubleday.

Bakan, David. 1979. *And They Took Themselves Wives*. New York: Harper & Row.

Bettelheim, Bruno. 1962. *Symbolic Wounds*. New York: Collier.

Biale, David. 1992. *Eros and the Jews: From Biblical Israel to Contemporary America*. New York: Basic.

Boyarin, Daniel. 1994. *A Radical Jew: Paul and the Politics of Identity*. Berkeley: University of California Press.

Brown, Francis, S. R. Driver and C. A. Briggs (eds). [1907] 1975. *A Hebrew and English Lexicon of the Old Testament*. Oxford: Clarendon.

Cassuto, U. 1967. *A Commentary on the Book of Exodus,* trans. Israel Abrahams. Jerusalem: Magnes.

Castelli, Elizabeth. 1991. '"I Will Make Mary Male": Pieties of the Body and Gender Transformation of Christian Women in Late Antiquity,' in *Body Guards: The Cultural Politics of Gender Ambiguity,* eds Julia Epstein and Kristina Straub. New York: Routledge. Pp. 49–69.

Childs, Brevard S. 1974. *Exodus*. Philadelphia: Westminster.

Clements, Ronald A. 1972. *Exodus*. Cambridge: Cambridge University Press.

Eilberg-Schwartz, Howard. 1990. *The Savage in Judaism: An Anthropology of Israelite Religion and Ancient Judaism*. Bloomington: Indiana University Press.

—— (ed.). 1991. *People of the Body: Jews and Judaism from an Embodied Perspective*. Albany: SUNY Press.

Friedman, Richard Elliot. 1987. *Who Wrote the Bible?* New York: Harper & Row.

Gevirtz, S. 1975. 'Of Patriarchs and Puns: Joseph at the Fountain, Jacob at the Ford,' *Hebrew Union College Annual* 46:33–54.

Jay, Nancy. 1988. 'Sacrifice, Descent, and the Patriarchs,' *Vetus Testamentum* 38/1:52–70.

——. 1992. *Throughout Your Generations Forever: Sacrifice, Religion, and Paternity*. Chicago: University of Chicago Press.

Kosmala, Hans. 1962. 'The "Bloody Husband,"' *Vetus Testamentum* 12:14–28.

Lévi-Strauss, Claude. 1963. *Structural Anthropology*, trans. Claire Jacobson and Brooke Grundfest Schoepf. New York: Basic.

——. 1973. *From Honey to Ashes*, trans. John and Doreen Weightman. New York: Harper & Row.

——. 1978. *The Origin of Table Manners*, trans. John and Doreen Weightman. New York: Harper & Row.

Malul, Meir. 1985. 'More on Pahad Yishāq (Genesis XXXI 42, 53) and the Oath by the Thigh,' *Vetus Testamentum* 35/2:192–200.

Mays, James L. 1969. *Hosea*. Philadelphia: Westminster.

Mellinkoff, R. 1970. *The Horned Moses in Medieval Art and Thought*. Berkeley: University of California Press.

Milgrom, Jacob. 1990. *Numbers*. Philadelphia: Jewish Publication Society.

Mollenkott, Virginia. 1986. *The Divine Feminine*. New York: Crossroad.

Morgenstern, J. 1925. 'Moses with the Shining Face,' *Hebrew Union College Annual* 2:1–27.

Noth, Martin. 1962. *Exodus*. Philadelphia: Westminster.

Pardes, Ilana. 1992. *Countertraditions in the Bible: A Feminist Approach*. Cambridge: Harvard University Press.

Propp, William H. 1987. 'The Skin of Moses' Face—Transfigured or Disfigured?' *Catholic Biblical Quarterly* 49/3:375–6.

Propp, William H. (forthcoming). 'The Bloody Bridegroom,' *Vetus Testamentum*.

Radcliffe-Brown, A. R. [1952] 1965. *Structure and Function in Primitive Society*. New York: Free Press.

Robinson, Bernard P. 1986. 'Zipporah to the Rescue: A Contextual Study of Exodus IV 24–6,' *Vetus Testamentum* 36/4:447–61.

Sarna, Nahum. 1970. *Understanding Genesis*. New York: Schocken.

——. 1989. *Genesis*. Philadelphia: Jewish Publication Society.

——. 1991. *Exodus*. Philadelphia: Jewish Publication Society.

Sasson, Jack. 1968. 'Bovine Symbolism and the Exodus Narrative,' *Vetus Testamentum* 18:380–7.

Saussure, Ferdinand de. 1966. *Course in General Linguistics*. New York: McGraw-Hill.

Smith, S. H. 1990. '"Heel" and "Thigh": The Concept of Sexuality in the Jacob-Esau Narratives,' *Vetus Testamentum* 40/4:464–73.

Stahl, Nanette. 1993. 'The Flawed Liminal Moment: Between Law and Narrative in the Bible' (Ph.D. diss.). University of California, Berkeley.

Trible, Phyllis. 1983. *God and the Rhetoric of Sexuality*. Philadelphia: Fortress.

Westermann, Claus. 1984. *Genesis* (3 vols), trans. John J. Scullion. Minneapolis: Augsburg.

Williams, Walter. 1986. *The Spirit and the Flesh: Sexual Diversity in American Indian Culture*. Boston: Beacon.

15

Sex and the Single Savior

Editor's Introduction

At the turn of the century, Albert Schweitzer wrote in *The Quest of the Historical Jesus* that 'there is no historical task which so reveals a man's true self as the writing of a Life of Jesus.' 'No vital force,' he continued, 'comes into the [Jesus] figure unless a man breathes into it all the hate or the love of which he is capable. The stronger the love, or the stronger the hate, the more life-like is the figure which is produced' (1910, 4). We already encountered Schweitzer's dictum in Graham Ward's theological rejection of assigning any particular sexuality to Jesus Christ (chapter 9), arguing, with Schweitzer, that such attempts tell us more about the erotic proclivities of the interpreter than Jesus' sexual nature. Dale Martin, a professor of New Testament, would have no disagreement on this point, although he offers a different hermeneutic conclusion on the question of the singularity of Jesus' sexuality.

In the chapter below, Martin introduces four distinct fields of the religious imagination that profess to know Jesus' sexuality: the patristic, the historic, the popular and the gay imagination. In each case, the quest for imagining Jesus' body comes with claims of historical accuracy; such claims, however, are less the result of historical reliability and more of sexual values of particular imaginations.

From early on, Christians were occupied with understanding the sensuous and sexual body of Jesus. Gnostic Christianity, for example, perceived the body of Jesus as accidental, a shell merely, that contained pure spirit. Such a body would neither suffer the pain of crucifixion nor enjoy the pleasures of sexuality – as a matter of fact, the famous Gnostic teacher Valentinus went so far as to imagine Jesus eating and drinking, but not defecating (see Meeks 1993, 137). Incarnational theology, on the other hand, believed in the 'real human flesh of the incarnate God' (Miles 2005, 4), and hence assumed that Jesus Christ would have been exposed to the same desires and pains as other human beings (though simultaneously freed from the corruption and necessities of the flesh). Incarnational theology became the accepted position in Christianity, and for the faithful it seemed only natural and reasonable to wonder how Jesus may have inhabited his male body. What could one possibly say about Jesus' manliness? How do the Gospels and early Christians portray him as a man? (See Moore and Anderson 2003; Green 1999; Loughlin 1998; Cline 1998; and Sean Gill, chapter 22.)

Almost every Christian epoch fueled anew the imagination: the majestic Christ in the waning Roman Empire and the *pantocrator* in the Byzantine world; the humanized Jesus of Renaissance paintings and the muscular Jesus of the Victorian age; the mangled body of Christ in European paintings after the 1918 war and the revolutionary Jesus of twentieth-century liberation theologies. In a study on religious art in contemporary American culture, David Morgan writes:

> Popular American piety from the second half of the nineteenth century to the first half of the twentieth century explored different experiences of Jesus as male ideal . . . Some viewed Christ as a gentle, effeminate, occasionally even homoerotic friend; other portrayed him as an ethereal, mystical ideal; and still others saw in him a rugged, violent revolutionary. (Morgan 1996, 251; also 1998)

Below, Martin takes a critical-hermeneutical look at the sexual imaginings of Jesus. In earlier works, he has examined gender and property relations in the thought of the apostle Paul, including the body (1990; 1995; on Paul's masculinity, also Mayordomo 2008; Larson 2004; Kahl 2000). He always places his biblical investigations into the larger context of late antiquity (2000; 2004; 2005).

Publications by the Same Author

Martin, Dale B. 1990. *Slavery as Salvation: The Metaphor of Slavery in Pauline Christianity*. New Haven: Yale University Press.

——. 1995. *The Corinthian Body*. New Haven: Yale University Press.

——. 2000. 'Contradictions of Masculinity: Ascetic Inseminators and Menstruating Men in Greco-Roman Culture', in *Generation and Degeneration: Tropes of Reproduction in Literature and History from Antiquity to Early Modern Europe*, eds Valeria Finucci and Kevin Brownlee. Durham: Duke University Press. Pp. 81–108.

——. 2004. *Inventing Superstition: From the Hippocratics to the Christians*. Cambridge: Harvard University Press.

——. 2006. *Sex and the Single Savior: Gender and Sexuality in Biblical Interpretation*. Louisville: Westminster John Knox.

Martin, Dale B. and Patricia Cox Miller (eds). 2005. *The Cultural Turn in Late Ancient Studies: Gender, Asceticism, and Historiography*. Durham: Duke University Press.

Further Reading

Cline, David J. A. 1998. '*Ecce Vir*: or, Gendering the Son of Man', in *Biblical Studies/Cultural Studies*, eds J. Cheryl Exum and Stephen Moore. Sheffield: Sheffield Academic Press. Pp. 352–75.

Green, Elizabeth. 1999. 'More Musings on Maleness: The Maleness of Jesus Revisited'. *Feminist Theology* 20:9–27.

Kahl, Brigitte. 2000. 'No Longer Male: Masculinity Struggles behind Galatians 3:28'. *Journal of the Study of the New Testament* 79:37–49.

Larson, Jennifer. 2004. 'Paul's Masculinity'. *Journal of Biblical Literature* 123/1:85–97.

Loughlin, Gerard. 1998. 'Refiguring Masculinity in Christ', in *Religion and Sexuality*, eds M. A. Hayes, W. Porter and D. Tombs. Sheffield: Sheffield Academic Press. Pp. 405–14.

Mayordomo, Moisés. 2008. 'Konstruktionen von Männlichkeit in der Antike und der paulinischen Korintherkorrespondenz'. *Evangelische Theologie* 68/2:99–115.

Meeks, Wayne A. 1993. *The Origins of Christian Morality: The First Two Centuries.* New Haven: Yale University Press.

Miles, Margaret R. 2005. *The Word Made Flesh: A History of Christian Thought.* Oxford: Blackwell.

Moore, Stephen D. and Janice Capel Anderson (eds). 2003. *New Testament Masculinities.* Atlanta: Society of Biblical Literature.

Morgan, David. 1996. 'The Masculinity of Jesus in Popular Religious Art,' in *Men's Bodies, Men's Gods*, ed. Björn Krondorfer. New York: New York University Press. Pp. 251–66.

——. 1998. *Visual Piety: A History and Theory of Popular Religious Images.* Berkeley: University of California Press.

Schweitzer, Albert. 1910. *The Quest of the Historical Jesus: A Critical Study of its Progress from Reimarus to Wrede*, trans. W. Montgomery. New York: Macmillan.

Sex and the Single Savior

DALE B. MARTIN

Jesus has been a figure of ambiguous sexuality. The vast majority of books about him have simply not raised the question of his sexuality. Was he married? Was he either accidentally or intentionally celibate? If he wasn't married, does that mean that he never experienced sexual intercourse? Did he experience sexual desires? If not, why not? If so, of what sort? Perhaps our traditions about Jesus include no reference to a wife or girlfriend because he simply was not attracted to women. Perhaps he found men sexually attractive. And of course I can't stop raising such questions without raising the question: Should we raise such questions?

Actually, I am less interested in Jesus' sexuality than in questions about whether or not that is a legitimate question and in how answers to such questions should be attempted. Is it illegitimate to raise questions about Jesus' sexual desires and activities? Some might argue that even to raise the question of Jesus' sexuality is to introduce anachronism. But who says anachronism is wrong? Why? Only if one is 'playing by the rules' of modern historical criticism can anachronism even be raised as a delegitimizing factor. Why should a modern person, a modern Christian or non-Christian, be worried about anachronism?

Once we have decided we are content that questions about Jesus' sexuality or singleness are admissible questions, though, we then must confront the problem of how to go about answering the questions. Most people have come to believe modern scholars, who mostly assume (they don't argue for it) that any possible right answers to questions about Jesus' sexuality will have to be settled by careful historical research. One of the purposes of this chapter is to challenge that assumption. I will pay attention to historical criticism, but only to situate it among several different interpretive methods. I will also attempt to highlight the weaknesses of historical criticism even when it is allowed to play by its own rules. I will show for one thing that history can give us no secure answer to the question of Jesus' singleness and sexuality. But I will also show that even the answers it can give are only the products of its imagination and have no right to delegitimize the answers supplied by other interpretive methods.

Though the number of possible interpretive methods that could theoretically be applied to my question is infinite, I will concentrate on just four: the popular imagination, the historical imagination, the patristic imagination, and the gay imagination. I want to make it quite clear that I privilege *none* of these imaginations. In fact, one of my most important points is that all of them *are* 'imaginations' that contemplate the singleness of Jesus in different ways, applying different criteria as to what will constitute a suitable answer within their own interpretive contexts. What I want to argue is that the day of the hegemony of historical criticism should be over. I am assuming for the most part a Christian interest in Jesus. And I am urging scholars to entertain the possibility—quite seriously—that several different ways of reading the Bible should be learned, taught, and practiced in the contemporary church and academy.

The Popular Imagination

First, the 'popular imagination.' The lack of clarity in Christian sources about Jesus' sexuality has left all sorts of avenues open for speculation in popular imagination. The Jesus of the novel and film *The Last Temptation of Christ*, to take just one example, is famously conflicted about sex and desire.[1] Not that he experiences much conflict about sexual orientation. He's fairly certain that he wants Mary and not Judas or the boys. The *Last Temptation* refers to Jesus' desire to live a completely 'normal' life of heterosexual fulfillment and family, if not with Mary alone, perhaps with more than one woman and several children. The struggle of Jesus here is against the very oddness or singularity to which he feels himself called. The premise of both the book and the film is that any departure from heterosexual coupling is abnormal. Jesus is queer only in that he feels that he must resist those very normal desires, and in the fact that he does indeed in the end resist them, as he must in order to become our Savior.

The huge popularity of the more recent novel by Dan Brown, *The Da Vinci Code*, adequately testifies to the hunger of the popular imagination for a rigorously heterosexual Jesus. As is thoroughly well known by now, the novel portrays a conspiracy to keep secret the 'historical fact' that Jesus and Mary Magdalene were sexually involved and produced offspring. Many people may have been offended by the notion, though it seems that many more have been intrigued and titillated. I'm sure many other New Testament scholars, as I have, have been inundated by questioners eager to have the novel's 'historical facts' confirmed. *The Da Vinci Code* is so captured by heterosexual normativity that it even turns the male 'Beloved Disciple' of the Fourth Gospel into a female Mary. The Jesus who would be acceptable to most modern Americans, of course, may indeed have been intimate with a disciple who *appeared* to be male, as long as he/she is 'truly' a woman.[2]

For alternatives to the heterosexual normativity of *The Last Temptation, The Da*

Vinci Code, or any of a number of other popular imaginations about Jesus, we may point to a few recent depictions, mainly in theatrical plays, in which Jesus is shockingly gay—shocking, that is, if we are to believe the tone of newspaper reports and protesters that often accompany the openings of such plays.[3]

But even in the popular imagination Jesus' sexuality is seldom unambiguous. Take *Jesus Christ Superstar*.[4] Here we have a Jesus, especially in the film version, who is a bit too mousey and vacillating to fit a decent American or British stereotype of muscular heterosexuality. He sings in a high, squeaky voice, swishes a bit too much in his gauzy, white gown, and seems as ambivalent in his erotic expressions toward Mary as he does toward Judas. Though Jesus in the film is caressed mostly by female camp-followers, both women and men writhe and moan as they wallow in the problem of not knowing 'how to love him.' Mary and Judas compete with one another in a duet of affective confusion. *Jesus Christ Superstar* is perhaps a bit more obvious than most in its portrayal of Jesus' ambiguous sexuality, but it is just one instance of the pervasive uncertainty in the popular imagination over what to do about Jesus' desires and possible sex lives.

Let's step back and note some underlying assumptions in the popular imagination about Jesus. We could even call these 'rules' of interpretation since they are like tacitly honored social agreements about what will count as a good as opposed to a bad understanding of Jesus' sexuality and singleness. First there is the assumption that Jesus *had* sexuality.[5] If the Gospels are relatively silent about Jesus' sexual desires, that need not preclude the popular imagination from wondering about it and supplying any missing information. But this is perfectly understandable: in our modern world, sexuality is everywhere, so why not in Jesus? To many modern persons, a man who experienced no sexual desire at all would not be a man. We *may* be able to imagine people who deny or control their desires and remain celibate. But not to experience desire at all renders someone, in our world, so abnormal as to be practically nonhuman. Thus, the popular imagination takes Jesus' humanity seriously.[6] In fact, it has been a regularity of popular treatments of Jesus to focus on his humanity, so they must imagine what his sexuality must have been. Second, we see that *most* of the time Jesus' sexuality is rigidly heterosexual, at least when it is made explicit in the portrait. If Jesus is agonized about sexuality, as he is in *The Last Temptation of Christ*, he must certainly be agonized about his desire *for women*. But we should also not be surprised when the portraits of Jesus show cracks in his heterosexual façade with the result that he comes across—even in those contexts in which he is ostensibly heterosexual—as sexually ambiguous. He is sometimes a bit effeminate; he seems to enjoy the company of his male disciples a bit more than some would think 'normal.' Thus, at least in three ways, the popular imagination reveals its own rules of interpretation: it must admit the constant reality of sexual orientation and desire; it must be dominated by assumptions about heterosexual normativity; and it must not be able completely to control the excess of sexuality within heterosexual normativity or to exclude homoeroticism.

The Historical Imagination

The previous examples represent, though, popular imagination. In the modern world, historical criticism has usually presented itself as the method that can overcome random diversity of interpretation and capriciousness of meaning. History, so the assumption has gone since the beginning of the modern period, can bring security of meaning—even perhaps singularity of meaning. With that modern goal of consensus of interpretation in mind, it is striking that there is so little consensus among biblical scholars about Jesus' sexuality and what to do with it. In the first place, the vast majority of scholars writing about the historical Jesus say absolutely nothing about his sex life or desires. In fact, one gets the feeling that the topic is for most of them rather embarrassing. When John Meier, as one of a very few, decides to address the question, he almost sheepishly admits that 'the mere act of asking whether Jesus was ever married will strike some readers as imprudent, others as vulgar, and still others as blasphemous' (Meier 1991, 332).[7] Apparently in our culture it is considered a bit radical, or perhaps only impolite, to raise questions about Jesus' sex life.

One scholar has in fact targeted that very embarrassment in his critique of traditional Christian notions about sexuality and his own argument that Jesus was probably married and experienced a 'normal' sex life. William E. Phipps has argued that within Judaism of Jesus' day, celibacy was rarely tolerated. Judaism required that Jewish men be married and engage in heterosexual intercourse. In Phipps's reconstruction, Judaism had a 'healthy' view toward sex in contrast both to surrounding Greco-Roman tendencies and to the later church (Phipps 1973; 1986). Thus it is almost certain that Jesus would have been married and sexually active.

In spite of Phipps's pretensions to objectivity freed from 'the distortion of sexuality in the Christian tradition,' his own historical imagination is quite limited. For one thing, as we will see, his view of ancient Judaism is simply inaccurate. But a more glaring error is Phipps's assumption of heterosexual exclusivity. At the beginning of his treatment of the sexuality of Jesus, for instance, he says that he will deal with 'the entire gamut of male-female relations' (Phipps 1973, 11). What about male–male relations? Or female–female relations—not to mention the variety of permutations and combinations we could otherwise imagine? Phipps therefore presents himself as advocating unbiased scholarship, untainted by traditional Christian neuroses about sexuality. But in the end he seems able to imagine only a Jesus who is 'normal,' that is, 'heterosexual.'[8]

Other scholars have pointed out the errors in Phipps's claims about ancient Judaism and have argued that in all likelihood Jesus was celibate. John Meier surveys Jewish texts from the Second Temple period and notes different Jewish groups and individuals who apparently practiced sexual asceticism for a variety of reasons. The Qumran community, he says, probably included at least some Jews who were celibate, though discerning precisely their reasons for avoiding marriage is difficult. Perhaps they held to a 'Sinai-covenant theology that demanded sexual abstinence in preparation for encounter with God (cf. Exodus 19.15).' Or they intended their actions as extending the rules for priestly purity to the entire community, 'which was a living temple worshipping God in the company of the angels.' Or perhaps they avoided sex as preparation for a holy war they expected to participate in along with heavenly powers arrayed against cosmic powers of evil. And it is possible, he admits, that basic misogyny, as is reflected in descriptions by Josephus and Philo, may have motivated the Qumran Jews, at least in part. In any case, Meier concludes that celibacy was practiced 'among certain marginal Jewish groups' (1991, 338–9).[9]

After rejecting some possible motivations for Jesus' choice of celibacy (priestly purity, holy-war ideology, misogyny) Meier guesses that Jesus may have intended his celibacy to be a puzzle to his contemporaries: 'Mirroring his parabolic speech, and like his easy fellowship with the socially and spiritually marginalized in Palestine, his celibacy was a parable in action, an embodiment of a riddle-like message meant to disturb people and provoke them to thought—both about Jesus and about themselves.'[10]

Dale Allison comes to similar conclusions.[11] After surveying different forms of ancient Jewish sexual renunciation, Allison suggests five different reasons for Jesus' celibacy. First, his dedication to his eschatological mission and the demands it would have made on its preachers discouraged marriage. Second, Allison notes that asceticism in millenarian groups sometimes is seen to separate the participant from 'the present world order,' often itself conceived as corrupt and corrupting.[12] Third, Jesus and his disciples offered their renunciation of the normal societal supports as rhetorical persuasion intended to convince others of the reality of their message that God himself would completely take care of their needs (Allison 1998, 206). Fourth, Jesus and his disciples intended their own renunciation as a prophetic, symbolic act of judgment on those who preferred to live lives of luxury and comfort.[13] And finally, their avoidance of sexual intercourse and family was a reflection of their belief that the coming eschatological society was already beginning to break into the current world through their own actions.[14] In opposition, therefore, to those who insist that Jesus must have been a 'normal' man who expressed his sexual desires and tendencies by the 'normal' means, Allison and Meier argue that in all probability Jesus was celibate, and that since the 'normal' in his society was defined at least in part by marriage and family, he was in this case not only single, but also singular.[15] He wasn't really 'normal' after all.

Neither Meier nor Allison (nor the vast majority of scholars) even entertains the possibility that Jesus may not after all have been sexually attracted to women. Meier, for example, believes that Jesus was not married and that this was a 'radical sacrifice' on his part. Is this so obvious? Meier's reconstruction is dependent on his assumption in the first place that Jesus did experience strong desires for sex, marriage, and family, and in the second place that those desires were heterosexual. Allison offers five different explanations for Jesus' celibacy (which raises the question of how satisfying a historical explanation can be that offers *five different* hypotheses)—and Allison never raises questions about Jesus' *desires*. Meier and Allison have made Jesus into an abnormal man with regard to his celibacy but a normal heterosexual with regard to his desires. In fact, if Phipps gives us a Jesus who is a normal heterosexual, Meier and Allison give us a Jesus who is an *abnormal* heterosexual: Jesus is heterosexual in his desires, yet he doesn't *act* on those desires. Jesus is singularly sexual: a queer heterosexual.[16]

Of course, there have been scholarly reconstructions of a very different sort, the most famous perhaps being Morton Smith's suggestions, based on the fragments of the so-called *Secret Gospel of Mark*. In one of the fragments Jesus raises a young man from the dead, causing the young man to 'love' Jesus deeply. In the other quotation, the young man is said to come to Jesus by night, naked except for a linen robe. Jesus spends the night with the young man, apparently initiating him into mysteries of esoteric knowledge.[17] Smith suggested that the fragment constituted evidence of ancient accounts of naked initiatory rites performed by Jesus himself with select male disciples, and Smith did not demur from opining that some homosexual activity may have constituted part of those initiations (Smith 1973a; 1973b).[18] Whatever one may think of Smith's hypothesis, one must admit that it would solve some conundrums. The significance of the naked young man in the canonical Gospel of Mark is just one such problem. Perplexing parallels between the Gospels of Mark and John constitute another. And the Jesus of Smith's reconstruction would go a long way toward explaining why Jesus may have never married.

I have no interest in arguing for any of these different proposals for Jesus' sexuality. I find certain assumptions undergirding each of them difficult to accept. What is more interesting for my purposes is how they illustrate what has been imaginable at different times with regard to the sexuality of Jesus—and what has been apparently unimaginable.

Nor do I believe that just practicing historical criticism more rigorously will clear up the ambiguity of Jesus' sexuality. Let us attempt, for the sake of illustration, a couple of thought experiments. First, let's argue the case for Jesus as a sexual ascetic. Christian tradition, including the evidence of the earliest Gospels, almost unanimously portrays Jesus without a wife or children. Furthermore, several sayings in the tradition imply that Jesus may have been nonmarried and maybe even a sexual ascetic, the main ones being the saying about eunuchs from Matthew (19.10–12) and the saying about the angels in heaven not being married (Mark 12.18–27 and parallels). From these and a few other hints, we *could* fairly postulate that Jesus was not married and that he was probably a sexual ascetic.

But in that case, Jesus must have been a very queer one. As I've mentioned, we now know of several different forms of Jewish asceticism current in Jesus' day. But Jesus fits none of them. The asceticism of the Dead Sea Scrolls, for example, is heavily implicated in their concerns about purity and the Temple, fastings, strict Sabbath observance, and obedience to a strictly interpreted Torah. Essenes also rejected the use of oil for anointing; bathed with cold water before meals and after relieving themselves; wore white clothing; enforced extreme physical modesty and dietary moderation; rejected animal sacrifice; and avoided the contemporary Temple cult. We find none of these concerns in the early Jesus movement.

To cite another example of Jewish asceticism, the sexual renunciation of Jewish Nazirites was pursued so that the ascetic might attain a 'priestly level of holiness' by avoiding, in the words of Steven Fraade, 'wine, grape products, contact with the dead, even of one's immediate family, and cutting of one's hair' (Fraade 1990, 213–23). Jesus seems to have been well-known for *not* avoiding wine or grape products; he had no compunction about physical contact with the dead; and though he seems at times to have avoided his family, he avoided them when they were alive and showed no concerns about their deaths at all; we have no hint that Jesus avoided cutting his hair, Hollywood and the history of Western art notwithstanding.

We could mention other examples, such as the 'Therapeutai' as described by Philo (*De vita contemplativa*), or, closer to home as far as Jesus was concerned, the asceticism of John the Baptist. But the impression in any case is that *if* Jesus was a Jewish ascetic, he can be fitted into *none* of the forms of Jewish asceticism known to us from his day. In almost every case, sexual asceticism is accompanied by dietary asceticism and the avoidance of wine or feasting. Usually, ascetics fast. Often, they withdraw to establish an uncontaminated life apart from normal culture. Asceticism often occurs as an intensified version of normal Torah observance. Most importantly, Jewish asceticism is almost always linked to heightened concerns for purity, often with the Temple playing a central role. In contrast, Jesus shows few concerns about purity or the Temple cult;[19] if Jesus taught anything about Torah, it was apparently a rather more liberal than strict interpretation; Jesus was apparently not an ascetic with regard to food or drink; he did not regularly fast or teach his disciples to fast; though he withdrew into the wilderness on occasion, Jesus did not in principle withdraw from society. Thus, though we can now admit that sexual asceticism was indeed practiced by Jews of Jesus' day, what we know about Jesus does not fit any of the forms of ascetic Judaism we know about. If Jesus was a sexual ascetic, he was a queer one.

Perhaps, though, we have here a clue that we are looking in the wrong direction. Since it is so difficult to place Jesus' assumed asceticism in an ancient Jewish context, and the evidence *that* he was a sexual ascetic is so slim (mainly an argument from silence), maybe it is safer to assume that Jesus was *not* an ascetic after all. Perhaps Jesus had nothing against sex and desire—even if he did have much against the ancient household, for which we have much more evidence. Perhaps Jesus never taught that sex itself was to be avoided. After all, a historical Jesus that so badly fits his environment may be too *queer* for good historiography. In other words, even when we play by the rules of modern historiography, we don't end up with satisfactory answers about Jesus' singleness—even by the standards of modern historiography: one of the central rules of modern historiography is that things must fit their historical context, that 'absolutely unique' entities in history must be viewed as suspect in their historical reconstruction. A celibate Jesus, if constructed according to our available evidence, does *not* fit his historical context well, yet we have no evidence that Jesus was anything *but* single, again by normal historiographical criteria of what counts as 'evidence.'

The Patristic Imagination

We've again ended up with a Jesus of ambiguous sexuality. Though we've searched through the popular imagination and the historical imagination, we've come up with nothing but a Jesus of uncertain sexuality. What if we turn our attentions to the writings of the early church fathers? May we find more secure answers in the Jesus of what we may call 'the patristic imagination'?

After all, I would think that the people who should be most concerned about the sexuality of Jesus would be Christians. And I would think that Christians would have little reason to allow modern historiography the right to settle the meaning of Jesus' desires. Invoking the Christian commitment to the 'communion of the saints' should imply, I think, that the voices of earlier Christians should be given at least as much attention as the relatively recent methods and opinions of modernism. So what can we discern about the sexuality of Jesus by reading the Fathers?

In spite of a very few early Christian voices to the contrary (Carpocratians, Manicheans?),[20] all the fathers who come to be accepted as 'orthodox' are agreed that Jesus was celibate. But that doesn't mean that the *meaning* of Jesus' celibacy was unambiguous or without problems.

First, it is remarkable that there is a noticeable reluctance among the Fathers to use Jesus as a *model* for celibate life.[21] Cyril of Jerusalem, for instance, as do many others, points to the *suffering* of Jesus as a model for Christian imitation, but when he wants a model for celibacy and virginity, he points to other Christians.[22] Basil the Great speaks of the imitation of Christ that is necessary for 'perfection of life' but does not mention celibacy; rather, he is thinking of Christ's gentleness, lowliness, long-suffering endurance, and death.[23] And Tertullian points to Christ as an example for Christian fasting—even though there is little portrayal in the Gospels of Jesus as fasting.[24] When the Fathers want an example of virginity, they much more often point to Mary as the model.[25]

In fact, Christ plays the role more often of the bridegroom than as a model for the celibate (see, for example, Elm 1994, 118–20). Tertullian rather confusingly uses Christ as a model both for virgins and for married persons, in the latter case to enforce one-time marriage. Christ, just like Adam 'before his exile,' was 'entirely unwedded,' 'entirely pure,' and can therefore serve as a model for virgins. But 'in spirit' Christ is a monogamist, 'having one church as his bride, according to the figure of Adam and Eve.'[26] Thus, as a virgin Christ is a model for virgins, as a monogamist he is a model for married persons. We end up with a rather queer Christ who is both a celibate virgin and a loyal husband.

Modern Christians may find many reasons to be less than enthusiastic, therefore, about the sexuality of Jesus as interpreted in the patristic imagination. And they may be even more uncomfortable when they pay attention to the *meaning* of Jesus' asceticism as interpreted by the Fathers. According to Gregory of Nyssa, the central issue in Christian conformity to Christ lies in his *apatheia*, his lack of passion, the absence of (the vice of) passion and desire.[27] Furthermore, Christ must have been perfect, and thus our model for perfecting ourselves. In the sexual ideology assumed by Gregory, sex represents lack or passion (that is, susceptibility to change), and thus Christ must not have been able to experience sex, any more than he could have experienced lack, change, and imperfection. Is this the meaning of sexuality that the church today wishes to promote?

Again, I must pass over other important patristic views about sex, such as the almost universal idea that even if marriage is not to be condemned, it is not equal to the 'higher calling' of virginity, or sentiments such as Origen's when he insists that Christians not pray in bed because that is where 'defiling sex' takes place.[28] The patristic imagination, in any case, much like both the popular imagination and the historical imagination, leaves modern Christians with more uncertainties and problems regarding the sexuality of Jesus than answers. Is there really anything here modern Christians should want to imitate? Is freedom from desire a Christian goal? Should we accept a hierarchy in which virginity is considered superior to sexual connection? Should sex be interpreted as signifying 'lack' and 'imperfection'? Do we want to promote detachment from the world and immutability as the highest virtues? And should we go along with the Fathers in viewing sex as defiling?

The Gay Imagination

With all this ambiguity surrounding Jesus' sexuality—whether in the popular imagination, the historical imagination, or the patristic imagination—is it any wonder that the gay imagination can so easily find a Jesus for itself? What happens if we read the Gospels through the eyes of the male homoerotic gaze? We may note, for starters, that there is practically no place in the Gospels where Jesus is said to 'love' a woman in particular The closest is when the Fourth Gospel tells us that Jesus loved Martha, her sister, and Lazarus (John 11.5), perhaps a *ménage à quatre*? Jesus' attraction to specific men, on the other hand, is explicit. Though he at first treated the 'rich young ruler' a bit abruptly, Jesus then 'looked on him and loved him' (according to Mark 10.21).[29] Even the people standing around surmised from Jesus' weeping that he must have loved Lazarus a great deal (John 11.36). And of course there is 'the disciple whom Jesus loved,' who is regularly close to Jesus, who lies practically on top of him at his last dinner, whom Jesus loves so much that he seems unwilling to allow him even to die (13.23–25; 21.20–22). For those unable to imagine anything erotic going on here, just consider what people would think if we took the 'beloved disciple' to be a woman (as has in fact been imagined, presumably by heterosexuals); in that case, most people wouldn't be able to resist the consequent erotic imaginings.[30] Finally, we have Jesus' last discussion with Peter in the Fourth Gospel, in which Jesus teases and flirts with Peter like a school girl: 'Do you *really* love me? Really? Really? Then prove it!' (21.15–19).

There are other sites of the sensual in the Gospels, but always with regard to men (is it significant that these occur almost entirely in John, the most homoerotic of the Gospels?). Thomas is invited to penetrate the holes in Jesus' body (John 20.24ff). Jesus dips his 'little piece' (*psômion*) in the gravy and places it in the hand of Judas (John 13.26). And though Jesus allows a woman to wash his feet (and we biblical scholars—who know our Hebrew—recognize the hint), when it is his turn, he takes his clothes off, wraps a towel around his waist, and washes the feet of his *male* disciples, again taking time out for a special seduction of Peter (John 13.1–11).[31] In contrast, when Mary later wants a hug, Jesus won't let her even touch him (John 20.17). (Jesus' *noli me tangere* is the Gospel version of Paul's homosocial slogan 'It is better for a man not to touch a woman'; 1 Cor. 7.1).

As these references imply, we needn't think of Jesus as actually 'having sex' (whatever *that* means these days) in order to see him as erotic and sexual. Any sexually experienced person knows that the most intense eroticism may be had by denying oneself consummation. Flirtation, titillation, intimacy, love taken to the edge of orgasm, are often sexually more intense than mere intercourse. May that explain the intensity of Jesus' passion? *If* we take him to be an ascetic after all (though, as we've seen, that is not at all certain), do we nonetheless see in him the erotic passion and desire of the sexually charged ascetic? But in that case *again*, Jesus is certainly not a normal man—not even a 'normal' *gay* man. He ends up again looking very singular—very queer.

The Nonfoundationalist Predicament—or Possibility

We have no direct and certain epistemological access to the 'real' Jesus. The popular imagination, the historical imagination, the patristic imagination, the gay imagination—all find both possibilities and limitations in what they are able to imagine concerning the sexuality of Jesus. That is perhaps not a matter of debate. What may be a matter of debate, though, are the two points I want to stress the most.

First, all of these different methods of interpretation are indeed 'imaginings.' We scholars and seminarians have all been taught by our training as modern exegetes that historical criticism, if not the only way to read texts, is the one method to which all other readings must bow. We may be willing to allow a preacher in a pulpit a few flights of allegory, narrative inventiveness, or modernizations, but in the end those fanciful interpretations must submit themselves to the more serious, secure, scholarly findings of historiography. This historiography need not be totally predictable or monolithic. Many exegetes, for example, have increasingly realized how difficult, if not impossible, it is to ascertain the 'author's intention' of 2,000 years ago—not to mention the fact that for biblical texts we often do not know who the author is (other than saying that the author is 'God,' which introduces fresh problems for discerning authorial intention). Even historical critics therefore have opened their minds enough to allow that perhaps attention to the author should be supplemented or even replaced by attentions to the ancient readers, or at least what we may imagine to have been the plausible understandings of ancient readers of the text. In other words, the reader's interpretations may have supplanted the author's intention in some contemporary interpretation, but in that case it is the *ancient* reader who is the criterion for better or worse interpretations. Most modern historical reconstructions still claim the right to judge between better and worse readings. I am insisting that that claim is theoretically naïve and theologically suspect. Moreover, historical critics should stop pretending that their own constructions of the text's meaning are any less 'imaginative' than any other. They just use a different kind of imagination.

My second crucial point is that *none* of these different imaginations can offer compelling reasons to claim the position of hermeneutical hegemony over the others. In other words, I am not advocating that the patristic imagination be allowed to displace the modern hegemony of historical criticism with a new hegemony of patristic criticism. Nor do I want to substitute the gay imagination for historical criticism or patristic interpretations. I see the nonfoundationalist (postmodern?) world of biblical criticism as one in which many different interpretive methods will vie with one another for our attentions, and in which students will not be considered well trained until they have been trained in several exegetical imaginations and until they demonstrate an ability to negotiate the labyrinth of the text (or the hypertext of the text) using several different reading strategies and different hermeneutical theories. In other words, I'm not in favor of letting 'narrative' criticism or 'canonical' criticism or any other one approach command center stage. In the nonfoundational hermeneutical world, there is no center stage.[32]

People who have not listened to me carefully when I have talked about this topic have sometimes thought that I was basically arguing for a 'gay' Jesus as the 'real' Jesus. Nothing could be a more egregious misunderstanding of what I am about. I am rather interested in shining a spotlight on several aspects of biblical interpretation. For one thing, I am making the uncontroversial point (at least it should be now uncontroversial) that all interpretation is subjective and interested, that people's interpretations of texts, even those about Jesus, are a product of who they are and where they live. Thus people come up with all sorts of ways to imagine the sexuality of Jesus. And of course that has a great deal to do with what they find imaginable about sex. As is the case with so many instances in all interpretation, how people interpret the sexuality of Jesus tells us more about the meaning of sex *for them* than for some 'real' Jesus freed from interpretation.

My other point, though, may be a bit more controversial. I refer to my insistence that there is nothing necessarily wrong with the fact that people interpret the Bible in many different ways and come up with widely varying Jesuses. It is part of the history of Christian interpretation—part of the way Christians have always made sense of their own sex and their very singular Savior. What makes my nonfoundationalist stance different from the foundationalism of modernism is my insistence that we can be no other way. We should learn from the facts of our contingency. If we need a hermeneutical theory at all (and perhaps we don't need one at all), we must come up with one that gives up on the search for security in interpretation in foundations outside the interpretive process itself. There is nothing 'out there' to referee our varying and even conflicting interpretations. There is nothing 'in the text' that can play the role of judge among us.

We have a right to think about the sex of Jesus, the sexuality of Jesus, the desires of Jesus, the singularity of Jesus. What none of us has a right to do, I am arguing, is to insist that he or she will supply *the* method of interpretation that will bring imagination to an end and silence the imaginations of others. For me, the sexuality and singularity of Jesus are significant issues. But the much more important issue is the question of interpretation itself in a nonfoundationalist world.

Notes

1 The motion picture was produced by Barbara De Fina, directed by Martin Scorsese, and released in 1988 by Universal Pictures and Cineplex Odeon Films. *The Last Temptation of Christ* (trans. P. A. Bien; New York: Simon & Schuster, 1960) is the English translation of *Ho Teleutaios Peirasmos* by Nikos Kazantzakis.

2 Dan Brown, *The Da Vinci Code* (2003). Much of the popularity of the novel, quite probably, is due to the false assertions made by the author that some of its

most controversial claims are actually based on historical 'fact' and good scholarship. That so many of these 'facts' are easily refuted by any real scholar of history
has meant that a virtual growth industry of books debunking Brown's claims has
also sprung up in the past few years. For a more 'literary' fictional version of Jesus'
heterosexual 'fulfillment' which predates both Kazantzakis and Brown, see the
novella by D. H. Lawrence, *The Man Who Died* (previously titled *The Escaped Cock*
. . . really!) (London: Martin Secker, 1931). In Lawrence's imagination, the crucified
Jesus awakes in the tomb, escapes, travels around, and eventually has a sexual relationship with a young woman in a precinct of the goddess Isis, finally finding in
heterosexual union the fulfillment he had always sought.

3 The appearance of Terrence McNally's *Corpus Christi: a Play* (New York: Grove
Press, 1988) was greeted by protests. For descriptions of the play, the protests, and
other similar events, see Goss (2002, 138–9, 171–6).

4 The film *Jesus Christ Superstar*, produced by Robert Stigwood and Norman
Jewison and directed by Norman Jewison, was a 1973 motion picture based on the
rock opera of the same name from the book by Tim Rice.

5 I don't mean by this to imply that most conservative, pious Christians assume
Jesus was sexual. As the conservative backlash against different popular treatments
of Jesus' sexuality demonstrate, many more traditional Christians are dismayed,
and sometimes react violently, when Jesus' sexuality is raised, even objecting
when someone points out that Jesus 'had a penis' (see Williams 1992). An interesting counterpoint to this is Leo Steinberg's (1983) argument that renaissance artists
emphasized the sexuality of Jesus, even 'pointing' to Jesus' genitals in paintings
precisely in order to highlight his humanness and even sex. It should be admitted, though, that not everyone has been convinced by Steinberg's interpretations.
Increasingly, in any case, a few voices are calling for Christians to consider the
sexuality of Jesus (his sexual desires and capabilities at least, and sometimes actual
sexual activity): see, for example, Timmerman (1994, 91–104); Beckford (1996).

6 This is precisely the argument H. W. Montefiore put forward many years ago,
apparently greeted by controversy, not only that Jesus' humanity meant that he must
have been a sexual being but also that we must at least entertain the possibility that
homosexual inclinations explain his apparent celibacy. See Montefiore (1968, 101–16,
esp. 109). The point about Jesus' full humanity is also made by Nancy Wilson, who
argues for a bisexual Jesus using arguments similar to those of Montefiore: *'it is very
important to deshame the fact that Jesus, as part of his humanness, part of the concept of
incarnation, was sexual'* (1995, 147; emphasis in original).

7 I find it interesting that when members of the 'Jesus Seminar' were polled
about the sexuality of Jesus, according to a report by Robert Funk, Roy Hoover,
and the Jesus Seminar, a majority of them said that Jesus was probably not celibate:
'They regard it probable that he had a special relationship with at least one woman,
Mary of Magdala.' See Funk, Hoover, and the Jesus Seminar (1993, 220–1). I find it
telling that heterosexuality was the majority assumption. I also wonder whether
this may be one indication [. . .] that the Jesus Seminar may not be representative of
the guild of biblical scholars as a whole.

8 For another such argument that Jesus must not have taught celibacy because
that would have been unthinkable in Judaism of his day, which commanded
marriage, see the work of a journalist (not a biblical scholar), Craveri (1969, 260).

9 Meier notes other sources that may shed light on the motivations or meanings of Jesus' own singleness. He mentions Jewish prophets such as Jeremiah, John
the Baptist, and others who molded themselves on 'the recycled Moses figure,' all

of whom may have avoided sexual relations as a result of experiencing a 'radical alteration' of their lives due to reception of divine revelation: 'The alteration, this being set apart by and for God's Word, is embodied graphically in the rare, awesome, and—for many Jews—terrible vocation of celibacy.' Or put differently, 'an all-consuming commitment to God's word in one's whole life precludes the usual path of marriage and child-rearing' (341).

10 Moreover, Meier thinks it likely that Jesus was motivated by 'his total, all-consuming commitment to proclaiming and realizing the kingdom of God' (1991, 342).

11 Pointing out that asceticism may often be found in movements motivated by eschatological fervor, both in the modern world and the ancient, Allison surmises that certain apparently ascetical statements attributed to Jesus are likely authentic and that Jesus taught sexual asceticism as part of his eschatological message. Jesus praises those who are eunuchs 'for the sake of the kingdom' (Matthew 19.12) 'because the approach of the kingdom requires of them a service that they might otherwise not be able to fulfill. Jesus and other celibates like him . . . have chosen their uncommon condition because, as heralds and servants of the approaching order, it is their primary duty to prepare people for its coming. There can be no time for marriage and children, no time for those consuming responsibilities. This is why, when Jesus calls others to the full-time job of fishing for people, he calls them to abandon their jobs, families, and money.' When in Mark 12.18–27, moreover, where he speaks of the resurrection, Jesus explains that resurrected persons will be like the angels and therefore not marry. So it would be sensible if Jesus and some of his disciples adopted celibacy as present participation in the imminent eschatological state. As Allison concludes, 'Indeed, such an individual might, as did so many Christian celibates later on, interpret his or her forswearing of sex in terms of realized eschatology: if one can make do without intercourse then this might be understood as one way of making present an eschatological circumstance' (1998, 189).

12 Religious celibacy reflects and reinforces 'estrangement from the normal structures of society' (Allison 1998, 204).

13 Their actions were intended as 'a warning that the normal course of things was about to change' (Allison 1998, 208).

14 'Jesus understood chastity as a replay of paradise and thus an anticipation of eschatological existence, in other words, as a proleptic recovery of "the glory of Adam"' (Allison 1998, 208).

15 One factor usually ignored by scholars is the question of the normal age of marriage for men in the ancient Mediterranean. Contrary to modern assumptions, men in the ancient world often did not marry until around the age of 30, for several reasons. First, most demographics of antiquity conclude that there were probably fewer eligible females than males of marriageable age. Men tended to marry much younger females, often even girls. Men of lesser means may have simply lost out in the competition for the fewer eligible females. Moreover, men sometimes put off marriage for financial reasons. In any case, if the Christian traditions about Jesus beginning his ministry around the age of 30 are true, we probably should not expect a man of his age to be already married. For age of marriage, see Lacey (1968, 106, 162, 284n38, 294n27); Hopkins (1965); Shaw (1987); and Saller (1994, 25–41). These studies are of Greek and Roman practices, but I know of no evidence that Jewish practices regarding age of marriage were substantially different.

16 I use the term 'queer' as has become popular in 'queer theory' since the 1990s. See, for example, Comstock and Henking (1997).

17 Though 'Clement' insists in his letter that certain words said by the Carpocratians to be in the text—'naked man upon [or next to, or with] naked man'—were not in the authentic version of the secret Gospel, 'Clement's' version itself is quite homoerotic enough.

18 There have been a very few other authors who have at least appropriated historical arguments to present a Jesus who is erotic with men (they sometimes even use the term 'gay'). See, for some examples, Williams (1992, 116–23) and Goss (2002, 114–22, 134–9).

19 In spite of the misnamed 'cleansing of the Temple' incident in the Gospels, I believe we can produce no firm evidence that Jesus was concerned to reform the Temple service.

20 See, e.g., Augustine, *On the Good of Marriage* 21 (26).

21 It sometimes does happen. Tertullian, for example, cites both Christ and Paul, though briefly, as examples to demonstrate the 'preference for continence' (*On Monogamy* 3). Gregory of Nazianzus speaks of both Christ and Basil as personal examples of virginity as well as promoters of it (*Panegyric on Basil* 62). But even though Jesus is used (rather oddly, sometimes) as a model, he seldom occurs as a model for Christian celibacy among the 'orthodox' fathers.

22 *Lecture* 13.23; 4.24. Jesus is also offered as an example that Christians should follow the proper 'order of things': 3.14.

23 *On the Spirit (De spiritu sancto)* 15.35.

24 Tertullian, *On Fasting* 8.

25 See Augustine, *De sancta virginitate.*

26 Tertullian, *On Monogamy* 5.

27 See Brother Casimir (1984, 349–79; esp. 354–5, 376).

28 For just one example, see Tertullian, *De sancta virginitate.* Interestingly in this document, given our attention to the way Christ's celibacy is used or not used as a model for Christian behavior, Tertullian treats Christ's virginity as basically the *only* one of his traits that all Christians do *not* imitate! Tertullian makes an important exception to a general *imitatio Christi* with regard to celibacy: see 27–28. For Origen, see references in Oulton and Chadwick (1954, 34–35).

29 In Mark he is just a man; in Matthew 19.20, he is said to be young; in Luke 18.18, he is said to be a ruler; only Mark has the part about Jesus loving him. The 'rich young ruler' is a conflation of all of them.

30 And thus, as pointed out above, the remarkable popularity of Brown's *Da Vinci Code.*

31 The Hebrew word for 'feet' was also a euphemism for 'genitals.'

32 For a clear and brief introduction to 'nonfoundationalism' and its relation to theology, see Thiel (1994) and the 'Introduction' in Martin (2006).

Literature

Allison, Dale C. 1998. *Jesus of Nazareth: Millenarian Prophet.* Minneapolis: Fortress.

Beckford, Robert. 1996. 'Does Jesus Have a Penis? Black Male Sexual Representation and Christology,' *Theology and Sexuality* 5 (September):10–21.

Brown, Dan. 2003. *The Da Vinci Code: A Novel.* New York: Doubleday.

Casimir, Brother. 1984. 'Saint Gregory of Nyssa: PERI TELEIOTHTOS—On Perfection,' *The Greek Orthodox Theological Review* 29:349–79.

Comstock, Gary D. and Susan E. Henking (eds). 1997. *Que(e)rying Religion: A Critical Anthology*. New York: Continuum.

Craveri, Marcello. 1969. *The Life of Jesus*. London: Panther.

Elm, Susanna. 1994. *'Virgins of God': The Making of Asceticism in Late Antiquity*. Oxford: Clarendon.

Fraade, Steven D. 1990. 'The Nazirite in Ancient Judaism (Selected Texts),' in *Ascetic Behavior in Greco-Roman Antiquity: A Sourcebook*, ed. Vincent Wimbush. Minneapolis: Fortress. Pp. 213–23.

Funk, Robert and Roy W. Hoover, and the Jesus Seminar. 1993. *The Five Gospels: The Search for the Authentic Words of Jesus*. New York: Macmillan.

Goss, Robert E. 2002. *Queering Christ: Beyond Jesus Acted Up*. Cleveland: Pilgrim.

Hopkins, Keith. 1965. 'The Age of Roman Girls at Marriage,' *Population Studies* 18: 309–27.

Lacey, W. K. 1968. *Family in Classical Greece*. Ithaca: Cornell University Press.

Martin, Dale. 2006. *Sex and the Single Savior: Gender and Sexuality in Biblical Interpretation*. Louisville: Westminster John Knox.

Meier, John P. 1991. *A Marginal Jew: Rethinking the Historical Jesus*, vol. 1. New York: Doubleday.

Montefiore, H. W. 1967. 'Jesus, the Revelation of God,' in *Christ for Us Today: Papers Read at the Conference of Modern Churchmen, Somerville College, Oxford, July 1967*, ed. Norman Pittenger. London: SCM Press. Pp. 101–16.

Oulton, John Earnest Leonard and Henry Chadwick (eds). 1954. *Alexandrian Christianity: Selected Translations of Clement and Origen: with Introduction and Notes* (Library of Christian Classics, vol. 2). Philadelphia: Westminster.

Phipps, William E. 1973. *The Sexuality of Jesus: Theological and Literary Perspectives*. New York: Harper & Row.

——. 1986. *Was Jesus Married? The Distortion of Sexuality in the Christian Tradition*. Lanham: University Press of America.

Saller, Richard. 1994. *Patriarchy, Property and Death in the Roman Family*. Cambridge: Cambridge University Press.

Shaw, Brent. 1987. 'The Age of Roman Girls at Marriage: Some Reconsiderations,' *Journal of Roman Studies* 77:30–46.

Smith, Morton. 1973a. *Clement of Alexandria and a Secret Gospel of Mark*. Cambridge: Harvard University Press.

——. 1973b. *The Secret Gospel: the Discovery and Interpretation of the Secret Gospel According to Mark*. New York: Harper & Row.

Steinberg, Leo. 1983. *The Sexuality of Christ in Renaissance Art and in Modern Illusion*. New York: Pantheon Books.

Thiel, John E. 1994. *Nonfoundationalism*. Minneapolis: Fortress.

Timmerman, Joan H. 1994. 'The Sexuality of Jesus and the Human Vocation,' in *Sexuality and the Sacred: Sources for Theological Reflection*, eds James B. Nelson and Sandra P. Longfellow. Louisville: Westminster John Knox. Pp. 91–104.

Williams, Robert. 1992. *Just As I Am: A Practical Guide to Being Out, Proud, and Christian*. New York: Crown.

Wilson, Nancy. 1995. *Our Tribe: Queer Folks, God, Jesus, and the Bible*. San Francisco: HarperSanFrancisco.

16

Biblical Interpretation as a Technology of the Self: Gay Men and the Ethics of Reading

Editor's Introduction

The gay male gaze is, as Dale Martin suggests in the previous chapter, one possibility of the religious imagination, though it, like other imaginations, does not provide a definitive answer about the historic Jesus. In this chapter, Ken Stone picks up on a related theme, asking questions about gay readings of biblical stories, here particularly of the Hebrew Scriptures/Old Testament. But rather than *gazing at* biblical texts (recall that 'gazing' fixes power relations; see chapter 10), Stone argues for an ethical relationship to the act of reading from a gay perspective. The difference could be described thus: whereas a gay male gaze (or *any* gaze for that matter) would claim a certain power over a text and also assume a stable gender identity, an 'ethics of reading' posits a dynamic interrelation between the interpretation of a biblical text and the formation of a gay self. Reading is seen as a practice that has an effect on the creation of the self – the self might become partially transformed through reading and, as the self transforms, new interpretive possibilities might open up, which, in turn, can open up new experiences for the self.

If this sounds 'Foucaultian', it is, and Stone acknowledges the influence of the French philosopher, particularly his concept of the 'technologies of the self.' Rather than reading the self as autonomous, the self is constituted by different practices, including practices of knowledge (among which one can count 'reading') and religious practices. In a 1980 lecture at Dartmouth, Foucault argued that religious practices are

> techniques which permit individuals to effect, by their own means, a certain number of operations on their bodies, on their souls, on their own thoughts, on their own conduct, and this in a manner so as to transform themselves, modify themselves and to attain a certain state of perfection, of happiness, of purity, and of supernatural power, and so on. (Quoted in Carrette 2000, 149)

Stone proposes that reading and interpreting biblical texts can be understood as a religious practice and that, as such, can transform and modify the reading subject. In the case of gay men, Stone argues that once the practice of reading coheres with the experiences of gay men as a marginalized group, they may actually find joy and strength in the homiletic, liturgical, exegetical and hermeneutical appropriations of biblical texts.

Stone has contributed to the discussion of homosexuality and the Bible in the past (1995; 1997). Rather than entering the debate between straight and gay Bible scholars that 'still fiercely rages over interpretative control of the biblical text' (Goss 2002a, 240), Stone addresses deeper hermeneutical problems related to the reading of biblical texts. In his recent scholarship, Stone has moved decidedly in the direction of queer studies, especially with *Practicing Safer Texts* (2005; also 2001; Goss 2002b; Moore 2001, 7–18).

In this chapter (first published in 1997), he discusses Comstock's *Gay Theology Without Apology* (1993) as an entry into his 'ethics of reading':

> As we might put it in the context of biblical interpretation, new subjects are constituted when biblical texts are read in new ways . . . The 'technology of the self' is thus not so much about the discovery or liberation of one's 'true' self but, rather, about the creation and recreation of the self in its variable relations with itself, with others, and with the world.

Publications by the Same Author

Stone, Ken. 1995. 'Gender and Homosexuality in Judges 19: Subject-Honor, Object-Shame?' *Journal for the Study of the Old Testament* 67:87–107.

——. 1996. *Sex, Honor and Power in the Deuteronomistic History*. Sheffield: Sheffield Academic Press.

——. 1997. 'The Hermeneutics of Abomination: On Gay Men, Canaanites, and Biblical Interpretation'. *Biblical Theological Bulletin* 27:36–41.

—— (ed.). 2001. *Queer Commentary and the Hebrew Bible*. Cleveland: Pilgrim; and Sheffield: Sheffield Academic Press.

——. 2005. *Practicing Safer Texts: Food, Sex and Bible in Queer Perspective*. London and New York: T&T International.

——. 2007. '"You Seduced Me, You Overpowered Me, and You Prevailed": Religious Experience and Homoerotic Sadomasochism in Jeremiah', in *Patriarchs, Prophets and Other Villains*, ed. Lisa Isherwood. London: Equinox. Pp. 101–09.

Further Reading

Carrette, Jeremy R. 2000. *Foucault and Religion: Spiritual Corporality and Political Spirituality*. London and New York: Routledge.

Comstock, Gary David. 1993. *Gay Theology Without Apology*. Cleveland: Pilgrim.

Goss, Robert E. 2002a. *Queering Christ: Beyond Jesus Acted Up*. Cleveland: Pilgrim.

——. 2002b. 'Homosexuality, the Bible, and the Practice of Safe Texts', in *Queering Christ*, Robert Goss. Pp. 185–203.

Moore, Stephen D. 2001. *God's Beauty Parlor: And Other Queer Spaces in and around the Bible*. Stanford: Stanford University Press.

Biblical Interpretation as a Technology of the Self: Gay Men and the Ethics of Reading

KEN STONE

The question of 'the ethics of reading' has been pressed at the intersection of two trends in contemporary biblical studies. Scholars influenced by liberation movements insist upon the ethical and political consequences of biblical interpretation (e.g. Schüssler Fiorenza 1988) while scholars influenced by literary theory acknowledge the role of reading in the production of meaning (e.g. Fowler 1991). The call for an integration of these trends, trends which we might designate, respectively, a focus on 'ethics' and a focus on 'reading,' has become increasingly common in biblical scholarship (see e.g. Jobling 1990; Weems 1991; Bible and Culture Collective 1995; Segovia and Tolbert 1995). Nevertheless, the two developments do not necessarily entail one another, and efforts to relate them often generate controversy.

Consider, for example, the proposal to focus upon 'some of the ways in which women reading *as* women can engage the biblical text' (Newsom and Ringe 1992, xviii; emphasis in original). Schüssler Fiorenza points out in response to this proposal that, apart from a feminist consciousness or method, 'reading *as a woman* does not produce a critical or liberating interpretation of the world.' Indeed, she cautions that such terminology may both 'reinscribe the cultural myth of femininity and womanhood' and evade differences that exist among women (Schüssler Fiorenza 1993, 14; also 1992, 4). In making this point, Schüssler Fiorenza forces biblical scholars to confront the difficulties associated today with the term 'essentialism' (see Fuss 1989). While some biblical scholars grapple with 'the ethics of reading' by locating readers in terms of their identity or experience, claims about an essential identity or common experience can elide differences which cut across the identity or experience in question (cf. Tolbert 1995a, 264–8; Bible and Culture Collective 1995, 241–4). At the same time, a recognition of this fact raises questions about the effect of critiques of identity and experience on those who have never been granted a legitimate identity and experience.[1] Hence, it may be useful to reformulate the question raised by critiques of essentialism in the following manner: What strategies for resistance remain when the identities and experiences which might serve as rallying points *for* resistance are *themselves* interrogated by a 'hermeneutics of suspicion' (Schüssler Fiorenza 1984, 15–18)?

The present essay examines this question in relation to gay male readers of the Bible.[2] At a time when biblical scholars claim 'that even in centres of institutional power there are no longer any arbiters of what may and may not be legitimately and fruitfully said about our texts' (Clines and Exum 1993, 13), I suggest that a confrontation between gay male readers and the discourse of biblical scholarship can be, indeed, 'fruitful.' Unfortunately, biblical scholars have managed to ignore almost entirely the production of knowledge taking place under such rubrics as lesbian and gay studies and queer theory.[3] An analysis of this lack of familiarity might itself be relevant to the question of the ethics of reading, for, as Eve Sedgwick notes, 'ignorance effects,' like effects of knowledge, can be deployed strategically in relation to power (1990, 4–8).

My argument, however, focuses on the possibility that reading strategies for marginalized readers (among whom I include gay men) need *not* entail the assumption that a monolithic identity, already in place prior to the moment of reading, simply precedes interpretation and leads necessarily to particular meanings. Rather, I wish to suggest that the subject of biblical interpretation does not only precede but is also formed, in part, through practices of reading. In order to speak about the gay male subject of biblical interpretation in this manner, I turn to Foucault's late work on the technology or practices of the self. I will not, however, comment on Foucault's corpus as a whole or discuss the many controversies that surround it (Dreyfus and Rabinow 1983; McNay 1992; 1994; Cook 1993; Castelli 1991). And, since part of my argument is that Foucault helps us to clarify *theoretically* developments that are *already taking place* in biblical interpretation, I look first at an example of reading that is in many respects far removed from both my argument and Foucault's work, though it does share with both of those projects the distinction of having been written by a gay male author.

Gary David Comstock devotes much of his book *Gay Theology Without Apology* to the relationship between gay men and biblical texts. Comstock does not ignore the question, 'What does the Bible say about homosexuality?'[4] However, he does go on to ask the very different question, 'What do gay men have to say about the Bible?' In the course of his discussion Comstock asserts at one point that 'we have been in all places at all times' without discussing adequately the problems involved in positing such a 'we' (Comstock 1993, 47). This claim could be criticized on grounds not altogether different from the objections of Schüssler Fiorenza cited above. For if it is difficult to assume that there is a transhistorical, cross-cultural essence of 'woman' shared by all women, it is also difficult to argue that there is an identity or experience shared by all gay men. Indeed, social constructionist analyses of modern concepts of 'the homosexual' indicate that assumptions about the transhistorical, cross-cultural validity of the term 'gay man' are perhaps even more problematic than similar assumptions about the term 'woman.' Even gay scholars often question whether there exists an experience of 'being gay' which can be described in isolation from specific social, historical and ideological contexts (e.g. Halperin 1990; Weeks 1985; 1991; D'Emilio 1983). It is at least clear that all known societies have had some sense of the differentiation of human beings on the basis of gender, whereas it is not at all clear that sexual desire has always and everywhere been a relevant mode of classifying individuals.

Nevertheless, several of Comstock's readings indicate that more is going on in his encounter with the Bible than simply a projection and reification of a presupposed gay identity. His most interesting interpretation in this respect concerns Vashti, the queen who appears in the first chapter of Esther. Comstock does not examine Vashti's story because of any obvious link to homosexuality. On the contrary, the book of Esther never refers to homosexuality; and the only influential gay-affirmative reading of Esther of which I am aware—namely, Sedgwick's treatment of the homosexual closet, discussed in relation to Esther's need to 'come out' as a Jew—mentions Vashti only in passing.[5]

Comstock approaches Vashti by acknowledging his difficulties in finding 'a role model in the Bible—someone to identify with and admire . . .' (1993, 49). Surprisingly, perhaps, Vashti is singled out by Comstock as one such character. When Vashti, summoned by the king, refuses to appear, the king's companions insist that she be punished, for the women of Persia may otherwise emulate Vashti's disobedience (thereby undermining, one supposes, Persian 'family values'). For Comstock, Vashti, 'a feisty, punished Queen,' is a character with whom gay men can perhaps identify. He finds her story to be one 'in which I find myself, in which I find a role model, someone to admire, to get excited about, to root for, to model my behavior after' (51).

Language about biblical characters as 'role models' for contemporary readers may strike the sufficiently disciplined biblical critic as naïve and ahistorical.[6] Nevertheless, it does shift the relation between reader and character from a relation of *being* to a relation of *becoming*. Comstock does not focus, here, on a character who is thought to be *like* gay male readers in any obvious sense.[7] Rather, he focuses upon a character who exhibits qualities toward which Comstock desires gay male readers to aspire. This emphasis on the *transformation* of gay male readers through their *emulation* of Vashti implicitly recognizes that 'gay identity' and 'gay experience' are not clearly identifiable and describable substances surviving unchanged across cultures, texts, and individuals. They are, rather, phenomena which Comstock is helping to create. I hasten to add that, by speaking about the 'creation' of gay identity, I am *not* suggesting that gay male readers are not 'really' gay or, worse, should 'choose' to be or live otherwise. The point is that the precise contours of this category, 'gay man,' are by no means clear, unchanging, or established on the firm foundation of nature or psychological type. They are, instead, being negotiated and renegotiated in a wide range of contexts, including instances of reading such as that performed by Comstock. I would also suggest that the same is true for the supposed opposite of the 'gay man,' namely, the so-called 'straight man' (cf. Katz 1995); that the same is true as well for other identity categories, even those such as race which are often taken as self-evident (cf. Omi and Winant 1994; Mercer 1994; Gates 1985; Davis 1991; Fuss 1989, 73–96; and Anderson 1995); and that this possibility needs to be taken seriously as biblical scholars grapple with the ethics of reading.

Some may object that we have assumed for far too long that readers should model themselves after biblical characters and that types for appropriate behavior exist in the Bible waiting to be emulated. To such an objection one must point out that, in fact, Comstock's interpretation is deviant in several ways, for he willingly transgresses a number of reading conventions. The most obvious of these transgressions has to do with gender. The character chosen as a role model by Comstock, a gay *man*, is a woman; and, while women who read are often encouraged to identify with male characters (cf. Schweickert 1986, 42), it is much less common—and even less frequently encouraged—for male readers to identify with female characters.

Comstock has relatively little to say about gender, but this identification across gender seems to be intentional. His ironic play upon Vashti's characterization—she is not just any woman, but a 'Queen'—is clearly aimed at an audience familiar with the social code whereby gay men are associated, though not unproblematically, with the so-called 'feminine' gender. A 'Queen,' after all, is a term widely used among gay men to refer to themselves, and often connotes not only male homosexuality as such (indeed, sexual activity is seldom at stake when the term is deployed) but also a particular style of life which willfully, even playfully, upsets expectations about gender identity and performance. Such language is not necessarily, and certainly not in Comstock's case, a reinforcement of traditional gender roles and stereotypes *for women*. Since, as Judith Butler argues, the 'institution of a compulsory and naturalized heterosexuality requires and regulates gender as a binary relation in which the masculine term is differentiated from a feminine term' (1990, 22–3), Comstock's reading can be read as a challenge to the ways in which such an institution is reinforced when male readers are discouraged from identifying with female characters. Comstock's identification with Vashti might therefore be considered a 'transgressive reinscription' (Dollimore 1991, 3) of the terms in which sex and gender are usually cast.

Indeed, Comstock's identification with Vashti does not ignore, but is rather based upon, a critical recognition of male dominance. Comstock admires Vashti precisely because she resists the order of the king; and this resistance signifies as resistance in relation to a patriarchal context. What Comstock valorizes as a gay man is not Vashti's characterization as a woman, but rather her characterization as a woman who resists patriarchy. In making Vashti the object of emulation, Comstock is not, I think, trying to deny gender. Rather, he is renegotiating his relation to the constraints and structures of his own context, repositioning himself over against the conventional authorities of that context just as Vashti repositions herself over against the king.

Moreover, Comstock transgresses not only the convention of gender identification but also that convention of reading which asks the reader to admire those characters which the dominant perspective within the narrative seems to admire. There are, after all, two queens in the text, and it is the second of these queens, Esther, who was probably intended as a model for readers. As Sidnie Ann White suggests, Esther's skillful maneuvering in a situation of relative powerlessness may represent something like 'the paradigm of the diaspora Jew, who was also powerless in Persian society,' a 'role model' for those 'seeking to attain a comfortable and successful life in a foreign society' (White 1992, 126). Thus, rare as it might be for male readers to identify with female characters, the book of Esther seems to invite such an identification in the case of Esther herself. Comstock, however, focuses upon Esther's 'foil' (White 1992, 127), acknowledging all the while that his chosen role model 'was not intended as a model for my or anyone else's liberation' (Comstock 1993, 56). He thus transgresses the norm of authorial intention not on the basis that such an intention cannot be known but, rather, on the basis that such an intention, even if inferred, may not be liberating.

Comstock is therefore led by his reading practice into a confrontation with certain ideas about biblical authority. In this respect his hermeneutic is rather different from the hermeneutic of those gay readers (e.g. Boswell 1980, 91–117) who argue that the negative evaluation of homosexuality that is based upon biblical texts is actually a product of post-biblical interpretation. Comstock is quite critical of such an apologetic approach to the biblical text, pointing out that 'biblical stories revolve largely around the concerns and control of powerful men and those who serve them' (1993, 51). Comstock, who is also the author of an analysis of violence against lesbians and gay men and of the biblical texts used to justify such violence (1991), knows that the Bible can be, in Mieke Bal's words, 'the most dangerous' book, 'the one that has been endowed with the power to kill' (1991, 14). It is no surprise, then, that he finds it necessary to become what Judith Fetterley calls 'a resisting rather than an assenting reader' (1978, xxii), to emulate the character who is punished for her disobedience while paying little attention to the book's heroes or heroines.

However, this difference between Comstock's position and the position of gay readers who take a more recuperative approach underscores the fact that there is no single, direct relation between social location and interpretation such that membership within a particular identity category necessarily leads to a particular interpretation. It is obvious that not all gay men read the Bible with Comstock's defiant attitude. Hence, while Comstock's reading can be linked to his self-nomination as gay, it is not a *necessary result* of that self-nomination.

Comstock, like an increasing number of biblical scholars, claims to approach the biblical texts 'from the point of view of my own experience' (1993, 4). Yet such a claim, while important, needs to be reconciled with the suggestion of Teresa de Lauretis that 'experience shifts and is reformed continually, for each subject, with her or his continuous engagement in social reality . . .' (1987, 18). If such engagement includes the practice of reading, then a theory of biblical interpretation must account for experience in a manner that does not simply posit a stable experience acting upon the interpretive process. Such a theory must also recognize that experience is often the *result* of reading, and that human consciousness and subjectivity can be formed and reformed, in part, through the practice of reading. As I have already hinted by calling attention to Comstock's use of Vashti as a 'role model,' Comstock himself implicitly acknowledges that the gay male subject is not (or not only) a pre-supposed subject that pre-exists biblical interpretation. It is also itself being produced by Comstock's reading, and by other readings of Comstock's reading, including my own.

Now in order to account for the most creative aspects of Comstock's reading while avoiding some of the assumptions that lead to the charge of 'essentialism,' and in order to link this account to discussions of 'the ethics of reading,' I suggest that we conceptualize biblical interpretation as one component of what Foucault called the 'technology of the self.' Toward the end of his life, Foucault began to speak less about the production of the subject through its subjection to relations of power and to focus instead upon the creation of the subject through processes of self-formation. This emphasis is referred to by one commentator as 'Foucault's turn toward subjectivity' (Cook 1993). Foucault became interested in those processes 'which permit individuals to effect by their own means or with the help of others a certain number of operations on their own bodies and souls, thoughts, conduct, and way of being, so as *to transform themselves* in order to attain a certain state of happiness, purity, wisdom, perfection or immortality'

(Foucault 1988a, 18; emphasis mine; Foucault 1985a, 367). He called these processes 'technologies of the self.'

Foucault developed his views of 'technologies of the self' through analyses of
the links established in those writings among ethics, modes of sexual conduct,
and conceptions of the self (see Foucault 1985b; 1985c; 1986; 1988a). He claimed
that, in some of these writings, 'the will to be a moral subject and the search for
an ethics of existence were . . . mainly an attempt to affirm one's liberty and to
give one's own life a certain form in which one could recognize oneself' and
'be recognized by others . . .' In contrast to conceptions of ethics which center
around what he called a 'code of rules,' Foucault was interested in uncovering
a different mode of ethical self-constitution. This alternative notion of ethics
caught Foucault's attention 'because, for a whole series of reasons, the idea of
a morality as obedience to a code of rules is now disappearing . . .' (Foucault
1988b, 49).

While Foucault developed his ideas through interpretations of ancient texts,
his research was carried out in relation to what he elsewhere called a 'history
of the present' (1977, 31). He used analyses of ancient texts to demonstrate the
contingency of some of *our* conceptions and to outline a conception of the
ethical subject different from our own. Foucault recognized that ethical self-
constitution always takes place in specific cultural and historical contexts and
that these contexts make particular patterns of self-constitution available to the
individual (see Foucault 1987, 11). He emphatically denied that ancient concepts
and practices could simply be transported into our own century, as is clear from
the following statement:

> The Greek ethics were linked to a purely virile society with slaves, in which
> women were underdogs whose pleasure had no importance, whose sexual
> life had to be oriented toward, determined by, their status as wives . . . The
> Greek ethics of pleasure is linked to a virile society, to dissymmetry, exclusion
> of the other, an obsession with penetration, and a kind of threat of being dis-
> possessed of your own energy, and so on. *All that is quite disgusting!* (Foucault
> 1984, 344, 346, emphasis mine; cf. 1988c)

What Foucault wished to reactivate was not the content of ancient beliefs but,
rather, the emphasis upon a type of ethics by which individuals, through 'intentional and voluntary actions . . . not only set themselves rules of conduct, but
also seek to transform themselves, to change themselves in their singular being,
and to make their life into an *oeuvre* that carries certain aesthetic values and
meets certain stylistic criteria' (1985b, 10–11). [. . .] Foucault also spoke of this
process of ethical self-constitution in terms of 'asceticism,' a word he used not
in the sense of 'self-denial' but, rather, to refer to 'an exercise of self upon self by
which one tries to work out, to transform one's self and to attain a certain mode
of being' (Foucault 1987, 2). He even spoke of a 'homosexual ascesis' as one goal
for the modern gay movement, urging a gay audience (with which he explicitly
identified) to '*work on ourselves* and *invent*, I do not say discover, *a manner of being
that is still improbable*' (1989, 206; emphasis mine).

Foucault connected the technology of the self to 'ethics' by playing upon the
relation between the 'ethics' and *ethos*. *Ethos*, he suggested, 'was the deportment

and the way to behave. It was the subject's mode of being and a certain manner of acting visible to others.' This mode of being was by no means of significance only for the isolated individual. Rather, 'Ethos implies also a relation with others ...' (1987, 6–7).[8] One acts upon and seeks to transform oneself in part by paying careful attention to and working upon one's relations with others; consequently, Foucault can speak of the process as 'an intensification of social relations' (1986, 53). This process involves an endless work, a ceaseless labor, and it is based upon what Arnold Davidson calls 'ethics as ascetics,' a sort of 'moral subjectivation' by which 'we constitute ourselves as moral subjects of our own actions' (1994, 65–6).

The 'technology of the self' is thus not so much about the discovery or liberation of one's 'true' self but, rather, about the creation and recreation of the self in its variable relations with itself, with others, and with the world. As several of Foucault's most perceptive readers note (e.g. Halperin 1995; Cohen 1988; Blasius 1994), this distinction underlies Foucault's comments about the modern gay movement and the constitution of gay male subjectivity. Foucault rejected the notion that sexuality and desire make up that aspect of human existence in relation to which one can decipher, or have deciphered, one's 'true' self (see Foucault 1978). He argued instead for a shift of focus from the discovery of one's *true* self to the constitution of *new* forms of existence:

> Another thing to distrust is the tendency to relate the question of homosexuality to the problem of 'Who am I?' and 'What is the secret of my desire?' Perhaps it would be better to ask oneself, 'What relations, through homosexuality, can be established, invented, multiplied and modulated?' The problem is not to discover in oneself the truth of sex but rather to use sexuality henceforth to arrive at a multiplicity of relationships ... [W]e have to work at *becoming homosexuals* and not be obstinate in recognizing that we are. (Foucault 1989, 203–04)[9]

Foucault's reference to 'becoming homosexuals' has influenced the language of a number of lesbian and gay writers who speak, for example, of 'becoming out' instead of 'coming out' (e.g. Phelan 1994, 41–56; Blasius 1994, 195, 203–04; cf. Cohen 1990). However, neither Foucault nor the lesbians and gay men influenced by him are referring to the etiology of homosexual desire.[10] What Foucault is talking about is the creation of new kinds of subjectivities through new practices, new forms of life, new attitudes, new technologies of the self. As he argues in another interview, 'It's not only a matter of integrating this strange little practice of making love with someone of the same sex into pre-existing cultures; it's a matter of *constructing cultural forms*' (Barbadette 1982, 36; emphasis mine).

Foucault included *reading* as one possible component of the 'technology of the self' (e.g. Foucault 1986, 48, 51), suggesting that what was 'essential' in the reading of a book was 'the experience which the book permits us to have.' The process of reading certain works and writing works of his own was undertaken in part, Foucault insisted, 'to prevent me from always being the same.' He also hoped that *his* readers would be transformed through the reading process, as is clear from the following comments about his use of history:

But the problem isn't that of humoring the professional historians. Rather, I aim at having an experience myself—by passing through a determinate historical content—an experience of what we are today, of what is not only our past but also our present. And I invite others to share the experience. That is, an experience of our modernity that might permit us to emerge from it transformed. Which means that *at the conclusion of the book we can establish new relationships with what was at issue* . . . (Foucault 1991, 33–4; emphasis mine)

The link made here between reading and subjective transformation coheres well with recent proposals that experience and subjectivity are themselves semiotic phenomena; or, as one proponent of such a view puts it, that 'human subjects' are 'not only . . . users of signs but also . . . themselves processes and products of semiosis' (Colapietro 1989, 47). Indeed, the overlap between Foucault's late work and a semiotic concept of the subject has been noted by Teresa de Lauretis in the course of her own attempt to develop a semiotic theory of experience and subjectivity. [. . .] Thus the technology of the self can be linked to, and may be an integral part of, signifying practices such as those discussed more explicitly by [. . .] de Lauretis (cf. 1994a; 1994b; 1984, 158–86).

Biblical interpretation, as one type of semiotic activity, is a technology of the self inasmuch as it is one route by which new experiences of self are created and recreated, 'contingently and continuously,' as de Lauretis insists (1994b, 304–05). It is one of the practices through which we constitute ourselves as ethical subjects, not necessarily in the sense that we must listen to the biblical texts for ethical admonitions, 'a code of rules,' but, rather, in the sense that our very existence as ethical subjects can be effected and modified through our variable interaction with texts which have, for better and for worse, assumed such a powerful position in our culture.

I thus argue that Comstock's use of Vashti's story is an enactment of biblical interpretation as something like a technology of the self. Like Foucault, Comstock is concerned about the formation of ethical subjects in a context where traditional sources of authority (including biblical authority) have been called into question and where new modes of existence must be created. And, like Foucault, Comstock hopes that, as a result of reading, gay men 'can establish new relationships' with something that is 'at issue' (Foucault 1991, 34). What is 'at issue' for Comstock is the traditional negative evaluation of gay men by religious authorities quoting biblical texts. In holding up Vashti and her disobedience, Comstock hopes to encourage resistance to those evaluations among his gay male readers. This resistance does not follow naturally from gay male identity or experience, however, but is an element of the ongoing formation of the gay male subject. Gay male subjectivity does not simply produce, but also emerges from, particular practices, including practices of reading. As Deborah Cook notes in her discussion of Foucault, 'Resistance makes possible new forms of subjectivity. By defining themselves differently vis à vis prevailing social-political norms in disciplinary society, subjects constitute themselves' (1993, 5). As we might put it in the context of biblical interpretation, new subjects are constituted when biblical texts are read in new ways (cf. Chopp 1995, 42–4).

Of course, the conceptualization of biblical interpretation as a technology of the self could account for quite traditional readings as well as non-traditional ones. Foucault noted that technologies of the self can differ from one another in several ways, including 'the kind of being to which we aspire when we behave in a moral way' (Foucault 1984, 355). The kind of being toward which Comstock aspires is, to play on his own words, a non-apologetic gay male subject. Comstock is interested in the transformation, through reading, of a particular group of readers. But this transformation takes place, I suggest, not so much by the recognition and affirmation of a presupposed, coherent experience and identity but, rather, by a *constitution* of experience and identity through the *ongoing construction* of cultural forms and subjectivities. This construction takes place, among other locations, at the site of reading insofar as gay readers are encouraged through their reading to respond to the authoritative sources of 'compulsory-heterosexuality' (Rich 1983) in the manner that Vashti responds to the authority of the king.

Thus, when we evaluate interpretations of biblical texts in relation to 'the ethics of reading,' it is necessary but not sufficient to ask whether such interpretations cohere with or express the experiences of marginalized peoples. We must also ask whether such interpretations open up possibilities for new experiences, new relationships (including new relationships to our religious traditions, as Comstock correctly realizes), and new forms of cultural existence, or, as Foucault might have put it, a new ethos. These experiences, these relationships, and these cultural forms will determine whether it will be possible to effect still more subjective, intersubjective, and material transformations. In this fashion, biblical interpretation as an ethical practice may help us to 'work on' and 'invent' those 'improbable' modes of being that Foucault desired (Foucault 1989, 206), that Comstock is creating, and that our world needs so desperately today.

Notes

1 These questions account in part for the discomfort felt by some feminist theorists with poststructuralist critiques of the subject. See e.g. Braidotti (1987), Benhabib (1995); cf. Tolbert (1995b, 309–11).

2 While gay men and lesbians share much in the context of 'compulsory heterosexuality' (Rich 1983), their problematic relation to the social categories 'male' and 'female' in this context makes it necessary, in my opinion, to consider their *differential* production as social subjects rather than subsuming them under the category of 'homosexuality.' Cf. de Lauretis (1991, iv–xi).

3 That such a production of knowledge does indeed exist is clear from the fact that it is impossible to list more than a small fraction of the relevant sources. To get started, see Abelove, Barale, and Halperin (1993); Warner (1993); de Lauretis (1991); Fuss (1991); and the sources cited in those works and throughout the present essay. The literature is much larger than this and is growing quickly.

4 For an important historical-critical discussion of this question, see Olyan (1994). For my own attempt to treat one aspect of this question in relation to anthropological categories, see Stone (1995).

5 Sedgwick's discussion (1990, 75–82) actually has less to do with the biblical book of Esther than with works by Proust and Racine which use Esther as a pre-text.

6 Lest my ironic use of the term 'disciplined' be misunderstood, I refer my reader to one of Foucault's most important texts (1977).

7 In his reading of the relationship between David and Jonathan (1993, 79–90), however, Comstock does follow such a procedure. This is a convenient point at which to note that *my reading* of Comstock's work is an *interpretation* of what I consider to be the most interesting section of his project, and does not entirely agree with all of his own statements or with all of his other discussions of biblical texts.

8 For a discussion of the 'ethos of lesbian and gay existence' which is explicitly indebted to Foucault, see Blasius (1994, 179–225).

9 Cf. similar statements by Foucault in Gallagher and Wilson (1987).

10 Although he is easily misunderstood on this point, Foucault specifies elsewhere that he has 'absolutely nothing to say' about what his interviewer calls 'the distinction between innate predisposition to homosexual behavior and social conditioning' (Foucault 1988d, 288). Cf. Blasius (1994, 195–6).

Literature

Abelove, Henry, Michele Aina Barale and David M. Halperin (eds). 1993. *The Lesbian and Gay Studies Reader*. New York: Routledge.

Anderson, Victor. 1995. *Beyond Ontological Blackness: An Essay on African American Religious and Cultural Criticism*. New York: Continuum.

Bal, Mieke. 1991. *On Storytelling: Essays in Narratology*, ed. David Jobling. Sonoma: Pole Bridge Press.

Barbadette, Gilles. 1982. 'The Social Triumph of the Sexual Will: A Conversation with Michel Foucault,' *Christopher Street* 6:36–41.

Benhabib, Seyla. 1995. 'Feminism and Postmodernism,' in *Feminist Contentions: A Philosophical Exchange*, ed. Linda Nicholson. New York: Routledge. Pp. 17–34.

Bible and Culture Collective. 1995. *The Postmodern Bible*. New Haven: Yale University Press.

Blasius, Mark. 1994. *Gay and Lesbian Politics: Sexuality and the Emergence of a New Ethic*. Philadelphia: Temple University Press.

Boswell, John. 1980. *Christianity, Social Tolerance, and Homosexuality*. Chicago: University of Chicago Press.

Braidotti, Rosi. 1987. 'Envy: or With My Brains and Your Looks,' in *Men in Feminism*, eds Alice Jardine and Paul Smith. New York: Methuen. Pp. 233–41.

Butler, Judith. 1990. *Gender Trouble: Feminism and the Subversion of Identity*. New York: Routledge.

Castelli, Elizabeth. 1991. *Imitating Paul: A Discourse of Power*. LCBI. Louisville: Westminster John Knox.

Chopp, Rebecca S. 1995. *Saving Work: Feminist Practices of Theological Education*. Louisville: Westminster John Knox.

Clines, David J. A. and J. Cheryl Exum. 1993. 'The New Literary Criticism,' in *The New Literary Criticism and the Hebrew Bible*, eds David J. A. Clines and J. Cheryl Exum. Sheffield: Sheffield Academic Press. Pp. 11–25.

Cohen, Ed. 1988. 'Foucauldian Necrologies: "Gay" "Politics"? Politically Gay?' *Textual Practice* 2:87–101.

——. 1990. 'Are We (Not) What We Are Becoming? "Gay" "Identity," "Gay Studies," and the Disciplining of Knowledge,' in *Engendering Men: The Question of Male*

Feminist Criticism, eds Joseph Boone and Michael Cadden. New York: Routledge. Pp. 161–75.

Colapietro, Vincent Michael. 1989. *Peirce's Approach to the Self: A Semiotic Perspective on Human Subjectivity*. Albany: SUNY Press.

Comstock, Gary David. 1991. *Violence Against Lesbians and Gay Men*. New York: Columbia University Press.

——. 1993. *Gay Theology Without Apology*. Cleveland: Pilgrim.

Cook, Deborah. 1993. *The Subject Finds a Voice: Foucault's Turn Toward Subjectivity*. New York: Peter Lang.

Davidson, Arnold. 1994. 'Ethics as Ascetics: Foucault, the History of Ethics, and Ancient Thought,' in *Foucault and the Writing of History*, ed. Jan Goldstein. Cambridge: Basil Blackwell. Pp. 63–80.

Davis, F. James. 1991. *Who is Black? One Nation's Definition*. University Park: Pennsylvania State University Press.

De Lauretis, Teresa. 1984. *Alice Doesn't: Feminism, Semiotics, Cinema*. Bloomington: Indiana University Press.

——. 1987. *Technologies of Gender: Essays on Theory, Film, and Fiction*. Bloomington: Indiana University Press.

——. 1994a. *The Practice of Love: Lesbian Sexuality and Perverse Desire*. Bloomington: Indiana University Press.

——. 1994b. 'Habit Changes,' in *More Gender Trouble: Feminism Meets Queer Theory*, *differences* 6/2–3:296–313.

De Lauretis, Teresa (ed.). 1991. *Queer Theory: Lesbian and Gay Sexualities*. *differences* 3.2.

D'Emilio, John. 1983. 'Capitalism and Gay Identity,' in *Powers of Desire: The Politics of Sexuality*, eds Ann Snitow, Christine Stansell and Sharon Thompson. New York: Monthly Review Press. Pp. 100–13.

Dollimore, Jonathan. 1991. *Sexual Dissidence: Augustine to Wilde, Freud to Foucault*. Oxford: Clarendon.

Dreyfus, Hubert L. and Paul Rabinow. 1983. *Michel Foucault: Beyond Structuralism and Hermeneutics* (2nd edn). Chicago: University of Chicago Press.

Fetterley, Judith. 1978. *The Resisting Reader: A Feminist Approach to American Fiction*. Bloomington: Indiana University Press.

Foucault, Michel. 1977. *Discipline and Punish: The Birth of the Prison*, trans. Alan Sheridan. New York: Random House.

——. 1978. *The History of Sexuality. Volume 1. An Introduction*, trans. Robert Hurley. New York: Random House.

——. 1984. 'On the Genealogy of Ethics: An Overview of Work in Progress,' in *The Foucault Reader*, ed. Paul Rabinow. New York: Pantheon. Pp 340–72.

——. 1985a. 'Sexuality and Solitude,' in *On Signs*, ed. Marshall Blonsky. Baltimore: The Johns Hopkins University Press. Pp. 365–72.

——. 1985b. *The Use of Pleasure*, trans. Robert Hurley. New York: Random House.

——. 1985c. 'The Battle for Chastity,' in *Western Sexuality: Practice and Precept in Past and Present Times*, eds Philippe Aries and Andre Bejin, trans. Anthony Forster. New York: Basil Blackwell. Pp. 14–25.

——. 1986. *The Care of the Self*, trans. Robert Hurley. New York: Random House.

——. 1987. 'The Ethic of the Care for the Self as a Practice of Freedom,' in *The Final Foucault*, eds James Bernauer and David Rasmussen. Cambridge: The MIT Press. Pp. 1–20.

——. 1988a. 'Technologies of the Self,' in *Technologies of the Self: A Seminar with Michel*

Foucault, eds Luther H. Martin, Huck Gutman and Patrick H. Hutton. Amherst: University of Massachusetts Press. Pp. 16–49.

——. 1988b. 'An Aesthetics of Existence,' in *Michel Foucault*, ed. Kritzman, pp. 47–53.

——. 1988c. 'The Return of Morality,' in *Michel Foucault*, ed. Kritzman, pp. 242–54.

——. 1988d. 'Sexual Choice, Sexual Act: Foucault and Homosexuality,' in *Michel Foucault*, ed. Kritzman, pp. 286–303.

——. 1989. 'Friendship as a Way of Life,' *Foucault Live: Interviews 1966–84*, ed. Sylvere Lotringer, trans. John Johnston. New York: Semiotext(e). Pp. 203–09.

——. 1991. 'How an "Experience-Book" is Born,' in *Remarks on Marx: Conversations with Duccio Trombadori*, trans. James Goldstein and James Cascaito. New York: Semiotext(e). Pp. 25–42.

Fowler, Robert. 1991. *Let the Reader Understand: Reader-Response Criticism and the Gospel of Mark*. Minneapolis: Augsburg Fortress.

Fuss, Diana. 1989. *Essentially Speaking: Feminism, Nature, and Difference*. New York: Routledge.

Fuss, Diana (ed.). 1991. *Inside/Outside: Lesbian Theories, Gay Theories*. New York: Routledge.

Gallagher, Bob and Alexander Wilson. 1987. 'Sex and the Politics of Identity: An Interview with Michel Foucault,' in *Gay Spirit: Myth and Meaning*, ed. Mark Thompson. New York: St. Martin's Press. Pp. 25–35.

Gates, Henry Louis, Jr. (ed.). 1985. *'Race,' Writing, and Difference*. Chicago: University of Chicago Press.

Halperin, David M. 1990. *One Hundred Years of Homosexuality and Other Essays on Greek Love*. New York: Routledge.

——. 1995. *Saint Foucault: Towards a Gay Hagiography*. New York: Oxford University Press.

Jobling, David. 1990. 'Writing the Wrongs of the World: The Deconstruction of the Biblical Text in the Context of Liberation Theologies,' *Semeia* 51:81–118.

Katz, Jonathan Ned. 1995. *The Invention of Heterosexuality*. New York: Dutton.

Kritzman, Lawrence D. (ed.). 1988. *Michel Foucault: Politics, Philosophy, Culture: Interviews and Other Writings 1977–1984*. New York: Routledge.

McNay, Lois. 1992. *Foucault and Feminism: Power, Gender and the Self*. Boston: Northeastern University Press.

——. 1994. *Foucault: A Critical Introduction*. New York: Continuum.

Mercer, Kobena. 1994. *Welcome to the Jungle: New Positions in Black Cultural Studies*. New York Routledge.

Newsom, Carol A. and Sharon H. Ringe. 1992. 'Introduction,' in *The Women's Bible Commentary*, eds Carol A. Newsom and Sharon H. Ringe. Louisville: Westminster John Knox. Pp. xiii–xix.

Olyan, Saul M. 1994. '"And with a Male You Shall Not Lie the Lying Down of a Woman": On the Meaning and Significance of Leviticus 18:22 and 20:13,' *Journal of the History of Sexuality* 5:179–206.

Omi, Michael and Howard Winant. 1994. *Racial Formation in the United States: From the 1960s to the 1990s* (2nd edn). New York: Routledge.

Phelan, Shane. 1994. *Getting Specific: Postmodern Lesbian Politics*. Minneapolis: University Minnesota Press.

Rich, Adrienne. 1983. 'Compulsory Heterosexuality and Lesbian Existence,' *Powers of Desire: The Politics of Sexuality*, eds Ann Snitow, Christine Stansell and Sharon Thompson. New York: Monthly Review Press. Pp. 177–205.

Schüssler Fiorenza, Elisabeth. 1984. *Bread Not Stone: The Challenge of Feminist Biblical Interpretation*. Boston: Beacon.
——. 1988. 'The Ethics of Biblical Interpretation: Decentering Biblical Scholarship,' *JBL* 107:3–17.
——. 1992. *But She Said: Feminist Practices of Biblical Interpretation*. Boston: Beacon.
——. 1993. 'Introduction: Transforming the Legacy of *The Woman's Bible*,' in *Searching the Scriptures. Volume I: A Feminist Introduction*, ed. Schüssler Fiorenza. New York: Crossroad. Pp. 1–24.
Schweickert, Patrocinio P. 1986. 'Reading Ourselves: Toward a Feminist Theory of Reading,' in *Gender and Reading: Essays on Readers, Texts, and Contexts*, eds Elizabeth A. Flynn and Patrocinio P. Schweickert. Baltimore: The Johns Hopkins University Press. Pp. 31–62.
Sedgwick, Eve Kosofsky. 1990. *Epistemology of the Closet*. Berkeley: University of California Press.
Segovia, Fernando F. and Mary Ann Tolbert (eds). 1995. *Reading From This Place: Volume 1: Social Location and Biblical Interpretation in the United States*. Minneapolis: Fortress.
Stone, Ken. 1995. 'Gender and Homosexuality in Judges 19: Subject-Honor, Object-Shame?' *JSOT* 67:87–107.
Tolbert, Mary Ann. 1995a. 'Reading for Liberation,' in *Reading From This Place*, eds Segovia and Tolbert, pp. 263–76.
——. 1995b. 'Afterwords: The Politics and Poetics of Location,' in *Reading From This Place*, eds Segovia and Tolbert, pp. 305–17.
Veyne, Paul. 1993. 'The Final Foucault and His Ethics,' trans. Catherine Porter and Arnold I. Davidson. *Critical Inquiry* 20:1–9.
Warner, Michael (ed.). 1993. *Fear of a Queer Planet: Queer Politics and Social Theory*. Minneapolis: University of Minnesota Press.
Weeks, Jeffrey. 1985. *Sexuality and Its Discontents*. Boston: Routledge.
——. 1991. *Against Nature: Essays on History, Sexuality, and Identity*. London: Rivers Oram.
Weems, Renita J. 1991. 'Reading *Her* Way through the Struggle: African American Women and the Bible,' in *Stony the Road We Trod: African American Biblical Interpretation*, ed. Cain Hope Felder. Minneapolis: Fortress. Pp. 57–77.
White, Sidnie Ann. 1992. 'Esther,' in *The Women's Bible Commentary*, eds Carol A. Newsom and Sharon H. Ringe. Louisville: Westminster John Knox. Pp. 124–9.

Fathers and Sons: Fragments from an Autobiographical Midrash on John's Gospel

Editor's Introduction

Jeffrey Staley's chapter gives us pause to ponder the extent to which biblical exegesis can go. Interweaving his personal relationship with his son with themes about father–son relationships found in the Hebrew Scriptures and the New Testament, Staley blurs styles, genre and methods. Is it exegesis? Is it poetry? Is it a diary? No matter how we like to classify his text, once we allow ourselves to be drawn into his textual world, we become witness to the multi-layered affection of a father as he tries to make sense of his contemporary experience through the lens of the biblical legacy.

Calling Staley's style an 'autobiographical midrash,' as he himself suggests, captures well the flavor of his writing. *Midrash*, the rabbinic mode of studying biblical texts, is a way of not only gleaning exegetical insight from the Torah but also understanding one's daily lives through the lens of Torah.

> The collapsing of time and history that is so characteristic of Midrash . . . should not be viewed as a matter of naïve anachronizing on the rabbis' part or as self-serving exploitation of Scripture for their own ends. Rather . . . bringing their own experiences to the interpretation of the words of Torah, and taking back from the Torah the language that allowed them to articulate their own experiences, the rabbis created a kind of mythical, timeless realm removed from the travails and injustices of contemporary history. (Stern 1992, xx)

The 'collapsing of time and history' as well as the interrelatedness of Scripture interpretation and the comprehension of one's own reality are very present in Staley's writing. Staley does not, however, remove himself from contemporary history (as Stern suggests for the rabbis), but places himself right in the midst of it, whether it is in the doctor's office of a modern hospital or at his son's bedside. Whereas, from a Jewish orthodox stance, midrashic writing has come to a close, Staley finds himself in a tradition of contemporary Jewish authors who continue to use midrash as a creative way of exploring biblical themes (in 1998, for example, a new journal was launched, called *Living Text: The Journal of Contemporary Midrash*). More strongly than traditional midrashic writing, Staley inserts his autobiographical voice, comparable to Alicia Suskin Ostriker's style in *The Nakedness of the Fathers* (1997). Ostriker writes:

Throughout history of the Diaspora, Jewish imagination has flowered through midrash – stories based on Biblical stories, composed not for a narrow audience of scholars, but for an entire community. It is this tradition to which I hope to belong. In midrash, ancient tales yield new meanings to new generations. Not surprisingly, many midrashists today are women . . . [and] I intend . . . to speak across Jewish/Christian boundaries, across male/female boundaries, and across the boundaries that separate past from present. (Ostriker 1997, xii–xv)

Like Ostriker, Staley crosses boundaries, and he does so from a Christian and a male perspective. Conscious of his gender and deliberate in transgressing traditional boundaries, he opens spaces for engaging the gospel with an exegetical style borrowed from Judaism and for directing our attention to the ambiguities of a father's experience.

Not coincidentally, Staley opens with a reference to Abraham and Isaac, the story of a father's attempted sacrifice of his son (Gen. 22), which has caught time and again the midrashic, literary, exegetical and psychological imagination. The story of the Akedah, as Genesis 22 is known in Judaism (Spiegel 1950), has been read in a variety of paradigmatic ways. It has often been used as a model to justify obedience to divine patriarchy and has equally often been criticized for its demand of blind obedience. Critical men's studies tend to read the Abraham–Isaac story as a text of terror for men and interpret its legacy through the lens of child abuse (Trible 1984; Culbertson 1992; Capps 1995). Staley's text does not deny the memory of such threats and fears, but he also manages to transform the sacrificial and abusive impulse into a relationship of love and care, yet without the pathos of sentimentality.

'Fathers and Sons: Fragments from an Autobiographical Midrash' also points to 'fatherhood' as an important topic within the study of men and religion, and one may want to read his contribution in comparison to Nelson (chapter 4), Moore (chapter 13), Eilberg-Schwartz (chapter 14), Lippy (chapter 23) and Capps (chapter 26; also Griswold 1993; Longwood 1996; Capps 2000). The slightly shortened version below is reprinted from *The Personal Voice in Biblical Interpretation* (1999a; for an expanded and revised version, see 1999b).

Publications by the Same Author

Staley, Jeffrey L. 1995. *Reading with a Passion: Rhetoric, Autobiography, and the American West in the Gospel of John*. New York: Continuum.

——. 1999a. 'Fathers and Sons: Fragments from an Autobiographical Midrash on John's Gospel', in *The Personal Voice in Biblical Interpretation*, ed. Ingrid Rosa Kitzberger. New York and London: Routledge. Pp. 65–8.

——. 1999b. 'Disseminations: An Autobiographical Midrash on Fatherhood in John's Gospel'. *Semeia* 85:127–54.

——. 1999c. 'Changing Woman: Postcolonial Reflections on Acts 16.6–40'. *Journal for the Study of the New Testament* 21/73:113–35 (revised and reprinted in *A Feminist Companion to Acts of the Apostles*, eds Amy-Jill Levine and Marianne Blickenstaff. Cleveland: Pilgrim, 2004. Pp. 177–92).

——. 2002a. '"Dis Place, Man": A Postcolonial Critique of the Vine, the Mountain, and the Temple in the Gospel of John', in *John and Postcolonialism: Travel, Space, and*

Power, eds Musa W. Dube and Jeffrey Staley. Sheffield: Sheffield Academic Press. Pp. 32–50.

——. 2002b. 'What is Critical about Autobiographical Biblical Criticism?' in *Autobiographical Biblical Criticism: Between Text and Self*, ed. Ingrid Rosa Kitzberger. Leiden: Deo Publishing. Pp. 12–33.

——. 2003. 'Manhood and New Testament Studies After September 11', in *New Testament Masculinities*, eds Stephen D. Moore and Janice Capel Anderson. Atlanta: Society of Biblical Literature. Pp. 329–35.

——. 2005. 'Reading "This Woman" Back into John 7:1—8:59: Liar Liar and the "Pericope Adulterae" in Intertextual Tango', in *Those Outside: Noncanonical Readings of Canonical Gospels*, eds George Aichele and Richard Walsh. London: T&T Clark. Pp. 85–107.

Further Reading

Capps, Donald. 1995. 'Abraham and Isaac: The Sacrificial Impulse', in *The Child's Song: The Religious Abuse of Children*, Donald Capps. Louisville: Westminster John Knox. Pp. 78–95.

——. 2000. *Men and their Religion: Honor, Hope, and Humor*. Harrisburg: Trinity Press International.

Culbertson, Philip. 1992. *New Adam: The Future of Male Spirituality*. Minneapolis: Augsburg Fortress (esp. chapters 3 and 4).

Griswold, Robert L. 1993. *Fatherhood in America: A History*. New York: Basic Books.

Longwood, Merle W. 1996. 'Changing Views of Fathering and Fatherhood: A Christian Ethical Perspective', in *Redeeming Men*, eds Stephen B. Boyd, Merle Longwood and Mark Muesse. Louisville: Westminster John Knox. Pp. 238–51.

Ostriker, Alicia Suskin. 1997. *The Nakedness of the Fathers: Biblical Visions and Revisions*. New Brunswick: Rutgers University Press.

Spiegel, Shalom. 1950. *The Last Trial: The Akedah*. New York: Behrman House.

Stern, David. 1992. 'Introduction', in *The Book of Legends: Sefer Ha-Aggadah: Legends from the Talmud and Midrash*, eds Hayim Nahman Bialik and Yehoshua Hana Ravnitzky, trans. William Braude. New York: Schocken Books. Pp. xvii–xxii.

Trible, Phyllis. 1984. *Texts of Terror: Literary-Feminist Readings of Biblical Narratives*. Philadelphia: Fortress.

Fathers and Sons: Fragments from an Autobiographical Midrash on John's Gospel

JEFFREY L. STALEY

Fragment One

'They answered him, "Abraham is our father".' John 8.39

And Abraham knew his wife, and she conceived and bore a son, and they named him Isaac. And Abraham lifted up his eyes and looked west. And he saw that the land of Indiana was good land, and he journeyed westward and settled there. Abraham Staley and Mary had two sons and two daughters. Abraham lived 77 years, and he died and was buried beside his wife beneath a grove of hickory trees near Cumberland, Indiana.

And Isaac knew his wife, and she conceived and bore a son. And they named him Abraham. Isaac and Lavinia had five sons and four daughters. Isaac lived 75 years and he died and was buried beside his mother and father, beneath the grove of hickory trees near Cumberland, Indiana.

And Abraham knew his wife, and she conceived and bore a son. And she named him Arlonzo. For she said, 'There have been far too many biblical names in this family.' And Abraham lifted up his eyes and looked west, and he saw that the land of Kansas was good land, and he journeyed westward and settled there. Abraham and Eliza had nine sons. Abraham lived 82 years and he died and was buried beside his wife in Ottawa, Kansas.

And Arlonzo knew his wife, and she conceived and bore a son. And they named him Lloyd. Arlonzo and May Belle had five sons. Arlonzo lived 91 years and he died and was buried beside his wife in Wellsville, Kansas.

And Lloyd knew his wife, and she conceived and bore a son. And they named him Robert. And there was a famine in the land, so Lloyd and Mary moved to the city. Lloyd and Mary had six sons and three daughters. And when they were old, lo, they lifted up their eyes and looked west. And they saw that the land of California was good land, and they journeyed westward and settled there. Lloyd lived 88 years and he died and was buried beside his wife in Atascadero, California.

And Robert knew his wife, and she conceived and bore a son. And they named him Jeffrey. And Robert lifted up his eyes and looked west from his home in Kansas, and he saw that the land of Arizona was good land, and he journeyed westward and settled there. Bob and Betty had four sons and two daughters. And Betty died and was buried at Immanuel Mission, on the Navajo Reservation. Then Robert took Esther for his wife, and they moved to Phoenix, a royal city, a miracle of glass and steel rising like a gigantic bird from hot desert ashes. And there they live, even until this day.

And Jeffrey knew his wife . . .

Fragment Two

'Very truly, I tell you, unless you eat the flesh of the Son of Man and drink his blood, you have no life in you.' John 6.53

And he said,
'This is my body;
take, eat ye all of it.
Run your tongue
over its soft round smoothness.
Breathe deep its heavenly scent.
Gaze long at its fragile opaqueness.
Cup it in your hands, caress it tenderly.
Nibble its outer edges
slowly, slowly.
Then swallow me whole.
Eat me up, up, up;
sup on me, one long,
everlastingly long sip—
dip in,
dine, thine.
Come to me,
oh come.
Come unto me,
on to me
now, now,
and I will give you rest.'
And it was so.
And he said,
'Here is my life blood
poured out for you;
drink deeply of it.
Remember me
in the rhythmic passages
of your life.
Wash your body
in my heavenly flow.
Find in its tingling flush
yourself
unearthed,
rebirthed.
A wriggling mass
of unumbilicled joy.'
And it was so.

And so she conceived and bore a son, and they named him Benjamin, for they said, 'It is a good name, a family name.'

Jeffrey and Barbara had one son and one daughter. And they are alive, even until this day.

Fragment Three

'In the beginning was the Word, and the Word was with God, and the Word was God.'
John 1.1

I have always wanted to be a father, just like in the beginning. But I wanted to be the father of a daughter first. A son could come later. Just give me the daughter first. My mother promised I would have the daughter first. Moments before she died I saw my daughter in her eyes—a translucent embryo in her last, silent tear that said, 'I'm sorry I will never get a chance to hold your baby girl in my arms.'

Now I have two children. A son and a daughter. But my mother was wrong. The son came first.

En arche en ho logos, kai ho logos en pros ton theon, kai ho logos en theos.

En can mean 'in, with, or by,' says Arndt and Gingrich's *A Greek-English Lexicon of the New Testament and Other Early Christian Literature*. And it can mean a host of other things too. It's like the Hebrew preposition *be*. The rabbis speculated about the meaning of the preposition *be* together with the noun *reshith* in Genesis 1.1. Does the expression mean 'in the beginning,' or 'with the first thing'? And if it means 'with the first thing,' then what is that first thing to which it refers? Maybe it refers to *hokmah*, said the rabbis. God made wisdom first, a female creature, and then everything else followed from her and was imprinted with her image. Perhaps John 1.1–18 is a fragment of a hymn to wisdom in which the feminine, Hellenistic *sophia* or the feminine, Semitic *hokmah* has metamorphosed into the masculine *logos*.

Some say that Christians, like those Jewish rabbis of old, also have a theology of prepositions. In argument with Calvinists and Roman Catholics Lutherans say the real body and blood of Jesus are given 'in, with, and under' the bread and wine. You are baptized *'en pneumati hagio'* says the author of Luke-Acts (Acts 11.16). But does the writer mean 'in the Holy Spirit,' 'with the Holy Spirit,' or 'by the Holy Spirit'? Entire Pentecostal denominations have been founded upon fine-line distinctions such as these. It's the difference, for instance, between telling my son, 'Go play *by* yourself for awhile' and telling him, 'Go play *with* yourself for awhile.' The distinction is crucial, but he doesn't seem to do much of either. Most often he is outside in the neighborhood, organizing games among his friends. My daughter, on the other hand, is more apt to play by herself and with herself.

'See dad, I have a little penis,' she announces proudly as she sits in the bathtub and spreads her labia apart.

'Well, kind of,' I say. I try to explain to her the difference between boys and girls. But she has already lost interest. She is busy blowing bubbles and trying to catch them in the palms of her hands.

I want to be right up front about this issue of gender in John, just as I have been with my children. Gender matters.

'*En arche en ho logos, kai ho logos en pros ton theon, kai ho logos en theos,*' writes the author of the Fourth Gospel. One feminine noun and two masculine nouns. And the two masculines, hiding behind the one feminine, have overpowered (*katelaben*) the feminine *sophia* and *hokmah* in the history of exegesis.

But if you take the masculine ending *'os'* from *theos* you simply have *'the.'* 'In the beginning was the *The.'* I like that. The terminal sigma, shaped like a slithering snake, is absent, and in its absence *theos* loses its masculine power.

In the beginning was the word—defrocked, emasculated, skinned, undone. And the word was with *the . . . the . . .* whatever—and the word was—whatever. Whatever the *os* will make it be. And mark my words, the *os* will make itself into something.

Fragment Four

'All things came into being through him, and without him, not one thing came into being.' John 1.3

That sneaky, sibilant sigma, shaped like a snake, is the one sound I could not say as a lisping boy of four. And not only at four. It would be 20 more years before my future wife finally taught me where to place my tongue.

'Like this,' she said, smiling encouragingly. And she opened her mouth into a wide *O*. So esses came spewing out of my mouth, just as if I were the Gihon Spring or the Euphrates River. And from that day forward the esses have not stopped coming.

Then one day a son came out. Right out of a wide, pulsating *O*. The unique child of his father. Half Chinese. The first non-Caucasian Staley child that I have been able to find in my family genealogy; the first non-Asian child in my wife's family. A wrong-headed child from the Staley-Wong family. His mixed up genetics are a metaphor for my own mixed up life.

The Father is in me and I am in the Father.[1]

In the beginning there was my son. And then three years later a daughter came along.

I always wanted the girl to come first. Just like in John 1.1, where the feminine *arche* precedes the masculine *logos* and *theos*. But for five generations in the Staley family boys have come first. I am not as different as my mother thought I would be, nor as different as I had hoped.

I watch my firstborn slowly poke a head through the widening *O*, into the great unknown. Before the child is waist deep in the world I hear the strong cry of life. Regardless of gender, the child will be strong and healthy. I helped make this child. I will teach this child—born, borne, bone of my bone and flesh of my flesh—about truth, about love, about the ways of the world.

Oh.

Boy.

It's a boy.

Fragment Five

'Look, here is the Lamb of God!' John 1.36

My newborn son's penis is huge. And it is not circumcised. He is not like me. What do I do now? I don't know anything about foreskins. This is America. American boys aren't supposed to be born with them. Snakes shed their skins. Baby boys shed their foreskins. Take him out behind the woodshed and have him skinned.

> What do you do with a foreskin?
> My son's is the first I've seen. Maybe we should cut it off.
> 'Do you want to make the first cut?' the doctor asks.
> *'What!'*
> 'You know, do you want to cut the umbilical cord? Lots of fathers do nowadays. It's kind of a ritual.'
> 'Oh. No, not really. You can cut it. I'll just watch.'
> Clip.

My daughter is different. We know she is a girl almost from the beginning. We saw her *in utero*, in a frontal position on the ultrasound. A head, two arms, trunk, two legs. No penis.

> 'Really?'
> 'Really. See?' says the doctor. 'Looks like a girl, all right!'

But just to be safe we pick two names: Allison Jean, if the sonogram is right; Stephen Isaac, if it has somehow missed an important part of human anatomy.

I was sicker than a dog when my daughter was conceived. My wife and I had been trying for months to have another child. The child should be born in summer, we decided, just like the first one, because I am a professor and will have the summer off to help with the new baby. So in September 1987 we begin baby making in earnest. But no baby. Now it is February, and I have a horrible cold.

> 'It's that time,' Barbara nudges me in the dark.
> 'Are you sure?'
> 'Yeah, I'm sure. I just took my temperature.'
> 'It can't be,' I groan, 'Not tonight. I can't even breathe!'
> 'But you've got to!' She whispers fiercely. And then she touches me.
> I know it's going to be hard, but I give it a try.

Much to our surprise a child is conceived that night. Our daughter will be born in October, mid-semester, just in time for midterms. Oh well, I don't sleep much then anyway.

Allison's umbilical cord is wrapped around her neck. It stretches taut, her heartbeat quickens. Her face begins to turns blue. With a quiet, urgent tone that sends chills down my spine, the doctor commands my wife, 'Stop pushing.' Then she slips a knife blade between my half-born daughter's neck and my wife's vagina. Carefully, slowly she cuts the cord. I am surprised at the rush of air that escapes my throat. I feel lightheaded and look for a chair.

The boy is red and smooth; soft, like crushed velvet. He nestles in my arms as I try awkwardly to hold his huge, swaying head. He is perfect, not one blemish or mole on his entire body. A spotless lamb of God.

My daughter is different. She is born with a wine-stain birthmark in the middle of her forehead. It is a special sign. A bright pink star.

A nurse, noticing my intense gaze, says encouragingly, 'It will fade with time.' But she misunderstands my staring. I want the star to stay.

> Star light, star bright,
> first star I see tonight;
> I wish I may, I wish I might,
> have the wish I wish tonight.

I inspect the rest of her body. Ten fingers, ten toes. An engorged vulva. She waits three minutes before she utters a sound.

> She has a beautiful round mole on her left buttock.
> —All things counter, original, spare, strange;
> Whatever is fickle, freckled (who knows how)—
> 'That mole will make some man happy one day,' I say, and my wife smiles.

His eyes try hard to focus on my face as I speak to him. I have talked to him many times in the past few months, as I nuzzled my wife's bulging belly. For seven months I have been calling him Katie, to help him become the girl I wanted first. But now I hold a boy in my arms and devise for him an impromptu oath as his eyes move around crazily in different directions.

'I know I will make many mistakes as a father,' I whisper in his tiny ear. 'I've never been one before now. But I promise that I will always love you.'

I silently pray that it will be true, for I have never been a father, and I had not been expecting a boy.

I carry him to the Alta Bates Hospital nursery, wrapped in a warm towel, where a nurse washes him off and lays him under a heat lamp, as though he were an entree to be served up from a cafeteria steam table.

This is my son. Hear him cry. A bleating little lamb.

I return to my wife's side, give her a kiss goodnight, and walk home alone to our two-room apartment on College Avenue in Berkeley. It is June 7, 1985. It is two o'clock in the morning. Even though I know that this will be my last chance in many months to get a good night's sleep, I lie awake for hours.

I am the father of a son: Benjamin (named for my favorite uncle, who was named for Benjamin Lamb, my paternal grandfather's maternal grandfather) Walter (named for my wife's father). A family name. Also a playful inversion of Walter Benjamin, a famous Jewish philosopher and literary critic whose writings I have recently read. My son's name is a subtle joke that no one in my family or my wife's family will ever catch. The son's father likes to pretend he is a famous New Testament literary critic. So the father gives his firstborn a famous name, turned upside down, just like the way he came into the world.

I have just finished writing a dissertation on the Gospel of John, and I will begin teaching that autumn in a tenure-track position at the University of Portland, in Oregon. I have a wonderful wife, a new son, and a new career. I know I will be a good provider, just like God was a good provider for his Son. I want to be like God. Tonight I feel like a god.

The world is a beautiful place. It is *my* place, *my* world. I have made it one person more beautiful than it was yesterday.

Fragment Six

'Moses gave you circumcision' (it is, of course, not from Moses but from the patriarchs) . . . John 7.22

Okay. We've had some time to think about it. Should we have our son circumcised? I am vacillating. Just a few hours ago he was a girl. I was sure of it. Now he is Benjamin, my son. And he has a foreskin.

My wife and I weigh the pros and cons of circumcision for seven days. Finally, her brother calls. 'Look, I had to be circumcised when I was twelve, because of an infection. It was pure hell. Junior high and all that. You should do it now, so he won't be forced to have it done later.'

How do you clean a foreskin? I don't know how to do it. If we don't have him circumcised he will be different from me, and I will be unable to help him.

On the eighth day we decide to have Benjamin circumcised. Just like a little Jewish boy.

He will look like me.
He will be like me.

I hold him down while the doctor straps his tiny arms and legs to a pad.

He will look like me.
He will be like me.

My son begins to cry. He doesn't like being tied down, naked and spread-eagled, like the Greek letter
X.[2]

Caught in the surgeon's finely woven web,
He fights to free himself.
In just a few moments it will be over, my son. Trust me.
You will be free. Free indeed.
I hear the bleating of a lamb.

Abraham is my father.
Abraham is my father.

'It won't really hurt, you know,' the doctor says reassuringly. 'I've done hundreds of these before. He won't remember a thing. Trust me. I'm a father, too.'

After properly cleansing the penis and pubis, the dorsal aspect of the prepuce is put on a stretch by grasping it on either side of the median line with a pair of hemostats (Yellen 1935, 147).

This boy should have been named Isaac, like his great, great, great, great grandfather.

Isaac, my son, I want to hear you laugh.
Laugh, boy! Laugh!

But the joke's on me. I have helped bind you to an altar of plastic and steel. You will be altered, and no divine voice will tell the doctor to put down his knife.

You are my son, but you don't look like me.
I want you to look like me. I want you to be like me. I want you to fit in. I don't want other American boys to laugh and stare at you in the gym or the bathroom when they see you naked, with a foreskin in your hands.

My eyes are on the doctor.
Steady, steady.

A flat probe, anointed with vaseline, is then inserted between the prepuce and the glans to separate adherent mucous membrane. The prepuce is then gently drawn backwards exposing the entire glans penis . . . In cases where the prepuce is drawn tightly over the glans, a partial dorsal slit will facilitate applying the cone of draw stud [the bell] over the glans. After anointing the inside of the cone, it is placed over the glans penis allowing enough of the mucous membrane to fit below the cone so that too much is not removed. The prepuce is then pulled through and above the bevel hole in the platform and clamped in place. In this way the prepuce is crushed against the cone causing hemostasis. We allow this pressure to remain five minutes, and in older children slightly longer. The excess of the prepuce is then cut with a sharp knife without any danger of cutting the glans, which is always protected by the cone portion of the instrument, leaving a very fine 1/32 of an inch ribbon-like membrane formed between the new union of the skin and mucous membrane. The pressure is then released. (Yellen 1935, 147)

No anesthesia is used.
It is finished.

Fragment Seven

'The Father loves the Son and has placed all things in his hands.' John 3.35

Watch my son writhe.
He is purple with rage and pain.

The application of two hemostats to the edges of the sensitive, unanesthetized prepuce, the application of a third crushing hemostat to the prepuce before cutting the dorsal slit, and the crushing of the entire circumference of the prepuce by turning a screw on the Gomco Clamp produces excruciating pain. Since Anand and Hickey's article in the *New England Journal of Medicine* (K. J. S. Anand and P. R. Hickey, 'Pain and Its Effects in the Human Neonate and Fetus,' 317 [1987]:1321, 1324, 1325), it can no longer be denied that pain is felt by the male infant during circumcision. Although the Gomco Clamp may have been designed to reduce the risk of bleeding, it has produced excruciating pain in every infant on which it is used. Even if anesthesia is used, the post-operative pain originating in a pleasure center can be expected to have serious untoward consequences. (Denniston 1996)

My son screams. He screams and he screams.
I cannot console him.

The Father is in me and I am in the Father.
The father loves the son and has placed all things in his hands.
In his hands.
In his tiny pink hands.
I am the father.
The son of far too many Abrahams.
But I am worse than them.
I pay someone else to take knife in hand and do what I cannot do.

During the biblical period (c. 1700 BCE–140 CE), the operator, or mohel placed a metal shield with a slit in it near the tip of the foreskin, so only the tip was removed. Often the mohel . . . pulled up on the outside of the foreskin before placing the shield. The result was that virtually all of the inner lining of the prepuce was preserved. This was known as Bris Milah.

The wonderful statue of David by Michelangelo appears intact but is in fact correctly represented because the future King David has been circumcised by the accepted procedure of the biblical era. Only the tip of his foreskin has been removed, fulfilling the covenant with Abraham (Genesis 17). (Denniston 1996; cf. Gairdner 1949, 1433)

Hours later I am still clasping my son's doll-like fingers.

Benjamin!
Benjamin!
I will always love you.
Jesus!
Sweet, sweet Jesus!
I'm sorry.
I am sorry.

Look at me! I'm wet with your sweat and tears.
You look like me.

You will be like me.
You will like me.

Fragment Eight

'Put your sword back in its sheath. Am I not to drink the cup that the Father has given me?' John 18.11

'Are you sure you want to go through with this?' my doctor asks as he enters the room where I lie, half naked, on an examining table.

My legs are spread apart, and my feet are in webbed stirrups, as though I am about to give birth. A sheet covers the lower part of my body.

A nurse comes in and cleanses my crotch with some orange, purifying liquid. Does she find my penis tiny? How does it compare with other penises she has seen? Does she ever take notes? I watch her eyes. She gives nothing away.

Do I want to go through with this?

Of course I do. I have two healthy children, one girl and one boy. And I have to put them through college someday. I can't afford to have any more children.

Through with this.

Hmmm . . . *Dia* with the genitaliave? Expression of agency? (With a note of urgency.) Or is it an ablative of accompaniment? Perhaps it should be *eis* with the accusative. The idea of limit, extent, direction toward, is important in this case.

'Yes, I want to go through with it.'
'Ouch!'
The doctor's needle pricks my skin at a very sensitive point.
'Did you feel that?'
'Yeah, whaddyya *think*?'

The doctor removes the sheet covering the lower half of my body, and I lean forward, propping myself up on my elbows. I watch as the doctor makes an incision in my scrotum and pulls out two tiny threads that connect my testicles to their ejaculatory ducts.

Ah, the vas deferens.

Truly, truly, I am a vine, and my *Doktorvater* is a vinedresser. He is removing every living branch from me so that I can no longer bear fruit.

I am thinking of Derrida and one of his many books—was it in *Dissemination* that he talked about the vastness of différance? I can't remember. I'm having problems concentrating on Derrida. I have a weird sensation in my anus, my derrière—

da . . . yes, right there—

as though someone is pulling an enormously long stringnified from it.

The doctor explains the surgery's aftereffects in response to my unvoiced anxieties.

'You'll be sore for a few days.'

'Don't do any lifting.'

'Take pain pills.'

'Oh, and be sure to wear an athletic cup—you know, a Jacquestrap—for at least forty-eight hours.'

I am a vine.

Clip.

I will never be the same. I am forever différant.

Clip.

The penis . . . is . . . is . . . mightier than the sword.

Fragment Nine

'Those who drink of the water that I will give them will never be thirsty.' John 4.14

I imagine a milky white, life-giving liquid seeping out onto the doctor's fingers.

From my side are flowing rivers of living water.

For ages, fathers and sons have drunk from wells like this. Jacob and his sons, for example. This liquid is a man's identity, the proof of his virility, masculinity, and power. I have been cut off from the land of the living.

Come, all you who are thirsty. Drink of me before I disappear.

A final drink.

To death, then.

Bottoms up. Derrière—da.

I go home and my wife makes a careful inspection of my body.

'Oh, my goodness, it has shrunk!'

She is worried.

'Is it supposed to look like that?'

I look down. It's true. My scrotum is black-and-blue and my penis is no larger than that of my four year-old son.

Within a few days, however, I'm a little kid, playing with myself again. Every few weeks I masturbate and ejaculate into a little plastic cup.

I put the top on the cup and take it to the hospital.

See what I can do?

'Am I dead yet?'

'No, not yet.'

The well is deeper than I thought.

Four months later the harvest comes, and I finally hear the response I have been waiting for.

'It is finished. You are dead.'

'Now you can go out and live again.'

Fragment Ten

'Very truly I tell you, the Son can do nothing on his own, but only what he sees the Father doing; for what the Father does, the Son does likewise.' John 5.19

A poem for my son, at five years old.

Jigsaw Puzzles
So like the father is the son,
matching color to color,
shape to shape,
with quickness and precision;
with flashes of intuition.
Surprises are interlocked
with carefully crafted solutions:
Sometimes he follows shadows to light,
or bright hues to near whites.
At other times, the mere
slippery force of gravity
pulls pairs together.
But, curiously, he does not begin with borders.
He leaves
without speaking,
those straight edges
which protect the slow-forming picture
from the chaos creeping
across the dining room table,
for another to shape and fit.

Fragment Eleven

'You search the writings because you think that in them you have eternal life; and it is they that testify on my behalf.' John 5.39

My son has decided to read my recent book, *Reading with a Passion,* for his sixth-grade book report. The class assignment is to read an autobiography, and since part of my book is autobiographical, he wants to write about me. I am not crazy about his idea, since it is difficult reading and he won't understand much of anything he reads. I think he thinks the assignment will be made easier if he reads about someone he knows. Still, I am pleased that he wants to read the book. After all, I gave him and my daughter Allison autographed copies when it first came out. I was hoping he would read the book sometime before I died. I just didn't expect him to try it when he was 11. [. . .]

Benjamin asked me to proofread his essay when he was done, and I did. I wrote at the top, 'Good work! You've done an excellent job!' in big round letters.

Now he is at my side, trying to get my attention.

'Dad, do you have any clothes I can borrow?'

'Why do you want my clothes?' I ask suspiciously.

'Well, tomorrow I have to do a class presentation about the autobiography I read, so I thought I would dress up like you.'

I go upstairs and rummage through my closet, finding a hat and shirt that he can wear. I discover an old transistor radio that I bought when I was 12 years old, and show that to him, too.

'I used to listen to "Yours truly, KOMA, Oklahoma City!" on this little radio.' I pat it and sing their signature ditty from 1964.

'That's where I heard the Beatles for the first time, you know. Out there on the reservation, thirty miles from the closest post office, Navajo girls used to come running over to listen to my Montgomery Ward radio whenever I yelled, "It's the Beatles!"'

'KOMA was the only rock 'n roll station we could pick up there in northern Arizona. I would fall asleep with the earphone stuck in my ear, and wake up in the morning to static.'

'Cool, Dad. Does it still work?'

'I don't know, let's try it. I haven't used it in about twenty years.'

We find a nine-volt battery, put it in the radio, and turn it on. Static. I turn the dial. Music. Maybe it's KOMA.

'She loves you, yeah, yeah, yeah!'

'Come on, Dad! That's a song by Alice in Chains!'

'Oh.'

'Hey, can I take this radio to school too?'

'Sure! Just don't lose it. It's one of the only things I have left from my childhood.'

'I'll take good care of it. Thanks, Dad!'

And he gives me a kiss.

Fragment Twelve

'While I was with them, I protected them in your name that you have given me, so that they may be one, as we are one.' John 17.12

He is my son. I am his father. I am in him and he is in me.

But my daughter is different. She is the intruder, the one that upsets the natural equilibrium. I am in her too, and she in me. But it cannot be the same. Even though we occasionally still sleep together, it cannot be the same as with my son. And I worry about that. I am hot and I sleep in boxer shorts. It's the niacin. I take it to control my cholesterol. But it sometimes gives me hot flashes, and I have felt overly warm ever since I started taking it more than two years ago. So I sleep half naked.

My wife is out of town, and my daughter sneaks into our bed at two o'clock in the morning.

'Daddy, I hear scary noises.'

I mumble some incoherent words and turn over.

Will she remember this night and other nights like it when she is 20, and will she accuse me of unspeakable acts?

I have never touched her that way. But there were times before she was born that I thought I might. And I was afraid. And so God gave me a son first.

I will not hold you, daughter of Abraham, for I might ascend. Even though I am old and you are my daughter, I might ascend. So I turn my back to you and hide the shame of my nocturnal ascensions. I feel safe with my back to you, my daughter. And so I will show you only my backside, fleetingly, as I glide by in the night. Only our toes will touch. For no one has ever seen the father. But the only son, who is close on the father's other side has made him known.

Fragment Thirteen

'Unless a grain of wheat falls into the earth and dies, it remains just a single grain; but if it dies, it bears much fruit.' John 12.24–25

My daughter is eight years old and we have just moved to Seattle. We have to find new doctors for our children, and now we are in the process of interviewing pediatricians for Allison. This is one my wife likes, and she wants me to meet her.

My wife and I are also somewhat concerned about the mole on Allison's bottom, the one that she was born with. It is no longer round and smooth as it was when she was a baby. It has grown larger. Now it is bumpy and asymmetrical.

'Allison is forty-nine inches tall, and weighs forty-eight pounds. Her blood pressure is 98 over 68. She's a healthy girl!' The pediatrician smiles reassuringly. 'Now, where's that mole?'

'Right—or is it her left buttock?' My wife looks at me with a question in her eyes. 'I can't remember.'

'It's on her left buttock,' I say without thinking. I know where it is. It has been mine for eight years.

—*All things counter, original, spare, strange;*
Whatever is fickle, freckled (who knows how).—

The new pediatrician does a careful inspection. 'We should really have it removed. The sooner the better, just to be on the safe side. Strange things can happen to moles like this when girls hit puberty.'

The doctor doesn't know that I have been saving this mark, this grain of wheat, and I am not ready to give it up.

'Will it hurt to take it off?' Allison asks. A worried frown crosses her face.

'Just a little. But not for long.'

I want to tell the doctor, 'You can't have it. It's not yours to take.' But the seed may not be dead, and I want my girl to live forever.

On July 7, 1997 the mole is removed. I squeeze my daughter's hand tightly as the doctor makes an incision, cuts out the mole, and sews up the remaining flaps of skin. My daughter is brave, she hardly cries.

The doctor saves the mole and sends it to the laboratory for testing.

'Just a precautionary measure,' she says cheerily.

The tests come back from the lab, and the doctor calls us to tell us the good news: the mole-seed is indeed dead.

In four months even my daughter's scar is gone. But she will always be to me a grain of wheat, sown and harvested before her time.

Fragment Fourteen

'*In a little while the world will no longer see me, but you will see me; because I live, you will also live. On that day you will know that I am in my Father, and you in me, and I in you.*' John 14.19–20

He still kisses me on the lips occasionally, this son of mine. And now he is nearly 12 years old. I thought the ritual would have ended long ago.

More and more often he just kisses me on the cheek. But there are times when only a kiss on the lips will do.

He started kissing me on the lips when he was about a year old. He would watch my wife and me kiss. Then he would mimic us, and we would laugh. Now I wonder when it will stop, when he will kiss me like this for the last time. He has no idea where and when the kissing began. And when it stops, he will probably forget that he ever did it. But I am his father, and I will not forget.

I don't want this kissing to stop, but I am afraid. What if someone sees us kissing like this, at our ages? What will they think?

He still sleeps with a night light on. Wrapped in San Francisco 49er blankets, he prays passionately each evening that God will keep him from bad dreams, and that God will keep his parents safe and alive until they are both 100.

When I am 100 and praying on my deathbed, I want my son at my side. I want to hold his head on my chest. I want to feel his warm lips on mine. I want to smell his sweet breath tickling my mustache.

I want my daughter to slip into the room and ask, 'Dad, can I crawl into bed with you?'

And I will say 'Yes, you may—just this once.'

I will not turn away from her, and she will hold me as close as I held her when we were both young. Then she will sing to me softly an old Beatles' lullaby—[3]

swift, slow; sweet, sour; adazzle, dim . . .
He fathers-forth whose beauty is past change . . .

I smile and drift off to sleep with no fear of bad dreams.

Even as the night light dims, I fear no evil, for thou art with me my daughter, my only begotten son.

Notes

1 Since I was unable to obtain permission to reprint the lyrics of the John Lennon and Paul McCartney song 'I Am The Walrus' (Northern Songs Ltd, 1967)—a song which shares certain theological motifs with the Fourth Gospel—I ask the reader

to begin humming the tune at this point in my essay (the lyrics to the song may be found at http://www.public.iastate.edu/trents/beatles/imwalrus.html; see also http://kiwi.imgen.bcm.tmc.edu:8088/public/rmb.html). Or better yet, put the song in your iPod and play it as background music while you read the remainder of the essay.

2 'According to the χ (the chiasmus) (which can be considered a quick thematic diagram of dissemination), the preface, as semen, is just as likely to be left out, to well up and get lost as a seminal différance, as it is to be reappropriated into the sublimity of the father. As the preface to a book, [the χ] is the word of a father assisting and admiring his work, answering for his son, losing his breath in sustaining, retaining, idealizing, reinternalizing, and mastering his seed. The scene would be acted out, if such were possible, between father and son alone: autoinsemination, homoinsemination, reinsemination' (Derrida 1981, 44–5).

3 Replay 'I Am The Walrus.'

Literature

Anand, K. J. S. and P. R. Hickey. 1987. 'Pain and Its Effects in the Human Neonate and Fetus,' *New England Journal of Medicine* 317:1321–9.

Denniston, George C. 1996. '"Modern" Circumcision: The Escalation of a Ritual,' *Circumcision* 1/1. Available online at http://weber.u.washington.edu/~gcd/CIRCUMCISION/.

Derrida, Jacques. 1981. *Dissemination*, trans., with an introduction and additional notes by Barbara Johnson. Chicago: University of Chicago Press.

Gairdner, D. 1949. 'The Fate of the Foreskin: A Study of Circumcision,' *BMJ* 2:1433–7.

Hopkins, Gerard Manley. 1967. 'Glory Be to God for Dappled Things,' in *The Poems of Gerard Manley Hopkins* (4th edn). New York: Oxford University Press.

Staley, Jeffrey L. and Rebecca G. 1997. 'Staley Family History'. Available online at http://www.u.arizona.edu/~rstaley/personal.htm.

Yellen, H. S. 1935. 'Bloodless Circumcision of the Newborn,' *Am. J. Obstet. Gynecol.* 30:146–7.

Part 5

Masculine Ideals in the Jewish and Christian Traditions

Religions not only conform to and legitimize normative ideals of manliness; they also challenge such ideals and create alternative pathways for men. Religious ideals of masculinity frequently originate as a counter-cultural impulse. However, since these ideals themselves often transform, over time, into new normative models invested with real and symbolic power, it is easy to forget their embattled origins. This part investigates the historical origins and contexts of some of these ideals, from late antiquity to modernity.

Individual men as well as homosocial communities, who, inspired by the religious imagination, defy gender expectations imposed by society, are at risk of being perceived as weak, odd, effeminized and, at times, queer. Calling upon divine legitimation, however, helps to avert the threat of emasculinization and to transform hitherto 'feminine' traits into manly virtues. Mathew Kuefler's chapter on the *miles Christi*, the soldier of Christ, illustrates well the symbolic reconfigurations that were necessary for Christian men in the first four centuries to claim a different kind of masculinity. Reinterpreting the values of patience, passivity, and humility as a person's true bravery and strength, Christianity subtly subverted the dominant Roman ethos of masculinity, eventually offering Roman men – at a time when the empire declined militarily, but Christianity ascended demographically – a way out of a crisis of masculine identity.

Michael Satlow also looks at ideals of masculinity in late antiquity, but his interest centers on Jewish men within emerging rabbinic Judaism. Like early Christianity, Jewish sources promoted self-restraint among rabbinic men, but unlike Christian men, the rabbis were not expected to practice sexual renunciation and asceticism. Instead, self-restraint was valued as a prerequisite for the study of Torah. 'Torah study is constructed as the masculine activity *par excellence*,' Satlow writes.

Virginia Burrus's exploration of the patristic imagination also remains within the same historical period. She investigates creedal statements of the early church fathers. Rather than looking at the practices of the body, Burrus examines masculine ideals through an analysis of theological metaphors.

Mark Jordan moves us into the Middle Ages, tracing the coinage of the term 'sodomy' to eleventh-century Christian theologians, a term over which there is much confusion, historically as well as contemporaneously. Jordan unpacks some of the convoluted history that has contributed to a persistent anti-homosexual discourse in Christianity.

Following Jordan's chapter, the historical analysis of religious ideals of masculinity leaps forward to modernity. Chapters 22 and 23 describe the resurgence of more reactive and combative forms of manliness as a response to secularization and the privatization of religion. Concerned about the decline of men's participation in the churches, nineteenth- and twentieth-century Christian men's movements tried to revitalize male religious commitments by attempting to re-masculinize the church. Sean Gill examines the Victorian ideal of a muscular Christianity, and Charles Lippy compares the Men and Religious Forward movement of the 1910s with the Promise Keepers of the 1990s.

18

Soldiers of Christ: Christian Masculinity and Militarism in Late Antiquity

Editor's Introduction

The study of the first 400 years of Christianity through a gender-conscious perspective has opened up new ways for understanding the diversity of Christian practices and beliefs. Feminist scholarship has long insisted on the gender-specific readings of texts and material artifacts in order to reconstruct women's lives during those formative centuries (for example, McNamara 1985; E. Clark 1986; 1999; G. Clark 1988; Cooper 1996). More recently, historical studies on men in early Christianity have followed suit, resisting dominant historiographies, which purported to be gender-neutral. Mathew Kuefler, historian at San Diego State University, is among these voices (see also the chapters by Virginia Burrus and David Brakke). In *The Manly Eunuch* (2001), Kuefler examines how the subordinated masculine ideology of Christianity was able to convince men adhering to the Roman hegemonic masculinity 'to transfer their allegiance' to the new Christian religion (2001, 6).

What is 'hegemonic masculinity'? Kuefler refers here to a theoretical concept that has gained prominence in critical men's studies since R. W. Connell first introduced it in 1995. Hegemonic masculinity 'recognize[s] *relations* between different kinds of masculinity: relations of alliance, dominance and subordination':

> These relationships are constructed through practices that exclude and include, that intimidate, exploit, and so on. There is gender politics within masculinity . . . Hegemonic masculinity can be defined as the configuration of gender practice which embodies the currently accepted answer to the problem of the legitimacy of patriarchy, which guarantees (or is taken to guarantee) the dominant position of men and the subordination of women . . . It is the successful claim to authority, more than direct violence, that is the mark of hegemony. (Connell 1995, 37, 77)

Applying hegemonic masculinity to late antiquity, Kuefler argues that the new Christian ideals of masculinity appealed to men of the old Roman elite. Though Christianity seemed, at first sight, to render men effeminate, soft and passive, it eventually succeeded in drawing Roman men into its new religious value system. Due to the decline of Roman power, traditional manly virtues could no longer be displayed on the actual battlefields. What before was measured by the success of military and political conquest became the spiritual triumph of a man's internal struggle.

Christian writers managed to subvert hegemonic definitions of Roman masculinity through the use of paradox that transformed what was formerly considered unmanly weakness into manly strength. Roman men found new political authority, for example, in the role of bishops, the latter asserting authority through the language of humility (*humilis* signified lowliness) and through the biblical (and gendered) metaphor of 'brides of Christ'. As 'brides of Christ', these Christian spokesmen were virtuous and manly, while the (male) adversaries of Christianity, especially heretics, were taunted as prostitutes who shamelessly flaunted their effeminacy.

It is important to remember that almost all sources available on the lives of men in antiquity are limited to the upper classes. Men of lower classes and men marginal to the Roman Empire easily disappear from the grasp of the historian. But the many documents of early Christianity, written and preserved by men and women conscious of the power of memory, give historians a chance to piece together a picture of how a subordinated masculinity eventually gained the status of hegemonic masculinity. Christian masculine ideals succeeded, Kuefler argues, because they reconciled the growing inconsistencies between manly ideals during the height of Roman imperial power and the social realities of men in the fourth and fifth centuries, when Rome's glory began to wane.

Kuefler's *The Manly Eunuch* not only examines the adjustments of male ideals within the increasingly hierarchically structured householder church but also discusses alternative models of masculinity, such as Christian and pagan notions regarding castration, eunuchs, holy transvestites and gender equality. Eunuchs, for example, subverted deeply rooted gender expectations, and self-castration was attractive even to some Christians, especially in Christian Byzantium (Ringrose 2003). Overall, however, the Christian discourse remained deeply suspicious of eunuchs, and in the end, visionaries of more gender-equal or genderless communities were not strong enough in numbers to redirect the course of the Christian householder church. The majority of Christian men continued to model themselves after the traditional *pater familias*.

It is primarily the householder church, not the eunuchs or other radical Christians, that is the topic of this chapter. Here, Kuefler explains how Christianity succeeded in transforming the manly ideal of *vita militaris* (virtue of military life) into a spiritual metaphor.

Publications by the Same Author

Kuefler, Mathew. 2001. *The Manly Eunuch: Masculinity, Gender Ambiguity, and Christian Ideology in Late Antiquity.* Chicago: University of Chicago Press.

——. 2003. 'Male Friendship and the Suspicion of Sodomy in Twelfth-Century France', in *Gender and Difference in the Middle Ages*, eds Sharon Farmer and Carol Brown Pasternack. Minneapolis: University of Minnesota Press. Pp. 145–81 (also reprinted in Kuefler 2006. Pp. 179–212).

—— (ed.). 2006. *The Boswell Thesis: Essays on Christianity, Social Tolerance, and Homosexuality.* Chicago: Chicago University Press.

Further Reading

Clark, Elizabeth A. 1986. *Ascetic Piety and Women's Faith: Essays in Late Ancient Christianity.* Lewiston: Edwin Mellen.

——. 1999. *Reading Renunciation: Asceticism and Scripture in Early Christianity.* Princeton: Princeton University Press.

Clark, Gillian. 1988. 'The Old Adam: The Fathers and the Unmaking of Masculinity', in *Thinking Men: Masculinity and Its Self-Representation in the Classical Tradition,* eds Lin Foxhall and John Salmon. London: Routledge. Pp. 170–82.

Connell, R. W. 1995. *Masculinities.* Berkeley: University of California Press.

Cooper, Kate. 1996. *The Virgin and the Bride: Idealized Womanhood in Late Antiquity.* Cambridge: Harvard University Press.

McNamara, Jo Ann. 1985. *A New Song: Celibate Women in the First Three Christian Centuries.* New York: Harrington Park.

Ringrose, Kathryn M. 2003. *The Perfect Servant: Eunuchs and the Social Construction of Gender in Byzantium.* Chicago: Chicago University Press.

Soldiers of Christ: Christian Masculinity and Militarism in Late Antiquity

MATHEW KUEFLER

Christian men of late antiquity shared with their pagan counterparts a desire to see themselves as manly, a desire also threatened by the military crisis of the Roman Empire. They also worried about the unmanly stance of victimhood. Out of that desire and because of those worries, Christian men fashioned for themselves the image of the soldier of Christ. From the martyrs, who represented the best and bravest soldiers of Christ, the image grew to encompass all Christian men, whose daily struggles against sin and temptation—against the unmanliness of vice within themselves—were identified as warfare against evil. These moral battles were sufficient to men and did not require further bloodshed in actual combat. Through the image of the soldier of Christ, Christian ideology was transformed in such a way that Christian men of the later Roman Empire might find manliness even in the midst of military collapse.

Patience and Pacifism

Christian writers were well aware of the disastrous military predicament of the Roman Empire in late antiquity. Indeed, they penned some of the most dramatic descriptions of the barbarian invasions. 'My voice sticks in my throat, and as I dictate, sobs choke my utterance,' cried the priest Jerome upon learning of the sack of the city of Rome in 410 at the hand of the Goths. 'The City which had taken the whole world was itself taken.'[1] Several decades earlier, the

Christian bishop Ambrose of Milan described the barbarian attacks with equal horror: 'How could you bear these things, I wonder, which we are compelled to endure, and what is worse, to behold: virgins raped, little children torn from the embrace of their families and thrown onto swords, bodies consecrated to God defiled . . . How could you tolerate them, I ask?'[2] And a half-century later, Sidonius Apollinaris used similar pathos, concluding that 'amid those calamities, that universal destruction, to live was death.'[3] Many more Christian writers echoed these sentiments.

Like pagan writers, Christian writers used the ravages of the barbarians to deliver indictments of the Romans and their moral character. Salvian of Marseilles, a priest writing about the middle of the fifth century in Gaul, claimed that God had permitted the attacks because of the Roman people's many sins. He wrote:

> Among chaste [*pudici*] barbarians, we are unchaste [*impudici*]. I say further: the very barbarians are offended by our impurities. Fornication is not lawful among the Goths. Only the Romans living among them can afford to be impure by prerogative of nation and name. I ask: What hope is there for us before God? We love impurity [*impudicitia*]; the Goths abominate it. We flee from purity; they seek it. Fornication among them is a crime; with us a distinction and an ornament.[4]

He concluded, perhaps responding to popular explanations, that 'it is not the natural vigor of their bodies that enables them to conquer us, nor is it our natural weakness that has caused our conquest.' Rather, he continued, 'the vices of our bad lives have alone conquered us.'[5] Salvian's comments were almost assuredly exaggerated for rhetorical purposes. Still, it reminds us that Christian writers linked the military catastrophe to their identity as Romans. (It also suggests that Christian writers might have highlighted the catastrophe for their purposes, which we will see were to highlight the futility of a military response to the crisis of the empire.)

Let us concentrate on the response of one Christian writer to the barbarian invasions. That writer was Augustine of Hippo, a Christian bishop in North Africa and one of the most prolific and most famous of early Christian writers, writing mostly in the first decades of the fifth century. His comments will be used as a linchpin in this chapter and as evidence of a careful Christian response to the military crisis of the later Roman Empire. From the example of Augustine, we will be able to situate more generally the shaping of Christian ideology by individual writers in response to the military crisis and to the challenge that this crisis posed to Roman masculinity.

Augustine certainly learned of the horrors of the barbarian invasions and the sack of the city of Rome in 410, and he drafted a series of sermons in order to console the Romans stunned by the implications of current events.[6] He was also aware of the accusation of some pagans that the Roman abandonment of the traditional gods was the cause of the military disasters of the empire. This accusation prompted Augustine to compose his lengthiest work, *De civitatis Dei* (On the City of God) following the sack. Augustine's reply to this accusation was twofold. First, he asserted that it was only *because* of the Christian god's providence that the destruction was somewhat mitigated.[7] Second, he demonstrated that the violence and victimization of warfare was nothing new to Roman history, but was a natural consequence of what he called 'the lust for domination' (*libido dominandi*) that had dominated the Roman cultural mentality.[8] Indeed, he maintained that the effects of war were always dire and among the greatest tragedies of human life.[9] (Such statements are an important antidote to much of the secondary literature on Augustine and war, which details his concept of the just and justifiable war but neglects to document his fundamental opposition to war.) Considering the emphasis on militarism among Roman men, it is curious that Augustine and his Christian contemporaries were able to distance themselves from the failure of the empire and from its militaristic tradition without at the same time sacrificing their masculine identity. Yet this is precisely what they did.

To understand how this distancing was possible, it is important first of all to appreciate the strong antimilitaristic tradition among the earliest Christians in the West. This antimilitarism appears especially in the hagiographical stories of individual Christians in the Roman army. One man named Maximilian, as he was inducted into the army at Tebessa in the Roman province of Mauretania in 295, refused to join, saying that 'I cannot wage war, I cannot do evil. I am a Christian.'[10] When the soldier Martin of Tours converted to Christianity in Gaul in about 356, he resigned when faced with battle, declaring that 'combat is not permitted to me.'[11] Such antimilitarism also found support among the earliest Christian writers of the West. Tertullian, writing in North Africa at the turn of the third century, took a rigid stance against Christian involvement in war.[12] Hippolytus of Rome took a similar position shortly afterward in decrees intended as binding on Christians.[13]

Scholars examining the Christian prohibition on military service have offered various explanations for it. Some see it as part of a general pacifism in early Christian ideology, which precluded any shedding of blood. Others see its origins in the Christian condemnation of idolatry, since occasional ritual worship of the emperor was required of all soldiers until the year 312, after which Constantine permitted Christians the free practice of their religion. There is no need to rehearse the arguments of these scholars, who all see a sea change after 312. All recognize that after that date—whether through a falling away from the early pacifism, or because of the end of emperor worship, or because of the growing Christian domination of public life—individual Christians regularly served as Roman soldiers, prayers were offered to the Christian god before battle, and Christian symbols replaced pagan ones on soldiers' shields and army banners.[14]

It is not necessary to reconcile entirely these opinions; rather, one must respect the possibility that different Christians held various viewpoints on the permissibility of soldiering according to diverse traditions of interpretation and specific cultural influences, and that these viewpoints might have contradicted each other. Still, it is also possible to see a broad path in Christian attitudes—both before and after the year 312—in which participation in war happened and was permitted and yet not encouraged.[15] From this perspective, it does not matter that there were numerous Christian soldiers in the Roman army from the second century onward, which seems indisputable. Nor does it matter that the army was thoroughly Christian by the end of the fourth century, which also seems likely. For it was not the Christian men of the army, but the men who refused to be made soldiers, men like Maximilian, or the soldiers who refused continued service, men like Martin, who were seen as the Christian ideal.[16]

Sources from the period after 312 confirm this antimilitarist ideal even while permitting Christian soldiering. Augustine declared that no sin was involved in soldiering as a profession, in a letter addressed to a Christian military commander, but even he felt war to be a necessary evil at best.[17] The bishop Paulinus of Nola in southern Italy attempted to persuade a Christian soldier to abandon his military career by appealing to his religious ideals.[18] Leo the Great, bishop of Rome in the middle of the fifth century, called military service 'free from fault,' although he believed that refusal to fight was a better option, and ordered that a public penance should be required for Christian soldiers after the end of their secular career.[19] Several church councils and bishops argued for a ban on former soldiers becoming Christian priests, precisely because the sinful nature of the former could not be reconciled with the special holiness expected of the latter.[20] These writers all recognized more or less that military service was a part of life for Christians of the later Roman Empire, but they also held up the refusal to participate in war as exemplary and as a higher ideal.

The Christian ambivalence toward military service, permitting it but recommending against it, stemmed in part from the reluctant reconciliation of Christian ideology to a militaristic society. But the ambivalence can also be better understood by placing it within the context of the tension between traditional and emerging ideals of masculinity. Military identity was seen as a sign of Roman manliness, but the Christian ideal of nonviolence—the virtue known as *patientia*, usually blandly translated as 'patience' but from the Latin *patiri*, 'to endure, suffer, submit to'—was in a real sense based on an ideal of passivity and of being a victim. Again, if we return to the earliest days of Christianity in the western Mediterranean, we see how central a theme this quality of patience was to Christians and how it was defended. Tertullian, who devoted a whole treatise to the encouragement of *patientia*, called it 'the height of virtue and manliness' (*summa virtus*).[21] Needless to say, this ideal of patient submission contrasted sharply with the myth of the Roman as bellicose aggressor, driven by the ideal of the *vita militaris*. Christian men of the western Mediterranean in the third, fourth, and fifth centuries had to step gingerly to find their way between these opposing ideals.

Let us look, then, at the tension between *patientia* and militarism in the Western Christian tradition to clarify what was at stake for men in the development of an ideology of being a victim. Cyprian, the mid-third-century bishop of Carthage in North Africa and one of the earliest Latin Christian writers, also devoted an entire treatise to the subject of *patientia*. He understood it as an attitude of forbearance to all of life's ills:

> When any man is born and enters the abode of this world, he begins with tears. Although even then inexperienced and ignorant of all things, he can do nothing else at his birth except weep. With natural foresight he laments the anxieties and labors of this mortal life, and at its very beginning, by weeping and lamentations his young soul testifies to the trials of the world which

he is entering. For he toils and labors as long as he lives here. Nothing else can relieve those who labor and toil more than the consolation derived from patience.[22]

It is easy to see how a philosophy offering such consolation could have been attractive to men of the later Roman aristocracy, fraught with a sense of their helplessness in the collapsing empire. The idealization of such impotence as the virtue of patience offered at least a method for Roman men to begin to make sense of their lives through Christian ideology. (One also hears more than a few echoes of Stoic thought in this ideal.) Cyprian, continuing in a later passage in the same work, touched on the very areas of upheaval in men's lives as examples where patience was most helpful: marriage and sexuality, wealth and power. He wrote:

It is that same patience which tempers anger, bridles the tongue, governs the mind, guards peace, rules discipline, breaks the onslaught of lust, suppresses the violence of pride, extinguishes the fire of dissension, restrains the power of the wealthy, renews the endurance of the poor in bearing their lot, guards the blessed integrity of virgins, the difficult chastity of widows, and the indivisible love of husbands and wives. It makes men humble in prosperity, brave in adversity, meek in the face of injuries and insults.[23]

In many ways, patience was a resignation to the life and lot of the later Roman male.

Christian writers did not describe *patientia* only in terms of passivity or resignation, however, but also with metaphors of triumph and success. Endurance in suffering was, as Cyprian and Tertullian reminded their readers, a virtue with many Biblical precedents. Indeed, Cyprian dealt at length with the model of patience provided by Jesus, who, he reminded his readers, had still overcome the world, and he equated patience with the Roman ideal of *firmitas* (steadfastness).[24] These metaphors of triumph and success became the foundation for the idealization of patience and a key to the transformation of Roman masculinity through Christian ideology.

The ideal of *patientia* is apparent, above all, in the deaths of the Christian martyrs who, during the time especially of the third-century persecutions, served in many ways as visible signs of Christian perfection. Indeed, the perfection of the martyrs came precisely from their willingness to become victims.[25] Cyprian claimed just that, giving the example of Stephen, revered as the first of the martyrs, 'who, in preceding by his most fitting death the martyrs that were to come, was not only a preacher of the Lord's suffering but also an imitator of His most patient [*patientissima*] gentleness.'[26] The more violent the attacks on Christians, Cyprian maintained, the more unresisting should be the individual's response.[27] In a letter to a friend, Cyprian addressed the persecutors directly on behalf of the Christian martyrs: 'no one of us fights back when he is apprehended, nor do our people avenge themselves against your unjust violence however numerous and plentiful.'[28]

The victimization embraced in Christian patience and martyrdom were obviously contrary to traditional Roman standards of masculine militarism. Pagan critics of Christianity were quick to point out the unmanliness inherent in such a willing acceptance of violence and death. Or at least, this is the viewpoint preserved in the hagiographical and historical sources of the martyrs—all written by Christians—in which the stigma of unmanliness is often included as an aspect of the pagan antagonism toward the Christian martyrs. When the martyrs of Lyons in 177 were brought into the arena just before their deaths, the crowd taunted them as lowborn (*agenneis*) and unmanly (*anandroi*).[29] When the soldier Martin of Tours refused to fight, his commander ridiculed his reluctance as unmanly cowardice, saying that 'it was fear of the battle which was to occur the next day that was causing him to refuse participation, not any religious motive.'[30]

Some Christian men were willing to accept this label of weakness and unmanliness as part of the humility required by patience and to leave the retribution for such attacks to God. As Cyprian wrote, the ultimate victory of God made the individual's victory unimportant.[31] Other men tried to find ways both to remain true to what they felt to be their Christian ideals and to counter pagan imputations of unmanliness, or perhaps also to allay their own concerns about their manliness. These men made frequent reference to the paradox of the Christian reversal of symbols, in which weakness was strength and defeat was victory, to create a manifesto for a new Christian masculinity. They embraced the paradox that a man might find military success even in *patientia*.

Militarism and Martyrdom

The number of Christian writers who attempted to defend their manliness, despite the seeming weakness and passivity of the Christian ideal of *patientia*, demonstrates how important the preservation of a masculine identity was to Christian men in late antiquity. The supreme act of Christian patience was to be martyred, and so it is in the accounts of the martyrs that the manliness of pacifist and patient Christians is most often invoked. Indeed, as we will see, the Christian martyrs were said to represent the new military ideal of masculinity.

As early as the beginning of the third century, Western Christian writers defended the manliness of pacifist Christians. 'For what wars should we not be fit,' asked Tertullian, 'even with unequal forces, we who so willingly yield ourselves to the sword, if in our religion it were not counted better to be slain than to slay?'[32] In other words, Christians would have made the best soldiers, exactly because of their steadfastness in facing suffering, had their religious beliefs not discouraged them from participating in war. In his account of the life of Martin of Tours, written two centuries later, Sulpicius Severus drew upon precisely the same motif, defending Martin's manliness despite his pacifism:

> Martin undismayed [by his military commander's charge of cowardice, noted above], was made all the bolder by the attempt to intimidate him. 'If my act is set down to cowardice [*ignavia*] rather than to faith,' he said, 'I shall stand unarmed tomorrow before our lines. In the name of the Lord Jesus and protected only by the sign of the cross, without shield or helmet, I shall penetrate the enemy's ranks and not be afraid.'[33]

Martin's bravery was never tested, Sulpicius noted, because God intervened and the enemy cancelled the battle. A similar story was also told of Victricius, a former soldier who became bishop of Rouen in Gaul in the early fifth century. Victricius was supposed to have faced torture gladly for his refusal to continue fighting in battle. Again, his courage was never tested, since God struck his torturer with blindness.[34]

The emphasis on the manliness of the martyrs can be seen, above all, in the military metaphors that Latin writers used to describe the martyrs, especially in the manly posture of the 'soldier of Christ' (*miles Christi*). The origins of this image are uncertain, though the phrase had been mentioned in earliest, Biblical Christianity, and there are other Roman, Hellenistic, and Jewish uses of the metaphor of life as a battle, some of which might have been in circulation in the western Mediterranean in the third century CE.[35] Among the Latin writers of late antiquity, though, the phrase 'soldier of Christ' was turned into the heart of a sophisticated (and complicated) defense of Christian manliness.

Tertullian was the first Christian writer to use the image of the soldier extensively, at the beginning of the third century, and he did so precisely in order to defend the manliness of Christians. Its first appearance occurs exactly in an apology for Christian victimization that Tertullian directed at pagan critics:

> It is quite true that it is our desire to suffer, but it is in the way that the soldier longs for war. No one indeed suffers willingly, since suffering necessarily implies fear and danger. Yet the man who objected to the conflict, both fights with all his strength, and when victorious, he rejoices in the battle, because he reaps from it glory and spoil. It is our battle to be summoned to your tribunals, that there, under fear of execution, we may battle for the truth. But the day is won when the object of the struggle is gained. This victory of ours gives us the glory of pleasing God, and the spoil of life eternal . . . Therefore we conquer in dying; we go forth victorious at the very time we are subdued.[36]

The paradox to which Tertullian alluded, that in the martyrs' seeming defeat they conquer, is simply the first instance of what would become a general theme in Latin Christian writings about masculinity: that true manliness is found in apparent unmanliness. In refusing to be soldiers, Tertullian argued, Christians were in fact showing themselves to be more militaristic and manlier than their pagan counterparts. The idea was a radical reworking of the traditional Roman military identity.

In a work addressed to the potential martyrs themselves, Tertullian returned to the same theme. He counseled those Christians imprisoned in the latest round of persecutions by the Roman government to count their hardships as a type of military discipline of their *virtus* for the battle ahead that was their approaching death. He wrote:

> No soldier comes out to the campaign laden with luxuries, nor does he go to action from his comfortable chamber, but from the light and narrow tent, where every kind of hardship and roughness and disagreeableness must be put up with. Even in peace soldiers inure themselves to war by toils and

inconveniences—marching in arms, running over the plain, working at the ditch, making the shield formation, engaging in many arduous labors. The sweat of the brow is in everything, that bodies and minds may not shrink at having to pass from shade to sunshine, from sunshine to icy cold, from the robe of peace to the coat of mail, from silence to clamor, from quiet to tumult. In like manner, O blessed, count whatever is hard in this lot of yours as a discipline of your manliness [virtus] of mind and body.[37]

His description is reminiscent of countless descriptions of the vita militaris.[38]

Tertullian's use of the military metaphor to describe Christians derived perhaps from some connection to the combination of militarism, masculine identity, and religion found in Mithraism.[39] Tertullian had a certain familiarity with the Mithraic religion and is one of our best sources of information about the cult in the West. [. . .] Tertullian explicitly contrasted the Mithraic soldier with the soldier of Christ, even while noting the similarities between the two images, complaining of how the enemies of Christianity ape certain religious truths.[40] The image of the Christian soldier, however, functioned for Tertullian in exactly the same manner as it had for the Mithraists. It gave a military flavor to religious devotion when describing the victory of individual salvation. In this context, Tertullian's use of the term solely to refer to martyrs, those individuals for whom the victory of salvation was assured, is noteworthy. Indeed, Tertullian in one passage called martyrdom a second baptism of blood instead of water, an image that also invites comparisons with the ceremony of initiation of Mithraism, called the taurebolium, in which initiates were drenched in the blood of a slaughtered bull.[41]

The soldier was also a uniquely masculine image, another parallel between Christian soldiering and the religion of Mithras (a religion that was open only to men). Christian writers were well aware of the masculine connotations of being a soldier of Christ when they described the martyrs, as we can see if we look at their descriptions of female Christian martyrs. Women were certainly among the early martyrs, and they were highly praised for their courage and willingness to suffer evil.[42] The fourth-century Christian historian Eusebius, for example, detailed at length the strength and courage of Blandina, a woman executed in Lyons in 177.[43] Nonetheless, at no point did he or any Christian writer of late antiquity ever call any woman a 'soldier of Christ.' (Paulinus of Nola is the only writer that even comes close to doing so, referring to Melania the Elder as 'a woman, inferior in sex, fighting for Christ (militans Christo) with the virtues of Martin,' but even he stopped short of using the expression miles Christi to describe her.[44])

The real importance of the soldier-of-Christ symbol, one might suppose, was not in its origins but in its uses for Western Christian ideology. The qualities that the ancient Romans had so admired in soldiers could be emphasized as the qualities that the Christian martyrs exhibited. For instance, a parallel might be easily drawn between the eagerness of soldiers for battle and the eagerness of Christians for martyrdom as equivalent indications of bravery, just as Tertullian did.[45] Tertullian's use of the term sacramentum (usually translated as 'sacrament,' but meaning a military vow of loyalty) for Christian baptism is another example of the implications of the military metaphor for Christian ideology. Several scholars have analyzed the military roots of this term in detail, noting among other facts that the term was by Tertullian's day already used to describe the rite of initiation into other religions, notably the Eastern mystery religions.[46] Such an oath of initiation had been part of the Mithraic religion, where the military aspects of the cult served to emphasize the analogy between the promise of participation in the religion and the oath of loyalty taken before war.[47] Tertullian made the same connection, writing to Christians that 'we were called to the warfare of the living God in our very response to the sacramental words [spoken at baptism].'[48]

The model of the Christian soldier carried important ramifications for masculine identity. As an ideal of manliness, the *miles Christi* could take on himself all of the military vocabulary of traditional masculinity: the bravery, endurance, and self-sacrifice even to the point of death, everything associated with the *vita militaris*. The difference between the secular soldier and the Christian soldier lay in his attitude toward victory. While a secular soldier who did not win the battles in which he fought was no good soldier, the Christian soldier won the battle by remaining passive in the face of violence and gained the victory in the very act of being defeated. In short, the figure of the soldier of Christ preserved for pacifist and suffering Christians a heroic and manly self-image in what might otherwise have been considered an unmanly action. Because of this paradox, Tertullian was able to suggest to Christians (all of whom in his day were potential martyrs): 'Let outrage be wearied out by your patience. Whatever that blow may be, conjoined with pain and contumely,' he declared, 'you wound that outrageous one more by enduring.'[49] [. . .]

The manly and militaristic image of the martyrs remained long after the period of persecution ended. Evidence of the continued popularity of the legends of the bravery and self-sacrifice of the martyrs comes especially from a poet of the early fifth century, Prudentius, who called his accounts of the martyrs *Liber peristephanon* (The Book of the Crowned). Even the title contains a military reference: victorious soldiers typically wore a crown of laurel leaves at their return home.[50] [. . .]

The manly image of the martyrs had other important uses. If the persecuted Christians could be depicted as manly, then the persecuting pagans could be equally depicted as unmanly. Accordingly, Tertullian contrasted the toughness or *duritia* of the deaths of true Christians in the arena with the effeminate softness or *mollitia* of the death in bed of even a pagan pseudomartyr such as Socrates.[51] The pagan also showed his true colors in the unmanly fury with which he persecuted Christians. So Prudentius, even while stressing the complete submissiveness of the martyr Romanus ('he goes unresisting, asks to be bound, and of his own accord turns his hands round behind him'[52]), nonetheless had the martyr-to-be ridicule his torturers precisely for their lack of manliness: 'What unmanly (*non virile*) strength! What effeminate (*molles*) hands! To think that in this long time you have failed to demolish the fabric of one poor perishing body!'[53] Leo the Great made repeated references to the weakness of the persecutors in a sermon written at Rome in the mid-fifth century for the feast of the martyrdom of Lawrence (again showing the popularity of the manly image of the martyrs long after the end of the persecutions). He said:

You gain nothing, you accomplish nothing, savage cruelty! The mortal matter is subjected to your inventions, but when Lawrence climbs to the sky, you lose. Your flames could not overcome the flame of the love of Christ, and the fire that consumed without proved weaker than the fire which burned within. Persecutor! You became the slave of the martyr when you raged against him [*servisti . . . cum saevisti*]; you added to his glory when you added to his suffering.[54]

Leo's manipulation of opposites only reinforced the general paradox of Christian masculinity.

Armed with their paradoxical masculinity, Christian writers could not only present their martyrs as heroic and manly, but also attack the pagan persecutors of their heroes as unmanly. Christian ideology thus absorbed much of the rhetoric of manliness and unmanliness in taking onto itself the image of military masculinity. By reversing the associations of the military metaphor and identifying manliness with pacifism, Christians helped to create a new masculine ideal, one that corresponded much more closely to Roman men's reluctance to engage in warfare.

The Interior Battle against Sin

From the martyrs, the image of the soldier of Christ was eventually extended, as the image of the *vita militaris* had been extended, to any man. Instead of battling physical persecutors, writers encouraged the Christian man to battle his interior weakness. In part, this reworking of the military image of Christian manliness was the necessary consequence of the end of persecution in 312, although references to the interior battle against sin predated the imperial edict of Christian toleration. The interiorization of the military image also permitted individual Christian men to see themselves as soldiers without having to face the supreme sacrifice demanded of the martyrs.

Cyprian of Carthage was an important participant in the extension of the notion of the soldier of Christ from martyrs alone to include all Christians. Although Cyprian wrote in a period of intensified persecution of Christians in North Africa in the middle of the third century, he relied much more on preparedness for martyrdom rather than death itself as defining the Christian soldier:

> For he cannot be a soldier fitted for the war who has not first been exercised in the field . . . It is an ancient adversary and an old enemy with whom we wage our battle . . . If he finds Christ's soldier unprepared, if unskilled, if not careful and watching with his whole heart; he circumvents him if ignorant, he deceives him incautious, he cheats him inexperienced. But if a man, keeping the Lord's precepts, and bravely adhering to Christ, stands against him, he must needs be conquered, because Christ, whom that man confesses, is unconquered.[55]

In this sense, any Christian individual, martyr or not, could be a soldier of Christ. Cyprian added that 'if persecution should fall upon such a soldier of

God, his virtue [or manliness, *virtus*], prompt for battle, will not be able to be overcome'; and that 'in persecution the warfare, in peace the purity of conscience, is crowned.'[56] Cyprian extended this metaphor at length, writing how 'the white-robed cohort of Christ's soldiers ... by a steadfast formation have broken the turbulent ferocity of an attacking persecution, prepared to suffer imprisonment, armed to endure death.'[57] Again, Cyprian's emphasis was always on the readiness for martyrdom. The use of the term *sacramentum* for baptism, which Cyprian adopted from Tertullian, helped to strengthen this idea that a military-type oath bound all Christians, whether martyr or not (and referring to Christians as a white-robed cohort did the same, since Christians wore white robes at baptism, a parallel with a soldier's uniform).

It is significant that it was Cyprian who first extended this military metaphor, given what we know of his personal history as bishop of Carthage. Instead of facing martyrdom in the Decian persecution of 249 to 250, he fled the city. This action was viewed as cowardice and as abandonment of his episcopal responsibilities by some, especially by a large group of near-martyrs called the confessors. The confessors had been imprisoned and sentenced to death, but had been freed after the period of persecution ended, before the sentences against them had been carried out. Revered as living 'soldiers of Christ' for their willingness to face death, their denunciation of Cyprian carried considerable weight. Cyprian returned to his episcopal duties, but for the remainder of his writing career he downplayed the authority of these confessors who criticized him.[58] The extension of the military image from martyrs alone to Christians may even have been a conscious strategy to deny to the confessors an important part of their authority. Cyprian's ideas were also a necessary rebuttal of those of Tertullian, who had written a treatise a century earlier opposing flight in persecution, describing it as cowardly and unmanly.[59] [. . .]

It was after the end of the period of persecution of Christians, though, in the fourth and fifth centuries, that the use of the symbol of the soldier of Christ for all men was especially popular and widespread. This is logical, since the risk of martyrdom no longer existed and Christian writers were faced with the choice of abandoning the metaphor or using it in a different way. This choice is the exact point of a fifth-century sermon of Leo the Great, who urged his Christian audience not to abandon the fortitude that they had acquired 'in the times when the kings of this world and all of the secular powers raged with a cruel impiety against the people of God,' but to 'be vigilant and beware of the perils which are born from the very quietness of peace.' He continued:

> The enemy himself, who was ineffective in open persecutions, now uses hidden arts to our destruction: so that those whom he did not make flee by striking them with afflictions, he now makes fall away by love of luxury ... The terror of proscriptions he has changed to the fire of avarice, and those whom he did not destroy with condemnations, he corrupts with lust.[60]

Leo considered the Christian who resisted lust and the love of luxury as brave and as true a soldier of Christ as the martyr who faced death. The Christian poet Commodian concurred: 'if you conquer by your good deeds, you are in that way a martyr.'[61]

It is easy to see how such an idea was attractive to Christian men, since it permitted any of them to view their daily struggles as part of a larger battle between good and evil. Such an idea made them the equivalent of the martyrs by being comparable followers of the 'commander of the heavenly army' (*dux caelestis militiae*), as Ambrose of Milan described Jesus in the late fourth century.[62] Each man might say to himself what Hilary of Arles is supposed to have said to his saintly predecessor as bishop in the fifth century: 'In truth, I believe that no one disputes that only the occasion of martyrdom was lacking in you, and not the spirit for it.'[63]

Similarly, a man's daily fight against sin and temptation might take on cosmic significance when construed in the fashion of a metaphysical war against the Devil and his armies. Already in the mid-third century, Cyprian often returned to the refrain that the true enemy of all Christians was the Devil, picturing him besieging the individual as a military commander might try to take a town. 'Circling about each one of us,' he wrote, 'and just as an enemy, besieging an enclosed people, he explores the walls and tries to find out if any part of our members is less stable and less faithful, by which he might, approaching, penetrate to the interior.'[64] [. . .]

Individual Christian participants in such battles, in turn, could perceive themselves as heroic fighters in an invisible but consequential war. By the middle of the fifth century, the seasons of the Christian churches and the commemorative feasts of the martyrs continually reminded Christian audiences of the military flavor of their lives. The theme of the war of the soul against sin could be found in virtually any writer preaching sermons on these occasions. Peter Chrysologus devoted a sermon entirely to the subject:

> [The Devil] conquers us in abundance, takes possession of us in pleasure, gorges himself at our feasts, and whenever luxury does not let go of us, lust arouses, a pagan procession carries us off, ambition compels us, wrath urges us, fury fills us, hatred kindles within us, desire inflames us, cares concern us, profits seize us . . . Then virtues die, vices live, pleasure runs forth, respectability perishes, mercy disappears, and greed abounds, confusion reigns, order succumbs, and discipline lies prostrate. These very things war against the soldier of Christ; these very things are the cohorts of Satan and . . . the legions of the Devil.[65]

What is being fought here, of course—lust, love of luxury, wrath and pride—are the vices that were long held to make a man effeminate. [. . .] The attack against the vices was nothing more than a war between *virtus* and *mollitia*. It was the battle to be a man. [. . .]

Christian writers generally recognized the irony in describing nonviolence in militaristic terms, but placed this within the context of the general paradox of Christian masculinity. Sulpicius Severus, in probably the most famous example of this disjunction of image and reality, had Martin of Tours say at his moment of conversion: 'I am a soldier of Christ; it is not permitted to me to fight.'[66] But a similar disjunction appears in the anonymous story of the martyrdom of Marcellus, killed in North Africa in about 300: 'it is not fitting that a Christian, who fights for Christ his Lord, should fight for the armies of this world.'[67] Peter

Chrysologus also emphasized the paradox of militarism in *patientia:* 'The meek warrior is to subdue the devil, the gentle victor is to reduce the pride of the world, the peaceful fighter is to blot out the discords of nations.'[68] But it was Tertullian who had first embraced this paradox: 'let [the Devil] find you armed and fortified with concord; for peace among you is battle with him.'[69]

One final point remains. Spiritual militarism left little concern for the actual state of the defenses of the empire, only of secondary importance in a symbolic universe that measured victory by internal rather than external success. As Ambrose wrote: 'The church conquers hostile forces not with physical weapons but with spiritual ones.'[70] It is with this in mind that we should return to Augustine's comments on war and violence with which we began the chapter, and in this context that we should situate the general Christian reaction to the disintegration of the Western Empire. Augustine, who believed that military service was permissible to Christian men, referred to the different battles waged by Christians. 'Some fight for you against invisible enemies by prayer,' he wrote in a letter written in 418 and after the sack of Rome, 'while you strive for them against visible barbarians by fighting.' Nonetheless, he left little doubt about which he considered to be the more important war, saying that the men who had renounced the world's battles enjoyed 'the highest self- discipline' and 'a more prominent place' before God.[71] Augustine wrote his own treatise on Christian patience at about the same time. In it, he reminded his readers of the experiences of the martyrs:

> In the body, they were fettered, they were imprisoned, they were beset with hunger and thirst, they were tortured, cut to pieces, lacerated, burned, butchered. Yet, with a faithfulness that remained unmoved, they subjected their minds to God while they suffered in the flesh whatever cruelty came into the minds of their assailants.[72]

In other words, the example of the martyrs could be used to see Christians through whatever kind of physical attacks they might face, even if the age of the martyrs had passed.

In fact, the age of the martyrs had not quite passed. The Christian associates of Augustine in North Africa were suffering tortures not only at the hands of brigands and barbarians, but also by bands of Christian renegades known as the Circumcellians, a splinter group of an already divided North African Christian population. [. . .] In correspondence with an Italian priest in 409—that is, a year before the sack of Rome—Augustine downplayed the attacks of the barbarians, even suggesting that 'the deeds of barbarians might be less destructive.'[73] [. . .] Yet, he continued by asking: 'What difference does it make whether they are set free from the body by fever or by the sword?'[74] Augustine demonstrated here how much the image of the soldier of Christ had come to be a moral rather than a physical one. In one of the sermons devoted to consoling Christians upset by the sack of Rome, Augustine contrasted the temporary sufferings of the victims at Rome with the eternal ones of the damned in Hell, for these were the true tortures to fear and the sufferings to be avoided.[75]

The manly self-image of Christian men did not depend on the successes of the armies of the Roman Empire but on the victories of an interior struggle, thanks to a redirection of the military image inward. Here was a masculine image that could no longer be threatened with a sinking into effeminacy by the collapse of Roman borders and the invasion of foreign troops, because it did not depend on outside variables such as these, but on the integrity of interior borders. Roman men who were Christians could continue to aspire to a *vita militaris* of steadfastness and courage and wage victorious wars of conquest, even in the final desperate years of the Western Empire and without ever picking up a sword, by redefining those wars in Christian terms of sin, suffering, and salvation.

Notes

1 Hieron. *Epist.* 127.12. (*NPNF* 6). Cf. idem, *Epist.* 123.15–16, 165.2. Abbreviations of ancient authors and some of their works are from the Oxford Latin Dictionary. If a translation is listed alongside the primary source, I used it in the text, and noted when I made changes to it. If no translation is listed, the translation is my own.

2 Ambrose *De excessu fratris Satyri* 1.32.

3 Sidonius Apoll. *Panegyricus . . . Avito* ll. 532–8. The address was delivered in 456. See also Hanson (1980).

4 Salvian *De gubernatione Dei* 7.6; cf. 4.12–14. I have replaced 'fornication of Goths' for *fornicatio apud illos* with 'fornication among them.'

5 Salvian *De gubernatione Dei* 7.23. Salvian also claimed (6.12–15) that the attacks of the barbarians were no worse than the morals of the Roman population.

6 August. *De excidio urbis Romae sermo;* August. *Sermo* 296 (ed. *PL* 38). See also the analysis by de Bruyn (1993, 405–21).

7 August. *De civ. D.* 1.1,7. Cf. Salvian *De gubernatione Dei* 7.1.

8 August. *De civ. D.* 3.14. Cf. Tert. *Apol.* 25; Min. Fel. *Oct.* 25.1–2. Elsewhere (*Contra Faustum Manichaeum* 22.74–8) Augustine described the lust for domination as more generally human, and war as something that God permitted to show that even earthly good things were given only at his disposal.

9 August. *De civ. D.* 19.7. Those authors who emphasize Augustine's role in the development of the Christian concept of just war include Bainton (1960, chap. 6); Russell (1975, chap. 1); Joblin (1988, chap. 3).

10 *Acta Maximiliani* 1.3.

11 Sulpicius Severus *Vita sancti Martini* 4.3.

12 Tert. *De idololatria* 19.1–3; idem, *De corona* 11. All of the works by Tertullian, except for *Adversus Marcionem*, are from the collected works *Opera* edited in the CCSL, vol. 1. See also Gero (1970, 285–98).

13 Hippolytus *Traditio apostolica* 16. This is an extremely problematic text; issues of its dating, authorship, and a comparative analysis with other early church regulations can be found in Cadoux (1982, 119–28).

14 The classic work arguing for a tradition of early Christian pacifism is Cadoux (1982). Modern representatives of this school include Bainton (1960, esp. chap. 5); and Windass (1962, 235–47). The classic argument for Christian antimilitarism as opposition more to idolatry than to bloodshed is Harnack (1905); for more recent scholarship arguing the same, see Helgeland (1974, 149–63). Emphasizing the shift from pacifism to militarism in Christianity after Constantine is Friesen (1986).

15 Ryan (1952, 1–32), sensibly argues for differing opinions among Christians.

16 On the presence of Christians in the Roman army of the second and third centuries, see Helgeland (1974); Hornus (1980, chap. 4). Heim (1991, 229–66) empha-

sizes the importance of a religious solidarity between the emperor and his troops, whether pagan or Christian. For excerpts from several accounts of military martyrs, see Helgeland, et al. (1985, chap. 9).

17 August. *Epist.* 189.4 (addressed to Boniface); cf. idem, *De libero arbitrio* 104.

18 Paulinus of Nola *Epist.* 25 (addressed to Crispianus).

19 Leo the Great *Epist.* 167.14.

20 See discussion in Hornus (1980, 190–3).

21 Tert. *De patientia* 1.7. An extended discussion of the concept of patience in Tertullian can be found in Rambaux (1979, chap. 6); and Fredouille (1972, chap. 7).

22 Cyprian *De bono patientiae* 12. I have changed the translator's 'anyone' for *unusquisque* to 'any man.'

23 Cyprian *De bono patientiae* 20.

24 Cyprian *De bono patientiae* 12, 16.

25 On the perfection of the martyrs, see Viller (1925, 3–25). On the willingness of Christians to face death, see Droge and Tabor (1992, esp. chap. 6).

26 Cyprian *De bono patientiae* 16.

27 Cyprian *De bono patientiae* 12.

28 Cyprian *Ad Demetrianum* 17. The translator has 'though' for *quamvis* where I have used 'however.'

29 Eusebius *Historia ecclesiastica* 5.1.35.

30 Sulpicius Severus *Vita sancti Martini* 4.4.

31 Cyprian *Ad Demetrianum* 17.

32 Tert. *Apol.* 37.5.

33 Sulpicius Severus *Vita sancti Martini* 4.5.

34 Paulinus of Nola *Epist.* 18.7.

35 The second-century author of the first letter to Timothy, writing under the name of the apostle Paul, used the phrase (1 Tim. 2.3, translated in the Latin Vulgate as 'bonus miles Christi Iesu'). On the military metaphor, see also Rom. 6.13; 2 Cor. 10.3–4; 1 Thess. 5:8. See Jaubert (1964, 74–84); Nielson (1961, 93–112); and Hobbs (1995).

36 Tert. *Apol.* 50, cf. idem, *De oratione* 19.

37 Tert. *Ad martyras* 3.1–3. I have changed the translator's *testudo*, left untranslated, to 'shield formation' (the *testudo* was a tortoiseshell, and by analogy, a temporary arch-shaped structure), and 'powers' for *virtus* to 'manliness.'

38 For late ancient examples see Kuefler (2001, 37–42).

39 The suggestion was first made by Harnack (1905, 58–9). See the more recent works by Demougeot (1961); and Rordorf (1969, 105–41).

40 Tert. *De corona* 15.

41 Tert. *Scorpiace* 6.9. In another place, Tertullian stressed the theme of individual salvation in defending the military images of the Old Testament to Marcion, the leader of a group of Christians who rejected the sacred quality of the writings of the Jewish Bible. Tert. *Adv. Marcionem* 4.20.

42 See Hall (1993); Jones (1993); and Frend (1978).

43 Eusebius *Historia ecclesiastica* 5.1.17–19.

44 Paulinus of Nola *Epist.* 29.6.

45 Tert. *Ad scapulam* 5.1–2.

46 Kolping (1948) provides a detailed list of classical uses of the term, as well as uses in early Latin translations of the Bible; see also Michaelides (1970), who points to the links between the uses of the term as military oath, as dedication or consecration to a purpose, and as a ritual sign of such a dedication in the mystery religions.

47 See discussion in Vermaseren (1963, 129–36). An exemplary text of such a Mithraic initiation is discussed by Cumont (1933, 151–60).

48 Tert. *Ad martyras* 3.1, cf. idem, *Scorpiace* 4.

49 Tert. *De patientia* 8.2. I have replaced the translator's 'outrageousness' for *inprobitas* with 'outrage.'

50 The heroic stance of the martyrs in the *Liber Peristephanon* has been noted and compared in style and content with various classical poets by Opelt (1967, 242–57); and Palmer (1989, chap. 5). A historical context is given by Fontaine (1980; 141–71). For a general treatment of Prudentius's works, their influences, and contexts, see Roberts (1993); and Malamud (1989). For more on the military martyrs see Kuefler (2001, 115–16).

51 Tert. *De animo* 55.

52 Prudent. *Perist.* 10 11. 69–70.

53 Prudent. *Perist.* 10 11. 801–3. I have replaced the translator's 'want of manly' for *non virile* with 'unmanly' and 'delicate' for *molles* with 'effeminate.'

54 Leo the Great *Sermo in natali sancti Laurentii martyri* (in *Sermones*) 85.4.

55 Cyprian *Ad Fortunatum, praefatio* 2. The differences between an actual martyr and a potential martyr are not always clear in early Christian usage; several scholars have examined the terminology of martyrdom. See Hoppenbrouwers (1961) who discusses inter alia the use of the term *miles Christi* in Tertullian (71–3), Cyprian (149–51), and anonymous, mid- and late-third-century acts of the martyrs (161; 175–6).

56 Cyprian *Ad Fortunatum* 13.

57 Cyprian *De lapsis* 2; cf. Cyprian, *Epist.* 10, 39, 58, 76.

58 For details and consequences of Cyprian's flight, see Hinchliff (1974); and Sage (1975). For more on the image of the soldier of Christ in the writings of Cyprian, see Capmany Casamitjana (1956); and Hummel (1946). Hummel notes (24), apparently without irony, the view of Cyprian that a Christian could be prepared for martyrdom even when he flees from persecution. On this theme, see also Nicholson (1989, 48–65). It should be noted that Cyprian refused to flee in the next round of persecutions and was killed.

59 Tert. *De fuga in persecutione* 10.2; see also Novatian *Epist.* 30.6.

60 Leo the Great *Sermo* 36.3, cf. 40.2, 18.1–2, and 39.

61 Commodian *Instructiones* 2.21. See also Malone (1950, chap. 2). We are not certain when Commodian lived and wrote, but his use of the image of martyrdom in this way may help to confirm a date for him in the period after the persecutions.

62 Ambrose *Expositio evangelii secundum Lucam* 1.14, cf. idem, *De Helia et ieiunio* 1.1. Tertullian was the first to refer to Christ as a military commander with the term *imperator* (Tert. *De exhortatione castitatis* 12, *De fuga in persecutione* 10); used also by Cyprian (*Epist.* 15.1 and 31.4–5) and Lactantius (*Div. inst.* 6.8).

63 Hilary of Arles *Sermo de vita sancti Honorati* 38.4.

64 Cyprian *De zelo et livore* 2. See also Hummel (1946, 56–90); Capmany Casamitjana (1956, 255–85).

65 Peter Chrysologus *Sermo* 12.3; cf. 38 (on the endurance of wrongs), 101 (on resisting fear of physical death), 116 (on warfare against vice), and 133 (on the apostle Andrew as a warrior in the heavenly army). Cf. Valerian *Homeliae* 15 and 16 (on the heroic example of martyrs), Leo the Great *Sermones* 18 and 39 (on the daily battle against vice), and Leo the Great, *Sermo in natali . . . Machaebaeorum* (on the example of the seven Maccabean brothers).

66 Sulpicius Severus *Vita sancti Martini* 4.3: 'Christi ego miles sum: pugnare mihi

non licit.' In a letter to Sulpicius Severus, his admirer Paulinus of Nola (*Epist.* 1.9) repeated this image back to him: 'Tu uero miles Christi.'

67 *Acta Marcelli* 4.3.

68 Peter Chrysologus *Sermo* 170.

69 Tert. *Ad martyras* 1. See also August. *De civ. D.* 22.9 and Leo the Great *Sermo* 54.4 *de passione* for other examples highlighting this paradox.

70 Ambrose *De viduis* 8.49. For more on Ambrose's attitude toward actual war, which he justified by separating the physical and spiritual realms, see Swift (1970, 533–43); and Heim (1974, 267–81).

71 August. *Epist.* 189.5.

72 August. *De patientia* 8.10. See also the analysis by Kaufman (1994, 1–14).

73 August. *Epist.* 111.1.

74 August. *Epist.* 111.6.

75 August. *De exeidio urbis Romae sermo* 4. See also idem, *Epist.* 127 and 228 for Augustine's reactions to the barbarian invasions.

Literature

Primary Sources

Acta Marcelli. Ed. and trans. H. Musurillo. *The Acts of the Christian Martyrs.* Oxford: Clarendon Press, 1972.

Acta Maximiliani. Ed. and trans. H. Musurillo. *The Acts of the Christian Martyrs.* Oxford: Clarendon Press, 1972.

Ambrose. *De excessu fratris Satyri.* Ed. in *Corpus Scriptorum Ecclesiasticorum Latinorum* (CSEL) 73 and trans. H. de Romestin, *Nicene and Post-Nicene Fathers* (NPNF) 10.

——. *De Helia et ieiunio.* Ed. and trans. M. Buck, *Patristic Studies* (PS) 19.

——. *De viduis.* Ed. F. Gori. Milan: Bibliotheca Ambrosiana, 1989. Trans. H. de Romestin, *NPNF* 10.

——. *Expositio evangelii secundum Lucam.* Ed. in *Corpus Christianorum, Series Latina* (CCSL) 14.

Augustine. *Contra Faustum Manichaeum.* Ed. in *CSEL* 25.1.

——. *De civitate Dei.* Ed. in *CCSL* 47–8. Trans. H. Bettenson, Landon: Penguin, 1972.

——. *De libero arbitrio.* Ed. and trans. F. Tourscher. Philadelphia: Peter Reilly, 1937.

——. *De patientia.* Ed. in *CSEL* 41. Trans. L. Meagher, *Fathers of the Church: A New Translation* (FC) 16.

——. *Epistulae.* Ed. in part in *CSEL* 57. Ed. in full in *Patrologia Latina* (PL) 33. Trans. in part J. Baxter, *Loeb Classical Library* (CL). Trans. in full Wilfrid Parsons, *FC* 12, 18, 30, 32.

——. *Sermones.* Ed. in *PL* 38. Trans. M. Muldowney, *FC* 38.

Commodian. *Instructiones.* Ed. J. Durel. Paris: Ernest Leroux, 1912.

Cyprian. *Ad Demetrianum.* Ed. in *CCSL* 3a. Trans. R. Deferrari, *FC* 36.

——. *Ad Fortunatum.* Ed. in *CCSL* 3. Trans. R. Wallis, *Ante-Nicene Christian Library* (ANCL) 13.2.

——. *De bono patientiae.* Ed. in *CCSL* 3a. Trans. R. Deferrari, *FC* 36.

——. *De lapsis.* Ed. and trans. M. Bévenot. Oxford: Clarendon Press, 1971.

——. *De zelo et livore.* Ed. in *CCSL* 3a. Trans. R. Deferrari, *FC* 36.

——. *Epistulae.* Ed. in *CSEL* 3.2. Trans. M. Bévenot. Oxford: Clarendon Press, 1971.

Eusebius of Caesarea. *Historia ecclesiastica.* Ed. G. Bardy, *Sources chrétiennes* (SC) 31 and 41. Trans. R. Deferrari, *FC* 29.

Hieronymus/Jerome. *Epistulae*. Ed. J. Labourt. 8 vols. Paris: Belles Lettres, 1949–63. Ed. and trans. in part F. Wright, *LCL*. Trans. in part P. Schaff and H. Wace, *NPNF* 6. Trans. in part C. Mierow, *ACW* 33.

Hilary of Arles. *Sermo de vita sancti Honorati*. Ed. M.-D. Valentin, *SC* 235.

Hippolytus. *Traditio apostolica*. Ed. B. Botte, *SC* 11.

Lactantius. *Divinae institutiones*. Ed. in *CSEL* 19. Trans. M. McDonald, *FC* 49.

Leo the Great. *Epistulae*. Edited in *PL* 54. Trans. E. Hunt, *FC* 34.

——. *Sermones*. Ed. R. Dolle, *SC* 200.

Minucius Felix. *Octavius*. Ed. in *CSEL* 2. Trans. R. Wallis, ANF 4.

Novatian. *Epistulae*. Ed. in *CCSL* 4.

Paulinus of Nola. *Epistulae*. Ed. in *CSEL* 29. Trans. P. Walsh, *Ancient Christian Writers* (*ACW*) 35–6.

Peter Chrysologus. *Sermones*. Ed. in *CCSL* 24a. Trans. G. Ganss, *FC* 17.

Prudentius. *Works*. Ed. and trans. H. Thomson, *LCL.*

Salvian of Marseilles. *De gubernatione Dei*. Ed. in *CSEL* 8. Trans. J. O'-Sullivan, *FC* 3.

Sidonius Apollinaris. *Works*. Ed. and trans. W. Anderson, *LCL*.

Sulpicius Severus. *Vita sancti Martini*. Ed. J. Fontaine, *SC* 133. Trans. G. Walsh et al., *FC* 7.

Tertullian. *Opera*. Ed. in *CCSL* 1. Trans. A. Roberts and J. Donaldson, 3 vols. *ANCL* 11–13. Edinburgh: T&T. Clark, 1869. Trans. in part W. Le Saint, *ACW* 13.

——. *Adversus Marcionem*. Ed. and trans. E. Evans. Oxford: Clarendon Press, 1972.

Valerian. *Homilia*. Ed. In *PL* 52. Trans. G. Ganss, *FC* 17.

Secondary Sources

Bainton, Roland. 1960. *Christian Attitudes toward War and Peace: A Historical Survey and Critical Reevaluation*. New York: Abingdon.

Cadoux, John C. 1982. *The Early Christian Attitude to War* (1919; reprint). New York: Seabury.

Capmany Casamitjana, Jose. 1956. *'Miles Christi' en la espiritualidad de san Cipriano*. Barcelona: Casulleras.

Cumont, Franz. 1933. 'Un fragment de rituel d'initiation aux mystères,' *Harvard Theological Review* 26:151–60.

De Bruyn, Theodore. 1993. 'Ambivalence within a "Totalizing Discourse": Augustine's Sermons on the Sack of Rome,' *Journal of Early Christian Studies* 1:405–21.

Demougeot, Emilienne. 1961, '"Paganus," Mithra et Tertullien,' in *Studia Patristica*, vol. 3, Texte und Untersuchungen zur Geschichte der altchristlichen Literatur, vol. 78. Berlin: Akademie-Verlag. Pp. 354–65.

Droge, Arthur, and James Tabor. 1992. *A Noble Death: Suicide and Martyrdom among Christians and Jews in Antiquity*. San Francisco: HarperSanFrancisco.

Fontaine, Jacques. 1980. 'Le culte des martyrs militaires et son expression poétique au IVe siècle: L'idéal évangélique de la non-violence dans le christianisme théodosien,' *Augustinianum* 20:141–71.

Fredouille, Jean-Claude. 1972. *Tertullien et la conversion de la culture antique*. Paris: Etudes Augustiniennes.

Frend, W. H. C. 1978. 'Blandina and Perpetua: Two Early Christian Heroines,' in *Les martyrs de Lyons* (177), eds J. Rougé and W. R. Turcan. Paris: CNRS. Pp. 168–86.

Friesen, John. 1986. 'War and Peace in the Patristic Age,' in *Essays on War and Peace: Bible and Early Church*, ed. W. Swartley. Elkhard: Institute of Mennonite Studies. Pp. 130–54.

Gero, Stephen. 1970. '*Miles Gloriosus:* The Christian and Military Service according to Tertullian,' *Church History* 39:285–98.

Hall, Stuart. 1993. 'Women among the Early Martyrs,' in *Martyrs and Martyrologies, Studies in Church History,* vol. 30, ed. D. Wood. Oxford: Blackwell. Pp. 1–21.

Hanson, R. P. C. 1980. 'The Church and the Collapse of the Western Roman Empire,' in *Aufstieg und Niedergang der Römischen Welt.* ed. Wolfgang Haase. Berlin: Walter de Gruyter. Pp. 910–73.

Harnack, Adolf. 1905. *Militia Christi. Die christliche Religion und der Soldatenstand in den ersten drei Jahrhunderten.* Tübingen: J. C. B. Mohr.

Heim, Francois. 1974. 'La thème de la "victoire sans combat" chez Ambroise,' in *Ambroise de Milan: XVIe centenaire de son élection episcopale,* ed. Y.- M. Duval. Paris: Etudes Augustiniennes. Pp. 267–81.

——. 1991. *Virtus. Idéologie politique et croyances religieuses au IVe siècle.* Berne: Peter Lang.

Helgeland, John. 1974. 'Christians and the Roman Army, A.D. 173–337,' *Church History* 43:149–63.

Helgeland, John, Robert J. Daly, and J. Patout Burns. 1985. *Christians and the Military: The Early Experience.* Philadelphia: Fortress.

Hinchliff, Peter. 1974. *Cyprian of Carthage and the Unity of the Christian Church.* London: Geoffrey Chapman.

Hobbs, Raymond. 1995. 'The Language of Warfare in the New Testament,' in *Modeling Early Christianity: Social Scientific Studies of the New Testament in Its Context,* ed. Philip Esler. New York: Routledge. Pp. 259–73.

Hoppenbrouwers, H. A. M. 1961. *Recherches sur la terminologie du martyre de Tertullien à Lactance* (Latinitas Christianorum Primaeva, vol. 15). Nijmegen: Dekker & Van de Vegt.

Hornus, Jean-Michel. 1980. *It Is Not Lawful for Me to Fight: Early Christian Attitudes Toward War, Violence, and the State,* trans. A. Kreider and O. Coburn. Scottdale: Herald.

Hummel, Edelhard. 1946. *The Concept of Martyrdom according to St. Cyprian of Carthage.* Washington, DC: Catholic University of America.

Jaubert, Annie. 1964. 'Les sources de la conception militaire de l'Église en 1 Clement 37,' *Vigiliae Christianae* 18:74–84.

Joblin, Joseph. 1988. *L'église et la guerre. Conscience, violence, pouvoir.* Paris: Desclée de Brouwer.

Jones, Chris. 1993. 'Women, Death, and the Law during the Christian Persecutions,' in *Martyrs and Martyrologies,* Studies in Church History, vol. 30, ed. D. Wood. Oxford: Blackwell.

Kaufman, Peter Iver. 1994. 'Augustine, Martyrs, and Misery,' *Church History* 63:1–14.

Kolping, Adolf. 1948. *Sacramentum Tertullianeum.* Regensberg: Regensbergsche Verlagsbuchhandlung.

Kuefler, Mathew. 2001. *The Manly Eunuch: Masculinity, Gender Ambiguity, and Christian Ideology in Late Antiquity.* Chicago: University of Chicago Press.

Malamud, Martha. 1989. *A Poetics of Transformation: Prudentius and Classical Mythology.* Ithaca: Cornell University Press.

Malone, Edward. 1950. *The Monk and the Martyr: The Monk as the Successor of the Martyr.* Washington, DC: Catholic University of America.

Michaelides, Dimitri. 1970. *Sacramentum chez Tertullien.* Paris: Etudes Augustiniennes.

Nicholson, Oliver. 1989. 'Flight from Persecution as Imitation of Christ: Lactantius' Divine Institutes IV.18, 1–2,' *Journal of Theological Studies* 40:48–65.

Nielson, E. 1961. 'La guerre considérée comme une religion et la religion comme une guerre,' *Studia Theologica* 15:93–112.

Opelt, Ilona. 1967. 'Der Christenverfolger bei Prudentius,' *Philologus* 111:242–57.

Palmer, Anne-Marie. 1989. *Prudentius on the Martyrs*. Oxford: Clarendon Press.

Rambaux, Claude. 1979. *Tertullien face aux morales des trois premiers siècles*. Paris: Belles Lettres.

Roberts, Michael. 1993. *Poetry and the Cult of the Martyrs: The Liber Peristephanon of Prudentius*. Ann Arbor: University of Michigan Press.

Rordorf, W. 1969. 'Tertullians Beurteilung des Soldatenstandes,' *Vigiliae Christianae* 23:105–41.

Russell, Frederick H. 1975. *The Just War in the Middle Ages*. Cambridge Studies in Medieval Life and Thought, ser. 3, vol. 8. Cambridge: Cambridge University Press. Pp. 16–39.

Ryan, Edward. 1952. 'The Rejection of Military Service by the Early Christians,' *Theological Studies* 13:1–32.

Sage, Michael M. 1975. *Cyprian* (Patristic Monograph Series 1). Philadelphia: Philadelphia Patristic Foundation.

Swift, Louis. 1970. 'St. Ambrose on Violence and War,' *Transactions and Proceedings of the American Philological Association* 101:533–43.

Vermaseren, Maarten Jozef. 1963. *Mithras, The Secret God*, trans. T. Megew and V. Megew. New York: Barnes & Noble.

Viller, Marcel. 1925. 'Martyre et perfection,' *Revue d'ascétique et de mystique* 6:3–25.

Windass, G. S. 1962. 'The Early Christian Attitude to War,' *Irish Theological Quarterly* 29:235–47.

19

'Try to be a Man': The Rabbinic Construction of Masculinity

Editor's Introduction

Sociological gender studies have emphasized that 'man' cannot be conceived of as a separate gender unless it is seen in relationship to 'woman'. 'Men' and 'women,' in other words, are meaningless categories unless one examines them in their complementarity and their oppositional pairing. 'That gender is not fixed in advance of social interaction, but is constructed in interaction,' writes Connell, 'is an important theme in the modern sociology of gender' (1995, 35). In this chapter, Michael Satlow applies this insight to rabbinic Judaism in late antiquity, arguing that masculine ideals were shaped in opposition to notions about womanhood.

In a study of masculinity in rabbinic Judaism, other interactions – besides the interaction between men and women – shape the construction and analysis of Jewish men as gendered beings. For one, on the historical level, there is an interaction between two religious renewal movements based on the Hebrew Scriptures as they evolve side by side in late antiquity: Christianity and Rabbinic Judaism. It would be a mistake to assume that Jewish and Christian men in the Roman Empire lived completely separate lives. Rather, their lives intersected in a shared geographic and political space, and they drew from the same sources of medical knowledge from which they derived their understandings of morality, gender, and the body (see, for example, Boyarin 1999; 2004; Diamond 2004). They differed, of course, in the kinds of moral and religious responses to the world they inhabited, but it is important to see those differences as a result of interaction – not separateness – between these groups. Rabbinic texts talking about Jewish men, in other words, are not only juxtaposing Jewish men and women but also interact with non-Jewish men from Hellenistic and increasingly Christian backgrounds. When Satlow addresses, for example, the issues of self-restraint and *yetzer* (desire, drive, inclination), he rightly locates the rabbinical textual sources within the context of non-Jewish philosophical and medical knowledge of the time.

Interaction happens on yet another level, and this level concerns the study of masculinity itself. The discussion of Eilberg-Schwartz (chapter 14) and of Daniel Boyarin (chapter 8) already illustrates the spectrum – and possible controversies – within the study of Judaism when gender is brought into play. In a chapter on 'Engendering Jewish Religious History', Miriam Peskowitz questions whether one can understand the development of Judaism 'without taking into account the presence and constructedness of gender'.

For instance, the very terminology of the subject – 'women and rabbinic Judaism' – implies that 'rabbinic Judaism' and 'women' are separate entities. Consequently, the study of 'women' is inadvertently kept marginal to the enterprise of studying rabbinic Judaism ... [and] it allows some scholars to continue to study 'rabbinic Judaism' without considering women and gender. (Peskowitz 1997, 21)

Satlow takes into account the issue of gender in rabbinic Judaism but, unlike Peskowitz and other Jewish feminists, he does not focus on women but men. He thus responds to the need to take gender seriously in Jewish studies, and he also responds to the call of Jewish feminism not to privilege men. Avoiding a 'masculinist lens' (Peskowitz and Levitt 1997, 3), he contextualizes the authoritative claims on 'being a man' in the Jewish sources of late antiquity.

A reader less familiar with the interpretation of ancient Jewish sources may find the chapter below somewhat challenging in its details. But if one keeps in mind that rabbinic constructions of masculinity are played out at the various levels of interaction – between 'man' and 'woman', between 'rabbinic Judaism' and 'Christianity', and between 'Jewish studies' and 'Jewish feminism' – then the world and words of the rabbis, to which Satlow invites the reader, seem less impenetrable. Satlow writes:

I argue that the rabbinic evidence repeatedly returns to a consistent construction of manhood, which is portrayed as directly in opposition to the construction of womanhood in these texts. For the rabbis, being a man means using that uniquely male trait, self-restraint, in the pursuit of the divine through Torah study. For the rabbis, as for their non-Jewish elite contemporaries, manhood was an acquired status that was always at risk, and was thus consistently a focus of anxiety.

Publications by the Same Author

Satlow, Michael L. 1994a. '"They Abused Him Like a Woman": Homoeroticism, Gender Blurring, and the Rabbis in Late Antiquity'. *Journal of the History of Sexuality* 5/1:1–25.

——. 1994b. '"Wasted Seed": The History of a Rabbinic Idea'. *Hebrew Union College Annual* LXV:136–75.

——. 1995a. 'Sex and Shame in Late-Antique Judaism', in *Asceticism*, eds Vincent L. Wimbush and Richard Valantasis. New York: Oxford University Press. Pp. 535–43.

——. 1995b. *Tasting the Dish: Rabbinic Rhetorics of Sexuality*. Atlanta: Scholars Press.

——. 2001. *Jewish Marriage in Antiquity*. Princeton: Princeton University Press.

——. 2006. *Creating Judaism: History, Tradition, Practice*. New York: Columbia University Press.

Satlow, Michael L., David Brakke and Steven Weitzman (eds). 2005. *Religion and the Self in Antiquity*. Bloomington: Indiana University Press.

Further Reading

Boyarin, Daniel. 1999. *Dying for God: Martyrdom and the Making of Christianity and Judaism*. Stanford: Stanford University Press.

——. 2004. *Border Lines: The Partition of Judaeo-Christianity*. Philadelphia: University of Pennsylvania Press.

Connell, R. W. 1995. *Masculinities*. Berkeley: University of California Press.

Diamond, Eliezer. 2004. *Holy Men and Hunger Artists: Fasting and Asceticism in Rabbinic Culture*. Oxford: Oxford University Press.

Peskowitz, Miriam. 1997. 'Engendering Jewish Religious History', in Peskowitz and Levitt, pp. 17–39.

Peskowitz, Miriam and Laura Levitt (eds). 1997. *Judaism since Gender*. New York: Routledge.

'Try to be a Man': The Rabbinic Construction of Masculinity

MICHAEL L. SATLOW

What does it mean 'to be a man'? Whereas in most societies at most times the determination of 'maleness' is straightforward (Does he have male genitalia? What is his chromosomal make-up?), locating the cultural constructions of 'manhood' is far more difficult. Many anthropologists have noted that in contrast to models that postulate a common psychology for all men, everywhere, all the time, constructions of manhood are varied and culturally dependent.[1] For example, the highly aggressive behavior necessary for retention of manhood for a male resident of Andalusian Spain can be contrasted to the sanctioned behavior of males of Tahiti. Unifying these diverse constructions of masculinity, however, is the common idea that manhood is an acquired state that males must fight both to attain and maintain. Because manhood is an achieved state, it can never be taken for granted: a male must be constantly proving that he is a man. 'The state of being a "real man" or "true man" [is] uncertain or precarious, a prize to be won or wrested through struggle' (Gilmore 1990, 1). Similar constructions of manhood are evident today throughout the circum-Mediterranean (see esp. Pitt-Rivers [1966] 1974, 19–77; Brandes 1980; Gilmore 1987, 2–21; Herzfeld 1985).

These anthropological approaches can be applied to late antique cultures. What, if anything, did it mean to the Greeks, Romans, Jews, and Christians of antiquity 'to be a man'? What are the contours of manhood in these societies? Is manhood constructed as something elusive, a 'prize to be won' or a culturally transformed state? Are there correspondences or divergences among the ideals of manhood that these overlapping groups constructed? For once, the fact that the vast bulk of the surviving literature from late antiquity was authored by elite men can help in answering these questions. Whether fictional, poetic, philosophical, religious, or moralistic, this literature, almost all written by elite males, often presumes assumptions of manhood.

This is no less true of rabbinic literature. Written and compiled over the course of five centuries (first to sixth centuries CE) by men who at least considered themselves members of the elite class, the literature of the rabbis can be mined for answers to this same question: to the rabbis, what did it mean 'to be a man'? Although the rabbis rarely address this topic explicitly, there are many places within this literature that reveal rabbinic assumptions about masculinity.

I argue that the rabbinic evidence repeatedly returns to a consistent construction of manhood, which is portrayed as directly in opposition to the construction of womanhood in these texts. For the rabbis, being a man means using that uniquely male trait, self-restraint, in the pursuit of the divine through Torah study. For the rabbis, as for their non-Jewish elite contemporaries, manhood was an acquired status that was always at risk, and was thus consistently a focus of anxiety. This construction of manhood did not arise from nothing; it only slightly reconfigures elements found in both Jewish Hellenistic writings and in the literature of the non-Jewish elite, especially moralists and philosophers. In order to contextualize the rabbinic evidence, I shall briefly review some roughly contemporaneous nonrabbinic constructions of masculinity. Finally, because the rabbis represent only a single (and probably numerically very small) class of Jews, I shall comment on how my understanding of the rabbinic construction of manhood compares with that of contemporaneous nonrabbinic Jews (see Cohen 1992, 157–73; Levine 1989).

Nonrabbinic Constructions of Masculinity

The rabbinic construction of masculinity derives from themes present in the pre-rabbinic Jewish wisdom traditions and non-Jewish (and Philonic) philosophy and medicine. Two themes in particular stand out in this literature. First, self-mastery is a prerequisite for a life of the mind (whether Torah study or the pursuit of wisdom); it is gendered as characteristically male. Second, the pursuit of the life of the mind also is gendered as a masculine activity. Together, these characteristics define what it means to be a man.

The importance placed on self-mastery by classical authors is well known. Philosophers and doctors frequently counseled elite men, who had absolute legal power over everything in their *potestas* ('authority,' 'dominion'), to control their passions and desires. As early as Aristotle, the lack of self-mastery was a sign of weakness, a characteristic that was soon gendered as feminine.[2] In both Greek and Roman society,

> gender hierarchy lies close to the heart of the discourse of self-mastery. Life is war, and masculinity has to be achieved and constantly fought for. Men are always in danger of succumbing to softness, described as forms of femaleness or servility.[3]

Only males had the capacity to exercise the self-control that, at least in the eyes of the philosophers and doctors, made them men.[4] It is likely that these same ideas migrated from Stoicism to the early church.[5]

Stowers has described the Jewish Hellenistic writers as presenting Judaism 'as a philosophy for the passions, a school for self-control' (1994, 58). Whether or not that was the real intent of these authors, they clearly assume that self-mastery was both important and a distinctly masculine trait. The *Testament of the Twelve Patriarchs* sees women as constitutionally unable to restrain themselves.[6] The *Testament of Job* most likely displays a uniform attitude that associates the female with the earthly and corruptible in contrast to the male, who is associated with the ethereal and spiritual.[7] In 4 Macc. 15.29—16.4, manliness is linked to reason, and is contrasted with the female characteristic of passion. Philo clearly sees the self-discipline necessary for efficacious philosophical study as a male virtue. He advocates an almost ascetic regimen that would help a man transcend his 'feminine,' corporeal aspect.[8] His comments on women consistently emphasize female lack of self-control, while his 'heroes' are all distinguished by their possession of this quality.[9] [. . .]

These themes are not confined to literature written in Greek. The fullest expression of these themes in a document originally written in Hebrew is Ben Sira. Ben Sira abounds with maxims about vigilance with regard to women and their sexual wiles and about exercising self-control.[10] According to Ben Sira, Wisdom's discipline will 'be a torment to [its follower], and her decrees a hard test' (4.17). Self-control is the conduct most becoming to the pursuit of Wisdom: 'Do not let your passions be your guide, but restrain your desires' (18.30). The author advises that one hold his wine 'like a man,' by which he means with restraint (31.25). As with the Jewish Hellenistic authors, Ben Sira sees self-restraint as the characteristically masculine activity that is a prerequisite for pursuit of Wisdom and Torah (see also Marböck 1971, 34–133).

This literature genders the pursuit of Wisdom and Torah study as masculine in two ways. First, as shown above, both activities require the masculine characteristic of self-restraint. Hence, these activities would be open to women only to the extent that they refrained from those activities that were gendered as appropriate for women. Second, both Wisdom and Torah are themselves, at least within the Jewish Hellenistic literature, gendered as female. Pursuit of Wisdom or Torah study, therefore, are presented as isomorphic to the erotic pursuit of a woman, an image that reinforces the masculine gendering of the activity. [. . .]

The presentation is slightly more complicated in Philo than in Wisdom of Solomon. Philo genders wisdom, or Sophia, as female; this, however, is a functional rather than ontological distinction (see Baer 1970, 65–6). Where Philo does portray Sophia as female, he does so only in order to illustrate one particular function of Sophia. Philo states:

As indeed all the virtues have women's titles, but powers and activities of consummate men. For that which comes after God, even though it were chiefest of all other things, occupies a second place, and therefore was termed feminine to express its contrast with the Maker of the Universe who is masculine, and the feminine always comes short of and is lesser than it. Let us then pay no heed to the discrepancy in the gender of the words, and say that the daughter of God, even Wisdom, is not only masculine but father, sowing and begetting in souls aptness to learn, education (*paideian*), knowledge, sound sense, good and laudable actions.[11]

Because Sophia occupies a second place to God, who is always gendered as a man, Sophia is functionally a female. In her relationship with humans, however, Sophia is ontologically a man. The gendering of Sophia is relative, depending upon the gender of Sophia's partner. This shifting use of gender stands in contrast to the Wisdom tradition, which constructs a manhood that involves an erotic attachment with the female wisdom through a disciplined life. Philo, nevertheless, clearly sees philosophy as an activity suitable only for the man, since 'the female gender is material, passive, corporeal and sense-perceptible, while the male is active, rational, incorporeal and more akin to mind and thought.'[12]

This sketchy survey points to a relatively uniform construction of manliness that was pervasive in Jewish and non-Jewish, Semitic and Greek elite groups in late antiquity. On a fundamental level all of these groups share the same conception of what it means to be a man: to exercise that (nearly) distinctly manly attribute of self-control in order to pursue Torah study, wisdom, or philosophy. This construction of manliness is very similar to that of the rabbis.

Rabbinic Constructions of Masculinity

The rabbis undoubtedly held that a penis made one male.[13] Those characteristics that make a male a man, however, are more elusive. While 'manhood' is rarely explicitly discussed in this literature, an examination of those passages that contrast the behavior, constitution, and responsibilities of men and women reveals two coherent themes. First, men are perceived as possessing the ability to control their desires and urges, whereas women are not. Second, because this quality of self-restraint is a prerequisite for Torah study, Torah study is constructed as the masculine activity *par excellence*. Thus for the rabbis the manly characteristic of self-restraint is necessary for acquisition of the manly virtue, Torah study; and it is the virtue of Torah study which leads to a relationship to God. For the rabbis, therefore, manliness is never secure; it is achieved through the constant exercise of discipline in pursuit of virtue, and vanishes the moment a male ceases to exercise that discipline.

Although desire and other carnal impulses (*yetzer*) threatened both men and women, only men are thought in rabbinic sources to have the ability to subdue those desires.[14] Whereas the 'warrior' (*gibor*) in the Hebrew Bible is the man of war,[15] to the rabbis he is the one who exercises self-restraint: 'Ben Zoma says . . . Who is a *gibor*? One who conquers his [evil] inclination, as it is written, "Better to be forbearing than mighty, to have self-control than to conquer a city" [Prov. 16.32].'[16] Self-restraint, like war, is constructed as a masculine activity.[17]

Many rabbinic stories revolve around male resistance of the *yetzer*. One (apparently Palestinian) tradition urges men, even when physically ill with love (or perhaps, lust) to resist.[18] A series of Babylonian stories illustrates both the power of the *yetzer* and the ability of holy men to resist temptation.[19] According to a tannaitic tradition, 'just as righteous men adjure their *yetzer* not to act, evil men adjure their *yetzer* to act.'[20] Men are portrayed as praying for God to help them control their *yetzer*. One tradition asserts explicitly that controlling the *yetzer* is a manly ability:

'Happy is the man who fears the Lord' [Ps. 112.1]. Happy is the man and not happy is the woman? R. Amram said in the name of Rav, 'Happy is the one who repents when [sic] he is a man.' R. Yehoshua b. Levi said, 'Happy is the one who overpowers his *yetzer* like a man.'[21]

Implicit in R. Yehoshua b. Levi's statement is the assumption that a woman cannot typically overpower her *yetzer*.[22]

That self-restraint is constructed by the rabbis as a manly activity is seen more clearly against rabbinic portrayal of women and their own sense of self-control. Women are consistently portrayed as lacking sexual self-control. Women are thought to have an evil inclination at least as strong as men's. According to one Mishna, 'A woman prefers one measure of material substance along with sex (*tiplut*) to nine measures of material substance and abstinence.'[23] According to one *baraita* (tannaitic teachings outside of tannaitic documents), when plied with wine, women will lose control to the point that they will sexually proposition animals.[24] The redactor of the Babylonian Talmud even goes so far as to suggest that a woman's sexual urge can seize her, making her unaccountable for her actions.[25] Because women are seen as sexually tempting to men and as unable to resist sexual advances, rabbis present them as posing a particular threat to male self-control.[26]

This latter supposition generates some of the rabbinic laws against 'seclusion' (*yihud*).[27] 'A man should not remain alone with two women, but a woman may be alone with two men.'[28] Why should a man be forbidden from remaining alone with two women, but not a woman with two men? Unlike women, men are assumed to be able to control each other: a single man may succumb to temptation, but if there are two men at least one will resist and prevent his fellow. Women, however, cannot prevent each other from sexual advances, because they cannot control their desires. As a *baraita* explains, 'What is the reason [that a man cannot be alone with two women]? As it is taught of the school of Eliyahu, because women are light-headed.'[29] Women are understood as constitutionally unable to exercise self-restraint.

One striking example can be further adduced to demonstrate that the rabbis used the category of self-restraint for gender constructions. Among the many eugenic suggestions found in rabbinic literature (primarily the Babylonian Talmud), male modesty and self-restraint in sexual intercourse are seen as the most common techniques for reproducing *men*. Controlled sex leads to male children, whereas, one can assume, uncontrolled sex leads to female children.

The Babylonian Talmud contains several eugenic suggestions. These passages, which outline how one can guarantee (righteous) male children, assume that the way in which one has sexual intercourse influences the sex and character of the child conceived.[30] Two of these passages strikingly link the production of males with manly control during intercourse. According to one of these passages, a woman will conceive a male child if she 'emits her seed' first:

(a) R. Yitzhak said in the name of R. Ami, 'If the woman emits her seed first she will bear a male. If the man emits his seed first she will bear a female, as it is written, ". . . When a woman who brings forth seed bears a male [she shall be unclean seven days] [Lev. 12.2].'''

(b) Our Rabbis taught: 'At first they would say that if the woman emits her seed first she would bear a male. If the man emits his seed first she would bear a female.' And the sages did not explain the matter until R. Zadok came and explained, "Those were the sons whom Leah bore to Jacob in Paddan-Aram, in addition to his daughter Dinah [Gen. 46.15]." The males depend on the females, and the females on the males.'

(c) 'The descendants of Ulam—men of substance, who drew the bow—had many sons and grandsons [1 Chron. 8.40].' Is a man able to increase sons and grandsons? Rather, it is because they restrained themselves on the stomach so that their wives would emit seed first, so that their children would be male. And Scripture attributes to them as if they increased sons and the sons of sons.

(d) And this is what R. Katina said, 'I am able to make all my children male.'[31]

(a) and (b) offer alternative examples of the same conclusion, that the timing of female 'emission of seed'—presumably orgasm—determines the child's gender. This opinion is found elsewhere in the Babylonian Talmud, attributed only to Palestinian sages.[32] According to R. Ami (a), this view is derived from the identification of female emission of seed with male children in Leviticus 12.2, while R. Zadok (b) derives it from the attribution of Jacob's sons to Leah and Leah's daughter to Jacob in Genesis 46.15. In (c), an anonymous exegesis of 1 Chronicles 8.40 is used to demonstrate the effectiveness of the maxims presented in (a) and (b). Here it is clear that the Talmud understands the suggestions of (a) and (b) to refer to self-control; (d) is attributed to a Babylonian sage, and has the same purpose—that of attributing to men the power to reproduce men.[33]

Assuming that 'emits her seed first' means 'have an orgasm,' this tradition links manly self-control during sex to the conception of male children. The longer the man controls himself, the more likely it is that his partner will emit her seed first, thus conceiving a male child. Moreover, the concern for female sexual pleasure as a demonstration of manly sexual competence is well attested in both anthropological literature and contemporaneous non-Jewish sources.[34] This text, therefore, links the conception of male children to two manly characteristics: the man's ability to control himself, and his ability to please his wife.

A second well-known story similarly links the conception of male children to manly self-control:

(a) R. Yohanan b. Dahavei said: 'The ministering angels taught me four things: Why are there lame [children]? Because they [the parents] "overturned their table." Why are there dumb [children]? Because they [the parents] kissed that very place [that is, had oral sex]. Why are there deaf [children]? Because they [the parents] talked during intercourse. Why are there blind [children]? Because they looked at that very place [that is, at the female genitals].'

(b) An objection: They asked Ima Shalom, 'Why are your children most beautiful?' She said to them: 'He does not "talk" to me either in the beginning of the night or at the end, but in the middle of the night, and when he "talks" he reveals a handbreadth and covers a handbreadth, and he is similar to one whom a demon[35] forces. And I asked him: "what is the reason?" And he said to me: "so that I will not think of another woman" and his sons are found to come into *mamzerut* (offspring of a forbidden union).'[36]

Manly modesty and self-restraint in sex reproduces men. The implication, of course, is that a man who allows himself to lose control during intercourse will produce female children. The difference could hardly be clearer: when males act like men they are responsible for the reproduction of males (who will be future men), but when they allow nature to 'take its course' and do not exercise their manly attributes during sex then females are conceived.[37]

According to a *baraita*, women are exempt from the obligation of Torah study. This exemption derives from a narrow exegesis of Deuteronomy 11.19: '"Teach them to your sons"—your sons and not your daughters.'[38] Why are women exempted from Torah study? The exegetical reason cannot stand alone; frequently the word 'sons' (*banim*) is interpreted by the rabbis to refer to all children.[39] In order to understand the gender-valence that Torah study holds, it is necessary to discern how Torah is understood as a masculine activity throughout rabbinic literature. It is my contention that Torah study is constructed as distinctly masculine because women were seen as lacking the self-discipline needed for this activity.

Among its many social functions, Torah study was seen as almost as effective as consideration of the day of one's death in combating the *yetzer*.[40] When feeling overwhelmed with desire, men should hastily get themselves to a study-house, for Torah study is the antidote to desire:

> 'And you shall place these words upon your hearts' [Deut. 11.18]—this says that words of Torah are like a life-saving remedy. A parable: [This is similar] to a king who was angry at his son, struck him hard, and placed a bandage on the wound. He said to him: 'My son, as long as this bandage is on your wound, you can eat whatever you want; drink whatever you want; bathe in either hot or cold water, and you will not be hurt. But if you remove it, immediately a sore will arise.' So too the Holy One said to Israel, 'My children, I created for you the *yetzer hara* (evil inclination), which nothing is worse than—"But if you do not do right" [Gen. 4.7]. When you are engaged in words of Torah, it will not rule over you, but if you separate from words of Torah, behold it will rule over you, as it is written [in the continuation of the verse], "sin crouches at the door."'[41]

As elsewhere in rabbinic literature, Torah study was seen as an antidote to desire. Yet the life of Torah study was represented as a difficult one that involves a substantial amount of individual deprivation.[42] Just as Torah study leads to self-restraint, self-restraint is a prerequisite for Torah study. Moreover, as Boyarin has shown, Torah study was represented in terms so erotic that Torah was in competition with women, vying for the time and energy of the Jewish man.[43] These references to Torah represent her as a demanding mistress. It is this representation of Torah as female, and the starkly sexual language often used to describe the Jewish man's relationship to it, that is relevant to this article. To my knowledge, Torah is never represented in rabbinic literature as 'male.' To pursue Torah is an unquestionably masculine (and, by definition, heterosexual) activity. And it is Torah study, with its self-reinforcing cycle of self-control, that presents the clearest path to God.

Within rabbinic literature, there are very few occurrences of phrases equivalent to the English phrase 'be a man,' which would indicate quite clearly what traits exactly are expected of men. Yet the few times that the phrase does occur is in the context of Torah study. At the end of a passage that details the characteristics necessary for successful Torah learning, the Mishna states, 'in a place where there are no men, try to be a man (ish).'[44] The only other place that this expression is found is in connection with a saying attributed to Hillel. This saying says that where people are not receptive to the Torah one should 'gather,' but where they are receptive, one should 'scatter' his Torah learning.[45] The Babylonian Talmud follows the citation of this tradition with a statement attributed to Bar Kappara: 'Where [goods] are cheap, hurry and buy. Where there is no man, there be a man (gibor)!'[46] While it is impossible to determine the original context of this statement (if it is genuine), the Talmud understands it to mean that when one is in a place with no scholars, one should teach, but where there is a wiser scholar one should refrain from teaching.[47] 'To be a man' in these passages means at least to teach (and could easily imply study as well) Torah. Another Palestinian tradition links 'being a man' to liturgical expertise.[48]

As with the sources on manly self-control, when this construction of the role of Torah study in carving out manly identity is placed in contrast with rabbinic dicta on female Torah commentary, the differences between the gender constructions are highlighted. All of the rabbinic comments that condemn female Torah study do so on the grounds that because a woman does not have the requisite amount of self-discipline, she will use her Torah knowledge for ill. The signal example of condemnation of female Torah study is R. Eliezer's statement that 'anyone who teaches his daughter Torah, [it is as if][49] he teaches her licentiousness (tiplut).'[50] The Talmud itself comments that R. Eliezer opposes teaching one's daughter Torah, because female Torah knowledge will make her temporarily immune from the sota ordeal, the test of the suspected adulteress described in Numbers 5.11–31. Because she knows that she is immune, she will be more likely to commit adultery. A tradition in the Palestinian Talmud expresses fear that a woman will use her knowledge of Torah to seduce unwary men.[51]

Here is the ultimate subversion of Torah knowledge: that women were seen as unable to engage in Torah study because they lacked the requisite self-control lends the so-called 'Beruriah traditions' their force. These traditions, scattered throughout rabbinic literature, involve a woman, sometimes identified as 'Beruriah,' who demonstrates knowledge of Torah and rabbinic law.[52] Regardless of the historical value (or lack of value) of these stories—that is, what they can tell us about the rabbinic education of women—the presence of a learned woman in the tradition serves a heuristic function.[53] The function of a learned female in most of these traditions is either to shame men or, in one case, to emphasize the danger of a woman, especially one thought to be learned in Torah. Thus, when a rabbi uses the example of Beruriah to shame a man who is of doubtful origin and who wants to learn Torah, he is essentially saying that 'you can not even equal the learning of a woman.'[54] Other traditions present her besting a Sadducee or rebuking a student—the force of both would have been to shame the men involved.[55] In another tradition one rabbi advises another to give wide berth to Beruriah, exchanging with her not a single word more than necessary.[56] Her knowledge of Torah, the passage implies, makes her a sexual danger. [. . .] Whenever rabbinic sources portray a woman learning Torah, there is a heuristic reason that depends upon the assumption that women, unlike men, do not learn Torah.

The Elusiveness of Rabbinic Masculinity

The rabbinic construction of masculinity posits men as polar opposites of women, and their traits as opposite those that they gender as 'feminine.' Whereas women are constructed as having little self-restraint and thus no true access to the primary means of a relationship with God (namely Torah study), the rabbis define men as almost the precise opposite. A woman is born a woman and no matter what she does she can never be anything but a woman. Manhood, however, is the result of a cultural transformation: a man can never lose his biological maleness, but he can lose his standing as a man. This model accounts well for the correspondences between rabbinic constructions of women and non-Jews. Gentiles, like women, are portrayed by the rabbis as totally lacking the ability to control themselves.[57] To be a woman or a Gentile is essentially to be in a natural state. To be a rabbinic man of God is to be transformed, to rule over those natural tendencies that women and Gentiles manifest.

A rabbinic tradition that combines this link between Gentiles and loss of self-control and the contrast of 'natural' and 'civilized' can be found in the Babylonian Talmud. According to the Mishna, a Jew should not leave an animal alone with a Gentile for fear of bestiality.[58] [. . .] Gentile men are portrayed as so lustful that when they fail in their attempt to commit adultery, they settle for an animal. They are so lustful because they were not 'civilized' at Sinai. By standing at Sinai, Israel lost its natural state of lust. Moreover, the text leaves unclear whether 'Israel' is meant to include Jewish women. Whether or not the rabbis would historically place women at Sinai, exempting them or even prohibiting women from Torah study (and thus continuing revelation) suggests a link between even Jewish women, lust, and a natural state.

Because the rabbis understand being a man as transcending nature, manhood is always at risk; it is always there to be lost. As noted above, Gilmore asserts that among many cultures manhood is a prize to be won and a status males usually must struggle to preserve; I argue that this also applies to the rabbinic construction of manhood. Two major forces always threaten to emasculate the rabbinic man: the *yetzer* and, to a lesser degree, the loss of Torah knowledge.

The body is seen as a battleground between the good and evil inclinations:

Rav said: 'The *yetzer hara* can be compared to a fly that sits between the two openings of the heart, as it is written, "Dead flies turn the perfumer's ointment fetid and putrid"' [Eccl. 10.1].
Shmuel said: 'It can be compared to a kind of thread . . .'
Our rabbis taught: 'In a person (*adam*) there are two kidneys. One counsels good, the other bad.'[59]

The *yetzer hara* dwells within a person, always waiting to wreak its havoc. Unchecked, the male *yetzer hara* was thought to increase in strength:

> At first, [the *yetzer hara*] is weak like a woman, and afterwards it gets stronger like a man. R. Akiba said: 'At first, [the *yetzer hara*] is made like a spider thread; later, it is made like the rope that drags the plow, as it is written, "Ah, those who haul sin with cords of falsehood and iniquity as with cart ropes"' [Isa. 5.18].[60]

The *yetzer* continually assails a man's defenses. Women, who share with men a strong sexual desire, are portrayed as presenting a particular threat to male sexual self-control, hence to their manhood.[61] A man must daily fight the same battle in order to preserve his status as a man. Letting the *yetzer* do its will unhindered for even a short while is to risk increasing the strength of the *yetzer* ultimately to the point of completely overwhelming the man. Constitutionally, women cannot defend themselves against this; but men must be aware of even the slightest temptation or provocation and battle it.

For the rabbis, Torah knowledge, like self-control, is never safe. Knowing something today is no guarantee that one will know it tomorrow. Without constant reinforcement, Torah knowledge is easily lost, and the price of that loss is high: 'R. Dostai b. Yannai in the name of R. Meir says: "Anyone who forgets a single thing of his learning, the Scripture accounts him as if he is liable with his life."'[62] By losing Torah knowledge, a man risks descending to the status of the *'am ha-aretz*, the common man who is just a little above the woman and Gentile.[63]

I think, therefore, that the several rabbinic sources that portray Israel or the patriarchs as feminine in contrast to the masculine job are best understood functionally rather than ontologically.[64] They do not set a model for how the rabbis see themselves and their endeavor as much as they provide a metaphor to describe God's power, which is never represented as feminine.[65] Whenever a metaphor shows the direct relationship between God and individuals or the people Israel, God is always the player with more social power: Lord/servant; king/subject; parent/child; man/woman. When, then, the rabbis seek a gendered metaphor to portray the relationship between God and any people or individual, it is not surprising that Israel is feminized. Similarly, this functional use of gendered characteristics for describing power relationships seems to me also to explain best the feminized representation of rabbis in relation to their rabbinic superiors. Rabbinic masters might be feminized in the portrayal of their relationship with God, but their students (*talmide hakamim*) are feminized in the portrayal of their relationship with their masters.[66] In both cases, a relative social hierarchy is being worked out. This portrayal, however, in no way confuses what to the rabbis were very clear gender lines.

For the rabbis, manhood is elusive. It is difficult to win and difficult to keep.[67] When a man relaxes his self-defenses, when he succumbs to his *yetzer*, he risks his manhood. Thus, it is not surprising that the rabbis linked femininity, loss of control, and male homoeroticism (see Satlow 1994, 1–25). Male homoeroticism, especially as the receptive partner in anal intercourse, is seen as merely the embodiment of the loss of control that turns a man into a woman. Manhood, for the rabbis, is a prize to be won and constantly rewon. [. . .]

Conclusions

I have argued throughout this article that for the rabbis, to be a man means to use that uniquely male trait, self-restraint, in the pursuit of the divine through Torah study. This conclusion appears to hold for all rabbis, early and late, Palestinian and Babylonian, and cuts across all rabbinic documents. For the rabbis, being a man is the opposite of being a woman, much in the same way that culture is constructed as opposite of nature. A woman is born a woman and no matter what she does, she can never be anything but a woman. A man, however, is the result of a cultural transformation: a man can never lose his biological maleness, but he can lose his standing as a man. Moreover, this rabbinic understanding of manliness is by no means unique. It is amply attested in pre-rabbinic Jewish sources as well as in contemporaneous non-Jewish sources drawn especially from elite intellectual circles. [. . .]

Notes

1 For an example of the essentialist position that there is a common core to the male experience, see Gregor (1985, 9).

2 Aristotle *Eth. Nic.* 1150b 20.

3 Stowers (1994, 45); his entire survey of this theme is excellent (42–82). My thanks to Shaye Cohen for this reference. See also Brown (1988, 9–12).

4 On the increasing tendency of all philosophies to emphasize male self-control, see Foucault (1988, 39–68). The Stoics advocated sexual equality in the pursuit of philosophy, but for someone like Musonius Rufus this occurred only when a woman abandoned those trails that were gendered as feminine. See Musonius Rufus 3 (Cora E. Lutz, trans., *Musonius Rufus: 'The Roman Socrates'* [reprint; New Haven: Yale University Press, 1947] 41); 4 (ET 42–9, on educating daughters); 6 (ET 52–7, on training). Note that in fragment 1, Musonius disapproves of the man who allows his body to become 'effeminate' (ET 34–5). On the Stoic attitude toward sexual equality, see Favez (1933, 1–8); Manning (1973, 170–7); and Colish (1985, 1.36–8). On Roman medicine and self-control, see Soranus *Gyn.* 1.30. Note that he also recommends virginity for women, but that he appears to assume that this would be much harder for women who had had intercourse than those who had not. See Foucault (1988, 105–23). On the idea of women being unable to control themselves, see Dixon (1984, 343–71).

5 On these themes in the early church, see Clark (1991, 221–45); Rousselle (1988, 129–40); and Meyer (1985, 554–70). On Stoic influence on the church, see Spanneut (1969); Colish (1985, 2). [. . .]

6 *T. Reub.* 5.1–7. See also *T. Judah* 13; *T. Joseph* 6.7, 10.2–3; *Ep. Arist.* 250. See further Hultgard (1991, 46–7).

7 See Garrett (1993, 55–70); see also Horst (1989, 99–113).

8 Philo *Sob.* 5; see also *Mos.* 2.68. For ascetic tendencies in Philo, see Fraade (1986, esp. 263–6); Horsley (1979, 38–40).

9 Philo *Abr.* 253 (Abraham); *Sob.* 65 (Jacob); *Ias.* 42–8 (Joseph); *Mos.* 2.68 (Moses). On Philo's description of women, see Sly (1990).

10 Sir 9:1–9; 19:2–3; 25:16–26; 36:21–25; 42:9–14. See further Trenchard (1982, 95–128); Camp (1991, 1–39).

11 Philo *Fug.* 51–52 (ET Supp. 2.15–16). See also *Abr.* 99–102.

12 Philo *Quaest. in Ex.* 1.8 (ET 5.37–79; modified). Wegner talks of Philo's 'inextricable nexus between rationality and masculinity' (1991, 47, also 48–9).

13 The emphasis on the penis as defining who is a man, which is of no small import in a legal system that assigns different liabilities to males and females, is most clearly seen in rabbinic discussions on those who have either male and female genitalia (*androgonos*) or no genitals at all (*tumtum*). A male can lack testicles and remain a male; he is simply a eunuch. On rabbinic definitions of the male see *m. Yebamot* 8.6; *t. Yebamot* 10.2; *b. Yebamot* 82b, 83b; *y. Yebamot* 8.6, 9d.

14 On the *yetzer*, see nn. 18–21 below. It is important here to differentiate between rabbinic constructions and reality. Rabbinic sources do mention in passing that some women could indeed control themselves, but this observation never penetrated to the level of gender construction. Shame, it appears, was one societal institution that promoted female chastity among Jews in late antiquity. See Satlow (1995b, 535–43).

15 For examples of *gibor* in the Hebrew Bible see Gen. 10.8; 2 Sam. 17.10; Jer. 46.12; and Amos 2.14. God too is described as *gibor* in Jer. 32.18.

16 *m. 'Abot* 4.1 (ET *The Mishna*, 1988, 4.368–369). All translations of rabbinic texts are my own. I have indicated the original texts on which the translations are based throughout. Translations of citations from the Hebrew Bible are from *Tanakh* (1985).

17 The word used in this tradition for 'conquer' (*kobesh*) also appears in Gen. 1.28, in which God exhorts both Adam and Eve to procreate, 'fill the earth, and conquer it.' One midrash expresses surprise that Eve too is commanded to 'conquer': 'A man restrains (*kobesh*) his wife so that she not go to the market, for every woman who goes out to the market is destined to fall (*lehikashel*), as it is written, "Now Dinah . . . went out [to visit the daughters of the land]" [Gen. 34.1]' (*Gen. R.* 8.12 [*Midrash Bereshit Rabbah* 1965, 66]; note the manuscript problems with this tradition). This tradition subverts both Gen. 1.28 and 34.1, while relying on a complex web of assumptions. Use of the word *lehikashel* implies some kind of sexual transgression. Thus, 'conquering' is understood as something that only a man can do, and should do to keep his wife (who lacks self-restraint) from wandering out and succumbing to sexual temptation (not rape, as in Genesis 34). The more common expression that denotes a man overcoming his *yetzer* is *mitgaber* ('to become master [or man] over'), which contains the same root as *gibor*. See, for example, *b. Meg.* 15b.

18 *b. Sanh.* 75a (with some variants at *y. Šabbat* 14.4, 14d and *y. 'Aboda Zar.* 2.2, 40d).

19 *b. Qidd.* 80b.

20 *Sifre Deut.* 33 (Finkelstein [1939] 1969, 60).

21 *b. 'Aboda Zar.* 19a.

22 According to Rashi's exploration of this passage, both traditions contrast a man in his youth to an older man, who no longer has the power he once had. I assume that this interpretation is occasioned by the odd syntax of Rav's tradition.

23 *m. Sot.* 3.4 (ET *Mishna* 1988, 3.240–241). See further Wegner (1988, 153–62).

24 *b. Ketub.* 65a.

25 *b. Kerub.* 51b, 54a; *b. Qidd.* 81b.

26 See, for examples, *m. 'Abot* 1.5; *m. Sot.* 1.5; *t. Sot.* 1.7; *Sifre Num.* 139; *y. Sot.* 3.4, 19a; *b. Šabbat* 62b (par. *b. Yoma* 9b); *y. Šabbat* 14.4, 14d (par. *y. 'Aboda Zar.* 2.2, 40d; *b. Sanh.* 75a). For a discussion of these passages, see Satlow (1995, 158–67).

27 See *t. Qidd.* 5.9–10. 14; *y. Sot.* 1.3, 16d; *b. Qidd.* 80b–81b. See further Epstein (1948, 68–75).

28 *m. Qidd.* 4.12 (ET *Mishna* 1988, 4.328–329).

29 *b. Qidd.* 80b. See also *b. Šabbat* 33b (women cannot be trusted with information); *b. Sot.* 32b; *Tanhuma vayikra'* 22 on Gen. 22.1.

30 On male modesty during sexual intercourse, see the discussion in Satlow (1995, 298–303).

31 *b. Nid.* 31 a–b.

32 *b. Ber.* 60a (R. Yitzhak b. Ami); *b. Nid.* 25b. (R. Yitzhak b. Ami), 28a (R. Yitzhak), 71a (R. Hama b. R. Haninah).

33 See also *b. 'Erubin* 100b.

34 See Galen, *De usu pertium* 14.6 (1968, 2.628–630). This approach continues throughout the Middle Ages. See Bullough (1994, 31–45).

35 MS Munich 95 reads, 'prince.'

36 *b. Ned.* 20 a–b.

37 See, for another example, the story of R. Yohanan whose sexual self-control is so strong, that women who merely look upon him conceive after his likeness (*b. Ber.* 20a). See the discussion on rabbinic eugenics in Satlow (1995, 303–13).

38 *Sifre Deut.* 46 (ET Finkelstein 1969, 104). See also *b. Qidd.* 29b; *y. Ber.* 1.3, 4c; *y. 'Erubin* 10.1, 26a.

39 For example, the commandment for a son to honor his parents is interpreted as referring to both children. See *b. Qidd.* 29b.

40 *m. 'Abot* 3.1.

41 *Sifre Deut.* 45 (ET Finkelstein 1969, 103–104). For other rabbinic comments on the efficacy of Torah study, see *b. Ber.* 5a; *b. Sukk.* 52a-b; *b. Qidd.* 30b: *b. Sanh.* 107a.

42 See *m. 'Abot* 6.4.

43 Boyarin (1993, 134–166). Several passages in the Babylonian Talmud juxtapose male sexual impropriety and Torah knowledge. See *b. 'Erubin* 64a; *b. Sot.* 4b.

44 *m. 'Abot* 2.6 (ET *Mishna* 1988, 4.359).

45 *b. Ber.* 6 (7).24. There is a close parallel in Aramaic at *y. Ber.* 9.8, 14d. See further Lieberman (1955, 1.125).

46 *b. Ber.* 63a. A close parallel, attributed to Hillel himself, can be found at *Sifre Zuta. Pinhas.*

47 See also the commentary of the *Tosafot. b. Sot.* 23b.

48 *Lev. R.* 23.4.

49 Some versions do not have this clause, which most likely migrated into the Mishna from the talmudic discussion on *b. Sot.* 21b.

50 *m. Sot.* 3.4 (ET *Mishna* 1988, 3.240).

51 *y. Sot.* 3.4, 19a.

52 *t. Kel. B. Qamma* 4.17; *t. Kel. B. Mes.* 1.6; *Sifre Deut.* 307; *b. Ber.* 10a (2); *b. 'Erubin* 53b–54a (2); *b. Pesah.* 62b; *b. 'Aboda Zar.* 18a–b (2).

53 On the tendency to approach these stories positivistically, see the sophisticated study of Goodblatt (1975). Boyarin (1993, 167–196, esp. 181–196) takes seriously the heuristic function of these stories as evidence for rabbinic ambivalence over female Torah study.

54 *b. Pesah.* 62b.

55 *b. Ber.* 10a; *b. 'Erubin* 53b–54a.

56 *b. 'Erubin* 53b. If Boyarin, following Rashi, is substantively correct that the enigmatic 'incident of Beruriah' mentioned at *b. 'Aboda Zar.* 18a–b refers to her being seduced by a disciple of her husband's, that may be another example of this function. Although Rashi sees her Torah knowledge as making her the target of the seduction, it is easy to imagine her Torah knowledge as leading to her own seduction of a man.

57 See, for examples, *b. Yebamot* 103a–b (par. *b. Hor.* 10b; *b. Nazir* 23b): *b. Qidd.* 49b; *b. Sanh.* 39b, 95b. For a discussion of this phenomenon, see Satlow (1995, 146–53). The underlying link between women and non-Jews may account for the three things for which a man should thank God each morning: that he was not created a non-Jew, an ignoramus (*bor*), or a woman. See *t. Ber.* 6(7).18. It is interesting to note that according to the Bible, it is Adam who is created from the earth, implying a more natural state. The rabbis deal with this by revaluing earth in their treatment of these accounts. See *Gen. R.* 17.8: *b. Nid.* 31b.

58 *m. 'Aboda Zar.* 2.1. See also *t. 'Aboda Zar.* 3.1.

59 *b. Ber.* 61 a. See also *b. 'Erubin* 18b.

60 *Gen. R.* 22.4 (*Midrash Bereshit Rabba* 1965, 210). See also *b. Sukk.* 52a; *b. Sanh.* 99b.

61 See *m. 'Abot* 1.5; *b. Sabbat* 62b (par. *b. Yama* 9b); *b. Ketub.* 51b, 54a, 62b; *b. Qidd.* 81b; *y. Kerub.* 1:8, 25d, 1:9, 25a; *y. Sanh.* 2:3. 20b.

62 *m. 'Abot* 3.8 (ET *Mishna* 1988, 6.365). See also *m. 'Abot* 3.7; *b. Menah.* 99b; *b. Ber.* 8b; *b. B. Qam.* 14b.

63 *b. Pesah.* 49b (partial par. *b. Sanh.* 90b). The tradition is placed in a series of *baraitot* that condemn *ame ha-aretz* ('people of the land,' 'common folk').

64 For what appears to be a modified ontological interpretation of these sources, see Eilberg-Schwartz (1994, 163–74), who cites examples of rabbinic traditions that feminize Adam, Abraham, Isaac, Jacob, Moses, and David. Nearly all of his examples are either directly from *Song of Song Rabbah* or are exegeses of verses from Song of Songs.

65 Even rabbinic representations of the *Shekina* do not contain feminine elements, despite the gender of the term. See Urbach (1975, 65).

66 Boyarin discussed rabbinic texts that feminize students in 'Dis/Owning the Phallus: Male Sexuality and Power in Early Christianity and Judaism,' a paper presented at AAR/SBL Annual Meeting, 1994. Boyarin's conclusions are different from the one presented here. Use of the term 'humility' in rabbinic literature also conforms to the model I argue for here: students should be humble before their social superiors (teachers) and all should be humble before God. My thanks to Jeffrey Rubenstein for bringing this to my attention.

67 Rabbinic Judaism, unlike many peoples, appears to show no knowledge of initiation rites. The *bar mitzva* does not appear to have been any kind of male initiation and circumcisions are performed when the child is so young that this too would not qualify as such a rite. To my knowledge, there is only a single text that might suggest a male initiation rite. In *Tanhuma vayikra'*22 on Gen. 22.1, in which Abraham is trying to trick Sara into letting him take Isaac to be sacrificed, he says that he is going to take Isaac to a place where they *mehankim* ('educate') youths. Elsewhere in rabbinic literature the term means to initiate through a process of teaching, a definition that would make little sense here (see *b. Nalir* 29a; *m. Yoma* 8.4).

Literature

Baer, Richard A. Jr. 1970. *Philo's Use of the Categories Male and Female.* Leiden: Brill.

Boyarin, Daniel. 1993. *Carnal Israel: Reading Sex in Talmudic Culture.* Berkeley: University of California Press.

Brandes, Stanley. 1980. *Metaphors of Masculinity: Sex and Status in Andalusian Folklore.* Philadelphia: University of Pennsylvania Press.

Brown, Peter. 1988. *The Body and Society: Men, Women, and Sexual Renunciation in Early Christianity*. New York: Columbia University Press.

Bullough, Vern L. 1994. 'On Being a Male in the Middle Ages,' in *Medieval Masculinities: Regarding Men in the Middle Ages*, ed. Clare A. Lees. Minneapolis: University of Minnesota Press. Pp. 31–45.

Camp, Claudia V. 1991. 'Understanding a Patriarch: Women in Second Century Jerusalem through the Eyes of Ben Sira,' in *'Women Like This': New Perspectives on Jewish Women in the Greco-Roman World*, ed. Amy-Jill Levine. Atlanta: Scholars Press. Pp. 1–39.

Clark, Elizabeth A. 1991. 'Sex, Shame, and Rhetoric: En-Gendering Early Christian Ethics,' *JAAR* 59:221–45.

Cohen, Shaye J. D. 1992. 'The Place of the Rabbi in Jewish Society of the Second Century,' in *The Galilee in Late Antiquity*, ed. Lee I. Levine. New York: Jewish Theological Seminary of America. Pp. 157–73.

Colish, Marcia L. 1985. *The Stoic Tradition from Antiquity to the Early Middle Ages* (2 vols). Leiden: Brill.

Dixon, Suzanne. 1984. '*Infirmitas Sexus*: Womanly Weakness in Roman Law,' *Tijdschrift Voor Rechtsgeschiedenis* 52:343–71.

Eilberg-Schwartz, Howard. 1994. *God's Phallus and Other Problems for Men and Monotheism*. Boston: Beacon.

Epstein, Louis M. 1948. *Sex Laws and Customs in Judaism*. Cambridge: Harvard University Press.

Favez, Charles. 1933. 'Une féminis le romain: Musonius Rufus,' *Bulletin de la Société de J'Etudes de Lettres* 20:1–8.

Finkelstein, L. (ed.). [1939] 1969. *Sifre on Deuteronomy*. New York: Jewish Theological Seminary of America.

Foucault, Michel. 1988. *The History of Sexuality: Care of the Self* (vol. 3), trans. Robert Hurley. New York: Random House.

Fraade, Steven D. 1986. 'Ascetical Aspects of Ancient Judaism,' in *Jewish Spirituality: From the Bible through the Middle Ages*, ed. Arthur Green. London: Routledge. Pp. 253–88.

Galen, 1968. *De usu pertium*, trans. Margaret Tallmade May (2 vols). Ithaca: Cornell University Press.

Garrett, Susan R. 1993. 'The "Weaker Sex" in the *Testament of Job*,' *JBL* 112:55–70.

Gilmore, David. D. 1987. 'Introduction: The Shame of Dishonor,' in *Honor and Shame and the Unity of the Mediterranean*, ed. David D. Gilmore. Washington, DC: American Anthropological Association. Pp. 2–21.

——. 1990. *Manhood in the Making: Cultural Concepts of Masculinity*. New Haven: Yale University Press.

Goodblatt, David. 1975. 'The Beruriah Traditions,' *Journal of Jewish Studies* 26:68–86.

Gregor, Thomas. 1985. *Anxious Pleasures: The Sexual Lives of an Amazonian People*. Chicago: University of Chicago Press.

Herzfeld, Michael. 1985. *The Poetics of Manhood: Contest and Identity in a Cretan Mountain Village*. Princeton: Princeton University Press.

Horsley, Richard A. 1979. 'Spiritual Marriage with Sophia,' *Vigiliae Christianae* 33:38–40.

Horst, Pieter W. van der. 1989. 'Images of Women in the Testament of Job,' in *Studies in the Testament of Job* (SNTSMS 66), eds Michael A. Knibb and Pieter W. van der Horst. Cambridge: Cambridge University Press. Pp. 99–113.

Hultgard, Anders. 1991. 'God and Image of Woman in Early Jewish Religion,' in

Image of God and Gender Models in Judaeo-Christian Tradition, ed. Kari Elisabeth Børresen. Oslo: Solum Forlag. Pp. 35–53.

Levine, Lee I. 1989. *The Rabbinic Class of Roman Palestine*. New York: Jewish Theological Seminary of America; Jerusalem: Yad Ben-Zvi.

Lieberman, Saul. 1955. *Tosefta ki-Fshuta: A Comprehensive Commentary on the Tosefta* (10 vols). New York: JTSA.

Manning, C. E. 1973. 'Seneca and the Stoics on the Equality of the Sexes,' *Mnemosyne* 26:170–7.

Marböck, Johann. 1971. *Weisheit im Wandel: Untersuchungen zur Weisheitstheologie bei Ben Sira*. Bonn: Hanstein.

Meyer, Marvin W. 1985. 'Making Mary Male: The Categories "Male" and "Female" in the Gospel of Thomas,' *New Testament Studies* 31:554–70.

Midrash Bereshit Rabbah. 1965. eds J. Theodor and H. Albeck (2nd edn). Jerusalem: Wahrmann.

Mishna, The. 1988. Ed. Chanoch Albeck (6 vols). Tel Aviv: Mosed Bialik.

Pitt-Rivers, Julian. [1966] 1974. 'Honour and Social Status,' in *Honour and Shame: The Values of Mediterranean Society*, ed. John G. Peristiany (reprinted 1974). Chicago: University of Chicago Press. Pp. 19–77.

Rousselle, Aline. 1988. *Porneia: On Desire and the Body in Antiquity*, trans. Felicia Pheasant. Oxford and New York: Blackwell.

Satlow, Michael L. 1994. '"They Abused Him Like a Woman": Homoeroticism, Gender Blurring, and the Rabbis in Late Antiquity,' *Journal of the History of Sexuality* 5:1–25.

——. 1995. *'Tasting the Dish': Rabbinic Rhetorics of Sexuality*. Atlanta: Scholars Press.

Sly, Dorothy. 1990. *Philo's Perception of Women*. Atlanta: Scholars Press.

Spanneut, Michel. 1969. *Le Stoicisme des pères de l'Église de Clément de Rome à Clement d'Alexandrie* (2d edn.). Paris: Seuil.

Stowers, Stanley K. 1994. *A Rereading of Romans: Justice, Jews, and Gentiles*. New Haven: Yale University Press.

Tanakh. 1985. Philadelphia: Jewish Publication Society.

Trenchard, Warren C. 1982. *Ben Sira's View of Women: A Literary Analysis*. Chico: Scholars Press.

Urbach, Ephraim E. 1975. *The Sages: Their Concepts and Beliefs*, trans. Israel Abrahams. Cambridge: Harvard University Press.

Wegner, Judith Romney. 1988. *Chattel or Person: The Status of Women in the Mishna*. Oxford: Oxford University Press.

——. 1991. 'Philo's Portrayal of Women—Hebraic or Hellenistic,' in *'Women Like This': New Perspectives on Jewish Women in the Greco-Roman World*, ed. Amy-Jill Levine. Atlanta: Scholars Press. Pp. 41–66.

20

Begotten, Not Made: Conceiving Manhood in Late Antiquity

Editor's Introduction

Like Mathew Kuefler (chapter 18), Virginia Burrus argues that a new Christian male subjectivity supplanted other notions of masculinity in late antiquity. Also like Kuefler, she states that Christian men adopted 'female' traits as manly virtues, while, at the same time, hurling unwanted traits as 'effeminizing' vices at their theological adversaries. The new Christian discourse on manhood eventually developed its own coercive power that presented itself as 'truth', while portraying Christian heretics as misbegotten, effeminized, and dangerous men.

Where Burrus differs from Kuefler's *The Manly Eunuch* is her emphasis on the use of theological metaphors in creedal debates of the church fathers. In these debates, a new conception of Christian masculinity became increasingly divorced from materiality. Whereas Kuefler focuses more on the interplay of ideological and material forces that shape theological debates about gender, Burrus's *Begotten, Not Made* (2000) – and her sequels *The Sex Lives of Saints* (2004) and *Saving Shame* (2008a) – engage in an intertextual theological reading of patristic, hagiographic, and martyrological sources.

The ideal Roman man, Burrus observes in *Begotten, Not Made* (from which this chapter is excerpted), fashions himself in rhetorical performances, while the new Christian patristic ideal of man is rooted in a transcendent, immutable order. 'Receding is the venerable figure of the civic leader and familial patriarch; approaching is a man marked as a spiritual father.' Part of her overall thesis is that the patristic fathers construct a male self that becomes insulated from its physical origins, the maternal body. The fathers most heavily involved in the trinitarian debates emphasized paternal generativity and directed their 'attention away from sons emerging in time from wombs, to sons eternally quiescent in fathers' loins; away from children born, to words uttered.' 'To be begotten a son,' Burrus summarizes, 'is to transcend maternal birth, and to transcend the flesh – to be made word – is to become man' (2000, 56–7). The complications, however, have just begun, since, paradoxically, such paternal generativity, in which the (spiritual) word is a substitute for the (material) womb, relies on discursive strategies that effeminize men.

As a feminist cultural historian of the early church, Burrus sets herself the task of unpacking the complexity contained in theological metaphors. In *Begotten, Not Made*, she focuses on select writings by Athanasius of Alexandria, Gregory

of Nyssa and Ambrose of Milan – the three fathers who were instrumental in
interpreting and spreading the Nicene trinitarian doctrine.

Burrus's writing demands the reader's full attention because, as she explains,
there is no simple story to tell. She wants to preserve the ambiguity and paradoxes of patristic texts, which inscribe a new masculinity increasingly separated
from material practices while they, at the same time, create images that blur
the boundaries between sexed and gendered roles. In her analysis of ancient
theological debates, Burrus seamlessly crosses over into contemporary thought
of (feminist) cultural critics such as Luce Irigaray, Hélène Cixous, and Michel
Foucault. Within her own discipline, she works in line with such scholars as
Peter Brown, Patricia Cox Miller, Derek Krueger, David Brakke (chapter 24) and
Daniel Boyarin (chapter 8).

Publications by the Same Author

Burrus, Virginia. 1995. *The Making of a Heretic: Gender, Authority, and the Priscillianist
Controversy.* Berkeley: University of California Press.
——. 2000. *'Begotten, Not Made': Conceiving Manhood in Late Antiquity.* Stanford:
Stanford University Press.
——. 2004. *The Sex Lives of Saints: An Erotics of Ancient Hagiography.* Philadelphia:
University of Pennsylvania Press.
——. 2008a. *Saving Shame: Martyrs, Saints, and Other Abject Subjects.* Philadelphia:
University of Pennsylvania Press.
——. 2008b. 'Torture and Travail: Producing the Christian Martyr', in *Feminist Companion
to Patristic Literature*, ed. Amy-Jill Levine. New York: Continuum. Pp. 56–71.
Burrus, Virginia and Catherine Keller (eds). 2006. *Toward a Theology of Eros: Transfiguring
Passion at the Limits of the Discipline.* New York: Fordham University Press.

Further Reading

Brakke, David. 1995. *Athanasius and the Politics of Asceticism.* Oxford: Clarendon.
Boyarin, Daniel. 1993. '(Re)producing Men: Constructing the Rabbinic Male Body', in
Carnal Israel: Reading Sex in Talmudic Culture, Daniel Boyarin. Berkeley: University of
California Press. Pp. 197–225.
Brown, Peter. 1978. *The Making of Late Antiquity.* Cambridge: Harvard University
Press.
——. 1988. *The Body and Society: Men, Women and Sexual Renunciation in Early
Christianity.* New York: Columbia University Press.
Miller, Patricia Cox. 1983. *Biography in Late Antiquity: A Quest for the Holy Man.*
Berkeley: University of California Press.
——. 2009. *The Corporeal Imagination: Signifying the Holy in Late Ancient Christianity.*
Philadelphia: University of Pennsylvania Press.
Krueger, Derek. 1996. *Symeon the Holy Fool: Leontius's Life and the Late Antique City.*
Berkeley: University of California Press.

Begotten, Not Made: Conceiving Manhood in Late Antiquity

VIRGINIA BURRUS

Graduate studies undertaken in Berkeley in the 1980s equipped me for professional play in that corner of church history known, rather pointedly, as 'patristics.' Formed by a discipline that bore the very name of the Father(s), I resisted what seemed to me its most punishingly patriarchal practice: the study of authoritative theological doctrine. I found an ally—as well as an alibi—in the version of late Roman religious history frequently tagged 'late antiquity' and particularly associated with the work of Peter Brown. Having already imbibed feminism at the subversive edges of my undergraduate classics curriculum, I also eagerly read the available writings of Elizabeth Clark and the few other women historians working on what we sometimes referred to (with both humor and a certain ferocity) as 'matristics.' The approaches of social and cultural history promised to open up room for women and other 'others' (historical and contemporary) in the field of ancient church history. Thus might an academic enterprise that had begun as the study of doctrine's 'Sitz im Leben' finally put the Fathers and their teachings in their place—possibly even cut them down to size. After all, they had been taking up almost all the space for a virtual eternity, and some of us were impatient for change. [. . .]

Much as I have tried to elude their authority, the Fathers have continued to loom large in my view, and I seem destined to be a perversely loving daughter (even when equipped with cutting edges). Why not, then, surrender to destiny? I have asked myself. Wrapping the patristic authors tightly in a 'context' has not, after all, diminished the sprawling literary body (evidently not yet a corpse) that remains at the center of ancient Christian historical studies. Thus, I have pursued a different strategy in these pages, encouraging the Fathers to grow and swell. I have let them overwhelm and engulf me. And then, with nowhere left to go, I have crawled into the skins of their lively and capacious texts. If I have brought my old interdisciplinary allies—'late antiquity' and 'feminism'—inside with me, I am finally also ready to confide in them about the mysteries of doctrine buried in the heart of the patristic corpus, to which I am bound (as it now seems to me) by ties of desire as well as discipline.

> It is a coarse view of history which can see nothing
> in it but the flash of swords. (Gwatkin 1882, 4)

Like the Arian marginalia that first cite, then dispute, and finally largely ignore the Nicene texts inscribed in the centers of the pages of a fifth-century manuscript (McLynn 1996, 477–93), the present study emerges as a series of digressive glosses on Henry Gwatkin's 1882 historiographic judgment. Gwatkin argued that 'ecclesiastical history'—including the history of Christian belief—could not remain insulated from 'secular history.' However, he also sharply resisted the reductive secularization of church history that would convert ancient theological debates into mere wranglings for power, lamenting the selectivity of vision that could descry only 'the flash of swords.' His own goal was, rather, to produce a single, inclusive, 'organic and indissoluble' account of the Nicene-Arian struggles, an account that would take seriously the extent to which ecclesiastical history was the 'counterpart of secular' history, both 'pervading it and permeated by it with the subtlest and most various influences' (Gwatkin 1882, 1).

To a scholar writing near the turn of the millennium, the totalism of Gwatkin's vision may seem not merely naïve but even sinister in its ambition. Yet it is perhaps easier than ever to sympathize with his insistence on the complexity of the causalities at work within a history that remains open-ended, as well as with his particular resistance to the foreclosures effected by narrowly politicizing interpretations of theological disputes. In this work, I have deliberately taken what might at first glance appear to be a 'coarse view of history' (in Gwatkin's terms), adding another layer to recent reassessments of the Arian controversy by writing a new chapter in the history of masculine gender.[1] Indeed, it is by attending closely to the rhetorical 'flash of swords' in the doctrinal debates of the fourth century that I hope to show how, in the late Roman Empire, theological discourse came to constitute a central arena in which manhood was not only tested and proven but also, in the course of events, redefined: when the confession of the full and equal divinity of Father, Son, and Spirit became for the first time the *sine qua non* of doctrinal orthodoxy, masculinity (I argue) was conceived anew, in terms that heightened the claims of patriarchal authority while also cutting manhood loose from its traditional fleshly and familial moorings. My aim is not, however, to *reduce* theological texts to sources for a cultural history of masculine gender but rather, precisely by *also* reading them as such, to enable the flashing swords of ancient manhood to vivify theological material that has become so deadeningly familiar that we can no longer perceive some of its most fascinating and indeed downright queer aspects. By opening our eyes to (re)conceptions of manhood, we gain deeper insight into the powerful paradox of God's singular multiplicity. The creedal formula 'begotten, not made,' gives birth to a sublime patriliny, as masculinized, sexualized, and pluralized theological metaphors are balanced against the one God's transcendence of a humanity defined by sexual difference and the generative flux of the flesh. [. . .]

Inevitably, then, what I have above named a redefinition of manhood becomes visible primarily through my own re-marking of the traces of gradual, ambiguous processes sometimes resistant to the inscription of boundaries and the recording of shifts in terrain that are so beloved by historians, cartographers of time. To map out a plot, to write history at all, is perhaps not only to force one's 'material' but also, and more to the point, to coerce one's readers. Yet every writer of history is herself first of all a reader of history, coerced but also actively struggling, writing *back,* remarking upon an always already marked page. Here, then, I add my marginalia to an ongoing historiographic tradition.

'We must . . . take up the neglected data,' writes Gwatkin (1882, 4). Must we not therefore take up the neglected matter of man? As we shall see, a decisive shift in ancient Mediterranean ideals of masculinity had taken place by the end of the fourth century. (Around this 'shift'—inscribed as a re-mark on Gwatkin's text—pivots the drama of my own historical narrative.) Furthermore, the production of a sophisticated and tightly interwoven body of Christian literary texts contributed powerfully to the consolidation of that broader cultural shift. The emergent corpus of 'patristic' writings, authored predominately by ascetic bishops deeply involved in the trinitarian controversies of their day, now stands on the near side of a chronological watershed that it initially helped to create: receding is the venerable figure of the civic leader and familial patriarch; approaching is a man marked as a spiritual father, by virtue of his place in the patrilineal chain of apostolic succession, and also as the leader of a new citizenry, fighting heroically in a contest of truth in which (as Gregory of Nyssa puts it) the weapon of choice is the 'sword of the Word.'

I am not really asking 'whether . . . a watershed was passed' (to borrow Peter Brown's phrasing) but instead 'what it is like for a great traditional society to pass over a watershed' (Brown 1978, 2). Rather than straining to prove that a change had in fact taken place (for this account of change is, after all, simply another version of a fiction that historians have been telling and retelling at least since Gibbon, indeed since late antiquity itself), I want to turn one aspect of this freshly remarked 'fact' into a problem, so as to make it a matter of curiosity— and it is perhaps no small undertaking to render the 'unchanging,' unmarked, genderless gender an object of curiosity or questioning. I want to ask 'what it is like' when certain of the more vociferous members of 'a great traditional society' succeed in both raising the stakes and gaining the upper hand in the ancient contest of men by adopting a radically transcendent ideal of manhood that commands more of the cultural authority of virility than the traditional roles of father or husband, soldier or statesman, orator or philosopher.[2] Such is the wager of many of the surviving anti-Arian texts. That wager, I am arguing, in large part pays off: the most stridently (and innovatively) dualistic and transcendentalizing theological assertions of the fourth-century Nicene Christians usher in a new era in the history of masculine gender. The assertion of the Son's absolute divinity and the divinization of humanity anticipated in his incarnation register their historical effect in the rigid discipline of fourth-century bodies resisting their own carnality, and in the sclerosis of words fixed in transcendentalized corpora of Scripture and creed, dogmatic commentary and liturgical text. A particular narration of salvation history, shot through with cosmological implications, sinks itself into the lives of those who incarnate it in the telling: as the Son attains full divinity in theological discourse, men begin to groom themselves for godliness, even as they also attempt, more audaciously than ever, to bring heaven down to the earthly city.

One of the paradoxes to be explored is the extent to which a hypertranscendent masculinity incorporated characteristics or stances traditionally marked as 'feminine'—from virginal modesty, retirement from the public sphere, and reluctance to challenge or compete on the one hand, to maternal fecundity and nurturance on the other. Indeed, feminization itself was frequently—though not inevitably—a device by which the new ascetic order of maleness distinguished itself from the female-identified carnal order it claimed to supersede. This was not an entirely unprecedented development in the history of the ancient Mediterranean. Nicole Loraux has argued that Homeric epic and later heroic legend perpetuate 'a tradition that . . . postulates that a man worthy of the name is all the more virile precisely because he harbors within himself something of the feminine' (1995, 8). She goes on to suggest that Plato, in resistance to an ideology of the classical polis that defined 'the man/citizen according to a notion of virility that is impermeable to anything feminine' (3), retrieved and partly transformed this heroic ideal of a manhood that encompasses the feminine, most notoriously in his use of the metaphors of pregnancy and birthing to articulate the intellectual potency of the philosophic man.[3] Carlin Barton has tracked broadly analogous patterns of resistance to the Roman Republican ideal of a hard (*durus*) or weighty (*gravis*) manhood, as these emerge in the period of the civil wars and early Roman Empire: 'In the besieged city one could sport. Now the "heavy" and "light" were equally weightless. The Roman male, liberated from rigid masculine sex roles, delights in the freedom of playing a slave and a woman' (Barton 1994, 92). In such a context, the transgressive fantasies of persecuted Jews and Christians, who imagine themselves 'mothers' giving birth in suffering to their own ultimate triumph over their oppressors begin to seem less marginal as cultural product.[4] The later subversions of classical ideals of civic manhood by a Christian elite under imperial patronage likewise contain echoes of the feminized virility of the wounded hero, echoes partly mediated by the Greek Platonic tradition and the early imperial fascination with figures of noble slavishness, triumphant victimization, and salvific suffering.[5] Or, to turn the argument the other way around: the particular 'heroism' of the Platonic philosopher and the Roman gladiator (as well as the Jewish and Christian martyrs) have been mediated for later readers—to a greater extent than is perhaps generally acknowledged—by a late-ancient Christian ascetic ideal of masculinity.[6]

Although the very notion of analyzing fourth-century trinitarian doctrine in terms of the history of masculine gender might seem impossibly 'coarse' to some, my intention is not to elide theological issues by suggesting that the long-enduring Nicene doctrine of God—with its explicit and virtually unprecedented preoccupation with the concepts of Fatherhood, Sonship, and the transcendence of the Spirit—is simply a residue of late ancient gender politics. [. . .] As a cultural historian interested in ideas about gender, I remark on what appears to me remarkable—namely, that Nicene Christianity's contested articulation of the roles of Father, Son, and Spirit emerges as one of the most potent sites for reimagining manhood in the late Roman Empire. As a historical theologian, I interrogate ancient worlds of Christian thought and language that continue to grip me with the stubborn force of long centuries of habit—my ambivalent engagement and even identification with this history being a matter of fact, as I perceive it, rather than a confession or an assertion, far less a complaint. 'Coarseness' is merely a ploy for disrupting a scholarly tradition that cannot imagine commingling talk of a trinitarian God with the delicate topics of human desire, fecundity, and the gendered body. What I strive for, finally, is not the drama of an apocalyptic exposé of history but rather the nuance of an attentive, inquisitive, and intimate reading of theological literature, a reading that preserves the subtle weave of the ancient texts more or less whole—if by no means leaving our understanding of them unchanged. [. . .]

I have suggested that this study may be read as an extended marginal gloss on a passage from Gwatkin's 1882 *Studies of Arianism*. But it is equally important to acknowledge that this study is written between and indeed sometimes layered over the lines of Peter Brown's *The Making of Late Antiquity* (1978). In that work, Brown argues that 'the locus of the supernatural had come to shift significantly' between the second and the fifth centuries, and he charts the effects of this shift on 'the claims of particular human beings to represent the supernatural on earth,' proposing that 'what gives Late Antiquity its special flavor is precisely the claims of human beings' (1978, 6, 16). Frequently positioning Christianity not as the cause but as the symptom of social and religious currents arising within ancient Mediterranean culture, Brown also assigns to Christianity a paradigmatic or even directorial role as *'impresario* of a wider change' (12). [. . .] Although initially also identified with bishops and emperors, the heroes who interest Brown most are, finally, the desert ascetics who quickly displace bishops and emperors in his text. 'Constantine, the "man of God" and his new [episco-pal] colleagues were not the only bearers of that title,' he notes. 'They were the younger contemporaries of men who had begun to carry the role in society of the "friend of God" yet one stage further . . . In the making of Late Antiquity, the monks of Egypt played a role more enduring than that of Constantine' (Brown 1978, 79–80). If Christianity is a metonym for late antiquity, the ascetic holy man is a metonym for late ancient Christianity, and Brown's making of late antiquity also makes the holy man. The desert is the new city, and the city remakes itself in the image of the desert, as the monk overtakes the bishop and an asceticized episcopacy displaces both philosophers and magistrates in their roles of civic leadership.[7]

My own narrative consciously replays Brown's at many points, an act of homage no less where it may seem least faithful. By proposing that readings of a restricted set of Christian theological texts might add up to a study of 'the making of late-antique *man,*' I am taking the considerable liberty of relabeling Brown's own accomplishment while also implicitly reproducing—indeed potentially intensifying—his positioning of Christianity as the *'impresario* of a wider change.' In repeating his narrative move, I do not intend simply to affirm Brown's assertion that Christianity is both distinctive relative to con-temporaneous paganism and prototypically 'late antique'; nor do I choose to criticize directly a narrative history of 'late antiquity' that consistently makes Christianization the central plot. It is in order to explore and expose its effects—rather than defend or dispute its accuracy—that I inhabit one contemporary, ambiguously secularized version of a story of Christian triumph, a story that, as Brown (among others) points out, was originally authored by the late-ancient Christians themselves.[8] My argument also implicitly cites Brown's plot insofar as I, too, am interested in the link between shifts in the roles of men and ideals of masculinity, on the one hand, and shifts in cosmology, on the other. For Brown, what 'makes' late antiquity is in large part the collective imaginative construc-tion of a new 'world,' or a novel way of imagining the universe, centered in the perceived closure of what had been a fluid and 'open frontier' between the human and the divine realms (Brown 1978, 65). According to his account, the new men of late antiquity, as 'agents of the supernatural,' emerge partly in order to negotiate the hard boundary between heaven and earth freshly inscribed on the map of the cosmos. These 'upstart heroes'—combining an exaggerated 'upperworldly' orientation with an almost unprecedented level of 'worldly' authority (1978, 16)—arise at the paradoxical joint of the newly estranged realms of heaven and earth.

While Brown's narrative will be foundational for my own in these ways and others, I will also overwrite some of the palimpsest's lines rather thickly, in the course of bringing out my own arguments. First, as I have already indicated, this work will deal extensively with the interpretation of theological texts and themes, focusing particularly on the sedimented language of late-fourth-century trinitarian discourse. To encroach very far into territory jealously guarded by historians of Christian doctrine is an act understandably avoided by many secular scholars of late Roman religion and culture, especially those interested in downplaying the often exaggerated uniqueness or centrality of Christianity in its late-antique setting. In addition, Christian anthropology and Christology have seemed far more useful to the more down-to-earth purposes of cultural historians than have the high reaches of the doctrine of God.[9] And yet, as I am suggesting, it is trinitarian thought—characteristically patrilineal in its preoccupations and transcendentalizing in its tactics—that reveals most fully and directly the impact of shifts in cosmology and social roles on the positioning of *men*.

Second, I must introduce an explicit and critical analysis of gender into the text, if Brown's making of late antiquity is to accommodate my own account of the making of late-antique man. Attentive to the realm of the performative in a culture in which the actors are almost always male and gender is the performance *par excellence*, Brown brightly illumines the shifting contours of manly roles played out in late antiquity, but for the most part he carefully avoids naming masculine gender as such.[10] In *The Making of Late Antiquity* he speaks generically of 'the claims of human beings,' and elsewhere in his writings he enlarges the category of 'holy men' to include 'holy women' as well—rhetorical strategies of inclusion that partly mask perduring gendered distinctions (historical as well as contemporary). Recently, however, Brown has remarked directly upon the 'stolid male identity' of the 'holy man' and begun to interrogate not only the exclusion of women from that 'highly public, even confrontational role' but also the transformation of masculine gender: the 'imaginative alchemy' by which a man 'turned . . . completely from the procreation that defined male gender in the normal world' might become, like an angel, 'an unfailing source of hyper-procreativity in the world around him' (Brown 1998, 356, 371). Thickening such a line of interpretation in order to mark more clearly the turning and bending of ancient norms of masculinity, I will seek both to reinhabit the world of the ancient texts and to extricate myself from the enveloping fabric of a male-centered 'late antiquity.' [. . .]

Finally, I will also continue to expand the view of late antiquity to encompass the 'settled communities' of the late empire, as these appear through the idealizing lenses of the bishops who inhabit them: the desert—despite its widespread metaphoric currency—was not the only theater, and its 'holy men' were not necessarily the most representative or revealing icons of 'late antiquity' or even of 'late antique Christianity.'[11] The ascetic authors with whom I am primarily concerned were preoccupied with the imaginative reinterpretation and reoccupation of the city, rather than with its abandonment. For these bishops, an already ancient version of patriarchy remained firmly in place, as the male body was not simply dissolved through its transformation into angelic status but rather subtly remolded to fit the context of a new patrilineage and novel modes of rhetorical competition and civic governance. Making such continuities visible so as also to clarify the variety of mutations taking place will involve shifting some of the emphases of a historiographic tradition heavily influenced by models of 'privatization' and the 'fall of the city.' Such models are partly driven by an otherworldly Christian teleology that may prove inadequate not only for the interpretation of 'late antiquity' more broadly but also for the interpretation even of Christianity's most outspoken ascetics. [. . .]

In order to put a new spin on the late-ancient revolution of manhood, I will sometimes find it necessary to veer away from the historical page altogether: this work is, finally, explicitly transgressive of even those wide-flung disciplinary boundaries that encompass the well-glossed and multilayered texts of both 'patristic' and 'late Roman' history. [. . .] Revoicing words received from the Fathers, I seek to capture late-ancient manhood's rays. [. . .] My aim is thus not simply to reflect (upon) masculinity flatly or 'objectively,' with the rote fidelity of one positioned as the mirroring object of the singular sex of man. Rather, reading mimetically while remaining in motion, I hope also to insinuate difference into the apparent sameness of the texts, frequently twisting the inexactitude of repetition into the service of parody. Such an interpretive technique functions as a disciplined refusal of the choice between the light and the serious, the faithless and the faithful, or the critical and the apologetic reading. A parodic reflection of and upon late-ancient theological writings will take the shape of a convex mimesis (Irigaray 1985a, 248), on the one hand, enhancing and exposing the swell of a 'masculine' discourse, while also conforming to the complex contours of concavity, on the other, giving a new turn to a tradition of theological speculation that thereby begins to curve in on itself, seeking the shining inner spaces of its own 'feminine' excesses (Irigaray 1985a, 143–4).

If ancient Christian writings have been understood to adopt a dominant strategy of transcendence in relation to sexual distinctions by allowing (some) women to join men in shedding their gender—an approach both criticized and effectively appropriated by their feminist interpreters[12]—I have now chosen also to read those works for the traces of sexual difference that are simultaneously created and negated, contained and excluded, within fourth-century trinitarian discourse. Reading and writing to mark and thereby make a difference turns out, however, to be an immensely difficult project, constrained by a theological tradition that appears to be fundamentally oriented toward the task of reproducing one and the same Man. Indeed, despite more than two decades of patristic scholarship devoted to the study of 'women' and the 'female,' the very attempt to shift the interpretive focus away from the category of the generic 'Man' toward that of the sexed 'man' meets with resistance at almost every turn. The theoretical problem presented by masculine gender, not only for late-ancient Christian discourse but also for the subsequent philosophical and theological tradition, has been framed by Irigaray, ironically, as the failure of an intellectualizing transcendence. The masculine subject of historical record is founded on the refusal to recognize the particularity of manhood; systematically mistaking the limit of his gender for a principle of universality, 'he dreams that he alone is nature and that it is up to him to undertake the spiritual task of differentiating himself from (his) nature and from himself' (Irigaray 1996, 41). [. . .]

The discipline required for the resexing of man involves the skills of both the critic and the lover. My own narrowly focused genealogical interrogation of late-ancient manhood will frequently intersect with Irigaray's wide-ranging analysis of the male subjectivity produced and transmitted in the texts of a European-centered philosophical tradition.[13] [. . .] Literary critic Helene Cixous is perhaps even more deeply committed to the explicit feminization and eroticization of language—or rather, more specifically, of writing—pursued not least through her elaborate reworking of a literary culture's heritage of metaphor and myth, in interpretations that themselves effectively dissolve the distinction between the figurative and the literal, text and body. Reading, according to Cixous, is 'writing the ten thousand pages of every page,' making the text 'grow and multiply,' 'making love to the text.' Reading and making love are 'the same spiritual exercise' (Cixous 1991, 24). Such a close identification of the sexual and the interpretive realms is also crucial to my understanding of my task. Reading the Fathers sensitively and responsively—but also assertively and without too much fear of the friction experienced in the encounter, so as finally to put the sex back into late-antique man—is for me necessarily an explicitly erotic, as well as a profoundly spiritual, practice. However, it is not, strictly speaking, a 'hetero-sexual' erotic practice. [. . .] [T]he goal is not to reproduce two sexes—which turn out to be no more than one—but rather to give rise to a 'sex which is not one'—that is, to a 'sex' that is multiple and fluid (Irigaray 1985b, 150). [. . .]

I have chosen to explore fourth-century masculinity by reading certain major works of three prominent and roughly contemporaneous Fathers—Athanasius of Alexandria, Gregory of Nyssa, and Ambrose of Milan—each of whom played a crucial role in defending Nicene trinitarian doctrine as the touchstone of 'orthodox' and 'catholic' belief. [. . .] Triadic patterns are, finally, also intended to hint at ways of reconceiving both masculine gender and trinitarian theology along paths neither sharply discontinuous nor straightforwardly in line with the patristic texts that have engaged me. In playing with various possibilities for casting Athanasius, Gregory of Nyssa, and Ambrose in the roles of Father, Son, and Spirit, respectively, I am attempting not only to reveal how narrative and figural representation shape and reshape a historiographic tradition—in this case, the story of the 'triumph' of Nicene orthodoxy—but also, and more importantly, to open space for ongoing reconceptions of divinity and the cosmos, transcendence and particularity. Such reconceptions might accommodate the fecundity of gendered desire and embodiment *differently*, while yet remaining in intimate—indeed fertile and transporting—conversation with the Fathers themselves. Framing this agenda is an ironic reclaiming of the Nicene assertion that the Son is 'begotten, not made,' by the Father, with its concomitant, paradoxical disavowal of any literalized biologism: interpreted as a sign of resistance to the frequently posited dichotomy of 'sex' and 'gender,' 'natural essence' and 'cultural construction,' this compact creedal formula may (I am suggesting) be fashioned anew as the linguistic matrix of a sublimely supple sexuality and a fluidly engendered transcendence.

Notes

1 Previous chapters of this history have been drafted by Michel Foucault (1985; 1986), whose influential study of the desiring subject in antiquity also results in an account of the masculine subject, owing to its mimetic reperformance of the exclusion of the female and the pathic from the domain of subjectivity.

2 Cooper (1996) calls attention to the extent to which this radically transcendent conception of manhood, along with the accompanying idealization of female virginity, represented the perspective of a minority 'faction' even within Christianity. She allows, however, that asceticizing reinterpretations of gender roles attained a kind of cultural hegemony in the late fourth century, evoking a variety of responses from 'traditionalist' Christians.

3 See also the account of Plato's antidemocratic appropriation of the female reproductive body in duBois (1988, 169–83).

4 On the 'femminization' (sic) of the (masculine) subject produced within Talmudic texts, see Boyarin (1997, 81–150). More focused reflections on gender and martyrdom can be found in Boyarin (1998). See also Moore and Anderson (1998) and Burrus (2008). Although its readings run deliberately against the grain of historical chrono-logic, Moore's study *God's Gym* is also directly relevant to the discussion of torturously produced and ambiguously feminized early Christian masculinities.

5 On the prevalence of positive representations of suffering in the Roman period, see Perkins (1995).

6 My argument here is partly anticipated by Gillian Clark (1988).

7 See also Brown's 1971 essay, 'The Rise and Function of the Holy Man in Late Antiquity' (1998), as well as his more extensive study of the rise of asceticism (1988). In *Power and Persuasion*, Brown argues that the philosopher was displaced as political agent by 'bishops and monks.' In *Authority and the Sacred*, Brown reconsiders whether the cultural prominence of the 'holy man,' as well as the asceticizing apocalyptic narrative that partly creates this figure, has not been overplayed in his earlier works; [. . .] here Brown does not so much demote as reinterpret the now-integrative figure of the 'holy man' as the icon of late antiquity.

8 Brown (1995, 4). See also the significant work of Cameron (1991).

9 Brown: 'Some Christian theological controversies of the late fourth and early fifth centuries show how the tide had turned' (1978, 98). Brown has in mind here the anthropologically focused Origenist and Pelagian debates, whose broader cultural implications are explored not only in Brown (1988) but also in Clark (1992). See also the brief but highly suggestive account of the fifth-century Christological controversies in Brown (1992, 152–8).

10 Brown (1988) is the most significant exception to this general rule; yet even this work subtly resists thematizing masculine gender per se.

11 See McLynn's suggestion that readers of Brown 'instinctively, but mistakenly, classify holy men in contradistinction to bishops' and his proposal that Brown's portrait of the holy man might serve more helpfully to illumine 'a continuum of "self-created" holiness' that would include many of late antiquity's more famous urban bishops as well as the ascetics of its hinterlands (McLynn 1998, 464).

12 See esp. Ruether's early essays (1974; 1979) and Clark (1986). While these works have been considerably extended by more recent studies, they have not, in my view, been superseded.

13 Philosophy being defined as 'the discourse on discourse,' in Irigaray (1985b, 74).

Literature

Barton, Carlin. 1994. 'All Things Beseem the Victor: Paradoxes of Masculinity in Early Imperial Rome,' in *Gender Rhetorics: Postures of Dominance and Submission in History,* ed. Richard C. Trexler. Binghamton: Center for Medieval and Early Renaissance Studies. Pp. 83–92.

Boyarin, Daniel. 1997. *Unheroic Conduct: The Rise of Heterosexuality and the Invention of the Jewish Man.* Berkeley: University of California Press.

——. 1998. 'Martyrdom and the Making of Christianity and Judaism,' *Journal of Early Christian Studies* 6/4:577–627.

Brown, Peter. 1978. *The Making of Late Antiquity.* Cambridge: Harvard University Press.

——. 1988. *The Body and Society: Men, Women and Sexual Renunciation in Early Christianity.* New York: Columbia University Press.

——. 1992. *Power and Persuasion in Late Antiquity: Towards a Christian Empire.* Madison: University of Wisconsin Press.

——. 1995. *Authority and the Sacred: Aspects of the Christianization of the Roman World.* Cambridge: Cambridge University Press.

——. 1998. 'The Rise and Function of the Holy Man in Late Antiquity, 1971–1997,' *Journal of Early Christian Studies* 6/3:353–76.

Burrus, Virginia. 2008. 'Torture and Travail: Producing the Christian Martyr,' In *Feminist Companion to Patristic Literature,* ed. Amy-J. Levine. New York: Continuum. Pp. 56–71.

Cameron, Averil. 1991. *Christianity and the Rhetoric of Empire: The Development of Christian Discourse.* Berkeley: University of California Press.

Cixous, Helene. 1991. 'Coming to Writing,' in *'Coming to Writing' and Other Essays,* ed. Deborah Jenson. Cambridge: Harvard University Press. Pp. 1–58.

Clark, Elizabeth A. 1986. *Ascetic Piety and Women's Faith: Essays on Late Ancient Christianity.* Lewiston: Edwin Mellen.

——. 1992. *The Origenist Controversy: The Cultural Construction of an Early Christian Debate.* Princeton: Princeton University Press.

Clark, Gillian. 1988. 'The Old Adam: The Fathers and the Unmaking of Masculinity,' in *Thinking Men: Masculinity and Its Self-Representation in the Classical Tradition,* eds Lin Foxhall and John Salmon. London: Routledge. Pp. 170–82.

Cooper, Kate. 1996. *The Virgin and the Bride: Idealized Womanhood in Late Antiquity.* Cambridge: Harvard University Press.

duBois, Page. 1988. *Sowing the Body: Psychoanalysis and Ancient Representations of Women.* Chicago: University of Chicago Press.

Foucault, Michel. 1985. *The Use of Pleasure: The History of Sexuality* (vol. 2), trans. Robert Hurley. New York: Random House.

——. 1986. *The Care of the Self: The History of Sexuality* (vol. 3), trans. Robert Hurley. New York: Random House.

Gwatkin, Henry Melvill. 1882. *Studies of Arianism: Chiefly Referring to the Character and Chronology of the Reaction Which Followed the Council of Nicaea.* Cambridge: Deighton, Bell.

Irigaray, Luce. 1985a. *Speculum of the Other Woman,* trans. Gillian C. Gill. Ithaca: Cornell University Press.

——. 1985b. *This Sex Which Is Not One.* Ithaca: Cornell University Press.

——. 1996. *I Love to You: Sketch of a Possible Felicity in History,* trans. Alison Martin. New York: Routledge.

Loraux, Nicole. 1995. *The Experiences of Tiresias: The Feminine and the Greek Man*, trans. Paula Wissing. Princeton: Princeton University Press.

McLynn, Neil B. 1998. 'A Self-Made Holy Man: The Case of Gregory Nazianzen,' *Journal of Early Christian Studies* 6/3:463–83.

——. 1996. 'From Palladius to Maximinus: Passing the Arian Torch,' *Journal for Early Christian Studies* 4/4:477–93.

Moore, Stephen. 1996. *God's Gym: Divine Male Bodies of the Bible*. New York: Routledge.

Moore, Stephen D., and Janice Capel Anderson. 1998. 'Taking It Like a Man: Masculinity in 4 Maccabees,' *Journal of Biblical Literature* 117/2:249–73.

Perkins, Judith. 1995. *The Suffering Self: Pain and Narrative Representation in the Early Christian Era*. London: Routledge.

Ruether, Rosemary. 1974. 'Misogynism and Virginal Feminism in the Fathers of the Church,' in *Religion and Sexism*, ed. Rosemary Ruether. New York: Simon & Schuster. Pp. 150–83.

——. 1979. 'Mothers of the Church: Ascetic Women in the Late Patristic Age,' in *Women of Spirit*, eds Rosemary Ruether and Eleanor McLaughlin. New York: Simon & Schuster. Pp. 71–98.

21

The Discovery of Sodomy

Editor's Introduction

With Mark Jordan's chapter, we move to the Middle Ages, to the time of crusaders and inquisitors, popes and knights, chivalry and romantic love. Ideals of masculinity, as they were constructed and invented during those centuries, were complex and contradictory, ranging from 'the body of the knight' and 'the young man in the service of the lord' as the 'ideal lay male body' (Dunlop 2001, 329) to ideals of courtly love that both engendered and also impeded affectionate male friendships (Kuefler 2006b), and to ecclesiastical enforcement of compulsory male celibacy (Ranke-Heinemann 1990; Barstow 1982).

> No doubt, masculine stereotypes that emerged during the Middle Ages still abound in contemporary culture. Sold as toys and expanded into 'master stories' by movies and comic strips, figures such as the knight, the crusader, the alchemist, the feudal lord, or the wandering minstrel are still powerful enough to subtly shape gender norms and expectations. More ambiguous than knights and minstrels, however, are religious stereotypes of medieval masculinity. (Wiethaus 1996, 48)

There is also a vivid modern imagination vis-à-vis religious medieval men, Wiethaus writes, which depicts them as 'power-hungry' hypocrites, 'well-hidden' lechers, or self-effacing monks. If, however, one 'scraped off the patina' of these images, we would discern medieval masculinities as contested and fragile constructions (Wiethaus 1996, 48).

Mark Jordan does just that. He scrapes off the patina of misconceptions about a particular medieval invention concerning masculinity: sodomy. As a concept and name, sodomy is an accusation hurled against same-sex genital activity, and it has become a shorthand for legitimizing the anti-homosexual impulse not only in Christian theology but also in 'European and American legislation, medicine, natural science, and manners' (Jordan 1997, 1). Jordan refutes the idea that 'sodomy', as the term is used today, can be traced to the biblical account of Sodom itself (Gen. 18 and 19); thus he does not engage in exegetical debates on whether that story is about homosexuality or, as Boswell and others have argued, about the sin of inhospitality. Instead, Jordan argues that 'sodomy was invented by medieval theologians'. It is a 'medieval artifact', he writes, and 'I have found no trace of the term before the eleventh century' (1997, 1).

This chapter is reprinted from *The Invention of Sodomy in Christian Theology* (1997). As the book's title suggests, Jordan is not interested in writing a history of homosexuality within the Christian West, as others have tried to do, such as Boswell in *Christianity, Social Tolerance, and Homosexuality* (1980; also Jordan 2006; Kuefler 2006a ; Brinkschröder 2006). Instead, as a historian of theology and a Christian theologian himself, Jordan researches the genealogy of *sodomia* as a sexual term in medieval theology. He aims at investigating the theological invention of 'sodomy' as a category for classifying behavior: as a theological category, it was used, first, to define particular sexual acts and, second, to judge and condemn them.

Scholars who have plowed the medieval field on issues of gender and masculinity have relied primarily on social-historical and literary approaches (for example, Bloch 1991; Bynum 1992; Lees et al. 1994; Kolve 1998). Jordan's genealogical investigation is also historically oriented, but he inserts a theological and ethical dimension fruitful for further research on medieval masculinities within the field of critical men's studies in religion.

Publications by the Same Author

Jordan, Mark D. 1997. *The Invention of Sodomy in Christian Theology.* Chicago: University of Chicago Press.

———. 2000. *The Silence of Sodom: Homosexuality in Modern Catholicism.* Chicago: University of Chicago Press.

———. 2002. *The Ethics of Sex.* Oxford: Blackwell.

———. 2003. *Telling Truths in Church: Scandal, Flesh, and Christian Speech.* Boston: Beacon.

———. 2005. *Blessing Same-Sex Unions: The Perils of Queer Romance and the Confusions of Christian Marriage.* Chicago: University of Chicago Press.

———. 2006. '"Both as a Christian and as a Historian": On Boswell's Ministry', in *The Boswell Thesis*, ed. Mathew Kuefler. Chicago: University of Chicago Press. Pp. 88–107.

Further Reading

Barstow, Anne Llewellyn. 1982. *Married Priests and the Reforming Papacy: The Eleventh-Century Debates.* New York: Edwin Mellen.

Bloch, Howard. 1991. *Medieval Misogyny and the Invention of Western Romantic Love.* Chicago: Chicago University Press.

Boswell, John. 1980. *Christianity, Social Tolerance, and Homosexuality: Gay People in Western Europe from the beginning of the Christian Era to the Fourteenth Century.* Chicago: The University of Chicago Press.

Brinkschröder, Michael. 2006. *Sodom als Symptom: Gleichgeschlechtliche Sexualität im christlichen Imaginären – eine religionsgeschichtliche Anamnese.* Berlin: Walter de Gruyter.

Bynum, Carline Walker. 1992. *Fragmentation and Redemption: Essays on Gender and the Human Body in Medieval Religion.* New York: Zone Books.

Dinges, Martin (ed.). 1998. *Hausväter, Priester, Kastraten: Zur Konstruktion von Männlichkeit in Spätmittelalter und Früher Neuzeit.* Göttingen: Vandenhoeck & Ruprecht.

Dunlop, Anne. 2001. 'Masculinity, Crusading, and Devotion: Francesca Casali's Fresco in the Trecenty Perugian *Contado'. Speculum* 76:315–36.

Kolve, V. A. 1998. 'Ganymede/Son of Getron: Medieval Monasticism and the Drama of Same-Sex Desire'. *Speculum* 73/4 (October):1014–67.

Kuefler, Mathew (ed.). 2006a. *The Boswell Thesis: Essays on 'Christianity, Social Tolerance, and Homosexuality'*. Chicago: University of Chicago Press.

——. 2006b. 'Male Friendship and the Suspicion of Sodomy in Twelfth-Century France', in *The Boswell Thesis*, ed. Mathew Kuefler. Chicago: Chicago University Press. Pp. 179–212.

Lees, Clare A., Thelma Fenster and Jo Ann McNamara (eds). 1994. *Medieval Masculinities: Regarding Men in the Middle Ages*. Minneapolis: University of Minnesota Press.

Ranke-Heinemann, Uta. 1990. *Eunuchs for the Kingdom of Heaven: Women, Sexuality and the Catholic Church*. New York: Doubleday.

Wiethaus, Ulrike. 1996. 'Christian Piety and the Legacy of Medieval Masculinity', in *Redeeming Men*, eds Stephen B. Boyd, Merle Longwood and Mark Muesse. Louisville: Westminster John Knox. Pp. 48–61.

The Discovery of Sodomy

MARK D. JORDAN

The credit—or rather, the blame—for inventing the word *sodomia*, 'Sodomy,' must go, I think, to the eleventh-century theologian, Peter Damian. He coined it quite deliberately on analogy to *blasphemia*, blasphemy, which is to say, on analogy to the most explicit sin of denying God. Indeed, and from its origin, Sodomy is as much a theological category as Trinity, incarnation, sacrament, or infallibility. As a category, it is richly invested with specific notions of sin and retribution, responsibility and guilt. The category was never meant to be neutrally descriptive, and it is doubtful whether any operation can purify it of its theological origins. There is no way to make 'Sodomy' objective.

Peter's coining of the term is the result of long processes of thinning and condensing. These processes made it almost inevitable that there would be an abstract term for this kind of sin, so specifically stigmatized. One process thinned the reading of the Old Testament story of the punishment of Sodom. That complicated and disturbing story was simplified until it told only the punishment of a single sin, a sin that could be called eponymously the sin of the Sodomites. Another process, more diffuse but no less important, had to do with grouping together a number of sins under the old Roman category of *luxuria*. *Luxuria* came to be seen as the source of sinfulness in a number of acts, many of them having to do with the genitals. Peter Damian's coinage can only be understood against these processes.

I said that they were processes of thinning and condensing. The essential thing to notice in the processes by which 'Sodomy' was produced is that they first abolish details, qualifications, restrictions in order to enable an excessive simplification in thought. Then they condense a number of these simplifications into a category that looks concrete but that has in fact nothing more concrete about it than the grammatical form of a general noun. The rather dry business of tracking words has in this case a useful reward. It allows one to see, in the microcosm of grammatical form, the tyranny of generalization that results in there being a category like the category 'Sodomy.' The history of the word 'Sodomy' is a history of the abuse of grammar, which is a reduction of thought.

Misreading Sodom

Many contemporary exegetes agree that the Hebrew Bible's story about the destruction of Sodom cannot be read as a lesson about divine punishment of same-sex copulation.[1] If any lesson is wanted from the story, the lesson would seem to be about hospitality. After all, the story in Genesis 19 is akin to the story of the Levite's concubine in Judges 19. A Levite and his party, on their way home from a trip to the concubine's father, are offered lodging by an old man in the town of Gibeah. But the house is surrounded by some townsmen who demand that the Levite be brought out to them (19.22). As he recounts the events later, the Levite understood that they intended to kill him (20.5). The Levite instead pushes out his concubine, who is gang raped throughout the night. She dies on the doorstep in the morning. After returning home, the Levite dismembers her body in order to send its pieces to the tribes of Israel as a bloody call for revenge. The Israelites assemble an army that finally succeeds in killing the inhabitants of Gibeah and nearby towns.

Both of the stories, the one about Sodom and the one about Gibeah, narrate a terrible violation of the obligations of host to traveler. In the case of Sodom, the violation is punished by divine destruction. In the case of the Levite's concubine, the violation becomes an occasion for concerted military revenge. But the story of Judges 19 does not issue in a long tradition of moral reflection, much less in the naming of a special sin. Christian theology did not become preoccupied with a 'sin of the Benjamites' (as the inhabitants of Gibeah were called), nor did European countries adopt penal statutes against 'Benjamy.' This is the more striking because the incidents at Gibeah are more horrible than the events surrounding Lot's hospitality to the angelic messengers in Sodom. The citizens of Sodom do nothing in the end. They are blinded by the angels, who then instruct Lot to hurry his family out of the city in view of its impending destruction. At Gibeah, there were no angels to rescue the sacrificed woman during the dark night of her torture. She has to suffer and then to die of her wounds. Nor does God punish Gibeah with fiery storm. The Israelite armies must do it themselves, after sustaining heavy casualties. Why is it then that the story of Sodom had such a long afterlife? How does it come to be misread so systematically and for so many centuries? The beginning of an answer lies precisely in the dramatic and total divine judgment executed on the city and its neighbors.

Sodom is already used by several books of the Hebrew Bible as an image. It is not always the same image. Most often Sodom is an image of utter destruction, of desolation.[2] It is thus a name for sudden divine judgment.[3] Sometimes Sodom is an image of a poisonous land, a land producing bitter fruit.[4] At other times it is an image for brazen or widespread sin.[5] When the sin is specified by biblical authors, it is a sin of arrogant self-indulgence or self-satisfaction. So Ezekiel:

'This was the iniquity of your sister Sodom: she and her daughters had pride, overabundance of bread, abundance, and leisure, but they did not extend their hand to the poor. They were raised up and they committed abominations before me' (16.49–50).[6] The two sentences are constructed in the familiar pattern of parallel repetition. The abomination is not a new sin; it is the sin of the previous sentence recapitulated.[7]

Sodom continues to be used as an image for divine judgment or barrenness in the few New Testament texts that mention it.[8] Indeed, there are only two passages in the New Testament that associate Sodom with sexual sins. After invoking Sodom and Gomorrah as examples of divine judgment, 2 Peter adds: 'Above all [God] will punish those who walk according to the flesh in the desire of uncleanness (*immunditia*) and who contemn authority' (2.10). The 'desire of uncleanness' might be construed as same-sex desire, except that a few verses later the text continues: 'They have eyes full of adultery and [are] unceasingly sinful' (2.14).

The other New Testament text is no less problematic. Jude 7–8 reads: 'Just as Sodom and Gomorrah and the nearby cities, fornicating and going after other flesh in the same way [as the aforementioned angels], were made an example, suffering the punishment of eternal fire, so too it will be with those who stain the flesh and spurn authority and blaspheme against majesties.' The angels here are, of course, not the good angels who came to stay with Lot in Sodom. They are the evil angels who abandoned heaven and are now imprisoned in hell. The author of Jude understands their sin as sexual, as analogous to fornication and seeking after other flesh. The last, mysterious phrase may be a reference to the sort of legend that appears in Genesis 6.1 about the 'sons of God' copulating with 'the daughters of men' (see Bailey 1955, 10–23). It seems certainly to reflect non-scriptural traditions that identified the sin of Sodom with sexual irregularity. In neither case does it refer necessarily to same-sex copulation. Moreover, in Jude these same sinners are guilty of taking bribes—a sin that exercises the author at greater length.

What is clear, I think, is that Sodom figures in the Christian Scriptures as the unsurpassed example of divine retribution. The challenge would seem to be that of figuring out what provoked it. The answer, as it appears in these lesser texts of the New Testament, is sexual. But within the Gospels, that is, in the mouth of Jesus, Sodom is not a reminder of a specific sin. It is a trope for divine wrath generally. Indeed, as Jesus is made to say several times, the sin of rejecting the gospel merits greater punishment than the sin of Sodom and Gomorrah—whatever exactly it was. So Sodom is at this point not yet a geographical name for a particular kind of sin. It is a memorial site that records God's power to judge. It refers not to specific human actions, but to a story that is to be remembered for its present pertinence. What happened at Sodom is not an exotic, foreign vice that cannot be mentioned. It is, on the contrary, a most articulate reminder of the consequences of rebelling against God. We remember the story of Sodom because we need to learn obedience from it.

With these considerations, if not from the simple inspection of passages, it should be clear that there is no text of the Christian Bible that determines the reading of Sodom as a story about same-sex copulation. On the contrary, there is explicit scriptural evidence that the sin of the Sodomites was some combination of arrogance and ingratitude. This evidence was not ignored by patristic exegetes writing in Latin. Indeed, many of Latin theologians continue to speak of the inhospitality of Sodom, of its pride and arrogance, even as they speak of its association with forbidden sex. I will not here try to prove that remark by a statistical survey of patristic scriptural commentary. Views about the sense of a group of texts become convincing not through numbers so much as by self-directed reading. I will instead offer a few highly visible passages from the theologians that would become most authoritative for the Latin Middle Ages. Traditionally, the four 'doctors' of the Western church were Jerome, Ambrose, Augustine, and Gregory the Great. Each wrote on the story of Sodom many times in different contexts. I select the most extended or instructive treatments as examples.

Jerome, master of the scriptural text and its renowned translator, not surprisingly preserves the widest range of readings. In his commentary on the passage from Ezekiel, for example, he paraphrases the prophetic teaching quoted above quite succinctly. The first of the crimes of Sodom and her daughters is pride.[9] Its primacy is supported by abundant quotation from the New Testament. The seedbed of this pride is abundance with leisure or, in words that Jerome takes from the Septuagint, 'the opulence of delicacies and of luxury.' The lesson is summed emphatically: 'The Sodomitic sin is pride, bloatedness (*saturitas*), the abundance of all things, leisure and delicacies.'[10] In another passage, from his commentary on Isaiah, Jerome adds to this list the feature of brazenness. Princes are said to be Sodomites when they publish their sins abroad, not taking any trouble to conceal them. The princes 'publicly proclaim' their sin 'without having any shame in blaspheming.'[11] On Jerome's reading of these texts, the sin of Sodom is brazen arrogance bred of opulence.

Elsewhere Jerome acknowledges that Sodom has taken on a variety of allegorical or spiritual meanings. So, for example, he reports a reading according to which Samaria and Sodom mean respectively 'heretics and Gentiles.'[12] He contests the heretical interpretation according to which Jerusalem, Samaria, and Sodom signify spiritual, animal, and earthly. Again, in defending the literal sense of Jude 7–8, he refuses to let Sodom mean this visible world.[13] But Jerome's most striking reference to Sodom comes in a letter on a practical matter. Can a woman whose husband is an adulterer and 'a Sodomite' count her marriage to him as dissolved?[14] Jerome's answer is a strong no. His phrasing of the question and his answer to it both make clear that to be an adulterer is different from being a Sodomite. They do not make clear what a Sodomite is. It involves some form of sexual irregularity, but it might well be sexual irregularity in the mode of copulation with the man's wife or with his mistress. With Jerome, then, we run the full scriptural range from the prophetic use of Sodom's arrogance through scriptural allegorization of it to its use to a specific but unstated sexual act.

In Ambrose the moral sense of Sodom begins to narrow around sexual or at least bodily sin. He does recognize that the threat against the angels was a violation of hospitality.[15] Elsewhere, though, and especially in his treatise *On Abraham*, he identifies Sodom straightforwardly with fleshly indulgence and lasciviousness.[16] The Sodomites were, he says, fierce and sinful, given to crimes beyond the mean of human wickedness. Their special province seems to be that of luxury (*luxuria*) and disordered desire (*libido*).[17] When Lot's wife turns back to look at the burning city, she is turning back to the impure region of lust.[18]

The evidence from Augustine is, as always, complicated. On the one hand, there are passages in which Sodom is understood as a sign of human depravity generally—of 'the pernicious society of humankind.'[19] The Sodomites were unclean and proud; they were blasphemers.[20] On the other hand, Augustine is quite clear that the citizens of Sodom wanted to rape the male angels. In his narrative of Old Testament history within the *City of God*, Augustine gives as reason for the destruction of Sodom that it was a place where 'debaucheries in men' (*stupra in masculos*) flourished by custom.[21] That is why Lot tried to offer his daughters instead. Better for men to violate women than to violate other men.[22] Another passage from the *Confessions* is much quoted by medieval theologians as being equally explicit, since Augustine there mentions the Sodomites in a condemnation of iniquities done against nature (*flagitia contra naturam*).[23] In fact, Augustine uses the story of Sodom in the *Confessions* only as an illustration of divine punishment. The crimes being discussed, the exact nature of which is unclear, are always and everywhere to be published as harshly as the Sodomites were punished.

With Augustine, then, we reach an explicit description of the sin of the Sodomites as the desire for same-sex copulation. It was a custom among them, and it was immediately understood by Lot as the reason for the demand that he hand over his guests. But even in Augustine the sin of the Sodomites is not just or merely same-sex desire. That desire is a symptom of the madness of their fleshly appetites, of the underlying delirium of their passions. The root sin of the Sodomites is not desire for same-sex copulation. It is rather the violent eruption of disordered desire itself. The distinction is crucial for Augustine but quickly lost in the readings of him.

One piece of evidence for the sexual fixation of the reading of Sodom comes in a poem written by an unknown author in fifth-century Gaul.[24] The poem narrates the whole story of destruction—from the infamy of Sodom's sin and the mission of the angels through the city's conflagration. The poem makes absolutely clear that Sodom was known for sexual irregularities and, indeed, for same-sex copulation. No male visitor could enter the city without fearing damage to his sex from a citizenry known for its 'mixed,' incestuous marriages, its rebellion against nature.[25] Lot even tries to reason with the crowd, a foretaste of theological reasonings to come, by arguing that no other animal gives way to same-sex desire. 'A woman is spouse to every [man],' he pleads, 'and never has anyone's mother been other than a woman.'[26] For the author of this poem, the men of Sodom not only like to rape strangers, they like to marry each other. In short, the sexual interpretation of Genesis 19 is now assumed. It has begun to fuel more and more vivid imaginations about what happened that night within the doomed city.

The last of the four Latin 'doctors,' Gregory the Great, treats Sodom theologically in two prominent passages. Together they show that alternate readings have been pushed out of the way by the sexual ones. Gregory knows the reading that Ezekiel gives to Sodom. He reproduces it as scriptural commentator and applies it in his own voice.[27] But when Gregory thinks of Sodom, his first thought is of sexual sin, not of pride or inhospitality. This is clearest in his *Moral Readings of Job,* a book that would enormously influence medieval moral theology. At one point in explicating Job, Gregory wants to gloss the image of sulfur. He thinks at once of the destruction of Sodom. 'That we should understand sulfur as signifying the stench of the flesh, the history of the holy Scriptures itself testifies, when it narrates that God rained down fire and sulfur upon Sodom.'[28] Sodom is punished for 'crimes of the flesh' (*scelera carnis*), for 'perverse desires arising from the stench of flesh' (*peruersa desideria ex fetore carnis*), for 'what they did from unjust desire' (*ex iniusto desiderio*). In his *Pastoral Rule,* Gregory makes the moral explicit: 'To flee from burning Sodom is to refuse the illicit fires of the flesh.'[29]

One other passage from Gregory must be mentioned. It is not theological so much as legal or administrative. The passage comes in a letter in which Gregory instructs one of his subordinates how to deal with a case of a priest who is accused of idolatry and of being 'stained by the crime of the Sodomite.'[30] Here, as in the earlier letter from Jerome, the meaning of the accusation is presumed. In both cases, it accompanies an accusation of idolatry. But I mention the letter now in order to emphasize a terminological point. Gregory writes 'the crime of the Sodomite.' In two tenth-century copies of the text, there is a telling scribal error. 'Of the Sodomite' becomes 'of Sodomy.'[31] This slip is the reason why a number of dictionaries will record Gregory's letter as the first appearance of the abstract term 'Sodomy.'[32] In fact it is not. The term appears after Gregory, and then as a scribal error. But its absence here is worth noting. If patristic readers of the Christian Bible fixed on a sexual interpretation of the sin of Sodom, they did not yet make up a word to single it out. The entire Latin interpretation proceeds through Gregory and beyond without the help—or hindrance—of that kind of abstraction. You would not know this from the English translations, of course, which tend to become particularly irresponsible when translating terms having to do with same-sex copulation. Some translators disappear into prim vagueness; others apply an overly precise and definitely modern vocabulary. Either tactic will obscure important features in the history of moral theology, such as the entire absence of an abstract category 'Sodomy' for some ten centuries of Christian theology.

We need to move forward in order to witness the birth of the term. But before we can do so responsibly, we have to pick up one other process that has run parallel to the misreading of Sodom. The passages from Gregory make two things clear. The first is that Latin exegesis had by the end of the patristic period fixed on a sexual interpretation of Sodomitic sin, even if it kept repeating the other interpretations offered by the Scriptures. In some passages, though not in all, the sin is specified as that of same-sex copulation. In most passages, it is stigmatized as a sin of corrupted, luxurious flesh. The second point, the one yet to be investigated, is that the interpretation of Genesis 19 has been taken up into a much larger system of moral teaching about a sin called *luxuria.* The scope of the teaching can be seen especially in Gregory. When Gregory speaks of Sodom and *luxuria,* he says something quite specific. For Gregory, *luxuria* is one of seven principal or capital sins. It has a certain rank among sins, and it has certain properties or consequences. The misreading of Sodom has intersected with the formation of Christian moral categorizations in the Latin-speaking West.

Baptizing Luxury

When Jerome chose the Latin *luxuria* to translate several different terms in the Old and New Testaments, he imported into Christian theology a moral category with a long Roman pedigree. That pedigree is more important for later Christians than the sense of the Hebrew or Greek terms that *luxuria* displaced. *Luxuria* recurs in Latin moral texts as the opposite of the stern virtues of the Republic.[33] It is often coupled with *licentia*, with the threat of social dissolution, the loosening of the bonds necessary to keep the city and then its empire intact. Whatever may have been the original Christian teaching on the dangers of the flesh, it arrived in the Latin-speaking portions of the empire both reinforced and distorted by the teaching of Rome itself.

The results of Jerome's choices appear in a number of passages. In his Latin Old Testament, *luxuria* is associated with drunkenness or gluttony and with sexual excess.[34] In his Gospels, it appears only once—in the description of the life of the prodigal son when he has run away from home to dissipate his wealth.[35] But the most the most important uses for later writers occur in the New Testament letters. *Luxuria* appears as one term in Paul's list of sins in Galatians. It follows immediately after fornication and uncleanness, just before idolatry.[36] In the letters ascribed to Peter, *luxuria* gets connected with blasphemy and the desires of the flesh.[37] And in Jude, just before the text that links the sin of Sodomy with lusting for alien flesh, *luxuria* is named as the sin of certain false teachers who have corrupted the word of God.[38] Already in Jerome's Latin Bible, then, *luxuria* covers an enormous range even as it begins to condense around the flesh as the site of opposition to God.

I jump forward now to Gregory the Great's *Moral Readings of Job*. That text will fix for medieval moral theology a certain view of *luxuria* and its place among the principal and most lethal sins. Gregory's schemes of classification are fairly straightforward. Seven chief sins spring from the malignant root of pride: vainglory, envy, wrath, sadness, avarice, gluttony of the stomach, and *luxuria*.[39] *Luxuria* comes last, not because it is least important, but because Gregory means to emphasize it. With malice and pride, it forms a trio of sins that particularly attack the human race.[40] It leads to idolatry and to one or another of its sibling sins along various causal chains.[41] The 'daughters' or consequences of *luxuria* are identified by Gregory as mental blindness, inconsiderateness, inconstancy, haste, self-love, hatred of God, passionate attachment to the present, and horror or despair over the future.[42]

These schemes and causal connections hardly suggest the flexibility of *luxuria* in Gregory's thought. It agitates the soul in countless ways—burns it, beats it, stimulates it, rushes through it.[43] *Luxuria* seems in such passages to mean self-indulgence, self-gratification. It is both of the flesh and of the heart, of deed and of thought.[44] Many fall because they rid themselves of fleshly *luxuria* only to fall into the inward *luxuria* of pride. So long as *luxuria* agitates the soul, salvation is impossible.[45]

At the same time, in adjacent texts, Gregory teaches that *luxuria* is what we would call a sexual sin. It is linked to the genitals.[46] More symbolically, Gregory says that it is tied to the 'loins' in men, to the 'umbilical,' that is, the center in women.[47] The devil holds these members in subjection and from them produces the salacious images and the physiological pulses that lead to acts of *luxuria*, outward or inward.[48] The sin is connected with effeminacy and animality.[49] It is symbolized by the ass, the pig, and the worm. Considered as fleshly sin, *luxuria* is described as staining, polluting, stinking.

Gregory's teaching on *luxuria* doubles the sin. On the one hand, it is a sin subject to indefinite modulation through the chambers of the body and the soul. It appears in one guise, then in another. Beaten down in the flesh, it returns through images projected from memory. If the memory of one kind of pleasure is successfully controlled, control itself may become an occasion for *luxuria*. On the other hand, the sin is housed in the genitals, a part of the body given over to demonic control. It flames out of those organs through specific channels of desire. It reaches out to fornication, adultery, to every perverse ordering of the flesh.

One way to ease this duality is to believe that Gregory means to elevate sexual sins to a unique prominence as cause of sin. The 'loins' would become the source of the whole of *luxuria*. There is something to this belief, but it ignores the differ- ent logic implicit in the two views of *luxuria*. The logic of generalized *luxuria* is the logic of mutation, infiltration, reactivation; the logic of genital *luxuria* is the logic of disruption, direct assault. This dual logic is not accidental. It is impor- tant to Gregory's argumentative strategy. To have a category that bridges the two logics, the two models of causality, is to have a category that can be used to prevent troublesome sins from being subjected to corrective analysis. *Luxuria* has two logics built into it by Gregory. If one is attacked, it can be retired while the other is brought into play.

There is more. The two logics are not deployed symmetrically. It is rather the case that the generalized *luxuria* is used to defend the genital one from criticism. To the charge that Gregory's teaching gives too much weight to genital sins, it can be replied that *luxuria* is much broader than that. It is more like Augustine's notion of disordered desire, a fundamental inversion in the will that shows itself in dozens of secondary disorders. But as soon as this expansive doctrine is advanced, Gregory will bring all of its weight to bear on genital sins, as if they alone were the fundamental inversion. Certain sins of the flesh are brought into the system of moral teaching at one level, then linked by the term *luxuria* to much graver dysfunction. This makes it easy enough to transfer the sense of gravity out, down to the sins of the flesh.

Whatever the doublings of Gregory's notion of *luxuria*, it is a relatively less potent device for moral reorganization—for moral condemnation—than the term 'Sodomy.' 'Sodomy' represents a level of abstraction beyond the slippage encoded within *luxuria*. Indeed, 'Sodomy' will have the advantage of carrying within it all the polemical resources of *luxuria* and more besides.

Fighting Words

We have followed so far two textual processes. The first is a thinning down of the reading of the story of Sodom. The other is a condensation of the ancient category of *luxuria* around what we would call sexual sins. The two processes overlap and then reinforce each other. The story of Sodom becomes a story about one particular form of *luxuria*. Still, the abstraction of the sin from the story and the moral explanation has not yet taken place. There has so far been no mention of the term *sodomia*, 'Sodomy.' [. . .]

The immediate ground for abstracting the essence of Sodomy was provided by attempts to classify particular acts for the sake of punishing them. The attempts are recorded in the early medieval books of penances. These penitentials seem to have been first compiled in Irish and Anglo-Saxon monasteries for the use of confessors.[50] They typically group together certain sins, which are carefully described, in order to assign appropriately graded penances for each kind. The books were popular from the seventh century onward, and they spread widely. They certainly spread into the church schools and administrative circles of Italy, where they seemed important enough to Peter Damian to require an extended refutation. If their influence was much diminished by the twelfth century, it was in part because their project of moral classification had been entirely appropriated by the common theological traditions.

It is no easy thing to draw inferences from the penitentials about sexual attitudes or practices, much less about theological reasoning on sexual matters. As Peter Damian will delight in pointing out, the penances assigned are hardly consistent indications of the gravity of the sin committed. More generally, penitentials were written for use in a comprehensive system of spiritual practices, monastic and nonmonastic. They had important relations to liturgy, and they need to be read with an eye to ritual functions as much as to juridical or descriptive ones. So I mention the penitentials here not as social records or even as pieces of coherent theology, but rather as samples of theological speech about same-sex acts.

Their speech is pertinent because it shows that by the seventh or eighth century, Sodom and its inhabitants were being mentioned as a way of designating a particular kind of sexual intercourse.[51] Some sections of the penitentials refer simply to 'Sodomites' as a class meriting a certain punishment.[52] Others speak more precisely of fornication 'in the Sodomitic manner' (*sodomitico more*), where the immediate context suggests a contrast with simple fornication.[53] Yet other passages speak more cryptically of the 'Sodomitic sin.'[54] There are a few lines in which descriptions of this sin are attempted, but they are not particularly helpful. The so-called *Penitential of Columbanus* describes fornication 'according to the Sodomitic custom [or style]' (*sodomitico ritu*) as sinning by having 'female intercourse' with a man.[55] This would seem to be an allusion to the Latin of Leviticus 18.21. Other passages do speak frankly of fornication 'in the rear' or 'between the legs,' but passages in which these frank descriptions are equated with the Sodomitic manner of fornication are not easy to find. Even in the penitentials, which are noted for their blunt speaking about sexual matters, references to Sodom or Sodomites are used both to conceal and to reveal. They reveal to those who already know what the geographico-biblical reference means. Otherwise they conceal.

There is a more important point about the speech of the penitentials. The prescriptions against Sodomitic intercourse are not the same as the construction of the category *sodomia*, for which the appearance of the abstract noun serves as an important index. What are the implications of abstracting an essence from a proper name? Again, what are the implications of abstracting from a historical name? To abstract an essence from a proper name is to reduce the person named to a single quality. All that you need to know about the Sodomites is that they practiced Sodomy. In this way, abstraction from a proper name is deeply connected with the project of essentializing persons. A term like Sodomy suggests, by its very grammatical form, that it is possible to reduce persons to a single essence, which can then be found in other persons, remote from them in time or place. This kind of essentialism is necessarily anti-historical. The isolated essence is to recur across time, like an Aristotelian species, never subject to evolution. As a recurring essence, it would seem to justify recourse to the same means of control in every case—to a punishment as near as one can get to the divine fires that poured down on Sodom. If such dramatic punishments are not available, then at least the sin should be subjected to relentless denunciation.

A polemical character is suggested in a curious way by the form of the word *sodomia*. Its ending is not a native Latin ending; it is borrowed from the Greek. Now *sodomia* is unattested in theological Greek, but the habit of coining abstract nouns from names was a habit the Latins learned from Greek theological polemics. Most of the name abstractions that appear before the Middle Ages are specifically Christian and specifically polemical. 'Christian' itself is a nominalized proper name, and one that was originally applied as a term of derision. Christian authors picked up the naming habit, it seems, and began to speak of such heresies as 'Arianism' or 'Sabellianism.' The abstractions serve an obvious polemical purpose. They allow a writer to reduce an opponent to a schematic caricature. Arian authors could protest that they did not recognize themselves in the caricatures of their views given by pro-Nicean polemicists. But the damage was done. The nuances and dialectical complexities of a teaching, the circumstances and motivations of particular teachers could be swept away in an attack upon a malignant essence, everywhere the same and everywhere to be combated.

I say 'malignant' deliberately, because the kind of transhistorical essentializing that goes into a name like 'Arianism' is much like bad medical reasoning. Ancient medicine in the Hippocratic and Galenic traditions, whether empirical or dogmatic, was marvelously attentive to particular variations of individual body, custom, season, situation. The diagnosis of a disease was precisely not an excuse to import a reductive explanation or to employ a pre-fabricated therapy. But the Hippocratic and Galenic traditions were for that very reason difficult to learn. The reaction against them, most famously expressed in the methodist or methodical school, wanted to make things easy by reducing complexities or particularities to a small scheme of invariant causes of disease. A disease, once identified, could be treated by the same treatment every time—and the treatments themselves would be few in number. The same logic of willed simplification is at work in coining terms like 'Arianism.' Such words are in effect slogans. They reduce an opposing position to an easy caricature, one that can be ridiculed or refuted memorably because briefly.

It is hard to say how many of these considerations were in Peter Damian's mind when he coined the term. Certainly he was thinking of analogies to Greek names for sins, because the sentence in which *sodomia* appears so emphatically is built around that kind of analogy: 'If blasphemy is the worst sin, I do not know in what way sodomy is any better.'[56] *Blasphemia, sodomia.* Linked grammatically, linked by the seriousness of the sin, linked by being terms most useful in polemic. *Sodomia* does not make its appearance as a neutral description of acts. It is a brand that burns condemnation into certain acts. It burns into them as well the presumption of a stable essence, a sameness found wherever the acts are performed. The sameness links those who perform them back to the criminals who suffered the most severe divine punishment.

That transition from acts to persons is perhaps what an essence does best. By coining an abstract term to group together a series of acts, Peter Damian has made the inference from acts to agent almost automatic. The acts display an essence, the essence of Sodomy. Where is that essence? Derivatively in the acts, fundamentally in the actor—the Sodomite who expresses his essence, his identity, by acting. The unity of the abstract essence, Sodomy, points back to the unity of the identity in Sodomites. They are no longer persons who perform a few similar acts from a myriad of motives and in incalculably different circumstances. They are Sodomites doing Sodomy. [. . .]

Notes

1 I will not here repeat the detailed arguments made by Bailey (1955) and recapped by Boswell (1980, 93–7).

2 Deut. 29.23; Isa. 13.19; Jer. 49.18, 50.40; Zeph. 2.9.

3 Lam. 4.6; Amos 4.11.

4 Deut. 32.32.

5 Isa. 3.9; Jer. 23.14.

6 Here and in what follows I translate into English from the Latin Bible known to the Middle Ages. My point in doing so is that I am principally interested in the scriptural texts as they were known to Latin theology. It was the Vulgate, and not the Hebrew or the Greek texts, that proved decisive for the construction of the category of Sodomy.

7 A similar interpretation is given in modern versions of Ecclus. 16.8: 'There was no reprieve for Lot's adopted home, abhorrent in its arrogance.' This does not occur in the Vulgate.

8 Matt. 10.15, Luke 17.29, Rom. 9.29.

9 Jerome *Commentaria in Hiezechielem* 5.16.48–51 (Glorie 75:205.663–4).

10 Jerome *Commentaria in Hiezechielem* 5.16.48–51 (Glorie 75:206.683–5).

11 Jerome *Commentaria in Esaiam* 2.3.8–9 (Adriaen 73:51.19–21).

12 Jerome *Commentaria in Hiezechielem* 5.16 (Glorie 75:204.597).

13 Jerome *Epistulae* 46.7 (Hilberg 336–8).

14 Jerome *Epistulae* 55.4(3) (Hilberg 492–3).

15 Ambrose of Milan *Hexaëmeron* 5.16.54 (Schenkl 32/1:181.10).

16 Ambrose of Milan *De Abraham* 1.3.14 (Schenkl 32/1:512.9), 1.6.55 (538.25), 2.6.25 (582.4).

17 Ambrose of Milan *De Abraham* 2.8.45 (Schenkl 32/1:599.9).

18 Ambrose of Milan *Explanatio psalmorum XII* ps.43 34.1 (Petschenig 64:286.18); *Epistulae* 4.11.21 (Faller 82/1:90.230).

19 Augustine *Quaestiones XVI in Matthaeum* 3 (Mutzenbecher 44B:120).

20 Augustinus *Sermo* 100 (Demeulenaere 83 = Migne *PL* 38:604).

21 Augustinus *De ciuitate Dei* 16.30 (Dombart-Kalb 48:535.3–5).

22 Augustinus *De mendacio* 7.10 (Zycha 41:429.4).

23 Augustinus *Confessiones* 3.8.15 (Skutella-Verheijen 27:35.3–7).

24 There is a very 'free' and rather fussy English rendering by S. Thelwall reprinted in Paul Hallam (1993, 191–7).

25 *De Sodoma* (Peiper 23:213.20–23).

26 *De Sodoma* (Peiper 23:215.49–50).

27 For example, *Moralia in Job* 30.18.60 (Adriaen 143B:1532.79).

28 Gregory the Great *Moralia in Job* 14.19.23 (Adriaen 143A:711.8).

29 Gregory the Great *Regula pastoralis* 3.27 (Rommel 382:452.80).

30 Gregory the Great *Registrum epistolarum* 10.2 (Norberg 140A:827.7–9).

31 The manuscripts called $e1$ (Milan, Bibl. Ambrosiana MS C 238 inferior, tenth century, from Bobbio) and $e2$ (Paris, Bibl. Nationale MS Nouvelles acquis. lat. 1452, tenth or eleventh century, from Cluny). See the apparatus for 10.2 (Norberg 140A:827.9).

32 Most authoritatively, Blaise, *Dictionnaire latin-français des auteurs chrétiens*, s.v. 'Sodomia.' The article 'Sodomy' in the *Encyclopedia of Homosexuality* confidently asserts that *sodomia* appeared 'around 1180 as a designation for the "crime against nature."' As will be seen, it appeared a century and a half earlier and preceded the preference for the term 'crime against nature.'

33 For some Roman texts on *luxuria* and a reading of them, see Edwards (1993, 176–206).

34 For example, Deut. 21.20, gluttony and drunkenness; Prov. 20.1, drunkenness; 2 Macc. 6.4, gluttony; Jer. 5.7, prostitution.

35 Luke 15.13.

36 Gal. 5.19.

37 1 Pet. 4.4, 2 Pet. 2.18.

38 Jude 4.

39 Gregory the Great *Moralia in Job* 31.45.87 (Adriaen 143B:1610.15).

40 Gregory the Great *Moralia in Job* 33.15.30 (Adriaen 143B:1700.22).

41 Gregory the Great *Moralia in Job* 33.38.67 (Adriaen 143B:1730.13); compare 25.9.24 (143B:1249.79).

42 Gregory the Great *Moralia in Job* 31.45.88 (Adriaen 143B:1610.34).

43 Gregory the Great *Moralia in Job* 3.31.60 (Adriaen 143:153.32), 'inflammat'; 9.65.98 (143:526.54), 'ignis'; 26.32.58 (143B:1497.20), 'pulsat'; 30.10.38 (143B:1518.87), 'stimulis'; 30.3.9 (143B:1497.20), 'fluxa'. Compare 32.14.20 (143B:1645.14–15) and 32.14.21 (143B:1645.40).

44 Gregory the Great *Moralia in Job* 21.2.5 (Adriaen 143A:1067.65).

45 Gregory the Great *Moralia in Job* 21.12.19 (Adriaen 143A:1079.19–24).

46 Gregory the Great *Moralia in Job* 7.28 (Adriaen 143:361.131); 31.45.89 (143B:1611.57).

47 Gregory the Great *Moralia in Job* 32.14.20–1 (Adriaen 143B:1645.10–37).

48 Gregory the Great *Moralia in Job* 21.2.5 (Adriaen 143A:1067.87–91).

49 Gregory the Great *Moralia in Job* 26.17.29 (Adriaen 143B:1287.86); 26.35.63 (143B:1314.7).

50 For a convenient survey of different studies of the genre, see Driscoll (1996).

51 For a survey of the teaching of many of the penitentials on sexual matters, see Payer, which contains a very useful list of passages on same-sex relations (1984, 135–9), and the analysis by Frantzen (1998, esp. 149–75, with the supplementary tables on 175–83).

52 To cite only a few examples, Wasserschleben (1958, 222 for Bede; 234 Egbert;

599 ps-Theodore); and Bieler (1963, 68 for Grove of Victory; 100 for Columbanus; 114 for Cummean).

53 Wasserschleben (1958, 532) (Vigilia).

54 Bieler (1963, 96) (Columbanus).

55 Bieler (1963, 102).

56 Peter Damian *Liber gomorrhanus* (Reindel 328.2–3).

Literature

Ambrose of Milan. 1897. *De Abraham*, ed. Karl Schenkl. Corpus Scriptorum Ecclesiasticorum Latinorum, vol. 32/1. Vienna: Tempsky.

——. 1968–1982. *Epistulae*, eds Otto Faller and Michael Zelzer. Corpus Scriptorum Ecclesiasticorum Latinorum, vol. 82, in three parts. Vienna: Hoelder-Pichel-Tempsky.

——. 1919. *Explanatio psalmorum XII*, ed. M. Petschenig. Corpus Scriptorum Ecclesiasticorum Latinorum, vol. 64. Vienna: Tempsky.

——. 1897. *Hexaëmeron*, ed. Karl Schenkl. Corpus Scriptorum Ecclesiasticorum Latinorum, vol. 32/1. Vienna: Tempsky.

Augustine. 1981. *Confessiones*, eds M. Skutella and L. Verheijen. Corpus Christianorum Series Latina, vol. 27. Turnhout: Brepols.

——. 1955. *De ciuitate Dei*, Corpus Christianorum Series Latina, vols 47–8. Turnhout: Brepols. Reproducing the text of the 4th edn of Bernardus Dombart and Alphonsus Kalb. Leipzig: Teubner (1928–1929).

——. 1900. *De mendacio*, ed. Joseph Zycha. Corpus Scriptorum Ecclesiasticorum Latinorum, vol. 41. Vienna: Tempsky.

——. 1980. *Quaestiones XVI in Matthaeum*, ed. Almut Mutzenbecher. Corpus Christianorum Series Latina, vol. 44B. Turnhout: Brepols.

——. 1994. *Sermo* 100, ed. Roland Demeulenaere, in 'Le sermon 100 de saint Augustin sur le renoncement,' *Revue Bénédictine* 104:77–83.

Bailey, Derrick Sherwin. 1955. *Homosexuality and the Western Christian Tradition*. London: Longmans, Green & Co; reprint, Hamden: Archon Books (1975).

Bieler, Ludwig. 1963. *The Irish Penitentials*. Scriptores Latini Hiberniae, vol. 5. Dublin: Dublin Institute for Advanced Studies.

Blaise, Albert. 1954. *Dictionnaire latin-français des auteurs chrétiens*. Turnhout: Brepols.

Boswell, John. 1980. *Christianity, Social Tolerance, and Homosexuality*. Chicago: University of Chicago Press.

De Sodoma [anonymous poem]. 1881. Ed. Rudolf Peiper. Corpus Scriptorum Ecclesiasticorum Latinorum, vol. 23. Vienna: Tempsky.

Driscoll, Michael S. 1996. 'Penance in Transition: Popular Piety and Practice,' in *Medieval Liturgy*, ed. Lizette Larson-Miller. New York: Garland. Pp. 212–63.

Edwards, Catharine. 1993. *The Politics of Immorality in Ancient Rome*. Cambridge: Cambridge University Press.

Encyclopedia of Homosexuality. 1990. Ed. Wayne R. Dynes et al. 2 vols. New York: Garland.

Frantzen, Allen J. 1998. *Before the Closet: Same-Sex Love from* Beowulf *to* Angels in America. Chicago: University of Chicago Press.

Gregory the Great. 1979–85. *Moralia in Job*, ed. Marc Adriaen. Corpus Christianorum Series Latina, vols 143–143B. Turnhout: Brepols.

——. 1982. *Registrum epistolarum*, ed. Dag Norberg. Corpus Christianorum Series Latina, vols 140–140A. Turnhout: Brepols.

——. 1992. *Regula pastoralis*, ed. Floribert Rommel. Sources Chrétiennes, vols 381–2. Paris: Éditions du Cerf.

Hallam, Paul. 1993. *The Book of Sodom*. London and New York: Verso.

Jerome. 1963. *Commentaria in Esaiam*, ed. Marc Adriaen. Corpus Christianorum Series Latina, vols 73–73A. Turnhout: Brepols.

——. 1964. *Commentaria in Hiezechielem*, ed. Francis Glorie. Corpus Christianorum Series Latina, vols 75–75A. Turnhout: Brepols.

——. 1910–18. *Epistulae*, ed. Isidor Hilberg. Corpus Scriptorum Ecclesiasticorum Latinorum, vols 54–6. Vienna: Tempsky.

Payer, Pierre J. 1984. *Sex and the Penitentials*. Toronto: University of Toronto Press.

Peter Damian. 1983. *Liber gomorrhanus=Epistola* 31, in *Die Briefe des Petrus Damiani*, vol. 1, ed. Kurt Reindel. Monumenta Germaniae Historica: Die Briefe der deutschen Kaiserzeit, vol. 4. Munich: MGH.

Wasserschleben, F. W. Hermann. 1958. *Die Bußordnung der abendländischen Kirche*. Graz: Akademische Druck- und Verlagsanstalt; original Halle: Graeger (1851).

22

Christian Manliness Unmanned: Masculinity and Religion in Nineteenth- and Twentieth-Century Western Society

Editor's Introduction

In the next two chapters, Sean Gill and Charles Lippy address the re-emergence of 'manly' ideals of masculinity in the Christian men's movements of modernity. These movements are reactions to the profound cultural, political and economic changes in Western society, which not only destabilized traditional gender roles and expectations but also increasingly separated religion as a private sentiment from the public arena.

With the beginning of the Enlightenment and secularization, religious ideals of masculinity that had been generated during centuries of Christian hegemony in Europe began to go out of fashion. Somewhat ambiguous male gender arrangements (such as eunuchs, celibates, homosocial monastic communities, vagrant prophets) – which, at times, even met the ire of religious authorities, forever suspicious of heresies – became increasingly the target of scorn and ridicule of secular elites. Religious men were branded as effeminized and sodomitic, and religious sentimentality was considered womanish, soft, even neurotic. No longer did men seek power, authority, and recognition in the ecclesiastical but in the secular realm. With the strengthening of nation states, nationalism, colonial expansion, and a belief in technological progress, new masculine models were needed: heroic ideals of men as rational, calculating, muscular, belligerent, and national beings.

Several Christian men's movements – fearing that 'women were co-opting the sacred' (Culbertson 2007, 65) – responded to the loss of male membership in the churches by re-masculinizing Christianity. An 'effeminized' church, these movements variously claimed, had little to offer to modern men, thus deepening the 'perceived crisis in masculinity' (Culbertson 2007, 65). A church catering to private and womanish religious sentiments would also lead to a loss of public morality. By reverting to martial and national virtues, Christian men's movements asserted man's rightful place within the church and aspired to re-inject a more 'manly' Christian morality into public discourse.

Sean Gill, in the chapter below, illustrates these new manly ideals by examining the Victorian phenomenon of 'muscular Christianity' (see also Hall 1994; Gill et al. 2000). What Gill observes with respect to the valorization of a blend of religious and nationalistic manliness in Britain is true also in other countries, such as in Germany the Catholic 'Men's Apostolate' (founded in 1910) or the Protestant 'Men's Service' founded in 1915 (see Bergen 1996; Fout 1996; Zwicker 2006; Blaschke 2008). Similarly, in the United States several Christian men's movements emerged from the churches and, occasionally, in opposition to the Church. In chapter 23, Charles Lippy will trace these sentiments in the 'Men and Religion Forward' movement of the early twentieth century as well as in the 'Promise Keepers' and the 'Mythopoetic Movement' of the 1990s.

In 'Christian Manliness Unmanned,' Sean Gill focuses on muscular Christianity. He opens his chapter with quoting Baden-Powell, the founder of the boy scouts, 'God made men to be men,' because it captures well the spirit of Victorian Christian manliness. Such seemingly 'unproblematic correlation between masculine identity and religion' in the nineteenth century (Gill et al. 2000, 1) has, in recent years, attracted the attention of scholars in literature, history and religion.

> [T]he connection between the growing cult of Victorian manliness and Evangelical and Broad Church forms of Christianity . . . [and] Charles Kingsley's advocacy of 'muscular Christianity' fed easily into the swelling strain of militarism and imperialism which characterized the second half of the [nineteenth] century . . . [and] reveal[ed] the transmutation of the ideal of the warfare of the Christian hero and martyr from a defensive and essentially internalized stance, to one that was much more public and offensive. (Gill et al. 2000, 3)

Publications by the Same Author

Gill, Sean. 1994. *Women and the Church of England from the Eighteenth Century to the Present*. London: SPCK.
——. 1998. *The Lesbian and Gay Christian Movement*. London and New York: Cassell.
——. 2000. '*Ecce Homo*: Representations of Christ as the Model of Masculinity in Victorian Art and Lives of Jesus', in *Masculinity and Spirituality in Victorian Culture*, eds Sean Gill et al. Pp. 164–78.
Gill, Sean, Andrew Bradstock, Anne Hogan and Sue Morgan (eds) 2000. *Masculinity and Spirituality in Victorian Culture*. New York: St. Martin's Press.

Further Reading

Bergen, Doris. 1996. 'The Manly Church', in *The German Christian Movement in the Third Reich*, D. Bergen. Chapel Hill: University of North Carolina Press. Pp. 61–81.
Blaschke, Olaf. 2008. 'Fältmarskalk Jesus Kristus: Religiös remaskulinisering i Tyskland' (Field Marshall Jesus Christ: Religious Remasculinization in Germany), in *Kristen manlighet: Män och religion i en nordeuropeisk kontext 1840 till 1940*, ed. Yvonne Maria Werner. Lund: Nordic Academic Press. Pp. 23–50.
Carroll, Bret E. 2000. '"A Higher Power to Feel": Spiritualism, Grief, and Victorian Manhood'. *Men and Masculinities* 3/1 (July):3–29.
Culbertson, Philip. 2007. 'Christian Men's Movements', in *International Encyclopedia of Men and Masculinities*, eds M. Flood, J. K. Gardiner, B. Pease and K. Pringle, London, New York: Routledge. Pp. 65–7.
Fout, John C. 1996. 'Policing Gender: Moral Purity Movements in Pre-Nazi Germany and Contemporary America', in *Redeeming Men*, eds Stephen B. Boyd, Merle Longwood

and Mark Muesse. Louisville: Westminster John Knox. Pp. 103–14.

Hall, Donald E. (ed.). 1994. *Muscular Christianity: Embodying the Victorian Age*. Cambridge: Cambridge University Press.

Kirkley, Evelyn A. 1996. 'Is it Manly to Be Christian? The Debate in Victorian and Modern America', in *Redeeming Men*, eds Stephen B. Boyd, Merle Longwood and Mark Muesse. Louisville: Westminster John Knox. Pp. 80–8.

Zwicker, Lisa F. 2006. 'New Directions in Research on Masculinity and Confession'. *Kirchliche Zeitgeschichte/Contemporary Church History* 19/2:315–35.

Christian Manliness Unmanned: Masculinity and Religion in Nineteenth- and Twentieth-Century Western Society

SEAN GILL

According to the founder and icon of the Boy Scout movement Lord Baden-Powell, in his book *Rovering to Success* published in 1922, God made men to be men. Clearly for Baden-Powell, as one of the last great exemplars of Victorian values, the relationship between religion and gender was as close as it was conceptually transparent. Whether men lived up to this God-given ideal of masculinity was another matter though, for he went on to warn his readers that 'we badly need some training for our lads if we are to keep up manliness in our race instead of lapsing into a nation of soft, sloppy, cigarette suckers' (quoted in Warren 1987, 203). As a field of study, the subject of religion and masculinity is a relatively recent one that sets out to explore the two relationships implied in Baden-Powell's text. First, it seeks to elucidate the ways in which religious doctrines, symbols, and practices function in the creation and maintenance of ideas about masculinity, as in Baden-Powell's assertion that God made men to be men. Second, it examines how social constructions of gender influence theological and doctrinal formulations; Baden-Powell's obviously already had a clearly defined ideal of what constituted acceptable male behavior, which in his view many of his contemporaries were far from attaining.

It is not hard to account for the recent growth of interest in these issues. Surveying recent work in gender studies in his study *Men, Masculinity and Pastoral Care,* Mark Pryce concludes that much of the literature talks of a crisis in masculinity and male identity. There is, he continues, 'a profound dissatisfaction among some men with the ways of being a man which are open to them,' while 'others speak of confusion amongst men as traditional masculine identity no longer seems socially acceptable or feels secure' (Pryce 1993, 6). According to the title of a recent BBC series, it is a bad time to be male. Masculine identity has, it seems, become anxiously self-reflexive.

Numerous explanations have been advanced to account for the malaise of modern manhood.[1] Economic and technological change, it is argued, has destroyed most forms of traditional employment dependent upon male brawn rather than on intellectual ability, leaving a disaffected underclass with no employment prospects and rendering the traditional model of the male bread-winner obsolete. The feminist movement, and changes in the relationship between the sexes at work and in the home, have also been held responsible for the crisis in male self-identity. Feminism has also advanced a devastating critique of the evils of patriarchy for which men are held responsible—evils which extend not only to the oppression of women but to the possible destruction of all life on earth. In this view the rape of women and the violation of the planet are both aspects of the same masculine pathology.[2] Women have also made demands upon men to improve their performance as fathers, not only by sharing more in the burdens of parenthood, but by being more emotionally involved in the upbringing of their children.[3] Criticisms of this kind are aimed at the very heart of traditional understandings of what it is to be a man. As Roger Horrocks puts it, patriarchal masculinity cripples men. Its message to them, he suggests, is 'conceal your weakness, your tears, your fear of death, your love for others . . . Dominate others, then you can fool everyone, especially yourself, that you feel powerful' (1994, 25).

In a climate of such agonized self-questioning, it is not surprising that, whereas to date, nearly all of the most fruitful scholarship in the field of religion and gender has concentrated upon the impact of patriarchy upon women's lives, attention is now focusing upon its effects upon men. As with feminist historical and theological studies, the intention is both to unmask those forms of past religious thought and praxis that have contributed to the pathological nature of contemporary masculinity, and to explore what spiritual resources may yet exist within the Christian tradition for its creative reconfiguration. However, if this is to be done successfully there are a number of methodological problems that need to be taken into account.

Conceptual and Methodological Problems in the Study of Christianity and Masculinity

Undoubtedly the most serious obstacle standing in the way of such research has been the androcentric nature of much traditional scholarship, which has problematized the feminine while treating the category of maleness as normative. This has meant that while the overwhelming bulk of historical writing has concerned the activities and preoccupations of men as agents in the past, there has been little if any appreciation that masculinity itself might be problematic. It makes little sense, for example, to consider the ways in which Augustine's sense of selfhood as a man in a patriarchal society and his conception of the majesty and power of God might be interrelated, if the relationship between the two, although flawed on the human side, is ultimately accepted as one of ontological congruence. By contrast, the fact that within the Christian tradition femininity has been conceptualized as the disruptive other has quite rightly been the spur to an immense amount of fruitful reenvisioning of the past.[4]

Yet even if we succeed in posing new questions of the Christian tradition, other difficulties arise. If we accept a social constructionist perspective and

realize that gender is not a biologically determined or God-given category, but
the product of social practices, then it follows that the ideal of masculinity is
a context-specific one that changes over time. But when we begin to ground
our discussion of the relationship between Christianity and masculinity in a
particular social context we are then faced with the further problem of deciding to what extent both religion and gender operate as independent variables.
Clearly as Western society has become more secular and more pluralist, the role
of Christianity in sustaining the gendered ordering of the public realm, and in
providing models of appropriate male behavior, is far less easy to identify than
in the more distant past.

Perhaps even more of a challenge is the task of locating the formation of gender
within the complex interplay of class, race, sexual orientation, and nationality.
To talk, for example, of a putative crisis of masculinity within advanced capitalist societies conceals as much as it reveals, since its impact upon white or black
working-class males or upon white-collar workers has been very different from
that experienced by those engaged in professional and managerial jobs. In seeking to understand the dynamics of gender relations in past societies, historians have found it helpful to employ the concept of hegemonic masculinity to
describe the attempts to impose a normative model of male conduct upon all
sections of society in order to sustain the power of particular social or racial
groups. Yet it is important to be aware that such ideological formulations are
by their very nature unstable, contradictory, and contested. For instance, the
role of Protestant Christianity in the creation of what Max Weber called a new
masculine model of 'worldly asceticism' suited to the needs of the capitalist
economy should not obscure the fact that this ideal clashed head on with the
very different mores of popular male culture (Weber 1976, 153–4). We need to
study masculinities rather than masculinity if we are to make sense of gender
construction.

We must also be aware of the dangers of studying masculinity in isolation.
As R. W. Connell has argued, 'masculinity and femininity are inherently relational concepts' (1995, 44), and this is true both in terms of cultural dynamics
and of the distribution of power in any given society. So far, it has been the case
that the majority of studies of the relationship between religion and masculinity in the formative period of nineteenth-century English capitalism have
concentrated upon single-sex male environments such as public schools and
the armed forces.[5] In the rest of this article I shall try to adopt a contextualized
and relational approach to two important nineteenth-century theological issues
which can shed light on the links between Christianity and masculinity: the
ideal of Christian manliness, and the depiction of Christ. In doing so I shall
focus largely, but not exclusively, upon the writings of one of the most influential nineteenth-century writers on masculinity, the novelist and Christian
Socialist, Thomas Hughes.

The Ambiguities of Muscular Christianity

1857 saw the publication of what has come to be regarded as one of the classic
expositions of the Victorian ideal of heroic Christian masculinity, Thomas

Hughes's novel *Tom Brown's Schooldays*. Closely associated with the ethos of the newly emergent English public school, the ideal of muscular Christianity exalted an anti-intellectual credo of schoolboy athleticism and adult male toughness perfectly attuned to the ethos of Victorian imperialism.[6] In one sense Hughes's commendation of the virtues of what he calls manfulness or manliness provides a good example of the way in which the gendered polarities operating within mid-Victorian society perpetuated an ideal of masculine power over and against what most Victorian Christians would have regarded as the more feminine virtues of gentleness and compassion. Thus at one point in the novel he delivers a panegyric upon the necessity of conflict waged in a righteous cause:

> After all, what would life be without fighting, I should like to know? From the cradle to the grave, fighting, rightly understood is the business, the real, highest, honestest business of every son of man. Every one who is worth his salt has his enemies, who must be beaten, be they evil thoughts and habits in himself or spiritual wickedness in high places, or Russians, or border-ruffians, or Bill, Tom, or Harry, who will not let him live in quiet till he has thrashed them. (Hughes 1989, 282–3)

And he goes on to reject an alternative Christian model of masculinity exemplified by the pacifism associated with the Quakers as impracticable. Such a passage can be read as a perfect example of the new enthusiasm for Christian militarism, which Olive Anderson has suggested derived from the cult of the pious soldier martyr such as Sir Henry Havelock who died at the relief of Lucknow during the Indian mutiny, and which was to reach its apotheosis in the death of General Gordon at Khartoum in 1885 (Anderson 1971).

Nor was Hughes alone in emphasizing the tougher, more masculine, aspects of the Christian faith, for there was widespread unease at the time that it was appealing far more successfully to women than to men. As the Reverend S. S. Pugh complained in his *Christian Manliness: A Book of Examples and Principles for Young Men* published by the Religious Tract Society in 1867, 'The Christian life has often been strangely and mischievously misapprehended as to this, so that men have come to think of it as a state of dreary sentimentalism, fit only for women, or for soft and effeminate men, not calling forth or giving room for the exercise of the sterner and stronger virtues' (Pugh 1867, 95).

Hughes's fellow Christian Socialist, the Anglican clergyman F. D. Maurice, was similarly anxious to repudiate what he called 'the passive or feminine character which has often been ascribed to the Sermon on the Mount,' and which, he went on, had 'been thought to discourage all the qualities which have been most conspicuous in heroes who have struggled for freedom' (Maurice 1969, 461).

Norman Vance has argued, however, that Hughes had serious reservations about the label 'muscular Christianity' (Vance 1985, 2), which came to be associated with his writings, and he suggests that the term manliness is a more appropriate way of describing the synthesis of moral and physical virtues that he sought to promote. More recently this view has been challenged by Donald Hall, who prefers the more traditional epithet 'muscular Christianity' commenting on 'the consistent, even insistent, use of the ideologically charged and aggressively poised male body' in the work of writers such as Hughes and Charles Kingsley (Hall 1994, 9). Such differences of interpretation arise in no small part from the ambiguities towards gender differentiation that exist within Hughes's writing, for it is certainly possible to find there a very different attitude towards masculinity and femininity from the one which we have so far been discussing. It is important to recognize, for example, that Hughes sought to stress that the courage implied in his ideal of Christian manliness was primarily not physical but moral. His ideal of heroism turns out to owe a great deal more to the Pauline ideal of spiritual warfare against the world, the flesh, and the devil than to any imperialist or neo-Darwinian vision of human competitiveness and aggression. This meant that in practice it was open to women as well as to men to embody it. Thus in the novel, although the father of the hero's school friend Arthur is the epitome of Hughes's ideal of Christian manliness as an Anglican clergyman working for little recognition in an economically depressed working-class parish, his wife shares fully in the hardships of his life and ministry. Finally, both together face the ultimate test of courage when called upon to visit the sick of the parish during an epidemic of typhus to which they both succumb but from which only she recovers.[7]

As Hughes was well aware this was no mere fictionalized account. Women were taking an increasingly active part in the life of the Victorian churches, particularly in the fields of philanthropy and overseas missions (see Prochaska 1980). In so doing they were exhibiting many of the qualities of courage, organizational flair and intellect which were supposedly the particular characteristics associated with masculinity. Hughes indeed recognized such qualities in his own wife, writing to his close friend the future Marquess of Ripon that he felt sure that his wife Fanny could 'be a wonderful parsoness'—a task that he regarded as 'the work which was Christ's special work on earth' (Wolf 1921, I:153). Yet the increasing participation of women in the life of the church—what has been described as the feminization of Victorian Christianity (Douglas 1978)—ran counter to the polarities of contemporary thinking about gender, and neither Hughes nor his fellow proponents of Christian manliness were able to resolve the contradictions that this dualism entailed. For example, Charles Kingsley dismissed the ideal of muscular Christianity associated with his novels as 'a clever expression, spoken in jest, by I know not whom,' but then went on to offer his own definition of what he called 'a healthy and manful Christianity, one which does not exalt the feminine virtues to the exclusion of the masculine' (Kingsley 1865, 5).

In Hughes's case the unresolved tension between inclusive and exclusive conceptions of gender is nowhere more evident than in the conclusion to his novel *Tom Brown at Oxford*, written as a sequel to his earlier best seller. Tom has been saved from the vices and frivolities of life by the love of a good woman, Mary Porter. When he laments that in marrying her he has unwittingly tied to himself 'a brave, generous, pitying angel,' she indignantly rejects the appeal to Coventry Patmore's image of woman as the Angel in the House insisting that she has made a free moral choice to share his hardships. When Tom enthuses that 'life should be all bright and beautiful to a woman,' she replies by asking if women have different souls from men, and if not why they should not share their highest hopes. Yet ultimately Hughes returns to a much more conventional view of the relationship between men and women:

> Cannot a woman feel the wrongs that are going on in the world? Cannot she long to see them set right, and pray that they might be set right? We are not meant to sit in fine silks, and look pretty, and spend money, any more than you are meant to make it, and cry peace where there is no peace. If a woman cannot do much herself, she can honour and love a man who can.

To which he replies that she has made him 'feel what it is that a man wants, what is the help that is meet for him' (Hughes 1861, III:307–08).

There are several reasons why Hughes's construction of an ideal of Christian manhood was an unstable one. For one thing, it was a class-based ideal whose applicability to working-class culture was far from obvious. Above all it depended upon an unambiguous understanding of the feminine against which it could be defined. Yet as Hughes was well aware, the role of Christianity in the lives of Victorian middle-class women was far from simple. If it limited them by the stereotypes of pious passive femininity that it promoted, it also empowered them to undertake much more dynamic public roles (see Malmgreen 1986, 6–7). By appealing to what were ultimately transcendent values beyond the structures of patriarchal society, Christianity destabilized the category of the feminine even as it attempted to define it, thereby calling into question any attempt to arrive at a coherent notion of Christian masculinity.

Ecce Homo: Victorian Masculinity and the Jesus of History

Nowhere are these strains more evident than in the numerous attempts that were made in the mid-Victorian era to produce a convincing human portrait of Christ with which both men and women could identify. Hughes's contribution to the genre, significantly entitled *The Manliness of Christ*, appeared in 1879. In it he labored to provide what turned out to be mutually incompatible solutions to two problems. As we have seen, a number of prominent Victorian Christians were expressing alarm that Christianity, by being increasingly identified with the supposedly feminine virtues, was ceasing to appeal to men. Thus Hughes refers in the introduction to his work to the lack of success of branches of the YMCA in reaching the young:

> Their tone and influence are said to lack manliness, and the want of manliness is attributed to their avowed profession of Christianity. If you pursue the inquiry, you will often come upon a distinct belief that this weakness is inherent in our English religion; that our Christianity does and must appeal habitually and mainly to men's fears—to that in them which is timid and shrinking, rather than to that which is courageous and outspoken. (Hughes 1879, 2)

At the same time, the numbers of increasingly active women in the church had also to be able to identify with Christ in a Protestant Christian culture which found no place for the cult of the Virgin Mary and of female saints. Where this did not occur the risk of alienation from orthodox Christian symbolism was a real one. As Florence Nightingale argued, women would never really be liberated until the day when 'there shall arise a woman, who will resume, in her own soul, all the sufferings of her race, and that woman will be the Saviour of her race' (quoted in Gill 1994, 140). Hughes therefore attempts to portray a Christ who combines the highest qualities of both masculinity and femininity—a man at once of 'absolutely unshaken steadfastness' and at the same time 'this most tender and sensitive of the sons of men—with fibres answering to every touch and breath of human sympathy,' a classic definition of the Victorian ideal of female gentleness (Hughes 1879, 143). The same hypostatic union of gendered opposites is also evident in the concluding peroration of *Tom Brown's Schooldays,* where the rhetoric of muscular Christianity sits uneasily beside that of submissive Christian femininity:

> Such stages have got to be gone through, I believe, by all young and brave souls who must win their way through hero-worship, to the worship of Him who is the King and Lord of heroes. For it is only through our mysterious human relationships, through the love and tenderness and purity of mothers and sisters and wives, through the strength and courage and wisdom of fathers and brothers and teachers, that we can come to the knowledge of Him, in whom alone the love, and the tenderness, and the purity, and the strength, and the courage, and the wisdom of all these dwell for ever and ever in perfect fullness. (Hughes 1989, 376)

How far such rhetorical strategies were successful is another matter given the Victorian rejection of any behavior by men deemed to be inappropriately feminine as effeminate. The *Westminster Review,* for example, dealt gingerly with the gender implications of Hughes's life of Christ, commenting that the spirit of Christ was not the spirit of an athlete, while hastening to add that 'we are far from saying that Jesus was not manly.'[8] As the leading exponent of the American social gospel movement, Walter Rauschenbusch, put it, 'there was nothing mushy, nothing sweetly effeminate about Jesus.' He was, he reassured his readers, 'a man's man' (quoted in Curtis 1990, 72).

One possible resolution of these difficulties lay in the appeal to the notion of chivalry, that interplay of masculine strength and feminine weakness that served to reinforce both ideals. As the Reverend Pugh explained to his readership of young men, Christ's gentleness was of a particular kind, and in following his example 'a man who is strong, who in fidelity and courage and self-reliance and self-mastery can keep the even tenor of his ways, can afford to be gentle without fearing to be suspected of weakness' (Pugh 1867, 123). Hughes's fellow novelist and Christian Socialist Charles Kingsley agreed, describing Christ's example of self-sacrifice as 'the true prowess, the true valour, the true chivalry, the true glory, the true manhood to which we should all aspire' (Kingsley 1865, 20). The appeal of chivalry to Hughes was equally strong. His grandmother knew and entertained the novelist Sir Walter Scott, one of the most influential figures in the development of the Victorian enthusiasm for the Middle Ages, and Hughes was an avid reader of his works. On one occasion, he recalled, while a student at Oxford he read selections from the novels to a 'broken-down old jockey' in an endeavor to get him to abandon the public house—though the result of this somewhat unusual form of temperance campaigning is not recorded (Mack and Armytage 1952, 116). Hughes's depiction of Christ as a man of 'most exquisite temper and courtesy' in his dealings with both rich and poor alike owes a great deal to the ideals of knighthood seen through the rose-tinted spectacles of Victorian neo-medievalism.[9]

The Legacy of Christian Manliness

In one sense it might be argued that little has survived of the context and assumptions that inform Hughes's wrestling with the problems of Christianity and masculinity. The ideal of heroic male chivalry did not, after all, survive the brutal realities of the Somme battlefields, and when D. H. Lawrence sought to engage with the Jesus of history in the 1920s, the result would have been unintelligible and deeply offensive to Hughes and his contemporaries. In revolt against what he regarded as the stifling and emasculating conventions of Victorian society, Lawrence rejected what he felt to be the infantilism and the dualism of flesh and spirit implied in conventional portrayals of Christ, substituting for them an image of the risen Lord as 'a full man, in full flesh and soul' who marries and has children.[10] Lawrence's rejection of the traditional image of Christ as an inadequate model for masculinity has in fact striking resemblances to the work of one of the gurus of the contemporary men's movement, Robert Bly. In Bly's Iron John Christ is also a problematic model of maleness on account of both his lack of sexuality and his weakness. While he is commended for his machismo at the point where 'he goes wild in the temple and starts whipping the moneylenders,' Bly argues that a new and more vigorous Christ is needed to which modern men can relate—'a religious figure, but a hairy one, in touch with God and sexuality, with spirit and earth' (Bly 1990, 249). Bly, and the new men's movement with which he is associated, reveal a deeply ambiguous response to feminism, accusing it of being partly responsible for the emasculation of men. One can find similar concerns voiced in fundamentalist Christian groups, such as the American men's movement Promise Keepers, whose appeal to a Christ at once new man and old is designed to reassert traditional ideals of male headship which they fear are being undermined by both feminism and liberalism (see Dyson 1997, 83). As Albert Schweitzer remarked in his great critical survey of the Victorian quest for the historical Jesus, 'There is no historical task which so reveals a man's true self as the writing of a Life of Jesus' (Schweitzer 1954, 4). In our day, no less than in Hughes's, the search to find and express that self remains both anguished and contentious.

Similarly it would be hard to maintain that we have solved the other problems of gender that made the Victorians so uneasy. The recent tormented debates within the church of England over the ordination of women reveal, among many other things, a great deal about our contemporary confusions and anxieties in this respect. Thus some opponents of the measure appealed to what were essentially Victorian notions of polarized and God-given gender identities. For instance, V. A. Demant, then Regius Professor of Moral and Pastoral Theology at Oxford, could argue that the divine Logos is in some sense inherently masculine because 'maleness is associated with law, order, civilisation, logos, clock time, and what Freud called the "super-ego." Femaleness is associated with nature, instinct, biological time, feeling, eros, and what Freud called the "id"' (quoted in Gill 1994, 248).

Yet even among those in favor of change, there were deep differences as to whether women's ordination was being advocated on the grounds of the unitary nature of masculinity and femininity in which reason, creativity and compassion were the common characteristics of both, or whether appeal was being made to specifically feminine qualities that men lacked and that women would bring to the church's ministry. What debates such as these suggest is that while we would do well to engage in what Foucault (1969) has termed the archaeology of knowledge, and thereby to uncover the origins of much of our contemporary thinking about masculinity, much more is at stake. No more than Thomas Hughes have we found answers to the troubling questions about Christianity and male identity with which his contemporaries would no doubt have said that he grappled so manfully.

Notes

1 There are good general accounts of this theme in Kimmel and Messner (1989), and Morgan (1992).

2 From among an ever growing literature see Plant (1989, 1–4); Primavesi (1991, 24–43); Ruether (1993, 13–23).

3 For a recent discussion of this question see Moss (1995).

4 For the relative neglect by scholars of masculinity as a problematic gender construct, and the reasons for this, see Morgan (1992, 26–30).

5 Examples of this genre include Mangan (1981) and Springhall (1977). An outstanding exception is Davidoff and Hall (1987).

6 For the cult of Victorian manliness see Newsome (1961) and Vance (1985).

7 Hughes, *Schooldays* (1989, 238–41).

8 *The Westminster Review* 57 (1880):547.

9 Hughes, *Manliness* (1879, 123). The theme of Victorian neo-medievalism is well covered in Girouard (1981).

10 Lawrence, 'The Risen Lord' (1968, 575). This essay was first published in 1929 and took up themes which had appeared in his more extended treatment of Christ, *The Man Who Died* (1925).

Literature

Anderson, Olive. 1971. 'The Growth of Christian Militarism in mid-Victorian Britain,' *The Journal of Ecclesiastical History* 86:46–72.

Bly, Robert. 1990. *Iron John: A Book About Men*. Reading: Addison-Wesley Publishing.

Connell, R. W. 1995. *Masculinities*. Oxford: Polity Press.

Curtis, Susan. 1990. 'The Son of Man and God the Father: The Social Gospel and Victorian Masculinity,' in *Meanings for Manhood: Constructions of Masculinity in*

Victorian America, eds M. Clynes and C. Griffin. Chicago: Chicago University Press. Pp. 67–83.

Davidoff, Leonore and Catherine Hall. 1987. *Family Fortunes: Men and Women of the English Middle Class, 1780–1850*. London: Hutchinson.

Douglas, Ann. 1978. *The Feminization of American Culture*. New York: Avon Books.

Dyson, Anthony. 1997. 'Carnal Knowledge: Men and Sexuality,' in *Sexuality and Spirituality in Perspective*, ed. M. Percy. London: Darton, Longman & Todd. Pp. 76–85.

Foucault, Michel. 1969. *L'archéologie du savoir*. Paris: Éditions Gallimard.

Gill, Sean. 1994. *Women and the Church of England from the Eighteenth Century to the Present*. London: SPCK.

Girouard, Mark. 1981. *The Return to Camelot: Chivalry and the English Gentleman*. New Haven: Yale University Press.

Hall, Donald (ed.). 1994. *Muscular Christianity: Embodying the Victorian Age*. Cambridge: Cambridge University Press.

Horrocks, Roger. 1994. *Masculinity in Crisis: Myths, Fantasies and Realities*. London: Macmillan.

Hughes, Thomas. 1861. *Tom Brown at Oxford* (3 vols). London: Macmillan.

——. 1879. *The Manliness of Christ*. London: Macmillan.

——. 1989. *Tom Brown's Schooldays*. Oxford: Oxford University Press.

Kimmel, Michael S. and Michael A. Messner (eds). 1989. *Men's Lives*. New York: Macmillan.

Kingsley, Charles. 1865. *Four Sermons Preached before the University of Cambridge*. London: Macmillan.

Lawrence, D. H. 1968. 'The Risen Lord,' in *Phoenix II. Uncollected, Unpublished and Other Prose Works by D. H. Lawrence*, eds W. Roberts and H. Moore. London: Heinemann. Pp. 571–7.

Mack, Edward C. and W. H. G. Armytage. 1952. *Thomas Hughes: The Life of the Author of* Tom Brown's Schooldays. London: Ernest Benn.

Malmgreen, Gail (ed.). 1986. *Religion in the Lives of English Women, 1760–1930*. London: Croom Helm.

Mangan, J. A. 1981. *Athleticism in the Victorian and Edwardian Public School: The Emergence and Consolidation of an Educational Ideology*. Cambridge: Cambridge University Press.

Maurice, Frederick Denison. 1969. *Social Morality: Twenty-one Lectures Delivered in the University of Cambridge*. London: Macmillan.

Morgan, David H. J. 1992. *Discovering Men*. London: Routledge.

Moss, Peter (ed.). 1995. *Father Figures: Fathers in the Families of the 1990s*. Edinburgh: HMSO.

Newsome, David. 1961. *Godliness and Good Learning*. London: Cassell.

Plant, Judith. 1989. 'Towards a New World: An Introduction,' in *Healing the Wounds: The Promise of Ecofeminism*, ed. J. Plant. London: The Merlin Press. Pp. 1–4.

Primavesi, Anne. 1991. *From Apocalypse to Genesis: Ecology, Feminism and Christianity*. Minneapolis: Fortress.

Prochaska, F. K. 1980. *Women and Philanthropy in Nineteenth-Century England*. Oxford: Clarendon Press.

Pryce, Marc. 1993. *Men, Masculinity and Pastoral Care* (Contact Pastoral Monographs, 3). Edinburgh: Contact Pastoral Limited Trust.

Pugh, S. 1867. *Christian Manliness: A Book of Examples and Principles for Young Men*. London: The Religious Tract Society.

Ruether, Rosemary Radford. 1993. 'Ecofeminism: Symbolic and Social Connections of the Oppression of Women and the Domination of Nature,' in *Ecofeminism and the Sacred*, ed. C. Adams. New York: Continuum. Pp. 13–23.

Schweitzer, Albert. 1954. *The Quest of the Historical Jesus* (3rd English edn). London: A. & C. Black.

Springhall, John. 1977. *Youth, Empire and Society: British Youth Movements, 1883–1940*. London: Croom Helm.

Vance, Norman. 1985. *The Sinews of the Spirit: The Ideal of Christian Manliness in Victorian Literature and Religious Thought*. Cambridge: Cambridge University Press.

Warren, Allen. 1987. 'Popular Manliness: Baden Powell, Scouting and the Development of Manly Character,' in *Manliness and Morality: Middle-Class Masculinity in Britain and America 1800–1940*, eds J. A. Mangan and J. Walvin. Manchester: Manchester University Press. Pp. 199–219.

Weber, Max. 1976. *The Protestant Ethic and the Rise of Capitalism*, ed. Anthony Giddens. London: George Allen & Unwin.

Wolf, Lucien. 1921. *The Life of the First Marquess of Ripon* (2 vols). London: John Murray.

23

Miles to Go: Promise Keepers in Historical and Cultural Context

Editor's Introduction

In the 1990s, both the evangelical Promise Keepers as well as the non-church-based mythopoetic men's movement succeeded in attracting thousands of men, gathering in sports stadiums and local support groups (Promise Keepers) and at lectures and weekend retreats (mythopoetic men). Whereas the mythopoetic movement appealed more to 'white, middle-aged, heterosexual' men of professional status (Messner 1997, 17), Promise Keepers intentionally sought to cross racial barriers, bringing together North American men of diverse social and ethnic backgrounds. Public attention peaked in the mid-1990s, perhaps best evidenced by two events at the Mall in Washington, DC: first, the Million Man March in 1995, which was organized by Louis Farrakhan of the Nation of Islam, gathering close to 900,000 people of mostly African-American descent; and, second, two years later, the 1997 'Stand in the Gap' rally, which was backed by the Promise Keepers and brought to the Mall about 600,000 people (Baker-Fletcher 1998; Poling and Kirkley 2000).

These movements followed different aspirations, with the Nation of Islam leader drawing attention to the plight of African-American men and their families, the evangelical Promise Keepers aiming at rejuvenating male participation in Christian churches and family life, and the archetypal mythopoetic movement encouraging men to rediscover and integrate their wild, untamed male nature. However, these movements, as sociologists of religion have repeatedly pointed out, pursued similar politics (see Williams 2001; Bartkowski 2004). Men were taken to task for their responsibilities within families (or their lack thereof) and, in exchange, were promised to regain dominance in their social networks, particularly in their homes. The 'mythopoetic men's movement and the Christian Promise Keepers', Michael Messner states, are 'strikingly similar':

Leaders of both share an aversion to what they see as a recent 'feminization' of men. The mythopoetic movement, though, is more apt to blame modernization for this feminization of men, whereas Promise Keepers is more apt to blame feminism, gay liberation, sexual liberation, and the 'breakdown of the family' for men's problems. Both groups see a need for men to retreat from women to create spiritually based homosocial rituals through which they can collectively recapture a lost or strayed 'true manhood.' And these movements are asserting men's responsibility to retake their natural positions of leadership in their communities. (Messner 1997, 16–17; also Clatterbaugh 1990, 85–103)

In this chapter, Charles Lippy looks at the Promise Keepers in the context of twentieth-century Christian men's movements. Following the historical sketch that Sean Gill started to draw in chapter 22, Lippy continues with the Men and Religion Forward movement of the early twentieth century and ends, like Gill, with a reference to Robert Bly, who has been a pivotal figure in the mytho-poetic movement.

Lippy presents a view of the Promise Keepers that is less skeptical than Messner's political assessment quoted above. The ideal Promise Keeper, Lippy writes, 'is sensitive, faithful, inclusive, and committed.' Though Lippy joins in rebuking male dominance, he calls 'attention to the ambivalence' contained in the messages of Promise Keepers about manliness. 'I submit', he writes, 'that Promise Keepers is simply trying to carve out a place for men in the domestic sphere that allows them to retain a male identity.' In *Do Real Men Pray?*, Lippy follows up on the question of whether male spirituality is 'distinct and distinc-tive', wondering what it would mean for 'a white Protestant American male . . . to be a Christian man' (Lippy 2005, 1).

With the beginning of the new millennium, Promise Keepers has declined in numbers and public visibility; in their stead, a new manifestation of an American Christian men's movement, called the 'GodMen', has picked up speed. GodMen is, like earlier movements, a parachurch phenomenon and not bound to a particular Christian denomination. GodMen is a network and forum for men to meet outside the church in order to liberate themselves from the ballast of what they call a 'feminization of mainline churches'. GodMen con-siders the Promise Keepers too soft. 'The syrup and the sticky stuff is holding us down,' commented a minister from Tennessee; and Rick Caldwell, global director of the affiliated Men's Fraternity, self-described the revivalist program as 'testosterone-friendly' (quoted in Jarvie and Simon, 2007). GodMen charges that the message conveyed by the church today boils down to God creating men for no other purpose than making them 'nice guys' – exemplified tellingly in Paul Coughlin's bestselling *No More Christian Nice Guy* (2005). Such unmanly attitudes, these spokesmen promise, will have to come to an end.

Publications by the Same Author

Lippy, Charles H. 1994. *Being Religious, American Style: A History of Popular Religiosity in the United States*. Westport: Praeger.

——. 2000. *Pluralism Comes of Age: American Religious Culture in the Twentieth Century*. New York: M. E. Sharpe.

——. 2005. *Do Real Men Pray? Images of the Christian Man and Male Spirituality in White Protestant America*. Knoxville: The University of Tennessee Press.

Further Reading

Baker-Fletcher, Garth Kasimu (ed). 1998. *Black Religion After the Million Man March: Voices on the Future*. Maryknoll: Orbis.

Bartkowski, John P. 2004. *The Promise Keepers: Servants, Soldiers, and Godly Men.* Piscataway: Rutgers University Press.

Clatterbaugh, Kenneth. 1990. *Contemporary Perspectives on Masculinity: Men, Women, and Politics in Modern Society.* Boulder: Westview Press.

Claussen, Dane S. (ed.). 2000. *The Promise Keepers: Essays on Masculinity and Christianity.* Jefferson: McFarland Press.

Coughlin, Paul. 2005. *No More Christian Nice Guy: When Being Nice—Instead of Good—Hurts Men, Women and Children.* Bloomington: Bethany House.

Donovan, Brian. 1998. 'Political Consequences of Private Authority: Promise Keepers and the Transformation of Hegemonic Masculinity'. *Theory and Society* 27/6:817–43.

Jarvie, Jenny and Stephanie Simon. 2005. 'What Would Jesus Do? Watch the Game: GodMen Espouses Macho Christianity', *Washington Post* (4 February):D5.

Messner, Michael A. 1997. *Politics of Masculinities: Men in Movements.* Thousand Oaks and London: Sage Publications.

Poling, James N. and Evelyn A. Kirkley. 2000. 'Phallic Spirituality: Masculinities in Promise Keepers, the Million Man March and Sex Panic'. *Theology and Sexuality* 12:9–25.

Williams, Rhys H. (ed.). 2001. *Promise Keepers and the New Masculinity: Private Lives and Public Morality.* Lanham: Lexington Books.

Miles to Go: Promise Keepers in Historical and Cultural Context

CHARLES H. LIPPY

In early February 1997, newspapers around the US were already carrying advance publicity for the Promise Keepers' 'Stand in the Gap' Sacred Assembly of Men. Organizers of this gathering, slated for October 4, 1997 in Washington, DC, hoped to draw more men than the 1995 African American Million Man March to a 'day of worship and prayer' that they said would involve men from 'every religion, culture, and race.'[1] After the event, published reports put the attendance at 700,000, but whether 'Stand in the Gap' matched or outdrew the Million Man March—or actually included men from every religion, culture, and race—is less important than the Promise Keepers phenomenon itself, for few efforts to advance the religiosity of American men in the twentieth century have attracted the attention given this movement. Nor have other efforts matched the number of men who have flocked to stadiums and arenas for Promise Keepers rallies. Estimates suggest, for example, that between one and one-and-a-half million men attended the nearly two dozen major rallies held by the Promise Keepers from late spring through early fall of 1996.

How can we understand this effort to boost the spirituality of American men? Most of the attempts to analyze Promise Keepers have come in the popular press where writers are prone to look at the movement as if it emerged *ex nihilo*. None to my knowledge has compared this burst of male religious enthusiasm with the 'muscular Christianity' of the early twentieth century, or with the Men and Religion Forward movement, a transdenominational venture to draw men into Protestant churches through a series of carefully planned mass rallies in 1911–12.[2] My thesis is that both Men and Religion Forward and Promise Keepers emerged in part as reactions to marked changes in gender roles both in religious culture and in American culture as a whole, and that each movement presumes an image of the ideal male—the religious man or the Promise Keeper—that identifies it as a product of its own time and place. Developing this argument requires some explication of precisely what each movement involves.

Men and Religion Forward owed its genesis to two men, Harry W. Arnold and Fred B. Smith.[3] Both were well aware of a statistic that remains a rule-of-thumb among analysts: that women outnumber men on the rolls of American religious groups by about a two to one margin. As the twentieth century opened, that meant there were '3,000,000 more girls and women in the churches of America than men and boys.'[4] (It perhaps goes without saying that this calculation was for white Protestants only.) Early in the century, Arnold put together a series of meetings in Maine designed to reach unchurched men. Several years later, Smith brought together a committee of 97 men from around the country to transform Arnold's vision for Maine into national reality.[5] Under their auspices, local events were planned in cities around the country, organized in each case by a local committee 'composed of the one hundred strongest men' in the city, a 15-member executive committee, and 11 subcommittees that handled the details.[6] Advance teams surveyed each city using the latest tools of the newly founded field of sociology to determine where the unchurched were and what specific needs existed in five areas: social service, boy's work, evangelism, Bible study, and missions. These five areas in time became part of the movement's logo, with each area represented by one point of a five-pointed star. To attract men and boys to these five areas of concern, the organization also developed a catchy slogan: 'More Men for Religion, More Religion for Men.'

On September 18, 1911 the Men and Religion Forward campaign opened, with meetings in Protestant churches across the country. Between then and the wrap-up 'Christian Conservation Congress' in New York in April 1912, eight-day meetings were conducted in 76 major cities, and smaller-scale rallies were held in more than 1,000 towns. Large auditoriums and theaters, including New York's Carnegie Hall, were rented for these occasions, which featured teams of men presenting 'the manly gospel of Christ . . . to men.'[7]

Like the later Promise Keepers rallies, Men and Religion Forward meetings were designed for men only. Except for an occasional separate gathering for mothers and a few cities that welcomed women to one or two meetings, women were specifically excluded. Why? Movement leaders apparently were intent on shattering the cultural connection between religion and emotion, between religion and the sphere of women that had been developing in the United States at least since the antebellum period. 'The gospel of Jesus of Nazareth—and its practical application to our practical daily life,' one often-repeated statement put it, will be 'presented calmly, sanely, logically, so that it will convince the average man, who is a man of sane, logical, common sense. Women have no part in this movement . . .'[8] The inference is clear: feminized religion was not logical; nor could it be presented calmly and sanely.

What was manly Christianity presented calmly and sanely? It was not a Christianity of piety and devotion, but one of efficiency, action, and engagement—particularly engagement in social service programs. Indeed, Men and Religion Forward speakers promoted an active, social Christianity so strongly that C. Howard Hopkins linked the organization to the social gospel movement (Hopkins 1940, 296). And Gail Bederman has pointed out that in Des Moines men who attended the movement's meetings helped establish a public shelter and worked to improve prison conditions, while elsewhere they 'concentrated on reforming garbage collection, inspection of water and milk, and improving communication with labor unions' (Bederman 1989, 450).

There remains considerable doubt whether the participants in Men and Religion Forward were smitten with the theology of the social gospel. One has the sense, rather, that there was a certain busy-ness in their activities simply because such busy-ness was considered manly and therefore not reflective of a sentimental, feminized religion. The idea was that men, simply because they were men, had to be physically engaged in some activity to be religious, and that what they did had to be executed in an efficient, businesslike manner.

Men and Religion Forward also emphasized social service work because its leaders recognized that emphasizing doctrine and belief could be divisive. At the start of the twentieth century, denominations placed greater significance on doctrine and on the distinctions between groups based on differences in belief. The religion of efficient social service advocated by Men and Religion Forward sought to overcome these divisions; its leaders hoped that men engaged in such activity would overlook differences of belief or would be too busy to allow them to get in the way.

The manly Christianity advocated by Men and Religion Forward can also be seen in a broader context as a product of and a response to the changes in gender roles that marked the late nineteenth century. As numerous scholars have noted, the Victorians saw the home as the locus of 'real' religion, and thus relegated vital piety to the sphere of women (see esp. McDannell 1986; Fishburn 1982; Douglas 1978). This feminization of the home had been underway since the antebellum period; what was new in the late nineteenth century was that men were increasingly employed outside the home in business and industry, where productivity and efficiency were coming to reign supreme. When the family was a working economic unit, generally in an agrarian context, men were responsible primarily to themselves and their families for what they did. Women, too, had an economic function that went well beyond their domestic role as homemakers. But in the emerging capitalist industrial society of the late nineteenth century, men who worked outside the home—although perhaps enjoying greater financial security and the leisure provided by regular hours of employment (even if much more than most would find acceptable today)—were now responsible to others. They had lost control over a vital part of their lives, a loss that must have been felt keenly, especially by those whose identity was molded in part by what we have come to call, since Max Weber, the 'Protestant work ethic.'[9] Compounding this loss, the ready availability of immigrants willing to work for low wages posed an additional threat to the sense of self-worth that workers derived from their jobs. In fact, as Gail Bederman points out, the economic transformations of the age 'were undermining Victorian ideals of self-restrained manhood' (Bederman 1995, 15).[10]

What did it mean to be a man in this new context? Where was a man to turn to find a sense of identity and direction? Not to the home, the domain of women, nor to the churches, which were dominated by women even if controlled by men. Some men sought refuge in fraternal lodges, though as Mark Carnes points out many of these lodges drew heavily on feminine imagery for their rituals (see esp. Carnes 1989; also Clawson 1989). Other men turned to 'muscular Christianity,' a movement rooted in British Christian Socialism that was popularized in English novels geared toward adolescent boys and men.[11] Others were influenced by the 'rough rider' image associated with Theodore Roosevelt, whose linking of masculinity with adventure and bellicosity contributed to the rising popularity of sports such as boxing and football.[12]

A parallel alternative, one more specifically religious, was offered by Billy Sunday, who left a professional baseball career to become an itinerant revivalist. He held meetings for men only in connection with some of his campaigns, peppered his sermons with lots of sports analogies because of their presumed appeal to men, and preached in the slang thought typical of casual male speech.[13] Sunday biographer Roger Bruns described the evangelist and his preaching:

> This was no dainty, sissified, lily-livered piety the crowd was hearing. This was hard-muscled, pickaxed religion, a religion from the gut, tough and resilient. Prayer here was a manly duty; faith was mountain-moving, galvanic. There was power in reverence, energy in belief. The tough guys were on the right side. This was not a place for weak-kneed, four-flushing boozers and sin-soaked infidels. (Bruns 1992, 15–16)[14]

Or as Sunday himself reportedly commented about the prevalent style of religion in his day, 'Lord save us from off-handed, flabby cheeked, brittle-boned, weak-kneed, thin-skinned, pliable, plastic, spineless, effeminate, ossified three-karat Christianity' (quoted in Bruns 1992, 138).

Men and Religion Forward offered another option for men who were uncertain of their role and status in society. With its strong emphasis on social service, the movement created its own image of what the American man should be. The man who was a worker in business and industry need not cede his identity to an employer on the job or to his wife in the home. Active physical labor—doing something—had once provided men with an identity. Men and Religion Forward offered exactly the same, only now men were encouraged to become involved in such efforts as reforming prisons, addressing child labor issues, or wrestling with the apparent increase of prostitution in the cities. In this way, religion could provide a viable identity for men. It was a religion of action, not contemplation, and its programs were executed with the same stress on productivity and efficiency that business lauded as hallmarks of success. But its emphasis on social service introduced an important new element into the process of 'remaking manhood' that marked this period.[15]

The religious man who was absorbed in active social service was also likely to become more involved with his home and family, not as ruling patriarch but as an equal partner with his wife. Traditional interpretation is so trapped by stereotypes that it is easy to overlook the movement in favor of what Margaret Marsh has called 'masculine domesticity' that was roughly contemporary with

Men and Religion Forward and complementary with its aims (Marsh 1988, 165–86). As Marsh has pointed out, advocates of masculine domesticity urged men to take greater interest in home and family now that the leisure created by regular work in industry was becoming more common. After all, the 'responsibility for the home is not [the woman's] alone,' wrote the male editor of *American Homes and Gardens* magazine in 1905, 'but is equally the husband's' (cited in Marsh 1988, 175). That same year, *American Homes and Gardens* proclaimed that 'there is no reason at all why men should not sweep and dust, make beds, clean windows, fix the fire, clean the grate, arrange the furniture . . .' (cited in Marsh 1988, 165). The magazine was talking about male domestic servants here, but its words could apply just as easily to the proverbial 'man of the house.'

One link between the call for masculine domesticity and Men and Religion Forward is provided by Martha Bruère, a professional home economist who wrote approvingly about both. Bruère and her economist husband did case studies of rural, urban, and suburban households, concluding in part that 'the home is man's affair as much as woman's . . . When God made homemakers, male and female created He them!'[16] And writing in *Collier's* magazine in 1925, she argued that a long-term result of Men and Religion Forward was that the churches were becoming 'defeminized' (just as she hoped the home would be) because male converts were equaling the number of female converts.[17]

Gail Bederman argues that the social service impulse fostered by Men and Religion Forward was rather short-lived, but that the movement to masculinize the Protestant churches was more enduring. Churches added athletics to their programs and became captivated in the 1920s by the image of Jesus as corporate executive popularized by Bruce Barton's best-selling *The Man Nobody Knows* (1925).[18] That appraisal tells one part of the story. Historians also point to the Great War as ending both the opportunity and impetus for the kind of reform associated with the social gospel movement and Men and Religion Forward. In addition, the Progressive movement sapped much of the religious energy for social reform by making reform the province of government (and launching the kind of government regulation under attack in many quarters at the end of the twentieth century). After the government seized the initiative in social reform, men who tried to find their identities in physical activity did so on the battlefields of World War One or, after the war, in sports, not in the urban slums.

Nonetheless Men and Religion Forward did provide white urban and suburban Protestant men with an opportunity to shape their identities as men through active social service. These 'Christian gentlemen,' to use Billy Sunday's phrase, took an activity that popular culture classified as feminine and recast it in masculine terms. The work required by the fading ideal of agrarian self-sufficiency generated physical strength that was presumed to signal strength of character. Now the work required by a religion of efficient social service would generate a moral strength that was presumed to signal strength of character as well. Seen in this way, the Christian man that Men and Religion Forward held up as a model was both traditional and a product of the times.

Just over three-quarters of a century after the Men and Religion Forward campaign, a cognate movement to promote male bonding and a masculine spirituality was founded by former University of Colorado football coach Bill

McCartney. Called Promise Keepers, this nondenominational parachurch organization held its first religious-renewal rally, attended by approximately 4,200 men, at the University of Colorado in 1991.[19] Like Men and Religion Forward, Promise Keepers is a movement by, for, and about men.[20] Unlike Men and Religion Forward, however, it is not intended as a one-time effort to attract men into the churches. Instead, Promise Keepers has seen itself from its inception as an ongoing ministry that will remain part of the American religious landscape. It began publishing its own magazine, *New Man*, in 1994, and it produces literature to help local groups organize and operate.

Most of the stated premises of Promise Keepers, particularly the Seven Promises at its ideological core, cannot be understood apart from McCartney's life experience. As a successful football coach, McCartney was an active participant in perhaps the one cultural institution in America that is racially inclusive, and his approach to football was even more inclusive than most. In fact, by the time he resigned his position in 1995 to devote himself full-time to Promise Keepers and related activities, he was the only Division I-A head coach whose staff had equal numbers of African American and white coaches.

At the same time, McCartney came to believe that in his fanatical desire to rise to the top of his profession and coach a national championship football team, he had failed his wife and family.[21] After all, his unmarried daughter had two children, each fathered by a different University of Colorado football player. McCartney also concluded that he was far from the only American workaholic absentee husband and father who believed that family life should revolve around his job.

Along the way, McCartney had also abandoned the Roman Catholic faith of his formative years. Instead, he found himself increasingly drawn to the charismatic, exuberant expression of faith promoted in churches associated with the Vineyard Christian Fellowship, founded by John Wimber. Wimber had long believed that 'signs and wonders' accompanied authentic ministry, and in time McCartney would look at the phenomenal growth of the Promise Keepers movement as evidence of the divine presence in its program.

Not surprisingly, given McCartney's spiritual journey and personal life, the Seven Promises trumpeted by Promise Keepers revolve primarily around God, race, and family. They are:

1 To honor Jesus Christ through worship, prayer, and obedience to God's Ward through the power of the Holy Spirit.

2 To pursue a vital relationship with a few other men, understanding that a man needs brothers to help him keep his promises.

3 To practice spiritual, moral, ethical, and sexual purity.

4 To build strong marriages and families through love, protection, and biblical values.

5 To support the mission of his local church.

6 To reach beyond any racial and denominational barriers to demonstrate the power of biblical unity.

7 To influence his world being obedient to the Great Commandment (Mark 12.30–31) and the Great Commission (Matthew 28.19–20).[22]

Like the meetings sponsored by Men and Religion Forward, Promise Keepers conferences feature a series of speakers who address stated themes. In 1996, the overall theme was 'Break Down the Walls'—referring to the barriers between men and God, men and their wives, men and their children, white men and African American men, and men and persons from other religious denominations. In keeping with McCartney's experience, the Seven Promises, and this theme, speakers at Promise Keepers rallies cross denominational and racial lines, and the staff running the Denver headquarters and the field offices in the US, Canada, Australia, and New Zealand is multiracial as well. (In fact, speakers and staff are often more multiracial than the audiences at the rallies.)

Just as important as the message of Promise Keepers is its delivery system, whose most visible manifestation is the stadium rally. Promise Keepers uses stadiums for these events deliberately. 'We hold conferences in stadiums because the stadium is safe and masculine. It puts guys together in a group. We [men] are all little boys [in a stadium],' said one Promise Keepers organizer.[23] The meetings themselves often take on the trappings of sports events. The first North Carolina conference was held at the Charlotte Motor Speedway. Before the meeting began, the crowd of 45,000 bounced beach balls in the stands and joined in responsive cheers from one side to the other: 'We love Jesus! Yes we do! We love Jesus! How about you?'[24] Later, the man warming up the crowd belted out, 'I've been wanting to say this all day: Gentlemen, start your engines! We're going to take a few laps for Jesus this weekend.' And during the meeting, the participants raised their arms and hands in unison, saying 'Praise God' in American sign language.[25]

Promise Keepers leaders insist, however, that the heart of the movement is not found in the stadium rallies but in local support groups, some established within local congregations and some for entire communities. There, it is hoped, men who have committed themselves to the Seven Promises will find nurture and support within a community of like-minded individuals. These support groups are led by what are called 'key men,' who provide a connection between local units and the national organization, following guidelines in an official handbook in executing local programs. One interesting feature of these local groups is that like Men and Religion Forward they downplay discussion of the particulars of religious belief that could bring conflict. Men called 'ambassadors' who recruit the local 'key men' and who serve as another connection to the field staff refrain from theological discussion since disagreement builds barriers rather than breaking them down. Buttressing barriers runs counter to the larger, more inclusive vision of Promise Keepers, although critics of a more separatist fundamentalist ilk have criticized Promise Keepers for failing to preserve doctrinal purity in order to attract more participants.

Since we are in the midst of the Promise Keepers explosion, historians cannot evaluate it as easily as Men and Religion Forward. Even leaders of the movement are cautious, for the national and local infrastructures are still relatively new. But it is possible to see that like Men and Religion Forward, the organization is both a product of and a response to changing gender roles. Some demographic data illuminate the cultural context. McCartney believed he had a stable, 'traditional' family before his personal world began to unravel. Yet statistics suggest that this image of the family no longer reflects empirical reality. Women do continue to outnumber men approximately two to one on the membership rolls of the churches. But between 1960 and 1995, the number of families maintained by women with no husband present grew by 171.9 percent, and the divorce rate grew by 197.5 percent. Further, between 1970 and 1994, the proportion of women over 20 who were employed full time rose from 32.4 percent of the labor force to 41.0 percent; if we include those employed part-time as well, the figures are 37.2 percent and 45.9 percent.[26]

These changes have a several important implications. First, men are no longer the heads of many families. Second, the women to whom the thousands in the stadiums and arenas renew their promises are not full-time housewives and homemakers as were most of the women in the background of Men and Religion Forward. These women have careers; they are no longer dependent on their husbands the way women in 1911–12 were. Third, if male workers at the time of Men and Religion Forward felt a loss of control because they were obligated to do their employers' bidding, the world of work was at least men's sphere. But the increasing number of women in the labor force means that this is no longer the case, and the impact of this shift is exacerbated by changes in the nature of work itself as the nation moves into a post-industrial, service-oriented economy. Not only is the world of work no longer men's sphere; it hardly seems to be anyone's sphere.

The result of all of these changes may not be another 'crisis' in masculinity, although data could be interpreted as evidence that men have once again lost control of the worlds they inhabit. But the changes in the typical family and household, the growth of the women's movement, and the shifting character of the labor force all raise questions about male identity, questions that are complicated for many men by the continuing belief (except perhaps in Pentecostal and charismatic circles) that expression of religious feeling is more appropriate for women than for them. As in the waning decades of the Victorian era, social and cultural changes require men to plunge into the process of 'remaking manhood.'

At the dawn of the century, images of 'muscular Christianity' competed with those of the physically active, socially involved religious man of Man and Religion Forward. So too, at the century's close, there are competing images of the kind of masculine identity that is most appropriate. One is clearly rather different from what Promise Keepers promotes. It is the 'Iron John' image explicated by poet Robert Bly (1990). In the conclusion to Manliness and Civilization, Gail Bederman connects 'Iron John' to Tarzan. Both have a raw, untamed quality and an almost feral strength, and both suggest that men must escape the constraints of civilization, in a forest or some other place that embodies primal purity, in order to experience their true nature. Unlike Tarzan, however, 'Iron John' also implies that once men have had this experience they can resume their cultural roles with a fresh sense of self.

Promise Keepers transforms this mosaic of images. It too suggests that finding male space is central to remolding masculine identity. Where can a man be a man? In a sports stadium. Where can a man be emotional? In a sports stadium in the company of other men. Where can a man be again in control of his own destiny? In a sports stadium in the company of other men at a rally organized and led by men. But Promise Keepers endows the new man with a rather different set of virtues. A news item in the *Atlanta Journal-Constitution* was close to the target when it noted that 'Promise Keepers combines the Jesus Saves preaching of Billy Graham with the male bonding message of Robert Bly, the call for racial conciliation of Martin Luther King, Jr., and the marital advice of Ann Landers.'[27]

What kind of religious man is the Promise Keeper, and how does he compare with the religious man advocated by Men and Religion Forward? Men and Religion Forward extolled an ideal man who was physically active and engaged in social service. The Promise Keeper is sensitive, faithful, inclusive, and committed; echoing the theme of the 1996 conferences, he breaks down walls and barriers—between spouses, within families, and across racial and denominational lines. These are rather different virtues than those advocated by Men and Religion Forward, but they are as bound to American culture at the close of the century as physical activity and social engagement were at the beginning of the century. They are virtues viable only in a post-industrial society where women and the ideals associated with feminization are not confined to the four walls of the home or the churches.

Men and Religion Forward fused a muscular Christianity with masculine domesticity. There are hints of that within Promise Keepers as well. Although criticized by some feminists for being patriarchal and macho because it calls for men to 'Take back the reins of spiritually pure leadership God intended them to hold,'[28] Promise Keepers also holds up as an ideal 'male and female leaders sharing the burden for their families and their community.'[29] Mary Stewart Van Leeuwen (1997) has called attention to the ambivalence in these seemingly contradictory claims. I submit that Promise Keepers is simply trying to carve out a place for men in the domestic sphere that allows them to retain a male identity, just as Men and Religion Forward and advocates of male domesticity did. Only now that masculine identity combines qualities of commitment and sensitivity with an inner sense that a man can be himself and retain control over his destiny only when he is at peace with God, wife, children, and neighbors. Men and Religion Forward linked physical strength with moral strength in its paradigmatic religious man; Promise Keepers links moral strength with inner strength in its ideal of masculine religious identity.

Students of American religious culture have nearly forgotten Men and Religion Forward and the call for masculine domesticity of the opening decades of the twentieth century. It remains to be seen whether a hundred years from now Promise Keepers will fare better. What is clear is that the last chapter has not been written in the saga of fashioning and marketing a spirituality that emerges from the religious, cultural, and personal worlds inhabited by American men. There remains much truth in the words written in 1923 by a poet who had a rather different vision than Robert Bly:

The woods are lovely, dark and deep
But I have promises to keep,
And miles to go before I sleep,
And miles to go before I sleep.[30]

Notes

1 Advertisement clipped from the *Chattanooga Free-Press* 2 February 1997.

2 Others have also looked to Men and Religion Forward for a useful historical analogue to Promise Keepers, but with a rather different construction than my argument suggests. The most helpful is an as yet unpublished paper by Scott Cormode presented at the annual meeting of the American Academy of Religion in 1996. See also Kirkley (1996, 80–8).

3 There is a dearth of analytical material on Men and Religion Forward. Particularly helpful in what follows were Bederman (1989) and Smith (1987).

4 'For Men,' *Christian Advocate* 86 (August 1911):1926.

5 Many of the speakers brought together for the Men and Religion Forward movement rallies later took their message overseas.

6 The standard model for these efforts is outlined in Men and Religion Forward, *The Program of Work* (New York: Association Press, 1911, 6). This text is an organizational manual published by the central office for local use.

7 Henry Rood, 'Men and Religion,' *Independent* 71 (1911):1364. Rood was the publicity chairman for the 97–man central committee overseeing the entire endeavor.

8 Henry Rood, 'Men and Religion,' *Independent* 71 (1911):1364.

9 Other approaches to this 'crisis' of male identity are offered in Filene (1974, chapter 3); Kimmel (1996, Part II); and Rotundo (1993).

10 I am indebted to Bederman's argument that masculinity or manliness is a historical, ideological process.

11 See the essays collected in Hall (1994). See also Norman Vance (1985).

12 We owe much of our understanding of this image to John Higham's influential essay 'The Reorientation of American Culture in the 1890s' (1970, 73–102).

13 Robert F. Martin (1996) analyzes this dimension of Sunday's revivalistic style.

14 The same point is made, albeit less colorfully, in the other two standard biographies of Sunday, Dorsen (1991), and McLoughlin (1955).

15 'Remaking Manhood' is the title of the first chapter of Bederman, *Manliness and Civilization* (1995). But see also Griffen (1990, 183–204).

16 Martha S. Bensley Bruère and Robert Bruère, *Increasing Home Efficiency* (New York: Macmillan, 1912, 291–2).

17 Martha Bensley Bruère, 'Are Women Losing Their Religion?' *Collier's* (Feb. 7, 1925):17.

18 Barton was clearly trying to create a stereotypical masculine Jesus who was popular with women but also a shrewd leader of men.

19 Most of the material written about Promise Keepers has appeared in newspapers and other popular media. For an insider perspective, see Trent (1996). See also 'The Promise of a Promise Keeper,' *Good News* (September–October 1995):12–17. For analysis, see Van Leeuwen (1997). More in the format of the expose is Donna Minkowitz, 'In the Name of the Father,' *Ms.* 6.3 (November–December 1995):64–71. Also see Jeff Wagenheim, 'Among the Promise Keepers,' *Utne Reader* 73 (January–February 1996):74–7; Edward Gilbreath, 'Manhood's Great Awakening,' *Christianity Today* 39.2 (February 6, 1995):20–8; and Joseph Shapiro, 'Heavenly Promises,'*U.S. News and World Report* (October 2, 1995):68–70.

20 The only women prominent at Promise Keepers rallies are those who testify via video about husbands who became more sensitive, took their roles as fathers more seriously, and did more around the house as a result of participating in the movement; others are part of the support staff.

21 McCanney relates much of his personal journey in his autobiography, co-authored with Dave Diles, *From Ashes to Glory* (Nashville: Thomas Nelson, 1995).

22 The promises are printed on brochures distributed to all who attend the conferences. They are explained in much greater detail in *The Seven Promises of a Promise Keeper* (Colorado Springs: Focus on the Family, 1994), a collection of essays by eighteen writers.

23 The speaker was not identified by name, but quoted in the *United Methodist Review* (August 9, 1996):9.

24 From the *Asheville Citizen-Times* (June 22, 1996):B2, taken from Associated Press wire service reports.

25 The photo was carried in the *Chattanooga Free Press* (June 23, 1996):A8.

26 Based on figures provided by the Bureau of Labor Statistics, US Department of Labor (1995).

27 *Atlanta Journal-Constitution* (June 27, 1995):B10.

28 Tony Evans, 'Spiritual Purity,' *Seven Promises of a Promise Keeper* (1994, 75).

29 H. B. London, Jr, 'The Man God Seeks,' *Seven Promises of a Promise Keeper* (1994, 142).

30 Frost (1967, 2:1083–4).

Literature

Barton, Bruce. 1925. *The Man Nobody Knows*. Indianapolis: Bobbs-Merrill.

Bederman, Gail. 1989. '"The Women Have Had Charge of the Church Work Lang Enough": The Men and Religion Forward Movement of 1911–1912 and the Masculinization of Middle-Class Protestantism,' *American Quarterly* 41.3 (September):432–65.

——. 1995. *Manliness and Civilization: A Cultural History of Gender and Race in the United States, 1880–1917*. Chicago: University of Chicago Press.

Bly, Robert. 1990. *Iron John: A Book about Men*. Reading: Addison-Wesley.

Bruns, Roger A. 1992. *Preacher: Billy Sunday and Big-Time American Evangelism*. New York: W. W. Norton.

Carnes, Mark C. 1989. *Secret Ritual and Manhood in Victorian America*. New Haven: Yale University Press.

Clawson, Mary Ann. 1989. *Constructing Brotherhood: Class, Gender, and Fraternalism*. Princeton: Princeton University Press.

Dorsen, Lyle W. 1991. *Billy Sunday and the Redemption of Urban America* (Library of Religious Biography), eds Mark A. Noll and Nathan O. Hatch. Grand Rapids: Eerdmans.

Douglas, Ann. 1978. *The Feminization of American Culture*. New York: Knopf.

Filene, Peter Gabriel. 1974. *Him/Her/Self: Sex Roles in Modern America*. New York: Harcourt, Brace, Jovanovich.

Fishburn, Janet Forsythe. 1982. *The Fatherhood of God and the Victorian Family: The Social Gospel in America*. Philadelphia: Fortress.

Frost, Robert. 1967. 'Stopping by Woods on a Snowy Evening,' in *The American Tradition in Literature*, eds Sculley Bradley, Richmond Croom Beatty, and E. Hudson Long. New York: Norton and Grosset & Dunlap (from the *Complete Poems of Robert Frost*, New York: Henry Holt, 1949).

Griffen, Clyde, 1990. 'Reconstructing Masculinity from the Evangelical Revival to the Waning of Progressivism: A Speculative Synthesis,' in *Meanings for Manhood:*

Construction of Masculinity in Victorian America, eds Mark C. Carnes and Clyde Griffen. Chicago: University of Chicago Press. Pp. 183–204.

Hall, Donald E. (ed.). 1994 *Muscular Christianity: Embodying the Victorian Age.* Cambridge: Cambridge University Press.

Higham, John. 1970. 'The Reorientation of American Culture in the 1890s,' in *Writing American History: Essays on Modern Scholarship.* Bloomington: Indiana University Press. Pp. 73–102.

Hopkins, C. Howard. 1940. *The Rise of the Social Gospel in American Protestantism, 1865–1915.* New Haven: Yale University Press.

Kimmel, Michael, 1996. *Manhood in America: A Cultural History.* New York: Free Press.

Kirkley, Evelyn A. 1996. 'Is It Manly to Be Christian? The Debate in Victorian and Modern America,' in *Redeeming Men: Religion and Masculinities,* eds Stephen B. Boyd, Merle Longwood and Mark W. Muesse. Louisville: Westminster John Knox. Pp. 80–8.

Marsh, Margaret. 1988. 'Suburban Men and Masculine Domesticity, 1870–1915,' *American Quarterly* 40:165–86.

Martin, Robert F. 1996. 'Billy Sunday and Christian Manliness,' *The Historian* 58.4 (Summer):811–23.

McDannell, Colleen. 1986. *The Christian Home in Victorian America, 1840–1900.* Bloomington: Indiana University Press.

McLoughlin, William G. 1995. *Billy Sunday Was His Real Name.* Chicago: University of Chicago Press.

Rotundo, E. Anthony. 1993. *American Manhood: Transformations in Masculinity from the Revolution to the Present.* New York: Basic Books.

Smith, Gary Scott. 1987. 'The Men and Religion Forward Movement of 1911–1912: New Perspectives on Evangelical Social Concerns and the Relationship between Christianity and Progressivism,' *Westminster Theological Journal* 49.1 (Spring):91–118.

Trent, John et al. 1996. *Go the Distance: The Making of a Promise Keeper.* Colorado Springs: Focus on the Family Publishing.

Vance, Norman. 1985. *The Sinews of the Spirit: The Ideal of Christian Manliness in Victorian Literature and Religious Thought.* Cambridge: Cambridge University Press.

Van Leeuwen, Mary Stewart. 1997. 'Servanthood or Soft Patriarchy? A Christian Feminist Looks at the Promise Keepers Movement,' *The Journal of Men's Studies* 5.3 (February): 233–61.

Part 6

Spirituality and the Intimate Body

In the study of male socialization, the lack of emotional and erotic expressiveness among heterosexual men is often lamented. In *The Men We Long To Be*, for example, Stephen Boyd writes: 'Masculine socialization and conditioning produce within us a desperate situation. Since we view the open expression of emotions as feminine, we develop only a limited ability to recognize and express them. This greatly obstructs our human need for intimacy' (Boyd 1995, 66; also Clark 1996; Dittes 1985; 1996). Similarly, James Nelson, who has tirelessly encouraged Christian men to broaden their erotic and spiritual receptivity, observes:

> We are easily confused about intimacy. Because we have genitalized so much of our sexual feelings, intimacy and sex seem to be one and the same. Thus, if we are heterosexual, we fear intimacy with other men because it seems to imply genital expression. And deep emotional intimacy with women threatens our masculinity, because we learned our first lessons about manhood by the process of breaking the erotic bonding with a woman, our mother. (Nelson 1992a, 107)

The lack of intimacy, as most therapists would confirm today, contributes to the paucity of men's relationships to others, whether they are wives, children, or male friends. Restrictive gender regulations in the Jewish and Christian traditions have certainly contributed to the fear of erotically charged intimacies outside of marriage. However, religious traditions have also offered resources for enriched intimate living, sometimes through symbolic reconfigurations and by charging the intimate body with moral signification and, at other times, through replacing human love with love for the divine (God, Torah, saints) and cultivating a spiritual yearning for mystico-erotic unions.

In this part, six contributors address the religious male body as an intimate body and explore the intersection of spirituality and sexuality. All six chapters move beyond the lamentation over male emotional paucity. They focus, instead, on particular aspects of how the male body, gay and straight, has been both problematized in the Jewish and Christian traditions as well as creatively employed in search of deepening spiritual experiences. David Brakke's study of the attitudes of the early Christian church toward nocturnal emission illustrates, among other things, that the patristic fathers did not shy away from theologizing the carnal male body. Examining the sexual discourse in late antiquity implicitly raises the question of whether the observable prudishness of many Christian congregations today is actually a modern phenomenon. Harry Brod raises equally evocative questions about the role and place of circumcision in contemporary Judaism, wondering about its centrality as a defining marker of Jewish identity. Donald Capps investigates the moral discourse concerning sexual practices in the nineteenth century, arguing that medical, religious, and public disapproval has shifted from masturbation to homosexuality in the twentieth century.

Finally, Ronald Long, Scott Haldeman and Donald Boisvert address the intersection of sexual intimacy and spiritual yearning from an openly gay perspective. The differences between these three authors could be briefly sketched in the following way: Ronald Long emphasizes an *aesthetical*-ethical dimension by acknowledging the eroticism of 'male beauty'; Haldeman uses a *liturgical*-ethical frame to understand gay sexual practices as ritual activity; and Boisvert's *devotional*-ethical stance allows him to link gay desire to sacred objects of admiration. All three authors move the issue of gay male intimacy beyond the confines of personal preference and toward a public discussion of right and caring relations in (religious) communities.

The spectrum of the intimate male body is, of course, not exhausted by these six contributions. For example, the question of male–male friendship is only marginally touched on and could have been expanded (see Clark 1996; Culbertson 1996; Doty 1996; Kuefler 2006). In the future, critical men's studies in religion must also pay more attention to the intersection of spirituality and the adolescent, disabled, chronically ill, abused and aging male body. A good example in this direction is the edited volume *The Spirituality of Men* (Culbertson 2002; also Thompson and Remmes 2002; Capps 1995; Nelson 1992b), in which male scholars of religion address the social, psychological, spiritual, and relational health conditions of men – concerns that, by and large, still fall under the exclusive domain of religious self-help literature and practical theology.

Literature

Boyd, Stephen B. 1995. *The Men We Long to Be: Beyond Domination to a New Christian Understanding of Manhood*. San Francisco: HarperSanFrancisco.

Capps, Donald. 1995. *The Child's Song: The Religious Abuse of Children*. Louisville: Westminster John Knox.

Clark, J. Michael. 1996. 'Gay Men, Masculinity, and an Ethic of Friendship', in *Redeeming Men*, eds Stephen B. Boyd, Merle Longwood and Mark Muesse. Louisville: Westminster John Knox. Pp. 252–62.

Culbertson, Philip. 1996. 'Men and Christian Friendship', in *Men's Bodies, Men's Gods*, ed. Björn Krondorfer. New York: New York University Press. Pp. 149–80.

——. 2002. *The Spirituality of Men: Sixteen Christians Write about their Faith*. Minneapolis: Fortress.

Dittes, James E. 1985. *The Male Predicament: On Being a Man Today*. Louisville: Westminster John Knox.

——. 1996. *Driven by Hope: Men and Meaning*. Louisville: Westminster John Knox.

Doty, William G. 1996. '"The Manly Love of Comrades": Mythico-Religious Models of an Athletics of Male-Male Friendship', in *Men's Bodies, Men's Gods*, ed. Björn Krondorfer. New York: New York University Press. Pp. 181–201.

Kuefler, Mathew. 2006. 'Male Friendship and the Suspicion of Sodomy in Twelfth-Century France', in *The Boswell Thesis*, ed. Mathew Kuefler. Chicago: Chicago University Press. Pp. 179–212.

Nelson, James B. 1992a. *Body Theology*. Louisville: Westminster John Knox.

——. 1992b. 'Men and Body Life: Aging as a Case Study', in *Body Theology*, James Nelson. Pp. 75–92.

Nelson, James B. and Sandra P. Longfellow (eds). 1994. *Sexuality and the Sacred: Sources for Theological Reflection*. Louisville: Westminster John Knox.

Robertson, C. K. (ed.). 2006. *Religion and Sexuality: Passionate Debates*. New York: Peter Lang.

Thompson, Edward and Kathryn R. Remmes. 2002. 'Does Masculinity Thwart Being Religious? An Examination of Older Men's Religiousness'. *Journal for the Scientific Study of Religion* 41/3:521–32.

24

The Problematization of Nocturnal Emissions in the Early Christian Church

Editor's Introduction

One of the vexing dilemmas for religious men who have pledged sexual abstinence has been the fact that they – who have learned to be in command of
their urges while awake – are unable to discipline their bodies while asleep.
Particularly, they seem to have little control over the one anatomical member
that most distinctively makes them male: the sexual organ.

> The unruly erectility of the penis constantly reminded [Christian] men of
> their weakness. For Augustine, man's lack of control over his vital organ was
> a sign of humanity's inherent sinfulness. Even renunciation of sexuality did
> not help man to gain total control over lust. Nocturnal emissions offered
> conclusive proof. Augustine, like many celibate men before and after him,
> was bewildered by nocturnally recurring, sensual memories which moved
> from the realm of dreams straight down to the pelvis. After confessing to
> involuntary carnal emissions, Augustine, exasperated, prayed to God, 'Grieve
> at my imperfect state . . . and perfect in me your mercies to achieve perfect
> peace' (*Confessions* X.30; cf. Miles 1992). The ultimate control of male virility
> was not in man's power but subject to God's mercy. (Krondorfer 1996, 7)

In chapter 3, we already read Foucault's interpretation of the Christian battle
for chastity, exemplified by John Cassian's monastic rules. 'All through this
battle against the spirit of fornication and for chastity,' Foucault writes, 'the
sole fundamental problem is that of pollution – whether as something that is
subservient to the will and a possible form of self-indulgence or as something
happening spontaneously and involuntarily in sleep or dreams. So important
is this that Cassian makes the absence of erotic dreams and nocturnal pollution a sign that one has reached the pinnacle of chastity.' David Brakke returns
to this issue in more depth and detail in this chapter, offering a comparative
analysis of different moral and theological attitudes toward nocturnal emissions. Looking at the textual evidence left by early church communities and
individual church fathers from the third to the fifth centuries and from three
different Mediterranean locations (Syria, Egypt and southern France), Brakke
explains and contextualizes the different theological responses to the male
anxiety over involuntary emissions.
  This chapter could have been placed next to the contributions of Kuefler
(chapter 18) and Burrus (chapter 20), since Brakke shares with them a historical

interest in the theological significance of the Christian body as well as in the gender politics of late antiquity. Brakke is part of what one might call a post-structuralist renaissance of late antiquity studies; some of this literature has already been cited (chapters 18 and 20), and here one must mention also the more recent works by Penn (2005), Masterson (2006), Schroeder (2007), Schott (2008), and Sizgorich (2008).

Brakke's 'Problematization of Nocturnal Emissions in Early Christianity' (first published in 1995) opens this section on male spirituality and intimacy because it concentrates on one aspect of the male body and its theological signification. By analyzing theological concerns about involuntary emission of sperm, Brakke historicizes the development of intimate discourse – a discourse that continued into the Middle Ages and modernity (see, for example, Braudy 1994; Leyser 1999), and may find echoes in the nineteenth-century debates on masturbation (see Capps, chapter 26).

Publications by the Same Author

Brakke, David. 1995a. *Athanasius and the Politics of Asceticism*. Oxford: Clarendon.
——. 1995b. 'The Problematization of Nocturnal Emissions in Early Christian Syria, Egypt, and Gaul'. *Journal of Early Christian Studies* 3/4:419–60.
——. 2001. 'Ethiopian Demons: Male Sexuality, the Black-Skinned Other, and the Monastic Self'. *Journal of the History of Sexuality* 10:501–35.
——. 2006. *Demons and the Making of the Monk: Spiritual Combat in Early Christianity*. Cambridge: Harvard University Press.
Brakke, David, Michael L. Satlow and Steven Weitzman (eds). 2006. *Religion and Self in Antiquity*. Bloomington: Indiana University Press.

Further Reading

Augustine. 1992. *Confessions*. Trans. Henry Chadwick. Oxford and New York: Oxford University Press.
Braudy, Leo. 1994. 'Remembering Masculinity: Premature Ejaculation Poetry of the Seventeenth Century' (Special Issue: *The Male Body*, Part 2). *Michigan Quarterly Review* 23/1 (Winter):177–201.
Krondorfer, Björn (ed.). 1996. *Men's Bodies, Men's Gods: Male Identities in a (Post-) Christian Culture*. New York: New York University Press.
Leyser, Conrad. 1999. 'Masculinity in Flux: Nocturnal Emission and the Limits of Celibacy in the Early Middle Ages', in *Masculinity in Medieval Europe*, ed. D. M. Hadley. London: Longman. Pp. 103–20.
Masterson, Mark. 2006. 'Impossible Translation: Antony and Paul the Simple in the Historia Monarchum', in *The Boswell Thesis*, ed. Mathew Kuefler. Chicago: Chicago University Press. Pp. 215–35.
Miles, Margaret R. 1992. *Desire and Delight: A New Reading of Augustine's Confessions*. New York: Crossroad.
Penn, Michael Philip. 2005. *Kissing Christians: Ritual and Community in the Late Ancient Church*. Philadelphia: University of Pennsylvania Press.
Schott, Jeremy M. 2008. *Christianity, Empire, and the Making of Religion in Late Antiquity*. Philadelphia: University of Pennsylvania Press.

Schroeder, Caroline T. 2007. *Monastic Bodies: Discipline and Salvation in Shenoute of Atripe*. Philadelphia: University of Pennsylvania Press.

Sizgorich, Thomas. 2008. *Violence and Belief in Late Antiquity: Militant Devotion in Christianity and Islam*. Philadelphia: University of Pennsylvania Press.

The Problematization of Nocturnal Emissions in the Early Christian Church

DAVID BRAKKE

Nearly 30 years ago, Mary Douglas observed of the ancient Israelites that 'the threatened boundaries of their body politic would be well mirrored in their care for the integrity, unity, and purity of the physical body' (Douglas 1966, 124; 1982, 65–81).[1] Borrowing this insight, recent scholarship in early Christianity has described with some precision how male Christian authors used the female body, particularly the body of the virgin, as the symbolic locus for reflection on the purity and integrity of the church. Especially during the fourth century, as Christianity became the favored religion of an Empire that had once persecuted it, the virgin's intact, unpenetrated body came to represent an ideal church undefiled by either heresy or its new status in the world (Brown 1988, 341–65; Burrus 1994). These Christian men appear not to have invested their own bodies with so much significance, yet the ritual impurity caused by a nocturnal emission—a matter of concern in Christian documents beginning in the third century—invites a mode of analysis similar to that so fruitfully applied to discourse on the female body, one that aims at recovering not merely theological ideas, but also the personal and communal boundaries that regulations surrounding such emissions were meant to create, modify, or eliminate.[2] When early Christian men discussed the significance of their nocturnal emissions, they engaged in a process of personal and communal self-definition, embodying different perspectives on the church's identity in the world, their own psychological and physical makeup, and the relationships among different groups within the Christian church.

It was the question of whether a man who had experienced such an emission should receive communion or not that gave rise to this reflection. This essay will study early Christian opinions on this subject by examining literature from three geographical settings: third- and fourth-century Syria (the *Didascalia Apostolorum* and the *Apostolic Constitutions*), third- and fourth-century Egypt (episcopal and monastic writings), and fifth-century Gaul (John Cassian[3]). This evidence reveals that, on the immediate question, Christians held nearly every conceivable position: some believed that such emissions were always defiling, others that they were never so, and still others that some emissions were defiling and some not. In every case, however, the manner in which authors problematized emissions reveals concerns about defining and modifying the identities of at least three personal and social 'bodies.' The holiness of the first body, the body of Christ on the altar during the Eucharist, prompted concern about a second body, that of the individual Christian male. This second body could be pure or impure and thus eligible or ineligible for contact with the holy eucharistic elements. Here a nocturnal emission could be directly relevant, for material had crossed the boundary that distinguished the body's interior and exterior: what belonged inside had come outside. This anomaly raised questions about the male body's integrity and about the relationship between what in the human personality could be called 'body' and what was not 'body,' but rather 'soul' or 'spirit.' Even more, the practical question to which nocturnal emissions gave rise was a matter of social definition: should a man be excluded from the community's ritual or not? Here the third body to be defined was once again the body of Christ, not the sacramental body on the altar, but rather the social body of the church gathered around the altar. How tightly should the boundary between the church and the world be maintained? What internal boundaries of differentiation within the church (for example, between monks and laymen) needed to be established, persevered, or eliminated?

One result of the following examination is that, while Douglas's formu-lation above provides the right questions for our study, a direct correlation between greater need to define social boundaries and greater anxiety about the integrity of the individual body does not obtain. Particularly when the group against which a community wishes to define itself is perceived to have such strong purity concerns, the lack of such concerns can become a mode of tight self-definition. A survey of the evidence ranging from third-century Syria, to fourth-century Egypt, to fifth-century Gaul does, however, reveal at least two general trends. At the level of the individual body, while our earliest documents reveal a desire to preserve the body's integrity from assault by external forces, this concern gave way to an effort to distinguish and relate the body and the soul, and finally to anxiety about the existence of divisions within the soul. At the level of the social body (the church), a similar narrowing of focus took place: while the Syrian Christians sought to differentiate the Christian community from competing Jewish and pagan groups, the Egyptian authors and Cassian concerned themselves with relationships within the church, between parish churches and monastic groups or between ascetics within a monastery. As the church grew, the anxieties that male leaders expressed about emissions became increasingly internalized, both in social and personal terms. Changing modes of self-definition produced increasingly meticulous modes of problematization in Christian analyses of wet dreams, but not necessarily more or less stringent teachings an the subject.

Of course, these analytical perspectives and conclusions, articulated by the historian and borrowed from symbolic and cultural anthropology, were not the terms in which the ancient Christians debated the problem of nocturnal emissions and admissions to the Eucharist. Behind their thinking lay primarily two bodies of knowledge: on the one hand, passages in the Christian Old Testament that dealt with purity issues;[4] on the other hand, medical literature that explained why such emissions occurred and how they could be prevented or stopped. [. . .]

Medical literature saw nocturnal emission as a problem and provided some early Christians with what we might call common knowledge about the causes and remedies for such emissions. An illustrative treatment is that of Soranus of Ephesus, who practiced medicine in Rome at the beginning of the second century and whose teachings were preserved by Caelius Aurelianus in the fifth century in his books, *On Acute Diseases* and *On Chronic Diseases*. Soranus said that a nocturnal emission is not itself a disease, but could lead to one, such as epilepsy, insanity, or another illness in which the body 'suffers agitation and is shaken' (Aurelianus 1950, 958). The conceptual links between an emission and such diseases as epilepsy were most likely the dissipation of virility represented by the discharge of semen and the loss of rational control represented by 'agitation' (dangers associated with all orgasms) (Rouselle 1988, 66). The immediate cause of the nocturnal emission was a *phantasia*, a dream image, which was itself the result either of prolonged sexual desire or of prolonged sexual continence (Aurelianus 1950, 958). Because nocturnal emission could develop into a worse problem, the doctor suggested remedial action of two kinds. First, the patient's mental images, his *phantasmata*, had to be turned away from sex to other interests, 'for the patient's sensations in waking life readily give rise to dream images in which the movements resemble actuality' (Aurelianus 1950, 960–1). This conception of dreaming and its terminology derive ultimately from Aristotle, for whom 'what the soul sees during sleep are the "appearances" (*phantasmata*) and "residual movements deriving from sense-impressions" previously when the soul—and the body—were awake.'[5] The connection between manipulation of one's vision and the health of one's soul is reminiscent also of the Stoic Epictetus' teaching that the 'task' of the true Cynic is 'the right use of his *phantasiai*,' by which he means 'impressions' in general.[6] Second, the patient's body, evidently too hot and moist, had to be made cold and dry. This could be accomplished in a variety of ways—placing a lead plate on the groin, injecting (cold) juices into the urethra—but particularly by prescribing a cold, drying diet (Aurelianius 1950, 960–3). These two notions—the connection between dream images and what one sees while awake, and the need for drying and cooling measures—found their way, along with other medical 'facts,' into the arguments of Christians, both those who considered emissions defiling and those who did not. It is to these Christians that I now turn.

Third- and Fourth-Century Syria

The *Didascalia Apostolorum* and the *Apostolic Constitutions* reveal that church leaders in Syria criticized Christians who abstained from the Eucharist during menstruation or after a seminal emission. The official opposition to such abstention is consistent from the early third century (c. 230), when the *Didascalia* was compiled, to the late century (c. 380), when the *Apostolic Constitutions* were written.[7] Nonetheless, the terms of the debate in Syria over the significance of nocturnal emissions shifted with the changing social position of the Christian church: from a small competitor with the emerging Jewish synagogue to the official religion of the Roman Empire.

The *Didascalia* does not use terminology specific to nocturnal emissions, but it seems reasonably clear that wet dreams were among the reasons why Christian men would not commune. The author begins his discussion of purity issues by condemning those who 'observe, in accordance with the second legislation, physical customs, both emissions and intercourse.'[8] Here the Syriac translator uses for 'emission' the general term *dûbâ'*, which he uses later to refer specifically to a man's seminal discharge.[9] When the author discusses menstruation, however, the translator uses the term *mardîtâ'*.[10] In the case of men, the author appears to mean by 'emission' any ejaculation apart from 'intercourse' since he pairs the two terms, as above, and concludes the entire discussion by listing as persons eligible to receive the Eucharist the following: 'a woman when she is in the way of women, a man when an emission comes from him, and a man and his wife when they have intercourse and rise up from one another.'[11] Thus, the author considers men who have had a seminal emission apart from intercourse to form a distinct category; although he does not speak explicitly of nocturnal emissions, it is reasonable to assume that they would have been included in this category.

The author of the *Didascalia* phrases the problem of whether men and women who have experienced emissions should commune in terms that reflect the nascent church's fragile position in an overwhelmingly pagan society. First, he considers whether sexual emissions leave the individual Christian's body vulnerable to demonic penetration; second, he accuses his opponents of applying to themselves Jewish practices no longer relevant to Christians. As to the first point, the author accuses those who do not commune of believing that intercourse, menstruation, or a seminal emission leaves them 'empty of the Holy Spirit' and thus ineligible to receive the Eucharist until the flow has stopped and (perhaps) they have bathed. The author, in reply, claims that Christians receive the Holy Spirit in baptism; only a moral failure will cause the Spirit to leave a baptized person, not a 'natural' emission or intercourse. [. . .]

In any case, early Syrian Christians debated the significance of nocturnal emissions, along with that of other bodily functions, in terms of defining the human body as a space open to outside forces. For them, Christian baptism bounded the body as a contained space occupied by the Holy Spirit and impenetrable to demons; Syrian Christians differed on what effect the body's functions, particularly those in which material crossed the boundary between the body's interior and exterior, had on the status of this defined space. [. . .] To the *Didascalia*'s author this boundary was not so vulnerable: as there were two kinds of spirits, there were two kinds of people. [. . .] The Christian community's extreme minority status in a society full of other gods ('unclean spirits') was reflected in this concern over the external boundary of the individual's body and its openness to demonic penetration. [. . .]

When, in the late fourth century, the compiler of the *Apostolic Constitutions* used the *Didascalia* to construct his own church order, he picked up on the theme of a general moral life and gave it primary emphasis. [. . .] The author of the *Apostolic Constitutions* (AC) expands on the *Didascalia*'s teaching that bodily functions such as menstruation and nocturnal emissions do not cause the Holy Spirit to abandon the baptized person; only moral transgressions can do that. The author conveniently provides a list of those moral failings that 'can defile a human being's soul': these include violence, adultery, and fornication.[12] The danger of a menstruant avoiding worship activities is not, as it was in the *Didascalia*, that she 'rescinds' her baptism, but that lack of attention to prayer and Scriptures makes a person more vulnerable to temptation from the devil.[13] While the *Didascalia* did not distinguish between defilement of the body and that of the soul, the *AC* focuses on the person's moral character, not what kind of spirit inhabits the body. The author of the *AC* is less interested than his predecessor in the physical definition of the individual body as a holy space: the theology that baptism separates the person from demonic spirits and places him or her under the Holy Spirit remains, but this idea has become a general moral principle and is no longer localized in the individual's physical body. In fact, the author explains that the Holy Spirit is 'inseparable' from the baptized Christian precisely because the Spirit 'is not in a place.'[14] The spirit still protects the Christian from unclean spirits, but it does so, not by 'sealing' the body, but by supervising one's moral life: 'The Holy Spirit remains with the one who does good, fills him with wisdom and understanding, does not permit an evil spirit to approach him, and keeps his goings under surveillance.'[15] The Syrian Christian who compiled the *AC* has turned away from the realistic piety of spirits battling to posses the human body that characterized the Syrian understanding of baptism in the third century. Remnants of that belief persist in his thought, but he uses it to make more generalized exhortations to proper moral conduct. A church more at home in the world has lost some of its interest in the possibility of demonic penetration of the body. [. . .]

Accordingly, the discussion of menstruation and nocturnal emissions in the *AC*, unlike that in the *Didascalia*, concludes with a general attack on the sexual morality of the 'pagans' and an exhortation to Christians to manifest their holiness through material fidelity. The author claims that Christians 'do not abuse lawful intercourse,' unlike the pagans, 'whose custom it is to act impiously in such matters.'[16] This statement acts as a segue to a traditional Christian condemnation of pederasty, adultery, and other sexual vices that are said to characterize the lifestyle of non-Christians. The concern for general sexual morality exhibited by the author of the *AC* is another indication of how the situation of the Syrian church has changed since the compilation of the *Didascalia* in the third century. Practices surrounding nocturnal emissions no longer serve to define the physical body as a holy space and the Christian church as distinct from the synagogue; the interest of the fourth-century redactor has turned way from these 'micro' issues to the more general problem of cultivating a distinctive Christian sexual ethic. Such an ethic, in the author's view, follows 'the will of God' and promotes attention to God; natural bodily functions, such as nocturnal emissions and menstruation, have nothing to do with such abstract goals and thus are of no concern to the Christian who would be pure. While our two Syrian compilers of the church orders both considered nocturnal emissions of no significance for the Christian, the terms in which they understood this issue changed with the character of the Christian communities. Although both authors were eager to distinguish Christians from other groups, either the Jewish community or pagan society in general, they did not express this need for self-definition in purity regulations, for, at least in the case of the *Didascalia*, it was precisely the Christian community's lack of such purity concerns that was seen as a mark of Christian difference from neighboring Jews.

Third- and Fourth-Century Egypt

Unlike their Syrian counterparts, leaders of the Christian community in Egypt found the meaning of nocturnal emissions to be more complex and thus did not rule out abstention from the Eucharist by men who had had wet dreams. From Egypt we have sources on this question roughly contemporary with our Syrian documents: the canonical letters of the third-century bishop of Alexandria Dionysius (248–265) and of Bishop Timothy I, who presided over the Alexandrian church in the late fourth century (381–385). Both men barred menstruating women from communing, but considered men who had had an emission a more difficult case. The reasoning of Timothy in particular reveals the development in Egypt of desert monasticism, with its greater interest in the individual's spiritual condition and its strong belief in the activity of demons. Monastic sources and Athanasius of Alexandria's *Letter to Ammoun* provide a glimpse into how the monastic life problematized nocturnal emissions for both monks and bishops.

Bishops Dionysius and Timothy, whose episcopal terms were separated by over a century, held precisely the same opinion on whether men who had had wet dreams should commune, but their different reasons for this opinion reflect an Egypt transformed by the monastic movement. Bishop Dionysius, writing in the middle of the third century, called the question of whether a menstruating women should commune 'superfluous': obviously she should not 'approach the holy table or touch the body and blood of Christ' since the woman with the 12-year flow of blood did not touch the person of Jesus, but only the edge of his garment (Mark 5.25).[17] Dionysius applied the logic of Temple purity to the Christian celebration of the Eucharist: 'The person who is not entirely pure both in soul and body shall be forbidden to enter into the holy and the holy of holies.'[18] Most early Christians saw their Eucharist as superior to and therefore analogous to the sacrifices that had been made in the Jewish Temple and so applied purity regulations to it and their Christian 'priests'; thus, Origen, among others, believed that clergy who had recently had intercourse with their wives should not preside at the Eucharist.[19] Here Dionysius, a student of Origen, simply extended this principle to menstruating women. Sexism was a factor in Dionysius's thinking, however, for he hesitated to apply the logic of purity consistently to sexual intercourse and nocturnal emissions, cases that involved men. Married persons, he said, 'ought to be their own independent judges' on whether and how often they should abstain from intercourse in response to Paul's advice in 1 Corinthians 7.5.[20] Similarly Dionysius advised men who had experienced an 'involuntary nocturnal emission' to 'follow their own conscience' and 'examine themselves whether they doubt concerning this or not.' Paul's opinion on the observation of food taboos, that 'the one who doubts is condemned if he eats' (Romans 14.23), provided the biblical support for this more pragmatic position. Dionysius concluded: 'Let everyone who goes in to God be of good conscience and confidence with respect to his own inner disposition.'[21] This appeal to the individual's conscience should not obscure Dionysius' overriding concern, which was not to measure the spiritual life of the individual, but to protect the sanctity of the Christian altar, the 'holy of holies.'

Over a century later, Bishop Timothy of Alexandria held the same formal positions as Dionysius, but for more psychologically complex reasons focused on the individual Christian's spiritual condition. On the question of whether a menstruating woman should commune, Timothy answered simply that 'she should not until she is purified' (until the menstrual flow had ceased?) and did not feel it necessary to provide any further justification for what must have become by then an accepted practice.[22] But on whether a clergyman ought to permit 'a layman who has had a dream' to commune, Timothy was not so absolute: 'If the desire for a woman underlies it [the wet dream], he should not. But if Satan is tempting him, so that through this pretext he will be estranged from communion with the divine Mysteries, he ought to commune, since the tempter will not stop attacking him at that time when he ought to commune.'[23] Like our Syrian authors, Timothy worried about the demonic—but not in terms of penetration of the body, as in the third-century *Didascalia*, rather in terms of temptation, as in the roughly contemporary *Apostolic Constitutions*. So too Timothy differs from his third-century Egyptian predecessor, Dionysius. While Dionysius had defended his reasoning on sexual purity issues solely by appeals to passages from the New Testament, new elements appear in the thinking of Timothy: a psychological concern about the 'desire' that a dream might indicate, and the possibility that Satan is using sexual dreams precisely to keep a man from receiving the Eucharist. Here the logic of Temple purity gave way to an interest in the spiritual condition of the individual man. [. . .]

Egyptian monks, like the bishops of Alexandria, were ambivalent on whether someone who had had an emission should commune or not, but they were not satisfied with the question as Dionysius had posed it, as a simple problem of the altar's purity: rather, the monks used their emissions as tools for the diagnosis of their own spiritual condition, as ways of discerning the complex interaction between soul and body. The period between Dionysius and Timothy saw the rapid rise, and development—and at times the end—of diverse new forms of asceticism for men, collectively known as monasticism (Goehring 1992). The monastic literature of fourth-century Egypt reveals a variety of experiments in Christian asceticism, programs of spiritual discipline that required the definition of boundaries within the human person (between soul and body, will and body, a 'spiritual body' and the present body) and within Egyptian Christianity (between monks and bishops, ascetic communities and local churches, male and female ascetics). Although hardly a prominent topic in this literature, nocturnal emissions provided one occasion for the negotiation of these emerging boundaries.

The letters attributed to the acknowledged (if not actual) founder of eremitical monasticism, Antony the Great, present a spiritual program in which the distinction between 'soul' and 'body' is a guiding principle and nocturnal emissions serve as a marker of the interplay between these aspects of the self. In the first of his seven letters, Anthony offered a statement on the 'motions' of the body and their purification through repentance, a teaching that monks considered so significant that they transmitted a portion of it separately in the sayings tradition.[24] [. . .] In Antony's treatment, not only does the nocturnal emission mark the boundary between soul and body and thus measure the monk's progress in properly co-ordinating these two aspects of himself; it also points to a more elusive boundary, that between the monk's present, earthly body and the transformed, spiritual body that belongs to the resurrection.[25]

The possibility of transforming the body through asceticism and thus of an end to nocturnal emission indicates that Anthony's own ascetic program—in spite of how Athanasius presented it later in his *Life on Antony*—must be understood within the theological and spiritual framework of Origen. In the words of modern scholars, for Anthony as for Origen before him, asceticism was a matter of 'refining and transforming the body, ultimately making it less material and more spiritual' (Rubenson 1990, 71); or, through the guidance of the Spirit, 'what is natural [to the body], on one level, must pass away for [its] true nature to exist' (Vivian 1993, 84). Origen believed that, through a process of education and spiritual healing, the human body could be transformed into the 'spiritual body' discussed by Paul (see Brown 1988, 167–8; Scott 1991, 150–64). It has been suggested that Origen's self-castration, if factual, would have feminized his physical attributes and thus have made him 'a walking lesson in the basic indeterminacy of the body' (Brown 1988, 169). [. . .]

The spirituality of Evagrius Ponticus represents an appropriation of Origen's legacy in the monastic setting far more subtle and complex than Antony's; for him, too, the nocturnal emission was a phenomenon at the boundary of soul and body, but with him the accompanying dream and its 'images' became the focus of attention.[26] Antony had suggested that some emissions were due to a 'natural motion' that belonged to the body but that required the soul's 'consent'; even such 'natural' emissions could be brought to an end if soul and body were 'purified' and thus the soul's consent eliminated. He had, however, left the mechanism of the soul's consent unexplained. In Evagrius' treatment, the images that made up the wet dream filled this role; how the soul responded to the images presented to it determined the degree of one's culpability in a wet dream. Even the visual quality of the images was significant: 'Natural motions of the body while sleeping, if not accompanied by images, indicate that the soul is somewhat healthy. But the formation of images is an indication of sickness: even faces without boundaries are a sign that the passion is old, but bounded ones that the wound is recent.'[27] Since he considered imageless emissions a sign of a soul that is only 'somewhat healthy,' it is likely that Evagrius shared Origen's and Antony's belief that emissions could be brought to an end entirely.[28] Indeed, like the doctors, Evagrius suggested that drying the body through a diet of reduced food and drink could reduce the number of dreams and emissions, although he gave this medical theory a theological justification involving Satan's use of excess moisture in the body.[29] Unlike Antony, however, Evagrius' primary interest was not in the emission itself, but in the images that accompanied it, particularly the degree to which these images were 'bounded.' [. . .]

For Antony and Evagrius, who were bringing the theological framework of Origen to bear on the new spiritual projects of desert monasticism, nocturnal emissions provided one occasion to explore the boundary between the soul and body and how an ascetic program could work between these two dimensions of the self. But a second boundary emerged with new clarity thanks to monastic attention to emissions: the social boundary between the individual monk and the local worshiping community. The monk who judged his emission to be defiling would abstain from the Eucharist, the ritual that expressed and created the solidarity of diverse Christians with each other and their bishop. The teaching of Dioscorus, a friend of Evagrius, illustrates this point:

Take care that no one who has pondered on the image of a woman during the night dare to approach the sacred Mysteries, in case any of you has had a [wet] dream while entertaining such an image. For seminal emissions do take place unconsciously without the stimulus of imagined forms, occurring not from deliberate choice but involuntarily. They arise naturally and flow forth from an excess of matter. They are therefore not to be classified as sinful. But imaginings are the result of deliberate choice and are a sign of an evil disposition. Now a monk must even transcend the law of nature and must certainly not fall into the slightest pollution of the flesh. [. . .] For how else will the monk differ from the worldly people? [. . .][30]

Here the teachings of Evagrius and Antony are condensed into a deceptively simple principle: a nocturnal emission required that a monk abstain from the Eucharist only if it was a symptom of a deeper problem ('an evil disposition') rather than a 'natural' expulsion of excess fluid. [. . .] This heightened attention to the boundary between soul and body contributed to the demarcation of the boundary between monastic and lay Christians. The attentive monk who took seriously the teachings of Antony, Evagrius, and Dioscorus would have been hard pressed to identify with confidence any emissions as insignificant. Voluntary absence from the Eucharist may have been a fairly regular feature of such a monk's discipline and could make plain the superiority of his ascetic life over the lay: 'For how else will the monk differ from the worldly people?' The monk played out his difference from ordinary Christians through his absence from the sacrament, based on his exceptional care for his spiritual health. Social tension between the local episcopally centered church and the desert-oriented monastic community could manifest itself in a monk's discipline.[31] [. . .]

From this perspective, it is no surprise to find a bishop, Athanasius of Alexandria, condemning in fierce language monks who considered nocturnal emissions to be defiling. In his *Letter to Ammoun*, Athanasius used language that he normally used for heresy ('nonsense,' 'irrationality,' 'ignorance') to describe the teaching of such monks, an indication of how threatening the bishop considered the monastic practice of eucharistic abstention.[32] [. . .] Athanasius feared that monks who were anxious about the polluting effects of nocturnal emissions might also condemn marriage. Such scrupulous monks must, he thought, question the goodness of the body and the legitimacy of 'the lawful use' of its sexual organs.[33] If any monks should have such 'unclean and evil questions' about the holiness of married Christians, Athanasius insisted that there were 'two ways in life': abstinence and married intercourse.[34] Interpreting the Parable of the Sower (Matthew 13.1–8 par.) as he did in other writings, Athanasius described a hierarchical unity of Christians in which the married person yields fruit 'thirtyfold' and the celibate 'hundredfold.'[35] In this way, Athanasius sought to make clear to Ammoun and his monastic disciples their essential connection to the wider church made up of ordinary Christians, a connection created and expressed in the celebration of the Eucharist.[36] Bishop Athanasius worried that monks who abstained from the Eucharist created too sharp a division between themselves and Christians who engaged in sexual activity; in his effort to break down this social boundary, he declared all emissions natural, involuntary, and so insignificant, thereby positing a stronger separation between the individual's soul and body. [. . .]

Unlike most of his ideas, Athanasius' opinion that nocturnal emissions were never defiling did not prevail in the Egyptian church, as Bishop Timothy's more ambivalent and, in fact, more monastic view on the subject reveals. Athanasius' refusal to see a close connection between a seemingly natural function of the body and the spiritual condition of a person's soul did not last in a Christian culture that became, even in its parish churches, increasingly oriented toward the monastic life as the superior form of Christianity—a transformation aided in no small way by Athanasius' own writings and theology. At the same time, Athanasius' anxiety over the distance between the monk and the church of married Christians reflected a moment in the history of Christian Egypt in which the relationships between monk and bishop, monastery and parish church, were still tense, unclear, and in the process of formation. Thus, when such matters were more settled, 30 years after Athanasius' uncompromising letter to Ammoun, Bishop Timothy was able to adopt a view on nocturnal emissions that was essentially that of the monks.

Fifth-Century Gaul

While emissions were by no means a central topic in Egyptian monastic literature, the same cannot be said of John Cassian's writings: here wet dreams are subjected to a level of analysis deeper and literally more micro-'scopic' than anything we have yet encountered. John Cassian wrote his *Institutes* and *Conferences* in Gaul around 419–30 initially in response to a request from a local bishop for guidance in establishing monasteries in his area.[37] Cassian had sojourned in Egypt during the 380s and 390s and presented his work as the teachings of Egyptian monks whom he had encountered there. In fact, he adopted authentic material from the spirituality of Egyptian desert monasticism—particularly that of Evagrius—to the climate and customs of Western Europe, as well as to the contentious theological environment of the western church in the early fifth century. In Cassian's extensive discussions of nocturnal emissions, the boundaries that so concerned Syrian and Egyptian Christians—those between the body and the demonic environment, between the soul and body, and between the monastic communities and the parish churches—were no longer primary. In his more restricted horizon of the monastery itself, Cassian's concern was to negotiate boundaries that defined the fully coenobitic lifestyle—those across which the individual monk was separated from and revealed to himself and his senior colleagues. Moreover, the perfectionism that Dioscorus believed distinguished the monk from ordinary Christians had been rendered problematic by Augustine's controversial doctrine that all human goodness is a gift of God's grace, not a result of human efforts. In brief, Cassian refined the Egyptian teachings that we saw in Evagrius, Antony, and Dioscorus: emissions themselves are not sinful, but they may indicate a deeper problem. Once again it is the question of abstention from the Eucharist that provides the immediate occasion for the topic.[38] [. . .]

Cassian distinguishes perfect chastity from mere continence. Continence is a matter of effort and simple avoidance of sin; the monk is, as it were, still at war with the vice of fornication. Chastity, in contrast, is a state of peace; it is the positive love of virtue, so that the monk, even while sleeping, remains unaffected by any movement of the flesh.[39] The monk's progress toward perfect chastity forms a progression of infinite and imperceptible steps, which Cassian reduces to seven. At what he calls 'the summit of chastity,' the monk achieves a state of such peace that he is no longer troubled by emissions at all; one of the few monks who Cassian knew to have achieved such a state was appropriately named Serenus.[40] Serenus received the gift of 'uninterrupted purity of the body' when, after his 'perpetual supplications and tears,' an angel visited him at night, opened his belly, and removed from it a 'fiery tumor.'[41] Monks, however, who have achieved high degrees of chastity, but have not reached this summit, experience emissions only at the intervals considered natural, approximately every two to four months.[42]

Emissions that occur more frequently than this natural pattern are suspicious and may be due to one of three causes.[43] The first is gluttony: eating too much of a diet too moist leads to a surplus of humors that must be expelled; this expulsion can take place long after the overeating occurred, so that monks who are well into their new programs of fasting can still experience emissions whose ultimate cause was gluttony. The second possible cause is what Cassian calls 'the mind's negligence': a lack of vigilance during the daytime over one's thoughts and images creates a reservoir of desires in hidden parts of the monk's psyche, desires that emerge, so to speak, only when the mind relaxes with sleep. This is the most serious problem: here a monk is indeed rendered ineligible for the Eucharist. The third possible cause is an attack by the devil: in order to keep a monk from the sacrament, the devil causes an emission. In this case, the monk should commune—but a monk can be sure that the devil is at work only if a team of senior monks discerns that the other two causes are not in play.[44] [. . .]

Nocturnal emissions are problematic, then, because they suggest the persistence of boundaries between a person's 'inside' and 'outside,' a distinction that precludes an entirely visible self. A nocturnal emission indicates, for example, that the monk has still not brought his inner self, the 'spirit' or 'heart,' into conformity with his outer self, 'the flesh': while the outer person may be chaste, the inner person may still be lustful.[45] Cassian quotes Basil as saying, 'I have not known a woman, but I am not a virgin.'[46] A wet dream suggests just this state of affairs: a monk whose apparent chastity conceals a heart not yet pure, not yet filled with 'fear of God and love of chastity.' Examining the possible causes for his nocturnal emission, the monk stands at 'the boundaries of flesh and spirit' (confinia carnis ac spiritus).[47] Moreover, even the monk's inner self, his soul or heart, may be divided, its integrity violated by the existence of what Cassian calls 'hiding-places' (latebrae): sectors of the psyche impenetrable to the monk's conscious probings, but nonetheless repositories for his lustful thoughts.[48] Only sleep can reveal the existence and contents of these depths of the self: 'It (an emission) is a sign of some sickness hidden inside, something hidden in the inmost fibers of the soul, something that nighttime has not produced anew but rather has brought up to the surface of the skin by means of sleep's restorative powers. It (nighttime) exposes the hidden fibers of the agitations that we have collected by feasting on harmful thoughts all day long.'[49] The goal of the monastic discipline is, by filling one's heart with fear of God and love for the virtues (particularly chastity), to remove such hiding-places from one's heart and to become completely open to one's own inspection. [. . .] Indeed, Cassian's stated goal that the monk should become wholly known and thus eliminate any unknown inner self must not obscure the socially productive nature of the self that remains stubbornly hidden. The nocturnal emission, inasmuch as it indicates that there are unknown regions of the self, demonstrates that the monastic community based on the guide–disciple relationship is still required. [. . .]

The condition of being wholly known to oneself therefore required becoming transparent also to other monks, eliminating through confession any traces of a private, inaccessible, and so dangerous self. The monk who experiences nocturnal emissions without his awareness, without any images, and only as frequently as nature calls for has achieved this completely transparent consistency of self: 'Without doubt such a man has attained that state in which he is found to be the same at night as he is during the day, the same in bed as he is at prayer, the same alone as in a crowd of people, so that he never sees himself in secret to be such that he would blush to be seen by other people, nor does that inevitable eye (of God) see in him anything that ought to be concealed from human sight.'[50] The goal is to become a totally visible person, a self whose shape is wholly determined by one's living in a monastic community. Cassian's ascetic program depends on the cultivation of a completely honest relationship with one's elder monastic guides. 'Everything, not only what is done but also what is thought,' Cassian insists, must be 'preserved for the elder's scrutiny.'[51] Only so will the monk learn the tested ways of discipline and escape the deceits of the devil. Concealment, by contrast, leaves one open to the devil's attacks: 'An evil thought, as soon as it is disclosed, grows feeble, and even before the verdict of discernment is offered the most foul serpent, which, so to speak, has been dragged out of its dark subterranean cave into the light by the bravery of confession, retreats, in a certain sense exposed to ridicule and disgraced. Its guilty suggestions prevail in us as long as they are concealed in the heart.'[52] The persistence of boundaries that conceal areas of one's self from others, which the nocturnal emission may indicate, undermines, yet also requires, the guide–disciple relationship. [. . .] Ultimately, of course, the monk's self is transparent to what we have seen Cassian call 'the inevitable eye': that is, the eye of God. The monk must live his life as through always under the scrutiny of God's gaze. Cassian suggests that monks can bring the frequency of their emissions into line with what he considers natural if, he says, 'we consider God to be inspecting and sharing knowledge not only for our secret acts, but also of all our thoughts, both during the day and at night.'[53] [. . .]

The image is one of God and the monk dwelling in a high watchtower, perpetually observing the monk's now virtuous self in a fifth-century anticipation of Jeremy Bentham's (and later Michel Foucault's) panopticon.[54] Here is Cassian's version of the patristic manipulation of 'the gaze,' whose appearances in John Chrysostom and Augustine have been so expertly described in recent scholarship (Clark 1991; Leyerle 1993). Augustine's rhetoric of shame invoked the image of God as the 'All-Seeing-Eye' and was socially reinforced through a procedure of public confession (Clark 1991, 235–40). Similarly, Cassian shamed his male ascetics with his image of God's 'inevitable eye,' observing the monk from the watchtower of Zion: this divine gaze was created and sustained in social terms through the organization of the monastery, with its demand for relentless self-disclosure to one's elders. Indeed, Cassian has Antony describe the process of discernment, in which elder monks scrutinize the thoughts and deeds of themselves and younger monks, as 'the eye and lamp of the body' (Matthew 6.22–23 par.), which 'sees through (*pervideat*) and illumines all of a person's thought and actions, discerning everything that we must do.'[55] Without this 'eye of discernment' (*oculus discretionis*), the monk's body becomes 'dark' (*tenebrosus*).[56] A nocturnal emission suggested an imperfection in the system of observation, a failure of the eye of discernment to see through a man, in that it possibly indicated the persistence of a monastic self that was dark and private, inaccessible to other monks and possibly even to himself. In this way, the wet dream justified Cassian's monastic organization precisely by announcing the monastery's failure to complete its purpose.

Cassian's program for the diagnosis of emissions gendered its practitioners in a complex manner. On the one hand, 'the omnipresent male gaze feminizes its objects of vision' (Clark 1991, 237; Leyerle 1993, passim), here the confessing monks. In Cassian's method of monastic discernment, the relationship that is formed between the subject and object of observation is coded as seer/seen, active/passive, elder/younger, even though the ages of the two monks involved may not have correlated with this scheme. [. . .] In Cassian's treatment, then, monastic attention to nocturnal emissions served to define social identity of the monastic community and the monk's identity as a self in community. The goal was to dissolve boundaries that preserve an independent monastic self and so to create a self transparent to the discerning eyes of the monk himself, of his elder colleagues, and ultimately of God. At the same time, the ignorance that an emission disclosed demonstrated the need for the monastic system of confession. Emissions that occurred only as nature requires—and even more, no emission at all—were a sign of the monastic community's perfection, its distance from ordinary Christians. Yet the monks were to remain humble even about this superiority by attributing all of it to God's grace. All of this is well captured by Cassian's image of the watchtower of Zion, whose height indicates its superiority to the surrounding terrain and whose function of continual observation indicates the breakdown of the private self that the monastic life was meant to achieve.

Conclusion

It would be inaccurate to speak of an early Christian 'tradition' about nocturnal emissions. [. . .] Nonetheless, one can speak of a trend in Christian discussions of the nocturnal emission toward greater interiorization of impurity at two levels, the individual body of the male Christian and the collective body of the church. First, at the level of the individual's body, the source of impurity was increasingly located within the man. In the third century, the author of the *Didascalia* had to oppose Christians who believed that emissions left them emptied of the Holy Spirit and thus vulnerable to penetration by demons, and Dionysius of Alexandria worried about the communicant's effect on the holiness of the altar. In both of these cases, the focus was on the interaction of the body with its external environment, whether a demonic world or the Christian 'holy of holies.' Fourth-century sources, however, such as the *Apostolic Constitutions*,

Evagrius, Athanasius, and Timothy of Alexandria, increasingly looked to the moral condition of the individual as the determinative factor in judging whether or not emissions defiled, although they reached different conclusions on these matters. Athanasius and the Egyptian monks explored the body's interaction not with its surrounding environment, but with the companion housed within it, the soul. With Cassian the interiorization of impurity in Christian thinking, already present in his teacher Evagrius, became complete; for him, it was certainly not the emission itself that defiled the monk, but the evil thoughts lurking within that the emission might indicate. [. . .]

A similar interiorization in the problematization of emissions occurred at the level of the corporate body of the church, reflecting the changing social position of the Christian community. While Syrian Christians sought to define the church as a space separate from the Jewish synagogue or from pagan society in general, in Egypt Dioscorus and Athanasius were preoccupied by an emerging division with the church itself—between the growing monastic communities and the developing network of parish churches. While ordinary Christians appeared in Cassian's work, he was more concerned to remove boundaries within the monastic community itself—specifically those that separated the monk from the discerning eyes of his elders, his God, and himself. As the church became increasingly dominant in its society, the challenges to its self-definition appeared increasingly internal. [. . .] Self-definition, both of the individual male and of the church, was the continuing theme in early Christian discussions of male purity. Male Christian authors seldom used the male body to think about the church's shape and integrity, but instead examined the body of the female virgin from this perspective often and in great detail. Nonetheless, it cannot be said that the male body never performed this symbolic function: the nocturnal emission provided one occasion for such reflection because the movement of material from one space to another, from an inside to an outside, from where it belonged to where it did not, graphically raised the question of what inside and outside were and who was where.

Notes

1   This essay considerably revises and expands the brief discussion of this topic in Brakke (1995, 90–9). Translations of ancient sources are my own unless a modern translator is cited.

2   Some ancient authors believed that women, like men, contributed sperm to conception and so experienced ejaculations and even nocturnal emissions; see Van der Horst (1990, 287–302, esp. 295–6), and Rouselle (1988, 27–32). But the Christians discussed here speak only of men experiencing nocturnal emissions: the church orders and canonical letters consider menstruation in parallel with wet dreams; the monastic literature is aimed primarily, if not exclusively, at male ascetics.

3   Editor's note: Chadwick (1968), referred to elsewhere in Brakke's article, is essential reading.

4   Two passages in the Septuagint address the problem of seminal emissions apart from intercourse, Leviticus 15.16–17 and Deuteronomy 23.11–12; see Harrington (1993, 91–4), and Cohen (1991).

5   Cox Miller (1994a, 43), citing Aristotle, *insomn.* 461a18–20 (Gallop 1990, 95).

6 Arrian, *Discourses of Epictetus* 3.22.20 (*LCL* 218.136).

7 On the sources, dating, and provenance of these documents, see Bradshaw (1992, 87–8, 93–5). The Syriac translation of the *Didascalia* may date to the sixth century or later. Also Brock (1979, 33).

8 *Didasc. ap.* 26 (Vööbus, *CSCO* [1979, 255]). On *Didascalia* and purity issues, see also Cohen (1991, 289–90).

9 *Didasc. ap.* 26 (Vööbus, *CSCO* [1979, 259, 262]).

10 *Didasc. ap.* 26 (Vööbus, *CSCO* [1979, 256, 258]).

11 *Didasc. ap.* 26 (Vööbus, *CSCO* [1979, 262–3]).

12 I cite the more recent edition of Metzger, *Constitutions apostolique*, *SC* 329 (1986). Here 27.8 (*SC* 329.380).

13 *Constitutions apostolique*, 27.6 (*SC* 329.380).

14 *Constitutions apostolique*, 27.2 (*SC* 329.378).

15 *Constitutions apostolique*, 27.5 (*SC* 329.380).

16 *Constitutions apostolique*, 28.1 (*SC* 329.378).

17 Dionysius of Alexandria, *ep. can.* 2 (Joannou 1963, 2.12). Ironically, the author of the *Didascalia* cited the same passage to make the opposite point, that menstruants commune (*Didasc. Ap.* 26 [*CSCO* 407.262]); cf. Cohen (1991, 290).

18 Dionysius of Alexandria, *ep. can.* 2 (Joannou 1963, 2.12).

19 Origen, *sel. in Ezech.* 7.22 (*PG* 13.793); Cohen (1991, 288–9, 298 n. 58). See Bohertz (1992, 183–211, esp. 184–9).

20 Dionysius of Alexandria, *ep. can.* 3 (Joannou 1963, 2.13).

21 Dionysius of Alexandria, 4 (Joannou 1963, 2.13–14).

22 Timothy I of Alexandria, *resp.* 7 (Joannou 1963, 2.244).

23 Dionysius of Alexandria, 12 (Joannou 1963, 2.247–8).

24 Anthony the Great, *ep.* 1 (trans. Derwas J. Chitry, *The Letters of St. Anthony the Great* [1975], 1–5); cf. *apophth. Part. Ant.* 22 (*PG* 65.84).

25 On desert asceticism as performative ritual, 'enacting the spiritual body in the here-and-now,' see Cox Miller (1994b, 137).

26 On 'images' in Evagrius in general, see Clark (1992, 65–84, esp. 80–3).

27 Evagrius Ponticus, *Practicus* 55 (in Guillaumont 1971, 628).

28 Evagrius, *Practicus* 55 (628–9).

29 Less drink and Satan, Clark (1992, 82), citing *apopth. patr.* (syr.) 2.655 (Budge 1934, 416–17). Less food: Evagrius Ponticus, *sententiae ad monachos* 11 (Gressmann 1913, 154).

30 *Hist. mon* 20 (Festugière 1961, 118–19; Russell 1981, 105).

31 On the difficult relationship between early monasticism and the wider church, see Rousseau (1978), and Greer (1986, 164–8).

32 Athanasius, *ep. Amun* (Joannou 1963, 2.64–5). For citations of places where Athanasius uses these words for 'heresies,' see Brakke (1995, 98); cf. Barnard (1993).

33 Athanasius, *ep. Amun* (Joannou 1963, 2.65.67).

34 Athanasius, *ep. Amun* (Joannou 1963, 2.69).

35 Athanasius, *ep. Amun* (Joannou 1963, 2.69).

36 And in baptism as well: Athanasius *ep. Drac.* 4 (*PG* 25.518).

37 I have used the editions of E. Pichery, *Conferences* (*SC* 42, 54, 64; 3 vols, Paris: Édition du Cerf, 1955, 1958, 1959), and Jean-Claude Guy, *Institutions cénobitiques* (*SC* 109; Paris: Édition du Cerf, 1965).

38 John Cassian, *inst.* 6.8 (*SC* 109.272); *coll.* 22.4 (*SC* 64.119).

39 Cassian, *coll.* 12.10–11, 16 (*SC* 54.136–140, 145–1462); Russell (1992, 8–10).

40 Cassian, *coll.* 12.7 (*SC* 54.131–3).

41 Cassian, *coll.* 7.2 (*SC* 42.245).

42 Two months: Cassian, *inst.* 6.20 (*SC* 109.284), where he admits that he is being lenient; four months: *coll.* 2.23 (*SC* 42.134).

43 Cassian, *coll.* 22.3 (*SC* 64.116–19); Russell (1992, 5–8).

44 Cassian, *coll.* 22.6 (*SC* 64.121–3).

45 Cassian, *inst.* 6.2 (*SC* 109.262–264); *coll.* 4.19 (*SC* 42.182–3); 12.8.11 (*SC* 54.133–5, 139); 22.3,6 (*SC* 64.117, 121).

46 Cassian, *inst.* 6.19 (*SC* 109.284).

47 Cassian, *coll.* 12.8 (*SC* 54.133).

48 Cassian, *inst.* 6.9, 11 (*SC* 109.271–4); *coll.* 12.7 (*SC* 54.132).

49 Cassian, *inst.* 6.11 (*SC* 109.274).

50 Cassian, *coll.* 12.8 (*SC* 54.134); Brown (1988, 231–2).

51 Cassian, *coll.* 2.10 (*SC* 42.120).

52 Ibid., (*SC* 42.20–122).

53 Cassian, *inst.* 6.21 (*SC* 109.286).

54 Foucault (1979, esp. 170–7, 195–228), discussing Bentham's *Panopticon* (see also Bentham [1787], 1962, 4.36–66).

55 Cassian, *coll.* 2.2 (*SC* 42.113–14).

56 Cassian, *coll.* 2.3 (*SC* 42.114).

Literature

Aurelianus, Caelius. 1950. *On Chronic Diseases*, ed. and trans. J. E. Drabkin (*On Acute Diseases and On Chronic Diseases*). Chicago: University of Chicago Press.

Barnard, Leslie W. 1993. 'The Letters of Athanasius to Amoun and Dracontius,' *SP* 26:354–9.

Bentham, Jeremy. [1787] 1962. *The Works of Jeremy Bentham*. New York: Russell & Russell.

Bohertz, Charles A. 1992. 'The Development of Episcopal Order,' in *Eusebius, Christianity and Judaism*, eds Harold W. Attridge and Gohei Hata. Detroit: Wayne State University Press. Pp. 183–211.

Bradshaw, Paul F. 1992. *The Search for the Origins of Christian Worship: Sources and Methods for the Study of Early Liturgy*. Oxford: Oxford University Press.

Brakke, David. 1995. *Athanasius and the Politics of Asceticism* (Oxford Early Christian Studies). Oxford: Clarendon.

Brock, Sebastian. 1979. *The Holy Spirit in the Syrian Baptismal Tradition* (Syrian Churches Series 9). Poona, India: Anira.

Brown, Peter. 1988. *The Body and Society: Men, Women, and Sexual Renunciation in Early Christianity*. New York: Columbia University Press.

Budge, Wallis E. A. (trans.). 1934. *The Wit and Wisdom of the Desert Fathers*. Oxford: Oxford University Press.

Burrus, Virginia. 1994. 'Word and Flesh: The Bodies and Sexuality of Ascetic Women in Christian Antiquity,' *JFSR* 10:27–51.

Chadwick, Owen (ed.). 1968. *John Cassian*, 2nd edn. Cambridge: Cambridge University Press.

Chitry, Derwas J. (trans.). 1975. *The Letters of St. Anthony the Great*. Oxford: SLG Press.

Clark, Elizabeth A. 1991. 'Sex, Shame, and Rhetoric: En-gendering Early Christian Ethics,' *JAAR* 59:221–45.

——. 1992. *The Origenist Controversy: The Cultural Construction of an Early Christian Debate*. Princeton: Princeton University Press.

Cohen, Shaye J. D. 1991. 'Menstruation and the Sacred in Judaism and Christianity,' in *Women's History and Ancient History*, ed. Sarah B. Pomeroy. Chapel Hill: University of North Carolina Press. Pp. 273–99.

Cox Miller, Patricia. 1994a. *Dreams in Late Antiquity: Studies in the Imagination of a Culture*. Princeton: Princeton University Press.

———. 1994b. 'Desert Asceticism and "The Body from Nowhere",' *JECS* 2:137–53.

Douglas, Mary. 1966. *Purity and Danger: An Analysis of Concepts of Pollution and Taboo*. London: Routledge & Kegan Paul.

———. 1982. *Natural Symbol: Explorations in Cosmology*. New York: Pantheon.

Festugière, A. J. (ed.). 1961. *Historia Monarchum in Aegypto: Edition critique du texte et traduction annotée* (Subsidia Hagiographica 34). Brussels: Société des Bollandistes.

Foucault, Michel. 1979. *Discipline and Punish: The Birth of the Prison*, trans. Alan Sheridan. New York: Vantage Books.

Gallop, David (ed.). 1990. *Aristotle on Sleep and Dreams: A Text and Translation with Introduction, Notes and Glossary*. Peterborough, Ontario: Broadview.

Goehring, James E. 1992. 'The Origins of Monasticism,' in *Eusebius, Christianity and Judaism*, eds Harold W. Attridge and Gohei Hata. Detroit: Wayne State University Press. Pp. 235–55.

Greer, Rowan A. 1986. *Broken Lights and Mended Lives: Theology and Common Life in the Early Church*. University Park: Pennsylvania State University Press.

Gressmann, Hugo (ed.). 1913. 'Nonnenspiegel und Mönchspiegel des Euagrios Pontikos,' *TU* 39.4.

Guillaumont, Antoine and Claire (eds). 1971. *Évagre le Pontique: Traite pratique ou Le moine, SC* 171. Paris: Éditions du Cerf.

Harrington, Hannah K. 1993. *The Impurity Systems of Qumran and the Rabbis: Biblical Foundations* (Society of Biblical Literature Dissertations Series, 143). Atlanta: Scholars Press.

Joannou, Periclés-Pierre (ed.). 1963. *Fonti: Discipline générale antique (IVe-IXe s.)*, 2 vols. Rome: Grotaferrata.

Leyerle, Blake. 1993. 'John Chrysostom on the Gaze,' *JECS* 1:159–74.

Metzger, Marcel. 1986. *Constitutions apostolique, SC* 329. Paris: Éditions du Cerf.

Rouselle, Aline. 1988. *Porneia: On Desire and the Body in Antiquity*, trans. Felicia Pheasant. Oxford: Basil Blackwell.

Rousseau, Philip. 1978. *Ascetics, Authority, and the Church in the Age of Jerome and Cassian*. Oxford: Oxford University Press.

Rubenson, Samuel. 1990. *The Letters of St. Anthony: Origenist Theology, Monastic Tradition, and the Making of a Saint* (Bibliotheca Historico-Ecclesiastica Lundensis 24). Lund: Lund University Press.

Russell, Kenneth. 1992. 'John Cassian on a Delicate Subject,' *Cistercian Studies* 27:1–12.

Russell, Norman. 1981. *The Lives of the Desert Fathers: The Historia Monarchum in Aegypto* (Cistercian Studies 34). Kalamazoo: Cistercian Publications.

Scott, Alan. 1991. *Origen and the Life of the Stars: A History of an Idea*. Oxford: Clarendon.

Van der Horst, Pieter Willem. 1990. 'Sarah's Seminal Emission: Hebrews 11:11 in the Light of Ancient Embryology,' in *Greeks, Romans, and Early Christians: Essays in Honor of Abraham J. Malherbe*, eds David L. Balch, Everett Ferguson, and Wayne A. Meeks. Minneapolis: Fortress. Pp. 287–302.

Vivian, Tim. 1993. '"Everything Made by God is Good": A Letter Concerning Sexuality from St. Athanasius to the Monk Amoun,' *Église et théologie* 24:75–108.

Vööbus, Arthus. 1979. *The Didascalia Apostolorum in Syriac, CSCO* 407. Louvain: Peeters.

Circumcision and the Erection of Patriarchy

Editor's Introduction

At the site of the human body, conflicting cultural values can clash. This is true not only for the Christian anxiety over nocturnal emissions but also for the Jewish anxiety over male circumcision. Performed on a Jewish boy on the eighth day from his birth, circumcision is a sign for the covenant between the people of Israel and God and has become almost synonymous with Jewish male identity. Performed as a ritual even among assimilated Jews today, it seems that the significance of circumcision as a religious rite has been shifting toward a cultural marking in modernity. To be a Jewish man means to be circumcised.

The prevalence of circumcision in the Jewish community has not hindered Jewish scholars interested in issues of gender and masculinity from raising critical concerns about the rite of cutting. 'Of all the bodily locations where God could have marked a covenant with the Israelites, why the penis?' asks Silverman in the beginning of his *History of Jewish Circumcision*. 'Why not a handshake?' (2006, xv). Various Jewish male scholars – among them Eilberg-Schwartz (chapter 14), Eric Silverman, Shaye Cohen, Leonard Glick, Lawrence Hoffman, Yoram Bilu and Harry Brod – have wrestled with this question, offering different historical explanations and contemporary viewpoints. Eilberg-Schwartz, for example, traces the rite of circumcision back to ancient Israelite notions of fertility, reproduction and genealogy.

> The elaboration of the rules around the body was in part an attempt to control a puzzling object . . . Absorbed by the legal particularities surrounding ejaculation, menstruation, and skin disease, those inside and outside the priestly community would have lost sight of the larger dilemmas that inhered in the priests' religious culture. It is for this reason that the body became one of the richest sources of symbols in the priestly community . . . [including] the circumcised penis [as] a symbol of the covenant, procreation, and patrilineal descent. (Eilberg-Schwartz 1992, 38)

Others, like Silverman (2006) and Cohen (2005), move their discussion of circumcision beyond the confines of the rite's biblical origin and show how the rationale for circumcision has changed and shifted within Jewish discourse over time – from the Talmudic debate to the Middle Ages, from Jewish enlightenment (*haskalah*) to the twentieth century. Variously cited for the purpose of distinguishing Jewish men from Jewish women (who are not circumcised), and Jewish men from Christian men (circumcision versus baptism), circumcision has been inextricably linked to Jewish identity. Studying the 'history of Jewish circumcision', then, is for Shaye Cohen also a study of the 'history of Jewishness' (2005, xii).

Circumcision as a bodily practice is imbued with contradictory impulses and steeped in polyvalent symbolism. 'To the extent that circumcision sacralizes male fecundity', observes Silverman, 'the rite carves an image of Jewish men *against* women and uterine fertility':

> But circumcision, too, represents a masculine embodiment of female plenti-tude. The rite celebrates masculinity by sustaining male privilege and conse-crating the male body while nonetheless hewing men into something other than themselves – into a type of woman. Circumcision trims the penis to con-tain but also to unleash phallic aggression and potency. The rite intentionally affixes an ever-present, lifelong, intensely physical reminder of the covenant on the most private part of a man's body. (Silverman 2006, xv)

Contested within Judaism itself, circumcision also became a source of exter-nal misconceptions of Judaism. Christianity saw it as a sign of femininity, and modernity diagnosed it as displaced castration. Beginning with the apostle Paul's allegorical reading of the rite as 'the circumcision of the heart' (Rom. 2.29), Christian anti-Jewish prejudice compared the inferior blood of the circumcision to the superior water of baptism, regarded the blood as punish-ment for rejecting Jesus as Messiah, and even claimed that Jewish men were menstruating (for a brief summary, see Silverman 2006, 162–4; also Geller 1999; Taylor 2000; Bynum 1992). Today, the contemporary medical anti-circumcision movement views the cutting as an unnecessary operation that accomplishes nothing but to harm infant boys. Leonard Glick, for example, is a proponent of this view (Glick 2005; see also Slavet 2007).

Harry Brod, whose thoughts on circumcision are reprinted below, navigates between these different voices. As a son of Holocaust survivors, he is keen-ly invested in maintaining a strong Jewish identity. Yet he wonders whether circumcising his own son was the right decision (see also Staley, chapter 17). Did he continue a practice fraught with patriarchal problems? 'For circumcision is above all a male-to-male transmission of Jewish identity, one that dramatically centers Judaism on fathers and sons and marginalizes mothers and daughters,' he writes. 'For this reason alone, if not also for so many others, it therefore requires full and frank discussion.'

Harry Brod has been actively involved in masculinity studies for more than two decades. Advancing the field on theoretical levels (1987; 1994), he has also contributed in significant ways to the discourse on Jewish masculinity (1988; 1995).

Publications by the Same Author

Brod, Harry (ed.). 1987. *The Making of Masculinities: The New Men's Studies*. London: Routledge.

——. (ed.). 1988. *A Mensch Among Men: Explorations in Jewish Masculinity*. Freedom: Crossing.

——. 1992. *Hegel's Philosophy of Politics*. Boulder: Westview.

——. 1992. 'Pornography and the Alienation of Male Sexuality', in *Rethinking Masculinity: Philosophical Explorations in Light of Feminism*, eds Larry May and Robert Strikwerda. Lanham: Littlefield Adams Quality Paperbacks. Pp.135–47.

——. 1995. 'Of Mice and Supermen', in *Gender and Judaism: The Transformation of Tradition*, ed. Tamar M. Rudavsky. New York: New York University Press. Pp. 279–93.

——. 2007. 'Circumcision', in *International Encyclopedia of Men and Masculinities*, eds M. Flood, J. K. Gardiner, B. Pease and K. Pringle. London: Routledge. Pp. 67–8.

Brod, Harry and Michael Kaufman (eds). 1994. *Theorizing Masculinities*. Thousand Oaks and London: Sage.

Brod, Harry, Cooper Thompson and Emmett Schaeffer (eds). 2003. *White Men Challenging Racism: 35 Personal Stories*. Durham: Duke University Press.

Further Reading

Bilu, Yoram. 2000. 'Circumcision, the First Haircut and the Torah: Ritual and Male Identity among the Ultraorthodox Community of Contemporary Israel', in *Imagined Masculinities: Male Identity and Culture in the Middle East*, eds M. Ghoussoub and E. Sinclair-Webb. London: Saqi Books. Pp. 33–63.

Bynum, Caroline Walker. 1992. 'The Body of Christ in the Later Middle Ages', in *Fragmentation and Redemption*, C. W. Bynum. New York: Zone Books. Pp. 79–117.

Cohen, Shaye J. D. 2005. *Why Aren't Jewish Women Circumcised?* Berkeley: University of California Press.

Eilberg-Schwartz, Howard. 1992. 'The Problem of the Body for the People of the Book', in *People of the Body: Jews and Judaism from an Embodied Perspective*, ed. Eilberg-Schwartz. Albany: SUNY Press. Pp. 17–46.

Geller, Jay. 1999. 'The Godfather of Psychoanalysis: Circumcision, Antisemitism, Homosexuality, and Freud's "Fighting Jew."' *Journal of the American Academy of Religion* 67/2:355–85.

Glick, Leonard B. 2005. *Marked in Your Flesh: Circumcision from Ancient Judea to Modern America*. New York: Oxford University Press.

Hoffman, Lawrence A. 1996. *Covenant of Blood: Circumcision and Gender in Rabbinic Judaism*. Chicago: University of Chicago Press.

Silverman, Eric K. 2006. *From Abraham to America: A History of Jewish Circumcision*. Lanham: Rowman & Littlefield.

Slavet, Eliza. 2007. 'Jewish American Circumcision: A Review Article'. *Theology and Sexuality* 13/3:319–26.

Taylor, Gary. 2000. *Castration: An Abbreviated History of Western Manhood*. New York: Routledge.

Circumcision and the Erection of Patriarchy

HARRY BROD

I have a cartoon that in a simple line drawing depicts a bearded man in a simple cloak standing on a mountain top, holding a staff and addressing a cloud hovering above him. The caption reads 'You mean you want us to cut the ends of our dicks off?'

That cartoon was sent to me years ago by my friend Michael Kimmel. He and Amy Aronson (both Jewish and married to each other) made the decision to not circumcise their son, about which he wrote a very fine article (Kimmel 2005). In it, he tells a story of a close friend of his, a child of Holocaust survivors, who did have his son circumcised. That was my story, and my decision was based on a story my mother told me.

My mother was a German Jew who lost all of her immediate family in the Holocaust. She told me that her brother had been on his way to escape when he was halted by Nazi soldiers at the train station. They identified him as a Jew by forcing him to pull down his pants, and they executed him.

As I struggled over whether to circumcise my son, that story kept coming back to me. Arguments against circumcision as an outmoded tradition that needlessly and unjustifiably inflicts pain on a helpless infant seemed compelling to me. But despite the powerfully persuasive arguments against it, I was simply unable to not circumcise my son. That felt to me like a betrayal of what my people, including specifically my uncle who I never got to meet, had died for. My feelings ran much deeper than the level of rational argument. The power of the non-rational was powerfully brought home to me.

For many Jews, the circumcised penis is the defining mark of being a Jew, certainly for males. Theologically speaking, this is simply an error, for Jewish identity is conferred by parentage or conversion, not by any sign on the body. Yet the idea that circumcision confers Jewish identity has a deep and powerful hold on many Jews, even those not otherwise particularly observant.

Let us follow time-honored rabbinic traditions, and consider how some of the standard sources one would typically adduce to address issues of the body in Judaism might be applied to the issue of circumcision, which has to be the quintessential issue of the Jewish male body, and thus of signal importance for Jewish men. But I should first note that, as obvious as it is to me that this issue is central for any serious reconsideration of Jewish masculinity, I appear to be in a distinct minority in contemporary Judaism in saying so. For example UJR Press, the publishing arm of the Reform Movement, published two collections of writings by and about Jewish men in 2008, as part of major initiatives the movement has undertaken to increase men's involvement in congregational life (Holzman 2008; Person 2008). (The problem is by no means unique to this movement or to Judaism, and there is a broad conversation among many concerned with religion in the United States about a perceived 'feminization' of religion, by which is meant an increasing absence of men from traditional congregation-centered religious life). Though circumcision comes up from time to time in passing, neither volume has a single essay focused on the topic. One can speculate on the many reasons for the omission, including a defensiveness arising from antisemitic overtones in the ways anti-circumcision arguments are sometimes framed, as well as other reasons I shall address shortly. Nonetheless, I find the silence quite striking.

One relevant classic source is from Leviticus (19.28): 'You shall not make gashes in your flesh for the dead, or incise any marks on yourselves: I am the LORD.'

The first part of the passage has become a classic source for the practice of cutting one's clothes rather than oneself as a sign of mourning. The second part gives me pause. Isn't circumcision incising a mark upon oneself, and therefore prohibited? Surely there must be powerful reasons for this practice, in the face of what seems a clear commandment that human flesh should be left intact. What, then, are the reasons given for circumcision?

One common justification should really not be given great, or perhaps even any, weight. The boy should *look like* his father, many insist, and this is held to be extremely important for his development, especially for the development of his Jewish identity. But it seems hard to justify cutting into and removing part of the flesh for the mere sake of appearance, given the principle of the sanctity of the intactness of the flesh suggested by the Leviticus passage and its standard application to the issue of tattooing. If being tattooed is such a serious transgression that it denies burial rights in Jewishly consecrated ground, as orthodox rulings state, then the injunction against defacing the body seems so strong that there surely must be more than aesthetic reasons for circumcision. Our text suggests that such a reason for the practice is not only insufficient, but probably illegitimate.

Health considerations are often used to justify circumcision. This line of reasoning raises two problems. First, this does not get one to Jewish circumcision. These reasons lead only to the medical procedure, but when performed without accompanying Jewish rituals this is Jewishly profoundly unsatisfactory. Further complications arise because certain Orthodox practices raise their own medical problems in the contemporary world, requiring the *mohel* to suck blood from the wound orally, raising the possibility of disease transmission (some versions of this Orthodox rite avoid direct contact, for example by sucking through a tube, but this is not universal).

Secondly, the medical evidence is far from clear, to say the least. Much if not most of the evidence suggests that circumcision offers no clear medical benefit. Most medical associations throughout the world, including in the US, now no longer support routine circumcision. Earlier views that the infant felt no pain during the procedure have been discredited. Claims that it helps to reduce the incidence of sexually transmitted diseases, infections and penile cancer have generally not been validated by scientific studies. The most notable exceptions are some very recent studies of HIV/AIDS transmission, which have led to the promotion of circumcision as a means to prevent the spread of HIV/AIDS in Africa.

Medical circumcision emerged as a common practice in the United States and England in the later Victorian period. The neonatal surgical procedure marked middle- and upper-class whites as 'modern,' where birthing practices became medicalized into the hands of male doctors in hospitals rather than female midwives in homes, and as distinct from lower-class and 'darker' immigrants who did not have access to 'modern' ways and generally did not circumcise. The regulation of sexuality emerged as a great cultural concern in this period, and the belief that circumcision inhibited sexuality made it an important part of major moral crusades against what were seen as sexual excesses, especially including masturbation.

If aesthetic and health considerations seem to not sufficiently justify the practice, we are left with cultural and religious reasons. The problem here is, there's never been agreement on precisely what these reasons are, and contradictory things are often said.

There is the purely traditionalist argument. We do it because we have always done it. The act has been hallowed through its passage from generation to generation. But this is unsatisfactory because the tradition itself has always asserted that meaning arises intrinsically in each ritual enactment, not merely derivatively as one link in a chain.

In the defining biblical text God says to Abraham:

I will make you exceedingly fertile, and make nations of you . . . Such shall be the covenant between Me and you and your offspring to follow which you shall keep: every male among you shall be circumcised. You shall circumcise the flesh of your foreskin, and that shall be the sign of the covenant between Me and you. And throughout the generations, every male among you shall be circumcised at the age of eight days. (Genesis 17.6, 10–11. Jewish Publication Society translation)

In this text circumcision is linked to fertility, as opposed to the Leviticus text cited earlier, which links bodily incisions to death. One important though not dominant strand of ancient rabbinic interpretation saw God's commandment to circumcise as intended to symbolize God's own acts of creation, described in Genesis as acts of separation which establish clear demarcations, conferring form on formlessness, creating meaning out of chaos. Circumcision's separation of the flesh is seen here as a symbolically re-creationist and meaning-making forming of the flesh.

The major strain of early rabbinic interpretation linked circumcision to blood sacrifice, emphasizing a different aspect of the procedure, focusing not on separating the foreskin from the penile shaft but on drawing blood in its removal. On this view, male genital bleeding, ritually enacted and controlled by men, is superior to female menstrual bleeding, occurring naturally and uncontrolled. The sacrifice of the foreskin is culture's triumph over nature, a view which leads toward the next interpretative strain.

In the further development of medieval Judaism the meaning of circumcision changed from symbolic (of either creation and reproduction or sacrifice) to actual, as it came to be seen as desexualizing, elevating men above their animal nature and subjugating their sexual impulses to their will. For many Jews, whether they are aware of it or not, the teachings of Maimonides *are* what they understand as the teachings of Judaism. The view of Maimonides, the preeminent Jewish philosopher and also court physician to the twelfth-century

Egyptian Muslim Sultan Saladin, was extremely influential in this as in so many matters. He celebrated the importance of circumcision because he believed it lessened sexual arousal and sensitivity in men.

To those of us familiar with modern intellectual traditions this sounds very Freudian. We would interpret the reasoning that circumcision lessens male sexual urges as Judaism's wanting men to sublimate (that is, to repress and re-direct) their sexual urges into religious ones. Or we might say, with more recent Freudian theorist Jacques Lacan, that circumcision represents the literal embodi-ment of male patriarchal authority or, in Lacanian terms, the inscription of the phallus (that is, the meaning we attach to masculinity) onto the penis (a mere bodily organ), marking the erection of patriarchy. In this theoretical tradition circumcision is seen as both masculinizing and feminizing, the former because the ritual emphasizes the importance of the penis/phallus, and the latter for the seemingly opposite reason, because the cut is seen as de-emphasizing the importance of the penis/phallus (see also my entry on 'Circumcision,' [Brod 2007]).

It is in this concept of patriarchy that I believe we have reached the real mean-ing of circumcision. For circumcision is above all a male-to-male transmission of Jewish identity, one that dramatically centers Judaism on fathers and sons and marginalizes mothers and daughters. For this reason alone, if not also for so many others, it therefore requires full and frank discussion.

Some may feel that this discussion has already been more frank than they would have liked, and may already have been made uncomfortable by such explicit discussion of penises. That is precisely the point. That which is undiscussed and hidden (or, in Freudian terms, unconscious) operates all the more powerfully precisely because of its hiddenness. The authority of men is reinforced by the taboo on discussing the specifics of the male body.

Judaism offers profound insights into the power of hiddenness. For we serve a hidden God, one with an unknowable name. When Moses asks of the burn-ing bush what he shall answer when Pharaoh asks who sent him, God does not really give Moses a name, but instead responds with the cryptic formula 'Ayeh Asher Ayeh' ('I Am-Was-Will Be Who/What I Am-Was-Will Be').

Ancient mystical and magical traditions in play here, older than Judaism itself, teach that knowledge of a name confers power over what is named. On one tra-ditional interpretation in this vein, God calls upon Adam to name the animals as a sign of humanity's dominion over the creatures of the Earth, though this is not the only way to interpret the story, and ecologically sensitive Judaism offers differing interpretations. Further, naming is by definition an act of sepa-ration—any name or definition works by establishing limits and boundaries, differentiating this from that. To name God would therefore be to limit God, contradicting Jewish teachings.

For Judaism the privilege of namelessness or hiddenness is God's alone. To respect the distinction between the human and the divine is therefore to deny such hiddenness to humans. Just as humans are called upon to honor God's hiddenness, so they are thereby called upon to reveal themselves.

To take to ourselves the privilege of hiddenness is thus to claim for ourselves an identity and authority that is God's alone. It is an almost idolatrous sort of arrogance, of hubris. But men do this all too frequently. They, and at this point

I must in all honesty say 'we,' hide our selves, our deepest and most honest thoughts and feelings, even from our loved ones, because we understand or intuit that knowledge is power, and to expose ourselves is to give others potential power over us.

Men need to surrender this patriarchal power and pretensions to near divinity in order to reclaim our humanity. These practices diminish men as well as women, as patriarchal imperatives to hide our selves from others lead us to hide even from ourselves. We suffer from a peculiarly male malady that psychologists are beginning to call 'alexithymia,' an inability to attach words to emotions—from the Greek and Latin: 'a' ('without')-'lexus' ('words')-'thymos' ('emotions'). When asked how we are feeling, we are often unable to articulate a response. Problems that cannot be named cannot be solved, and so we stay locked inside our emotional straitjackets, suffering higher rates of heart attacks, ulcers, suicides and early deaths because of the emotional pressures that necessarily remain unreleased because they remain unrevealed. Our salvation lies in our surrender of patriarchal privilege.

We have traveled far in this discussion of the Jewish male body. I have used our reluctance to discuss the penis, its hiddenness, as a metaphor for the hidden dimensions of the male soul, seeing in both the maintenance of patriarchal authority by cloaking masculinity in mystery. Our world is deeply gendered. The cultural dichotomy between mind and body corresponds to a dichotomy between the masculine and the feminine, with women coming to be seen as stupefied bodies, i.e. 'sex objects,' and men becoming disembodied intellects. Emphasizing the embodiedness of men therefore de-privileges rather than re-privileges men. It is egalitarianism, not exhibitionism.

Attention to the male body will not only help empower women, as it reveals the hiddenness of male privilege, but it is in men's real human interests too. For example, seeing men as essentially minds rather than bodies creates role models of Jewish men as scholars rather than athletes. This is not to in any way diminish the value of the ideal of the Jewish scholar, but rather to lament how Jewish men have not as fully developed the potential of their bodies, to our great loss.

I intend through this essay to challenge as patriarchal not only the practice of circumcision, but also more broadly our reluctance to discuss the secrets men keep and the rituals by which their power is kept, and to call for their full and frank discussion. I do not presume to know what the results of that discussion will be. I do presume to know that we will be the better for having it.

I could and perhaps should end here, but I began with a personal perspective, and feel called upon to end on one as well. The decision to circumcise my son is behind me, so when I now think about this issue in personal terms it is in terms of the decision my children may be called upon to make. In my thoughts now is not so much the story with which I began, but more a quote from British writer E. M. Forster, who wrote: 'If I had to choose between betraying my country and betraying my friend, I hope I should have the guts to betray my country.' Mindful of the pain of circumcision, for me this translates into: 'If I had to choose between betraying my tradition and betraying my son, I hope I would have the guts to betray my tradition.'

I wish for my children the courage to confront the question.

Literature

Barth, Lewis M. (ed.). 1990. *Berit Mila in the Reform Context*. USA: Berit Mila Board of Reform Judaism.

Brod, Harry. 2007. 'Circumcision,' in *International Encyclopedia of Men and Masculinities*, eds M. Flood, J. K. Gardiner, B. Pease, and K. Pringle. London: Routledge. Pp. 67–8.

Cohen, Shaye J. D. 2005. *Why Aren't Jewish Women Circumcised?* Berkeley: University of California Press.

Gollaher, David L. 2000. *Circumcision: A History of the World's Most Controversial Surgery*. New York: Basic Books.

Hirji, Hassan, Rodger Charlton and Siddharth Sarmah. 2005. 'Male Circumcision: A Review of the Evidence,' *The Journal of Men's Health and Gender* 2/1:21–30.

Hoffman, Lawrence A. 1996. *Covenant of Blood: Circumcision and Gender in Rabbinic Judaism*. Chicago: University of Chicago Press.

Holzman, Michael G. (ed.). 2008. *The Still Small Voice: Reflections on Being a Jewish Man*. New York: URJ Press.

Kimmel, Michael S. 2005. 'The Kindest Un-Cut: Feminism, Judaism, and My Son's Foreskin,' in *The Gender of Desire: Essays on Male Sexuality*, Kimmel. Albany: SUNY Press. Pp. 175–84.

Knights, Ben. 2004. 'Men from the Boys: Writing on the Male Body,' *Literature and History* 13/1:25–42.

Mark, Elizabeth Wyner (ed.). 2003. *The Covenant of Circumcision: New Perspectives on an Ancient Jewish Rite*. Hanover: Brandeis University Press.

Person, Hara E., with Carolyn Bricklin, Owen Gottlieb and Melissa Zalkin Stollman (eds). 2008. *The Gender Gap: A Congregational Guide for Beginning the Conversation about Men's Involvement in Synagogue Life*. New York: URJ Press.

Silverman, Eric. 2006. *From Abraham to America: A History of Jewish Circumcision*. Lanham: Rowman & Littlefield.

From Masturbation to Homosexuality:
A Case of Displaced Moral Disapproval

Editor's Introduction

Donald Capps, professor of Pastoral Theology, has written several books on men and religion. He once described himself as a 'psychobiographer' of men like Augustine, John Henry Newman, Abraham Lincoln and Jesus (Capps 1995, 97; 1990; 2000b). He also writes on religion and the childhood and adolescence of boys (for example, 2007a). In this chapter, Capps presents an intriguing thesis, namely that the nineteenth-century reprobation of masturbation has been supplanted by the twentieth-century condemnation of homosexuality.

To contextualize Capps's argument, it is helpful to briefly look at the history of masturbation. Parallel to the modern use of the sexual term *sodomia*, which Jordan traced to the eleventh century rather than to the Bible (chapter 21), the modern meaning of masturbation cannot be captured fully by the biblical term onania, a term that is for many synonymous with the story of Onan who, according to Genesis 38, wasted his semen and thereby displeased God. Rather, masturbation as a recognizable sexual activity does not come into existence until the Enlightenment. This, at least, is Thomas Laqueur's argument in his extensive study, *Solitary Sex: A Cultural History of Masturbation* (2003).

> Modern masturbation can be dated with a precision rare in cultural history. It was born in, or very close to, the same year as that wild and woolly and profoundly self-conscious exemplar of 'our' kind of human, Jean-Jacques Rousseau ... The crucial moment is around the late seventeenth or early eighteenth century, when the sin [of masturbation] ... became into its own ... [M]asturbation became so central to the history of the self in relation to the broader cultural history of the last two hundred years ... [because] modern culture encourages individualism and self-determination and is threatened by solipsism and anomie ... Masturbation is the sexuality of the self par excellence. (Laqueur 2003, 13, 19, 20–1)

Masturbation has been met with moral unease even before the eighteenth century, as evident, for example, in the penitential manuals of the fifteenth century. However, masturbation as a solitary sexual act became a serious predicament only at the dawn of modernity, because, according to Laqueur, it could be named as such only when the 'self' emerged as an autonomous being. Such autonomy was welcomed as a new freedom of the individual but also feared for its potential to lead to social anarchy and anomie. Autoerotic sexuality – conceivable as a distinct entity among sexual sins only when the autonomous self emerged – became the lightning rod for a host of anxieties, and was variously vilified as self-pollution, self-abuse, onanism, perverted self-love, or arrested development. Only after the Freudian revolution, Laqueur argues, did a cultural shift occur. Masturbation was now valued as an adult, non-pathological, pleasurable activity. 'Beginning in the 1950s, picking up energy with the feminism of the 1960s and early 1970s, with the subsequent sex wars, and with the worldwide gay movement of the last quarter of the century, it would become an arena of sexual politics and for art across a wide spectrum of society' (2003, 22). Due to this cultural change across the social spectrum, even theological reassessments of masturbation as a positive sexual practice were possible – though, admittedly, rare (see Haldeman 1996; also Nelson 1992, 34–5).

Whereas Laqueur sees a parallelism in the acceptance of masturbation and homosexuality in the twentieth century, Capps argues that the heterosexual Christian mainstream shifted its moral disapproval from masturbation to homosexuality. In his concluding remarks, Capps encourages his contemporary readers to cast off negative attitudes toward homosexuality – just as society had shed its nineteenth-century worries about masturbation.

Publications by the Same Author

Capps, Donald. 1995. *The Child's Song: The Religious Abuse of Children*. Louisville: Westminster John Knox.

——. 1997. *Men, Religion, and Melancholia*. New Haven: Yale University Press.

——. 2000a. *Men and Their Religion: Honor, Hope, and Humor*. Harrisburg: Trinity Press International.

——. 2000b. *Jesus, a Psychological Biography*. St. Louis: Chalice Press.

——. 2007a. 'The Making of the Reliably Religious Boy'. *Pastoral Psychology* 55/3 (January):253–70.

——. 2007b. 'Augustine's Confessions: Self-Reproach and the Melancholy Self'. *Pastoral Psychology* 44/5 (May):571–91.

——. 2007c. 'The Homosexual Tendencies of King James: Should this Matter to Bible Readers Today?' *Pastoral Psychology*; 55/6 (July):667–99.

——. 2007d. 'Shame and the Solitary Way'. *Pastoral Psychology* 56/1 (September):3–8.

——. 2008. 'The "Religiously Mediated Change" of 11 Gay Men: A Case of Unexceptional Sublimation'. *Pastoral Psychology* 57 3/4 (November):125–46.

Capps, Donald and James E. Dittes (eds). 1990. *The Hunger of the Heart: Reflections on the Confessions of Augustine*. Society for the Scientific Study of Religion, Monograph Series 8.

Further Reading

Haldeman, Scott. 1996. 'Bringing Good News to the Body: Masturbation and Male Identity', in *Men's Bodies, Men's Gods*, ed. Björn Krondorfer. New York: New York University Press. Pp. 111–24.

Laqueur, Thomas W. 2003. *Solitary Sex: A Cultural History of Masturbation*. New York: Zone Books.

Nelson, James B. 1992. *Body Theology*. Louisville: Westminster John Knox.

From Masturbation to Homosexuality: A Case of Displaced Moral Disapproval

DONALD CAPPS

Those who engage in homosexual acts are now being singled out, especially in the religious culture, as moral reprobates, whereas in the nineteenth century and early decades of the twentieth century, they shared this dubious honor with those who engaged in self-masturbatory practices. Masturbation no longer receives the attention that it formerly received, having virtually fallen off the moral opprobrium radar screen. As a result, those who engage in homosexual acts bear a greater burden as the object of moral disapproval than before, and homosexual behavior receives much greater scrutiny, is the subject of much more moral and theological debate, and is the target of considerably greater moral condemnation than previously. Immanuel Kant, the nineteenth century German philosopher, identified masturbation, homosexual acts, and sodomy (sexual acts with other species) as the three major sexual 'crimes' against our 'animal nature' (1963, 169). If masturbation is no longer subject to moral disapproval, and sodomy is a relatively rare occurrence, this leaves homosexual acts as the unrivaled focus of sexual moral condemnation, at least as far as these three 'crimes' are concerned.

In *Whatever Became of Sin*, Karl Menninger, perhaps the most influential psychiatrist of the mid-twentieth century, notes that masturbation, long considered the 'great sin of youth,' is barely mentioned, much less discussed, today. Prior to the late twentieth century, however, 'Almost no other activity was so regularly condemned and punished as erotic self-stimulation, autoeroticism. For centuries, school children, prisoners, sailors, and slaves were savagely punished when detected in or even suspected of "the solitary vice" of "self-abuse"' (Menninger 1977, 31). [. . .]

Menninger notes that, while the moral taboo against masturbation is thousands of years old, and attempts at deterrence by punishment have gone on for centuries, a strong 'intimidation curb' from the medical profession began about 250 years ago. A famous book by an unknown author (Menninger suggests that he was a 'quack' doctor), bearing the title, *Onania, or The Heinous Sin of Self-Pollution*, published in 1716, went through 80 editions. Forty years later a renowned and universally respected Swiss physician, Samuel Tissot, took up the same theme in a book that claimed a direct causal relationship between masturbation and various physical diseases and mental disorders. Titled *Onania, or a Treatise upon the Disorders Produced by Masturbation*, it had a profound effect on medical thought, resulting in numerous medical articles on masturbation. [. . .]

Nineteenth-Century Views on Masturbation: The Case of William James

If masturbation is no longer held to be the heinous crime against the body it was once held to be, the obvious question is why and how this happened. Why did moral disapproval of masturbation decline? There are various reasons for this decline, and an attempt to identify all or even most of them would require a much more extensive investigation into the history of masturbation than is possible here. However, one important reason for this decline is that, in the first decades of the twentieth century, psychiatrists and other doctors began to challenge the view that masturbation causes physical disease, mental disorders, and moral degeneracy. A minority view at first, this challenge gained support through the 1930s and 40s. By mid-century the view that masturbation causes physical disease, mental disorders, and moral degeneracy was thoroughly discredited. By now, the fact that virtually the whole medical community in the nineteenth century assumed that masturbation had these effects is almost beyond belief. [. . .]

Beginning in the early decades of the nineteenth century, masturbation was deemed a major cause of mania, melancholy, and dementia. In *The Varieties of Religious Experience* (1982; originally published in 1902), William James includes an account of his experience in his late twenties of 'the worst form of melancholy,' that of 'panic fear.' In his case, this was a sudden attack of 'horrible fear of my own existence' (160). Simultaneously, there arose in his mind 'the image of an epileptic patient I had seen in the asylum, a black-haired youth with greenish skin, entirely idiotic, who used to sit all day on one of the benches, or rather shelves against the wall, with his knees drawn up against his chin, and the coarse gray undershirt, which was his only garment, drawn over them enclosing his entire figure. He sat there like a sort of sculptured Egyptian cat or Peruvian mummy, moving nothing but his black eyes and looking absolutely non-human' (160). At that moment, James felt his image of the youth and his own panic fear coalescing, and realized, to his utter horror, that the 'shape' he had seen in his mind was potentially himself: 'There was such a horror of him, and such a perception of my own merely momentary discrepancy from him, that it was as if something hitherto solid within my breast gave way entirely, and I became a mass of quivering fear' (160). The fear was 'so invasive and powerful' that had he not 'clung to scripture-texts like "The eternal God is my refuge," etc., "Come unto me, all ye that labor and are heavy-laden," etc., "I am the resurrection and the life," etc., I think I should have grown really insane' (161).

In her biography of James, Linda Simon suggests that the 'mental patient James recalled was notable because he suffered not from the common pathology of moral insanity (alcoholism and excessive masturbation, for example) but from epilepsy, which, although often misdiagnosed and misunderstood, could not be cured by strengthening a patient's will. An epileptic patient was at the mercy of his own biology' (1998, 125). This would seem to suggest that James did not associate his own crisis with his struggle, perhaps unsuccessful, [. . .] to 'hold in check certain bad habits, tendencies to "moral degradation" (another allusion, probably, to auto-eroticism)' (201). However, in *Manhood at Harvard*

(1996), Kim Townsend contends that James himself believed that masturbation was the cause of the young mental patient's madness. He notes:

When a man fears or experiences the dissolution of his financial and professional and public life, it would not be surprising if his private or intimate or sexual life seemed to lack all purpose or definition as well. How specifically James was applying the diagnosis to himself we cannot say, but into his darkest imaginings there seems to have come the figure—perhaps the very figure a nineteenth-century medical student [like James himself] might have in mind—of a man driven insane by masturbation. (Townsend 1996, 52)

[. . .] Townsend acknowledges that it may seem far-fetched to attribute James's experience of 'quivering fear' to his unsuccessful struggle to curb his masturbatory habits, but he notes that 'when [James] was a boy he was told about the dire consequences of "that horrible pollution" by his own father—and when the appropriate time came, he duly passed on his father's warnings to one of his sons. "If any boys try to make you do anything dirty," he told him when he went off to boarding school, "either to your own person, or to their persons . . . you must both preach and smite them. For that leads to an awful habit, and a terrible disease when one is older"' (1996, 53–4).

Noting that James determined to do something about his habit of 'self-abuse' by setting out on a course of 'moral hygiene,' Wendy Graham points out that he was therefore very much in tune with the moral leaders of his time:

William's reflections on moral hygiene should be read in light of nineteenth-century descriptions of sexual neurasthenia and masturbatory insanity. Samuel Tissot's 1758 text on onanism inaugurated a booming market for publications of this kind. William Acton's *The Functions and Disorders of the Reproductive Organs* was widely available after its publication in 1857, and his ideas were rapidly disseminated by boarding school administrators, priests, and doctors, as Ed Cohen explains: 'As the topic of frequent sermons, lectures, advice sessions, and disciplinary actions, masturbation became a primary focus for the enactment of pedagogical authority over middle-class adolescent boys.' (Graham 1999, 41)

[. . .] Graham's discussion of masturbation occurs within a larger consideration of William James's brother Henry's struggle with his homosexual desires. She notes that William, owing to his medical training and his position as an instructor in physiology and psychology at Harvard, served throughout his life as Henry's informal consulting physician. In that capacity, he must have advised his brother to control his homosexual desires, and for essentially the same reasons that he sought to control his own masturbatory urges. In any case, 'Henry's fears of psychological, physical, and moral disintegration carried greater weight' in 'his renunciation of physical passion' than did 'codes of respectable behavior' (Graham 1999, 44).

Medical Treatment of Masturbation

The medical journals of the late nineteenth century were replete with articles describing surgical and other procedures designed to eradicate masturbation. Writing in *The Boston Medical and Surgical Journal* in 1883, Dr Timothy Haynes described a surgical procedure that he had developed for curing 'hopeless cases of masturbation and nocturnal emissions.' Indicating that he has frequently been called upon to care for victims of self-abuse, his normal procedure is to help the 'perverted' state of mind of the victims by counseling marriage and even, at times, the immorality of a mistress. But some cases are so utterly desperate, the individual so destroyed mentally and physically, that he began to wonder whether some help could be provided even at the expense of the procreative powers. Judging the scar of castration to be an intolerable stigma, he developed a less extreme surgical procedure, which involved removing parts of the spermatic duct. He would make an incision midway between the external inguinal ring and the testis. This incision provided access to the duct, from which a half inch was cut off, and the 'slight' wound was then closed with a suture. [. . .]

In *The Therapeutic State* (1984), Thomas Szasz discusses an article published in the *New Orleans Medical and Surgical Journal* in 1879 in which the author, Dr B. A. Pope, describes the case of a 14-year-old boy whose 'syndrome' was allegedly caused by masturbation. The patient's presenting problem was the loss of sight, together with anemia and mental weakness. Judging that his blindness had a 'cerebral' or mental cause, as the retina and optic papillae appeared healthy, Pope proceeded to ask the boy about his masturbatory habits. He extracted a 'confession,' though with 'great difficulty,' and got the patient to promise to discontinue the habit. Thereupon, he injected morphine into his arm, and a month later the boy was dismissed from treatment, the very 'picture of health,' his sight restored and 'every type of anemia and mental imbecility' eradicated (Szasz 1984, 348–9).

Szasz contends that the case history presented by Dr Pope is nothing but a 'caricature' of medical diagnosis. [. . .] In Szasz's view, Dr Pope's 'diagnosis' of the 14-year-old boy is not science—he establishes no causal connection between the boy's masturbatory habits and his symptoms. Instead, it is pure rhetoric. What belief in the pathogenic powers of masturbation rested upon was the absence of a clear distinction between distress and disease.

Masturbation: Convenient Scapegoat

Because Szasz's main concern in *The Therapeutic State* was to challenge contemporary arguments that masturbation is therapeutic (for him, the medical profession has no more basis for claiming its therapeutic value now than it previously had in claiming its pathogenic powers), he did not develop his critique of the earlier pathogenic view in detail. However, in a recent article, 'Remembering Masturbatory Insanity' (2000), he returns to the subject, noting that, from the very beginning of scientific medicine, masturbation (or 'self-abuse') was a handy scapegoat when medical practitioners could not identify the cause of a

particular disease: 'By the end of the 1700s, it was medical dogma that masturbation causes blindness, epilepsy, gonorrhea, tabes dorsalis, priapism, consti-
pation, conjunctivitis, acne, painful menstruation, nymphomania, impotence,
consumption, anemia, and of course insanity, melancholia, and suicide' (Szasz
2000, 2). Among the widely accepted treatments of masturbation, the most
important were restraining devices and mechanical appliances, circumcision,
cauterizing of the genitals, clitoridectomy, and castration. He notes that as
recently as 1936, a widely used pediatric textbook recommended some of these
methods. The primary 'beneficiaries' of these treatments were children and the
insane, who were then, as now, the ideal patients because they were powerless
against their relatives and doctors, unable to resist 'being fitted with grotesque
appliances, encased in plaster of Paris, having their genitalia cauterized or de-
nerved, or being castrated—for their own good' (2).

In a concluding section of his paper bearing the heading, 'Error or Arrogance?'
Szasz suggests that this scapegoating of masturbation provides a valuable
warning against similar abuses of power today. Noting that young males have
always experienced and displayed nocturnal emissions, the manifestations of
normal pubertal male genital physiology, what was it that turned these emissions into dreaded 'symptoms' of dangerous 'spermatorrhea'? The same thing
that in our own day has turned youthful male exuberance into the dreaded
symptoms of dangerous attention deficit disorder, namely, 'parental annoy-
ance and anxiety combined with medical imperialism and furur therapeuticus'
(2000, 3). In Szasz's view, these are not innocent medical errors. Instead, the
belief in masturbatory insanity and its treatment 'enhanced the identity and
self-concept of the believers. Ostensibly, such beliefs assert facts; actually, they
credential believers' (4). Thus, 'none of psychiatry's classic mistakes—from
masturbatory insanity and its cures, to the disease of homosexuality and its
compulsory treatment with "aversion therapy," and to the attention of the cause
of schizophrenia to reverberating circuits in the frontal lobes and its cure with
lobotomy—are innocent errors' (4). Rather, these are instances of arrogance, the
abuse of power. [. . .]

Twentieth-Century Views: Masturbation as Immoral and Sinful Behavior

Most important for our purposes here, however, is the fact that, as the view of
masturbation as the cause of various physical diseases and mental disorders
was being abandoned in the first several decades of the twentieth century, the
view that it is immoral—a vice or sin—showed little sign of abating. Freud is
instructive in this regard. As Szasz shows, Freud did not view masturbation
as a cause of mental insanity, but he did contend that neurasthenia (a condition whose symptoms include lack of motivation, feelings of inadequacy, and
psychosomatic symptoms) may be traced back to a condition of the nervous
system caused by excessive masturbation or frequent emissions (Szasz 1984,
349). Freud also considered masturbation 'perverse' because 'it has given up
the aim of reproduction and pursues the attainment of pleasure as an aim
independent of it' (349). Thus, masturbation is problematic on moral grounds

because it departs from conventional, genital, heterosexual intercourse aimed at procreation. Menninger notes that when one of Freud's own sons came to him with worries about masturbation, he issued a strong parental warning against engaging in the practice, and this, according to another of Freud's sons, led to an estranged relationship between them (1977, 34). [. . .]

Menninger notes that Havelock Ellis, author of a multi-volume text on the psychology of sex and cited by Freud in his lectures at Clark University in 1909 as having coined the term 'autoeroticism' (Rosenzweig 1994, 428), complained in 1901 that Tissot's book on the disorders produced by masturbation had 'raised masturbation to the position of a colossal bogey, and accused Tissot of combining his reputation as a physician with religious fanaticism' (Menninger 1977, 33). To Ellis, it was clear that a major force behind the pathologizing of masturbation was the religious culture of the time. Thus, while the association of masturbation with various physical diseases and mental disorders declined in the first several decades of the twentieth century, its association with immorality and sinfulness did not.

Citing his own experience of growing up in America at the turn of the century, Menninger notes that 'in America the masturbation taboo has always been, until recently, very explicit.' It was never a crime, but it was considered a moral offense of such seriousness that many authorities joined hands in insuring its prohibition: 'To help stem the temptation of evil-doing, threats or inflictions of dire punishment were commonly made to children by all and sundry' (1977, 34). Parents looked for the slightest evidence of the sin, and school teachers were on the alert for it: 'To an extent difficult for the present-day reader to grasp,' masturbation was 'the *major sin* for middle- and upper-class adolescents a century and less ago' (35). Because it was secretly indulged in by the vast majority of adolescents, it was 'an ever-present, easily reached source of guilt feelings, often exploited by religious leaders. Consider the emotional conflict in a boy (or girl), instructed in the faith, that Jesus, the good man, the Son of God, died "for your sins," whose chief preoccupation was his propensity for repeating this dreadful act' (35).

What made it especially dreadful was the fear that one would be found out (either because one was directly observed engaging in masturbation or because one's body began to manifest one or more of its telltale signs). And, of course, religious leaders emphasized that God knows our 'secret sins,' that nothing can be hidden from the omniscient, all-knowing Father. Menninger notes that he once witnessed 'a large room full of university men bowed on their knees in prayer for forgiveness and for strength to resist the temptation of (this) sin' (35).

Masturbation as Sin: Disappearance or Displacement?

But, then, Menninger claims, an 'amazing circumstance' occurred 'sometime soon after the turn of the present [i.e., twentieth] century.' This ancient taboo, 'for the violation of which millions had been punished, threatened, condemned, intimidated, and made hypocritical and cynical—a taboo thousands of years old—vanished almost overnight! Masturbation, the solitary vice, the SIN of youth, suddenly seemed not to be so sinful, perhaps not sinful at all; not so dangerous—in fact, not dangerous at all; less a vice than a form of pleasurable experience, and a normal and healthy one!' (1977, 36). Menninger views this 'sudden metamorphosis in an almost universal social attitude' toward masturbation as 'more significant of the changed temper, philosophy, and morality of the twentieth century than any other phenomenon that comes to mind' (36). When the view that masturbation is a sin 'disappeared,' it seems that all sin other than crime disappeared along with it: 'This, in a way, now seems regrettable. For masturbation lost its quality of sinfulness through a new understanding, but there was no new understanding of ruthlessness or wastefulness or cruelty' (36). To be sure, 'a small amount of the disapproval of masturbation may have been displaced by previously undervalued "sins" such as those mentioned, but, in general, it seems as if the great phenomenon of a deadly sin suddenly disappearing—and disappearing "without anyone noticing it"—affected our attitude toward other disapproved behavior' (36).

Two points need to be made regarding the contention that the view of masturbation as sinful suddenly disappeared soon after the turn of the twentieth century. First, Szasz's account of attitudes toward masturbation in the twentieth century presents a very different and, in my judgment, far more accurate picture. In his reconstruction, there was a fundamental change in social attitudes toward masturbation, but it occurred during and after the sexual revolution of the 1960s. He views William Masters and Virginia Johnson's *Human Sexual Response*, published in 1966, and their subsequent book, *Human Sexual Inadequacy*, published four years later, as especially influential in this regard. If Samuel Tissot's book on onanism played a major role in shaping nineteenth-century attitudes toward masturbation, these books by Masters and Johnson had a similar influence in the latter decades of the twentieth century. While Freud had contended that the aim of sexual activity is reproduction, and that a sexual activity is perverse if it 'pursues the attainment of pleasure as an aim independent of it,' Masters and Johnson 'maintain the opposite view—namely, that the aim of human sexuality should be the procuring of pleasure' (Szasz 1984, 338). Thus, masturbation is not only acceptable, it is also highly recommended (e.g., for release of tension), and the problem that may require treatment is not engagement in masturbation but the failure to experience pleasure through masturbation.

Of course, there were members of the therapeutic community—Szasz included—who did not endorse this new understanding of masturbation. Szasz's opposition was based on his contention that, even as psychiatrists had no business endorsing the view that masturbation is immoral, neither do they have any warrant—scientific or otherwise—for endorsing the idea that it is a healthy activity. Many religious leaders also opposed it. However, Szasz quotes the following declaration by the evangelist, Ruth Carter Stapleton, sister of former President Carter, in the *Atlanta Journal* in the early 1980s: 'The Lord wants us to experience whole, complete lives, and He offers this gift (masturbation) to each of us as we surrender to Him' (Szasz 1984, 346). A clearer indication of how the moral and theological landscape had changed is difficult to imagine. It did not, however, happen overnight—as Menninger claims—and it did not occur shortly after the turn of the twentieth century. If there were indications of changing attitudes at that time, the 'almost universal' change to which Menninger refers took another 60 years.

Second, Menninger indicates that, for the most part, masturbation as an immoral or sinful behavior simply disappeared, that is, there was little displacement of the moral disapproval of masturbation onto other behaviors that are, in his view, clearly sinful. Rather, the disappearance of masturbation as a sin reflects the 'changed temper, philosophy, and morality of the twentieth century' (Menninger 1977, 36). I would agree that moral disapproval of masturbation was not displaced onto ruthlessness, wastefulness, or cruelty. However, in my view, such a displacement did occur in the last several decades of the twentieth century, a displacement of moral disapproval of masturbation onto homosexual behavior. As moral disapproval of masturbation has declined, moral disapproval of homosexual behavior has actually increased. Moral disapproval does not simply 'disappear.' Rather, it gets displaced. It is as though there is a constant amount of moral disapproval in American society, and if it ceases to be directed toward one behavior and its practitioners, it shifts on another behavior and *its* practitioners.

The Displacement of Moral Disapproval

The argument that the moral energy directed against masturbation was displaced onto a new object of moral disapproval, homosexuality, makes sense at a purely theoretical level, as the psychoanalytic theory of displacement refers to the redirection of an emotion or impulse from its original object (e.g., a person or idea) to another. It also assumes that this is an unconscious process, that the person (or, in this case, the religious culture) that engages in this displacement is largely unaware of the fact that it has done so. It knows, of course, what and who are its current targets of moral disapproval. But the original target of its moral disapproval is a distant memory. On the other hand, the two objects need to have something in common—while being sufficiently distinctive—for the displacement to do its work. Since, as we have seen, masturbation and homosexual behavior *do* have something in common that is deemed very important by those who engage in moral disapproval of both (i.e., the fact that both are sexual activities that do not serve the purpose of reproduction), homosexual behavior becomes a useful target for those who, for one reason or another, have relinquished their moral disapproval of masturbation. The fact that one of these behaviors is a solitary act (mutual masturbation between heterosexuals was rarely if ever included in the moral case against masturbation) while the other involves sexual behavior between two individuals enables the displacement to work, as this serves the purposes of insuring that the connection between them will remain unconscious. (The purpose of this article is to bring it to consciousness.)

The Mishandled Sex Life

Empirical support for this theoretical argument is provided by a book by
Leslie D. Weatherhead, published in 1932, entitled *The Mastery of Sex Through
Psychology and Religion*. While Weatherhead was an English clergyman, his
book was published in New York as well as London, and went through at least
11 printings between 1932 and 1947 (the year my copy of the book was published). [. . .] [It] has chapters on the mistake of silence and ignorance about
sexual matters, on comradeship and flirting, on the true approach to marriage,
on the unhappy marriage, on the question of birth control (which Weatherhead
strongly endorses), a message to those who do not marry, on the mishandled
sex life, on sex and society, and on healthymindedness. The chapter that most
concerns us here is chapter eight, 'The Mishandled Sex Life,' which covers the
subjects of masturbation or self-abuse, inversion or homosexuality, fetishism,
sadism and masochism, scoptophilia and exhibitionism, and venereal disease.
(Weatherhead seems not to be aware of the double entendre in the word 'mishandled'.) At 44 pages, it is the longest chapter in the book, and over half of the
chapter (26 pages) is devoted to masturbation. The section on homosexuality
ranks second, but at 7 pages it is about 27 percent the length of the masturbation
section. This suggests that when Weatherhead's book first appeared (1932), masturbation was by far the most important topic requiring treatment in a chapter
on the mishandling of one's sex life. Not only was homosexuality a very distant
second, but the fact that Weatherhead devoted nearly half as many pages each
to fetishism and venereal disease, and more than half as many to sadism and
masochism, suggests that homosexuality was not a subject that he felt was of
concern to his typical reader. This attitude is reflected in his citation of authors
whose statistics on the prevalence of the practice of masturbation ranged from
95 to 99 percent, though he states that 'my own experience would go to show
the percentage much lower, both in men and women, but much higher than
most people imagine' (Weatherhead 1947, 122). In contrast, while he asserts that
homosexual behavior is 'an exceedingly common one especially among unmarried women,' it is probably the case that 'true homosexuals are not more than 3
per cent of the population' (152).

    In his discussion of masturbation or self-abuse, Weatherhead distances him-
self from the view promoted 'in olden days—not so very olden either' that this
practice is 'the blackest of all possible sins' and that anyone 'who practiced it
was pretty sure of hell' (123). He notes that 'our grandfathers, including our
medical grandfathers,' taught that it was 'not only a dreadful sin, but that it also
had physical and mental consequences which were terrible; these consequences
being regarded as the just punishment of God for human wickedness. It was
said that the victim of this habit invariably brought disease upon himself and
that if he did not speedily check it he would go mad. Asylums were said to be
full of people brought there by this cause alone' (123). Evidence that such views
were still held in Weatherhead's own day was a youth's query of Weatherhead
whether it is true that the substance of the brain runs down the spinal column
and escapes with the seminal fluid. Another believed that it made entering into
marriage immoral because it rendered its victim impotent.

    Weatherhead assures his readers that, fortunately, 'most of what was held to be true in regard to masturbation, physically, psychologically, and theologically, we now know to be vulgar nonsense' (124). Physically, its effects are negligible: 'A person may masturbate daily for twenty years and suffer no more physical disability than a slight and temporary devitalization' (124). On the other hand, we cannot so easily dismiss the psychological consequences of masturbation, for 'masturbation in the adult is nearly always due to a maladjustment to sex and its continuance maintains such maladjustment' (124). He largely faults 'the Victorian taboo on the discussion of sex problems' as the primary cause of such maladjustment, as the reason for it is due less to the act itself and more to 'the false emotions with which it has been surrounded,' emotions 'the intensity of which are out of all proportions to the seriousness of the habit' (124). These emotions are guilt, shame, inferiority, self-loathing, horror, and, above all, fear.

But however much he regrets the sexual maladjustment that arises from the false emotions generated by 'the Victorian taboo,' Weatherhead believes that there is another consideration that needs to be brought to bear. There is the theological question whether or not masturbation is a sin. While condemning the older theological view that masturbation has dire consequences (e.g., that anyone who practices it may go to hell for this), he considers it potentially sinful to the degree that it conjures up 'mental pictures.' It is not the mental pictures per se, but what one does with them that determines whether masturbation is a sinful act. Because these pictures 'come from the depths of the unconscious mind,' we have no moral responsibility for the mere fact that they appear. We do, however, have responsibility for what our conscious mind does with them. It isn't necessary that we act on these pictures in the world around us. Rather, 'masturbation becomes sin when such thoughts are *deliberately entertained*' (his emphasis). Thus, what makes masturbation sinful 'is not the act itself, but the conscious reliving of imaginative pictures conjured up by the mind which accompany the act and produce the first stirrings of sex excitement' (126). He cites the case of a young man who masturbated five or six times a day and on every occasion 'the act was accompanied by the working out of an imaginative scene in which he took a lustful part' (126–7). He notes in this connection Jesus' condemnation of the imaginative 'looking' on a woman with intent to seduce her as 'a way of committing adultery' (127).

Weatherhead sees two dangers in the conscious entertaining of such imaginative scenarios. One is that a person may dwell on these mind pictures so long that one has no self-control when circumstances similar to the fantasy present themselves. The other is that one may come to believe that the mental picture has actually occurred, and this can lead to false allegations of seduction or rape. Not surprisingly, Weatherhead implies that men are more susceptible to the former danger while women are more prone to the latter.

While he views masturbation with conscious fantasy as sinful, he cautions that it is 'no worse in the sight of God than, say, to lose one's temper' (130). He also notes that everyone who has come to him for help has nearly always suffered from 'an exaggerated sense of guilt,' often referring to masturbation as 'the unpardonable sin' (130). He cannot believe that a sin that only harms the person who engages in it 'can be so bad in the sight of Heaven as a sin such as spiritual pride' (130). The 'social cruelty' that results from such pridefulness is far worse, in his view, than masturbation, which normally harms only who engages in it.

Weatherhead believes that masturbation is curable, and he sets forth a series of suggestions in this regard under the three headings of the psychological, religious, and physical. I will not discuss these suggestions in detail, but I do want to draw attention to his observation, under the heading of the psychological, that masturbation is an expression of narcissism, and for this reason is a form of 'misdirected' sexual energy. Defining narcissism as 'a psychological term which means a self-love that has become morbid,' he encourages the adult masturbator to view the habit as a means of satisfying 'an undeveloped, infantile self-love' (Weatherhead 1947, 134). Thus, he advises looking for and identifying one's hidden, thwarted, egoistic desires, and to redirect them toward more adult expressions of sexual desire. As the prevailing psychoanalytic view of homosexuality was that it, too, is narcissistic (Freud wrote in 1917: 'Homosexual object-choice originally lies closer to narcissism than does the heterosexual kind. When it is a question, therefore, of repelling an undesirably strong homosexual impulse, the path back to narcissism is made particularly easy' [Freud 1966, 530]). Weatherhead was aware, no doubt, that he was making an indirect association of masturbation and homosexuality, both of which are thus contrasted with mature heterosexuality.

Under the heading of the religious, Weatherhead suggests that because sex and religion are closely associated, religion provides excellent means for the sublimation of the desire to masturbate. He recommends training one's mind to focus on the face of Christ when it wants to picture sex fantasies, and notes that the picture of Christ blessing the little children, or as smiling and radiant, is better than picturing him as sad, anguished, and covered with thorns. [. . .]

Innate and Acquired Homosexuality

Weatherhead views 'inversion' or homosexuality as another example of the 'misdirection' of the sexual instinct, for the 'sex energies, instead of going out to the member of the opposite sex, are directed towards a member of the same sex' (Weatherhead 1947, 148). He identifies two forms of homosexuality, innate and acquired, and acknowledges that in its present state psychological science can do little to help those who are afflicted with the innate form. Alleviation through the use of hypnosis has been somewhat successful, but 'the word ["talking"] cure could not fairly be used' (149). Thus, treatment is generally directed to the deflecting of the sexual energies, the avoidance of all sex stimulation and the removal of the guilt-feelings which make the homosexual of this class feel a kind of outcaste or leper (149). In other words, the sexual energies are redirected (i.e., sublimated) and 'feelings of self-loathing and revulsion' are challenged on the grounds that this is a 'congenital abnormality,' probably 'due to remote prenatal causes' (149), and therefore neither vice nor sin.

Acquired homosexuality is more akin to masturbation in that it is not an innate 'psychological disharmony,' as is innate homosexuality, but a 'practice' in which one 'indulges' with members of the same sex. Weatherhead focuses on the question of whether such practices are wrong among consenting adults. Citing the case of a woman of 40 who considered herself 'married' to a young girl of 18, he advances three points in favor of the argument that it is, in fact, wrong. First, any 'perversion—here differing from a sublimation—always makes exceedingly difficult and frequently impossible the redirection of the sex energies to the biological [i.e., reproductive] channel if ever the way is opened up' (150). While the 40-year-old woman could respond to this objection that this does not concern her, it *does* concern the 18-year-old girl 'who has a reasonable expectation of normal marriage.' It is 'not right to do fellow beings an injury even if they welcome the injury' (150). Weatherhead does not say whether he would therefore be approving of a sexual relationship between two post-menopausal women.

Second, the fact that the older woman raised the question with him indicated her 'uneasiness of mind,' and subsequent inquiry showed that her uneasiness derived not from outmoded taboos but from the fact that her 'religious feelings were hurt,' as her behavior was inconsistent with her 'ideals and aspirations' (151). That these hurt feelings, ideals, and aspirations were shaped to a significant degree by the outmoded taboos is a point that Weatherhead neither considers nor addresses.

Third, and most potent for Weatherhead, is the psychological argument that in 'inverted practices' the 'sex instinct is roused and yet is not satisfied.' He compares it to bringing a hungry man to a hotel grill room so that he can smell the food, then not allowing him to eat it. To 'stimulate each other's sex instinct constantly and deny that instinct harmonious satisfaction is a practice fraught with peril indeed' (151). While not wanting to seem 'alarmist,' he observes that very few people have any idea of what an awakened and unsatisfied sex desire can do: 'The passion becomes sometimes uncontrollable and may lead in extreme cases to that unpleasant kind of nervous disorder called nymphomania in women and satyriasis in men.' He 'has seen cases of nymphomania—uncontrollable passion in women—and I can only say I do not want to see another. Women of good birth and breeding have been driven by it to give themselves to anybody and even to have relations with animals to satisfy the pangs aroused within them' (152). Here, Weatherhead makes a causal connection between homosexuality and sodomy [. . .].

Weatherhead believes that unless the 'inversion' is innate, the very same methods recommended for the cure of masturbation may effect a cure for acquired homosexuality. He recognizes that it may be more resistant to treatment, and that in many cases the most that can be done 'is the removal of morbid emotions and self-loathing, the reduction of sexual hyperaesthesia [i.e., unusual or pathological sensitivity of the skin], the fear that inversion is a sign of mental deficiency and the strengthening of the patient's spiritual life so that he may not cause others to acquire the perversion or endanger their well-being' (154). Significantly, his argument that masturbation may be sinful when it is accompanied by a conscious entertaining of mental scenarios is avoided in the case of both forms of homosexuality. In fact, he contends that the 'modern attitude must not be to label inversion as a loathsome vice . . . but as a psychological disharmony the causes of which we must investigate and the sufferers from which, with pity and skill, we must try to help' (154). Of course, he does not normalize homosexuality, nor does he even consider the argument that homosexual behavior may be an expression of adult sexual desire and of 'harmonious satisfaction' in its own right. But the fact that masturbation is so singularly and unqualifiedly narcissistic; that it typically involves the conscious entertaining of lustful mental pictures that may either be acted out in the real world or affect one's ability to discriminate between what is real and what is imagined; and that it is so universal, makes it an especially pernicious practice, even to a person like himself who wants to set aside the 'old taboos' and view it from the perspective of 'a modern attitude.'

The Redirection of Moral Disapproval

If, for Weatherhead, the primary forms of 'the mishandled sex life' are masturbation and homosexuality, and if, for Menninger, masturbation has 'disappeared' as a major sexually related sin, it should not surprise us if the moral disapproval directed against masturbation should be directed instead toward homosexual behavior. As Weatherhead himself emphasizes, the other forms of misdirected sexuality (fetishism, sadism and masochism, scoptophilia—or voyeurism—and exhibitionism) are primarily matters that require more 'technical' discussion than is appropriate for a text whose intended readership are young persons, their parents, and the clergy. That is, they clearly fall within the domain of psychiatry. He does not make similar caveats with respect to masturbation and homosexuality, thus implying that these two forms of misdirected sexuality are the concern of nonspecialists. This, in fact, is precisely the situation we find today. While nonexperts may continue to defer to the specialists on fetishism, scoptophilia, and so forth, they do not hesitate to express their opinions and views on homosexuality. (They sometimes invoke 'studies' by 'specialists' to buttress these opinions.) Lack of expertise—much less a personal self-identification as homosexual—is no deterrent to making one's views known on this particular form of 'misdirected' sexuality. Homosexuality is therefore the only issue, aside from masturbation, that remains from Weatherhead's forms of 'mishandled sex life' for the nonspecialists who wish to engage in moral disapproval. It alone satisfies the need to engage in the 'social cruelty' fueled by spiritual pride. Weatherhead's view that persons who are 'dreadfully shocked' by sex scandals are perhaps engaging in 'a form of sex-gratification' may also apply to many who are currently engaged in morally inspired attacks on persons who engage in homosexual practice. In any event, the one virtue of the view of masturbation as a sinful act is that it aroused the vast majority of members of the religious culture to be morally introspective (even if this introspection was itself misdirected), whereas the current focus on homosexual behavior as sinful enables the vast majority of contemporary members of the religious culture to externalize their sense of sinfulness and engage, instead, in moral disapproval of others.

Conclusion

The very year that Dr Pope reported on his use of morphine to cure a 14-year-old boy of masturbation, and exactly 100 years *before* evangelist Ruth Carter issued her rather stunning theological endorsement of masturbation in the *Atlanta Journal* (1979), Mark Twain delivered a brief, satirical talk on masturbation before a small group of American expatriates in Paris. The talk was considered so scandalous that it did not see print until 85 years later. Here is an excerpt from this talk:

> Cetewayo, the Zulu hero, remarked, 'A jerk in the hand is worth two in the bush.' The immortal Franklin has said, 'Masturbation is the mother of invention.' He also said, 'Masturbation is the best policy.' Michelangelo said to Pope Julius II, 'Self-negation is noble, self-culture is beneficent, self-possession is manly, but to the truly grand and inspiring soul they are poor and tame compared to self-abuse.' (Quoted in Szasz 1984, 351)

Menninger views Havelock Ellis as 'brave' and 'far-visioned' for having complained in 1901 that Samuel Tissot's supposedly scientific views on masturbation were heavily influenced by 'religious fanaticism.' But Twain had made essentially the same point several decades earlier. What could have been a liberating word was instead silenced.

This history should be instructive for those who have moral and/or religious objections to homosexual behavior. As we have seen, these objections have essentially the same moral basis as previous objections to masturbation, that is, that the primary purpose of sexual activity is reproduction, and neither masturbation nor homosexuality meet this criterion. [. . .] May we expect that the religious culture will soon abandon its moral disapproval of homosexual behavior? Freud's suggestion that the leadership structures of the army and the church are remarkably similar (1960, 32–9) bears on this question, as it appears that these two inherently traditionalist and conservative institutions tend to view this issue in remarkably similar ways and to use very similar procedures in handling cases of 'deviance' from the prescribed—that is, heterosexual—norms. Whether this similarity is grounds for hope or despair may depend on social forces beyond the control of either institution. But, in any event, these two institutions have rarely in the past been numbered among the vanguard as far as the abandonment of long cherished traditions of privilege and prejudice is concerned. As the suppression of Mark Twain's 1879 satire on masturbation would seem to suggest, the religious institutions, in taking themselves—and their deliberations—so seriously (see Saraglou and Jaspard, 2000), tend, in the end, to make *themselves* a laughingstock, fair game for ridicule and the all-too-familiar charge of moral hypocrisy. [. . .]

Literature

Freud, Sigmund. 1960. *Group Psychology and the Analysis of the Ego*, trans. J. Strachey. New York: Bantam Books.

———. 1966. *Introductory Lectures on Psycho-Analysis*, trans. and ed. J. Strachey. New York: W. W. Norton.

Graham, Wendy. 1999. *Henry James's Thwarted Love*. Stanford: Stanford University Press.

Haynes, Thomas, M.D. 1883. 'Surgical Treatment of Hopeless Cases of Masturbation and Nocturnal Emissions,' *The Boston Medical and Surgical Journal* 109 (July–December issue).

James, William. 1982. *The Varieties of Religious Experience*. New York: Penguin Books.

Kant, Immanuel. 1963. *Lectures on Ethics*, trans. L. Infield. New York: Harper & Row.

Menninger, Karl. 1977. *Whatever Became of Sin?* New York: Hawthorn Books.

Rosenzweig, S. 1994. *The Historic Expedition to America (1909): Freud, Jung, and Hall the King-Maker*. St. Louis: Rana House.

Saraglou, V. and J.-M. Jaspard. 2001. 'Does Religion Affect Humour Creation? An Experimental Study,' *Mental Health, Religion and Culture* 4:33–46.

Simon, Linda. 1998. *Genuine Reality: A Life of William James*. New York: Harcourt Brace & Company.

Szasz, Thomas. 1984. *The Therapeutic State: Psychiatry in the Mirror of Current Events*. Buffalo: Prometheus Books.

——. 2000. 'Remembering Masturbatory Insanity.' *Ideas on Liberty* 50 (no. 5): 35–6.

Townsend, Kim. 1996. *Manhood at Harvard: William James and Others*. New York: W. W. Norton.

Weatherhead, Leslie D. 1947. *The Mastery of Sex Through Psychology and Religion*. New York: The Macmillan Company.

Receptivity and Revelation:
A Spirituality of Gay Male Sex

Editor's Introduction

Within a span of seven years, Scott Haldeman, professor of worship, published two theological essays on the intimate male body: 'Bringing Good News to the Body: Masturbation and Male Identity' (1996) and 'Receptivity and Revelation: A Spirituality of Gay Male Sex' (2003). Both appeared in edited volumes on the religious dimension of masculinity and sexuality, and it is the latter piece which is reprinted below.

These two essays are emblematic of an embodied theology that is deeply confessional. The theological imagination is called upon in an effort of collapsing the spiritual and the sexual; sexual practices, Haldeman implies, are essential for the making of the male self.

Both 'Good News' and 'Receptivity' reveal a general body-positive attitude and a liberationist theological stance. Like James Nelson before (chapter 4), Haldeman does not condemn or control the erotic male body but wants to celebrate it and expand the sexual and religious imaginary. His language is intentionally direct. He does not want to escape to the safety of sparse metaphoric allusions or to employ a 'language of romance,' which would 'risk layering the topic with suffocating gauze' (Haldeman 2003, 221).

> I masturbate. I do it often and in a variety of ways. I do it most often in the shower . . . I touch my body, all of it, to wash, yes, but also simply to touch. Sometimes I linger. Sometimes my touch takes on an urgency that corresponds with a feeling of excitement inside that manifests itself in an erection . . . Then, my body tenses. My pelvis begins to rock. The muscles in my arms and legs contract. Blood comes to the surface of my body; my chest and face redden. And I come. Release. (Haldeman 1996, 111–12)

> To return to the practice itself, I like playing the receptive role in sex . . . First, as I play with my lover, I begin to feel a sense of anticipation. He attends to me, and I to him. As he wraps around me, lays upon me, or comes up behind, his erection touches my body, and I shudder. I sense my permeability, abandon notions of self-protectiveness, and I let him cross the membrane of my skin. (Haldeman 2003, 222–3)

Sexual practices that have been condemned, loathed, silenced, prohibited, and punished by religious, state and medical authorities are described in

Haldeman's essays in an unapologetic style that aims at healing. It is a language of care, not of provocation.

Publications by the Same Author

Haldeman, Scott. 1996. 'Bringing Good News to the Body: Masturbation and Male Identity', in *Men's Bodies, Men's Gods*, ed. Björn Krondorfer. New York: New York University Press. Pp. 111–24.

——. 1998. 'American Racism and the Promise of Pentecost'. *Liturgy: Journal of the Liturgical Conference* 14/4 (Summer):34–50.

——. 2001. 'The Welcome Table: Worship that Does Justice and Makes Peace'. *Liturgy: Journal of the Liturgical Conference* 17/1 (Summer):4–13.

——. 2003. 'Receptivity and Revelation: A Spirituality of Gay Male Sex', in *Body and Soul: Rethinking Sexuality and Justice-Love*, eds Marvin Ellison and Sylvia Thorson-Smith. Cleveland: Pilgrim. Pp. 218–31.

——. 2006. 'Beyond Idealization: The Role of Liturgy in the (Trans-)Formation of Racialized Identities in the United States'. *Studia Liturgica: An International Ecumenical Review for Liturgical Research and Renewal* 36/1:109–23.

——. 2007a. *Towards Liturgies of Reconciliation: Race and Rites among African American and European American Protestants*. Aldershot, UK: Ashgate.

——. 2007b. 'No Easy Peace: Cultural Diversity, American Racism, and Christian Worship'. *Call to Worship: Liturgy, Music, Preaching, and the Arts* 41/2 (Fall):33–45.

——. 2007c. 'A Queer Fidelity: Reinventing Christian Marriage'. *Theology and Sexuality* 13/2 (Spring):173–88.

Further Reading

Bersani, Leo. 1988. 'Is the Rectum A Grave?', in *AIDS: Cultural Analysis, Cultural Activism*, ed. Douglas Crimp. Cambridge: MIT Press. Pp. 197–222.

Boisvert, Donald L. 2004. 'The Lover and the Activist: Understanding Gay Male Sanctity', in *Sanctity and Male Desire*. Donald L. Boisvert. Cleveland: Pilgrim. Pp. 198–212.

Comstock, Gary David. 1993. *Gay Theology Without Apology*. Cleveland: Pilgrim.

Goss, Robert E. 2002. 'Is There Sex in Heaven?', in *Queering Christ: Beyond Jesus Acted Up*, Robert E. Goss. Cleveland: Pilgrim. Pp. 72–87.

Receptivity and Revelation:
A Spirituality of Gay Male Sex

SCOTT HALDEMAN

I am becoming a gay man. This is a life-long project and a large part of my work in this current phase of my life. Each day, each hour, each encounter, I must choose to be out or not, to be proud or ashamed, to be courageous or fearful, to 'flame' or to 'play it straight.' Each day I must choose to face and fight the stigma of tradition, society, and church, or allow it to eat away a bit more of my energy, my life. Each day, while the seminary for which I work is committed to the full inclusion of sexual minorities in the life of the church and society, the homophobia of other institutions threatens the meaningful work and livelihood of both myself and my partner, and so I must choose how much to put us at risk, calculate who knows whom, choose discretion or openness.

Each day, under such circumstances, I practice my own version of a gay life. I demonstrate my affection to my lover, kissing him goodbye in the kitchen since the porch seems too exposed, reaching carefully for his hand lest the couple behind us in the theater notice, searching out safe places to be together, reveling in each other's bodies at home, seeking yet more intimacy, exploring yet unfound pleasures. Each day, as well, I think socially, politically, theologically, ecclesiologically, and liturgically in queer ways, from a margin. Each day, too, I do things like read, prepare lectures, exercise, wash dishes, commute, and get ready for bed.

In all these things I, like you, practice who I am becoming.[1] I practice being gay as I practice being a teacher, a scholar, a father, and a spouse. I practice these things in relation to the choices available and the constraints that impinge on those choices.[2] In some ways, I am confined by the meanings given to notions of being 'gay,' 'male,' 'partner,' 'father,' 'liturgist,' 'white,' 'academic,' and many other labels, which I claim with more or less comfort. I negotiate them, too, accepting, rejecting, or most often making some sort of compromise with these images, categories, and boxes that are available, here and now, to me and the mechanisms that enforce them. Laurel Schneider challenges us to turn from a natural law understanding of sexual identity to a queer one in which identity is understood as communal and the norms governing behaviors are more about relational effect than the protection of static identity categories. She puts the matter this way:

> So whether I *am* a lesbian or *choose* to be one is relevant only in terms of what I ultimately do in community with being one. How, for instance, does being lesbian [or refusing to be lesbian] make me a better, more whole person working toward a better, more honest and peaceful world? . . . Does being a lesbian give me strength to love others more deeply and courageously? If the designation helps me with that—and in my case it does—so much the better. (Schneider 2001, 30–1)

Therefore, we must consider our practices in terms of their effects and choose, without ignoring real constraints, what will make us better neighbors and friends, more attuned to the needs of others and our world.

I reflect here on a few things revealed to me while 'on the bus.' While recognizing the roots of my queer self in earlier days, I have been 'in the life' for only a short while. In these few years of being 'out,' my eyes have opened to many new aspects of myself, of being human, of community, and of justice and faith. I focus here on one practice and, actually, on only one aspect of one practice, namely sex. Because sexual practices are particularly significant to gay male identity and at the same time culturally despised, they function as a locus of debate. Sex with another man is also particularly meaningful to me in ways that oppose hegemonic interpretations and, thus, is a compelling topic for me. However, a few caveats are in order.

First, I consider sex only as I know it, meaning sex involving myself and another man. This is rather limited in scope, surely, but necessary to keep as concrete as possible. In other words, I am not attempting to define revelatory aspects of sex generally, nor do I make any claim to speak for other queer folk, the term I use as shorthand for lesbian, gay, bisexual, and transgender people and other sexual minorities in a heterosexist society. I make no claim of insight into sex between women, sex between all men, or sex even of the other person with whom I have had sex. I simply cannot tell you what sex between men means, much less what sex in general means, but only about what some sex acts have meant and are continuing to mean to me, a white academic with leisure to think on such things, lately out, once married to a woman, and now in a long-term relationship with a man.

What I hope to accomplish by looking critically at my particular story is to encourage readers to reflect on their stories and thereby engender mutual learning through dialogue. This is both a methodological and epistemological claim. In other words, first I contend that articulation of the particular leads not so much to generalizations, but to conversations among those who bring their particularities to voice. And, second, our knowledge, limited by social location and perspectival horizon, is grounded in bodily experience and grows in analytical power only through recognition of these limits and in joining with others in critically appreciative dialogue. In other words, I reject the opportunity to impose my insights on others or define their experience. At the same time, I accept responsibility to consider the implications of my norms and values for others in a social system that coerces many through physical and social violence in order to protect the security and privilege of a few.

Second, as the title of this essay indicates, I believe sex is revelatory. By this I do not mean that when I am in bed, I regularly experience theophanies, the sensible presence of the divine, as witnessed to in Scripture: God in a burning bush that is not consumed, in cloud, fire, earthquake, and wind, or in the sound of sheer silence. Nor in light of Romans 1.18–32, a central text used to keep queer folk from ordination and full participation in the churches, do I consider my human lover a god. What Paul condemns here is idolatry, a temptation as much for heterosexuals as it is for queers. As far as I can tell, this has not been an issue in my own relationship, for as much as I love my 'husband,' I do not associate him with God.

Revelation, instead, has come to me in a way that I would call sacramental. Material, embodied, sensory experiences mediate, but do not delimit in themselves, particular, partial, and fragile aspects of divine reality, divine grace, and divine love. By sacramental experience, I am referring to something akin to an icon through which one sees, as through a portal, something of the attributes of God. In Christian tradition, material objects mediate God's presence as they are used communally and ritually to remember God's past saving activity and to imagine and rehearse God's promised future. Less traditionally but no less faithfully, in the commingling of bodies, I feel deeply and tangibly, yet fragilely and fleetingly, something of divine love. Sex as revelation is about mediated knowledge of God, about encountering God, in partial, momentary glimpses, through the act of encounter with my lover.

Third, my title indicates that I intend to outline a spirituality of gay male sex. Again, my claims are humble. My purpose is to evoke, not limit the reflections of others. But what is spirituality these days, other than a very slippery term? I like Don Salier's definition that Christian spirituality is 'living at full stretch' (1984/1996, 1) evoking Irenaeus's ancient claim, paraphrased as 'the glory of God is a human being fully alive' ('Against Heresies,' 1989, 490). Spirituality means the sum of life in relation to God and neighbor, comprising how one lives in this world and not simply a yearning for something beyond it. This way of life is inescapably relational and directed toward life abundant both in history and in hope of God's coming reign.

Finally, what aspect of my sex life am I talking about? Shall I employ the language of romance and risk layering the topic with suffocating gauze? No, while seeking not to offend or discomfort, I want to be clear that I am speaking about what I have learned in moving in a sexual sense from top to bottom. Already there are problems of euphemism: these words may imply a static structuralism that I neither promote nor experience. Over four years ago, in a flash of emotional and relational chaos, I found myself in an unexpected place of receptivity, a place where I now feel at home as I have felt in no other place in my life. In bed with another man, I have found myself not as the Leviticus code defines it, 'lying with another man as with a woman,' but as one the authorities considered unworthy even of condemnation, the receptive partner in gay male intercourse (Lev. 8.22). Opening myself to receive another physically has revelatory—spiritual, ethical, and theological—value for me, even as it is also a new source of pleasure, a practice that deepens relationality, and an inversion of my former self-understanding. By continuing to practice receptivity in a sexual sense, I am forming and being formed as a new person. I am finding this person more and more to be the one I want, for moral and ethical reasons, to become.

Am I condemning, along with the Levites, those on top? By no means. Am I positing that this act, this role, has better moral quality than others? By no means. While eschewing moral relativism, I understand human thought and behavior as profoundly ambiguous, enough so to be both potentially life-giving and revelatory, a locus of grace if practiced in mutual love and respect and, if not, potentially destructive, divisive, and death dealing. For this reason, all we do is in constant need of critical reflection and reform. My claim, then, is that playing the receptive role in sex can be healthy and healing, while it can also be destructive and harmful. Like other human practices, it involves risk. Andrea Dworkin sees penetration as colonization,[3] and I do not dispute that it can be for many women and some men, and yet it is not always so. It can also be a moral good even though condemned and rendered illegal in many locales inside and outside the United States. In addition, am I at risk for defining myself by this one practice, the dread of sodomy? Probably, but this is a risk worth taking in order to oppose the forces of hate and fear that threaten my living and loving and the lives and loves of countless others.

To return to the practice itself, I like playing the receptive role in sex. Moreover, on occasion, I experience it not so much as a desire, but as a physical need like hunger or thirst. As I receive and hold the other, I find myself feeling complete, whole, and yet yearning for more—more justice, more mutual respect, and more well-being for myself, my partner, communities near and far, and the whole world. For me, being receptive in sex is sacramental, and what sacramental occasions offer, in a proleptic sense, is fragile but real satisfaction and a promise of an ultimate, complete satisfaction of our deepest and best yearnings.

I would like to name and then expand upon four movements of anal intercourse. First, as I play with my lover, I begin to feel a sense of anticipation. He attends to me, and I to him. As he wraps around me, lays upon me, or comes up behind, his erection touches my body, and I shudder. I sense my permeability, abandon notions of self-protectiveness, and let him cross the membrane of my skin. He enters me. I am full of him, allowing him to touch me deep inside while holding him with my body. After we have rocked together, moved as closely as we possibly can, and found a rhythm that suits us both, he cums. I usually want him to stay inside me, hold me close, and share those final throes of orgasm, to partake and absorb him. Finally, in the moments and, on good days, for hours afterwards, I feel my openness, the stretching of my body to fit another, and be filled.

There you have an account of a despised practice. What religious traditions define as an unforgivable evil is an act in which I find life. How to explain the discrepancy? It is not enough to note it and move on. Too much is at stake: the vocations and very lives of my brothers and of my sisters, too.

For Leo Bersani, 'the rectum is a grave' (1987). In trying to understand society's revulsion toward anal sex during the escalating North Atlantic AIDS crisis, especially as it ravaged the population of men who have sex with other men, he notes how the victims of this scourge were portrayed as if they were killers. Anal sex was seen not merely as a risky behavior for transmitting a virus, but as the primary disease itself. Without subscribing to his ahistorical reading of anal sex, we can sense the threat felt in the larger culture about any man submitting to penetration in this 'blame the victim' stratagem. Contrary to my own experience, opening oneself to receive a male lover threatens masculine identity, something evidently so fragile that it must be protected by force. This disdain for anal sex between men shows both the depth of misogyny and the cultural mandate to define men as those who penetrate rather than are penetrated. Although I reject equating the experience of women as receptive sexual partners with that of men, the notion is found in scriptural descriptions of the penetrated man acting 'as a woman.' Other cultural slights imply that he has 'lost his manhood' and been 'feminized.' Such metaphors are long standing and apparently devastating to many men, outside of and within the gay community. The fear of feminization has given license to the bashing and rape of gay men, similar to ways in which misogyny is enforced through the rape of women. Within the gay community, this stigmatizing of receptive (male) sex has led to the development of more or less static sexualized categories, such as 'top' and 'bottom,' so that, perhaps, men may claim a more secure identity within a subculture of gender ambiguity that both reflects and subverts hegemonic definitions of masculinity.[4]

Better vocabulary for talking about sex and power is needed, and Susan Kippax and Gary Smith provide us with help (2001, 413–34). They recognize that phallocentric norms have deep-seated effects on contemporary Western society and on any cultural structures based on a static, hierarchical binary system of value: that penetration is power and the penetrated powerless, that one is either male or female, dominant or submissive, the inserter or the receptacle, active or passive—the latter in each dyad being, of course, also lesser. At the same time, Kippax and Smith have also found that in a major ethnographic survey in Australia gay men describe anal intercourse in ways that contest this static dualism. These men deploy new descriptors, such as active passivity, versatility, powerful receptivity, and pleasurable vulnerability.

Keeping this in mind, I seek interpretations of my own practices that contest the violence and disdain of heteronormativity, challenge static understandings of power, postures, and roles in sex and other human interaction, and help overturn phallocentric anthropologies. While acknowledging that I may find only what I am looking for, I seek complex, flexible, and ethically self-conscious ways of construing and criticizing my own behaviors. Without fostering naïve romanticism about the democracy of gay sex, my own sense of receptivity is not about being passive, but of fully participating in an act of mutual pleasuring. It is not about abandoning my maleness, but about reinventing it. It is not about surrendering control, but often about being very much in control, even while playing a supposedly submissive role. In any case, I understand control not as the exercise of power over the other, but about mutual care, intensity of sensation, and conscious role playing. Desiring and being desired, while practicing a healthy vulnerability, can be mutually pleasurable, as well as empowering and healing.

To gain a clearer understanding of how sexual receptivity contributes to spirituality, consider the phases of the sex act noted above. First, I assume a posture in which I can be entered. Second, the boundary of my skin is crossed. Third, I receive and am filled by another. Fourth, we commune in intimate embrace and movement, reaching toward ecstatic release. I take these four as spiritual values. They are touchstones for other parts of my life, as well. In other words, I am being formed in new ways by practicing this posture of openness and vulnerability, this permeability, this rhythm of emptying and being filled, and this regular, embodied communion. I will expand on each before concluding.

A Posture of Vulnerability

I am a student of ritual. As Ron Grimes notes, ritual is embodied, so ritual studies must attend to posture. 'A posture is not only one's manner of physical comportment (how one parks the body so to speak),' he writes, 'but also one's attitude—one's manner or style in the world. Attitude denotes the spiritual component of posture' (1993, 39). Other practices sustained over time also shape our attitudes and spirituality. Grimes uses the language of sexual posture to describe two competing liturgical styles. I find in my own sexual postures a new sympathy for what he calls liturgical supinity, forms of worship and ritualization that arise from the ground and from human need as opposed to those imposed, as it were, from the sky as unquestionable, what Grimes calls 'erect.' Suspicious of forms that 'render domination beautiful,'[5] I seek attitudes of prayer that tell the truth in all its complexity and stretch toward relationships of mutual respect and justice. So, too, I am suspicious of 'sacred' forms that claim divine inspiration and thereby exclude styles of prayer based in local culture, discourage criticism, and serve to maintain unjust power relationships. I want to encourage the construction of rites that suit particular communities in dialogue with, but not in slavish imitation of, inherited tradition.

Supine myself, I tarry for my sisters and brothers, desiring that we construct together ways of ritualizing that empower holy acts, such as gathering, story-telling, washing, eating, anointing, giving thanks, and raising cries of want and need. Yet I do so as a man, a recognition made all the more necessary because of Grimes's own heavily gendered undertones. As a man, I place myself in the vulnerable position of supinity. I do so with a strong sense of security, based on the trustworthy relationship in which I practice this posture, but also on the privilege and power at my disposal that allows me to speak up and act for myself, should violation occur. Many who have had trust betrayed, who know about sexual and other kinds of violence, and who have been forced into supin-ity, may find such a posture too problematic to assume voluntarily.

I honor the need both for self-protection and for a wide variety of practices that may contribute to building human community. Yet, because I remain con-vinced of my own need for trust and vulnerability, I place myself at the other's disposal, including the community, in order to foster richer, more honest, and more transformative forms of rehearsing the reign of God together. All this takes place in the context of worship and as worship. As Grimes concluded before a group of mostly male liturgical scholars, 'If you choose to embody and practice [the metaphor of supinity], it will stretch muscles you did not know you have. And you may be sure, you will be sore the next day' (1993, 58). Being supine can invite pain, literally and metaphorically, yet such a posture feels right and good to me. In it, I foster an attitude that avoids domination, engenders dialogue, and risks even the betrayal of trust in the hope of reconciliation and the increase of justice.

Permeability

Culturally considered, the anus is a place of dirt and discomfort. By allow-ing another person to approach this part of your body, you risk giving offense and being rejected as dirty, smelly, and ugly. Furthermore, opening to receive another into your body means risking pain and perhaps even harm. Such risks may also lead to pleasure, intimacy, and healing. Allowing another to come inside encourages me, in other places and times, to risk listening deeply to others across lines of difference, to touch and be touched in risky yet promis-ing ways. No doubt there are other ways out of the trap of hyper-masculine invulnerability, but living with permeable rather than rigid and unyielding boundaries is surely one. For instance, we may learn the value of risking peace rather than penetrating the enemy's defenses with smart bombs or to absorb the wisdom of others rather than imposing only irrefutable arguments upon them. Transgressing taboos against sodomy encourages me to reconsider the labels I paste upon others, denying them freedom to be truly themselves. Practicing permeability, I find myself more open and flexible as I try to live justly in communities of difference.

Of course, there are limits to risk-taking. I practice such permeability only in a relational context of deep trust. While some may find pleasure in inflicting pain, even sadomasochism and bondage require establishing clear lines of communication, including signals of approaching boundaries between what is pleasurable and what is violation. With the rise of 'bare-backing' (anal sex without condoms) among younger gay men, safe sex practices must again be encouraged, so that risk-taking does not lead to loss of yet another generation to AIDS. Adopting attitudes of permeability, while also being realistic about the possibilities of violation and transmission of a deadly virus, may encourage in us a fierce passion and yearning for abundant life, not a denial of suffering and death.

Emptying and Being Filled

The practice of being filled has helped me discover things about God. God's phallus as metaphor is not the problem it once was.[6] While the maleness of God remains central in Scriptures and so in theologies, it is now possible to relate in more playful and yet serious ways to these narratives. Ken Stone points out how the book of Hosea portrays God as the husband of Israel in ways that support sexist control of female sexuality, and yet this divine husband is also the cuckold. The power metaphor is broken, allowing space for queer images and, perhaps, queer lives (Stone 2001, 116–39).

The Bible's almost exclusively masculine images for the divine present a lopsided and dangerous picture, one that many women refuse to accept as normative because it justifies their entrapment in second-class citizenship in church and society. Certainly we ought not confine ourselves to the tales of ancestors for knowledge about God. We must continue to imagine God in new language that allows her to escape any attempts to confine her divine freedom. However, my delight in allowing my male lover to fill me allows me, analogously, to delight also in the intimate approach of the God who is imaged as male in Scripture. As Ted Jennings helps us see, this God also delights in the seductive dance of his beloved, David (2001, 36–74). I can delight in God as 'he' melts, molds, fills and uses me, as that most hilarious of hymns, 'Spirit of the Living God,' puts it. At the same time, I do not and cannot forget that God is *not* my male lover, does not literally seduce me, and also delights in others who find their pleasure and affirmation in different acts, bodily-based analogies, and relational metaphors. However, in practicing receptivity, I allow myself the pleasure of being overwhelmed by God who delights in me and wishes my good. This provides balance to other notions of God that I hold dear, invites my attentiveness to God's presence in and around me, and shatters the categories that have allowed keepers of tradition to confine the divine for too long.

Communion

Finally, the deep physical intimacy of sex with my lover echoes and deepens my understanding of communion. In bed, I give myself fully to our embrace and synchronized movement. I take him in, hold him deep, and partake of his touch and very being. This embrace has little other purpose than mutual pleasure. Queer love, despised and supposedly unproductive, is, in fact, often gratuitous and extravagant like the love of God in creation and redemption, like the kenosis of Jesus in his sojourn with us and his torture and death, and like the overwhelming love that graces the dead with new, incorruptible life.[7] The church as the embodiment of God on earth is charged to get on with discovering, celebrating, and living the promised era of wholeness, peace, and justice. For that work, Jesus promises his presence as people gather about the table. As Augustine, paraphrased, says about the table: 'See there, it is you, you upon the table, you the bread broken, the wine poured.' In other words, we are what we eat, this bread, this body. Communion is about ingesting, absorbing, and assimilating self to other, other to self, very God of very God, we, the body of Christ. Communing in bed or at table, I become more and more the lover and the beloved. I become more me, more in union with my male lover, with my neighbors, with the stranger, and with God. More and more love is rising, melts, overflows. More and more love.

Conclusion

I practice receptivity in sex and also in life. It is shaping me, as other things I do also shape me, but as a condemned practice, to do this is to practice transgression. Still fire and brimstone have not consumed me, and although surely the Day of Judgment is coming, I feel confident of divine approval of my doing of this act. While I do not deny the possibility of self-deception, and although biblical and theological traditions give little support, the inward and outward dimensions of my life grow richer, truer, and more whole in ways I take as indications of rightness. Perhaps God is not a lover of static structure or of hierarchies of values and set orders. Looking from the margins, from below in a physical and a social sense, I see a divine self that is more playful and more serious, quite uninterested in notions of purity, and yearning to become a new thing among us, a communion in which all will dance a wild dance of joy and passion. Therefore, I plan to continue assuming a supine posture and to practice permeability, emptying and being filled, and communion, joining gladly in this impure dance of passion.

Do my reflections spark responses in you? If so, I have accomplished my purpose, to encourage not so much agreement as your own desire to reflect on your own practices, sexual and otherwise, in relation to the whole of your lives. Despite hypocrisy, rationalization, and brokenness, what we humans do remains the clearest indicator of who we truly are. All practices exist in relationship to every other, not in anything resembling coherence, and yet the full spectrum of our doing shapes who we are becoming. So, too, our practices are shaped by, and shape, our notions of self, community, and God. Through our practices we are revealed, just as God reveals her divine self in glimpses of uncontainable glory. So, too, our practices are becoming; they are flawed and in need of critique and reform. None of us has it perfect. While, as Tom Driver (1977) has written, 'All my experience is Word of God for me,' such words are partial, fragile, and not (yet) wholly trustworthy. They must be sorted out in terms of their contribution to wholeness, justice, and truth. Therefore, we must find better, more honest, and more revelatory ways to talk together about what we do and why we do it, as well as what we condemn and what we value, if we are to 'find and follow pathways of freedom' (Driver 1998, v).

Notes

1 A provocative discussion of the role of 'practice' in human life comes from Pierre Bourdieu (1977, 72–95), who proposes that human beings learn how to act with competence in their society through a complex system of practices that are defined and constrained by a particular cultural field. He uses the term *habitus* to designate the dispositions that enable people to know what to do in a variety of situations that they encounter in life. This *habitus* does not determine one's choice since one can act inappropriately or otherwise violate social norms, but it does shape deeply one's self-understanding – body, mind and imagination – so that the range of choices available are defined according to the structures of the culture in which one lives.

2 In a critical assessment of Bourdieu's notion of *habitus*, Judith Butler (1999, 113–28) writes of the depth of coercion involved in enforcing particular interpretations of human identity ('being called a "girl" from the inception of existence is a way in which the girl becomes transitively "girled" over time') and of instances of resistances to such habituations, such as using terms of insult (e.g., 'black' and 'queer') as efficacious slogans for liberative social movements.

3 See Dworkin (1987). While her critique of heterosexual intercourse as a means of reinforcing patriarchy is relentless and compelling to a degree, in her fourth chapter entitled 'Communion,' she turns, I note with some surprise, to the novels and essays of James Baldwin in order to describe this same act, but now between men, as an act of grace, 'the intensity and magnificence of violent feeling transformed into tenderness' (60).

4 I reflect upon some ways in which masculinity is practiced among gay men in an unpublished paper, 'Resistance and Replication: Gay Men, Male Gender Roles and "The Chute,"' presented at the 1999 annual meeting of the American Men's Studies Association, Vanderbilt University.

5 This phrase is inspired by the poetry of Adrienne Rich (1981, 3–5).

6 While grateful for his insights on gender identity and worship of a lone male deity by male devotees, here I play on the title of Eilberg-Schwartz's *God's Phallus* (1994).

7 Seubert (1999, 71) discusses the generativity of homoerotic relations based upon the pure gift of self, as a distinct yet parallel value to the traditionally recognized procreative generativity of heteroerotic relations.

Literature

Bersani, Leo. 1987. 'Is the Rectum a Grave?' in *AIDS: Cultural Analysis, Cultural Activism*, ed. Douglas Crimp. Cambridge: MIT Press. Pp. 197–222.

Bourdieu, Pierre. 1977. *Outline of a Theory of Practice*, trans. Richard Nice. Cambridge: Cambridge University of Press.

Butler, Judith. 1999. 'Performativity's Social Magic,' in *Bourdieu: A Critical Reader*, ed. R. Shusterman. Oxford and Malden: Blackwell. Pp. 113–28.

Driver, Tom. 1977. *Patterns of Grace: Human Experience as Word of God*. San Francisco: Harper & Row.

——. 1998. *Liberating Rites: Understanding the Transformative Power of Ritual*. Boulder: Westview Press.

Dworkin, Andrea. 1987. *Intercourse*. New York: The Free Press.

Eilberg-Schwartz, Howard. 1994. *God's Phallus: And Other Problems for Men and Monotheism*. Boston: Beacon.

Grimes, Ronald. 1993. *Reading, Writing, and Ritualizing: Ritual in Fictive, Liturgical, and Public Places*. Washington, DC: The Pastoral Press.

Irenaeus. 1989. 'Against Heresies,' in *The Ante-Nicene Fathers* (vol. 1), eds A. Roberts and J. Donaldson. Grand Rapids: Eerdmans.

Jennings, Ted. 2001. 'YHWH as Erastes,' in *Queer Commentary and the Hebrew Bible*, ed. Ken Stone. London and New York: Sheffield Academic Press. Pp. 36–74.

Kippax, Susan, and Gary Smith. 2001. 'Anal Intercourse and Power in Sex Between Men,' *Sexualities* 4/4:413–34.

Rich, Adrienne. 1981. *A Wild Patience Has Taken Me This Far*. New York: W. W. Norton.

Saliers, Don. 1984 and 1996. *Worship and Spirituality*. Akron: Order of St. Luke.

Schneider, Laurel. 2001. 'What If It Is a Choice? Some Implications of the Homosexuality Debate for Theology,' *The Chicago Theological Seminary Register* 91/3:23–32.

Seubert, Xavier John. 1999. 'But Do Not Use the Rotted Names: Theological Adequacy and Homosexuality,' *The Heythrop Journal* 40 (January):60–75.

Stone, Ken. 2001. 'Lovers and Raisin Cakes: Food, Sex and Diving Insecurity in Hosea,' in *Queer Commentary and the Hebrew Bible*, ed. Ken Stone. London and New York: Sheffield Academic Press. Pp. 116–39.

The Sacrality of Male Beauty and Homosex

Editor's Introduction

The fear of intimate relationships, writes gay theologian J. Michael Clark, is not limited to heterosexual men but is affecting gay men as well (chapter 6). Competitive sexual prowess, he laments, is favored over against relational mutuality among gay men.

> Nongay men may actually be *envious* of the same sex intimacy and friendship they *perceive* among gay men, while, conversely, gay men wrestle with the threat of their socialized masculinity which such intimacy causes for them. Male-male competitive relational models certainly complicate gay male relationships and even their friendships, particularly if such men are *sexually* competitive. (Clark 1992, 27; italics in original)

Neither straight nor gay men can escape their male socialization under patriarchal conditions, Clark argues. Hence, gay men, too, suffer from lack of intimacy. 'Our masculine socialization precluded many of us from any deeper erotic pleasure than fleeting accumulations of genital experience' (Clark 1996, 253). As remedy, Clark advocates 'loving self-criticism' and genuine mutuality among gay men as well as a de-genitalization of sex and a de-ghettoization of gay lives. 'Afraid our emotions and interior life will be derided as sissified,' he writes, 'we become "emotionally constipated." We are taught not to be emotional and not to share emotions.' And, with a reference to the work of Ronald Long, Clark laments that the 'gay subculture only reinforces this message' (Clark 1997, 321).

Ronald Long presents a different view of gay sexuality as a way of becoming intimately male. He disagrees with Clark's assumptions about the potentially detrimental effects of the gay ghetto, arguing that a genuine and indigenous gay theology can only be envisioned in the ghetto as a space protected from external pressures. He questions Clark's suspicion that all sex outside of relational intimacy is destructive. He disputes the idea that promiscuous sex is necessarily tied to patriarchal values, which turn sexual partners into mere sex objects. 'We need a shift in perspective in order to be able to see "promiscuous sex" . . . with an appreciative eye,' Long writes (1994, 25). Cruising, tricking and sexual attraction are interactions in which gay men come into their 'own masculine maleness' (33). Degenitalization, he claims, would miss the point of gay sexual intimacy: 'it remains a fact that an erect male wants his erection touched' (35).

The disagreements between Long and Clark illustrate the different ethical assessments on how to think about the spiritual and sexual needs of gay men within a religious framework. Whereas Clark focuses on the ethical commitments of mutuality that accompany sexual pleasure, Long embraces the aesthetization of male beauty as a key difference between gay (promiscuous) desire and heteronormative regulations of sexuality (also Dutton 1995; Doty 1996; Luciano 2001).

In this chapter, first published in 1996, Long builds upon a Foucaultian understanding that sexuality – more than merely a sexual act – is a practice embedded in discourse that defines one's identity. A same-sex act, hence, does not make a gay man; only a broader practice of living constitutes gay identity, including a 'coming out' experience and a differently practiced sexuality.

Gay pride and gay courage—the courage to be gay—is rooted in the discovery of the holiness and sacrality of male beauty and gay sex. To be gay, in its deepest dimension, is in fact a religious vocation.

Publications by the Same Author

Long, Ronald E. 1994. 'An Affair of Men: Masculinity and the Dynamics of Gay Sex'. *The Journal of Men's Studies* 3/1 (August):21–48.

——. 1995. 'Toward a Phenomenology of Gay Sex: Groundwork for a Contemporary Sexual Ethic', in *Embodying Diversity: Identity, (Bio)Diversity, and Sexuality*, eds J. Michael Clark and Michael Stemmeler. Las Colinas: Monument Press. Pp. 69–112.

——. 1996. 'The Sacrality of Beauty and Homosex: A Neglected Factor in the Understanding of Contemporary Gay Life'. *The Journal of Men's Studies* 4/3:225–42; reprinted in 1997, *Que(e)rying Religion: An Anthology*, eds Gary David Comstock and Susan E. Henking. New York: Continuum. Pp. 266–81.

——. 2004. *Men, Homosexuality, and the Gods: An Exploration into the Religious Significance of Male Homosexuality in World Perspective*. New York: Harrington Park Press.

Further Reading

Clark, J. Michael. 1992. *Masculine Socialization & Gay Liberation: A Conversation on the Work of James Nelson and Other Wise Friends*. Arlington: The Liberal Press.

——. 1996. 'Gay Men, Masculinity, and an Ethic of Friendship', in *Redeeming Men*, eds Stephen B. Boyd, Merle Longwood and Mark Muesse. Louisville: Westminster John Knox. Pp. 252–62.

——. 1997. 'Doing the Work of Love: I. Men's Studies at the Margins'. *The Journal of Men's Studies* 5/4 (May):315–31.

Doty, William G. 1996. 'Baring the Flesh: Aspects of Contemporary Male Iconography', in *Men's Bodies, Men's Gods*, ed. Björn Krondorfer. New York: New York University Press. Pp. 267–308.

Dutton, Kenneth R. 1995. *The Perfectible Body: The Western Ideal of Male Physical Development*. New York: Continuum.

Luciano, Lynne. 2001. *Looking Good: Male Body Image in Modern America*. New York: Hill and Wang.

The Sacrality of Male Beauty and Homosex

RONALD E. LONG

Urvashi Vaid (1995) has recently summoned lesbians and gay men to explore what they stand for and represent, a task that is, to my mind, essentially a theological one. Theology—or, more precisely, religious reflection—is the public cultural enterprise by which humankind tries to establish for itself what it should finally be about and how. The nascent enterprise that is gay theology seeks not to articulate what traditional theology has had to say about homosexuality, but rather to give voice to what can and should be said ethically and religiously on the basis of gay experience. Gay theology, then, seeks to make a contribution to the general discussion that it is uniquely empowered to make. The reflections that follow have really grown out of my attempt to discover why the works of my pro-feminist and queer colleagues in this enterprise strike me as failing to make good on the promise of a distinctively gay contribution. However, what follows is finally an essay in what scholars call 'method,' my most sustained effort to date to discern the work of gay theology. The essay is comprised of three 'acts.' Act One develops a critique of the Foucaultian reading of gay identity that enables me to suggest that coming out can most comprehensively be understood as religious in character. Act Two develops an idea of religion in virtue of which the description of gay life as religious makes sense, and suggests a way of going about articulating the distinctive 'religiosity' of gay life. Act Three further refines the suggested method in a short discussion of how Clark's (1993; Clark and McNeir 1992) 'pro-feminist gay theology' and Goss's (1993) 'queer theology' miss the mark. I conclude with a brief characterization of the kind of contribution gay theology as I envision it stands poised to make.

'Coming Out'—An Act of Courage

Sometimes at a gathering like the annual Morning Party on Fire Island, where, in the clear light of the noonday sun, so many half-clad, smiling gay men have swarmed on the beach and are dancing to the beat of a common rhythm, it is easy to forget how much courage it takes to live an 'out' gay life. The reality of the context of gay life does not, however, disappear, even as it recedes from view. For, in our society, to live as an out gay man is to dare to live a life that is meaningful to oneself in spite of real risk to social (and even bodily) security.

It takes courage to recognize and to own one's difference from others and one's deviation from expectation. It takes courage to recognize that one's erotic interests and experimentation constitute neither a phase, nor something that can be chalked up to one night's drunkenness. It takes courage to own one's 'deviant' desires as an authentic expression of who one is. It takes courage to announce one's difference to the world, and it takes courage to live one's difference in the world.

Much of contemporary American society is not comfortable with homosexuals or homosexuality. Indeed, however tolerant some segments of American society may have become, society in general makes known that it prefers homosexual chastity, and expects homosexual invisibility. If homosexuals don't 'flaunt' their homosexuality, no one needs to be aware of the homosexuals around them. 'Don't ask, don't tell'—the code formulation of the current military policy respecting homosexuals in the military—actually captures the *modus operandi* of the general society. Richard Mohr (1994) is right. Society expects homosexuals to treat their homosexuality as their private 'dirty little secret.' In the general social praxis, homosexuality has the abject status equivalent to flatulence in an elevator—something everyone knows is there, but something no one will ask about or own up to (Mohr 1994, 113). And it is finally this abject status that even the boy who first begins to notice his 'difference' would want to avoid.

To be 'out of the closet,' however, to be 'gay' instead of merely 'homosexual,' is to refuse complicity in a social practice that would treat one's homosexuality as a dirty little secret about which one ought finally to be ashamed. It is to live one's homosexuality as humanly meaningful and downright respectable, social prejudice notwithstanding. Indeed, the out gay man does *not* live *as if* his homosexuality were respectable; he lives on the basis of an assumed respectability—social opinion notwithstanding. To come out is, of course, not a single act, but the beginning of a process. No one, on just coming out, knows what exactly the professional and personal cost that living as an out gay man will exact. But daring to live in a world that may exact personal, professional, legal, and indeed bodily punishment for living as an out gay man takes courage.

My point is that it takes courage to assume the moral high ground by coming out, and it takes courage to begin to dare to live a life that makes one so obviously vulnerable. And, unless one can understand the grounds of this courage, one has not yet understood the meaning of homosexuality in and for our day. The thinking of many contemporary gay activists and gay academics is rooted in the thought of the late Michel Foucault. While this is not the place to engage the thought of Foucault in any detail, a brief sketch at this point will enable us to see why his approach fails to account for the epiphany of the courage to come out of the closet and live as an out gay man.

Foucault's work constitutes a series of assaults on the 'culture of authenticity.' For Foucault, there is no core 'self' that uses cultural forms to discover, express, and reveal itself. Rather, the self—or better, subjectivity—is an emergent reality determined by those very cultural forms and practices. Subjectivity is the product of learning to think and handle the self in terms of the social practices and conceptualities of the culture in which a person lives. We become aware of ourselves as 'subjects' as we conform, adapt, transgress, or otherwise contest the labels that are available in our society for self-description. To be a prisoner, for example, is not a biological given. But rather, learning to think of and handle the self as a prisoner is a product of one's imprisonment under the watchful eyes of one's guards. Subjectivity, then, is a product of subjection by the culture.

Foucault thinks of 'having sexuality' rather like he thinks of 'being a prisoner.' Under the tutelage of catholic Christendom, the West learned the habit of self-examination. Under the tutelage of nineteenth-century medical classificatory science and the emergence of the psychological 'sciences,' modern Westerners have learned to examine the self in search of its biologically determined 'sexuality.' We see ourselves as 'having a sexuality' that needs to be 'expressed,' not because we have a sexuality that must be expressed, but because we have learned to think that we do.

For Foucault, the idea of having a sexuality is so historically anomalous as to be trivial. But the 'discursive practices' associated with sexuality are particularly burdensome for those who learn to think of themselves as homosexual. Within the regime of sexuality, homosexuality—a term invented in the nineteenth century—is an abnormality and perversion. To see someone as 'homosexual' then is to see them as a 'freak.' Seeing someone as a 'homo,' a freak, is a strategy by which the normals effectively disenfranchise and silence the homosexual: a homosexual is someone who does not need to be listened to, for he is but a freakish formation, a mad man. For Foucault, to think of and handle the self as homosexual is ultimately to become an accomplice in the self's own oppression.

However, because categorizations of people ('identities') position them within systems of power in a society, subordinate status can easily breed insubordination and resistance. In the form of resistance that Foucault calls a 'reverse discourse,' the prisoner may assert, 'Yes, I'm a prisoner—but, I'm not ashamed of it. I'm proud of it. I refuse to think of myself as societal refuse.' So too the homosexual may declare. 'Yes, I am homosexual. And I'm proud . . . I am a gay man!' ('Gay' here figures into the discourse of sexuality as the 'reinscription' of the category 'homosexual.') Although it is difficult to see that the 'resistance' offered by the discredited and oppressed is anything but an impotent protest, lacking in transformative potential, Foucault finds such resistance healthy and ethically sound.

Indeed, Foucault's concerns in the end turn out to be ethical ones. His analyses are meant to subserve and make possible ethical creativity. 'From the idea that the self is not given us, I think that there is only one practical consequence: we have to create ourselves as a work of art' (quoted in McNay 1992, 351). I question whether subjectivity, as he earlier characterized it, is the kind of thing that can exercise the kind of creativity Foucault endorses; but whether Foucault the ethicist actually outruns Foucault the analyst is a matter I will leave to the experts in Foucault's thought. It suffices in this context to consider how such 'self creation' looks under the regime of the discursive practices of sexuality. In the first instance, Foucault—and Foucault's 'queer' followers—bid us 'invent' new discursive practices that can ideally avoid the social dominations the discourse of sexuality involves. Second, the self-identified homosexual, for instance, is not to allow society to determine what being a homosexual means, nor what a homosexual lifestyle should look like. The gay man is to make of his homosexuality what he will! The person then, or more specifically, the person's body becomes the locus for a contest over the meaning of the person, the site for a contest of wills between society and the individual. Unfortunately, in Foucault, the quarrel seems to me to be about nothing more than who is in control. Foucaultian freedom fails to carry the weight and heft of a morally admirable individuality, but reveals itself to be rooted in nothing more than what my forbears would have called 'sheer cussedness,' a mere 'againstness.' Foucaultian ethics finally bids us become moral dandies, not self-determining individuals—rugged or otherwise.

In sum, it seems to me that Foucault's *oeuvre* fails the gay community in two respects. The suggestion that an identity based on sexuality is a trivial matter is an affront to the courage gay men show in coming out as gay men. Second, and more importantly, gay pride is more than an assertion of power. Moral integrity is trivialized to the extent it cannot be seen as grounded in something other than sheer willfulness. Foucault, as Charles Taylor has noted, seems to draw on the idea of 'authenticity' that he otherwise repudiates (1992, 61). And his repudiation blinds him to the conditions for 'authentic existence'—to those horizons of significance external to the self that guarantee the meaningfulness of the self's choices—as well as to those 'internal' conditions whereby choice becomes 'meaningfully mine.' It is the latter blindness that concerns me here. The problem, as I see it, is the lack of a fully rounded understanding of individuation in the Foucaultian project. In particular, I think Foucault can be faulted for overestimating the determinateness and determination of language, and underestimating the determinateness and the determination of the body. Simply put, Foucault attends to how people talk, not to what they may be saying.

In the first instance, Foucault operates with a sense that creation, and by extension self-creation, is a matter of imposing one's will on an alien material. In such a perspective, an artistic medium is mere material, mere matter, an alien substance that the artist can bend to his will. It is because the body of the self is analogously understood as having a certain alien independence of the self that it can thus become the site of a war between the self's will and the 'will' of the culture. Eliot Deutsch (1992), it seems to me, has presented a much more compelling account of artistic creation. An artistic creativity that exercises a willfulness over its material makes for bad art. Good art results from an artistic creativity that contains a humility before and respect for its medium. Rather than imposing an alien will on a foreign material, a truly creative artist gives form to a creation that is integrally related to the potentialities of the medium. For such an act, Deutsch proposes the image of 'cooperative control'; and creativity becomes an act of 'working with, rather than coercive control over, the principles or structure of a medium' (1992, 158). By extension, self-creation could be understood as a co-operation with the material (body) that is an inchoate— but not formless—proto-self. Neither the self nor its body should be understood as a mere cipher, only the site of the assertion of a cultural or an individual will to power.

Moreover, so busy is Foucault in attending to the system wherein the word 'gay' signals a diagnosis that he remains deaf to what gay men may in fact be saying by identifying themselves as gay. It is inadequate to think that people simply plug into or get caught up in the discursive practices of their society. And the relations of power implicit within such discursive practices remain but one factor as people negotiate their way by and with the socially mediated identities available to them. Indeed, it is helpful to see the way people position themselves within the 'systems' at hand as complex sets of negotiations—in the course of which the person achieves definition, and discourses and discursive practices *may be altered*. That is to say, people 'use' cultural forms to achieve meaning; 'meaning' is not exhausted in the forms themselves. Specifically, I would argue that identities are best understood as strategic acts of self-interpretation by which a self brings itself into determinate focus. [. . .]

In short, I hold that an understanding of contemporary 'gayness' cannot avoid the issue of gay subjective selfhood. However, if being gay is a way of creating the self in its individuality in accordance with the tendencies of the self's individual material, it would seem that the ways of being gay would be as numerous as the different individuals who understand themselves as gay. However, if the word 'gay' is not to lose all determinateness, we must allow for the possibility of common patterns of usage among some gay men. We must at least hypothesize that there is some shared core that grounds a gay identity for at least most—if not all—gay men. Without ruling out idiosyncratic usage, this line of thinking will allow us to see much of the plurality in gay life as evidence, not necessarily of different meanings of the word 'gay,' but of different ways of being gay. But where might we find such a core? [. . .] A personal remembrance might help us here.

Sometime after his diagnosis with AIDS, my now deceased lover Jim let it be known that he was no longer interested in talking or thinking about men— much less interacting with them—in the ways that had 'gotten him into trouble.' As the illness progressed, it became probable that, at some point, Jim would have to undergo a diagnostic spinal tap. Spinal taps, he had heard, were painful; and he dreaded and feared the prospect of having to have one. Eventually, the day came when he would have to undergo the procedure. While weekending at the cabin in the country we owned at the time, Jim had his first seizure. The local rural hospital was unaccustomed to AIDS patients and did not know what to do with him. It was decided to send him by ambulance back to a New York City hospital for whatever treatment would be necessary. Jim was to be met there by his friend Merle, since I had to go back to the cabin and gather the cats before heading back to the city in the car. By the time I got there, Merle told me that Jim had already had the dreaded spinal tap. When I asked him how he had fared with it, Merle told me that Jim's doctor had turned out to be a real hunk, and Jim had just 'melted.' He even joked about whether Jim had even noticed the 'discomfort'—that misnomer for pain so rampant in the medical community—of the procedure. I breathed a sigh of relief, and I recognized the Jim I had taken as a lover, the gay Jim who had returned if only for a moment.

The story, it seems to me, points to a susceptibility—indeed, an erotic receptivity—to masculine beauty at the heart of many a gay man. And it is this receptivity I argue that grounds a gay identity for most gay men. The theme of male beauty is a vastly underplayed theme in current theory. I would here place it in the forefront of analysis. Being gay is not simply a matter of erotic interest in other males, but of a responsiveness to the beauty of other males, a responsiveness that includes the sexual. For gay men, I submit, there is a compulsion in a magnificent male that commands attention and solicits . . . the word 'worship' will suffice for the moment. And sexual interest here may be seen as a mode of such worship. But there is more. Brian McNaught relates how many in his workshops own up to living 'for the nod of acceptance from someone better looking' (1988, 67). That is to say, many gay men confess to drawing strength from the attention—an attention that can range from a nod to a lay—from someone who is good-looking. Further, to be gay is minimally to find sex with other men one finds attractive a captivating prospect. And while there may be a few gay virgins, gay men typically seek out, enjoy, and find life-affirming sex with other men.

But the mere acknowledgment of the presence of such an erotic responsiveness to masculine beauty as part of oneself does not a gay man make. Nor does it ground the courage to come out. The gay man is one who finds that these realities are to a great extent his anchors to life and to the world at large—and one who treats them as foundational realities for a good life by giving them prominence in how he goes about leading his personal life. [. . .] Lastly, to echo the clarion shout of an earlier generation, an assertion we have not heard loud and clear for some time now, 'Gay is Proud!' The gay man refuses the abject status that society seeks to assign him. He refuses to be ashamed of what is so deeply important to him. But these are refusals that are part of his discovery of gay dignity, gay pride. His love for male beauty and his love for males, these are not things to be ashamed of, but venerable realities to be celebrated and revered. Indeed these things are realities, the neglect of which is felt to result in the impoverishment of life, the very essence of 'sacrality.' A gay man is one who recognizes and lives by the 'sacrality' of masculine beauty and homosex. And 'coming out' is a gay man's refusal to live a life that belies the sacrality of what he holds sacred.

Herdt and Boxer have recently described the discovery of that gay 'pride' that grounds the act of coming out as a species of 'moral conversion' (1993, 18–24)—the breakthrough to a valuation in spite of social prejudice and pressure to the contrary. Conversion may be prompted in a number of ways. We are social beings and have a tendency to join with those we like in seeing the world through their eyes. But even if our conversion was a product of coming to see things the way our friends do, no conversion is long lasting in which one does not come to experience for oneself the appropriateness and the deep satisfactions of the new life the conversion has made possible. As theologian Gordon Kaufman observes, even coming to believe in God is above all a matter of the discovery of the 'fittingness' of the life that faith in God implies (1972, 226–56). The words of a theologian here serve to remind us—whether we preface the word with 'moral' or not—that conversion is part of the vocabulary of religion. In his essay for the 1993 Gay Pride issue of *The Village Voice*, Richard Goldstein argued that the religious right is correct in sensing a religious challenge in the gay rights/gay liberation movement. Being gay, he suggests, is itself a 'faith' (1993, 26). I think he is right. Gay pride and gay courage—the courage to be gay—is rooted in the discovery of the holiness and sacrality of male beauty and gay sex. To be gay, in its deepest dimension, is in fact a religious vocation.

Being Gay as a Religious Vocation

The suggestion that being gay is a religious option has important political repercussions in a society for whom freedom of religion is a constitutional guarantee. But the suggestion that being gay is itself a religious phenomenon must surely sound strange to many a contemporary Western ear. Isn't religion a matter of faith—or at least belief—in a worshipful reality designated by the word 'God'? And hasn't religious belief—and Western religious belief, in particular—always found homosexuality the mark of irreligion and divine defiance? This is not the occasion to disavow ourselves of those Western prejudices that inhabit a full appreciation of the religious dimensions of human existence. I do, however, want to suggest a way of viewing religion in the light of which the claim for a religious dimension to gay life makes sense. [. . .]

Just as every boy comes to realize that just having a penis does not qualify him as 'being a man,' so being fully human is something other than our mere biological endowment. Our humanity, our humanness, our humaneness, is rather a direction in which the biological is channeled and cultivated. A religious tradition is a clustering of a culture's historical answers to the question about what makes us fully human, in essence providing strategies for self- and group-cultivation.

Typically, any given religious tradition will isolate certain focal realities that it understands we neglect at our peril and honor to our good. Indeed, what makes any given focal reality sacred is the perception that 'synchronicity' with the sacred reality is the condition for full and significant life. That is not to say, however, that sacral realities are necessarily 'worshipful.' Santayana taught us to recognize two distinct modes of religious 'reverence,' distinguishing 'piety' from 'worship' on the basis of the moral standing of the object of reverence (1982, see esp. 177–213). Piety, Santayana argued, is a recognition and honoring of the *sources* of our lives and the steadying of our lives by that attachment (179). But piety—since it can be directed towards such things as one's ancestors, one's parents, one's nation, or nature itself—is perfectly consonant with moral imperfection in the object of piety. 'Worship,' on the other hand, is the ascription of absolute worth, the recognition of the revered reality as absolutely good. Religion is thus not to be understood exclusively as a relation with a worshipful 'god'—but rather as one's relations with any revered reality. It follows, then, that a group's or an individual's religious life is pluriform, constellated by the multiplicity of things revered and whatever pattern of hierarchy in which those realities are ordered—which may or may not include a relation with a morally perfect sacred reality. This is an important point; for, when I claim that being gay is religious in character, I am not claiming that being gay is *the* religion of gay men. Gay life is not a cult in that sense—nor does it involve the recognition of a sacrality that is 'jealous' of other sacred realities. Rather, while the valuation of male beauty and homosex that anchors gay life is itself religious, it is a reverential tie that will probably take its place among other sacred ties.

However, religion is not a mere matter of recognizing sacred realities. Any given religious tradition will not only isolate certain focal realities, synchronicity with which makes life full and meaningful, but will also sketch the way of moving about in a sacred manner that constitutes such 'synchronicity' with the sacral realities; and will in turn offer certain basal self-understandings, 'identities,' derived from such sacred movement (cf. Obenchain 1994, 126–9). A religion is above all a path for life. The Buddhist who bows before an image of the Buddha understands himself not as honoring an individual, but expressing his respect for Buddhahood, a potentiality of all humans (or in some cases all beings) and devoting himself to the cultivation of his own 'enlightenment.' So he sits down in the posture of the Buddha imaged before him and proceeds to meditate as part of the path to Buddhahood. [. . .]

If speaking of the religious dimension or character of gay life is at all valid, as I think the fruitfulness of the reflections that follow will show, it will mean that no understanding of gay life that is blind to its religious dimension, its implicit spirituality, will be adequate. Second, if understanding gay life requires an appreciation of the spirit of gay life, the characterization of gay life as religious further suggests a strategy for understanding that spirit, namely along the lines required for the appreciative understanding of any religious form. [. . .] [I]f we are to appreciate how and why male beauty and homosex are found to be sacred, and what being gay means in light of that sacrality, we must attend to the way that gay men go about living with, for, and by those sacral realities that gay men as gay men live by and for, in short, how they ritualize their lives in relation to masculine beauty and homosex.

But where should we look for the ritualization of gay life? Once again, an analogy from the 'recognized' religions comes to our aid. At the expense of a certain facetious characterization, it seems to me one can speak of Buddhism as proffering a salvation of 'attitude adjustment.' The Theravadin Buddhist tradition (the Buddhism 'of the elders') has always insisted that such a massive attitude adjustment—an adjustment that is not merely a temporary relaxation, but a final transformation however variously described—requires a full-time occupation. For the Theravadin tradition, then, only monks stand a chance of realizing a 'nirvanic psychology.' Yet, it is interesting to observe that in a country like Sri Lanka, which is identifiable as a Theravadin Buddhist society, so many people who would not hesitate to identify themselves as Buddhists do not practice the kind of religious discipline that is characteristic of monks seeking to realize 'nirvana.' And this has tempted some observers to postulate two separate religious systems as operative—the religion of the laity and those 'monks' who function chiefly, if not exclusively, to provide the rituals the laity seek, and the very different religion of the meditative monks. As William LaFleur has noted, however, what the observer misses is the common conviction that any human life is a sequence of lives (1988, 105). While the villager may seek the aid and blessings of the various Hindu-derived divinities and Buddha-figures [. . .], her quest for the goods of this life and a better life next time around can be understood as one step in the quest for a life in which one is free to become a mediating monk. That is, although no villager may explicitly desire to be a monk, it is the monk's pursuit of nirvana that is the 'point' of the good life the villager seeks. In a similar way, I would argue, it is life as it is ritualized in the gay ghettos that is the distinctively 'gay' way of relating to the sacrality of male beauty and man-to-man sex. Gay men, of course, find themselves in a variety of social locations and have a plurality of personal agendas. Not every gay man aspires to live in the ghetto—nor do they aspire to live like ghetto gays. Nor should they. There are many ways of living as gay men. Nevertheless, I am arguing that the life style of the ghetto gays constitutes a paradigmatically determinant 'gay' way of relating to the sacred realities of gay life. To invoke another image I have exploited in another place, what is characteristically gay is the ability to own the ghetto, if not as home, at least as 'hometown' or 'home base'—and to welcome ghetto gays as fellow worshippers at the altar of male beauty and man-sex. [. . .]

But the gay ghettos should not be seen as areas to which gays have been relegated, but rather as sections where gays flock to be with other like-minded individuals, places where they are free to be 'gay' with one another. As a matter of social history, these gay areas have been built upon and expanded from the sociality of the gay bars. While originally it was the walls of the bar that allowed gays to gather together in a space far from the disapproving glances of the wider world, the walls of the bars no longer function chiefly to isolate gay fraternization from the eyes of passers-by, for visible gay communities have grown up around them, and gay socializing is publicly visible on the streets around the bar. While one might be tempted to think of gay areas as 'sections' or 'neighborhoods,' the label 'ghetto' emphasizes that these are sacred precincts whose separation expresses the social inversion they represent. As Woodhouse (1993, 28) argues, in the wider life of the city, gays are exceptional and invisible. However, in the ghetto, gayness is taken for granted—invisible because of its very 'normalcy.' At the same time, however, because it is the place where gays congregate as gays and freely interact as fellow gays, it is the place where 'gay-ness' becomes determinate and recognizable, hence visible. It is the place, then, where what is distinctively gay is free to make itself manifest. Since the 'ghetto' is not just a neighborhood, but a communal life that has grown around the bars and the baths, and the bars and the baths are the institutions that in turn pro-vide a determinate sexual delivery system, sexuality is manifested as founda-tional to 'gay' life—and the pursuit of sex associated with the bars and the baths is to be understood as the determinative ritualization of the gay religion of male beauty and mansex.

Envisioning an Indigenous 'Gay' Theology

The men of the gay ghetto have by and large been abandoned, if not betrayed, by many an activist and academic alike. Indeed, the 'schools of thought' that have begun to emerge out of the gay community all seem to share a common disaffiliation from the gay ghetto. Typically, 'assimilationists' are calling for the legitimization of gay marriage. I, for one, am unsure how many gay men are actually clamoring for 'gay marriage' as such. Rather, of more immediate con-cern are those particular rights and privileges that married partners enjoy that are especially problematic for gay couples especially in the age of AIDS: the right of inheritance, the right to be counted as 'immediate family' who can visit in the hospital and determine the direction of care, the right not to be kicked out of an apartment when one's lover has died, and so forth. While conservative liberals (or is it liberal conservatives?) like Andrew Sullivan (1995) seem to be content with giving gay men the option of marriage, spokesmen for gay coupling like Bruce Bawer (1993) seem to hope that the option of marriage or some form of socially sanctioned gay union will prove to be a way of domesticating the ghetto. The ghetto—or particularly the promiscuous lifestyle characteristic of the ghetto and the gay subculture—is for these latter types an embarrassment, as well as an impediment to social and political progress. From here, it is but a short step to viewing the lifestyle of the gay ghetto as symptomatic of a mascu-line difficulty with monogamous intimacy that is itself the product of a diseased process of masculine socialization in a dreadful hegemonic hetero-patriarchal order—in sum, a short step to the 'gay' feminism of a J. Michael Clark (cf. 1992) and a John Stoltenberg (1993).[1]

The political leverage gained by the disavowal of the ghetto is obvious. If the 'gay (read: ghetto) lifestyle' is typical of only some gays, then the (religious) right's intolerance of gays based on their rejection of the 'gay lifestyle' is undermined. I prefer to allow the ghetto the moral high ground: men in the ghetto, it seems to me, are much more honest about some elements of our common life, knowledge of which the general culture prefers not to acknowledge. Second, the gay ghetto may be pioneering a workable life that the general culture would do well to share.

'Queers,' as a group, seem far less bothered by ghetto promiscuity than ghetto particularity. They are troubled by the way gay and lesbian politics tends to 'privilege' issues of sexuality over those of race, class, and gender. They are dismayed by the way so many gender misfits are marginalized by the 'gay mainstream.' Fearful that self-discrimination, the acknowledgment of one's uniqueness and difference, entails social discrimination, they have tried to invent a non-exclusionary identity that forges a solidarity (at least in name) among all the marginalized and oppressed.[2] As a matter of practice, queers are driven to root out any political incorrectness that would threaten the integrity of any actual or potential coalition with other marginalized groups. Indeed, for queer thinkers like Robert Goss, political action entails the purgation of all the hated -isms of our time from the group as well as the world at large. Unfortunately, the fusion of horizons involved in such coalitional politics tends to dissolve, rather than celebrate, difference. And as the difference sexuality makes is blended into a generic 'being different,' the power of sexuality so important to the gay ghetto is conscripted as but an instrument in a total revolutionary transformation of the world on behalf of all the marginalized—the contours of which remain unclear. 'Queer' identity and politics represent, I am suggesting, a flight from particularity; I, in contrast, would affirm particularity. Indeed, it seems to me that the appeal to principles on behalf of the interests of a particular group, principles to which other interest groups may in turn appeal, is a wiser course of action than the attempt to create a common identity and a fusion of interests.

All these strategies—assimilationist, feminist, and queer—represent, I would argue, the intellectual equivalent of throwing out the baby with the bath. Both the disavowal of the ghetto and the dissolution of ghetto particularity results in a loss of power. In distancing oneself from the ghetto, one loses the ability to address the gay community as a loyal patriot, and the ability to address the community at large from a richly 'gay' perspective. And this is as true of the nascent enterprise of gay theology as any other. If the word 'theology' can at all be salvaged in our era, theology can no longer be thought an exclusively—or even primarily—a church matter, but should rather be thought of as the public enterprise of taking stock, in which an individual or a culture reflects critically on its direction in life. Likewise, gay theology is not the clarification of what the churches and synagogues have taught and do teach about homosexuality, but rather the exploration of what can and should be said religiously on the basis of gay experience, thereby making a distinctively gay contribution to the general discussion. While neither J. Michael Clark nor Robert Goss seek to interpret gay life in terms of 'church' tradition, each seeks to interpret gay life in the light of a school of thought whose roots lie outside the gay community. Each can appreciate gay life finally only insofar as gay men can be inducted into a revolution for a utopia of a feminist and/or liberationist (queer) imagination. If theology is a matter of 'testing' the spirits by which people live, it depends upon appreciative discernment. But, in their urgency to speak a prophetic word to the gay community, both Clark and Goss bypass the moment of appreciation, with the result that they speak to and at the gay ghetto, rather than with and for it. In addition, each of their 'theologies' fails to make good on the promise of making a distinctively gay contribution to the general cultural debates of our time. [. . .]

I resolutely maintain that it is only in an appreciative understanding of the ghetto's sexually promiscuous celebration of male beauty that gay theology will find its distinctive voice and power.[3] A gay theology that roots itself in the ghetto and seeks to appreciate the wisdom by which the ghetto lives stands uniquely poised to contribute to the general culture wars of our time in at least the following ways.

First, historically, most of humankind has operated with a sense that sexual penetrability was either puerile or womanly behavior. What characterizes modern ghetto homosexuality, however, is the rise of what I would call the 'butch bottom'—a willingly penetrable masculine male—as a social type. Since the butch bottom challenges us to think of sexual penetrability as an aspect of adult, masculine behavior, the gay ghetto is thus in the vanguard of helping us to 'rethink' what masculinity can and should mean in our time (cf. Long 1994). Indeed, we might even begin thinking of the ghetto as a men's movement beachhead.

Second, promiscuity is typically understood as a form of sexual 'abuse,' that is, using another as a sex object—with relational sex posed as its opposite. Since ghetto sexual practices invite seeing intimate sex as a cultivated form of promiscuity, we are summoned to new ways of thinking ethically about sex (cf. Long 1994; 1995). And last, ghetto gays take the body so seriously that even its appearance is significant, thus perhaps taking the Christian idea of embodiment with a seriousness that Christian culture has never dared to. Ghetto body seriousness forces a reopening of the question of the importance of the physical appearance in human life in a culture so fearful of the evils of 'lookism,' and an opening of the question about the importance of display.

If, as I have suggested, gay life is in large part about the power of masculine beauty, and the conjoint quests to have (sexually) and to be a beautiful man, it is astounding that those who have taken on themselves the task of gay theology should turn such a blind eye to its reality. A gay theology that has not yet begun to ask what the power of male beauty is and means to a gay man, why sex with a beautiful man—who may or not be an intimate other—is so important, and why it is so important to be found attractive has not yet found its ownmost subject matter. If, as I have argued, the gay ghetto is a privileged access to gay life *qua* gay, then the first order of business should be the exploration of how and why life in the ghetto should and does appeal to and seem to promise fulfillment for the men who flock there to live and socialize for a shorter time or longer.

The way to go about understanding what masculine beauty means is, first of all, to investigate how and why men pursue beauty in the way that they do in the ghetto. The rituals of the gay bar (and the attendant practice of 'tricking' that the bars facilitate) and the gym, I submit, are the keys to understanding the meaning that beauty holds for ghetto gays. Such a line of inquiry—indeed religious inquiry—is not without precedent. Plato mapped out a spirituality of ascent, starting with the 'love' of a beautiful boy, while the Sufis developed a theology of the 'witness' in support of the practice of *shahid bazi* (Schild 1990, 1264). Each of these approaches is, of course, rooted in the experience of visual contemplation, of gazing lovingly. The task of probing the meaningfulness of (sexual) interaction with a beautiful man and of the cultivation of personal physical beauty remains in its infancy. However, if we approach it, seeking less to instruct and reform than to understand, we may find that gay men live out a wisdom that may help us to a more adequate approach to the wider questions of our day. We may in fact discover that ghetto gays have more to teach than to learn.

Notes

1 Unfortunately, to the extent the assimilation of gay and feminist perspectives tends to root homophobia in a devaluation of the feminine, profeminist gay thought perpetuates that old stereotype of the gay man as effeminate queen.

2 Cohen's question goes to the heart of queer concern: 'How can we affirm a relational and transformational polities of self that takes as its process and its goal the interruption of those practices of differentiation that (re)produce historically specific patterns of privilege and oppression?' (1991, 89). The fear is of a 'totalizing sameness' imposed by a particular identity.

3 Comstock (1993) inquires as to the conditions in which a gay man, with no loss to his integrity, might come to terms with (religious) tradition. Religious traditions and realities – even Jesus himself – become religiously available only when they are friends and not parental authorities. Comstock draws his strength to treat traditional religious authority in this way, it seems to me, because of his anchorage in gay community, tradition, and culture. The ghetto here comes into view, but remains unexplored.

Literature

Bawer, Bruce. 1993. *A Place at the Table: The Gay Individual in American Society*. New York: Poseidon.

Clark, J. Michael. 1993. *Beyond Our Ghettos: Gay Theology in Ecological Perspective*. Cleveland: Pilgrim.

Clark, J. Michael and Bob McNeir. 1992. *Masculine Socialization and Gay Liberation: A Conversation on the Work of James Nelson and Other Wise Friends*. Arlington: The Liberal Press.

Cohen, Ed. 1991. 'Who are "we"? Gay "Identity" as Political Emotion,' in *Inside/Out: Lesbian Theories, Gay Theories*, ed. D. Fuss. New York: Routledge. Pp. 71–92.

Comstock, Gary David. 1993. *Gay Theology Without Apology*. Cleveland: Pilgrim.

Deutsch, Eliot. 1992. *Creative Being: The Crafting of Person and World*. Honolulu: University of Hawaii.

Foucault, Michel. 1990. *The History of Sexuality: An Introduction*, trans. R. Hurley. New York: Vintage Books.

Goldstein, Richard. 1993. 'Faith, Hope and Sodomy: Gay Liberation Embarks on a Vision Quest,' *The Village Voice* (June 29):21–30.

Goss, Robert. 1993. *Jesus Acted Up: A Gay and Lesbian Manifesto.* San Francisco: HarperSanFrancisco.

Herdt, Gilbert and Andrew Boxer. 1993. *Children of Horizons: How Gay and Lesbian Teens are Leading a New Way Out of the Closet.* Boston: Beacon.

Kaufman, Gordon. 1972. *God the Problem.* Cambridge: Harvard University Press.

La Fleur, William R. 1988. *Buddhism: A Cultural Perspective.* Englewood Cliffs: Prentice Hall.

Long, Ronald. E. 1994. 'An Affair of Men: Masculinity and the Dynamics of Gay Sex,' *The Journal of Men's Studies* 3:21–48.

——. 1995. 'Toward a Phenomenology of Gay Sex: Groundwork for a Contemporary Sexual Ethic,' in *Embodying Diversity: Identity, (Bio)Diversity, and Sexuality,* eds J. Michael Clark and Michael Stemmeler. Las Colinas: Monument Press. Pp. 69–112.

McNaught, Brian. 1988. *On Being Gay: Thoughts on Family, Faith and Love.* New York: St. Martin's Press.

McNay, Lois. 1992. *Foucault: A Critical Introduction.* New York: Continuum.

Mohr, Richard D. 1994. *A More Perfect Union: Why Straight America Must Stand Up for Gay Rights.* Boston: Beacon.

Obenchain, Diane B. 1994. 'Spiritual Quests of Twentieth-Century Women: A Theory of Self-Discovery and a Japanese Case Study,' in *Self as Person in Asian Theory and Practice,* eds R. T. Ames, W. Dissanayake, and T. P. Kasulis. Albany: SUNY Press. Pp. 125–168.

Santayana, George. 1982. *Reason in Religion* (vol. 3). New York: Dover Publications.

Schild, Maarten. 1990. 'Sufism,' in *Encyclopedia of Homosexuality,* ed. W. Dynes. New York: Garland. Pp. 1261–4.

Sullivan, Andrew. 1995. *Virtually Normal: An Argument about Homosexuality.* New York: Knopf.

Stoltenberg, John. 1993. *The End of Masculinity: A Book for Men of Conscience.* New York: Dutton.

Taylor, Charles. 1991. *The Ethics of Authenticity.* Cambridge: Harvard University Press.

Vaid, Urvashi. 1995. *Virtual Equality: The Mainstreaming of Gay and Lesbian Liberation.* New York: Anchor Books.

Woodhouse, Reed. 1993. 'Five Houses of Gay Fiction,' *The Harvard Gay and Lesbian Review* (Winter):23–29.

29

Sanctity and Male Desire:
Sebastian and Tarcisius

Editor's Introduction

In the past decades, openly gay scholars in religious studies have recovered the history and experiences of gay lives. They have investigated discourses on sex and gender, defended their sexual orientation against public hostility and against biblical scripturalism, and critiqued heteronormativity.

A subgenre of writing within gay religious scholarship has focused on the experience of gay men in view of their religious upbringing in a particular tradition as well as of their current devotional practices. In these texts, auto-biographical insertions and confessional revelations blend with historical, phenomenological and ethical musings. Donald Boisvert's 'Sanctity and Male Desire,' reprinted below from his work with the same title (2004), falls into this genre of gay devotional writing. Boisvert argues that Catholic male saints elicit both devotion and desire, and he illustrates this with the help of St Sebastian and St Tarcisius. Their stories and images, just as many other hagiographies, contain an eroticism that can be recovered from beneath a more repressive Catholic culture.

Being raised Catholic himself, Boisvert situates his essay within a larger argument about Roman Catholicism as being homophobic as well as 'homoerotic and campy' (2004, 8; also Jordan 2000; Goss 2002a). 'In intensely Catholic cultures,' Boisvert writes, '[saints] are clothed and bathed, covered with flowers or dripping in bright red droplets of blood, gaudy and almost comical in their painted features, and lit by the reflective glow of a thousand votive candles' (2004, 19). Boisvert translates the passionate and sensuous devotion to saints observable in Catholic piety into the specific dynamics between a gay devotee and his object of admiration.

Boisvert, in his own words, is 'engaged in a process of "queering" hagio-graphy', recasting 'a limited number of male saints . . . as gay icons' (2004, 207). For example, the story of Sebastian as martyr and saint as well as his depiction in Christian art contain queer elements. Hence, the martyred body in its icono-graphic form is subjected to the gay male gaze (for a different approach to martyrology, see Castelli 2004). Boisvert's devotional-hagiographic approach differs from a discursive-theological critic issued by other gay and queer scholars (see, for example, the February 2008 issue of the international Catholic journal *Concilium*; also Steinhäuser 1998; Jordan 2003; Reck 2008). Sharing similari-ties with Goss (chapter 12), he expresses a Catholic yearning for intimacy and spirituality that is quite distinct from Protestant-leaning authors (see Johnson, chapter 11; Haldeman, chapter 27; also Gorsline 1996). Gay men socialized in Catholicism draw on a different religious imaginary than their Protestant counterparts.

Broadly speaking, Boisvert's project follows a Foucaultian framework with its shared interest in an archaeology of knowledge – except that, in Boisvert's case, the knowledge unearthed is less related to discursive formations and more to an embodied knowing of desire.

Publications by the Same Author

Boisvert, Donald L. 2000a. *Out on Holy Ground: Meditations on Gay Men's Spirituality*. Cleveland: Pilgrim.

——. 2000b. 'Men, Muscles and Zombies: A Partial Response to Michelangelo Signorile'. *Theology and Sexuality* 16 (March):9–20.

——. 2004. *Sanctity and Male Desire: A Gay Reading of Male Saints*. Cleveland: Pilgrim.

——. 2005. 'The Spirit Within: Gay Male Culture as a Spiritual Venue', in *Gay Religion*, eds Edward R. Gray and Scott Thomas. Walnut Creek: AltaMira Press. Pp. 351–66.

——. 2006. 'Talking Dirty about the Saints: Storytelling and the Politics of Desire'. *Theology and Sexuality* 12/2:165–80.

——. 2007. 'Homosexuality and Spirituality', in *Homosexuality and Religion: An Encyclopedia*, ed. Jeffrey S. Siker. Westport: Greenwood Press. Pp. 32–44.

Boisvert, Donald L. and Robert E. Goss (eds). 2005. *Gay Catholic Priests and Clerical Sexual Misconduct: Breaking the Silence*. Binghamton: The Haworth Press.

Further Reading

Barzan, Robert (ed.). 1995. *Sex and Spirit: Exploring Gay Men's Spirituality*. San Francisco: White Crane.

Castelli, Elizabeth A. 2004. *Martyrdom and Memory: Early Christian Culture Making*. New York: Columbia University Press.

Concilium: Internationale Zeitschrift für Theologie. 2008. [Theme:] Homosexualitäten, eds Regina Ammicht Quinn, Marcella Althaus-Reid, Erik Borgman and Norbert Reck (44/1, February).

Gorsline, Robin Hawley. 1996. 'Facing the Body on the Cross: A Gay Man's Reflections on Passion and Crucifixion', in *Men's Bodies, Men's Gods*, ed. Björn Krondorfer. New York: New York University Press. Pp. 125–45.

Goss, Robert E. 2002a. *Queering Christ: Beyond Jesus Acted Up*. Cleveland: Pilgrim.

——. 2002b. 'Finding God in the Heart-Genital Connection: Joe Kramer's Erotic Christianity', in *Queering Christ*, Robert E. Goss. Pp. 56–71.

Jennings, Theodore W. 2003. *The Man Jesus Loved: Homoerotic Narratives from the New Testament*. Cleveland: Pilgrim.

Jordan, Mark D. 2000. *The Silence of Sodom: Homosexuality in Modern Catholicism*. Chicago: University of Chicago Press.

——. 2003. *Telling Truths in Church: Scandal, Flesh, and Christian Speech*. Boston: Beacon.

Reck, Norbert. 2008. 'Gefährliches Verlangen: Die katholischen Diskurse über gleichge-schlechtliche Sexualität'. *Concilium* 44/1 (February):7–19.

Steinhäuser, Martin. 1998. *Homosexualität als Schöpfungserfahrung: Ein Beitrag zur theologischen Urteilsbegründung*. Stuttgart: Quell Verlag.

Sanctity and Male Desire: Sebastian and Tarcisius

DONALD L. BOISVERT

Martyrs, particularly those from the beginnings of Christianity, occupy a special place in the pantheon of saints. They were, in fact, the first saints. Their tombs, on the outskirts of Roman cities, were at the origin of what became known as the cult of the saints (see Brown 1981). The stories of their lives became paradigmatic for all subsequent writings and legends about saints. Very often, the more gruesome and glorious the descriptions of their martyrdom, the more inspiring their legends were thought to be. There was a colorful sadistic streak to much of this, as though religious piety were a function of voyeurism. It has often been said that it was 'the blood of the martyrs,' the earliest witnesses to the faith, that nurtured the soil upon which the Christian church grew and spread throughout the Roman world. There is undoubtedly much truth to this, as would understandably be the case for the fallen heroes of any secular or religious revolution. These early martyrs, standing at the very heart of the military and political colossus that was Rome, gave powerful credence to the universalist claims of the emerging Christian faith by negating defiantly the religious and political monopoly of the empire's gods, including the emperor himself. It was divine vindication by persecution.

In the self-conscious and defensive American Catholicism of the 1950s and 1960s, not only were we called to Christian sanctity; we were also urgently summoned to martyrdom. I recall, during my high school days, having seen a rather hysterical book decrying the ravages of atheistic communism. Vivid parallels were drawn between the Christian martyrs and what those living under such a political regime had to endure. I remember one particularly compelling image of people being whipped by soldiers and set upon by ravenous dogs. The implication was that 'the Commies' would do to us what Roman emperors did to the Christians if we allowed any subversion of the American way of life. Good was American; evil was Russian. It was simplistic but terribly effective propaganda. I knew nothing of Karl Marx and his perceptive and humane critique of injustice back then, but I sensed that all this hysteria was somehow a bit much.

The Christian martyrs, for me, had much more to do with hungry lions and mad emperors than with anything else. As stereotypical as this imagery might have been, it was, in fact, little more than a series of horror stories filling the wild imaginings of an impressionable Catholic boy. Horror, whether real or invented, both attracts and repels. Religious horror is particularly insidious in this regard. Under the veneer of pious and saintly devotion often lingers the sadistic streak of ruthless power being acted out. The dead, martyred victim emerges as the one saved, and more importantly in the case of Jesus himself, the one through whom such salvation is possible. The 'monster' remains absolute in his claims upon the martyr and upon our imaginations, just as Nero stands secure yet enthralling in his legend as a bloodthirsty tyrant.

The iconography of martyrdom had a great deal to do with my response. I once visited a wax museum that showed a series of scenes of early Christian martyrs in a coliseum encircled by apparently ravenous lions and tigers, while others were hiding in the catacombs. The effect was eerie, even though the display was a bit tattered and dusty around the edges. I tried to imagine what it might be like to be in their position, and I didn't care for the feeling. It made me feel afraid and vulnerable, not at all confident in my faltering abilities to imitate them to the death. Years later, on two separate occasions, I visited some of the original catacombs on the outskirts of Rome. My response was very different. These were times of spiritual recollection for me. I also recall, as an altar boy, being brought on a day-trip to a chapel in a small Quebec village which claimed to have the largest collection of early Christian relics in the world. It was overwhelming and slightly tacky. Every square inch of wall space had some glassed-in piece of bone affixed to it. We played a game, trying to figure out which martyred saint fit with which bone. The anxieties of our Catholic youth had much more to do with the weird and anonymous bones of dead people than it did with the heavenly aspirations of long-forgotten martyrs.

What they were said to have done to some female martyrs was truly hideous, having to do, no doubt, with the usual projections of thwarted male sexual craving: the cutting of breasts and gouging of eyes, the spikes in the flesh, and the raw assaults upon puerile virginity. Male martyrs, by comparison, were assured of somewhat more decent deaths by such 'manly' instruments as arrows, knives, stones, wild beasts, and fire. Yet invariably, they were bare-chested in their pictures and often wore only a loincloth, as a shining, androgynous angel hovered above them with the martyr's palm. The ways in which Catholics were taught to envision the deaths of their martyrs had as much to do with sexual role-making and gender normativity, including homoerotic projections, as it did with hagiographic musings or just plain theology. Among the male martyrs, there were some given as models or patrons for different masculine stations in life, whether one was a military man or nothing but a simple altar boy. Such was the case for both Sebastian and Tarcisius. Martyrs can also be, and very much are, a reflection of social structure and class, just as they display subtle cultural readings of sexuality and gender.

The suffering and death of the martyr is what brings them glory and, by extension, what brings us, as believers, the promise and hope of an equally sublime afterlife. What is particularly striking about depictions of martyrdom, however, is the almost obligatory and strangely attractive equation of pain and ecstasy, of agony and beatitude. Much of this has to do with a uniquely Christian take on suffering as a redemptive fact of life, particularly if it is accepted with open arms. An equally significant variable is found in the Christian understanding of the erotic life as something which, even though it remains highly suspect, opens up a certain measure of spiritual freedom. From our postmodern stance, the torturous throes of martyred bodies can appear erotic in the extreme, as indeed they were always meant to be. From these ambiguous images, desire is born, be it desire for spiritual union or the more problematic desire for sexual coupling.

Few Christian saints have exerted such pervasive influence in the realm of cultural production as Saint Sebastian. In the history of art, even to this very day, his image is encountered quite regularly. His story has inspired drama, music, film, and literature, both pious and secular, and the paintings of him are literally legion. His iconography is immediately recognizable: a semiclad youth, well proportioned, tied to a tree or standing with his arms bound above his head, pierced by arrows and gazing heavenward. It is the arrows that give him away, for legend has it that this was how they attempted to kill him. If one did not know the story, one could not tell that Sebastian, in his semi-naked state, was, in fact, a member of the Roman military elite. His legend therefore symbolizes the historic encounter between Roman paganism and sectarian Christianity, and tells how the latter effectively subverted the former from the inside. Sebastian was, in his origins, an engaging figure of cultural and religious controversy, and he remains so (see Ressouni-Demigneux 2000).

In his classic study of gay male visual imagery in photography and film, *Hard to Imagine*, cinema scholar Thomas Waugh, writing about the decades following World War Two, states:

> The martyr, however, not the angel, is perhaps the most characteristic mythic carryover from the Glamour Generation. Photographers of the fifties such as Tobias and Lynes offered more than their share of crucifixions, and Pasolini hammered in more nails on every set. But Saint Sebastian towered above all, transformed by pre-Stonewall artists from a minor saint of the thirties into a profoundly rooted bellwether of fifties and sixties erotic sensibilities. The images of the martyr—or in sexual subcultural terms, the masochist— reverberate through the work of this entire generation, inextricably fusing eroticism with the representation of pain. After all, 'passion' really means suffering, etymologically speaking, as theorists of the melodrama, that other great genre of the fifties, keep reminding us. Influenced by Cocteau, artists such as Genet, Anger, Lynes, Tobias, and Jutra all articulated intensely desir- ous erotic images of the passive receiver of sexualized violence or power play. (Waugh 1996, 145)

Waugh touches upon one of the more significant, yet too often misunderstood, aspects of Saint Sebastian's iconography: that of his compelling and recur- ring stature as a homoerotic ideal. It is Sebastian's physicality, above all, that captures one's attention. Here is the male body at its most beautiful and erotic ravaged by arrows—unambiguous symbols of phallic power and dominance— but still translucent and desirable in its grace and elegance. Here are stark death and sadism, but ennobled to the point of sexual hunger. Here is the martyred military saint who feeds (and affirms) our fantasies about swarthy Roman legionnaires. Here is male desire in its simplest and most eloquent manifesta- tion, at once victimized and glorified. The image of Saint Sebastian carries a complex symbolism having to do with the hunger of men for men and its nec- essary corollary of power and pain. Sebastian is a paradigmatic queer, which is why one of the most famous Renaissance portraits of him was painted by Sodoma, and why he can also be represented as a sailor, that other great homo- sexual icon, by twentieth-century French painter Alfred Courmes,[1] or by the more contemporary kitsch artists-photographers Pierre et Gilles. Perhaps the most significant literary reference to Sebastian is Yukio Mishima's *Confessions of a Mask* (1958), which undoubtedly says more about the Japanese author's own tortured homosexuality than it does about the place of Sebastian in the literature of the East. Mishima's passages where he uses the image of the pierced saint as a source of nascent erotic desire are beautifully arousing.

The actual legend of Sebastian is at once reflective of the essence of Christian martyrdom, yet quite fantastic in its originality. The iconography that has sprung up around it is equally ambiguous. Martyred under the co-emperor Diocletian (reigned 284–305), some stories refer to him as the emperor's favorite, a sort of sexual plaything. This hints at the question of physical beauty, though its historical accuracy is far from certain. Already, however, there is a homoerotic subtext in the construction of the legend. It is claimed that he resisted Diocletian's advances, thereby courting death. The far more common version—certainly more normative in terms of its theological and sexual template—states that he used his privileged position to convert upper-class Roman citizens, especially fellow military officers, and also to comfort Christians facing death. Regardless, he was condemned to death by being shot with arrows. The story goes that he survived and was nursed back to health by another saint, Irene. He once again confronted the Roman emperor for his paganism, and this time was martyred in a far more prosaic fashion by clubbing. His body was thrown in the open sewer of Rome. He was 'twice-killed.' This gives him very special curative and restorative powers in the popular religious imagination. After Saints Peter and Paul, he is the third patron of the Eternal City, thus placing him at the very center of Catholic religious geography.[2]

Popular devotion to Saint Sebastian became widespread in Europe because of successive waves of the plague. In fact, he was the saint prayed to as a defense against it. Two reasons can explain this: the fact that he was able to survive his first martyrdom, and therefore was seen as a source of healing; and perhaps more significantly, because the symbolism of arrows was linked to the widespread imagery of the plague 'piercing' individuals as a punishment from God. The phallic undertone—the sexual ravaging by the hypermasculinized deity—cannot be underestimated here. The twin concepts of *eros* and *thanatos* (sex and death) have always stood in harmony, spurring artistic production as well as the most obtuse forms of spiritual and erotic ecstasy. Equally important, they have fixed the contours of the religious imagination, which is why Sebastian, in his flirtatious half-naked pose transfixed by the instruments of phallic death, resonates so powerfully in Christian hagiography, and why he stands so proudly at the center of gay culture. Sebastian is an even more necessary saint for gay men today. The time of AIDS is still upon us, and this saint, in his therapeutic and healing powers, becomes a patron, the one who would protect us from 'the gay plague,' so named by those who reject us with disdain and spite. Perhaps his religious potency could become our political force, and his prophylactic energy our haven of salvation.

The male body is certainly not something easily handled by religion. In its wild unpredictability and its phallic energy, it is a body most often ignored. As opposed to the female body, which is a source of intense wonder and sadistic control because of religion's oppressive heteronormativity, male physicality remains deeply suspect despite its all too apparent theological and ritual visibility. In the Christian tradition, the omnipresent image of the crucified god-man wearing only a loincloth is powerfully negated by the antigenital theology that surrounds his person. This portrait stands in vivid opposition to that of his mother, Mary, whose very identity is founded on her sexual omnipotence, even though it is a sublimated and virginal one. There are really only two other Christian saints whose sexuality defines their attributes so intimately: Mary Magdalene, who was said to be a whore and can therefore be depicted as nothing but naked flesh and flowing hair, and Sebastian, who was perceived as queer and can be represented beautifully bare-chested while being sodomized passively and ecstatically by arrows. The other important aspect of Sebastian portraiture is the ethereal beauty of the face. He is shown as handsome and young, at times slightly androgynous. Once again, as in the case of Saint Michael the Archangel, there is a clear and persistent ambivalence with respect to what constitutes masculinity, and how it can be represented both theologically and iconographically.

The wonder of the Saint Sebastian story is its elasticity, the fact that it has such a powerfully homoerotic subtext which, while so often negated, still manages to titillate. This subtext—especially in the eye of the informed, queer beholder—transforms the religious into a source of masculine desire. One can certainly pose two distinct gazes upon the story. The first is the typically hagiographic one of a confrontation between paganism and Christianity, with the defiant martyr being subjected to hideous torture and death while eagerly awaiting his heavenly reward. The second can give rise to all sorts of intriguing possibilities. What if Sebastian was, in fact, the emperor's favorite because of his physical beauty? Presumably, this means that he was no longer a virgin, and that he had already allowed himself to be seduced, physically and emotionally, by the allure of paganism. Was his death caused by his conversion to Christianity, or rather because he refused, for whatever obscure moral reason, no longer to give in to sexual demands of a particularly exciting sort? Was the martyrdom decreed by a jealous lover who chose death by arrows as a symbolic way of reaffirming and avenging his sexual conquest?

The very posing of these questions makes possible a queer Sebastian. It is not so much the official hagiographic discursive framework as the subtly hinted-at potentiality that actualizes the legend. If Sebastian were the lover of the emperor, and even if he were a Christian, then his martyrdom assumes a wholly different dimension. It is no longer exclusively a matter of sectarian Christianity confronting pagan arrogance, but rather of a struggle between two men desiring and possessing each other, to the ultimate destruction of one of them. In the end, it becomes a paradigmatic story about the hidden homoerotic and homophobic underpinnings of power and the destruction they can blindly wreak. The transpierced saint emerges not as a virtuous and straight Christian icon, but ultimately as a vulnerable and vindicated queer one. Queering Sebastian, though the artistic and hagiographic traditions may allow it, still entails a process of appropriation.

A few years ago, on the occasion of the Catholic jubilee, I visited the catacombs of Saint Sebastian on the outskirts of Rome, off the Appian Way. This is reputed to be the place where he was buried, and a major church stands on the site. Apart from the actual site of his tomb, surrounded by graffiti in honor of Saints Peter and Paul, whose remains were believed to have rested here temporarily, the highlight is the chapel dedicated to him containing a beautiful white marble statue of a Sebastian reclining in death from a drawing by the great sculptor Bernini. It is a strikingly attractive piece of religious art, at once ambivalent and arousing. A young, handsome male figure, half-naked and perfectly proportioned, lies on his side, with one hand covering his chest. Longish, curly hair surrounds a head slightly elevated, reclining on the breastplate and helmet of a Roman military officer. The almost naked body is covered sensuously by a rippling piece of cloth, leaving his sinewy legs and chest exposed, while three golden arrows protrude almost lovingly from his chest, biceps, and thigh. The saint looks as though he were asleep, or just napping after a bout of lovemaking. I was mesmerized. Here I was, standing at the site of Saint Sebastian's burial, totally engrossed by the beautiful yet saintly body represented by the statue. I prayed and lit a candle, kneeling in silent and holy adoration before this translucent image of masculine beauty.

My own engagement with the figure of Saint Sebastian arises from the sheer visual pleasure of contemplating a handsome male wearing only a loincloth. Mine is decidedly a fetishistic gaze. If he were a contemporary model strutting Calvin Klein underwear in some ad, the image would be equally arousing. Completely naked men do not engage me as powerfully, though they certainly can be beautiful. Men in underwear bespeak the dormitories and locker rooms of my boarding school days, my father sitting at home, my boyfriend in bed. They give voice to nostalgia and innocence. There is nothing more masculine or alluring than underwear, nothing more private or hinting at the secret vices of forbidden pleasure.

Sebastian remains my icon. I have pursued his image in several of the world's great museums, my eyes ever alert at a distance to the raised arms and pierced torso. I go on pilgrimage, seeking, like a talisman, the comforting embrace of his ecstatic, saintly gaze. I examine carefully the pose of the body and the position of the instruments of death, those arrows so firm yet flirtatious in their murderous intentions. I can recognize the different styles of Sebastian iconography, and the periods in which they were painted. I peer at the loincloths, hoping to detect in each the timid outline of the holy tumescent member. My eyes reach out to enfold and embrace the martyr, to heal his sacred wounds, to place his dying head on my comforting shoulder. Desire speaks. If only he were mine. If only he were my saint, my man, my lover.

A considerably less well-known saint, though an important one in the pantheon of young Catholic martyrs, is Tarcisius. As a seminarian, I recall the wooden statue of him that stood near our dining room. It always had a light shining on it. The statue was of a boy our age dressed in the short Roman toga, with a shawl around his shoulders and his hands clasped underneath. This was an obvious reference to his death. He was carrying the Eucharist to sick Christians in Rome when he was set upon by a mob demanding to see what was hidden so carefully beneath his cloak. Legend has it that rather than give up the consecrated host to be desecrated, he accepted martyrdom.

The statue was meant to inspire us in our young vocations. The seminary was run by a religious order dedicated to the cult of the Eucharist, and the example of Saint Tarcisius suggested that we should be equally prepared to die defending the body and blood of Christ, or at least that we should be as pious and single-minded in our devotion to them. I always found this young Roman martyr a bit of a puzzle. His story is virtually unknown, so little can be said about him. How he may have lived, if he was a recent convert, or even if he really did die the way it is claimed—all these questions remained unanswered, almost as though it was up to a boy's wild imaginings to fill in the gaps. The model of Saint Tarcisius was also suggestive of the special place which boys occupied in the Catholic cultic hierarchy, that of the altar boy.

Prior to the reforms of Vatican II, only boys were allowed to serve at the altar. This was a form of privilege, a copy of the men-only regulations governing the ordained clergy. Altar boys were really miniature priests in drag. When I was 12, I would wake up at 5:00 on snowbound winter mornings to serve the 6:00 a.m. mass at my parish church. It was quite the thrill for me to walk around in a cassock and surplice, pretending to be a priest. In a way, I was preparing for my days in the novitiate when I was obliged to wear the cassock, even though, by then, I had rejected it in a spirit of liberal defiance. As an altar boy, I learned all my responses to the prayers in Latin by rote, and every gesture for serving the celebrant was meticulously choreographed. We were an elite in the parish. I felt I was participating as a significant player in what it truly meant to be a Catholic, with all the campy ritualistic performance that this implied.

Altar boys, or minions like Tarcisius serving the central Catholic ritual that is the mass, reflect the subtle homoerotic ambivalence of institutionalized Catholicism. Altar boys are servants of celibate men, malleable vessels for the transmission of sexualized men-only values. The mass, at that time, was an intensely charged *mise-en-scène*, an erotic stage of masculine desire and possibility. The distance from the sacristy to the altar, with all that the former implied by way of whispered and secretive gropes, was not that great; the latter simply extended and ritualized the ever-present erotic charge of the former. Of course, I was not conscious of any of this while I was playing at the altar. My heart was intent solely on serving the priest to the best of my ability. My thoughts were turned to the mysteries of the transubstantiation—to the apparent wonder of the god-man becoming bread, and to my desire to eat him and make him one with my body. But I was grateful for the presence of these older men around me, and I shivered with delight and childish expectation when they sheltered me in their fatherly arms. Now, many years later, I am reminded of the sweet and sorrowful story entitled 'The Priest and the Acolyte,' long attributed to Oscar Wilde, but written by John Francis Bloxam (1997, 263–74). It tells the moving tale of a priest/minister and a very young altar boy who discover love together, though death invariably comes between them. Though my times as a server at mass were certainly not as melodramatic, nor as erotically charged, they still fired my imagination as sites for the acting out of my priestly desires and potential vocation. I was serving celibate men in order to be like them some day, carriers and servants of an overwhelmingly wondrous and mysterious power.

What Tarcisius makes possible by way of a model of gay sanctity is his proximity to the cult of masculine power and privilege. That is what we were being taught by his statuesque representation in the seminary. We were encouraged to be boys serving men under the guise and duty of religious ritual. We were called to an active engagement and identification with the paternal figures of our childhood and adolescence. We were the receptacles of the spectacle of male desire, and Tarcisius's utter passivity in the face of his own extinction was a model of life held out to us. We too, like him, should be willing to lay down our lives for the raw privilege of ingesting the body and blood of the male of males. We too, like a scout or a military cadet, should always stand prepared to serve and, by implication, 'to service.' Saint Tarcisius, the effeminate and uncertain boy-martyr, patron of first communicants and other liminal religious categories, silent and willing victim of rapacious pagan violence, was, for us and for our seminary mentors, a conduit of sublimated pedophilic delight and promise. He was the servant of servants, the boy not quite sure of where he stood.

There is another sense in which the figure of Saint Tarcisius evokes the sweet memories of queer Catholic youth. His death was the result of an encounter with a roaming gang of nameless Romans. We can let our imaginations run wild. Was he, in fact, beaten up by Roman teenagers intent not so much on desecrating the host, as on jeering the boy for his oddness and difference? Was this really an attempt at gang rape gone amiss? Did the young martyr die because he was protecting the unplucked blossom of his virginal anus? Has the legend been transformed from the image of one defending his corporeal integrity to that of the young saint safeguarding the new Christian god's sacred body and blood? The metamorphosis does not appear so strange after all. Many of us undoubtedly remember encounters with the bullies of the schoolyard in our youth. Though perhaps not as violent as what happened to Saint Tarcisius, we knew we were being picked on because our secret desires were dangerous. The bullies certainly knew it, which is why they wanted us so desperately and why they had to erase this knowledge with the bloody blows of their clenched fists. To allow, for one passing moment, the possibility of same-sex desire to emerge was to undermine a fragile masculine identity.

Martyrdom requires a victim and an executioner. Its discourse is that of power and altruism in synchronic, almost fluid exchange. When the symbol of the martyr is charged with latent homoerotic potential, as is the case with both Saint Sebastian and Saint Tarcisius, this power is at once political and sexual, and the altruism becomes vividly, powerfully paradigmatic. Martyrdom is an exemplary tool for spiritual transformation. Its potency is its very vulnerability, a vulnerability that exhorts and engenders change. For gay men, the queer martyr is, in sum, the queer man divinized, the faggot forever beaten and crushed, yet who thereby attains a state of immortal release and perfection. The queer martyr is ultimately a call to arms, an angry cry against a deadening, homophobic culture.

Perhaps Sebastian and Tarcisius really had known each other. Perhaps they were boyfriends once upon a time. [. . .]

Notes

1 See *Saint Sébastien dans l'histoire de l'art depuis le XVe siècle* (Paris: Éditions Jacques Damase, 1979), preface by François Le Targat.

2 See *Saint Sébastien: rituels et figures* (Paris: Éditions de la Réunion des musées nationaux, 1993).

Literature

Bloxam, John Francis. 1997. 'The Priest and the Acolyte,' in *Pages Passed from Hand to Hand: The Hidden Tradition of Homosexual Literature in English from 1748 to 1914*, eds Mark Mitchell and David Leavitt. New York: Houghton Mifflin Company. Pp. 263–74.

Brown, Peter. 1981. *The Cult of the Saints: Its Rise and Function in Latin Christianity*. Chicago: University of Chicago Press.

Mishima, Yukio. 1958. *Confessions of a Mask*. New York: New Directions.

Ressouni-Demigneux, Karim. 2000. *Saint-Sébastien*. Paris: Éditions du Regard.

Waugh, Thomas. 1996. *Hard to Imagine: Gay Male Eroticism in Photography and Film from Their Beginnings to Stonewall*. New York: Columbia University Press.

Part 7

Gender, Justice, and Community

The concept of hegemonic masculinity, which has been like a red thread throughout this volume (see chapter 18), points to the simultaneous existence of both dominant and marginal masculinities in Judaism and Christianity. Dominance presumes access to power and authority that is denied to others; inevitably, such power differentials lead to questions about justice concerning communal and gender relations.

> We cannot ignore class, religious, ethnic, or sexual differences among men that have led to numerous forms of repression and persecution of men in Christian history. We only need to recall the oppression of peasants during the feudal system, the persecution of heretics during the Inquisition, the enslavement of Africans during colonization, the antisemitic assault on Jews, and the homophobic retaliation against gender transgressors to realize how many men and women have been marginalized, victimized, and brutalized by the dominant forces of European Christian cultures. (Krondorfer 1996, 3)

Boyd, Longwood and Muesse conclude their volume on *Redeeming Men* on a similar note. They call on the need for further thinking about 'the personal and political dimensions of male experience' under the 'theological rubric of justice and love':

> We see emerging ethical visions of friendship (power-in-community) – across social barriers involving gender, race/ethnicity, sexual orientation, class, age, and species – wherein there develop structures of accountability to and within more inclusive communities . . . In this revisioning of both justice and love, [men can] draw on a variety of religious and spiritual traditions in service of the common good. (Boyd, Longwood and Muesse 1996, 288–9)

The final part of the *Critical Reader* returns to the political dimension of unjust gender systems as they affect the intersection of religion and masculinity. The term 'political' here is not used in any narrow sense – as referring, for example, to the implementation of specific social policies – but broadly as a commitment to counteract the effects of dominant masculinities, which obstruct, inhibit, derail or paralyze an auspicious life within communities that appreciate and welcome differences.

The five concluding chapters pay attention to social, cultural, and discursive mechanisms that render particular groups invisible and marginal. The groups chosen in this section include gay men in religious studies scholarship (Krondorfer) and the LGBT community in South America (Musskopf). They also include men whose ethnicity has rendered them a minority (Baker-Fletcher; De La Torre; Musskopf) as well as women who suffer from male abuse within particular social and cultural settings (De La Torre; Poling). Aware of feminist, womanist, *mujerista* and queer voices, these five scholars – like so many others in this volume – merge their analytical skills with a sense of responsive account-ability in order to rectify unjust gender relations.

Literature

Boyd, Stephen B., Merle Longwood and Mark Muesse (eds). 1996. 'Where Do We Go From Here? Some Concluding Remarks', in *Redeeming Men*, eds Stephen Boyd, Merle Longwood and Mark Muesse. Louisville: Westminster John Knox. Pp. 285–93.

Ellison, Marvin M. and Sylvia Thorson-Smith (eds). 2003. *Body and Soul: Rethinking Sexuality and Justice-Love*. Cleveland: Pilgrim.

Krondorfer, Björn. 1996. 'Introduction', *Men's Bodies, Men's Gods*. New York: New York University Press. Pp. 3–26.

Nonn, Timothy. 1996. '"I Took it like a Man": Survival and Hope among Poor Men', in *Redeeming Men*, eds Stephen B. Boyd, Merle Longwood and Mark Muesse. Louisville: Westminster John Knox. Pp. 156–68.

Who's Afraid of Gay Theology?
Men's Studies, Gay Scholars, and
Heterosexual Silence

Editor's Introduction

At the 2006 annual gathering of the American Academy of Religion, Krondorfer presented a paper on the heterosexual silence vis-à-vis gay religious studies scholarship. His paper, revised and expanded, was published a few months later in the journal of *Theology and Sexuality*, and it is reprinted below. In 'Who's Afraid of Gay Theology?' the author probes five clusters of anxieties that, according to his thesis, have contributed to the heterosexual neglect of the research advanced by gay scholars in religion. It calls on heterosexual male scholars to reflect upon their anxieties, which span from professional indifference to the fear of pollution.

The intended primary audience for this criticism is the heterosexual scholarly community. Calling for more dialogue, however, may trigger anxieties also in the gay scholarly community, since any genuine and sincere debate inevitably opens the door to critical engagement and thus renders the minority discourse of gay scholarship vulnerable to the potential hazards of (heterosexual) mainstreaming.

Further debate was sparked when the editors of *Theology and Sexuality* decided to invite additional voices into the dialogue in a subsequent volume. '[Krondorfer's] research,' they write, 'revealed that straight men with an interest in masculinity and a sympathetic approach to gay rights were just as unlikely to refer to gay scholarship in their work as more conservative male scholars':

> While acknowledging that his findings were of preliminary nature and that further research would be profitable . . . [his] arguments, we believe, are worthy of consideration. In the interest of a debate that rightly begins among male scholars but has implications for all concerned theologians, we now publish four significant responses. (Walton and Stuart 2007, 79–80)

The responses were written by straight and gay men (Livingston; Longwood; Haldeman; Musskopf), followed by a rejoinder (Krondorfer 2007c). This exchange eventually led to another round of dialogue in 2008 at a second AAR panel, titled 'Across the Great Divide: Men, Masculinities, and the Challenge of Gay Religious Scholarship'. Responding to the panelists – who included Donald Boisvert, Ronald Long, Merle Longwood and Paul Collins – Krondorfer proposed replacing the language of the 'great divide' with the image of a river. Tagging on to an idea developed by Norbert Reck (2008), he envisions a river in which gay, straight, and queer men swim together. Rather than floating in separate canals – one labeled, 'for gay men only'; the other, 'for straight men only' – men in their multiplicity of sexed and gendered identities would plunge into the same river of ever-changing desires. Such a river, Krondorfer muses, 'is not a "main stream,"but a source of ever refreshing water with different currents, surges, rapids, occasional torrents, or caressing ripples':

> Dialogue does not imply 'mainstreaming.' Whereas dialoguing 'across the great divide' conjures up an inert landscape of ravines, canyons, gaps, walls, fences – a landscape of hurdles that need to be overcome, bridged, climbed over or torn down – dialoguing while swimming is an activity marked by fluidity. The river is not an image of sameness but of continuous change and permeability.

Publications by the Same Author

Krondorfer, Björn (ed.).1992. *Body and Bible: Interpreting and Experiencing Biblical Narratives*. Philadelphia: Trinity International Press.

——. 1995. *Remembrance and Reconciliation: Encounters Between Young Jews and Germans*. New Haven: Yale University Press.

——(ed.). 1996. *Men's Bodies, Men's Gods: Male Identities in a (Post-) Christian Culture*. New York: New York University Press.

——. 2002. 'Revealing the Non-Absent Male Body: Confessions of an African Bishop and a Jewish Ghetto Policeman', in *Revealing Male Bodies*, eds Nancy Tuana et al. Bloomington: Indiana University Press. Pp. 245–68.

——. 2004. 'Mel Gibson's Alter Ego: A Male Passion for Violence'. *CrossCurrents* 54/1 (Spring):16–21.

——. 2006. 'Nationalsozialismus und Holocaust in Autobiographien protestantische-Theologen', in *Mit Blick auf die Täter*. B. Krondorfer, K. von Kellenbach and N. Reck. Gütersloh: Gütersloher Verlagshaus. Pp. 23–170.

——. 2007a. 'World Religions, Christianity', in *International Encyclopedia of Men and Masculinities*, eds M. Flood, J. K. Gardiner, B. Pease and K. Pringle. London and New York: Routledge. Pp. 658–60.

——. 2007b. 'Who's Afraid of Gay Theology? Men's Studies, Gay Scholars and Heterosexual Silence'. *Theology and Sexuality* 13/3:257–74.

——. 2007c. 'Rejoinder: Navigating Through Troubled Language'. *Theology and Sexuality* 14/1:108–12.

——. 2008a. 'Eunuchen oder Viagra? Frühchristliche Männlichkeitsideale als zeitgenössische Irritation', in *Theologie und Geschlecht: Dialoge Querbeet*, eds Heike Walz and David Plüss. Münster: LIT. Pp. 57–71.

——. 2008b. 'Textual Male Intimacy and the Religious Imagination: Men Giving Testimony to Themselves'. *Literature and Theology* 22/3 (September):265–79.

Further Reading

Haldeman, Scott, 2007. 'On Writing Religion, "Gay" and "Straight"'. *Theology and Sexuality* 14/1:95–9.

Livingston, David J. 2007. 'Overcoming Heterosexual Anxiety before Gay Theology'. *Theology and Sexuality* 14/1:81–8.

Longwood, Merle W. 2007. 'Response to Björn Krondorfer's "Who is Afraid of Gay Theology?"' *Theology and Sexuality* 14/1:100–05.

Musskopf, André S. 2007. 'Who is not Afraid of Gay Theology?' *Theology and Sexuality* 14/1:89–94.

Reck, Norbert. 2008. 'Das Politische in der schwulen Theologie: Befreiung von der Homosexualität'. *Werkstatt Schwule Theologie* 14/2 (May):165–85.

Walton, Heather and Elizabeth Stuart, 2007. 'A Silence that Speaks Louder than Words'. *Theology and Sexuality* 14/1:79–80.

Who's Afraid of Gay Theology? Men's Studies, Gay Scholars, and Heterosexual Silence

BJÖRN KRONDORFER

There are two important forums in the United States where the scholarly discourse on men and masculinity in religion and theology is advanced: the Gay Men's Issues in Religion group and the Men's Studies in Religion group, both housed in the American Academy of Religion (AAR).[1] [. . .] These two groups have occasionally offered joint sessions and sometimes drawn on similar audiences. Largely, however, they separate along the lines of gay and heterosexual. This is true in at least two ways: first in regard to each group's implicit assumptions of the themes, objects and subjects to be studied; second, in regard to each group's identity politics, that is, the sexual identity of the majority of each group's leadership, steering committees and audience.

I am offering this as an observation and not (yet) as criticism. As a matter of fact, there are many good reasons why two groups with perspectival differences should focus on issues of men, male gender, and masculinities. Given the numerous publications that have emerged in gay religious studies and (heterosexual) men's studies in religion, there is enough food on the academic table for both groups to feast on. Each has been instrumental in establishing recognizable new fields and each is struggling with its own particular sets of problems and dilemmas. What is still missing, however, is a more strongly developed scholarly partnership—a partnership based on critical engagement of each group's methodologies, research agendas, and mutual and divergent interests.

That such a partnership of mutuality does not yet exist is, I believe, largely a result of the absence of heterosexual responses to gay scholarship in religion and theology. This absence is mirrored in the unspoken division of labor between the Gay Men's Issue in Religion and the Men's Studies in Religion groups. Such silence, of course, is not limited to these discrete organizational units of know-ledge at the AAR. The homosexual/heterosexual divide in men and masculin-ity studies points to larger cultural forces at work, many of which, I will argue, are rooted in heterosexual anxieties.

When examining this divide I do not presume that straight and gay men (and their scholarship) constitute a binary position.[2] Yet, the separation as reflected in the AAR is not purely accidental. The heterosexual silence vis-à-vis gay theology—and I am focusing here on *gay theology*, though I believe that my observations apply also to the larger field of gay men's issues in religion[3]—requires some critical probing.

Gay and Heterosexual Men's Studies in Religion

When gay studies met religion and theology more than 20 years ago, it had to overcome a whole range of resistances that heterosexual men did not have to confront, namely the experience of 'coming out' publicly over against a long religious and cultural history of silencing, discrimination, physical harass-ment, and legalized violence. Not surprisingly, as Robert Goss summarizes in *Queering Christ* (2002, 239–42), when gay theology appeared in the 1950s, it began defensively and apologetically (e.g. McNeill 1976; Horner 1978) before it was able to embrace a liberationist theological paradigm in the 1980s and early 1990s (e.g. Clark 1989; McNeill 1988; 1995; Goss 1993; Comstock 1993; see also Schneider 2000). In the mid-1990s, gay theology expanded into a more dif-ferentiated field with a variety of methodological and comparative approaches; currently it discusses the stability and fluidity of its boundaries in conversation with feminism, LGBT, and queer studies (Goss 2002).

Heterosexual men's studies, in contrast, did not develop under such antago-nistic conditions. Missing the existential urgency and activist momentum char-acteristic of the history of gay religious studies (rooted, among others, in the devastating HIV/AIDS calamity), heterosexual men's studies in religion has not acquired the same identifiable profile. Yes, it has been awarded a separate entry in the second edition of the *Encyclopedia of Religion*, mentioning 'gay and queer studies' under the rubric of 'Men's Studies in Religion.' But in this entry, its 'object of inquiry' is vaguely defined as '"men" as gendered beings in relation to religion,' further stating that 'the precise delineations of this inquiry [are] not yet determined.'[4] Its profile, in other words, is not yet as clearly recognizable as feminist, womanist, lesbian, gay, or queer studies in religion.

Heterosexual men's studies in religion may, perhaps, envy the manifest sexu-al identity concerns that frame, guide, and make visible gay studies in religion and theology. But such taxonomic envy—if it indeed exists—is, of course, the envy of the benevolent outsider, who has not participated in the daily struggles and suffering of a socially marginalized group. Gary Comstock's brief allusion to those struggles in his introduction to *Gay Theology Without Apology* serves as one example—a very restrained example: 'When I was working on this book,' Comstock writes,

I was finding firm ground on which to stand as an openly gay man; I had been ordained and was employed as a college chaplain and professor. These accomplishments were not gained without problems, obstacles, rejections, setbacks, and worry, but enough people helped at key times to produce a positive outcome. (1993, 5)

Gay theology, as this passage demonstrates, knows its own victories and defeats.

As gay theology moved from silence and apologetics to adopting an affirmative and liberationist voice, it also evolved from a minority discourse to an academically established new field. As such, it has come to face a new dilemma. Like so many other fields of knowledge emerging from marginalized groups, gay theology has been caught in its own 'minoritizing rhetoric'—a term Allen Frantzen used in his article 'Between the Lines: Queer Theory [and] the History of Homosexuality.' Once 'established as a field,' gay theology became 'ghettoized as a field' (1996, 260): For gay men only! Looking at how little attention gay theology has received in the research, publication, footnotes and bibliographies of heterosexual men's studies, one begins to grasp the scope of this problem.

It can be argued that, to some extent, both gay men's studies and (heterosexual) men's studies in religion have been ghettoized. Like other specialized fields of knowledge, they share the postmodern fate of academic specialization where a small circle of like-minded people end up talking to each other and fail to reach a larger audience. For a ghettoized minority discourse to break free from its external restrictions and self-imposed limitations, it would have to become integrated into larger fields of knowledge. The danger, of course, is that such integration may diffuse the difference and distinctiveness of a 'minoritized' discourse and thereby mute its identity.

Currently, however, this danger does not loom large. Far from it. Given the current cultural climate with its gender backlash and its entrenchment of normative masculinity and revivification of martial masculine ideals, the need for focused groups on critical men's studies in religion and theology remains strong. What is, however, in our power to change—and what is still lacking—is to develop a stronger scholarly partnership between gay and straight men's studies in religion.

Minimally, gay and straight scholar can become active partners in helping to de-ghettoize the other—a point that Michael Clark had already raised in his 'A Gay Man's Wish List for the Future of Men's Studies in Religion' (1999, 269). Such partnership has to be based on recognized mutuality, an ethical claim I want to hold on to even in light of the fact that a power differential exists between gay men's and heterosexual men's studies in terms of scholarly discourse, social positioning, and heteronormative privileging. There is no reciprocal relationship yet. To put it simply: While gay theologians have read, acknowledged and responded to the research outside their own field, heterosexual men's studies in religion does not critically engage with the scholarship of their gay peers. I suspect that heterosexual men interested in the field of male gender have read some gay men's scholarly publications, but the latter are rarely acknowledged, and a sustained critical engagement is as good as absent.

A number of indicators confirm the existence of such heterosexual silence: For one, my colleagues in gay theology have unanimously confirmed in e-mail correspondences that their work has received little to no public 'heterosexual theological attention.'[5] Second, neither mainstream, peer-reviewed journals nor heterosexual scholars rush to review gay religious and theological scholarship. Mark Jordan's *Invention of Sodomy* (1997) and its sequel *The Silence of Sodom* (2000) are the exception. They were reviewed substantially in journals like *Speculum, Church History, Signs, JAAR, American Historical Review,* and *Theological Studies.*[6] Gary Comstock's works received limited attention, often in smaller church-related journals and magazines, and so did Robert Goss's work;[7] Comstock, Jordan, and Clark are featured in a review article of the *Religious Studies Review* (Schneider 2000);[8] but there is almost complete silence, for example, around the work of Ron Long, Donald Boisvert, and others.[9]

There are, of course, serious limitations about these two indicators. To begin with, most academics are chagrined that their work does not receive the attention it deserves—it is a frustration that comes with the profession. Hence, personal correspondences may tell us something about subjective experience but not necessarily objectively verifiable facts. With respect to book reviews, there is the problem that the sexual identity and identification of the reviewer is, in most cases, not known (at least publicly), so that it would be difficult to draw conclusions about heterosexual silence by just counting the number of reviews. In addition, as far as evaluating scholarly work goes, the sexual orientation or identity of a particular reviewer ought not to matter, and we may not want to pay any heed to it.

But there are patterns that are not just purely accidental. First, gay religious and theological work is often reviewed in the form of short entries in various book lists and book notes outside religious studies journals.[10] Second, biblical and historical scholarship on homosexuality receives more attention than ethical and theological works.[11] Third, books that follow what I call a gay confessional or gay devotional style have found almost no echo in the academic mainstream, like Boisvert's books on gay saints and gay spirituality (2000; 2004).

More reliable indicators of heterosexual silence are monographs and edited volumes by heterosexual authors that address men's studies in religion, including issues of homosexuality. As a general rule, they do not mention the significant work that has been done in gay theology. For example, Van Leeuwen's *My Brother's Keeper* (2002)—a blend of psychological and social science approaches to masculinity while informed by Christian ethics—does not mention gay theological scholarship at all, even when homosexuality and religion are discussed. The author acknowledges, however, authors like Stephen Boyd, Harry Brod, Michael Kimmel, Kenneth Clatterbaugh, mythopoetic men, NOMAS, and the Promise Keepers. Walter Wink's edited *Homosexuality and Christian Faith* (1999), which is geared toward an educated Christian lay audience, does not make reference to any gay scholarly voices. Donald Capps's *Men and their Religion* (2002), with its short discussion of Freud's understanding of homosexuality, also lacks any inclusion of gay theological works. Though these books are just a representative sample, I doubt that a more systematic survey will come to fundamentally different conclusions. Mind you: these and other authors are not from the homophobic religious right but represent the liberal-minded world that is generally supportive of gay men.

Not to paint too bleak a picture, I should mention two positive examples: for one, James Nelson, who has inspired and supported gay theologians with his emphasis on a sex-affirmative body theology (Nelson 1978; 1992; see also Clark 1992); second, Stephen Boyd, who credits in *The Men We Long to Be* (1995) gay men and gay theologians for raising his awareness about homophobia and the unhealthy dearth of intimacy between heterosexual men. Nevertheless, a sustained analysis of the scholarship of their gay peers remains absent also in these two works.

Edited volumes in the field of (heterosexual) men's studies in religion have indicated their gay-friendly agenda by including gay scholarly voices, like *Redeeming Men*, edited by Boyd et al. (1996),[12] and my own *Men's Bodies, Men's Gods* (Krondorfer 1996a). These volumes follow a pluralistic model, arranging different voices side by side rather than engaging them analytically or through dialogue across the homosexual/heterosexual divide.

So the question remains: Who is afraid of gay theology? In light of the availability of gay scholarly resources, why such striking absence of heterosexual responses? Gay scholarship in religion and theology can still count more predictably on the ire of conservative folks than on a nuanced, non-homophobic critique by their heterosexual colleagues. Though many heterosexual male scholars might agree with their gay colleagues that a critique of the heterosexual-normative framing of religious and theological issues is necessary and that a vision of full equality of all humans is desired, their silence continues to speak loudly.

Clusters of Anxiety

Let me suggest a few explanations arranged in five clusters. Each of them, I believe, expresses particular anxieties:

1. *Indifference:* Heterosexual men—because of their social and hermeneutical position of privilege—do not have to engage with the particularities of gay theology. Individuals may feel for the plight of their gay colleagues, but their own research agendas do not coincide with those of their gay peers. Gay theology neither speaks to their lived experience nor is it advantageous to their professional careers. One could argue, of course, that heterosexual men ought to pay more attention to gay religious scholarship since homosexuality—if nothing else—is continually at the center of public discourse and in the public imagination. But usually this is not the case with regard to their professional work and research. Perhaps we can call this indifference an anxiety about one's professional reputation.

2. *Boundary Violations:* Many gay religious studies scholars do not frame their work within traditionally defined disciplines. Such a transcending of disciplinary boundaries mirrors a need to break out of the mold of traditionally gendered roles and heteronormative identities. Hence, such a 'transcending' is at the core of many gay theologians and religious scholars. It reflects the need to piece together, support, and preserve a wholeness of gay identity that has been so seriously fragmented by and disallowed in hegemonic religious discourse. Michael Clark, for example, introduces his *Masculine Socialization &*

Gay Liberation as a book that 'cannot be constructed as if it were merely a traditional academic text' because the issues 'require the testimony of our lived
experiences' (1992, 4). Jim Mitulski, in the Foreword to *Queering Christ*, lauds
Robert Goss for 'changing the boundaries' and for 'creating an entirely new
discipline . . . no longer content to reform Christianity' but to 'reinvent it' (Goss
2002, viii).

Transcending disciplinary boundaries—a trend that becomes even more
pronounced as gay studies embrace queer studies—can be read as 'transgression.' In terms of academic methodology, what is transgressed is disciplinary
territoriality, which, in turn, offers peer-reviewed journals and mainstream
scholars an excuse to ignore and overlook such scholarship. Perhaps we can
speak of a methodological anxiety. But methodological reservations only get us
so far in explaining heterosexual silence—for, surely, one can judge and evaluate published research in terms of what it sets out to do, whether it accomplishes
its task, whether it uses sources correctly and whether its rationale and arguments are persuasive. Such a procedure does not yet imply a personal agreement or disagreement with a particular work's thesis, findings or conclusions.
Even if the scholarship is weak, there is a need to point out flaws and engage in
a debate.

3. *The Gay-ing of Religion:* Religious historians of homosexuality have recovered, reclaimed and reassessed the place of same-sex eroticism in Christianity's
past, and they have raised complex issues of historiography when dealing with
primary texts of specific eras. Certainly, John Boswell's groundbreaking work
(1980) would have to be mentioned in this context, to which heterosexual and gay
academic communities responded with both excitement and furor (see Kuefler
2006; Goss 2002, 240). The publicity that Boswell's work received is still reflected
in the relative public visibility and success of Mark Jordan's more recent historical study on sodomy in the Middle Ages (1997).

Some gay theologians picked up historical themes to blend them into their
personal, ethical, and speculative writings; by doing so, they have been gay-
ing (or homosexualizing) religious spaces and religious figures. In the process,
historiography has shifted often to gay hagiography.[13] Monastic and religious
orders are reclaimed as potential or actual gay spaces; male saints and Jesus
in his divinity and maleness have become objects of gay erotic desire and the
embodied imagination. Goss (2002) and Jordan (2000) have, for example, written
in revealing and provocative detail about the homoeroticism, homodevotion-
alism, and repressed or enacted homosexual desires in monastic orders and
Catholic seminaries—'a honeycomb of closets,' as Jordan has called the Catholic
Church (2000, 199). The savior figure of Jesus and various male saints have been
subject and object of the desiring homosexual gaze and of active gay fantasy
life (see, for example, Gorsline 1996; Boisvert 2004). Much would need to be said
about this in a separate article, but let me here only suggest the kind of anxieties it can trigger among heterosexual men. As regards the gay-ing of religious
spaces, it causes anxiety about institutional purity and authority; as regards the
gay-ing of religious figures, it raises anxiety about spiritual purity and idolatry. As a result, this kind of gay appropriation of the sacred is prone to hostile
reactions.[14]

4. *Autobiographical Insertions:* Gay religious studies scholars often insert auto-biographical material in their texts. Like Clark, they reflect and respond to lived experiences of gay men. Boisvert, for example, writes in *Sanctity and Male Desire* that he comes to his topic on 'how saints can instill desire' as a 'gay scholar of religion' and that his 'book constitutes a theological reflection on my life experi-ence' (2004, 7); Goss introduces *Queering Christ* as representing 'nearly a decade of reflection as a queer Christian theologian' and remarks that he will 'weave narrative details from my own life' into the essays. 'Sexual theology,' he writes, 'involves always the texts of our lives' (2002, xiv, xv). Gary Comstock, to men-tion a final example, introduces *Gay Theology Without Apology* as a discussion of Christian Scripture and traditions in 'my own terms, that is, from the point of view of my experience' (1993, 4). Each of these works then proceeds to include autobiographical passages as well as personal life stories of their friends and lovers.

Autobiographical insertions always render an author vulnerable—we know this since Augustine's *Confessions*: when speaking intimately about his bod-ily needs and spiritual failures, the Roman-African bishop of late antiquity expressed repeatedly his fear of being ridiculed by the reader.[15] Not surprisingly, homophobic or otherwise gay non-friendly responses have jumped on autobio-graphical insertions and turned them against their authors. Robert Lockwood of the Catholic League serves as one example. In a web-based review of Mark Jordan's *The Silence of Sodom*, Lockwood accuses him of 'ugly stuff that speaks more of the path Jordan has taken in life and his obsessions, rather than any kind of an honest view;' it is a 'book of opinion—outrageous opinion—based on little more than the author's own fantasy life.'[16]

Beyond homophobic polemics, even the liberal, gay-friendly heterosexual outsider may perceive the insertion of the personal voice as violating academic standards. But more to the point, such insertions are experienced conceptually and emotionally as 'othering,' since the experiences described are not their own. We have to imagine the reading experience of heterosexual men as ambivalent since it can de-stabilize their identity. On the one hand, gay theology opens a window into a male world different from the straight man's own sexuality—an uncanny experience, since it is othering and yet familiar. On the other hand, the reading of gay autobiographical passages may feel like eavesdropping on an intimate conversation, and one may wonder whether one should continue to listen. It may trigger the moral qualm in response to voyeuristic anxieties: fear of trespassing into the intimate territory of another, yet desire for observing the unknown while remaining invisible. Such invisibility is lost once heterosexual men respond to and engage with gay theology in the public arena. The voyeur-istic anxiety is, in other words, an anxiety about publicity, about being 'outed' publicly as a consumer of gay intimacy in gay religious writings.

5. *Erotic Confessions:* Autobiographical insertions often adopt a confessional mode. What is revealed are not only autobiographical data but intimate details of gay erotic and sexual life. Several books and articles describe in fairly explicit details gay sexual desires and practices, especially, though not exclusively, in a genre that I suggest we call gay devotional or gay confessional scholarship. Goss, who describes his own sexual experiences in *Queering Christ*, writes: 'With

the risk of self-confession, I will use myself as text, not place myself as judge' (2002, 81). Similarly, Clark writes that 'self-disclosure has increasingly been a hallmark in the progression of my own work in men's studies' (1997b, 316). Ron Long (1997), Donald Boisvert (2000), Philip Culbertson (2006), Scott Haldeman (1996; 2003), and others have followed such self-confessional modes.

Let me suggest a hypothesis: I believe that as long as the loving care among and between gay men is described in gay theology within a framework that resembles the embodied theology of James Nelson, who has put a sex-friendly agenda into the center of his Christian ethics of love, the non-homophobic heterosexual reader still treads on safe grounds. There may even be some envy, as Clark suggests: 'Nongay men may actually be *envious* of the same sex intimacy and friendship they *perceive* among gay men' (1992, 27; emphasis in original). Yet, rarely does such envy get acknowledged by heterosexual men. When, however, gay theology claims that the divine can be found in the loving experience of male–male penetration, the level of heterosexual anxiety rises sharply, perhaps to degrees of homosexual panic. Goss, for example, writes:

> Men lying joyfully on their backs with their feet ecstatically in the air or in a variety of receptive postures arouses fears among heterosexual men, but for gay men, it signifies receptivity, trust, intimacy, vulnerability, and spirituality. Anal sex carries profound human as well as spiritual meanings. Penetrating another man or getting penetrated by another are powerful, intimate, and spiritual experiences. (2002, 79)

Indeed, the image of male–male penetration goes to the core of heterosexual stability, a threat so deep, I think, that it can hardly be spoken, visualized, imagined, or engaged with—even within the safe distancing that academic discourse can provide. Inserting a heterosexual voice into gay reflections on the theological, ethical, and spiritual dimensions of bottoms and tops, fisting, or 'barebacking' (i.e. unprotected anal sex)[17] is, at this point, close to impossible. It may signify most sharply the current heterosexual/homosexual divide. An active engagement of the current heterosexual discourse on men and religion with, for example, Long's ethical claim of the liberationist potential of considering 'bottoms' (men penetrated by other men) as a new masculine ideal is difficult to imagine. 'To entertain the possibility of the fully masculine bottom,' Long writes, 'is to begin to think about gender and masculinity in a new way. In turn, masculine gay bottoms can be thought of as the avant-garde for a new way of being a "real" man in the world' (2004, 144). Boisvert writes in *Out on Holy Ground*: 'This openness to a willful condition of receptivity in the sexual act is, I would argue, one of the distinguishing marks of gay male sexuality, something not always readily understood and accepted in a heterosexist, patriarchal culture' (2000, 116; on gay men's receptivity, see also Haldeman 2003). The phrase, 'something not always readily understood' is, of course, rather an understatement.

Outlook

Perhaps these and similar anxieties would first have to be addressed before heterosexual and gay men's studies in religion can move to a partnership of mutuality. But as long as heterosexual men do not acknowledge gay religious and theological scholarship, they do not have to address those anxieties. Thus, heterosexual self-discernment continues to remain absent. Certainly, the closer a heterosexual reader moves from the more abstract, methodological reservations to the emotionally charged, de-stabilizing grounds of gay erotic intimacy, the greater the fear of social pollution and contamination, even among heterosexual men who perceive themselves as non-homophobic. It is feared that wrestling academically with the content, methodology, and theory of gay religious scholarship would associate the heterosexual man with the homoerotic visions and gay sexual desire presented in their writings. Engaging publicly with gay theology would shift the position of the heterosexual reader from invisible consumption to public visibility. The fear of social pollution and contamination (even among largely non-homophobic men), then, is threefold: it is a fear of gay men themselves; it is also a fear about the de-stabilization of one's own heterosexual identity; but most importantly, it is a fear of how one is perceived among one's own heterosexual professional peers. It is a fear of other heterosexual men.

Recognizing these fears, we must move forward. Non-homophobic heterosexual responses to gay theology are necessary and beneficial for gay men, for heterosexual men, and also for our scholarship. Heterosexual men's studies must learn about and from gay religious studies. Equally, gay theology would benefit from the critique of non-homophobic heterosexual readers, because they can bring a fresh view on some of its methodological impasses and unquestioned assumptions. As insiders/outsiders, heterosexual men may be less restrained by the limits of a minoritizing rhetoric that may have slipped into the new field of gay religious studies. To offer but one example in need of further exploration: Heterosexual men might want to assess and contextualize the strong emphasis in gay theology on the links between eros and divine, the sexual and the spiritual. The almost unquestioned divinization of gay sexual experiences—today almost a trope in gay devotional writings—can benefit from being critically examined within the historical context of modern conceptualizations of pleasure and modernity's eschatological expectations.

The playing field for the critical study of men and masculinity in religion, whether from gay, heterosexual, or queer perspectives, is still wide open, with plenty of ground and territory to explore together, precisely because all bring differently lived experiences to the naming and analysis of issues and problems. It might be worthwhile to start a conversation by deliberately not seeking the most basic common comfort zone but, instead, by studying models and practices of masculinity that sit comfortably neither with heterosexual men's studies nor gay men's studies in religion. The history of Christianity (let alone other religious traditions) provides numerous alternative models of masculinities that strike a discomfiting note among twenty-first-century men. Let's just name the once highly valorized ascetic impulse of celibacy or the once celebrated, yet ambiguously experienced eunuch.[18]

There is so much more to say. This is just a beginning.

Notes

1 The 2006 AAR-membership is at about 11,300, of which 960 members are from countries outside the United States and Canada.

2 The debate about the social construction of gender (gender identity, gender roles, sexual desires, etc.) and the emergence of queer studies have amply demonstrated that any such binaries are constructed themselves. This article does not engage theoretical issues on whether and how one can speak about homosexuality and heterosexuality as fixed categories or whether these differences need to be seen as continuum and gradient. Part of the debate would be, of course, the question of whether homosexuality is a natural variant of sexuality (and hence one would engage a liberationist paradigm to assert a public and protected space for a marginalized and oppressed group) or whether gay identity is itself socially constructed and hence, to a certain degree, only definable against the heterosexual norm (or, vice versa, the heterosexual can define himself only against the homosexually constructed man). Queer theory would push the latter. For a debate about differences between queer theory and homosexual scholarship, see Schneider (2000), who favors the former, and Frantzen (1996), who favors historians of homosexuality over queer theorists.

3 Themes and topics relating to Christianity—in practice, theory and theology—have dictated the agenda of the Gay Men's Issues in Religion group for a long time. But the group, as many other sections at the AAR, has over time expanded to include comparative religious perspective. See Long (2004) and Leyland (1998) as two book samples that reflect the comparative expansion.

4 Krondorfer and Culbertson (2004); for another 'archival' entry of similar but narrower content, see Krondorfer (2007).

5 This phrase was used by Goss in an e-mail correspondence with the author (Feb. 7, 2006).

6 Jordan's *Invention of Sodomy* was reviewed by William Percy in the *American Historical Review* 103/2 (April 1998), John Baldwin in *Speculum* 74/2 (April 1999), Lynn Staley in *Church History* 67/4 (Dec. 1998), Laurel Schneider in *Religious Studies Review* 26/1 (2000), and James Keenan, S.J. in *Theological Studies* 59/2 (June 1998) and in the *Journal of Homosexuality* 36/2 (1998). His book, *Silence of Sodom*, was reviewed by Melissa Wilcox in the *Journal of the American Academy of Religion (JAAR)* 70/4 (Dec. 2002), James Keenan, S.J. in *Theological Studies* 62/1 (March 2001), George Piggford in *Canadian Literature* 175 (Winter 2002), and Amy Hollywood in *Signs* 76 (2001). His *Telling Truth in Church* was reviewed, for example, by Krondorfer in *JAAR* 73:1 (March 2005) and Beverly Wildung Harrison in *Conscience* (Autumn 2003).

7 For example, Comstock's *Gay Theology Without Apology* was reviewed in *Conscience* 14 (Winter 1993); his *Unrepentant, Self-Affirming, Practicing* is part of Laurel Schneider's review article on several gay and queer books (2000), is mentioned twice again in the *Religious Studies Review* (vol. 24, April 1998; and vol. 23, April 1997), and in *Theology Today* 53 (January 1997); *A Whosoever Church* was reviewed in *Christian Century* (March 27, 2002) and, briefly, in *The Other Side* (July/August 2001). Robert Goss's *Jesus Acted Up* was reviewed in *Conscience* 14 (Winter 1993), his edited work *Take Back the Word* in *The Journal of Religion* 82/10 (2002), and *Queering Christ* in the gay magazine *Lambda Book Report* (Nov.–Dec. 2002).

8 Clark's early work was reviewed occasionally by *Lambda Book Report* (Nov. 1991; March 1993; and Jan. 1994); *Defying Darkness* (1997a) received one review in the *Religious Studies Review* 24 (July 1998), and *Beyond Our Ghettos* one review by Ron Long in JAAR 63/4 (Winter 1995).

9 For Boisvert's main books (2000; 2004) or for Long, no entries are found in the *Book Review Index* (Detroit, New York: Thomson & Gale). Boisvert's and Goss's edited book *Gay Catholic Priests and Clerical Sexual Misconduct* (2005) is briefly reviewed in two issues of *Conscience* (26/4, Winter 2005; and 27/1, Spring 2006).

10 In such lists, these books are not so much reviewed as announced. They include publications like *Publishers Weekly, Book World, The Booklist, Reference and Research Book News, Library Journal, Choice, TLS Time Literary Supplement, Kirkus Review, Multicultural Review* and *The Gay and Lesbian Review Worldwide.* Outside of peer-reviewed religious studies journals, *Lambda Book Report* carries occasionally reviews of gay religious scholarship. Jordan's work, for example, was also (briefly) reviewed in places like *Virginia Quarterly Review* 77 (Winter 2001) and 73 (Autumn 1997), *Commonweal* 127 (Sep. 8, 2000) and 124 (Oct. 24, 1997), the online *Medical Review* (May 1999), and *Canadian Literature* (2002).

11 Though it needs to be stated that, for example, Ken Stone's *Queer Commentary and the Hebrew Bible* (2001) has also not received any entry in the *Book Review Index*, numerous works of heterosexual and gay scholars alike have advanced our understanding of biblical texts and homosexuality, at times with no strongly pronounced perspectival differences and with no obvious identifiable sexual identity markers. See, for example, the work of William Countryman (1988; see also Countryman and Riley 2001), Martin (1995; 2006), Culbertson (1992), and Moore (1996; 2001). For a brief discussion and a more complete list of works in biblical studies, see Goss (2002: 240; esp. ftns. 4 and 5).

12 For reviews of Boyd's work by a heterosexual and a gay scholarly voice, see Krondorfer's review of *Redeeming Men* in *The Journal of Men's Studies* 5:4 (May 1997) and Clark's review of *The Men We Long to Be* in *The Journal of Men's Studies* 5:2 (Nov. 1996).

13 In queer studies, the proclivity to 'queering' religious texts, figures, and spaces is even more pronounced, because queer theorists seek to 'locate the sexual . . . where we don't expect it,' as Frantzen writes. 'Essays in queer theory disclose the sexual content of texts that seem neutral, "queering" them by exposing their unexamined homosexual content and heteronormative biases' (1996, 260). For the queering of (male) religious texts in antiquity, see, for example, the work of Burrus (2000; 2004) and, from a Jewish perspective, Boyarin (1993; 1997). For the 'queering' of biblical texts, see Stone (2001; 2005) and Moore (1996; 2001). See also Comstock and Henking (1997).

14 See also Boisvert's 'Talking Dirty about Saints' (2006), which is a rejoinder and response to the criticism and scrutiny that his manuscript *Sanctity and Male Desire* (2004) received during the publication process with Pilgrim Press.

15 On the issue of vulnerability in male autobiographical and confessional writings, with references to Augustine, see Krondorfer (1996b; 2002).

16 Published July 2000 (www.catholicleague.org/research/silence_of_Sodom. html), retrieved July 2006. Goss reports (e-mail correspondence with author, Feb. 7, 2006) on similarly unkind, Web-based reviews by the Catholic League of his *Queering Christ* (not found on web in July 2006) and by Mother Angelica's Eternal Word Network of *Jesus Acted Up* (could not be independently verified when searching the net, July 2006).

17 For a description of some of the practice of barebacking as intimate and sacred, see Goss (2002, 83).

18 For celibacy, see, for example, Burrus (2000; 2004) and Stewart (1998, 62–84). In some future piece, I would want to explore 'celibacy' as a sexual choice rather than a

coerced repression of sexuality. In its ideal form, a life of voluntary celibacy requires a constant and detailed verbalization of one's most intimate erotic and sexual sensations. Without such a continuous self-discerning discourse on one's sexuality—as John Cassian, for example, required as part of his monastic rules (Cassian 1997)—celibacy would indeed be just an externally imposed rule. For eunuchs in Western Christianity, see Kuefler (2001), and in Byzantine Christianity, Ringrose (2003). For an interesting interpretation of the 'eunuch' in the Gospel of Matthew, see Anderson and Moore (2003).

Literature

Anderson, Janice Capel, and Stephen D. Moore. 2003. 'Matthew and Masculinity,' in *New Testament Masculinities*, eds Stephen Moore and Janice Chapel Anderson, Semeia Studies 45 (Atlanta: Society of Biblical Literature). Pp. 67–91.

Boisvert, Donald L. 2000. *Out on Holy Ground: Meditations on Gay Men's Spirituality*. Cleveland: Pilgrim.

——. 2004. *Sanctity and Male Desire: A Gay Reading of Saint*. Cleveland: Pilgrim.

——. 2006. 'Talking Dirty about Saints: Storytelling and the Politics of Desire,' *Theology & Sexuality* 12/2:165–80.

Boisvert, Donald L. and Robert Goss (eds). 2005. *Gay Catholic Priests and Clerical Sexual Misconduct: Breaking the Silence*. Binghamton: Haworth Press.

Boswell, John. 1980. *Christianity, Social Tolerance, and Homosexuality: Gay People in Western Europe from the Beginnings of the Christian Era to the Fourteenth Century*. Chicago: University of Chicago Press.

Boyarin, Daniel. 1993. *Carnal Israel: Reading Sex in Talmudic Culture*. Berkeley: University of California Press.

——. 1997. *Unheroic Conduct: The Rise of Heterosexuality and the Invention of the Jewish Man*. Berkeley: University of California Press.

Boyd, Stephen B. 1995. *The Men We Long to Be: Beyond Domination to a New Christian Understanding of Manhood*. San Francisco: HarperSanFrancisco.

Boyd, Stephen B., Merle Longwood and Mark Muesse (eds). 1996. *Redeeming Men: Religion and Masculinities*. Louisville: Westminster John Knox.

Burrus, Virginia. 2000. *'Begotten, Not Made': Conceiving Manhood in Late Antiquity*. Stanford: Stanford University Press.

——. 2004. *The Sex Lives of Saints: An Erotics of Ancient Hagiography*. Philadelphia: University of Pennsylvania Press.

Capps, Donald. 2002. *Men and Their Religion: Honor, Hope, and Humor*. Harrisburg: Trinity Press International.

Cassian, John. 1997. *The Conferences*, trans. and annotated by Boniface Ramsey, O.P. New York: Newman Press.

Clark, J. Michael. 1989. *A Place to Start: Toward an Unapologetic Gay Liberation Theology*. Dallas: Monument Press.

——. 1992. *Masculine Socialization & Gay Liberation: A Conversation on the Work of James Nelson and Other Wise Friends*. Arlington: The Liberal Press.

——. 1993. *Beyond Our Ghettos: Gay Theology in Ecological Perspective*. Cleveland: Pilgrim.

——. 1997a. *Defying Darkness: Gay Theology in the Shadows*. Cleveland: Pilgrim.

——. 1997b. 'Doing the Work of Love: I. Men's Studies at the Margins,' *The Journal of Men's Studies* 5/4 (May):315–31.

——. 1999. 'A Gay Man's Wish List for the Future of Men's Studies in Religion,' *The Journal of Men's Studies* 7/2 (Winter):269–73.

Comstock, Gary David. 1993. *Gay Theology Without Apology*. Cleveland: Pilgrim.

——. 1996. *Unrepentant, Self-Affirming, Practicing: Lesbian/Bisexual/Gay People within Organized Religion*. New York: Continuum.

——. 2001. *A Whosoever Church: Welcoming Lesbians and Gay Men into African American Congregations*. Louisville: Westminster John Knox.

Comstock, Gary D. and Susan E. Henking (eds). 1997. *Que(e)rying Religion: A Critical Anthology*. New York: Continuum.

Countryman, William L. 1988. *Dirt, Greed and Sex: Sexual Ethics in the New Testament and their Implications for Today*. Philadelphia: Fortress.

Countryman, William L. and M. R. Riley. 2001. *Gifted by Otherness: Gay and Lesbian Christians in the Church*. Harrisburg: Morehouse.

Culbertson, Philip. 1992. *New Adam: The Future of Male Spirituality*. Minneapolis: Fortress.

——. 2006. 'Mothers and Their Golden Sons: Exploring a Theology of Narcissism,' in *Religion and Sexuality: Passionate Debates*, ed. C. K. Robertson. New York: Peter Lang. Pp. 209–38.

Frantzen, Alan. 1996. 'Between the Lines: Queer Theory, the History of Homosexuality, and Anglo-Saxon Penitentials,' *The Journal of Medieval and Early Modern Studies* 26/2 (Spring):255–96.

Gorsline, Robin H. 1996. 'Facing the Body on the Cross: A Gay Man's Reflections on Passion and Crucifixion,' in Krondorfer 1996, pp. 125–45.

Goss, Robert E. 1993. *Jesus Acted Up: A Gay and Lesbian Manifesto*. San Francisco: HarperSanFrancisco.

——. 2002. *Queering Christ: Beyond Jesus Acted Up*. Cleveland: Pilgrim.

Haldeman, Scott. 1996. 'Bringing Good News to the Body: Masturbation and Male Identity,' in Krondorfer 1996, pp. 111–24.

——. 2003. 'Receptivity and Revelation: A Spirituality of Gay Male Sex,' in *Body and Soul: Rethinking Sexuality and Justice-Love*, eds Marvin Ellison and Sylvia Thorson-Smith. Cleveland: Pilgrim. Pp. 218–31.

Horner, Tom. 1978. *Jonathan Loved David: Homosexuality in Biblical Times*. Philadelphia: Westminster.

Jordan, Mark D. 1997. *The Invention of Sodomy in Christian Theology*. Chicago: University of Chicago Press.

——. 2000. *The Silence of Sodom: Homosexuality in Modern Catholicism*. Chicago: University of Chicago Press.

——. 2003. *Telling Truths in Church: Scandal, Flesh, and Christian Speech*. Boston: Beacon.

Krondorfer, Björn (ed.). 1996a. *Men's Bodies, Men's Gods: Male Identities in a (Post-) Christian Culture*. New York: New York University Press.

——. 1996b. 'The Confines of Male Confessions: On Religion, Bodies, and Mirrors,' in Krondorfer 1996a. Pp. 205–34.

——. 2002. 'Revealing the Non-Absent Male Body: Confessions of an African Bishop and a Jewish Ghetto Policeman,' in *Revealing Male Bodies*, eds Nancy Tuana et al. Bloomington: Indiana University Press. Pp. 247–68.

——. 2007. 'World Religions, Christianity,' in *International Encyclopedia of Men and Masculinities* (1 vol.), eds M. Flood, J. K. Gardiner, B. Pease, and K. Pringle. London and New York: Routledge. Pp. 658–60.

Krondorfer, Björn and Phil Culbertson. 2004. 'Men Studies in Religion,' in *Encyclopedia of Religion*, 2nd edition (vol. 9), ed.-in-chief Lindsay Jones. Detroit and New York: Macmillan. Pp. 5861–5.

Kuefler, Mathew. 2001. *The Manly Eunuch: Masculinity, Gender Ambiguity, and the Christian Ideology on Late Antiquity*. Chicago: University of Chicago Press.

Kuefler, Mathew (ed.). 2006. *The Boswell Thesis: Essays on 'Christianity, Social Tolerance, and Homosexuality.'* Chicago: University of Chicago Press.

Leyland, Winston (ed.). 1998. *Queer Dharma: Voices of Gay Buddhists*. San Francisco: Gay Sunshine Press.

Long, Ronald E. 1997. 'The Sacrality of Beauty and Homosex: A Neglected Factor in the Understanding of Contemporary Gay Life,' in eds Gary David Comstock and Susan E. Henking. Pp. 266–81.

———. 2004. *Men, Homosexuality, and the Gods: An Exploration into the Religious Significance of Male Homosexuality in World Perspective*. New York: Harrington Park Press.

Martin, Dale B. 1995. *The Corinthian Body*. New Haven: Yale University Press.

———. 2006. *Sex and the Single Savior: Gender and Sexuality in Biblical Interpretations*. Louisville: Westminster John Knox Press.

McNeill, John J. 1976. *The Church and the Homosexual*. Kansas City: Sheed Andrews and McMeel; reissued 1993, Boston: Beacon.

———. 1988. *Taking a Chance on God: Liberating Theology for Gays, Lesbians, and their Lovers, Families, and Friends*. Boston: Beacon.

———. 1995. *Freedom, Glorious Freedom: The Spiritual Journey to the Fullness of Life for Gays, Lesbians, and Everybody Else*. Boston: Beacon.

Moore, Stephen D. 1996. *God's Gym: Divine Male Bodies of the Bible*. New York: Routledge.

———. 2001. *God's Beauty Parlor: And Other Queer Spaces in and around the Bible*. Stanford: Stanford University Press.

Nelson, James B. 1978. *Embodiment: An Approach to Sexuality and Christian Theology*. Minneapolis: Augsburg.

———. 1992. *Body Theology*. Louisville: Westminster John Knox.

Ringrose, Kathryn M. 2003. *The Perfect Servant: Eunuchs and the Social Construction of Gender in Byzantium*. Chicago: Chicago University Press.

Schneider, Laurel. 2000. 'Homosexuality, Queer Theory, and Christian Theology,' *Religious Studies Review* 26/1 (January):3–12.

Stewart, Columba. 1998. *Cassian the Monk*. Oxford: Oxford University Press.

Stone, Ken (ed.). 2001. *Queer Commentary and the Hebrew Bible*. Sheffield/Cleveland: Sheffield Academic Press/Pilgrim.

———. 2005. *Practicing Safer Texts: Food, Sex and Bible in Queer Perspective*. London: T&T Clark.

Van Leeuwen, Mary Stewart. 2002. *My Brother's Keeper: What Social Sciences do (and don't) tell us about Masculinity*. Downer's Grove: Intervarsity Press.

Wink, Walter (ed.). 1999. *Homosexuality and Christian Faith: Questions of Conscience for the Churches*. Minneapolis: Fortress.

Critical Theory, Deconstruction, and Liberation

Editor's Introduction

'There are times when the black man is locked into his body,' wrote Frantz Fanon famously in *Black Skin, White Mask* (1967, 225). This black body is also locked into the larger history of colonialism and the continuing politics of skin color within a racially unjust system. Seen through the eyes of a hegemonic 'white' masculinity, the black man is at once invisible and a threat – a male body charged with sexual prowess but kept politically impotent, a body admired for its strength, yet exploited for cheap labor.

All of the above is true, and none of it is true. Layers of adverse stereotyping, historical experiences, symbolic configurations and class discrimination have created twisted and knotted discourses on race, religion and masculinity that are difficult to untangle. 'The black body remains an ambiguous object in our society, still susceptible to whatever meanings the white gaze assigns to it' (Johnson 1995, 610; also Gordon 1996; Brown-Douglas 1999). Hence, it is all the more important that a critical men's studies in religion approach gets its hands on the knots of racial discourse and assists in disentangling the warped ideas around men of 'color'. In this chapter, Baker-Fletcher argues forcefully for men's studies to engage in such a task. Elsewhere, he writes:

> African American communities of the United States are still suffering from the continuing effects of racial discrimination, class exploitation, and gender discrimination that have affected our existence since the Middle Passage. There is a sameness to black existence that transcends the specific historical differences between slavery and our time. (Baker-Fletcher 1996, 89)

As a Christian theologian, Baker-Fletcher is operating with the analytical tools of deconstructionism but also embraces the constructionist perspectives of Africentrism and womanist theology. His goal is to empower black people in the United States. Africentric ideas, on the one hand, led him to articulate the 'XODUS Journey', a combination of the biblical exodus and the '"X" honoring the spiritual-cultural journey of Malcolm X.' XODUS is an extrication from the history and ideology of white impositions, a journey toward a 'space suitable for the flourishing of the bodies, souls, minds, and spirits of all African people' (Baker-Fletcher 1996, 66; also 1995; Munir 1996; Butler 2002). Womanist theology, on the other hand – which brings black women's experiences to the task of theological interpretation (Cannon 1988; Townes 1993; Williams 1993)

– has motivated Baker-Fletcher to apply a gender-conscious theological reading to the black male experience. Together with his wife Karen Baker-Fletcher, a womanist theologian herself (1998; 2007), he has co-written *My Sister, My Brother: Womanist and Xodus God-Talk* (1997).

Publications by the Same Author

Baker-Fletcher, Garth Kasimu. 1995. *Xodus: An African American Male Journey.* Minneapolis: Fortress.

——. 1996. 'Black Bodies, Whose Bodies? African American Men in XODUS', in *Men's Bodies, Men's Gods*, ed. Björn Krondorfer. New York: New York University Press. Pp. 65–93.

—— (ed). 1998. *Black Religion After the Million Man March: Voices on the Future.* Maryknoll: Orbis.

——. 2000. *Dirty Hands: Christian Ethics in a Morally Ambiguous World.* Minneapolis: Augsburg Fortress.

Baker-Fletcher, Garth Kasimu and Karen Baker-Fletcher. 1997. *My Sister, My Brother: Womanist and Xodus God-Talk.* Maryknoll: Orbis.

Further Reading

Baker-Fletcher, Karen. 1998. *Sisters of Dust, Sisters of Spirit: Womanist Wordings on God and Creation.* Minneapolis: Augsburg Fortress.

——. 2007. *Dancing with God: The Trinity from a Womanist Perspective.* St. Louis: Chalice Press.

Brown-Douglas, Kelly. 1999. *Sexuality and the Black Church: A Womanist Perspective.* Maryknoll: Orbis.

Butler, Lee H., Jr. 2002. 'Xodus to the Promised Man: Revising our Anthropodicy', in *The Spirituality of Men*, ed. Philip Culbertson. Minneapolis: Fortress. Pp. 257–69.

Cannon, Katie G. 1988. *Black Womanist Ethics.* Atlanta: Scholars Press.

Gordon, Lewis R. 1996. 'Can Men Worship? Reflections on Male Bodies in Bad Faith and a Theology of Authenticity', in *Men's Bodies, Men's Gods*, ed. Björn Krondorfer. New York: New York University Press. Pp. 235–250.

Fanon, Frantz. 1967. *Black Skin, White Mask.* New York: Grove Press.

Johnson, Charles. 1993. 'A Phenomenology of the Black Body' (Special Issue: *The Male Body*, Part One). *Michigan Quarterly Review* 32/4 (Fall):599–614.

Munir, Fareed. 1996. 'Malcolm X's Religious Pilgrimage: From Black Separatism to a Universal Way', in *Redeeming Men*, eds Stephen B. Boyd, Merle Longwood and Mark Muesse. Louisville: Westminster John Knox. Pp. 62–76.

Pollard, Alton B, III. 1996. 'Magnificent Manhood: The Transcendent Witness of Howard Thurman', in *Redeeming Men*, eds Stephen B. Boyd, Merle Longwood and Mark Muesse. Louisville: Westminster John Knox. Pp. 222–33.

Townes, Emilie M. 1993. *Womanist Justice, Womanist Hope.* Atlanta: Scholars Press.

Williams, Delores S. 1993. *Sisters in the Wilderness: The Challenge of Womanist God-Talk.* Maryknoll: Orbis.

Critical Theory, Deconstruction, and Liberation

GARTH KASIMU BAKER-FLETCHER

The 'birth' of men's studies in religion was a very intentional and creative response to the perceived lack of a self-conscious, scholarly study of men. It came in the wake of a proliferation of studies on the psychosocial and cultural [de]formations of women. At such a turning point, the field of men's studies needs to remember its *reactive* birth, lest it become as covertly ideological as the NAAWP (National Association for the Advancement of White People). While striving to become a respected (read 'objective') academic discipline, we often fail to acknowledge the challenge of feminists and womanists who ask us, 'Hasn't the entire history of academic studies been a covert and unconscious men's studies program?' The project of men's studies must deconstruct its reactive birth and not avoid it, precisely because we see ourselves as *self-consciously studying males, without an evil intent.* Not to do so leaves us in a dishonest position, morally and intellectually. Further, it continues the kind of claims of disrespecting women's voices that traditional patriarchal studies exemplified.

Building on the formal works by Krondorfer (1996) and Boyd, Longwood and Muesse (1996), I believe there are several methodological approaches to 'men's studies.' Broadly speaking one can say that they fall into about six general kinds of approaches:

1. *Descriptive* studies that try to flesh out the historical development of various kinds of masculinities by utilizing the paradigm of human sciences.

2. *Marginalized Other* studies (or 'Group-Specific' as named by Boyd and Longwood) with the eruption of the subjugated voices of previously silenced men, for example, African American, gay, Latino, Native American, and other Two-Thirds World men.

3. *Traditionalist* approaches that seek to re-capture a 'lost' sense of 'authentic' manhood. Often these studies have an ambivalent relationship towards feminist critiques of sexism; citing the sense of loss of a 'deep masculine' as one of the regrettable consequences of the women's movement in contemporary society. Promise Keepers is an excellent example of how traditionalist men have formed a conservative populist movement.

4. *Essentialist* approaches seek to revivify and re-ground males in a notion of an 'essence' of masculinity deeply rooted in our psyches. Also ambivalent toward feminist movements, the aim of essentialist approaches (like that of Robert Bly's *Iron John*) is to undo the enervation of masculinity that often is attributed to contemporary women's movements as well as to the stresses of a post-capitalist, high-tech era.

5. *Pro-Feminist/Womanist/Mujerista* approaches promote critique of traditional normative views of 'being a man' as sexist, exclusionary, and hierarchical. This approach deconstructs cultural practices of manhood as inimical to women, children, and ultimately men themselves.

6. And *Healing Psychology* approaches place the academic discourse of men's studies into active dialogue with disciplines of psychology and psychotherapy. This approach is quite diverse in seriousness of academic endeavor. It includes everything from kitsch self-help manuals and men's magazines sold at magazine-counters to serious scholarly research and theory. Pastoral psychologists like Robert Moore, Edward Wimberly, and James Poling are representative authors of this type. Their work expresses concern for helping males to overcome the stresses of adjusting to the pressures of contemporary re-formulations of male roles, manhood, and expectations in the family.

Mass marches like that of the Million Man March of October 1995 and the Promise Keepers March of October 1997 could be considered examples of a kind of movement consciousness among males. What is difficult to determine is the extent to which these mass marches represent a groundswell of the millions of men in the United States. On the day of the 'Stand in the Gap' Promise Keepers March (or 'gathering' as they preferred to call it), C-Span reported that more than 53 percent of its respondents supported the goals of the Promise Keepers. If one puts any stock in reading responses on the Internet, it is shocking how much of the Promise Keepers Web site has negative testimony about the Nation of Islam, Louis Farrakhan, and the Million Man March. One man, Gary Thomas, reports alleged strong-arm tactics and threats weighed against African American evangelical pastor John Jenkins of First Baptist of Glendarn Maryland.

My work has tended toward pro-feminist/womanist/*mujerista* approaches. I examine the fundamental problematic of maleness in relationship to the majority of cultures on the globe—that of patriarchy. Clearly men's studies cannot become what Cornel West would call a 'think analysis' without dealing critically with methodologies and approaches that bolster patriarchy. Insofar as the discipline of men's studies in religion does not deal with the historical project of patriarchy as its central and fundamental problematic, it fails as a critical theory. The 'work' of men's studies ought to be akin to that of liberationists—to deconstruct previously unquestioned categories and methodologies that legitimate systemic injustice. As long as men's studies has not taken seriously feminist/womanist/*mujerista* critiques of male sexism and systemic global patriarchy, it can easily fall prey to the powerful co-opting energies of normative traditionalist ideals of masculinity. A thorough deconstruction of 'men's studies' may reveal that we cannot justify remaining as 'men's studies,' but ought to move toward a 'gender studies' model, lest we unintentionally bolster the already embedded power of systemic patriarchy. The critical, deconstructive *telos* ought to have the possibility of creating a new academic space for making gender studies a genuine source of critical creativity. The cultural power of reinstating what is close to a traditionalist (read 'patriarchal') form of masculinity must be taken with utmost seriousness.

A simple description of the historical trajectory of sexist maleness, or even an uncritical 'listening' to the voices of 'Marginalized Other' men, can lead to a kind of *laissez faire* attitude toward dehumanizing forms of being a male human being. For example, I once heard a West African male ostensibly 'describe' the rituals of scarification and female genital mutilation as equivalently painful rites 'necessary' for adult initiation and cultural survival in West Africa. I believe that scars on one's face (male) are not morally 'equivalent' to the massive physical destruction caused to a woman's body in the female rites of initiation, and would contest that such rites are *fundamental* to tribal survival. My argument (and that of most of the womanists) was not welcomed, however, because the unspoken 'norm' of the conversation was to 'listen' without critique to his supposedly 'objective description.' Cries of 'cultural imperialism' were quickly sounded, and so the atmosphere of debate was quickly squelched.

A deconstructive and critical theory of men's studies should answer the charge of cultural imperialism. In my view, however, critique of sexist practices is *transcultural*. Fighting against violent, mutilating, abusive misogyny ought to be a 'universal' or *normative* principle. I am willing to embrace such a norm as necessary, at least at this point for men's studies *because* a deconstructed analysis of this West African would have probably revealed a strongly ideological traditionalist approach masquerading as 'descriptive.' A deconstructive approach insists on the rights of women to be treated at all times and all places as fully human and equal beings. The point of uplifting the humanity of women for men's studies is one way that *all men* can insure a necessary and healthy openness to self-criticism.

Self-criticism is not 'p.c.' (politically correct), but is another important norm necessary in the deconstruction of misogynist forms of masculinity. It has a strongly deconstructive function, keeping open the possibilities of change. To hold to a norm of self-critique is to recognize and nurture a 'becoming' aspect of our humanity. I believe that such a deconstruction of masculinity may be more fruitful than attempting to revive some 'lost sense' of 'deep masculinity.'

Most important, self-criticism aims at preventing the facile energies of preclusion regnant in so many 'discussions' about different kinds of masculinities. In my work, *Xodus: An African American Male Journey* (1995), I contend that it is by insisting upon the norm of self-criticism that one articulates an openness to the becoming/unfolding aspect of humanity that is what it means to be on an 'Xodus Journey.' Although directed primarily to pan African males, the Xodus Journey posits the concept that males can grow into more humane embodiments of humanity by intentionally incorporating feminist/womanist critiques of sexism. As such, Xodus is a kind of universalist discourse, dealing with an element of 'essentialism,' namely, that of our common humanity.

In *Xodus*, I attempt to engage both a historical approach toward the development of the iconography of black males in the United States; and a cultural studies critique of how this iconography of the clown, the pervert, and the worker were continually subverted and recast by black males themselves. I reinterpret black men's lives from within our own creative resistance. So doing, *Xodus* opens a new theo-ethical space for self-critical reflection on the possibilities of being an anti-sexist, inclusive, 'Becoming Body-Self.'

At the same time an Xodus conception of masculinity recognizes the important work that the healing psychology approach of men's studies provides for many males, especially males from disenfranchised and socially marginalized ethnic-cultural groups. With feminists and womanists, an Xodus masculinity takes care to note the ways in which ideas of humanity inimical to the flourishing of one-half of the human race wind up crippling the fullness of all humanity. High rates of stroke, heart attacks, and intestinal illnesses are but prominent indications of the deep 'price' men pay for conforming to patriarchal expectations of manhood. *Men need to be redeemed from our traditions, practices, and uncritical visions.* So the gains of learning about how our psyches and practices must be transformed by healing energies need to be combined with a liberating vision.

In the end holistic attempts to envision masculinity like Xodus must query about our constructive *telos.* Is the goal of all this study activism toward social change? Is the goal to be more fully humane, compassionate human beings who happen to be male? Is the goal our ability to believe in and act out of a fully co-operative partnership of equity with women? If one could answer, 'all of the above,' then perhaps we might be able to move on to the final question of 'means.'

Deconstruction operates most effectively as a razor-sharp 'means' toward a reconstructive end. In *Xodus,* I symbolize this deconstructive activity as a 'journey' whereby we recognize the necessity for stripping away layers of emotion-denying, abusive practices that have become the edifice of the Hall of Masculinity (as my colleague Victor Anderson calls it). The Journey of Xodus is not a deconstruction without a reconstructive intent, it is just suspicious of what might well be called *premature reconstruction.* Part of the criticism that the Xodus project brings to efforts like that of Promise Keepers and the Million Man March is the Journey Deconstruction of masculinity, precluded by facile turns to clichéd 'pillars' of the Hall of Masculinity. You know these 'pillars'; they include, 'the man is the HEAD of the family,' or 'the real problem of our country is that *men* are not acting like *men.*' On the Journey, it is important to viciously, gleefully, and yet carefully exorcize the hidden sexist presuppositions of such statements and sentiments that seem to flow so easily from 'Men's Movement' folks—no matter what ethnicity, religion, or class.

On the Xodus Journey, I have chosen three historic figures for partners—Malcolm X, Martin Luther King, Jr., and Howard Thurman. The most overtly deconstructive of contemporary Western White Supremacy is Malcolm X. His humorous portrayals of both conscious and unconscious racism are classics for all men and women in their transgression of the constrictions of propriety as it is defined by the etiquette categories of an oppressive society. From Malcolm I learn that the Xodus Journey must be unrelenting in its vocal opposition to all attempts to subvert and reinsert the old ways. Yet Malcolm was a rabid sexist whose rigid definitions of gender-defined roles only began to change at the very end of his life. His patriarchy must not be imitated, even as he profoundly teaches deconstruction of supremacist tactics.

For a broader view of multiculturalism and the necessity of deconstructing capitalist oppression, we need to turn to Martin Luther King, Jr. King's deconstruction of capitalism's devices of 'divide and conquer' were so threatening to the 'powers that be' in 1968 as he planned the Poor People's March in Washington, DC, that he was assassinated! At the same time, King's vision of a Beloved Community has a deconstructive *telos* worth maintaining in our time. In *Xodus Journey,* I see King's Dream as a militant Christian reinterpretation of the possibilities of a truly democratic society.

From Howard Thurman we may learn that the Journey must deconstruct the separative categories of domination-over-nature that have been wedded to idealized patriarchy. Ideally, says contemporary patriarchy, nature is but a resource we 'use.' Thurman deconstructs this assumption by establishing the mystical, theological, and cosmological commonality of all that exists. Seeking to assert the Community of All, Thurman's mystic vision of communion debunks categorical atomism, political separatism, and anti-ecological economics. A powerful deconstruction of homophobic maleness can be built upon this common foundation.

The womanist vision of whole communities of people as espoused by Emilie Townes, Karen Baker-Fletcher, and Katie Cannon form other deconstructive partners on the Journey. Their deconstructive contribution is a reminder to all who deign to commit themselves to the norm of *Xodus Journey* that listening to the Sisters, the outspoken, brilliant, and fiercely loving women from around own 'corner' remains key to liberation. From womanist criticism I learn to listen to how I 'sound' and 'act' despite my best intentions. No matter how self-critical the *Journey of Xodus*, we have not accomplished our inclusive, non-sexist vision! The Journey continually humbles because it deconstructs facile assumptions of accomplishment. Even the best intentions of 'pro-feminist/womanist/*mujerista*' males does not mean that we have 'arrived' at the place of non-sexism! No male in our time can stand settled before the Journey's deconstructive sweep.

Men's studies in religion must continue to posit the necessity of deconstruction in order to be a liberating critical theory. Born in the turmoil of redefining the humanity, gendered functions, and essences of women and men, men's studies must clarify itself as an *explicitly anti-patriarchal discourse.* In order to keep open its constructive theoretical aims, men's studies ought to aim toward becoming 'gender studies.' Under this rubric, women and men can be brought together who are interested in transforming our common humanity. In vigilance, such a deconstructed men's studies/gender studies would model a very different kind of masculinity. Being suspicious of premature reconstructions of popular celebrations of 'new' masculine ideals, these difficult next steps must be taken with courage.

Literature

Baker-Fletcher, Kasimu G. 1995. *Xodus: An African American Male Journey.* Minneapolis: Fortress.
Boyd, Stephen B., W. M. Longwood and M. W. Muesse (eds). 1996. *Redeeming Men: Religion and Masculinities.* Louisville: Westminster John Knox.
Krondorfer, Björn (ed.). 1996. *Men's Bodies, Men's Gods: Male Identities in a (Post-) Christian Culture.* New York: New York University Press.

32

Beyond Machismo: A Cuban Case Study

Editor's Introduction

'I am a recovering *macho*, a product of an oppressive society.' So begins Miguel De La Torre's reflections on masculinity within a Latino/Hispanic context. In this society, 'gender, race and class domination do not exist in isolated compartments . . . [but] are created in the space where they interact and conflict with each other, a space I will label *machismo*.'

De La Torre is a Christian ethicist. Born in Cuba before the Castro Revolution, he came as an infant with his refugee family to the United States. After a career in a real estate company in Miami and an involvement in local politics, De La Torre decided to attend Southern Baptist Theological Seminary. Experiencing, in his words, a 'lack of opportunities within the church structure due to ethnic discrimination', he continued his education in social ethics, focusing on the intersection of religion, race, class and gender oppression, especially as it applies to Latino and Latina religiosity within the United States, the Caribbean and Latin America.

Parallel to Baker-Fletcher's threefold grounding in critical theory, Africentrism and womanist theology (chapter 31), De La Torre names as his resources post-colonial theory, Latino religiosity and *mujerista* theology. Like womanist theology, *mujerista* theology is a theology of liberation for women of a particular ethnic background within the United States. It refers to the theological embedding of a liberation praxis of and for Latina women (see Isasi-Díaz 1993). When De La Torre analyzes *machismo* within the contours of colonialism, sexism, racism and classism, he brings to the issue of Latino masculinity a historical perspective, a critical assessment and an ethical pronouncement.

Religious studies scholars have occasionally applied the concept of *machismo* to male behavior outside of the Hispanic communities (for example, Muesse 1996; Rosenstock 2003), but for De La Torre *machismo* is a challenge particular to the Latino male experience. Taking an activist stance, he also points to the need of social and individual healing (De La Torre 2003; 2004a; also Lloyd Moffett 2008; Welland and Ribner 2008). Echoing Mary Daly's 'house of mirrors', he concludes: 'Our task as Hispanic ethicists is to move toward dismantling *machismo*, to go beyond *machismo*, by shattering the illusions created in our hall of mirrors.'

Publications by the Same Author

De La Torre, Miguel. 2002. *Reading the Bible from the Margins*. Maryknoll: Orbis.

——. 2003. *La Lucha for Cuba: Religion and Politics on the Streets of Miami*. Berkeley: University of California Press.

——. 2004a. *Doing Christian Ethics from the Margins*. Maryknoll: Orbis.

——. 2004b. *Santería: The Beliefs and Rituals of a Growing Religion in America*. Grand Rapids: Eerdmans.

—— (ed.). 2004c. *Handbook on U.S. Theologies of Liberation*. St. Louis: Chalice Press.

——. 2007. *A Lily Among the Thorns: Imagining a New Christian Sexuality*. San Francisco: Jossey-Bass.

De La Torre, Miguel and Edwin David Aponte (eds). 2006. *Handbook of Latina/o Theologies*. St. Louis: Chalice Press.

De La Torre, Miguel and Gaston Espinosa (eds). 2006. *Rethinking Latino(a) Religion & Identity*. Cleveland: Pilgrim.

Further Reading

Gaston Espinosa, Gaston, Virgilio Elizondo and Jesse Miranda (eds). 2005. *Latino Religions and Civic Activism in the United States*. New York: Oxford University Press.

Isasi-Díaz, Ada María. 1993. *En la Lucha: Elaborating a Mujerista Theology*. Minneapolis: Fortress.

Lloyd Moffett, Stephen, 2008. 'Holy Activist, Secular Saint: Religion and the Social Activism of César Chávez', in *Mexican American Religions: Spirituality, Activism and Culture*, eds Gastón Espinosa and Mario García. Durham: Duke University Press. Pp. 106–24.

Muesse, Mark W. 1996. 'Religious Machismo: Masculinity and Fundamentalism', in *Redeeming Men*, eds Stephen B. Boyd, Merle Longwood and Mark Muesse. Louisville: Westminster John Knox. Pp. 89–102.

Rosenstock, Bruce. 2003. 'Messianism, Machismo, and "Marranism": The Case of Abraham Miguel Cardoso', in *Queer Theory and the Jewish Question*, eds Daniel Boyarin, Daniel Itzgovitz and Ann Pellegrini. New York: Columbia University Press. Pp. 199–227.

Tamez, Elsa. 1987. *Against Machismo*. Oak Park: Meyer-Stone Books.

Welland, Christauria and Neil Ribner. 2008. *Healing From Violence: Latino Men's Journey to a New Masculinity*. New York: Springer Publishing Company.

Beyond Machismo: A Cuban Case Study

MIGUEL DE LA TORRE

I am a recovering *macho*, a product of an oppressive society, a society where gender, race and class domination do not exist in isolated compartments, nor are they neatly relegated to uniform categories of repression. They are created in the space where they interact and conflict with each other, a space I will label *machismo*. The understanding of *machismo* fully considers sexism, heterosexism, racism, ethnocentrism, and classism. All forms of oppression are identical in their attempt to domesticate the Other. The sexist, who sees women playing a lesser productive role than men, transfers upon the non-elite male Other effeminate characteristics, placing him in a feminine space for 'easy mounting.'

This article explores the multidimensional aspect of intra-Hispanic oppression by unmasking the socio-historical construction of *machismo*. Usually, disenfranchised groups construct well-defined categories as to who are the perpetrators and who are the victims of injustices. All too often, we who are Hispanic ethicists tend to identify oppressive structures of the dominant Eurocentric culture while overlooking repression conducted within our own community. I suggest that within the marginalized space of the Latino/a community there exists intra-structures of oppression along gender, race, and class lines, creating the need for an ethical initiative to move beyond what Edward Said terms 'the rhetoric of blame' (1994, 14, 96, 228–30). Specifically, this article will present a paradigm called *machismo*, which explicates intra-Hispanic oppression. [. . .]

The *Machismo* Paradigm

To be a man, a *macho*, implies both domination and protection for those under you, specifically women. It becomes the *macho*'s responsibility, his burden, to educate those below his superior standards. Because of my gender, I confess my complicity with sexist social structures, a complicity motivated by personal advantages.[1] All things being equal, I prevail over women in the marketplace, in the church community, and within our Hispanic community because I am male. It is neither my intention to speak for women about their oppression, nor to provide them with the necessary pedagogy to achieve liberation. Several, although unfortunately not enough, *mujerista* theologians are presenting this voice.[2] My contribution to the discourse must be limited to how I, as a male, as a *macho*, facilitate the oppression of the gendered Other.

Because sexism reflects one aspect of *machismo*, it is appropriate to expand the meaning of this term to include all forms of oppression imposed on those who fail to live up to the manly standards of being a white, elite, Cuban male.[3] *Machismo* is as much about race and class as it is about gender. For Cubans, seriously dealing with patriarchal structures must be the first stage in the process of dismantling all forms of oppression, providing for the liberation and possible reconciliation of all, including women.

History is forged through one's *cojones* (balls). Women, non-whites and the poor fail to influence history because they lack *cojones*, a gift given to *machos* by the ultimate *Macho*, God. To call a man *lavándole los blumes de la mujer* (one who washes his wife's bloomers) is to question his *machismo*. 'El colmo' (the ultimate sin) is to be called a '*maricón*' (a derogatory term meaning queer or fag), the antithesis of *machismo*. We, white Cuban elite males look into Lacan's mirror and recognize ourselves as *machos* through the distancing process of negative self-definition: 'I am what I am not.' The formation of the subject's ego constructs an illusory self-representation through the negation of *cojones*, now projected upon Others, identified as non-*machos*. Ascribing femininity to the Other forces the construction of female identity to originate with the *macho*. In fact, the feminine Object, in and of itself, is seen as nothing, apart from a masculine Subject who provides unifying purpose.

The resulting gaze of the white Cuban elite male inscribes effeminacy upon Others who are not *macho* enough to 'make' history, or 'provide' for their family, or 'resist' their subjugation to the dominant *macho*. Unlike in the United States, sexual identity for Cubans is defined in terms of masculinity, not in terms of gender. Women are 'the not male.' When the gendered Other demonstrates hyper-*macho* qualities, she can be praised for being *macho*. This was the case with both General Maceo, who was black, and his mother, thus both were described *macho*.[4]

The phallic signifier of *machismo* is located in the *cojones*. For Cubans, *cojones*, not the penis, become our cultural 'signifier of signifiers.' The Other, if male, may have a penis, but lacks the *cojones* to use it. I conquer, I subdue, I domesticate *por mis cojones* (by my balls). A distinction is made between *cojones*, the male testicles, and *cojones*, the metaphoric signifier. Power and authority exhibit *cojones*, which are in fact derived from social structures, traditions, norms, laws, and customs created by *machos*, who usually are white and rich.

From one perspective, no one has *cojones*. The *macho* lives, always threatened by possible loss of his *cojones*, while the non-*macho* is forcefully deprived. The potent symbolic power invested in the *cojones* both signals and veils white elite Cuban male socioeconomic power. Constructing those oppressed as feminine allowed white Cuban men with *cojones* to assert their privilege by constructing oppressed Others as inhabitants of the castrated realm of the exotic and primitive (see Grosz 1990, 115–45). Lacking *cojones*, the Other does not exist, except as designated by the desire of the one with *cojones*. Like a benevolent father (*el patrón*), it becomes the duty and responsibility of those with *cojones* to care for, provide for, and protect those below. The castrated male (read, race and class Other) occupies a feminine space where his body is symbolically sodomized as prelude to the sodomizing of his mind.

The non-*macho* becomes enslaved by the inferiority engraved upon their flesh by the Cuban ethos. Likewise, the *macho* is also enslaved to his own so-called superiority that flows from his *cojones*. While the non-*machos* are forced to flee from their individuality, the *macho* must constantly attempt to live up to a false construction. Both are alienated, both suffer from an obsessive neurotic orientation, and both require liberation from their condition. For Cubans, Gutiérrez's 'preferential option for the poor' must be expanded to include a preferential option for those castrated by the *macho*, be they women, homosexuals, Taínos, Africans, Chinese, or the poor.

How did our neurotic state develop? Cuba, unlike other Latin American nations who enslaved the indigenous people, reduced the Taínos to near extinction. To replace this vanishing population, Mayans and Africans were imported as slaves. Later, Chinese began to take their place. The Cuban concern was the acquisition of cheap labor. Hence, slave merchants did not bother bringing women, contributing to a predominately male society. By the same token, the white overlords were also mostly men, searching for gold and glory. Cuba was a stopping off point to somewhere else. Those passing through were on their way to discover their riches on the mainland. Few women accompanied these *conquistadores*. Since the beginning of Cuban European history, its population lacked sufficient number of women of any color. This absence of women contributed to the creation of an excessively male oriented society, where weaker males (non-*machos*) occupied 'female' spaces. They washed; they cooked; they 'entertained.'

Cuba was the last Latin American nation to gain its independence from Spain. Rather than having a century of nation building, Cuba spent the nineteenth century preoccupied with military struggles, contributing to her hyper-*macho* outlook. The physical bravado that characterized a century of bloody struggle for independence fused manhood with nationhood. *Machismo* became ingrained in the fabric of Cuban culture. Both sides of the Florida Straits proclaim the same message: *Patria* is real man's work.[5] Women, gays and blacks are not *macho* enough to construct *patria*.[6] Hence Cuba, a predominantly black nation, is ruled by a predominantly white hierarchy, while in Miami, the Cuban American National Foundation (CANF) was established by 50 white business-*men* organizing to create a post-Castro Cuba. Exilic Cuban anthropologist Behar describes the amalgamation of *machismo* with nationhood when she writes:

> In seeking to free Cuba from its position as a colony of the United States, the Cuban Revolution hoped to redeem an emasculated nation. Manhood and nationhood, in the figure of the Cuban revolutionary hero, were fused and confused ... Manhood is an integral part of the counterrevolution too. As Flavio Risech points out, 'neither *revolucionario* nor anticommunist *gusano* (worm) can be a *maricón*' ... If national identity is primarily a problem of male identity, how are Cuban women on both sides to write themselves into Cuban history? (Behar 1999, 12)

With colonization by the United States immediately following independence from Spain, Cuba continued in its emasculated status. The long United States' military occupation, the Platt Amendment, and the transformation of La Habana into a whorehouse for Anglo consumption meant Cubans lost their manhood, their *machismo*. To regain *machismo*, Cubans learned how to imitate the oppressor by enhancing our forms of domination of non-*machos*, specifically women. We, who came to the United States as infants or small boys, now seek to reinstate our *machismo*. The first generation of Exilic-Cuban adolescent boys experienced both peer and parental pressure to 'prove their manhood.' *Machismo* means to be sexually ready for anybody, anywhere, anytime (see, for example, Lumsden 1996, 31). Conquering *la americanita* (the North American girl) became an adolescent ritual of *machismo*. Exilic Cuban boys were encouraged to date the *americanita* to prove their manhood, as long as they remembered to marry *la cubanita* (Cuban girl).

The generations of Exilic Cubans who arrived in this country as children were forced to navigate simultaneously both sexual maturation and cultural adaptation. Both these processes, as Gustavo Pérez Firmat points out, became interwoven so that gender and cultural identity became integrated. Thus, cultural preference merges with sexual preference. In trying to become a mature man in exile, both regression and assimilation remain constant temptations as I attempt to construct my identity on the hyphen in Cuban-American (see Firmat 1994,

41–5). To Firmat's description of the attempt to live on the hyphen, I would add the sexual conquest of the *americanita*. For as Fanon points out, 'When my restless hands caress those white breasts, they grasp white civilization and dignity and make them mine' (Fanon 1967, 63; also McClintock 1995, 362). Conquering the *americanita* provided an opportunity for the Exilic *macho* to converse with the dominant culture from the position of being on top (pun intended).

To tell a man not to be a *maricón* also means 'don't be a coward.' Cuban homophobia differs from homophobia in the United States. We do not fear the homosexual; rather we hold him in contempt for being a man who chooses not to prove his manhood. Unlike North Americans, where two men engaged in a sexual act are both called homosexuals, for Cubans only the one that places himself in the 'position' of a woman is the *maricón*.[7] Only the one penetrated is labeled *loca* (crazy woman, a term for *maricones*).[8] In fact, the man who is in the dominant position during the sex act, known as *bugarrón*, is able to retain, if not increase, his *machismo*.

While visiting the home of an Exilic Cuban radio commentator (who contributes to the anti-Castro rhetoric common on Miami's airwaves), I noticed a statue proudly displayed on his desk. The statue was of a cigar smoking Fidel Castro on all fours with his pants wrapped around his ankles while a standing Ronald Reagan sodomized him. In the mind of the sculptor and the Cuban men who see the statue, Ronald Reagan is not in any way a homosexual. Quite the contrary, the statue celebrates the *machismo* of Reagan who forces Castro into a non-*macho* position.

Carlos Franqui, director of *Radio Rebelde* and one of Castro's 12 disciples who came down from the mountain in 1959 to serve as editor of the newspaper *Revolución*, describes how *machismo* affects politics. He wrote:

> [The politics of gang warfare in the mid-1940s is] disguised as revolutionary politics. Actually, it was a collective exercise in *machismo*, which is its own ideology. *Machismo* creates its own way of life, one in which everything negative is feminine. As our Mexican friends Octavio Paz and Carlos Fuentes point out, the feminine is screwed beforehand . . . [*Machismo's*] negative hero is the dictator (one of Batista's mottoes was 'Batista is the Man'), and its positive hero is the rebel. They are at odds in politics, but they both love power. And both despise homosexuality, as if every *macho* had his hidden gay side . . . The two brands of *machismo*, conservative and rebel, are quite different. The conservatives (generals, soldiers, police) always defend the establishment, while the rebels attack it. Nevertheless, both groups share the same views about morality and culture. They hate popular culture, and all the Indian and black elements in it. Anything that isn't white is no good. (Franqui 1984, 150)

Sexism

Machismo moves beyond the oppression of women. Although a detailed review of the Cuban patriarchal system would reveal a multitude of examples showing how sexism maintains women's repression, this article will instead examine how the overall conquest of 'virgin land' was made possible by the initial conquest of female bodies. Cuban *machismo* and the establishment of *patria* (Motherland) occurred within the zones of imperial and anti-imperial power. Here, land and nationalism are gender. The land requiring subjection is assigned a female body. Several postcolonialist scholars perceive nationhood as resting on this male projection of identity (see Mason 1990; McClintock 1995; Spurr 1993; and Todorov 1984). The construction of *patria, la Cuba de ayer* or *Cuba Libre*, along patriarchal lines, can be understood as a gender discourse. For Resident Cubans, Fidel Castro serves as the father figure, *el senor*. For Exilic Cubans, the late Mas Canosa was the head of the household, *el patrón*. Below both exists feminine land, needing the masculinity of those who will construct *patria* upon her.

Earlier, the first creation of Cuba required the reduction of women to the status of representational objects.[9] As Mörner (1967) suggests, the European conquest of the so-called 'New World' began with the literal sexual conquest of the native American woman. Todorov recounts an incident involving Miguel de Cuneo who participated in Columbus's second journey. Cuneo attempted to seduce an indigenous woman given to him by Columbus. When she resisted, he whipped her and proceeded to rape her (Todorov 1984, 48–9). The image of land and woman merge. Another example illustrates how Columbus saw the world. To him, the world 'is like a very round ball, and on one part of it is placed something like a woman's nipple' (Todorov 1984, 16). The concept of 'virgin land' represents the myth of empty land. If land is indeed virgin, then, according to McClintock, the indigenous population has no aboriginal territorial claim, allowing for the colonizer 'the sexual and military insemination of an interior void' (McClintock 1995, 30).

The first European to gaze upon the naked female body of the indigenous people and the virgin land under their feet was Christopher Columbus.[10] Mason shows that Columbus's first reaction was not to the lack of political organization of the island's inhabitants nor to the geographical placing of these islands within the world scheme. Rather, by eroticizing the naked bodies of these inhabitants, visions of Paradise were conjured up, with Columbus receiving the Amerindians' awe and love. Columbus and his men are invited to penetrate this new erotic continent, which offered herself without resistance.[11] These naked bodies and 'empty' land merge the sexual and the economic preoccupations of the would-be colonizers (see Mason 1990, 170). Virgin land waits to be inseminated with man's seed of civilization. A reconstruction and reversal exposing the hidden transcripts of oppression through *machismo*, provides a fundamental step toward dismantling Cuban oppression as manifested on both sides of the Florida Straits. On our way to that task, we must address next the issue of racism.

Racism

Race is not a biological factor differentiating humans, rather, it is a social construction whose function is the oppression of the Object-Other for the benefit of the Subject. Racism against the Cuban's Others (Amerindians, Africans, Chinese, and any combination thereof) is normalized by the social structures of both Resident and Exilic Cubans. Because domination of a group of people by another is usually conducted by the males of the dominant culture, it becomes crucial to understand the construction of this domination as seen through the eyes of the oppressor. Our patriarchal structure projects unto my 'darker' Other the position occupied by women regardless of the Other's gender. For this reason, it is valid to explore Cuban racism as a form of *machismo*.

By examining the Spaniard's domestication of the Taínos (of the Arawakan nation), I will expose the original typology of intra-Cuban oppression. As previously mentioned, the *macho* subdues virgin land, relegating her inhabitants to landlessness. According to Kant, 'When America was discovered . . . it was considered to be without owners since its inhabitants were considered as nothing.'[12] The gendering of Taíno men as non-*machos* occurred early in the conquest, and provides a prototype for all subsequent forms of Cuban oppression.

By 1535 Gonzalo Fernández de Oviedo, chronicler of the colonization venture, referred to the Amerindians as sodomites in the Fifth Book of his *Historia General y Natural de las Indias* (General and Natural History of the Indies). There exists no hard evidence as to homosexuality among the aborigines, but de Oviedo claims anal intercourse by men with members of both sexes was considered normal (see Mason 1990, 56–7). In a report given to the Council of the Indies by the first bishop of Santa Marta, Dominican friar Tomás Ortiz wrote, 'The men from the mainland in the Indies eat human flesh and are more given to sodomy than all generations ever' (Gómez [1552] 1946, 155–294; quoted in Rivera-Pagán 1992, 137). Juan Suárez de Peralta, a resident of Mexico in the late sixteenth century, describes with obvious distaste the inverted patriarchal of Amerindian society when he writes:

> The custom [of the Amerindians is] that the women do business and deal with trade and other public offices while the men remain at home and weave and embroider. They [the women] urinate standing while the men do so seated; and they have no reluctance to perform their natural deeds in public.[13]

By the eighteenth century, the supposed prevalence of homosexuality among the Amerindians was assumed. Like other 'primitives' of the world, the typical Amerindian was regarded as a homosexual and an onanist, who also practiced cannibalism and bestiality. These sins against nature threatened the institution of the patriarchal family and by extension, the very fabric of civilized society. The supposed effeminacy of Amerindians was further demonstrated by emphasizing their lack of bodily hair and pictorially displaying their supposedly small genitals. Simultaneously, the Amerindian woman was portrayed with excessive masculine features and exaggerated sexual traits, justifying the need for *macho* Spaniards to enter the land and restore a proper, phallocentric social order (see Mason 1990 67, 173).

By constructing people of the periphery as non-*machos*, one assigns them a function in life: service to the Spaniard *machos*. Colonization becomes a form of sexism, the domestication of the indigenous male Other as woman. Thus, Sepúlveda illustrates the masculine superiority of Spaniards to Amerindians by saying that they relate 'as women to men' (Rivera-Pagán 1992, 135). This feminine space constructed for Amerindians was established through brutality. By linking sodomy to cannibalism and bestiality, the Spaniards justified their treatment of Amerindians; the latter were seen as violators of both divine rule and the natural order of both men and animals. The enslavement of the Amerindian was God's punishment for sins and crimes committed against nature.

Spaniards, seeing Taínos in the position of women, waged a ruthless war against *el vicio nefando* (the nefarious sin—a euphemism for sodomy; see Lovén 1935, 529). This crusade was waged with righteous indignation on the part of the colonizers, who had the Amerindians castrated and forced to eat their own dirt-encrusted *cojones* (see Iznaga 1986, xviii–xix). So also, conquistador Vasco Núnez de Valboa had 40 Amerindians thrown to the dogs on charges of sodomy (Mason 1990, 56). Spanish *machismo* entailed contempt and rage toward the non-*macho*, which displayed itself in barbarous acts. [. . .] According to the *licenciado* Gil Gregorio, the only hope for the Amerindian was acquiring civilization by working for the Spaniards so that they could learn how to live 'like men' (Pagden 1982, 49). Meanwhile, their not being *machos* allowed the Spaniards to take Amerindian women and daughters by force, without respect or consideration of their honor or matrimonial ties (Las Casa 1988, 156).

Cuba's African population also was categorized as feminine. Undergirding the construction of race is the perception that blacks are non-*machos*.[14] Quoting various anthropologists of his time [. . .], Fernando Oritz, the Cuban sociologist, classified humans into two groups: active or masculine, and passive or feminine. Using morphology, he decided that African skulls reveal feminine characteristics (Ortiz 1975, 60, 88). *Machismo* manifested as racism can be observed in the comments of the nineteenth-century Cuban theologian José Augustín Caballero, who wrote, 'In the absence of black females with whom to marry, *all* blacks [become] masturbators, sinners and sodomites' (quoted in Lumsden 1996, 50). Until emancipation, the plantation ratio of males to females was 2:1, with some plantations imbalances reaching 4:1 (see Knight 1970, 76–8; Pérez 1988, 87). Usually, black women lived in the cities and towns. Hence, slave quarters, known as *barracónes*, consisted solely of men, creating the reputation of their non-*macho* roles as voiced by Caballero. Skewed sex ratios made black males the targets of the white master who as *bugarrones* could rape them. The wives and children of the male slave were also understood to be the master's playthings.

Paradoxically, while the African man was constructed as a non-*macho*, he was feared for the potential of asserting his *machismo*, particularly with white Cuban women. White women who succumbed to the black man, it was thought, were not responsible for their actions because they were bewitched through African black magic (see, for a case study, Ortiz 1973, 325–30). Thus, attraction becomes witchcraft and rape. Likewise, the seductive *negra* (Negress) was held responsible for compromising the virtues of white men.[15] Fanon captured the white Caribbean's sentiments when he wrote:

As for the Negroes, they have tremendous sexual powers. What do you expect, with all the freedom they have in their jungles! They copulate at all times and in all places. They are really genital. They have so many children that they cannot even count them. *Be careful, or they will flood us with little mulattoes* . . . One is no longer aware of the Negro but only of a penis; the Negro is eclipsed. He is turned into a penis. *He is a penis*. (Fanon 1967, 157–9; emphasis added)

The African-Cuban may be a walking penis, but a penis that lacks *cojones*. White Cubans projected their own fears and forbidden desires upon the African-Cuban through a fixation with the black penis which threatened white civilization. The black penis was kept separate from power and privilege that come only through one's *cojones*. Casal documents this white Cuban fixation with the black penis in recounting oral history of blacks being hung on lampposts by their genitals in the central plazas throughout Cuba during the 1912 massacre of blacks (Casal 1989, 472). The massacre was fueled by news reports of a so-called black revolt leading to the rape of white women. This peculiar way of 'decorating' the lampposts perfectly expressed the sexual mythology created by Cuban white racism.

In this analysis we must also include Asians. Asian laborers were brought to Cuba as 'indentured' servants, an alternative to African slavery. Landowners were not necessarily interested in obtaining new slaves. Their concern was to procure domesticated workers. Although Coolies were technically 'free,' their conditions were as horrific, if not worse than slavery.[16] Many died during the long voyage to Cuba, ironically, on the same ships previously used to transport Africans. As in slave-ships, an iron grating kept Coolies separated from the quarter-deck. Cannons were positioned to dominate the decks in the event of a rebellion. A Pacific version of the Middle Passage was thus created. In some instances, almost half the Coolie 'cargo' perished in transport.[17]

Cuban structures of white supremacy constructed the Coolie laborer similarly to African slaves. Like Africans, few Chinese women were transported to Cuba. Market demand dictated the need for young men, not women, to work the sugar fields. According to a 1861 Cuban census, there were 34,834 Chinese in Cuba; of these, 57 were women. By 1871, out of 40,261 Chinese in Cuba, only 66 were women.[18] As with Africans, the lack of women created the construction of Chinese sexual identity as homosexual. The Cuban ethnologist Ortiz credits the Chinese for introducing homosexuality (as well as opium) in Cuba. For Martinez-Alier, the consequence of rejection by the white and black woman led society to conclude the Chinese succumbed to 'unspeakable vices,' a euphemism for sodomy (Martinez-Alier 1974, 79; also Franqui 1984, 146).

The Cuban Asian, African, and Amerindian share a sacred bond. These three represent God's 'crucified people,' victims in the expansion and development of capitalism, who literally bear the sins of the modern world. As crucified people, seen as the feminine Other by *machos*, they provide an essential soteriological perspective in Cuban history (see Ellacuría 1993, 580–1). [. . .] The theme of solidarity between the crucified God and the suffering of the non-*machos* [. . .] leads to atonement for the *macho* perpetrators. [. . .]Through the emancipation of the non-*macho*, crucified people liberates the rest of society.

Classism

The Amerindian, African, and Asian were constructed as feminine for the benefit of the *machos*. Similarly, those who were poor, regardless of their whiteness, were also seen as being emasculated. Whatever wealth Cuba produced was accomplished by the sweat, blood, and corpses of God's crucified people.

If Amerindian, African, and Asian represent the oppressed elements of our culture, then our Spaniard and Anglo roots represent the oppressive elements. Classism among Cubans can be understood as a manifestation of *machismo* whereby a dialectic is created between the subject (Spaniard and Anglo men) and the object (Amerindian, African, and Asian), consisting of the continuous progressive subordination of the object for the purposes of the subject. Writing of the narrative process by those with *cojones* constructs non-Europeans as a secondary race, which needs civilization to be mediated through the paternal white hands of the *macho*.

The *macho* subject sees himself in the mirror of commodity purchasing as one able to provide for family, thus strengthening the patriarchal system. For Exilic Cubans, Cuba's economic difficulties proved Castro's inability to provide. Castro thus forfeits his role as *patrón*, as the head of family. Remembering *la Cuba de ayer* as economically advanced, like the United States, justifies the need to reeducate Resident Cubans in a post-Castro Cuba so as to return to her former glory. Their inability to provide demonstrates the Resident Cubans' lack of manhood. Like children, they require instruction in the ways of freedom and capitalism. The relationship Exilic Cubans hope to reestablish is one where Miami positions itself 'on top of' La Habana.

Historically, the highest rung of Cuba's social hierarchy was occupied by whites, divided into a variety of stratified economic classes. Regardless of the degree of whiteness, all enjoyed equal political privileges: namely, the right to own as many slaves as desired, and the right to acquire wealth in any manner whatsoever. The apex consisted of whites born in Spain, called *peninsulares*, who dominated the property market. They also dominated the commercial sector and held the majority of colonial, provincial, and municipal posts. They were preponderant in the Cuban delegation to the Spanish parliament, and in the military and the clergy. They represented the majority of high court presidents, judges, magistrates, prosecutors, solicitors, clerks, and scribes. More than 80 percent of the *peninsular* population was qualified to vote, compared to 24 percent of the entire Cuban population (Knight 1970, 88–9; Olson and Olson 1995, 13; Pérez 1988, 135, 152). The *peninsulares* saw themselves in Lacan's mirror as *machos*, while viewing the white *criollos* (those born on the Island) as effeminate and culturally backward. A frequent *peninsular* charge against the *criollos* was their effeminacy, their non-*macho* position (see Paquette 1988, 48, 91).

Below the *peninsular* in the social hierarchy were these same white *criollos*. Antagonism between them and the *peninsulares* was checked by a shared racial fear. At the bottom of the white stratum were the *monteros* or *guajiros* who lived in the shadows of the white elite. While their lifestyle economically differed little from the slaves, *peninsulares* and white *criollos* conferred upon them the distinction of being superior to all the non-whites. Valuing their elevation above blacks, they served as vigilantes during 'slave revolts,' showing intense viciousness in their suppression of blacks (Knight 1970, 177; Olson and Olson 1995, 12; Paquette 1988, 43).

After the Spanish-American War, a dependency relationship with Cuba developed. It was, then, on the safe domain of Cuban land that the United States first launched its venture into world imperialism. Maturing as an empire, the United States was less interested in acquiring territory than in controlling peripheral economies to obtain financial benefits for the center. A dependency relationship with Cuba, masked under the guise of New World independence, was preferable to incorporating an 'effeminate' people into the Union. Theodore Roosevelt and his virile 'rough riders' helped establish the myth of United States' masculinity later incarnated as John Wayne and the Marlboro man. Attributing effeminacy to the Cubans justified the economic control of the Cuban periphery. Secretary of War Elihu Root, referring to Cuba, said it best: 'It is better to have the favors of a lady with her consent, after judicious courtship, than to ravish her' (Peréz 1995, 39).

On March 16, 1889, an article published in *The Manufacturer* questioned whether the United States should annex Cuba. Developing a case against it, the author writes:

> The Cubans are not . . . desirable. Added to the defects of the *paternal* race are *effeminacy* and an aversion to all effort, truly to the extent of illness. They are helpless, lazy, *deficient in morals*, and *incapable by nature* and experience of fulfilling the obligations of citizenship in a great and free republic. Their lack of *virile strength* and self-respect is shown by the apathy with which they have *submitted* to Spanish oppression for so long. (Martí 1977, 229; emphasis added)

According to *The Manufacturer*, Cuban submission to Spain identified the Cubans as an emasculated people, unworthy of being accepted into the *macho* Union.

The economic result of colonialism was the reduction of *machos* to effeminate positions. The 1959 revolution was an attempt to reclaim our masculinity. Likewise, the exilic experience for those of us who came to the US was in part the establishment of our *machismo* in terms of North American paradigms, accomplished through the capture of Dade County's political, social, economic and cultural power structures. To my mind, white Cuban men with power and privilege in both communities continue to benefit from repressive social structures built around the concept of *machismo*.

Conclusion

When *machos* gaze upon the Other, what do they see? How we 'see' them defines our existential selves as *machos*. To 'see' implies a position of authority, a privileged point of view. [. . .] The Latino elite *macho* understands who he is when he tells himself who he is not. *Machos* as subjects are defined by contrast with the seen objects: Amerindians, Africans, Asians, women, and the poor. In defining what it means to be a *macho* by emphasizing the differences with Others, one reflects established power relations which give meaning to those differences. [. . .] When the *macho* looks at himself in Lacan's mirror, he does not see a *maricón*; hence he projects what he is not into his Other, defining himself as a white, civilized *macho*. The power of seeing becomes internalized, naturalized, and legitimized in order to rationalize the dominant culture's position of power. Our task as Hispanic ethicists is to move toward dismantling *machismo*, to go beyond *machismo*, by shattering the illusions created in our hall of mirrors.

Notes

1 According to Shute, sexism names social structure and systems where the 'actions, practices, and use of laws, rules and customs limit certain activities of one sex, but do not limit those same activities of other people of the other sex' (1981, 27).

2 *Mujerista* theology is both a response to the sexism existing within our Hispanic community and the racial, ethnic and class prejudice existing within the Anglo feminist community who ignores the fundamental ways white women benefit from the oppression of women of color. See Isasi-Díaz (1993) and Aquino (1992). For Exilic Cuban women, see García (1996).

3 *Machismo* has recently become a popularized term. Although it is used synonymously with sexism, it originally referred to a celebration of conventional masculinities. The term *machismo* is neither solely associated with the oppression of women, nor solely used in a pejorative sense. *Machismo* described the values associated with being a man, a *macho*. Similarly, the celebration of female attributes is known as *hembrismo*. See Lumsden (1996, 217). A popular Cuban saying is '*soy tan hembra como tú macho*' (I am as much woman as you are man).

4 Antonia Maceo, Cuba's black general during the Wars for Independence, not only symbolized the hopes of Cuba's blacks, but embodied the *macho* qualities of honor, bravery, patriotism and the best that Cubans can hope to be. His exploits on and off the battlefield served as testimony to his testosterone gall creating the Cuban compliment '*Como Maceo*' (Like Maceo) said while upwardly cupping one's hand as if to weigh the enormity (of one's *cojones*).

5 Lumsden quotes Castro as stating, Revolutionary Cuba 'needed strong men to fight wars, sportsmen, men who had no psychological weakness' (1996, 53–4). Additionally, in a 1965 interview with *El Mundo*, Samuel Feijoo, one of Cuba's most prominent revolutionary intellectuals stated, 'No homosexual [represents] the revolution, which is a matter for men, of fists and not of feathers, of courage and not of trembling' (61). Likewise, Exilic Cubans consider *patria* building the task of real men of valor.

6 Between 1965 and 1968 thousands of artists, intellectuals, hippies, university students, Jehovah Witnesses, and homosexuals were abducted by the State Secret Police and interned, without trial, in Military Units for Assistance to Production (U.M.A.P), reeducation labor camps. Because they were dissidents to the normative gaze, they were constructed as homosexuals as illustrated by the slogan posted at the camp's entrance: 'Work will make man of you.'

7 For a more detailed discussion on the construction of Cuban homosexuality, see Arguelles and Rich (1989), Boogaard and Kammen (1985), Lumsden (1996), and Risech (1995).

8 Missing from this analysis is the space occupied by lesbians, known by Cubans as *tortilleras* (derogatory term translated as dyke). For lesbians, as well as homosexual men, the adage '*se dice nada, se hace todo* (say nothing, do everything)' remains the accepted closeted norm of the Cuban community.

9 Spaniards' understanding of racism was unlike the North American, which passed laws prohibiting racial mixing. For Spaniards sexual relations were as natural as breathing or eating. Spaniard men took indigenous women as bed-partners, concubines or wives. The children of these unions, claimed by the Spaniards as their own, took their father's name. It is estimated that by 1514, 40 percent of Spanish colonizers had indigenous wives. By 1570, in accordance with the Council of Trent elevation of marriage to a sacrament, the Crown forbade married men from traveling

to the Americas for more than six months without their family. This resulted with more single men heading west, stimulating a rise of a miscegenate population. See Mörner (1967, 35–52) and Sauer (1966, 199).

10 The entry in Columbus's travel diary for Thursday, October 11th reads: 'Immediately [the morning of Friday the 12th, after land was sited at 2:00 a.m.] they saw naked people, and the admiral went ashore in the armed boat . . . The admiral called two captains . . . and said they should bear witness and testimony how he, before them all, took possession of the island . . . They [the land's inhabitants] all go naked as their mothers bore them, and the women also . . . they were very well built, with very handsome bodies and very good faces' (Columbus 1960, 22–4).

11 Columbus records indigenous accounts about an island called Matino believed to be entirely peopled by women; see his entry January 15, 1493 (Columbus 1960, 150–1). Rather than visiting it, Columbus returns to Spain, possibly indicating that he and his crew have had their fill of native, erotic women.

12 Immanuel Kant, 'Zum ewigen Frieden' (in *Schriften von 1790–1796 von Immanuel Kant*, Berlin: Bruno Cassirer, 1914, 444); quoted in Rivera-Pagán (1992, 11).

13 Juan Suárez de Peralta, *Tratado del descubrimiento de las Indias* (Mexico, 1589, 5); quoted in Pagden (1982, 174–6).

14 In spite of *machismo* positioning the black man as a woman, it must be noted that within Cuban African culture, sexism also is prevalent. Ibos girls are taught to obey and serve men while boys learn to look down at their mothers. The *machista* ethos of the *abakuá* only allow intercourse if the man is on top and is the only one who is active. See Lumsden (1996, 47, 221–2), Sosa (1984, 50–51), and Casanova and Abréu (n.d., 16–17).

15 Quoting Gunnar Myrdal (*An American Dilemma*, New York: Harper & Row, 1944), Ortiz (1975, 87–8) shows how the myth of the black man's overly extended penis (when compared to the white man) and the white woman's small clitoris (when compared to the black woman) creates a need for precautions lest the white woman be damaged, as well as spoiled.

16 I use the word Coolie to refer to the Chinese laborer because this word best describes their social location of oppression. The word Coolie is composed of two Chinese characters, *coo* and *lie*. *Coo* is defined as 'suffering with pain;' *lie* means 'laborer.' Hence the Coolie is the 'laborer who suffers with pain,' adequately describing their condition in Cuba.

17 The first shipment of Coolies by Waldrop and Company sailed from Amoy on February 7, 1853 with 803 Chinese and arrived in La Habana with only 480. In 1859, the Spanish frigate *Gravina* embarked with 352 Coolies and arrived with 82. See Corbitt (1971, 16, 54). For a graphic documented description of the suffering and humiliation caused by their brutal treatment by 'civilized' Cubans, see Lanpin (1876) and Scott (1985, 3–124).

18 See Thomas (1971, 188). By 1942, the Chinese Consulate in Cuba had 18,484 Chinese registered, of which 56 were women. Social and legal regulations forbade African (or white) and Asian intermarriage. See Corbitt (1971, 114–15).

Literature

Arguelles, Lourdes and B. Ruby Rich. 1989. 'Homosexuality, Homophobia, and Revolution: Notes Toward an Understanding of the Cuban Lesbian and Gay Male Experience,' in *Hidden From History: Reclaiming the Gay and Lesbian Past*, eds Martin

Bauml Duberman, Martha Vicinus, and George Chauncey. Markham, Ontario: New American Library. Pp. 27–43.

Aquino, María Pilar. 1992. 'Doing Theology from the Perspective of Latin American Women,' in *We are a People: Initiatives in Hispanic American Theology*, ed. Roberto S. Goizueta. Minneapolis: Fortress. Pp. 79–105.

Behar, Ruth. 1995. 'Introduction,' in *Bridges to Cuba*, ed. Ruth Behar. Ann Arbor: University of Michigan Press. Pp. 1–18.

Boogaard, Henk van de and Kathelijine van Kammen. 1985. 'Cuba: We Cannot Jump over Our Own Shadow,' in *IGA Pink Book, 1985: A Global View of Lesbian and Gay Oppression and Liberation*. Amsterdam: COC. Pp. 29–41.

Casal, Lourdes. 1988. 'Race Relations in Contemporary Cuba,' in *The Cuban Reader: The Making of a Revolutionary Society*, ed. Philip Brenner, William M. LeoGrande, Donna Rich, and Daniel Siegel. New York: Grove Press. Pp. 471–86.

Casanova, Manuel Martínez, and Nery Gómez Abréu, no date. *La sociedad secreta abakuá*. Santa Clara, Cuba: Universidad Central de Las Villas.

Columbus, Christopher. 1960. *The Journal of Christopher Columbus*, trans. Cecil Jane. New York: Clarkson N. Potter.

Corbitt, Duvon Clough. 1971. *A Study of the Chinese in Cuba, 1847–1947*. Wilmore: Asbury College.

Ellacuría, Ignacio. 1993. 'The Crucified People,' in *Mysterium Liberationis: Fundamental Concepts of Liberation Theology*, eds Ignacio Ellacuría and Jon Sobrino, trans. Phillip Berryman and Robert R. Barr. Maryknoll: Orbis. Pp. 580–603.

Fanon, Frantz. 1967. *Black Skin, White Masks*, trans. Charles Lam Markmann. New York: Grove Press.

Firmat, Gustavo Pérez. 1994. *Life on the Hyphen: The Cuban-American Way*. Austin: University of Texas Press.

Franqui, Carlos. 1984. *Family Portrait with Fidel: A Memoir*, trans. Alfred MacAdam. New York: Random House.

García, María Cristina. 1996. *Havana USA: Cuban Exiles and Cuban Americans in South Florida, 1959–1994*. Berkeley: University of California Press.

Gómez, Francisco López de. [1552] 1946. 'Historia General de las Indias (1552),' vol. 22, *Biblioteca de Autores Espanoles*, ed. Enrique de Vedía. Madrid: Ediciones Atlas.

Grosz, Elizabeth. 1990. *Jacques Lacan: A Feminist Interpretation*. London: Routledge.

Iznaga, Diana. 1986. 'Introduction,' to Fernando Ortiz, *Los negros curros*. La Habana: Editorial de Ciencias Sociales. Pp. xviii–xix.

Isasi-Díaz, Ada María. 1993. *En la Lucha: Elaborating a Mujerista Theology*. Minneapolis: Fortress.

Knight, Franklin W. 1970. *Slave Society in Cuba During the Nineteenth Century*. Madison: The University of Wisconsin Press.

Lanpin, Chen. 1876. *Chinese Emigration*, trans. A. Mac Pherson and A. Huber. Shanghai: The Imperial Maritime Customs Press.

Las Casa, Bartolomé de. 1988. 'Historia de las Indias,' in *Two Worlds: The Indian Encounter with the European 1492–1509*, ed. and trans. S. Lyman Tyler. Salt Lake City: University of Utah Press.

Lovén, Sven. 1935. *Origins of the Tainan Culture, West Indies*, trans. anonymous. Göteborg: Elanders Bokryckeri Akfiebolag.

Lumsden, Ian. 1996. *Machos, Maricones and Gays: Cuba and Homosexuality*. Philadelphia: Temple University Press.

Martí, José. 1977. 'Manufacturer's Do We Want Cuba?' in José Martí, *Our America: Writings on Latin America and the Struggle for Cuban Independence*, ed. Philip S.

Foner, trans. Elinor Randall, Juan de Onís, and Roslyn Held Foner. New York: The Monthly Review Press. Pp. 228–30.

Martinez-Alier, Verena. 1974. *Marriage, Class and Color in Nineteenth Century Cuba: A Study of Racial Attitudes and Sexual Values in a Slave Society.* London: Cambridge University Press.

Mason, Peter. 1990. *Deconstructing America: Representations of the Others.* New York: Routledge.

McClintock, Anne. 1995. *Imperial Leather: Race, Gender and Sexuality in the Colonial Contest.* New York: Routledge.

Mörner, Magnus. 1967. *Race Mixture in the History of Latin America.* Boston: Little, Brown.

Olson, James S. and Judith E. 1995. *Cuban Americans: From Trauma to Triumph.* New York: Twayne Publishers.

Ortiz, Fernando. 1973. *Los negros brujos: Apuntes para un estudio de etnología criminal.* Miami: New House Publishers.

———. 1975. *El engano de las razas.* La Habana: Editorial De Ciencias Sociales.

Pagden, Anthony. 1982. *The Fall of Natural Man: The American Indian and the Origins of Comparative Ethnology.* Cambridge: Cambridge University Press.

Paquette, Robert L. 1988. *Sugar is Made with Blood: The Conspiracy of La Escalera and the Conflict between Empires over Slavery in Cuba.* Middletown: Wesleyan University Press.

Pérez, Louis A. Jr. 1988. *Cuba: Between Reform and Revolution.* New York: Oxford University Press.

———. 1995. *Essays on Cuban History: Historiography and Research.* Gainesville: University Press of Florida.

Rivera-Pagán, Luis N. 1992. *A Violent Evangelism: The Political and Religious Conquest of the Americas.* Louisville: Westminster John Knox.

Risech, Flavio. 1995. 'Political and Cultural Cross-Dressing: Negotiating A Second Generation Cuban-American Identity,' in *Bridges to Cuba: Puentes a Cuba*, ed. Ruth Behar. Ann Arbor: The University of Michigan Press. Pp. 57–71.

Said, Edward W. 1994. *Culture and Imperialism.* New York: Vintage.

Sauer, Carl Ortwin. 1966. *The Early Spanish Main.* Berkeley: University of California Press.

Scott, Rebecca J. 1985. *Slave Emancipation in Cuba: The Transition to Free Labor, 1860–1899.* Princeton: Princeton University Press.

Shute, Sara. 1981. 'Sexist Language and Sexism,' in *Sexist Language: A Modern Philosophical Analysis*, ed. Mary Vetterling-Braggin. Boston: Littlefield, Adams, and Company. Pp. 23–33.

Sosa, Enrique. 1984. *El carabalí.* La Habana: Editorial Letras Cubanas.

Spurr, David. 1993. *The Rhetoric of Empire: Colonial Discourse in Journalism, Travel Writing and Imperial Administration.* Durham: Duke University Press.

Thomas, Hugh. 1971. *Cuba: The Pursuit of Freedom.* New York: Harper & Row.

Todorov, Tzvetan. 1984. *The Conquest of America: The Question of the Other*, trans. Richard Howard. New York: Harper & Row.

A Gap in the Closet: Gay Theology in the Latin American Context

Editor's Introduction

In this chapter, André Musskopf introduces the reader to the struggles of gay liberation in the ecclesiastical and theological context of Brazil and, by extension, also of Latin America (see RIBLA 2007). As a theologian, Musskopf places the struggle of LGBT people into the tradition of liberation theology. The latter always relates the biblical call to justice to contemporary social and political situations. It links God's liberating intervention in human history and God preferential option for the poor with people's solidarity with the oppressed and a commitment to grass-roots communities.

Although it is within the Latin American countries that liberation theologies have emerged, they are, according to Musskopf, sadly lacking when it comes to addressing gender injustice and to supporting gay and lesbian people. 'In Latin-American theologies,' he states, 'gay people are not yet seen as theological subjects.' This chapter, first presented at a panel of the American Academy of Religion in 2004 and subsequently published in a German translation, aims at making the presence of gay people in Latin America visible as subjects within the church and theology.

Musskopf does not simply lament the discrimination LGBT people experience in Latin America but actively contributes to a still small but growing corpus of writings on sexual theology in the Portuguese and Spanish languages. It is a project that shares similarities with the work of Marcella Althaus-Reid, a Latin American theologian. She wants to move from feminist liberation theology to what she calls an 'indecent theology':

Our point of departure is the understanding that every theology implies a conscious and unconscious sexual and political praxis, based on reflections and actions developed from certain accepted codifications ... Indecent theology is a theology which problematises and undresses the mythical layers of multiple oppression in Latin America, a theology, which, finding its point of departure at the crossroads of Liberation Theology and Queer Thinking, will reflect on economic and theological oppression with passion and imprudence. (Althaus-Reid 2000, 2, 4; also 2005)

Publications by the Same Author

Musskopf, André S. 2004a. 'Queer: Teoria, Hermenêutica e Corporeidade', in *Teologia e Sexualidade: Um ensaio contra a exclusão moral*, ed. J. Trasferetti. Campinas: Átomo. Pp. 179–212.

———. 2004b. 'Além do arco-íris – Corpo e corporeidade a partir de 1 Co 12.12–27 com acercamentos do ponto de vista da Teologia Gay', in *À flor da pele*, eds M. J. Stroher, W. Deifelt and A. S. Musskopf. São Leopoldo: Sinodal, CEBI, EST. Pp. 139–68.

———. 2005a. *Talar Rosa: Homossexuais e o ministério na Igreja* [Pink Robe: Homosexuals and the Ministry in the Church]. São Leopoldo: Oikos.

———. 2005b. 'Identidade masculina e corporeidade: Uma abordagem queer', in *Corporeidade, etnia e masculinidade*, eds M. J. Stroher and A. S. Musskopf. São Leopoldo: Sinodal. Pp. 80–107.

———. 2005c. 'Homens e ratos! Desconstruindo o modelo hegemônico de masculinidade e visibilizando modelos alternativos construídos nos corpos de homens em Gênesis 38'. *Revista Estudos Bíblicos* 86:57–65.

———. 2006. 'Biblia, sanación y homosexualidad', in *Revista de Interpretação Bíblica Latino-Americana* (RIBLA 49). Quito: RECU. Pp. 88–100 .

———. 2007. 'O filho pródigo e os homens gays: Uma releitura de Lucas 15, 11–32 na perspective das teorias de gênero e sexualidade', in *Re-Imaginado Las Masculinidades* (RIBLA 56). Quito, Ecuador: RECU. Pp. 98–110.

———. 2008a. 'Veadagens teológicas', in *(Re)leituras de Frida Kahlo: Por uma ética estética da diversidade machucada*. Satan Cruz do Sul: EDUNISC. Pp. 101–20.

———. 2008b. 'Se Deus é homem o homem é Deus?', in *Teologia Feminista: Tecendo fios de ternura e resistência*, eds Lucia Weiler, Raquel Pena Pinto and Sandra Maria Pires. Porto Alegre: ESTEF. Pp. 96–104.

Further Reading

Althaus-Reid, Marcella. 2000. *Indecent Theology: Theological Perversions in Sex, Gender and Politics*. London and New York: Routledge.

———. 2005. *From Feminist Theology to Indecent Theology: Readings On Poverty, Sexual Identity and God*. London: SCM Press.

RIBLA (Revista de Interpretación Bíblica Latinoamericana). 2007. *Re-Imaginado Las Masculinidades* (RIBLA 56). Quito, Ecuador: RECU.

Sifuentes-Jauregui, Ben. 2002. *Transvestism, Masculinity, and Latin American Literature: Genders Share Flesh*. New York, Basingstoke: Palgrave Macmillan.

Rodriguez, Juana. 2003. *Queer Latinidad: Identity Practices, Discursive Spaces*. New York: New York University Press.

A Gap in the Closet: Gay Theology in the Latin American Context.

ANDRÉ S. MUSSKOPF

Homosexuality has become one of the most controversial issues in contemporary Western societies. After the black and feminist liberation movements, the visible and articulated presence of gay and lesbian groups has shaken the structures of Eurocentric, androcentric, and also heterocentric societies. These groups and their challenges have been assimilated or silenced, but have rarely accomplished structural changes. The battle for civil and human rights questions not only the social and cultural principles but also ecclesiastical organization and practice as well as the theological discourse in which they are grounded.

In general, public discussions on these issues are further advanced than in the churches. In several countries, some rights (like civil unions or marriage) are already guaranteed constitutionally. However, the recognition of those rights by the churches has occurred much later. In the case of the historic Protestant churches, their attitude has been more of pastoral respect and tolerance than recognition and a valuing of the homosexual experiences. By looking at homosexuality as sexual deviation or sin, the presence of homosexuals has not yet challenged the heterocentric structure of church and society. As a consequence, theological reflections from the gay perspective are still marginalized. They are hidden 'in the closet.' The closet, besides marking the personal lives of many men and women who do not identify themselves with heterosexuality, serves as a paradigm for my theological work. To get to the table where theological discussions occur, it is necessary to 'come out of the closet' and run the risks that such a coming-out may have on personal, communal and social levels. It is necessary to have the courage to open the doors of the closet time and again and to confront the discourse that causes marginalization. Gay theology happens in the space between the darkness of the closet and the few flashes of light. It is from this place that it reflects about faith and claims its theological and religious citizenship.

Though advances have been made in the Latin America context, invisibility of gay theological work still prevails. Gay theology is still in the closets of our universities and seminaries, of our private libraries and publishing houses. However, gay theology wants to 'come out of the closet' and dares to call itself by its name.

Opening (Some) Closets

During the 1960s, a 'new historical period' took place (especially in the Roman Catholic Church) that carried great promises of renewal. With the creation of CELAM in 1955 (Latin American Episcopal Council), which diminished the isolation of different Latin American churches, the Cuban Revolution in 1959, which exposed the social relations of exploitation and domination, and the Second Vatican Council in 1962, a renewed sense of openness filled Latin America and provided doctrinal elements that enabled new theological reflection. The church became aware of its particular identity, setting the grounds for the development of liberation theology, an effort to articulate a 'new historical (and theological) subject' (see Beozzo 1993; Dussel 1979).

During this period two important books were published, namely Paulo Freire's *Pedagogia do Oprimido* (1970) and Gustavo Gutiérrez's *Teología de la Liberación* (1971). They influenced a whole generation of theologians as well as educators. Just about the same time the so-called second wave of the feminist movement was articulated. Mary Daly's books *The Church and the Second Sex* (1968) and *Beyond God the Father* (1973) translated the implications of women's liberation to the theological and ecclesiastical situation. In Latin America the articulation of a feminist liberation theology, even though its own beginnings can be traced back to the mid-1970s, occurred during the 1980s when it established a dialogue with feminist theologians from so-called First World countries. In the 1990s, it adopted gender categories and theories to deepen its analysis of the social structures and the theological implications of those structures (Brunelli 2000). Along with those social and theological movements, James H. Cone published in 1969 *Black Theology and Black Power*, responding to the African-American movement that rose to prominence through the work of Martin Luther King Jr. and Malcom X. Black theology is also developed now in Latin America, such as in the *Consultas sobre Cultura Negra e Teologia* (Consultations about Black Culture and Theology) promoted by Atabaque (Guasá 2001; Mena-Lopez and Nash 2004).

This is the larger context within which the modern homosexual movement emerged. At the end of the 1960s this movement was already well organized in different parts of the world and had its unifying event in the Stonewall rebellion. In Latin America, and especially in Brazil, the effects of this worldwide movement were also felt. After the amnesty in 1979 during the dictatorial regime in Brazil (1964–85), people who returned from exile brought with them new ideas. In 1978, for example, the newspaper *Lampião* was founded. *SOMOS* (Group of Homosexual Affirmation) was founded in 1979, and the *Ação Lésbico-Feminista* (Lesbian-Feminist Action) in 1980. They became the central groups of the Brazilian homosexual movement (Trevisan 2000, 335–51). Yet, despite the chronological proximity of these movements, the homosexual experience has not impacted theological reflections in the same way as did liberation theology for the poor, feminist theology for women, and black theology for people of African descent. Homosexuality remained linked to a rigid sexual moral code and to a negative interpretation of specific biblical texts.

The Closets of Gay Theology

By the end of the 1970s, a few books had been published in North America that defined themselves as gay theology.[1] Their reflections were based on theological and epistemological principles developed in liberation theologies. But in the Brazilian and Latin American context the development of an articulated gay theology is still incipient. There are studies in anthropology and sociology that try to establish and analyze the connection between homosexuality and the religious experience, but in the theological field such analysis remained limited to the study of biblical texts or to the area of pastoral counseling. Often, these reflections have been carried out by people who 'sympathize' with the homosexual cause rather than by gays and lesbians themselves. Despite the fact that during the 1990s a debate occurred in liberation theology that diversified and specified the question of who 'the poor' really are, gay theology was not yet recognized as an emerging new theology, whereas feminist, black, indigenous, and pentecostal theologies were.

In Latin American theologies, gay people are not yet seen as theological subjects. Bock, in his doctoral thesis, reviews liberation theology of the 1990s and points to the emergence of new theological subjects, such as women, African descendents, and indigenous peoples. There is only one reference that mentions homosexuals as victims of exclusion and marginalization in modern society (Bock 2002, 141).[2] Ivan Perez Hernandez finds a few fleeting references in writings by Frei Betto (1990), Luis N. Rivera Pagán (1995) and Ofelia Ortega (1996). According to Perez-Hernandez:

> Even if Betto, Rivera Pagán and Ortega's declarations are very encouraging, they are in the context of what Libânio and Murad describe as the first step in the process of elaborating a 'new theological approach.' As we have seen, the voices of homosexuals of both sexes, bisexuals, transsexuals have been invited to speak; the voices themselves struggle to speak; the voices need to speak. But those voices have not yet articulated clear and systematic homoerotic discourses that enrich even more the branches of new liberation theologies in Latin America and the Caribbean. As I admit that such initiatives are just starting to come up, I believe they have not yet moved up to now but in the level of exploration. (2004, 127–8)

In 2003, the *Comunidad de Educación Teológica Ecuménica Latinoamericana y Caribeña* (CETELA—Latin American and Caribbean Community of Ecumenical Theological Education) held its 7th Theological Journey in which, for the first time in the history of this organization, gay theology was acknowledged and invited to the table. But there was much anxiety concerning the invitation to sit at the table along with Afro-Latin-American, feminist, pentecostal, indigenous, and 'classic' liberation theologians. Yet, the participation of gay theology at this event was a benchmark in the Latin American context. The final message of this forum read:

> ... we feel the need to continue the task of deconstruction of theological and educational theories and methods, which under the patriarchal visions, ethnocentrism, violence, myths excluding of others, anthropocentrism, knowledge centralism, heterosexism and homophobia, constitute impediments for life to flourish. (Ulloa 2004, 454)

Perhaps this passage gives the impression that very little has been achieved, but it was an important beginning. Publishing companies, seminaries and theological schools are still not really interested in making public the fact that they support the creation and publication of materials in gay theology. Much of what gay theologians and scholars have produced over the last 10 to 20 years remains hidden in the libraries. Master's and Ph.D. theses are still waiting for the good intentions of publishing houses or, when published, are hidden in back shelves of bookstores and absent from book catalogues. Invisibility is still a strong feature of Latin American gay theology. However, a lot has been produced in the last two decades and forms the basis of a Latin American Gay Theology.

Opening the Closets of Gay Theology

First of all, after the rise of the AIDS pandemic, innumerable NGOs were created and offered also a home for gay and lesbian activist groups. This is not different from other parts of the world, where AIDS was considered a 'homosexual disease.' In these spaces, where gay people could safely meet and discuss politics and social action, theological concerns also found a place. Theological discussions took place about the perpetuation of the marginalization of the gay community and of people living with HIV/AIDS. They resulted in the production of many pamphlets and booklets that talked about religious traditions, questioned traditional teachings that considered homosexuality a sin and HIV/AIDS a punishment of God, and reflected in biblical interpretations from the gay experience and from living with HIV/AIDS. These pamphlets and booklets (sometimes translated from English) are a practical example of liberation theology's methodology and represent well what has been produced on gay theology in Latin America. There is hardly any NGO that does not have some material on spirituality, religious teachings, and Bible interpretation.

The second setting for the development of gay theology is the growing LGBT congregations. Metropolitan Community Churches, in Portuguese called *Igreja da Comunidade Metropolitana*, have at least one congregation in every Latin American country. And other religious groups are emerging and establishing a network through initiatives such as the *LGBT South Cone Christian Groups Meeting (Encuentro de Grupos Cristianos GLTTB del Cono Sur)*, which met in 2002 in Buenos Aires and in 2003 in Montevideo. The theology being produced in these LGBT religious spaces throughout Latin America is varied and ecumenical, very alive and proactive. Even though to be a gay Christian is still considered odd among religious communities as well as gay activist communities, most of those groups understand part of their mandate—and thus of their theological reflection—to be active in the community, to fight against all kinds of prejudices, to love and care for all, and to be hospitable to those who are discriminated against. Through sermons, liturgies and social activism, those congregations and groups create and live another way of gay theology in Latin America.

Though these practices may not agree with a theology that is thought of only as an academic endeavor or rational and systematic reflection, it is essentially where liberation theology arose and on which grounds feminist theology was built. But even in the academic world, theologians have researched and written on the issue of gay theology. Some examples:

- Ivan Perez-Hernandez, Cuban Ph.D. Candidate at the University of Chicago, who does his research on Gay Liberation Theology and the absence of sexual minorities from the discourses of liberation theologies.
- Mario Ribas, a Brazilian theologian who wrote his thesis on *Scripture, Tradition, and Reason in the Debate on Homosexuality within Anglicanism*; he continues his research in South Africa, entitled *Towards a Post-Colonial Sexual Theology: A Critical Approach to the Heterosexual Paradigms of Dogmatic*.
- Tomaz Dixon Hanks, who has been living for many years in Argentina, has been active in *Other Sheep*, producing and translating materials on homosexuality and religion. He has published several books, including *The Subversive Gospel*, for which there is not yet an edition in Spanish.
- Johannes Hopman from Holland who has lived in Chile for significant parts of his life. He wrote his thesis on *Guilt, Christianity and Homosexual Identity* at the Gender Studies Department of the Universidad de Chile.
- Manuel Villalobos Mendoza from Mexico who wrote his thesis on *Appeal to the Biblical Tradition in Contemporary Discussions of Homosexuality* at the Catholic Theological Union at Chicago.
- José Trasferetti, a Brazilian Moral Catholic theologian, who has published books on ethics and pastoral work and homosexuality.

Most of those theologians are part of an informal network of gay theologians in and from Latin America. There are many others. It shows—to the surprise of many—that there is actually something called gay theology in Latin America. [. . .]

A Gap in the Closet

A Gap in the Closet: Proposals for a Gay Theology (Musskopf 2002) was the first Latin American publication that named itself in this particular area of studies.[3] In contrast to other books and articles that deal with homosexuality, it starts its theological thinking grounded in the gay experience while aware of the exclusion of gay people from church and academia.

A Gap in the Closet was written in the context of the Evangelical Church of Lutheran Confession in Brazil (IECLB). It was seen as a 'coming out' declaration and a scandal (after all, who would write a book on gay theology if not a gay man?). It resulted in an impediment to ordination. From a gap in the closet at the Lutheran Seminary in Southern Brazil it grew to a gap in the closet in Latin American theology.

A Gap in the Closet is a starting point for discussion and for beginning a more consistent and solid construction of what could be a Latin American gay theology. Perhaps, just pronouncing the words 'gay theology' is enough to open closets and to be respected in the theological (academic) world. The book is one more step in the 'coming out' process that complements and expands what other companions have been working for, many times in silence and incognito. The daily lives of many gay and queer people in Latin America, given the cultural, political, and religious context, make 'coming out' still a difficult and painful process. Thus, the phrase 'a gap in the closet' stands for this risky and frequently courageous efforts to name a theology that so many times 'does not dare to say its name' (based on a Brazilian expression, 'the love that does not dare to say its name').

The book starts with the question of why a gay theology was not born during the theological renewal of the 1970s, and why the experience of gay people was not taken into account when liberation from oppressive systems was discussed. [. . .] Liberation theology, like any traditional theological discourse, avoided getting into sexual issues because it did not seem relevant when compared to issues of poverty. The book counters such tendencies by taking into account the experience of being excluded from and oppressed by a heteronormative society. It does so by narrating the life histories of three gay men, building on their experiences when constructing a theology.

The starting point is the silence in which the lives of those men are embedded. This silence is broken through dialogue, leading to a deep sense of embodiment and body presence and enabling a renewed understanding of Jesus Christ's incarnation while also forging a new Christology. In this dialogical process, a re-reading of tradition and biblical interpretation—tools which kept sexuality confined to the heterosexual paradigm—are important. Positions defended by the fathers of the church regarding sexuality and homosexuality are put into context. Guilt is dissipated, and a new understanding of sin as related to homophobic and heterosexist system develops. Biblical readings go beyond mere justifications of the homosexual experience by deconstructing texts of terrors and by looking for affirming biblical messages. Experiences of 'coming out' are paralleled to 'justification by grace through faith.' Discovering that there is nothing one can do to earn God's love and mercy enables gay men to start a journey to build an identity around the experience of being gay, thus fulfilling what it means to be made in the image of God. 'Justification' no longer depends on a heterocentric society, but liberates the person to 'come out' as a child of God. Finally, the experience of having multiple partners is evaluated in this context, leading to a new construction of a sexual ethics based on friendship.

Queer Theory: A Critical Horizon

Queer theory is not yet widely known in Brazil and Latin America. But it has found a home, for example, in the academic setting of the Brazilian Association of Homoculture Studies. Denilson Lopes writes:

> In the Brazilian case, if we cannot speak of a field yet, we can also not proceed as if nothing had been done. If the basis for the emergence of gay and lesbian studies takes us to the constitution of what Foucault called king sex in the second half of the 19th century and the need to demarcate between a heterosexuality and a homosexuality . . . the works that have been done by Brazilian and Brazilianist History, Anthropology and Psychoanalysis, in the sense of getting to know better Brazilian sexuality, are of vital importance.

This research has not yet moved beyond the level of exploration and beyond translating what has been produced in North America and Europe. Mario César

Lugarinho uses the expression 'Teoria Homossexual' to translate queer theory to Portuguese.

> The investigation then requires a wide interdisciplinary network that may range from the medical and sanitary discourse to philosophy, sociology or, even, theology. In order to do that the concept of homoculture, the extended network of social and cultural relations that build up the homosexual identity, was coined. (Lugarinho 2003, 11)

The use of the word 'gay' in theology is not without problems and limitations, but it still allows the articulation of a group of people in the fight for their social and religious recognition and it gives visibility to this historically excluded, and socially and politically discriminated group. In this sense, to use this word is a political option. The use of the English word 'gay' in some way softens the impact that 'queer' might have in North America. The world's biggest Gay Pride Parade of São Paulo, for example, has chosen to call it the LGBT Pride Parade in 2004. The 'G' stands, of course, for gay and the experience of homosexual males. But it is impossible to unify all the male homoerotic relations under this term. The intimate-erotic-affectionate relationships between men are much more diverse and multiple than the term 'gay' is able to express. Its use runs the risk of essentializing or naturalizing a new group. To coin contextual words, concepts, and categories is one of the most urgent challenges for this discussion. Categories that speak to the experience of being an outsider in Latin American heterocentric society need to be strong enough to articulate the challenges real Latin Americans face. But when put within the critical horizon of queer theory, the term 'gay' allows in Latin America the eruption of a new historical (and theological) subject, which is able to question the heteronormative discourse and which creates gaps, so that a multiplicity of sexualities finds entry into theoretical and theological constructions.

Queer Theory and Gay Theology: Building Bridges

While most affirmative religious and theological discourses on homosexuality have argued for the inclusion of homosexuals, they have based their argument on a static concept of identity. An example of this is the argument centered on a 'homosexual nature' equivalent to a 'heterosexual nature.' This creates a binary from which queer theory wants to break away. According to Laurel Schneider,

> Queer scholars in religion have the task of complicating the warring positions without loosing sight of the obstacles that remain for those they would help . . . Queer Theology needs both the critical limit that queer theory offers and the prophetic inclusion that liberationists require. At the end, total inclusion may mean that neither homosexuality nor the heterosexual norm will remain intact. In fact, it is possible that there is no Christianity for queers, although there might be a queer Jesus. (2000, 11)

If there has been little produced formally regarding a Latin American gay theology, even less has been done to seek dialogue between gay theology and queer theory. It became evident in the context of the Second Conference of the Brazilian Association of Homoculture Studies in May, 2004. Out of a total of 180 papers presented at the conference, there was only one session with five papers under the subject of 'Homosexuality and Religion.' Only one of those papers was in the field of theology, all the others addressed the relation between homosexuals and the churches (from fields as varied as sociology, anthropology, psychology and communication).

The application of queer theory in theology ruptures a universalizing discourse (Althaus-Reid 2001). It breaks away from creating a naturalized or essentialized theology based on gender, sex, race ideologies. The construction of a gay theology becomes possible as part of a polyphony of theological voices, assuming its partiality as well as its particular and historical experience of gay men.

Queer Context: Brazilian Religiosity and Sexuality

Research in church history has shown the paradoxical situation of Latin America's Christianization. The sixteenth-century European mercantilist colonialism was followed and blessed by the mission of the church. Church and state united to dominate indigenous people and bring them the good news and civilization. Colonial Christianity joined European countries' mercantilist politics in seeking the higher good of salvation for the 'primitive people.' With the rise of slave traffic, African peoples were brought to the continent, who were eventually converted. The infantilization, barbarization, and demonization of the culture and religious experiences of enslaved and indigenous people helped the church to expand its dominion and to civilize and domesticate them. Despite the suppression and erasing of original religions, many of the subjugated people's religiosity remained alive through syncretic and popular religious practices.

The biggest challenge for Latin American theology today is to reflect theologically on religious plurality. The notion of interdependence generated by the ecological crisis makes dialogue between different religions an imperative (for example, Gutiérrez 2000; Altmann 2000; Teixeira 2000). Religious plurality/diversity is increasingly recognized as a trait of Latin America religiosity. According to Adilson Schultz, this religiosity is also marked by simultaneity and ambiguity. The emergence of African and indigenous religions does not represent the displacement of a group of people from one religion to another, but a simultaneous experience of different religious traditions.

> To claim a legitimate status for the ambiguity category in theology puts our relation with God on a more human level, freeing us from the weight of perfection, certainty and total assurance of faith. To say that our relation with God and of God with us is ambiguous imprints in faith and theology the perspective of provisionality, of fragmentarity. (Schultz 2001, 104)

The colonized reality of Latin America did not only leave its mark on religiosity but also in the configuration of sexualities. Studies on colonization show

how sex is a component of the domination of people and cultures. Sexuality is a way to reinforce domination and, in the case of Latin America, to affirming white European supremacy. Sexual relationships serve to demarcate the boundaries of race and gender between colonizers and colonized people (Stoler 2002). The configuration of Brazilian sexuality is also a result of the colonial enterprise and carries on the ambiguities of this history.

> A people born of an embryo of Portuguese prisoners and criminals left here, which was blended with indigenous peoples and, later, with Africans brought as slaves. This 'people,' of uncertain configuration, lives in search for itself, lost in between great distances where the Portuguese language causally became the mother tongue. (Trevisan 2000, 46–7)

Brazilian sexuality is multiple, diverse, and ambiguous, and can be seen in the popularity of Carnival. 'In Carnival, the instincts don't ask for permission to pass by; people dance, sing, fuck, fight, steal, and kill themselves in the same movement turned voracious . . . Opening its way in the heart of our misery, we can find this undeniable taste for licentiousness, plentiful during Brazilian life and history' (Trevisan 2000, 58).[4] The ambiguity of Brazilian sexuality is also evident in general cultural expressions (theater, literature, music). This brief description of Brazilian sexuality and religiosity points to a possible contribution of queer theory to the construction of a Latin American theology, in which ambiguity and simultaneity are correlated to *queerness*.

Gay theology, in the critical horizon of queer theory, presents itself as a valuable hermeneutic of ambiguity/simultaneity, which is built upon the concept of queer embodiment. It does not ignore differences of specific theologies but allows for an encounter and dialogue in complex networks of relationships, where matters of race, ethnic origin, sex, gender, sexuality, and class are intertwined.

Notes

1 The first example of this kind of literature is probably Oberholtzer (1971).

2 The author refers to J. R. Regidor, *Libertação e alteridade: 25 anos de história da Teologia da Libertação*.

3 I am referring to publications in Latin America available either in Spanish or Portuguese. It is important to acknowledge publications in other countries and languages, such as Althaus-Reid (2001), which have not yet been translated.

4 I refer to Gilberto Freyre. For another study of Brazilian sexuality and Carnival, see Green (2000).

Literature

Althaus-Reid, Marcella. 2001. *Indecent Theology*. London: Routledge.

Altmann, Walter. 2000. 'O pluralismo religioso como desafio ao ecumenismo na América Latina,' in *Sarça ardente*, ed. L. C. Susin. São Paulo: Paulinas. Pp. 391–414.

Beozzo, José Oscar (ed.). 1993. *A Igreja latino-americana às vésperas do concílio*. São Paulo: Paulinas.

Betto, Frei. 1990. 'Has Liberation Theology Collapsed with the Berlin Wall?', *COELI*, 57:3–7.

Bock, Carlos. 2002. *Teologia em mosaico* (doctoral thesis). São Leopoldo: EST.

Brunelli, Delir. 2000. 'Teologia e gênero,' in *Sarça ardente*, ed. L. C. Susin. São Paulo: Paulinas. Pp. 209–18.

Cone, James H. 1969. *Black Theology and Black Power*. New York: Seabury.

Daly, Mary. 1968. *The Church and the Second Sex*. New York: Harper.

——. 1973. *Beyond God the Father*. Boston: Beacon.

Dussel, Enrique. 1979. 'Dinámica de la opción de la Iglesia por los pobres (1968–1979),' in *La Iglesia latinoamericana de Medellín a Puebla*. Bogotá: Codecal/Cehila. Pp. 7–58.

Freire, Paulo. 1970. *Pedagogia do oprimido*. Rio de Janeiro: Paz e Terra.

Green, James. 2000. *Além do Carnava: A homossexualidade masculina no Brasil do século XX*. São Paulo: Ed. Unesp.

Guasá-Grupo de Teologia Afroamericana. 2001. *Teologia Afroamericana y hermenéutica bíblica*. Bogotá: Guasá.

Gutiérrez, Gustavo. 1971. *Teologia de la Liberación: Perspectivas*. Salamanca: Sígueme.

——. 2000. 'Situação e tarefas da Teologia da Libertação,' in *Sarça ardente*, ed. L. C. Susin. São Paulo: Paulinas. Pp. 49–77.

Lopes, Denilson. *Estudos gays e Estudos literários*. http://www.ufrj.br/pacc/beatriz.html.

Lugarinho, M. C. 2003. 'Universidade GLS,' in *Folha de São Paulo*, Caderno Mais! (March 30):10–12.

Mena-Lopez, Maricel and Peter T. Nash. 2004. *Abrindo sulcos: Para uma Teologia Afro-Americana e Caribenha*. São Leopoldo: Sinodal.

Musskopf, André. 2002. *Uma brecha no armário: Propostas para uma teologia gay*. São Leopoldo: EST.

Oberholtzer, Dwight W. 1971. *Is Gay Good? Ethics, Theology and Homosexuality*. Louisville: Westminster Press.

Ortega, Ofelia. 1996. 'Theological Education,' in *Dictionary of Feminist Theologies*, eds L. Russel and J. Shannon Clarkson. Louisville: Westminster John Knox.

Perez-Hernandez, Ivan. 2004. 'Teologías de la Liberación y minorías sexuales en America Latina y el Caribe,' in *Teologia e sexualidade*, ed. José Trasferetti. São Paulo: Átomo. Pp. 103–29.

Rivera Pagán, Luis N. 1995. 'El SIDA: Desafío a la Conciencia Cristiana,' in *Los Sueños del Ciervo: Perspectivas Teológicas desde el Caribe*. San Juan/Quito: Programa de Educación y Teología del Concilio Evangélico de Puerto Rico/CLAI. Pp. 53–68.

Schneider, Laurel C. 2000. 'Homosexuality, Queer Theory and Christian Theology,' *Religious Studies Review* 26/1:3–11.

Schultz, Adilson. 2001. *Misturando espíritos* (master's thesis). São Leopoldo: IEPG.

Stoler, Ann L. 2002. *Carnal Knowledge and Imperial Power: Race and the Intimate in Colonial Rule*. Berkeley: University of California Press.

Teixeira, Faustino. 2000. 'A interpelação do diálogo inter-religioso para a Teologia,' in *Sarça ardente*, ed. L. C. Susin. São Paulo: Paulinas. Pp. 415–34.

Trevisan, João Silvério. 2000. *Devassos no paraíso*. Rio de Janeiro: Record.

Ulloa, Amílcar. 2004. *Teologías de Abya-Yala y formación teológica*. Bogotá: CETELA.

34

The Cross and Male Violence

Editor's Introduction

The Achilles heel of any masculinity studies, including the critical study of men in religion, remains the issue of (sexual) violence and (domestic) abuse, and it is therefore apt to conclude the *Critical Reader* with Poling's chapter on male violence and a central religious symbol for Christianity, the cross. After all, it is in the effort of securing the integrity of people's lives and bodies that the critical study of men and masculinities in Judaism and Christianity finds its grounding, motivation, and *raison d'être*.

Although male violence is as much a secular as a religious issue, the Christian and Jewish traditions have frequently been part of the problem rather than its solution. Patriarchal, imperial, and colonial structures, in which religions are caught up, have certainly contributed to the perpetuation of violence (Brown and Bohn 1989); yet, even within religious traditions that have been excluded from hegemonic power relations, like Judaism, intra-communal male violence persists (Graetz 1995; Enger and Gardsbane 2005). Hence, the feminist critique of men in general, and men's movements in particular (Hagan 1992; Ruether 1992), has insisted on keeping the issue of violence on the front burner.

> Early Women's Liberation writing emphasized the family as the site of women's oppression ... [but] Western feminism's picture of men shifted from the domestic patriarch consuming unpaid labour to focus on men's aggression against women. Women's shelters spread awareness of domestic violence ... seeing men's sexuality as pervasively violent. (Connell 1995, 41)

Christian feminist scholars, confronted with the whole spectrum of male violence (from harassment to rape in the ministry, at the work place and at home), have located sexual violence in the religious traditions themselves: in biblical narratives, patriarchal church structures, misogynist dogma, androcentric liturgies and religious symbols. The symbolization of suffering as a redemptive act, as articulated in theologies of the cross and in Christologies, has increasingly come under critique (for example, Brock 1989; Brock and Parker 2002). In this chapter, Poling picks up on this theme by examining the effects of the cross on questions of violence as they concern Christian women and men. As a symbolic reminder of a violent death, does the cross resist and counteract (male) violence? Or does it impose on the (female) victims of violence a silent and submissive suffering that harms?

'We need to know,' Poling writes, 'how religion functions at the level of conscious and unconscious formation of perceptions and behaviors; that is, how the symbols, ideas, and rituals about God oppress or liberate the human spirit using the criteria of theology itself . . . [I]f certain forms of theology increase the suffering of women and children by refusing to address issues of rape and sexual violence, then we must raise prophetic voices to protest such theologies.'

Poling aims at using the resources within Christianity to oppose those dynamics in religion and theology that cause and legitimize violent behavior. His critique, then, is not against religion itself, but against certain forms of religiosity. He actively and constructively contributes to rectifying a social ill, and grants religion the power of the creative and ethical imagination with which to overcome male violence against women.

Publications by the Same Author

Poling, James N. 1991. *The Abuse of Power: A Theological Problem*. Nashville: Abingdon.

———. 1996. *Deliver Us From Evil: Resisting Racial and Gender Oppression*. Minneapolis: Fortress.

———. 2002a. *Render Unto God: Economic Vulnerability, Family Violence, and Pastoral Theology*. St. Louis: Chalice Press.

———. 2002b. 'Masculinity, Mimetic Violence, and Christian Theology', in *The Spirituality of Men*, ed. Phillip Culbertson. Minneapolis: Fortress. Pp. 113–31.

———. 2006. 'Preventing Family Violence: An Educational Model'. *Pastoral Psychology* 54/4 (March):377–91.

Poling, James N. and Marie M. Fortune. 1994. *Sexual Abuse by Clergy: A Crisis for the Church*. Decatur: Journal of Pastoral Care Publications.

Poling, James N. and Christie Neuger (eds). 2003. *Men's Work in Preventing Violence Against Women*. New York: Haworth Press.

Further Reading

Adams, Carol J. and Marie M. Fortune (eds). 1995. *Violence Against Women and Children: A Christian Theological Sourcebook*. New York: Continuum.

Brock, Rita Nakashima. 1989. '"And a Little Child will Lead Us": Christology and Child Abuse', in *Christianity, Patriarchy, and Abuse: A Feminist Critique*, eds Brown and Bohn. New York: Pilgrim. Pp. 42–61.

Brock, Rita N. and Rebecca Ann Parker. 2002. *Proverbs of Ashes: Violence, Redemptive Suffering, and the Search for What Saves Us*. Boston: Beacon.

Brown, Joanne Carlson and Carole R. Bohn (eds). 1989. *Christianity, Patriarchy, and Abuse: A Feminist Critique*. New York: Pilgrim.

Connell, R. W. 1995. *Masculinities*. Berkeley: University of California Press.

Enger, Cindy and Diane Gardsbane (eds). 2005. *Domestic Abuse and the Jewish Community*. New York and London: Routledge.

Graetz, Naomi. 1995. 'Rejection: A Rabbinic Response to Wife Beating', in *Gender and Judaism: The Transformation of Tradition*, ed. Tamar M. Rudavsky. New York: New York University Press. Pp. 13–23.

Hagan, Kay Leigh (ed.). 1992. *Women Respond to the Men's Movement*. San Francisco: Pandora.

Monk-Shepherd, Rosa. 2003. 'Male Sex Offenders: A Distorted Masculinity? A Theological Exploration of Possible Links'. *Feminist Theology: The Journal of the Britain and Ireland School of Feminist Theology* 11/2 (January):236–43.

Ruether, Rosemary R. 1992. 'Patriarchy and the Men's Movement: Part of the Problem or Part of the Solution?', in *Women Respond to the Men's Movement*, ed. Kay Leigh Hagan. San Francisco: Pandora. Pp. 13–18.

The Cross and Male Violence

JAMES NEWTON POLING

Male violence against women is a global problem. Every year, all around the world, grassroots organizations and women's networks raise awareness and inspire change through imaginative action to overcome different forms of violence against women. Such awareness and action campaigns have brought about the World Council of Churches' 'Decade to Overcome Violence (2001–2010),' the worldwide campaign entitled 'On the Wings of a Dove,' and annual events such as '16 Days of Activism Against Gender Violence' and the United Nations International Day for the Elimination of Violence against Women.[1] Witnesses from every culture and continent are reporting high levels of physical assaults, rapes, and emotional control of women by actions of individual men who are fathers and husbands, as well as other relatives, both male and female, and by official government decrees and actions. War, poverty, and massive migrations make the world and the home even more dangerous places for women and their children because they destroy the order and discipline of local communities. Throughout most of the church's history, however, male violence against women has not been thematized as a theological and ethical problem. I will argue in this essay that understanding and challenging the history of interpretation of the cross is one way to prevent male violence against women, and that this is a particular obligation of the present generation.

The cross of Jesus Christ was a violent event and its interpretation over the centuries has been ambiguous. For men who live in patriarchal societies, the cross gives mixed messages. On the one hand, the cross is a symbol that legitimizes male dominance in human community. For many centuries, the cross has been symbolic of the church's authority as a patriarchal institution. Jesus died as a man on the cross and brought salvation for humankind. Therefore, most churches have argued, only men can serve as governors and ritual leaders in the church, modeling a form of governance for all society, including the family. Theologians have taught that male headship over women is established by God the Father and his only Son, Jesus, and any challenge to male dominance is a challenge to God himself. One can see the cross as a symbol of a natural patriarchal order that must be supported by the interactions of men and women.

On the other hand, the cross is a symbol of accountability for men, a sign that God rejects domination and brings judgment on those who engage in violence.

In his Pentecost sermon, Peter encouraged his listeners to identify with those who were responsible for the cross: 'Jesus of Nazareth . . . you crucified and killed by the hands of those outside the law . . . God has made him both Lord and messiah, this Jesus whom you crucified . . . Repent and be baptized every one of you in the name of Jesus Christ so that your sins may be forgiven and you will receive the gift of the Holy Spirit' (Acts 2.23, 36, 38). In the passion narratives, the religious and political authorities are unmasked as villains more concerned about power and control than about justice and love. In the end of the biblical story these villains are discredited by the resurrection and the birth of an evangelistic church that the authorities cannot control. One can interpret the cross as a judgment on all forms of domination and violence that exist in human societies, including male domination and violence against women. 'The discipleship of the cross makes a . . . difficult demand: the application of nonviolence to every sphere of life.'[2]

Observing these two interpretations of the cross, how can we counter the negative effects of male dominance and its effects on the health and salvation for women and men and encourage interpretations of the cross that give priority to safety for women and accountability for men? This is a question for practical theology, an academic theological discipline with the task (one among others) of evaluating Christian doctrines and practices in terms of their consequences for individuals and communities of faith in dialogue with other branches of theology concerned with questions of truth.[3] In other words, the ways that Christian doctrines and practices affect the everyday lives of ordinary people need to be considered alongside questions of truth; that is, whether the doctrines and practices conform to the revelation of God in Scripture, history, and rational thought.

Clarice Martin, black womanist New Testament scholar, describes the difference between hermeneutics of truth and hermeneutics of effects:

> 'Hermeneutics' is not simply a cognitive process wherein one seeks to determine the 'correct meaning' of a passage or text. Neither are questions of penultimate truth and universality solely determinative of meaning. Also of essential importance in the interpretive task are such matters as the nature of the interpreter's goals, the effects of a given interpretation on a community of people who have an interest in the text being interpreted, and questions of cultural value, social relevance, and ethics. (Martin 1993, 25)

'What is at stake in hermeneutics is not only the "truth" of one's interpretation, but also the effects interpretation and interpretive strategies have on the ways in which human beings shape their goals and their actions.'[4] This form of hermeneutics involves a rhythm or dynamic interplay between biblical texts from the canon and the lived faith and experience of communities of faith. An interpreter cannot understand Jesus by studying the Bible in isolation, but must be immersed in a community of faith that practices the faith today. Without participation in a practicing community of faith today, one cannot comprehend the spirit of Jesus in the past or the present. The truth of Jesus in Scripture is revealed in ongoing discipleship in the name of Jesus.

The Cross and Violence against Women

The vocation of practical theologians is to understand how the stories, teachings, and practices of our religious institutions affect persons. We need to know how religion functions at the level of conscious and unconscious formation of perceptions and behaviors; that is, how the symbols, ideas, and rituals about God oppress or liberate the human spirit using the criteria of theology itself. If the ideas and practices of religious communities are damaging individual believers and their families according to Christian norms, then we have a responsibility to bring these realities to the attention of religious leaders for reexamination. For example, if certain forms of theology increase the suffering of women and children by refusing to address issues of rape and sexual violence, then we must raise prophetic voices to protest such theologies. If certain ideas and practices liberate persons, leading to healing and transformation, and bringing about a more just society for everyone, then we need to bring that feedback to our religious communities. For example, if some survivors of violence against women find Jesus to be a faithful companion in their journey toward healing, we need to understand their piety and bring it to the attention of the church.

Religious rituals and beliefs that shape practices of the church over many years become models that consciously and unconsciously influence our inner reality.[5] Figures in these dramas become internal objects that organize our religious experiences. How does the cross influence the religious imagination of believers? In the story of the cross, there are various figures available for the religious imagination. 'In the final scenes of the story we see the defecting disciples, the disillusioned crowd, and the hostile authorities, all juxtaposed to Jesus, who alone goes the way of the cross' (Myers 1988, 121). Thus, one has many options for reading oneself into the story. One can identify with Jesus, the innocent righteous one who was unjustly killed by his enemies. Many people find Jesus to be a compassionate figure who understands their own suffering and reveals a God who is compassionate with those who suffer. One can identify with the disciples who were frightened for their own lives and betrayed their loyalty to Jesus by denying and hiding from Jesus' enemies. One can identify with the religious and political leaders who persecuted Jesus and were responsible for his death. Or one can identify with the crowd who worshiped him but turned against him in the end.

According to narrative theory, any and all of these religious identifications are possible in the story of the cross.[6] We need to understand how these identifications can lead to ambiguous interpretations of the cross—as a symbol that legitimizes male dominance and violence against women and as a symbol of accountability for men.

One example of the cross as a symbol that legitimizes male violence against women is clergy sexual abuse, which has become the focus of so much public attention in the last decade. The most common scenario of clergy sexual abuse is a male clergyman with a female parishioner or with a child.[7] What happens when pastors and counselors sexualize their ministry relationships? A sexual relationship between a male clergyman and a female parishioner replicates the drama between a patriarchal God and an obedient, self-sacrificing Jesus standing in for a sinful humanity. A relationship that was supposedly based on the healing needs of the parishioner becomes reversed so that the parishioner serves the sexual needs of the clergyman. In religious terms, the clergyman has taken the place of God who is all-knowing, all-powerful, and all-loving, and the parishioner has taken the place of Jesus who takes on the sins of humanity, submits her will to God's, and sacrifices her life unto death on the cross for the sake of the relationship.[8]

In family violence, a similar drama is enacted. Given the negative and conflicting images of women in many churches and their responsibility to be obedient to an all-loving Father God and his Son Jesus, Christian faith means that men are closer to God than women, that the proper relationship of women to men is subservience, and that the traditional values of submission and obedience are the essence of Christian faith. The following are quotes from women who grew up as incest victims in Christian homes and their report of they learned from the Christian teaching they received:

> You must love your neighbor. Not much attention was paid to standing up for yourself (Ellen). You must always be the first to forgive and you must do so seventy times seventy times (Judith). You must always serve, serve God. Sexuality before and outside of marriage is bad (Margaret). Faith and standing up for yourself are conflicting concepts (Theresa). You must sacrifice your own needs and wants, you mustn't resist, mustn't stand up for yourself, must serve God, mustn't be your own person with your own ego (Amy). (Imbens and Jonker 1992, 271)

The images of Jesus' obedience to God, his sacrifice of his life for the Father God, and his ongoing service to divine authority are references to the cross. What is troubling about these illustrations is that certain interpretations of the cross clearly create the occasions for sexual and physical abuse of women and children because of their images of the Trinitarian God in relationship to human families. Survivors of abuse are saying that an abusive God and abusive clergymen do not contradict the church's theology. The images of abuse are inherent in the symbols themselves. A church that preaches God's love but projects the evil of the world onto women and other marginalized groups is preaching an abusive God (see Poling and Fortune 1994, 39–40).

The Cross and Accountability for Male Violence

In contrast to these examples, many contemporary theologians argue that the identification of the poor with the suffering of Jesus on the cross gives the cross power for survival and liberation in situations of oppression. Sharon Thornton's *Broken Yet Beloved: A Pastoral Theology of the Cross* draws on theologians Dorothee Soelle and Douglas John Hall: 'The cross stands as a powerful symbol of the suffering of people and of their yearning to know love' (2002, 115; see Hall 1996; Soelle 1995). She gives many examples of oppressed people, especially women, who feel God's solidarity with their suffering when they meditate on the cross. One example is Mercy Amba Oduyoye from Nigeria: 'Women in Africa know that they will need to be ready to risk even death in order to resist death . . .

"They face the cross in the hope that the humanity of women will rise from the silence and peace of the graveyard'" (Thornton 2002, 108). For those who are oppressed, the cross is empowering since it moves the suffering person toward community and empowerment.

> For those who suffer historical injuries ... [the cross] reveals the political, ideological, and economic factors that impact people adversely ... Seeing the relationship between one's own suffering and the social conditions that create and perpetuate it can help people find new descriptions and alternative meaning for themselves. (Thornton 2002, 117)

Likewise, Thornton suggests that the cross can be a symbol of liberation for those who are responsible for the suffering of others.

> For those who hold power over others in a particular society, the political cross speaks the word of judgment and demands change, usually in the form of relinquishment of power and control, followed by acts of reparation for past wrongs ... It pronounces judgment in the hope for *metanoia* on the part of the abusers. Judgment speaks the word that only God is God, and no one else is God. (2002, 116–17)

This interpretation is close to my own understanding of the cross. [. . .] Jesus died on the cross because of his solidarity with the oppressed people of his time and his courage to confront the forces of domination and violence. He died as a direct result of his commitment to justice and his resistance to evil (see Poling 2002, 205–08). Because of his faithfulness to his loving commitment to the people, Jesus revealed the loving justice of God, the creator of the universe. In Christ, we see God as a god of love, power, and justice who never abandons those who suffer because of evil forces. At the same time, Jesus becomes a model for human belief and action. Because Jesus was faithful and showed God's faithfulness, we can have courage in difficult situations to stand up for justice and love. The cross can empower us to engage in ethical actions in solidarity with those who are vulnerable. Thus, the cross discloses the nature of God and empowers those who believe in God. [. . .] [It] does not resolve the many ambiguities of the cross, nor counteract the many ways in which the cross has become a sanction for personal and military violence over the world. But perhaps it gives a way to help us understand why the cross continues to be a redemptive and comforting symbol for some persons who are oppressed and for some persons with power who seek to become nonviolent. We must continue to work to discern the truth and the effects of the cross in the lives of Christian communities and not settle for an interpretation that solves only our personal confusion.

The issue for this essay is whether the cross can function for men as a symbol of liberation from the false consciousness that protects our power and privilege and hides our pain and suffering. Theologian Ellen Wondra suggests that, in disclosing the relationship between God and humanity, Christology functions in two ways: manifestation and proclamation. In *manifestation* Jesus Christ provides a firm foundation for faith and practice. Jesus is "'the decisive re-presentation" of God and of the authentic character of human existence'

(Wondra 1994, 96). This is a hermeneutics of confession that trusts personal and corporate experiences with Jesus. In *proclamation* Jesus Christ shatters all theology and religious experience: 'Here, the sacred or divine is encountered as a power that shatters, defamiliarizes, or stands over against the human as the radically other which is nonetheless like the self' (97). This is a hermeneutics of suspicion that suspects all authoritative theological interpretations and interpreters, including oneself. In this distinction Wondra helps us understand the cross in faith communities as authentic manifestations and proclamations of the reality of human and divine life.

Jesus is the Christ because he is the manifestation of the transformation of humanity in the struggle to resist dehumanization, *and* he is the definitive re-presentation of the only God who saves. In the Christ, redemption of all existence is accomplished in principle, but it will be actualized only fully in the future. Thus, the incarnation of God in Jesus the Christ is simultaneously revelation of what has always been the case, vindication of this enduring if concealed and distorted reality, and promise and prophecy of its greater future fulfillment (see Wondra 1994, 326).

Research on this subject brings me to two Christological statements. First, the cross is the form of Jesus' resistance to evil as a *manifestation* that human resistance to evil can be trusted because it is the image of God in humans. Faith in Jesus thematizes resistance as a manifestation of 'the true relation between the divine and the human (and so the true nature of both divine and human)' (Wondra 1994, 315). Jesus resisted the evil of his day, even to death on a cross, and raises to ontological status human resistance to evil. *Jesus' resistance to evil discloses that resistance to evil is a fundamental attribute of God and humans.* The cross means that we can trust our own resistance to evil as an essential aspect of the image of God in our lives. [. . .]

Second, the mystery of Jesus' life, death, and resurrection is a *proclamation* that God is a mystery that is beyond all human understanding. *Jesus' relational love and power reveal the mystery of God's Otherness and proclaim that multiplicity and ambiguity are fundamental attributes of divine and human life.*[9] Jesus' death on the cross is a mystery that confronts us with the reality of a God who cannot be understood. [. . .] How do I experience the transformation of Peter who was a fearful coward in one story and a courageous preacher willing to risk his life in another story? How did he change from one kind of person to another? The answer is found in a personal encounter with the living Christ, a transforming moment in which one feels part of the larger relational web, a moment of losing one's self for the greater good, a liminal moment when everything looks different and one embraces a new identity. This second-order change does not come just from one's own sense of goodness and resistance to evil, but from an encounter with a living spirit that gives reason for living and dying. [. . .]

[W]e can hope the church will continue to tell the biblical stories in a way that confirms his emerging identity as a disciple of Jesus Christ who has the courage of his convictions to see another way besides patriarchy and male dominance. And I pray that men of all ages and cultures will begin to see other ways of being human and male that can be part of the new community God is bringing into history.

Notes

1 World Council of Churches, Project on Overcoming Violence Against Women (www.wcc-coe.org/). See also www.overcomingviolence.org, a Web site of the WCC (Web sites accessed April 4, 2006).

2 Myers (1988, 257) argues for a nonviolent interpretation of the cross. See also Poling (2002, 187–9).

3 For other definitions of practical theology, see Poling (1991, 186–91); and Poling and Miller (1985, 62–99).

4 Martin (1993) here quotes from Lunden et al. (1985, x, xi).

5 I am using a psychoanalytic model of interpretation; see Poling (1991, 75–91) for elaboration.

6 For more detail on narrative theory, see Doehring (1995, 141–52).

7 While the majority of victims are women and girls, a significant number of men and boys are also victims of clergy sexual abuse.

8 Paragraph from Poling and Fortune (1994, 39).

9 This section is taken from Poling (1996, 157–9). For more elaboration, see also Poling (2002, 198–211).

Literature

Doehring, Carrie. 1995. *Taking Care: Monitoring Power Dynamics and Relational Boundaries in Pastoral Care and Counseling*. Nashville: Abingdon.

Hall, Douglas John. 1996. *Confessing the Faith: Christian Theology in a North American Context*. Minneapolis: Fortress.

Imbens, Annie and Ineke Jonker. 1992. *Christianity and Incest*, trans. Patricia McVay. Minneapolis: Fortress.

Lunden, Roger, Anthony Thistleton and Clarence Walhout. 1985. *The Responsibility of Hermeneutics*. Grand Rapids: Wm. B. Eerdmans.

Martin, Clarice J. 1993. 'Black Theodicy and Black Women's Spiritual Autobiography,' in *A Troubling in My Soul: Womanist Perspectives on Evil and Suffering*, ed. Emilie M. Townes. Maryknoll: Orbis. Pp. 13–36.

Myers, Ched. 1988. *Binding the Strong Man: A Political Reading of Mark's Story of Jesus*. Maryknoll: Orbis.

Poling, James. 1991. *The Abuse of Power: A Theological Problem*. Nashville: Abingdon.

——. 1996. *Deliver Us from Evil: Resisting Racial and Gender Oppression*. Minneapolis: Fortress.

——. 2002. *Render unto God: Economic Vulnerability, Family Violence, and Pastoral Theology*. St. Louis: Chalice Press.

Poling, James and Marie Fortune. 1994. *Sexual Abuse by Clergy: A Crisis for the Church*. Decatur: Journal of Pastoral Care Publications.

Poling, James and Donald Miller. 1985. *Foundations for a Practical Theology of Ministry*. Nashville: Abingdon.

Soelle, Dorothee. 1995. *Theology for Skeptics: Reflections on God*, trans. Joyce L. Irwin. Minneapolis: Fortress.

Thornton, Sharon G. 2002. *Broken Yet Beloved: A Pastoral Theology of the Cross*. St. Louis: Chalice Press.

Wondra, Ellen K. 1994. *Humanity Has Been a Holy Thing: Toward a Contemporary Feminist Christology*. Lanham: University Press of America.

List of Contributors

Garth Kasimu Baker-Fletcher is Associate Professor of Religion at Texas College, Tyler, Texas. He has written widely on the subject of men's studies, including a book co-written with Karen Baker-Fletcher.

Daniel Boyarin is the Hermann P. and Sophia Taubman Professor of Talmudic Culture in the Departments of Near Eastern Studies and Rhetoric at the University of California, Berkeley. Besides his numerous books, he is series editor (with Virginia Burrus and Derek Krueger) of *Divinations: Rereading Late Ancient Religion*.

Donald L. Boisvert is Senior Lecturer in the Department of Religion at Concordia University, Montreal. Former co-chair of the Gay Men's Issues in Religion group of the American Academy of Religion, his current research interests include saints, gender, and sexuality in Catholic popular culture, and religious aspects of contemporary gay culture.

John Boswell was Professor of History at Yale University. He received his Ph.D. at Harvard University. In 1990, he became the A. Whitney Griswold Professor of History and chaired the Yale History Department for two years. He died in 1994.

Stephen B. Boyd (M. Div. and Th.D. from Harvard Divinity School) is the J. Allen Easley Professor and Chair in the Department of Religion at Wake Forest University. He teaches courses on the history of Christian thought and gender studies. He has served as co-chair of the Men's Studies in Religion group of the American Academy of Religion and as president of the American Men's Studies Association.

David Brakke is Professor of Religious Studies at Indiana University, Bloomington. He studies the history and literature of ancient Christianity, with special interests in monasticism, Gnosticism, and Egyptian Christianity. He serves as the editor of the *Journal of Early Christian Studies*.

Harry Brod is Professor of Philosophy and Humanities at the University of Northern Iowa. His new and forthcoming book is tentatively titled, *Superman is Jewish? How Comic Book Superheroes Came to Serve Truth, Justice and the Jewish-American Way*.

Virginia Burrus is Professor of Early Church History at Drew University's Theological School, where she has taught since 1991. Her interests in the field of ancient Christianity include the following: gender, sexuality and the body; martyrdom and asceticism; ancient novels and hagiography; orthodoxy and heresy; histories of theology and historical theologies.

Donald Capps is William Harte Felmeth Professor of Pastoral Psychology at Princeton Theological Seminary. He has served as editor of the *Journal for the Scientific Study of Religion* and as president of the Society for the Scientific Study of Religion. He has received an honorary doctorate from the University of Uppsala.

J. Michael Clark and his partner, Bob McNeir, live in the western North Carolina mountains near Asheville. In 1988, he founded the Gay Men's Issues in Religion group at the American Academy of Religion. Pioneering an unapologetic gay liberation theology, his expertise includes gender and ecotheology, AIDS and theodicy, men's studies, and gay sexual ethics. He has taught religious studies, gender studies, and college composition at Warren Wilson College since 2001.

Philip L. Culbertson was Professor of Pastoral Theology at the University of the South, Tennessee, and St. John's Theological College, Auckland, New Zealand. He is now an independent scholar in Palm Springs, California. His current research interests include the construction of masculinity in the Old Testament.

Mary Daly has taught for 33 years as Associate Professor in the Department of Theology at Boston College. She holds a Ph.D. in Religion (St. Mary's College) and two additional Ph.D.s in Sacred Theology and in Philosophy (University of Fribourg, Switzerland).

Miguel De La Torre is presently Associate Professor for Social Ethics and director of the Peace and Justice Institute at Iliff School of Theology in Denver. Since obtaining his doctorate in 1999, he served as director to the *Society of Christian Ethics* and co-chair of the Ethics Section at the American Academy of Religion. A scholar-activist, he has written numerous articles in popular media and has served in several civic organizations.

Howard Eilberg-Schwartz held positions in the Religious Studies Departments of Temple University, Philadelphia, and Stanford University. An ordained rabbi, he headed the Jewish Studies Program at San Francisco State University before he left the academic profession.

Michel Foucault was Professor of History and Systems of Thoughts at the Collège de France. He held the positions of director of the Institut Français in Hamburg and the Institut de Philosophie at the Faculté des Lettres in the University of Clermont-Ferrand. Lecturing around the world, he left an impact on almost every discipline in the Humanities. He died in 1984.

Sean Gill received his Ph.D. in Bristol. He was appointed Lecturer in the Department of Theology and Religious Studies at the University of Bristol, UK, in 1976. He was subsequently Senior Lecturer and head of the department before retiring in 2005. His main research interests are in the areas of religion, gender, and sexuality.

Robert E. Goss has been pastor and theologian of MCC in the Valley, North Hollywood, California, since June 2004, serving the LGBTQI as well as the Leather and Fetish community in Los Angeles. Goss received his Th.D. in Comparative Religion from Harvard University, specializing in Indo-Tibetan Buddhism and Christian Theology. He teaches in the Religious Studies Department at CSUN and also at Claremont School of Theology. He served as co-chair of the Gay Men's Issues in Religion group of the American Academy of Religion. He won the 2000 Templeton Course Prize in Religion & Science, and served on the National Advisory Board of the Center for Lesbian and Gay Studies in Religion and Ministry of the Pacific School of Religion.

Scott Haldeman is Assistant Professor of Worship at Chicago Theological Seminary, Chicago, Illinois. Specializing in the history, theology, and practice of US Protestant worship, he is also interested in the less formal ways human beings ritualize themselves in relation to various categories of identity, such as gender and sexuality.

Jay Emerson Johnson is an Episcopal priest and teaches theology at Pacific School of Religion (PSR) and the Church Divinity School of the Pacific (CDSP). He is also the Director of Academic Research and Resources at PSR's Center for Lesbian and Gay Studies in Religion and Ministry. He served for six years as the co-chair of the Gay Men's Issues in Religion group and is a member of the editorial board of the journal *Theology & Sexuality*. Currently working on queer theory and constructive theological work, he co-edits a forthcoming three-volume collection of essays under the title *Queer Religion*.

Mark D. Jordan is Asa Griggs Candler Professor of Religion at Emory University. He has published on medieval medicine, ancient rhetorics, and gay film, and is currently at work on a book about the rhetoric of queer adolescence in American churches.

Björn Krondorfer is Professor of Religious Studies at St. Mary's College of Maryland, and chair for the Department of Philosophy and Religious Studies. His field of expertise is religion and culture, with an emphasis on gender studies, cultural studies and Holocaust studies. He co-chaired the Men's Studies in Religion group of the American Academy of Religion and edited the *Cultural Criticism Series* of Oxford University Press. He is on the editorial boards of the online *Journal of Men, Masculinities and Spirituality* and *theologie.geschichte*. He is a member of the *Christian Scholars Group on Jewish-Christian Relations*, and was guest professor at the Institute of Theology at Berlin's Freie Universität in 2007–08.

Mathew Kuefler is Professor of History at San Diego State University. His interests include the history of marriage, childhood, and homoeroticism in late antiquity and the early Middle Ages. He is the editor of the *Journal of the History of Sexuality*.

Charles H. Lippy is the LeRoy A. Martin Distinguished Professor of Religious Studies Emeritus at the University of Tennessee at Chattanooga. He holds degrees from Dickinson College, Union Theological Seminary, and Princeton University. He has written or edited more than twenty books dealing with American religion, and will become in 2009 the president of the American Society of Church History.

Ronald E. Long is Associate Professor in the Program in Religion at Hunter College/City University of New York. He holds degrees in Religion from Kenyon College and Columbia University. A former Fulbright Scholar in philosophy in Germany, he has also taught Humanities at Columbia and Religion at Vassar College. Most of his writings have focused on men's and particularly gay men's issues in religion. Currently, he explores connections between gay rights and animal rights, and the spiritual dimensions of life within the gay community, including modern sport and ballet.

Dale B. Martin is Professor of New Testament and Christian Origins. Before joining the Yale faculty in 1999, he taught at Rhodes College and Duke University. He was an associate editor for the revision and expansion of the *Encyclopedia of Religion* (2005). Interested in topics related to the ancient family, gender and sexuality in the ancient world, and ideology of modern biblical scholarship, he currently works on issues in biblical interpretation, social history, and religion in the Greco-Roman world. He has held fellowships from the National Endowment for the Humanities, the Alexander von Humboldt Foundation (Germany), the Lilly Foundation, the Fulbright Commission (USA-Denmark), and the Wabash Center for Teaching and Learning in Theology and Religion.

Stephen D. Moore is Professor of New Testament and chair of the Graduate Division of Religion at the Theological School, Drew University, Madison, New Jersey. Beside his work on biblical studies, the male body and queer theory, he pursues his research in postcolonial studies and early Christianity.

André S. Musskopf holds a master's degree in theology and is currently a Ph.D. candidate at the Graduate Ecumenical Institute of the Escola Superior de Teologia in São Leopoldo, Brazil. He is a member of the Brazilian Association of Studies of the Homoculture (ABEH) and of the American Academy of Religion. He co-organized the first Latin American Congress on Gender and Religion ('Corporeidade, etnia e masculinidade'/Embodiment, Ethnicity, and Masculinity) and the 'Latin American Dialogues' with the Ninth Assembly of the World Council of Churches. His interests include systematic theology, feminist studies, gender and queer theories, masculinities and homosexuality.

James B. Nelson is Professor Emeritus of Christian Ethics at the United Theological Seminary of the Twin Cities. Author of numerous articles and books on Christian theology and sexuality, he also served on many committees and task forces on issues of human sexuality, including the *Sexuality Information and Education Council of the United States* (SIECUS), and the State of Minnesota Task Force on AIDS.

James Newton Poling is an ordained minister in the Presbyterian Church (USA), a pastoral psychotherapist, and Professor of Pastoral Theology, Care, and Counseling at Garrett-Evangelical Theological Seminary, Evanston, Illinois. He is the author of many articles and books on violence and abuse.

Michael L. Satlow is Associate Professor of Religious Studies and Judaic Studies at Brown University. He specializes in the history, literature, religion, and culture of Jews in antiquity, having written extensively on issues of gender, sexuality and marriage. He is currently examining Jewish piety in antiquity and is developing an Internet accessible database of inscriptions from Israel/Palestine.

Laurel C. Schneider is Professor of Theology, Ethics, and Culture at Chicago Theological Seminary. Originally from New England, she studied at Dartmouth College, Harvard Divinity School (M.Div.), and Vanderbilt University (MA/Ph.D.). She lives in Chicago with her partner and two dogs.

Jeffrey L. Staley is a Lecturer in the Department of Theology and Religious Studies at Seattle University, Seattle, Washington. His current research interests include Gospels and film, and Chinese American history.

Ken Stone is Professor of Bible, Culture and Hermeneutics at Chicago Theological Seminary. He edited *Queer Commentary and the Hebrew Bible*, which won a Lambda Literary Award.

Graham Ward reads English and Theology at Cambridge University. He taught theology, philosophy, and critical theory at both Oxford and Cambridge Universities. He is currently the head of the School of Arts, Histories and Cultures at the University of Manchester and also Professor of Contextual Theology and Ethics. His latest book with Michael Hoelzl, *The New Visibility of Religion*, was the fruit of a four-year, British Academy-backed research project examining the return of religion to the public sphere in contemporary Europe. Most recently he is translating the German political theorist and constitutional lawyer, Carl Schmitt. For eight years he was the executive editor of the journal *Literature and Theology*.

Acknowledgments of Sources

My gratitude goes to publishers for permission to reprint in full or in part earlier versions of chapters published previously as follows below. Every conceivable effort has been made to obtain permissions; any errors or omissions brought to the publisher's attention will be corrected in the next edition.

Chapter 1, by Mary Daly, is an excerpt from her *Beyond God the Father: Toward a Philosophy of Women's Liberation*, copyright © 1973, 1985 by Mary Daly, reprinted by permission of Beacon Press, Boston, and Quartet Books, London.

Chapter 2, by John Boswell, is an excerpt of his 'Introduction' in *Christianity, Social Tolerance, and Homosexuality* (Chicago: University of Chicago Press, 1980).

Chapter 3, by Michel Foucault, is a reprint of 'The Battle for Chastity' in *Western Sexuality*, trans. Anthony Forster, eds Philippe Ariès and André Bejin (Oxford: Basil Blackwell, 1985).

Chapter 4, by James B. Nelson, is a reprint of a shortened version of chapter 6 in his *The Intimate Connection: Male Sexuality, Masculine Spirituality* (Philadelphia: Westminster John Knox Press, 1988).

Chapter 5, by Stephen B. Boyd, is a reprint of 'Trajectories in Men's Studies in Religion: Theories, Methodologies, and Issues,' *The Journal of Men's Studies* 7/2 (1999):265–8, with permission by the Men's Studies Press, Harriman, TN.

Chapter 6, by J. Michael Clark, is a reprint of 'A Gay Man's Wish List for the Future of Men's Studies in Religion,' *The Journal of Men's Studies* 7/2 (1999):269–73, with permission by the Men's Studies Press, Harriman, TN.

Chapter 7, by Laurel C. Schneider, is a shortened version of her 'Homosexuality, Queer Theory, and Christian Theology,' *Religious Studies Review* 26/1 (January 2000):3–12. Permission granted by Blackwell Publishing.

Chapter 8, by Daniel Boyarin, is based on parts of his 'Prologue' and 'Introduction' in *Unheroic Conduct: The Rise of Heterosexuality and the Invention of the Jewish Man* (Berkeley and Los Angeles: University of California Press, 1997), approval by author and copyright © 1997, The Regents of the University of California.

Chapter 9, by Graham Ward, is a reprint of a shortened version of his 'The Displaced Body of Jesus Christ,' in *Radical Orthodoxy: A New Theology*, eds John Milbank, Catherine Pickstock, and Graham Ward (London: Routledge, 1999, 163–81).

Chapter 10, by Philip Culbertson, was first published as 'Designing Men: Reading the Male Body as Text,' *Journal of Textual Reasoning* 7 (1998). Permission granted on behalf of the *Journal of Textual Reasoning*.

Chapter 11, by Jay E. Johnson, was originally published in *A Rainbow of Religious Studies* (Gay Men's Issues in Religious Studies Series, Vol. 7), eds J. Michael Clark and Robert E. Goss (Dallas: Monument Press, 1996, 55–80).

Chapter 12, by Robert E. Goss, is a reprint of a shortened version of chapter 11 in his *Queering Christ: Beyond Jesus Acted Up* (Cleveland: Pilgrim Press, 2002, pp. 223–38). Permission granted by Pilgrim Press through the Copyright Clearance Center.

Chapter 13, by Stephen D. Moore, was originally published as a longer version as 'True Confessions and Weird Obsessions: Autobiographical Interventions in Literary and Biblical Studies,' in *Taking it Personally: Autobiographical Biblical Criticism*, eds Janice Capel Anderson and Jeffrey L. Staley, *Semeia* 72 (1995):19–50. Copyright Society of Biblical Literature, all rights reserved, reprinted by permission.

Chapter 14, by Howard Eilberg-Schwartz, is a reprint of chapter 6 of his *God's Phallus and Other Problems for Men and Monotheism*, copyright © 1994 by Eilberg-Schwartz, reprinted by permission of Beacon Press, Boston.

Chapter 15, by Dale B. Martin, is a reprint of chapter 7 in his *Sex and the Single Savior: Gender and Sexuality in Biblical Interpretation* (Louisville: Westminster John Knox Press, 2006).

Chapter 16, by Ken Stone, was originally published as 'Biblical Interpretation as a Technology of the Self: Gay Men and the Ethics of Reading,' in *Bible and Ethics of Reading*, eds Dana Nolan Fewell and Gary A. Phillips, *Semeia* 77 (1997):139–55. Copyright Society of Biblical Literature; all rights reserved, reprinted by permission.

Chapter 17, by Jeffrey Staley, is excerpted from his 'Fathers and Sons: Fragments from an Autobiographical Midrash on John's Gospel,' in *The Personal Voice in Biblical Interpretation*, ed. Ingrid Rosa Kitzberger (New York, London: Routledge, 1999, 65–85).

Chapter 18, by Mathew Kuefler, is a shortened reprint of chapter 4 in his *Manly Eunuch: Masculinity, Gender Ambiguity, and Christian Ideology in Late Antiquity* (Chicago: University of Chicago Press, 2001).

Chapter 19, by Michael L. Satlow, is excerpted from his '"Try To Be A Man": The Rabbinic Construction of Masculinity,' *The Harvard Theological Review* 8:1 (January 1996):19–40.

Chapter 20, by Virginia Burrus, is excerpted from her 'Prologue' in '*Begotten, Not Made': Conceiving Manhood in Late Antiquity* (Stanford: Stanford University Press, 2000), copyright © 2000 by the Board of Trustees of the Leland Standford Jr. University.

Chapter 21, by Mark D. Jordan, is a reprint of chapter 2 of his *The Invention of Sodomy in Christian Theology* (Chicago: Chicago University Press, 1997).

Chapter 22, by Sean Gill, is a reprint of his 'Christian Manliness Unmanned: Some Problems and Challenges in the Study of Masculinity and Religion in Nineteenth- and Twentieth-Century Western Society,' in *Is There a Future for Feminist Theology?*, eds Deborah F. Sawyer and Diane M. Collier (Sheffield: Sheffield Academic Press, 1999, 160–72); by kind permission of Continuum International.

Chapter 23, by Charles H. Lippy, is a reprint of his 'Miles to Go: Promise Keepers in Historical and Cultural Context,' *Soundings* 80/2–3 (Summer/Fall 1997):289–304.

Chapter 24, by David Brakke, is a reprint of a shortened version originally published as 'The Problematization of Nocturnal Emissions in Early Christian Syria, Egypt, and Gaul,' *Journal of Early Christian Studies* 3:4 (1995):419–60; copyright © The Johns Hopkins University Press. Reprinted with permission of The Johns Hopkins University Press.

Chapter 25, by Harry Brod, is a revised version of his 'Circumcisional Circumstances: Circumspecting the Jewish Male Body,' reprinted from *Jewish Choices, Jewish Voices: Body*, copyright © 2008 by Elliot Dorff and Louis Newman, published by The Jewish Publication Society, with the permission of the publisher.

Chapter 26, by Donald Capps, is excerpted from his 'From Masturbation to Homosexuality: A Case Study of Displaced Moral Disapproval,' *Pastoral Psychology* 51/4 (March 2003):249–72.

Chapter 27, by Scott Haldeman, is a reprint of 'Receptivity and Revelation: A Spirituality of Gay Male Sex,' in *Body and Soul: Rethinking Sexuality and Justice-Love*, eds Marvin Ellison and Sylvia Thorson-Smith (Cleveland: Pilgrim Press, 2003, 218–31). Permission granted by Pilgrim Press through the Copyright Clearance Center.

Chapter 28, by Ronald E. Long, is a reprint of a shortened version of his 'The Sacrality of Male Beauty and Homosex: A Neglected Factor in the Understanding of Contemporary Gay Reality,' *The Journal of Men's Studies* 4/3 (1996):225–42, with permission by the Men's Studies Press, Harriman, TN.

Chapter 29, by Donald L. Boisvert, is a reprint of chapter 2 in his *Sanctity and Male Desire: A Gay Reading of Saints* (Cleveland: The Pilgrim Press, 2004, 39–52). Permission granted by Pilgrim Press through the Copyright Clearance Center.

Chapter 30, by Björn Krondorfer, is a reprint of 'Who's Afraid of Gay Theology? Men's Studies, Gay Scholars, and Heterosexual Silence,' *Theology and Sexuality* 13/3 (2007):257–74. Permission granted on behalf of the Journal of Theology and Sexuality.

Chapter 31, by Garth Kasimu Baker-Fletcher, is a reprint of his 'Critical Theory, Deconstruction and Liberation,' *The Journal of Men's Studies* 7/2 (1999):275–80, with permission by the Men's Studies Press, Harriman, TN.

Chapter 32, by Miguel De La Torre, is a reprint of a shortened version of his 'Beyond Machismo: A Cuban Case Study,' *The Annual of the Society of Christian Ethics* 19 (1999):213–33, with permission by Georgetown University Press.

Chapter 33, by André S. Musskopf, is a revised version of a paper presented in 2004 at the Gay Men's Issues in Religion group of the American Academy of Religion; a German translation was published in *Werkstatt Schwule Theologie* 12/3–4 (2005).

Chapter 34, by James Newton Poling, is a reprint of a shortened version of his 'The Cross and Male Violence,' in *Cross Examination: Readings in the Meaning of the Cross Today*, ed. Marit A. Trelstad, copyright © 2006 Fortress Press. Reprinted by special permission of Augsburg Fortress Publishers.